Cetanā and the Dynamics of Volition in Theravāda Buddhism

Cetanā and the Dynamics of Volition in Theravāda Buddhism

NALINI DEVDAS

MOTILAL BANARSIDASS PUBLISHERS
PRIVATE LIMITED • DELHI

First Edition: Delhi, 2008

© Nalini Devdas
All Rights Reserved

ISBN: 978-81-208-3363-0

MOTILAL BANARSIDASS
41 U.A. Bungalow Road, Jawahar Nagar, Delhi 110 007
8 Mahalaxmi Chamber, 22 Bhulabhai Desai Road, Mumbai 400 026
203 Royapettah High Road, Mylapore, Chennai 600 004
236, 9th Main III Block, Jayanagar, Bangalore 560 011
Sanas Plaza, 1302 Baji Rao Road, Pune 411 002
8 Camac Street, Kolkata 700 017
Ashok Rajpath, Patna 800 004
Chowk, Varanasi 221 001

Printed in India

BY JAINENDRA PRAKASH JAIN AT SHRI JAINENDRA PRESS,
A-45 NARAINA, PHASE-I, NEW DELHI 110 028
AND PUBLISHED BY NARENDRA PRAKASH JAIN FOR
MOTILAL BANARSIDASS PUBLISHERS PRIVATE LIMITED,
BUNGALOW ROAD, DELHI 110 007

Dedication

To the memory of my mother, Annamma Devanandan,

my husband, A. G. Devdas,

and the guardian angel of my childhood, Kezia Ethel Munson.

Acknowledgements

This work is the fruition of over two decades of study, teaching and discussion with students in the Department of Religion at Carleton University, Ottawa, Canada. Many people have helped me in my study of Buddhism and supported me with friendship throughout these years. To all of them I make my offering of joyful gratitude.

I thank my father, Professor Paul David Devanandan and Professor C.T. Krishnamachari at Madras Christian College, who set me on the way, and all my other teachers—most especially Mrs. Tomoko Kodama at the Ottawa School of Art, with whom my association has been the longest and most fruitful.

My study of Theravāda Buddhism was greatly enriched by rigorous and interesting work with two of my graduate students, Angela Sumegi and Daniel Veidlinger. I express my gratitude to them, and to my colleagues Professor L.M. Read and Professor Cyril Williams for their strong support and interest in my work. I thank Dr. Harsha Dehejia for sharing with me his knowledge of Indian Art, and for helping me to bring this work to fulfilment.

I especially wish to thank members of the staff in the Interlibrary Loans Department at Carleton University for finding the books I needed for my research.

This work is a revised version of my Ph.D. thesis, submitted to the Department of Religion at Concordia University, Montreal, in 2004. It was a privilege to be able to study Pāli with Professor Steven Collins and Saṁskṛt with Professor Richard Hayes. I thank Professor Leslie Orr, the supervisor of my thesis, and Professor Mathieu Boisvert for their generous help and support.

I am grateful to Professor Angela Sumegi, Dr. Prabhakar Thyagaraj, Zsolt Sumegi and Ian McCrorie for their helpful comments on parts of this work, and to Elizabeth Dwivedi,

Evelyn Huer, and Felicetta Celenza for valuable editorial help. In spite of all my efforts, this work would never have been completed without the help of Louise Benoit, Ildiko Sumegi and Shawn Roske, who typed and edited the manuscript. I especially thank Ildiko Sumegi for the care with which she worked on the manuscript and Shawn Roske for completing the typing and editing with expert skill. I also thank Chitra Arcot for preparing the Index.

I conclude by thanking those who share my earliest memories. My sister and brother have never failed to challenge me intellectually and support me with love. I thank my dear extended family of cousins, nieces, nephews and their children. I offer my thanks to three women who have inspired me with their zest for life: my aunt Saraswathi Lakshmanan, and my friends Elizabeth Huggins and Savitri Devenesan.

Table of Contents

A Note on Transliteration

In this work, the plural of Pāli terms is indicated by the addition of 's'. The Pāli term itself appears in italics. For example, the plurals of *cetanā* and *citta* appear as *cetanā*s and *citta*s.

Abbreviations

I have used the Pali Text Society editions of Pāli texts. References to Pāli sources, except in the cases of those named below, are given by the abbreviation of the source used followed by a Roman numeral indicating the volume number and an Arabic numeral indicating the page. References to the *Dhammapada*, the *Theragāthā*, the *Therīgāthā*, and the *Sutta-nipāta* are given by an Arabic numeral indicating the verse number. References to the *Visuddhimagga* are given by chapter and verse. The Upaniṣadic sources are taken from S. Radhakrishnan, *The Principal Upanishads* (London: George Allen and Unwin, 1953). I have followed Radhakrishnan's system of numbering. The abbreviation of the *Upaniṣad* is followed by a Roman numeral indicating the section and an Arabic numeral indicating the verse. References to the *Yoga-sūtra* and the *Vyāsa-bhāṣya* are given by chapter and verse. The editions of the *Yoga-sūtra* and the *Vyāsa-bhāṣya* are those found in T.S. Rukmani, *Yogavārttika of Vijñānabhikṣu: Text with English translation and critical notes along with the text and English translation of the Pātañjala Yogasūtras and Vyāsabhāṣya* (New Delhi: Munshiram Manoharlal, 1981-89).

A. *Aṅguttara-nikāya*

AA. *Aṅguttara-nikāya commentary (Manorathapūraṇī)*

Abhk. *Abhidharmakośa-bhāṣya*

AbhkA. *Abhidharmakośa-bhāṣya commentary (Sphuṭārthā of Yaśomitra)*

Abhs.	*Abhidhammattha-saṅgaha*
Asl.	*Atthasālinī* (*Dhammasaṅgaṇi commentary*)
A.U.	*Aitareya Upaniṣad*
Bhg.	*Bhagavad-gītā*
B.U.	*Bṛhadāraṇyaka Upaniṣad*
C.P.D.	*A Critical Pāli Dictionary*, ed. V. Trenckner. Continued by D. Anderson, H. Smith, and others. (Copenhagen: Royal Danish Academy of Sciences and Letters, 1924-)
C.U.	*Chāndogya Upaniṣad*
D.	*Dīgha-nikāya*
DA.	*Dīgha-nikāya commentary* (*Sumaṅgalavilāsinī*)
Dhp.	*Dhammapada*
Dhs.	*Dhammasaṅgaṇi*
I.U.	*Īśā Upaniṣad*
K.U.	*Kaṭha Upaniṣad*
Ks.U.	*Kauṣītaki Upaniṣad*
Kvu.	*Kathāvatthu*
KvuA.	*Kathāvatthu commentary* (*Kathāvatthuppakaraṇa-aṭṭhakathā*)
M.	*Majjhima-nikāya*
MA.	*Majjhima-nikāya commentary* (*Papañcasūdanī*)
Mil.	*Milindapañha*
M.U.	*Muṇḍaka Upaniṣad*
Mt.U.	*Maitrī Upaniṣad*
Nt.	*Nettippakaraṇa*

P.E.D.	*Pali-English Dictionary*, ed. T.W. Rhys Davids and W. Stede (New Delhi: Oriental Books Reprint Corporation, 1975. Originally published in 1921-25 by the Pali Text Society, London)
Ps.	*Paṭisambhidāmagga*
P.T.S.	Pali Text Society
P.U.	*Praśna Upaniṣad*
Ṛg.	*Ṛgveda*
S.	*Saṁyutta-nikāya*
SA.	*Saṁyutta-nikāya commentary (Sāratthappakāsinī)*
S.E.D.	*A Sanskrit-English Dictionary*, ed. M. Monier-Williams (Oxford: Clarendon Press, 1809)
SK.	*Sāṁkhya-kārikā of Īśvarakṛṣṇa*
Sn.	*Sutta-nipāta*
S.U.	*Śvetāśvatara Upaniṣad*
Tha.	*Theragāthā*
Thi.	*Therīgāthā*
T.U.	*Taittirīya Upaniṣad*
Ud.	*Udāna*
VB.	*Vyāsa-bhāṣya*
Vbh.	*Vibhaṅga*
Vin.	*Vinaya-piṭaka*
Vsm.	*Visuddhimagga*
VsmA.	*Visuddhimagga commentary (Paramattha-mañjūsā)*
Y.S.	*Yoga-sūtra of Patañjali*

Introduction:
Cetanā in Modern Theravāda Scholarship

A verse from the *Dhammapada*, treasured by Buddhists, seeks to distil the entirety of Buddhism in a few terse phrases:

Refraining from all evil,
Pursuing what is good,
Cleansing one's own mind:
That is the teaching of all the Buddhas.[1] (Dhp. 183)

Practitioners and scholars of Theravāda Buddhism would agree with the central message of this verse, which upholds volition and self-effort as the very core of the teaching of the Buddhas. Nevertheless, whereas modern Theravāda scholarship has contributed much to a deeper understanding of the concept of "absence of a soul" (*anattā*), the notion of *kamma*, the epistemological views put forward in the Pāli texts, and the techniques of *vipassanā* meditation, less attention has been devoted to an investigation of the concept of volition in Theravāda. The purpose of this work is to explore how the Theravāda tradition approaches and perceives the processes of volition, and more specifically, to trace the connotations of *cetanā*, the term that is most often translated as "volition". The fundamental question that needs to be addressed is how Theravāda interprets the process of choosing between possibilities, deciding on a goal, and initiating goal-oriented action, without going against its central principle that all mental processes are governed by causes and conditions. Equally basic is the question of how Theravāda interprets the dynamics of volition in the context of *kamma.*

In the *Sutta* literature, perhaps the best-known statement where the term *cetanā* occurs is the definition of *kamma* given by the Buddha (A. III. 415). The Buddha begins by affirming that he declares *cetanā* to be *kamma* (*cetanāhaṁ bhikkhave kammaṁ vadāmi*). The next part of the definition explains why activity (*kamma*) of body, speech, and mind that carries moral values and produces karmic consequences is regarded as *cetanā.* The Buddha points out that exercising *cetanā,* a person performs *kamma* through body, speech, and mind (*cetayitvā kammaṁ karoti kāyena vācāya manasā*).[2] *Cetanā* is here related to a verb that signifies "to think" or "to intend".

The nuances of meaning assigned to the term *cetanā* affect the interpretation of the Buddha's definition of *kamma.* The question is whether Theravāda conceives of *cetanā* primarily as a cognitive function identified with intention, assessment of possibilities and choice of goals or as a factor of dynamic energy that produces goal-directed action in the organism. If cognitive processes of forming an intention and conative capacities of initiating action coalesce in *cetanā,* it becomes necessary to examine how these factors are synthesized in the Theravāda view of volition. From the perspective of Theravāda psychology, it is not possible to discover the nature of *cetanā* without penetrating the connections that *cetanā* has to *citta* and to *saṅkhāra. Citta* conveys Theravāda's holistic view of consciousness. *Saṅkhāra* has a wide range of meanings, but primarily signifies the "constructive activity" of consciousness, through which mental factors are brought together in such a way as to effectuate acts of body, speech, and mind.

The main primary sources for analyzing the import of *cetanā* as a psychological term are the first four *Nikāyas* of the *Sutta-piṭaka* (*Dīgha-nikāya, Majjhima-nikāya, Saṁyutta-nikāya,* and the *Aṅguttara-nikāya*), the *Dhammasaṅgaṇi,* the *Vibhaṅga,* the *Kathāvatthu*, the commentaries to these texts, and the *Visuddhimagga*. Of the texts of the *Khuddaka-nikāya*, the *Theragāthā*, the *Therīgāthā*, the *Sutta-nipāta*, the *Udāna*, the *Itivuttaka*, and the *Dhammapada* include poetry and statements that are regarded as accounts of the personal experiences of the earliest followers of the Buddha's teachings. These texts, therefore, offer an experiential dimension to the Theravāda view of the dynamics of volition. The *Milindapañha* contains an important definition of *cetanā* and discussions of the relationship between intention and act. The *Nettippakaraṇa* includes an analysis of the relationship between *kamma* and *cetanā*. These two texts are included in the *Khuddaka-nikāya* in Burma, though not in Sri Lanka. The *Vinaya-piṭaka* presents, in addition to detailed accounts of how monastic rules are to be applied, significant statements that bring into sharp focus the Theravāda position on the relationship between purposive thought or intention and act. In this work I use the term *Abhidhamma* to refer, not only to the *Abhidhamma* literature of the Theravāda tradition, but also, in a more general sense, to a system of thought based on the theory of *dhammas* and on a specific method of classifying physical and mental states. This method of classification reaches its fullest and most detailed exposition in the *Visuddhimagga*, the *Atthasālinī*, and the *Abhidhammattha-saṅgaha*, a manual that modern scholars maintain was probably composed between the tenth and early twelfth centuries.

The texts named above can be viewed as a unified whole in spite of the fact that they were composed over a long period of time. The reason for treating these texts as a single integral whole is that they fall within a single scholarly tradition named Theravāda. Collins has shown very convincingly in his article "On the very idea of the Pāli canon" that rather than equating the "Pāli canon" with "Early Buddhism" and regarding the Pāli canon as the textual basis for the development of the Theravāda school of Buddhism, we should see the Pāli canon as a product of the Theravāda school.

The Pāli canon also includes a large narrative literature consisting primarily of the *Jātaka* texts. The Theravāda tradition itself perceives a symbiotic relationship between the narrative literature and the scholarly tradition of the *Abhidhamma:* the cosmological speculations in the narrative literature and the stories relating to various dimensions of human experience have an impact on how students of *Abhidhamma* approach the psychological and ethical discussions in these scholarly texts; and the scholarly tradition, in turn, seeks the aid of the narratives for the communication of its psychological and ethical ideas to the general populace. I have not included the narrative sections of the Pāli canon in my investigation of *cetanā.* If I had started with the aim of describing the range of meanings ascribed to the term *cetanā* in general usage and the development of the term in the culture that developed in India and Sri Lanka during the period when the *Tipiṭaka* was composed, it would have been essential to address the narrative literature and the monastic tradition as presented in the *Vinaya-piṭaka.* However, my purpose is to focus more narrowly on philosophy and psychology, as these disciplines are understood in Theravāda. All references to "the Theravāda tradition" in this work, therefore, are limited primarily to the first four *Nikāyas*, the *Abhidhamma* texts, and the commentaries pertaining to them.

Tradition has it that the Pāli texts and the commentaries were brought to Sri Lanka during the reign of the Indian emperor Aśoka and preserved there orally. Although there is much controversy regarding the precise dates of Aśoka, it is generally agreed that he reigned during the middle of the third century B.C.E. According to the traditional account in the *Dīpavaṁsa* and the *Mahāvaṁsa*, the commentaries were translated into Sīhaḷa-bhāsā (the language of Sri Lanka) and enlarged by a line of Sri Lankan teachers, who added their own interpretations. During the reign of King Vaṭṭagāmaṇī Abhaya (between 29 and 17 B.C.E.), the decision was made that these texts and their commentaries should be written down.[3] The crux of the argument put forward by Collins is that there is no way of correctly gauging to what extent the collection of texts that was committed to writing in the first century B.C.E. would have resembled the Pāli canon as we have it today. Collins agrees with those who hold that the Pāli canon—as a closed list of scriptural texts—did not come into existence until the time of the great commentator Buddhaghosa (fifth century C.E.). Collins holds that in the first century B.C.E. the monks of the Mahāvihāra monastery in Sri Lanka decided to translate the Sīhaḷa commentaries into Pāli and to commit texts and commentaries to writing in the form of a single collection of Pāli texts so that they could hold on to their claim to be the sole custodians of Buddhism in Sri Lanka.

The argument put forward by Collins gives support to the method of approaching the texts of the Pāli canon as a single organic whole when interpreting any of the primary concepts of Theravāda. Nevertheless, it is important to keep in mind the approximate time periods in which different groups of texts were composed. Recent scholarship has challenged the generally accepted date of around 486 B.C.E. for the passing away of the Buddha. The revised dating of between 375 and 355 B.C.E. suggested by Heinz Bechert in his article "The Date of the Buddha Reconsidered" has been supported by Erdosy with archaeological data.[4] Both Bechert and Erdosy argue that the Buddhism that prevailed at the time of Aśoka was very similar to the Buddhism that developed immediately following the *parinibbāna* of the Buddha; therefore, they conclude that the dating of the Buddha's life must be revised to bring it closer to the reign of Aśoka. Since passages from Pāli texts are quoted in the Aśokan edicts, it is accepted that at least the core of what came to be the Pāli canon was well established at the time of Aśoka. Erdosy suggests that the Buddha was living and teaching at the time of the composition of the earliest sections of the *Sutta-piṭaka* and the *Vinaya-piṭaka.* However, the late dating of the life of the Buddha by Bechert and

Erdosy remains controversial, and this issue cannot be settled until more work is done on the early period of the history of South Asia.

The *Sutta-piṭaka* was passed down orally by *bhāṇakas* ("reciters") who specialized in individual *Nikāyas*. Von Hinüber points out that the first four *Nikāyas* of the *Sutta-piṭaka* reflect a cultural environment significantly earlier than that of the *Vinaya-piṭaka*. However, he goes on to say that not much success has been achieved in separating earlier and later layers in the *Sutta* literature.[5] The earliest section of the *Vinaya-piṭaka* consists of the main monastic rules, which were probably drawn up during the Buddha's life or very soon after his *parinibbāna*. Most of the *Vinaya-piṭaka* was completed before it was brought to Sri Lanka in the time of Aśoka (about 250 B.C.E.). It is generally agreed that the books of the *Abhidhamma-piṭaka* grew out of tabulated summaries (*mātikās*) of the main topics of what came to be accepted as the Buddha's teachings. A large part of the *Dhammasaṅgaṇi*, the earliest of the *Abhidhamma* texts, was probably available at the time of the third council, which was held during the time of Aśoka, according to accounts given in the Theravāda tradition.[6] Since the *Dhammasaṅgaṇi* already classifies mental states precisely and extensively, distinguishing them into categories of "wholesome" (*kusala*), "unwholesome" (*akusala*), and "ethically indeterminate"(*avyākata*), the dating of this text is important for understanding the development of the psychological categories of the *Abhidhamma* system.

According to von Hinüber, Buddhaghosa's dates are no earlier than 370 C.E. and no later than 450 C.E.[7] Modern scholarship agrees with the Theravāda tradition that the Pāli commentaries to the first four *Nikāyas* were composed by Buddhaghosa, together with the *Visuddhimagga*.[8] Though the tradition also attributes the authorship of the commentary to the *Vinaya*, called the *Samantapāsādikā*, and the *Atthasālinī* to Buddhaghosa, there is reason to doubt that the former was composed by him.[9] Modern scholars are generally of the opinion that Buddhaghosa was the "initiator" but not the actual author of the *Atthasālinī.*[10] In several passages of his own commentaries, Buddhaghosa refers to older Sīhaḷa commentaries as well as to the opinions of earlier teachers. He saw his work as a commentator, not solely as an individual endeavour, but as his participation in the monastic community's shared task of preserving and passing down the tradition.

This brief survey indicates that the primary sources for an investigation of the connotations of *cetanā* were composed during a time-span of nearly a thousand years. However, throughout that period the Theravāda tradition tried to preserve its own coherence and consistency. Theravādins perceive the *Suttas* as the source of inspiration for the development of their tradition and as the fundamental point of reference to which the composers of the later Theravāda texts continually returned. The *Abhidhamma* is seen as the explication and elaboration of what is implicitly contained in the Pāli *Suttas*. The tradition maintains that the commentators preserve a consistent line of interpretation. Furthermore, the Theravāda tradition is unified by a firm adherence to the causal theory of conditioned origination (*paṭicca-samuppāda*) throughout its history. Though the main themes of the *Suttas* are elaborated in precise detail, enlarged, and interpreted in the *Abhidhamma* and the commentarial literature, since this development takes place within the boundaries of the theory of conditioned origination, Theravāda remains a unified whole.

Following the Theravāda way of approaching the Pāli texts as a single whole, in seeking to draw out the connotations of a given psychological term, I have depended on the method of juxtaposing and comparing various passages in which that term appears. This method of studying how the term is utilized in different textual contexts should lead to an understanding of the semantic range of the term. At the same time, this procedure of comparing passages in which the psychological term occurs should reveal the nuances of meaning that the term acquired in relation to various discussions regarding mental processes that are contained in the Pāli texts. Discussions related to the description and analysis of the mental processes that constitute consciousness continued to preoccupy the Theravāda tradition throughout the period in which the Pāli texts were composed. This procedure of investigation is modelled after the method that Rune Johansson puts forward in two of his works: "*Citta, Mano* and *Viññāṇa*—A Psychosemantic Investigation" and *The Dynamic Psychology of Early Buddhism.* However, whereas Johansson rarely refers to the *Abhidhamma* texts or the commentarial literature but bases his inferences primarily on a comparison of passages in the *Suttas*, the procedure in this work is to see how the later texts approach and interpret the psychological concepts introduced in the *Suttas*. My primary concern has been to reflect on psychological terms such as *citta*, *cetanā*, and *saṅkhāra* as they occur in the texts and to allow the meaning of a term to emerge by setting up dialogues, as it were, between different passages where the term occurs. In the same manner, I perceive an on-going dialogue between the psychological issues raised by modern scholars of Theravāda and the psychological concepts delineated in the Pāli texts. In order to examine the interpretation that modern scholars give to passages in the *Suttas* where *cetanā*, *citta*, or *saṅkhāra* occur, I have compared their interpretations with the explanations of these same passages given in the *Abhidhamma* texts and in the commentaries.

I take *cetanā* to be a "psychological" term in the Theravāda tradition. This approach to *cetanā* implies that the Theravādins had well-formulated theories about the nature of consciousness and that they saw *cetanā* as a mental factor with distinctive characteristics, functioning in a specific manner in the continuum of consciousness. Moreover, from a Theravāda perspective, "psychological" implies data that can be observed through the techniques of "mindfully" observing one's own physical and mental states. The Theravāda tradition holds that skill in the observation of mental states grows with practice, but Theravāda does not claim that the entire contents of the mind are observable or that the observations are always accurate. It should be added that the texts show that those who developed and practised these techniques of observation were critically aware that the world-view and the state of mind of the subject condition the process of observation and the data so obtained. The Buddha, his disciples, and later *Abhidhamma* teachers developed their psychological concepts on the basis of the watchful attention they gave to the mental development of the novices placed in their care and their observation of the behaviour of many types of people who came to them for counsel.

In order to elucidate the meaning of key psychological concepts in Theravāda, I have discussed parallel concepts in the *Upaniṣads*, in two texts of the Yoga tradition, namely the *Yoga-sūtra* and the *Vyāsa-bhāṣya*, and in some early Jaina texts. None of these texts can be dated precisely. However, most of them fall within the time period when the texts of the Pāli Canon and their commentaries were being composed. Though the earliest of the principal *Upaniṣads* can be assigned to the period between the seventh and the sixth centuries B.C.E., these texts were composed over a long period of time, and the latest of them were not completed until the beginning of the Common Era.[11] The *Yoga-sūtra* of Patañjali in its present form is assigned to the second or third century C.E., and its earliest available commentary, the *Vyāsa-bhāṣya*, is placed in the period between the fifth and sixth centuries C.E.[12] It is generally agreed that the Jaina tradition developed from the groups of ascetics known in the *Suttas* as the *Nigaṇṭhas*. Nātaputta, who is mentioned in the *Suttas* as the preeminent *Nigaṇṭha* teacher is none other than the Jaina Tīrthaṅkara, Vardhamāna Mahāvīra. The first text that systematizes the Jaina teachings into a philosophical system is the *Tattvārtha-sūtra*, which was composed in the period between 150 C.E. and 350 C.E.[13]

Comments on *cetanā* in the *Abhidharmakośa-bhāṣya* (fifth century C.E.) are also very helpful in interpreting its functions as a mental factor. Since the *Abhidharmakośa-bhāṣya* was composed under the strong influence of the non-Mahāyāna Sarvāstivāda-Vaibhāṣika School, the Sarvāstivāda classification of mental states was incorporated into this text.[14] All the early schools of Buddhism that possessed an *Abhidharma* gave much importance to the classification of mental states.[15] In those passages of the *Abhidharmakośa-bhāṣya* where *cetanā* is defined and described as an observable mental state, there is no specific reference to the distinctive doctrines of Sarvāstivāda or to the Idealist views of Yogācāra. Comparison with the description of *cetanā* in the *Abhidharmakośa-bhāṣya* is helpful in elucidating how the relationship of *cetanā* to the cognitive processes of the *citta* and to the dynamic processes of *saṅkhāras* is conceived in the Theravāda *Abhidhamma.* There are obvious problems of scholarship in selecting a few texts outside the Theravāda tradition for a comparative study of psychological concepts, while ignoring other texts. Nevertheless, it is equally problematic to discuss the Theravāda tradition as if it were an isolated entity and make no acknowledgement of the rich cultural landscape in which it was nurtured in its formative period.

Approaches to the Concept of Volition in Modern Theravāda Scholarship

The pioneering work of C.A.F. Rhys Davids in Buddhist psychology is often forgotten. The attention of scholars has been concentrated, almost exclusively, on her controversial interpretation of the Theravāda notion of the absence of a permanent and separate self (*anattā*). The great care that she devoted to the study of psychological concepts in Theravāda is evident in her translation of the *Dhammasaṅgaṇi*, entitled *A Buddhist Manual of Psychological Ethics.* This work, which was published as early as 1900, contains a long introductory essay and valuable notes in which some key psychological terms of Theravāda are discussed in detail. C.A.F. Rhys Davids focuses on two points with regard to the concept of volition in Theravāda Buddhism: first, she distinguishes between Pāli terms that indicate motivation that is not ethically loaded and those terms that signify morally reprehensible dynamic desire; and second, she stresses that conditioned origination precludes the concept of an autonomous and controlling "will".[16]

In her article "On the Will in Buddhism", published in 1898, C.A.F. Rhys Davids argues that Buddhism has often been misinterpreted as a pessimistic doctrine that aims at suppressing all forms of willing. According to her, the reason for such misinterpretation is that translators have used the same words to translate those Pāli terms that signify the basic motivational capacity of the organism to initiate goal-oriented endeavour and those terms that express morally reprehensible craving. For example, she notes that the Pāli texts employ the term *viriya* and its synonyms to express dynamism that is not in itself morally qualified, but can be directed towards goals that may be either morally good or morally evil. Such terms, she says, express ardent striving, zealous endeavour, sustained effort, and persistent aspiration. She maintains that when the texts want to indicate the resolve to act that is characterized by moral values (in contrast to basic motivation that initiates action without carrying moral values), they either employ distinctive, morally weighted terms or they qualify a term signifying simple conation in such a manner as to make it a carrier of moral values. She points out, for example, that the morally neutral conative function indicated by *chanda* (desire to act) becomes *chanda-rāga* when the texts seek to convey morally reprehensible sensual passion. Furthermore, C.A.F. Rhys Davids shows that the Pāli texts are filled with terms indicating goal-oriented aspiration, especially in contexts where the Buddhist disciplines leading to liberation from sorrow are elucidated. She maintains that a preeminent feature of Buddhist ethics is that far from suppressing volition and desire to act, it regards the cultivation of these mental functions to be absolutely necessary for any progress towards the achievement of the goals that it upholds in its teachings.

It is significant that the term she prefers to translate as "desire" is the morally neutral *chanda* (defined as desire to act, *kattukāmatā*, at Vsm. XIV. 150), and not the morally reprehensible *taṇhā* (which she renders as "craving" or "thirst").[17] *Chanda*, according to the *Abhidhamma* method of classification, is a term signifying the basic impetus to act that can be directed either towards worldly objects of sensual pleasure (*kāma-chanda*) or towards the training that leads to liberation from sorrow (*dhamma-chanda*). C.A.F. Rhys Davids argues that desire in the sense of an impetus to act that is energized by emotions such as enthusiasm or zeal should be distinguished from desire in the sense of unwholesome greed for objects. In her article "On the Will in Buddhism" she notes that the *Suttas* and *Abhidhamma* texts abound in terms like *ussāha*, *tulanā*, and *padhāna* (which she translates, respectively, as "zeal", "pondering", and "struggle"). These terms convey not only energetic effort, but also heart-felt motivation, courageous persistence, and enthusiasm.

By translating *chanda* as "desire", C.A.F. Rhys Davids challenges what she perceives as a tendency among translators of her time to pick a psychological term that denotes just basic impetus to act and employ it to render a range of Pāli terms that signify morally blameworthy mental states. She provides lists of translated terms to prove that the single English word "desire" is used to translate as many as seventeen Pāli terms, all of which convey, not desire in the sense of wish to act in a particular manner, but morally reprehensible obsessive desire.[18] Her contention is that since the unqualified term *chanda* signifies desire in the sense of wish to act (*kattukāmatā*), it should be distinguished from terms indicating unwholesome (*akusala*) greed or lust.

In highlighting the distinction between terms that are meant to indicate morally neutral goal-oriented dynamism and those that point to morally reprehensible states, C.A.F. Rhys Davids, in fact, is drawing attention to the remarkable care and precision with which mental states are classified, analyzed, and defined in the *Abhidhamma* system. In her Introductory Essay and notes to her translation of the *Dhammasaṅgaṇi*, in her valuable editorial comments to S.Z. Aung's translation of the *Abhidhammattha-saṅgaha*, and in her *The Birth of Indian Psychology and Its Development in Buddhism*, she not only makes the reader aware of why she chooses certain English equivalents for Pāli terms, but she also alludes to fascinating discussions regarding the translation of Pāli terms between herself and Burmese *Abhidhamma* scholars of that time. *Cetanā* was evidently one of the terms that were discussed at length.

In *The Birth of Indian Psychology and Its Development in Buddhism*, C.A.F. Rhys Davids presents her own perspective on the Theravāda concept of will. The thrust of her argument is that whereas the essence of Theravāda practice is the application of will in the quest for the full development of human potential, the Theravāda system of thought has neither a fully developed concept of will nor a noun and verb that are the exact equivalents of "will" and "to will". She adds that she had not found another scholar who agreed with her that Buddhism is a "gospel of Will" that is vigorously upheld in a situation where there is no adequate term for will.[19] However, in some of her works[20] C.A.F. Rhys Davids expresses her conviction that the Buddha saw in *Dhamma* a volitional energy profoundly at work in the hearts of human beings, urging them towards an ideal of moral perfection. Her interpretation of *Dhamma* comes close to the concept of a will that has the inherent power to transform and govern all aspects of the human mind.[21]

It becomes clear in *The Birth of Indian Psychology and Its Development in Buddhism* that the way she defines will includes three criteria, none of which she finds in the semantic range of the psychological terms of Theravāda. First and foremost, she conceives of will as the arousal of the entire personality and the orientation of the whole self towards a goal. She believes will to be fundamental to a person, functioning as energy expressive of a person's very nature, whether that person is ignorant or enlightened. In her judgement, terms such as *viriya* and *padhāna* (which she renders as "energy" and "concentrated effort") do not signify a fundamental, self-expressive ability to initiate action, but only indicate modes of exerting the capacity to motivate action.

The second criterion implicit in the definition of will that C.A.F. Rhys Davids puts forward is that volition must be an autonomous capacity: it cannot be either a correlate of emotion or a subordinate expression of discursive thought. In her opinion, the mind's purposive deliberation does not guide the functioning of the will, but rather follows volition and expresses what the will has already chosen to do. She says that the "idea" of the goal that arises in a person's mind, in fact, is a purpose or plan that gives intellectual shape to what a person wills. She maintains that in the *Upaniṣads* and in the Pāli *Suttas*, she encountered only "mixed terms" expressing the blending of volition with coefficients of cognition or emotion or both, but could not find a term that precisely expresses what one is and what one chooses to become. She perceives will as energy that emerges from the very core of one's being and manifests itself as the capacity to choose one's mode of development. The third criterion implicit in her argument is that "will", by definition, signifies a "self-directing". She maintains that there can be no fully-developed concept of will in Buddhism because there is no concept of a self that is the agent of intention and action. She concludes that there can be no adequate concept of "will" when there is no idea of a "willer".[22]

This criticism of the Theravāda approach to the concept of will put forward by C.A.F. Rhys Davids cannot be countered by looking for loopholes in her argument. The discussion has to be reopened by starting with different premises and a different definition of will than what she puts forward. She maintains that the will must be regarded as capable of sustaining itself and as fundamental to the personality. Because of its teaching of conditioned origination, Theravāda cannot posit an autonomous will endowed with the inherent capacity to initiate action in the organism, to control bodily processes, and to transform mental states. Furthermore, she conceives of the will as a fundamental, self-initiating energy that can be clearly demarcated from emotional and cognitive coefficients. Theravāda posits the interdependence of the five aggregates[23] that comprise the physical and mental processes of the human organism. As a consequence, Theravāda cannot accommodate the concept of a "will" that is an autonomous capacity functioning without cognitive and emotive admixture. Those who disagree with C.A.F. Rhys Davids maintain that while Theravāda does not posit a central self or an autonomous will, it succeeds in demonstrating that there are factors of consciousness that initiate action and give direction to the personality, though they function within the limits of conditioned origination. In the *Atthasālinī* and the *Visuddhimagga*, *cetanā* is defined as the leader among the conditioned mental factors that produce goal-directed action (Asl. 111-112; Vsm. XIV.135).

Writing nearly twenty years after C.A.F. Rhys Davids ended the main part of her work, H.V. Guenther interprets *cetanā* to be the primary motivational drive in the mind. Guenther presents his definitions of the terms "drive", "motive", and "volition" in his work *Philosophy and Psychology in the Abhidharma*, first published in 1957. These definitions occur in the course of his analysis of the definition of *cetanā* given in the *Atthasālinī* (Asl. 111). He maintains that *cetanā* should be viewed, not as "volition", but as a "drive". He goes on to explain that a drive is to be defined as a stimulus that causes persistent activity in several parts of the organism, and that a motive is to be conceived as a stimulus that supports activity until the stimulating impetus is brought to cessation. According to

Guenther, then, the distinctive characteristic of motivation is the capacity to arouse activity in different areas of the body and mind simultaneously, and to impel that activity towards a goal. In contrast with the two terms "drive" and "stimulus", "volition" is defined by Guenther as the cognitive process of deliberating and deciding upon a course of action. Guenther interprets volition to be a process that arrives at a choice or makes a decision but rarely exhibits the capacity to initiate action in order to make that choice effective.

In Guenther's view, stimulus, drive, and motivation, in contradistinction to volition, are aspects of the capacity to initiate action. According to Guenther, motivation derives its power, not from any preceding cognitive process of making a choice, but from its invariable association with "emotional tensions".[24] He describes emotional tension as the condition that arises when there is an interaction between feelings, which assign specific values to physical and mental states, and the bodily changes in muscles and organs that correspond to these feelings. He describes strong motivations as those that are aroused by stimuli that are associated with strong emotional tensions and are capable of generating a broad spectrum of actions in the organism.

Guenther's strongly stated unambiguous analysis is helpful because it draws attention to two key issues that should be kept in mind when applying modern theories of motivation to the interpretation of Theravāda. The first relates to the separation that Guenther makes (especially in his definitions of "volition" and "drive") between the cognitive processes by which decisions are made and the conative functions by which goal-oriented actions are initiated. The cardinal teaching of Theravāda, however, is the interrelatedness of all physical and mental states, which implies mutual conditioning and interdependence among the cognitive process of purposive thought, the motivating drive of the emotions, and the mind's capacity to initiate action. The second issue relates to Guenther's reluctance to ascribe motivational capacity to cognitive factors. Theravāda, however, clearly endows some cognitive processes with the capacity to initiate action. For example, Theravāda assigns a leading role to the cognitive factors of right understanding (*sammā-diṭṭhi*), mindfulness (*sati*) and wisdom (*paññā*) in the motivational processes of the Eightfold Path[25].

Another approach to the Theravāda view of volition is found in Rune Johansson's interpretation of psychological concepts in the *Suttas*. In *The Dynamic Psychology of Early Buddhism*,[26] Johansson defines motivation in terms of "needs" that manifest themselves as "homeostatic deficiencies" in different parts of the body. He reduces all forms of motivation to "needs" occurring in different facets of life. He maintains that even intellectual and aesthetic needs can be traced to a physiological basis, although he does note that these types of needs are formed through complex processes of learning and conditioning. When Johansson distinguishes between motivation and volition, he defines the latter as "will power", by which he means the special rigorous effort put forth to fulfil a need under difficult circumstances. In his view, volition is nothing more than the intensification of motivational endeavour, and there can be no deployment of "will" without the experience of a want. In applying his theory of motivational needs to Theravāda, he acknowledges the Theravāda position that no physical or mental state can claim primacy since all factors in the organism are interdependent. Nevertheless, though he agrees that in the Theravāda view all mental and physical states are mutually conditioning factors, his interpretation of the Theravāda concept of volition is finally influenced by his conviction that certain factors that have the status of "needs" override other mental states and claim the primary role in governing motivation.

Johansson's comment on the "enumerations" or lists of motives in the *Sutta* texts[27] is significant for the light that it sheds on the Theravāda approach to the dynamics of volition. Johansson stresses that these lists do not distinguish between cognitive, emotive, and dynamic terms as modern schools of psychology do. He points out that the lists include these motivational factors: delusion (*moha*), understanding (*paññā*), and faith (*saddhā*), which can be regarded as cognitive terms, as well as fear (*bhaya*), shame in doing wrong (*hiri*), and fear of the consequences of committing evil deeds (*ottappa*), which can be classified as emotive terms. These cognitive and emotive terms are juxtaposed with dynamic terms, such as greed (*lobha*), wish to act (*chanda*), passion (*rāga*), and energy (*viriya*), which are regarded as motivational factors in modern systems of psychology. Furthermore, the *Sutta* lists include terms such as systematic attention (*yoniso-manasikāra*) and rightly directed mind (*sammā-paṇihitaṁ cittam*), which concern method of acting rather than motivation to act. According to Johansson, this overlapping of cognitive, emotive, and dynamic factors shows that in Theravāda psychology, all mental processes are considered to be capable of motivating action to a greater or lesser degree. He concludes that Theravāda does not accept the notion of a "tragic conflict" between emotion-charged drives that impel the organism to act and cognitive factors that form intentions, but are incapable of initiating action. Here Johansson takes the position that Theravāda Buddhism, far from separating the cognitive, emotional, and dynamic aspects of experience, actually attributes a capacity to initiate action to obviously cognitive factors. However, as he proceeds with his discussion, he reverts to his position that Theravāda consistently finds the primary basis for the arising of motivation in the overriding urgency of experienced needs.

According to Johansson, Theravāda holds that in an actual motivational situation, the personality is impelled by a need that becomes more urgent than other needs. He holds that other factors, including processes of reflective thought, then take the subordinate role of reinforcing that primary need. For example, he perceives *vitakka* (thought, reflection, application of the mind) to be a "needful" activity that serves to buttress the capacity to initiate goal-directed action. Johansson seems to disregard the argument that in Theravāda, processes of reflection and cognitive determination are regarded as factors that can assess, evaluate, and control motivational needs, especially through training in mindfulness and understanding. If mental processes are ultimately subordinated to "needs", it is difficult to see how cognitive functions can be trained to mindfully contemplate all motivational needs (both mental and physical, both wholesome and unwholesome) and to look upon them as transitory, devoid of autonomous selfhood, and liable to produce sorrow. In support of his interpretation, Johansson refers to a passage in the *Aṅguttara-nikāya* (A. I. 264-265) where the following two opposed motivational situations are described: in one situation, a person hankers after previously enjoyed objects; in the second, a person understands the harmful consequences of such pursuits and refrains from them. According to Johansson's interpretation of this passage, thought and understanding (*paññā*) cannot directly counter a harmful desire. Understanding can only play a role in motivation by evoking a "counter-desire", presumably, the desire to avoid painful consequences. Johansson maintains that it is by virtue of the capacity to find and support a counter-desire that cognitive factors acquire the capacity to neutralize the initial harmful desire. Johansson adds that once the counter-desire begins to exert its neutralizing capacity, wise understanding can "strengthen the counterforce" by consciously analyzing and repeatedly recollecting the sorrowful consequences of the harmful desire.[28]

When Johansson maintains that Theravāda explains motivation primarily in terms of desires and counter-desires, he underrates the role that Theravāda assigns to cognitive factors, such as systematic attention (*yoniso-manasikāra*), thought, deliberation (*vitakka*, *vicāra*), and mindful observation (*sati*), in the processes of forming and implementing intentions. Mindfulness and systematic attention are regarded as techniques that can be cultivated in such a way that they become capable of evaluating and choosing between needs. According to Theravāda, it is through the evaluation and renouncing of all needs and counter-needs that the *arahant* ultimately attains liberation from sorrow.

The interpretation of the Sri Lankan scholar Padmasiri de Silva differs from that of both Guenther and Johansson. He approaches the psychological concepts of Theravāda from the psychological perspectives put forward by Freud. In his work *An Introduction to Buddhist Psychology*, published in 1979,[29] de Silva defines motivation broadly as a cycle that covers three aspects of behaviour: mental factors that motivate behaviour, the behaviour motivated by mental factors, and the goals towards which such behaviour is directed. He shares Johansson's view that terms like "motive", "drive", and "want" connote some physiologically based condition of deficiency that initiates action in the organism. However, he is more firm and consistent than Johansson in maintaining that in the Theravāda view, cognitive processes that form purposes and action-initiating processes that implement purposes become fused in forming motives.

Though Padmasiri de Silva maintains that Theravāda conceives of the personality as a dynamic unity, he accepts that the "tripartite division" of the mind into cognitive, dynamic, and affective aspects can provide a conceptual structure for analyzing the Theravāda interpretations of complex mental processes. For the sake of such analysis, he correlates the aggregate of feeling (*vedanākkhandha*) with the affective aspect of experience, the aggregate that assembles mental resources and "constructs" goal-oriented activities (*saṅkhārakkhandha*) with the dynamic aspect of the mind, and the two aggregates of perception and cognition (*saññākkhandha* and *viññāṇakkhandha*) with the cognitive aspect. At the same time, he insists that the interpenetration of the three dimensions of experience is a pivotal concept in Theravāda. Since he holds that the four mental aggregates (feeling, perception, the constructive activities of the mind, and cognitive awareness) are present in all mental experiences, he argues that a process of volition does not function separately, but acts in collaboration with all other mental processes.[30] Unfortunately, de Silva does not offer a definition of volition. In fact, he maintains that "will" is a "semantically troublesome" term, and he concludes that its vagueness makes it inapplicable in interpreting the more minutely analyzed and diversely classified Buddhist terms. Here he echoes the sentiments of Guenther, who maintains that the term "volition" should be discarded forthwith since it masks much confusion. However, de Silva does use the term "volition" while discussing the nature and function of *saṅkhāra.* In this context he assigns to "will" the specific function of "deliberation" or purposive thought. Thus, de Silva distinguishes volition from motivation by defining volition as a thought process applied in deciding on a goal and motivation as "dynamism" manifesting itself in the capacity to initiate action to fulfil that goal. He maintains that both the cognitive features of volition, which manifest as purposive deliberation, and the dynamic energy of motivation become fused in the processes of the *saṅkhārakkhandha.*

Yet another modern view of how Theravāda conceives of volition is seen in the work of Joanna Macy. Her approach to the psychological concepts in Theravāda is based on her innovative interpretation of the idea of conditioned origination. In her work *Mutual Causality in Buddhism and General Systems Theory: The Dharma of Natural Systems,*[31] first published in 1991, Joanna Macy develops her analysis of the dynamics of volition in Theravāda against the background of the central principles of general systems theory. By arguing that the causal principle of *paṭicca-samuppāda* (conditioned origination) signifies systems of causes and effects in mutually dependent relationships and by seeking to demonstrate that *paṭicca-samuppāda* repudiates a unidirectional, linear view of causality, she posits viable parallels between Theravāda Buddhism and general systems theory.[32]

Joanna Macy emphasizes that the general systems view interprets the personality to be a dynamic, open system that is in constant interaction with a personal world. As an open system, the personality receives a flow of information that it processes in the form of perceptions, thoughts, and volitions; and its internal structure constantly transforms, and is transformed by, that information.[33] Macy notes that the general systems view stresses the capacity of the organism to modify its own components in a manner that facilitates the adjustments that it makes to impacts from the environment. This view holds that it is not the information received from the environment that determines or makes changes to behaviour, but what happens to that information when it is processed by the mind. It is posited that behaviour is continually modified through interactions between the information that the mind receives and the changes that the mind itself undergoes as it assimilates and responds to that information.

In the context of the general systems view, Macy defines motivation as the quest of the organism for internal coherence and for meaning in relation to the environment. She points out that according to this view, cognition and motivation mutually generate, nourish, and support each other. By utilizing the gestalts and structures that it has previously developed, the mind strives towards meaning in its cognitions, and this cognitive quest for meaning affects the way a person decides to act. The volitional responses, in their turn, influence and transform both outward behaviour and the mental structures through which sensory data are sorted, sifted, and transformed to achieve personal meaning.[34] It follows that our actions not only affect the external circumstances of our lives, but they also put forth a "reflexive dynamic" so that they shape and mould the very personality structures that produced them. It is this idea that personality and willed action mutually produce each other that dominates Macy's interpretation of *kamma* in Theravāda.

Although Macy does not offer definitions of "will", "volition", and "intention", it becomes obvious from her discussion that in her view, *cetanā* signifies the interweaving of cognitive and motivational factors in the act of making a choice. She stresses the transformative effect that the process of deciding has on the cognitive factors that are making the decision, on the motivational factors that are implementing the decision, and on the emerging personality as a whole. She maintains that *cetanā* and etymologically related Pāli terms signify purposive thought functioning as a process of personal involvement with the environment. Macy concludes that since the mind's capacity to know and the mind's capacity to initiate goal-oriented action involve each other, an act of knowledge is a "transactional process" whereby the mind becomes morally responsible for its interactions with the environment. In other words, Macy's interpretation of mutual causality seeks to demonstrate that cognition is not a process that is devoid of moral values. If the mutual conditioning of cognition and volition is accepted, this implies that knowledge carries moral responsibility because what we know and how we know affect what goals we choose and how we implement action to attain those goals.

Furthermore, Joanna Macy makes the principle of mutual causality the basis of her interpretation of the Theravāda practice of developing insight (*vipassanā*) through the cultivation of mindfulness (*sati*). The idea of mutual causality enables her to deal with the question of how Theravāda can validate its position that the cognitive function of mindfully observing the processes of one's own body and mind can have the motivational capacity to effect changes in attitude and behaviour. She interprets insight meditation as a practice where one learns to direct attention, not to what we perceive, but to how we perceive things, so that there is a growing awareness of how volitions, feelings, and perceptions arise interdependently and influence each other. In her interpretation of the disciplines of mindfulness and insight, Macy acknowledges that even the practice of insight into conditioning cannot avoid being conditioned by the structures and habit patterns of the mind. Nevertheless, from the systems perspective, she emphasizes that the processes of insight (*vipassanā*) have a "recoil effect": they begin to exert their influence on those very structures of the mind from which they arose. Macy argues that though even the practice of insight into the processes of conditioning is conditioned by the concepts, emotions and motivational capacities that are present in the mind, nevertheless, the awareness of conditioning casts its enlightening influence on those very same concepts, emotions and motivational patterns. As a consequence, a dynamic exchange is set up between the increasing experiential awareness of conditioning and the volitional capacities of the mind. Macy concludes her argument by pointing out that gradually, when the insight into conditioning influences volition more strongly, patterns of behaviour towards others and towards the shared environment also begin to change. Through the practice of mindfulness, a person gains the "eye of wisdom" (*paññā-cakkhu*) and no longer sees the world through eyes of greed and hate.[35]

Macy's concept of mutual causality offers refreshing insights into the psychological concepts of Theravāda. At this juncture, however, it is necessary to look more closely at her interpretation of *paṭicca-samuppāda*. Macy refers to several passages in the Pāli texts that can be interpreted to signify the "reciprocity of causal factors" and the interdependence of causes and effects, like sheaves of reeds holding each other in place. Nevertheless, there are other passages, especially those describing motivational processes, where it seems that the configuration of factors that forms the motivating cause must be well in place before it can be followed, subsequently, by the behaviour that constitutes the effect. Johansson lays out, in the form of charts, narratives from the *Sutta* texts spelling out the specific events through which a person strives towards a goal.[36] These charts are meant to show that the stages by which behaviour is transformed follow each other as causes and effects in a unilinear temporal sequence. Whether these accounts of motivational processes are taken as descriptions or as prescriptions, the emphasis is not on the reciprocity of cause and effect but on the notion that when the causal conditions are well established, the effect follows in due course, as a manifestation of the principle of conditioned origination. Furthermore, Joanna Macy's use of the term "structures" in relation to mental processes requires further elucidation than she has offered. In the *Suttas* and *Abhidhamma*, *saṅkhāras* are not defined as structures, dispositions or habit patterns that somehow remain intact in the mind, in spite of change and conditioning. In the *Abhidhamma* method of classification and in the commentarial literature, *saṅkhāras* are described as conditioning and composing processes by which the mind brings together its resources in such a way that they produce goal-directed activities.

Some Modern Interpretations of *Cetanā*

The equivalents of *cetanā* found in modern works on Theravāda are "volition", "will", "motive" or "drive", and "intention". Unfortunately, it is not always clarified in these works why the author has chosen a particular term as the equivalent of *cetanā*. What is apparent, however, is that there is no consensus about the precise connotations of *cetanā*. The basic question that emerges is whether *cetanā* should be perceived primarily as a conative function with inherent dynamism and the capacity to initiate action, or as a cognitive function expressed as purposive intellection. Of the scholars discussed above, C.A.F. Rhys Davids interprets *cetanā* to be purposive thought, Guenther most emphatically declares *cetanā* to be a dynamic drive, and de Silva argues that although *cetanā* is primarily a cognitive function expressing purposive deliberation, it is linked with conative energy within the configuration of a mental disposition (*saṅkhāra*).

C.A.F. Rhys Davids gives a frank account of her own frustrations in seeking to probe the significance of *cetanā*. She says that "groping by etymology" in her early research, she found *cetanā* to be "too intellectual" to be equated with will.

Since *cetanā* is an action noun derived from the verb *ceteti* ("to think", "to intend"), she concluded that *cetanā* conveys purposive thought rather than the impetus to initiate action. She felt that *cetanā* should not be equated with "will" because she defined will as autonomous self-expressive dynamism. Nevertheless, in her translation of the *Dhammasaṅgaṇi,* entitled *A Buddhist Manual of Psychological Ethics* and first published in 1900, she translated *cetanā* as "volition" at the persuasion of Burmese *Abhidhamma* scholars. She came to feel very uncomfortable about having done so; and in *The Birth of Indian Psychology and Its Development in Buddhism,* she stresses her problems in rendering *cetanā* as "will" or "volition". Her conclusion is that *cetanā* is purposive thought preceding an act.[37] In this context, she turns to the Buddha's definition of *kamma,* where he says that *cetanā* is to be equated with *kamma* since a person performs action of body, speech, or mind after having engaged in a process of *cetanā* (*cetayitvā*) (A. III. 415). According to the interpretation that C.A.F. Rhys Davids gives, *cetayitvā* signifies the goal-oriented thinking that precedes and prepares the way for physical, verbal, or mental action.

Whereas C.A.F. Rhys Davids links *cetanā* with thought processes involved in making decisions, Guenther interprets *cetanā* to be a drive that puts forth goal-oriented action. His rendering of *cetanā* as "motive" or "drive" must be set in the context of his emphasis on the creative nature of the continuum of consciousness. He points out that Buddhism regards consciousness, not as a passive recipient of sensory impressions, but as that which is creative and capable of shaping the world in its own way.[38] In Guenther's interpretation, *cetanā* is the motivating impetus that stimulates the mind and impels it to act. Guenther's interpretation of the Buddha's statement "I regard *cetanā* as *kamma*" follows from the view that the mind is dynamic and creative. According to Guenther, *kamma* is a universal principle that displays itself in a rhythmic process that repeatedly "heaps up" energy and "develops" it towards the production of an effect that brings about the discharge of the accumulated energy. Following this line of argument, Guenther maintains that "*cetanā* and Karma are synonymous" since both terms denote the drive that keeps the individual bound to the rhythm of "accumulating" and releasing energy. In Guenther's view, motivating energy is accumulated in the form of dispositions and tendencies, and "released" in the form of acts. He regards *cetanā* as the "stimulus, motive, or drive" that brings about the release of energy in the form of acts.

Like C.A.F. Rhys Davids, Padmasiri de Silva regards *cetanā* as purposive deliberation, but he posits that *cetanā* is inseparably linked with conative dynamism within the complex configuration of a mental habit or disposition.[39] According to de Silva, within a mental disposition (*saṅkhāra*) the two following factors are fused together: "volition" (*cetanā*) that functions as purposive thought and "dynamism" (*abhisaṅkhāra*) that initiates action to make the purposive deliberation effective. Since he perceives mental disposition to be a complex function where goal-oriented thought (*cetanā*) and goal-effectuating dynamism are blended, he suggests that an appropriate rendering of *saṅkhāra* would be "directed disposition".

Similarly, David Kalupahana maintains that in Theravāda Buddhism mental dispositions are regarded as the basis of all volitional processes. In his work *Ethics in Early Buddhism*, which was published in 1995, Kalupahana argues that the Buddha's concept of will is in perfect accord with his teaching of the Middle Way.[40] According to Kalupahana's interpretation, the Buddha avoided the idea of an autonomous individual will, which is one extreme, as well as the notion that human persons have no power of choice and decision, which is the other extreme. The Middle Way posits that although there is no sovereign will, there are "tendencies" (*saṅkhāra*) in the personality that make it possible for a person to plan and initiate actions. Kalupahana maintains that the *saṅkhāras* can even chart a new course that triumphantly moves against (*paṭisotagāmī*) the present course taken by mental processes. He concludes that Theravāda rejects the notion of a single controlling energy that may be termed "will" and affirms the presence in the mind of a whole collection of dispositions that perform the function of directing action.

Kalupahana stresses that since these dispositions arise and gradually develop from the decisions and the behaviour of the past, they cannot be regarded as autonomous or self-generating. He maintains that the *Suttas* give the following "psychological explanation" of the three-way relationship conjoining decision-making (*cetanā*), mental dispositions (*saṅkhāra*), and intentional action (*kamma*) involving moral responsibility. Purposive thoughts and processes of decision-making generate actions; decisions and actions begin to form tendencies and dispositions that constitute the gradually shaped "character" of a person; and "character" becomes the basis of future decisions and future behaviour. This statement can be seen as Kalupahana's response to the declaration of C.A.F. Rhys Davids that the notion of "will" is meaningless when no "willer" is affirmed. According to Kalupahana, the gradually forming mental dispositions and tendencies constitute a "will", and acts are "willed" by dispositions that have been formed through previous conscious decisions, intentional acts, and chosen mode of life. Kalupahana holds that *cetanā* signifies an immediate intention or decision to act that emerges from a mental disposition.

By claiming that *saṅkhāras*, functioning as dispositions, enable a person to make choices and arrive at decisions, Kalupahana seeks to give an account of the Theravāda concept of volition that is entirely faithful to the principle of conditioned origination. Nevertheless, his interpretation of *saṅkhāra* as "disposition" or "tendency" and his concept of "will" as a configuration of dispositions are not without problems. Since dispositions are constituted of mental habits, they cannot transcend the processes of conditioning through which they have originated.

It is difficult to see how functions such as making difficult choices, controlling motives, and changing habitual behaviour can be performed by habits, dispositions, or tendencies. These functions require thought processes endowed with the capacity of assessing different possibilities and critically reflecting on alternative choices. Dispositions, by their very nature, repeat the habits of the past; left to themselves, they do not envision new ways of thought and behaviour.

Cetanā and the "Ethicization" of the Idea of *Kamma*

In *The Way to Nirvāṇa: Six Lectures on Ancient Buddhism as a Discipline of Salvation*, first published in 1917, La Vallée Poussin maintains that the Buddhist definition of *kamma*—according to which *kamma* comprises both volition (*cetanā*) itself and the acts of body, speech, and mind that stem from volition—signals a break from a purely ritualistic understanding of *kamma* and marks the attainment of a significant stage in the history of Indian thought.[41] This pronouncement by La Vallée Poussin needs to be qualified. The thrust of the teaching in the *Upaniṣads* is that knowledge of Brahman leads to liberation from the sorrow of rebirth, not the performance of great sacrifices that bring abundant karmic merit (B. U. I. 4.15; M.U. I. 2.8-10). Steven Collins explains that the process of the "ethicization" of the idea of *kamma* had already begun in the teachings of Yājñavalkya (B. U. IV. 4.5). According to his interpretation, Buddhism's contribution was to complete the "ethicization" by making volition or intention (*cetanā*), rather than solely the manifest act, the crucial causal factor in the process of *kamma*.[42] Winston King, James Paul McDermott, and Richard Gombrich have added their voices to the idea that the identification of *kamma* with *cetanā* brought about the ethicization of *kamma*.[43]

Gombrich goes much farther than King or McDermott in the claims that he makes for the process of ethicization in early Buddhism. According to Gombrich, the "great innovation" of the Buddha was the "internalization" of *kamma*, and this innovation was achieved by locating the moral quality of any act in the "intention" (*cetanā*) behind it.[44] Taking a sociological perspective, Gombrich argues that the Buddha's achievement was to replace the notion of specific sets of duties that differed from caste to caste with a "universal" criterion of right and wrong based on the moral quality of the intention (*cetanā*). Furthermore, Gombrich maintains that as a result of vesting ethical value in intention (*cetanā*), Theravāda emphasizes individual responsibility and regards "individual conscience" as the "final authority" in moral judgments. The above statement suggests that Gombrich regards "conscience" as a volitional agency in the individual mind that can control mental processes and function as the source of moral intentions. Gombrich's concept of individual conscience is close to the notion of will that C.A.F. Rhys Davids sought in Theravada Buddhism but failed to find. Since Theravāda Buddhism maintains that all aspects of the human personality are impermanent and conditioned, it leaves no room for the idea of a sovereign individual conscience that ultimately controls intention and behaviour. Gombrich himself points out that early Buddhism, like the other early religious traditions of India, gave great importance to education, training, and the influence of society, family, preceptors, and friends. The emphasis was on teaching moral values through training, rather than on invoking an autonomous conscience that functions as the inner guide.

It is evident that there is no consensus among modern scholars of Theravāda with regard to the concept of *cetanā*. C.A.F. Rhys Davids regards *cetanā* as purposive thought emerging from the cognitive processes of the continuum of consciousness (*citta).* Guenther defines *cetanā* as a conative drive that impels action. Kalupahana considers *cetanā* to be a present decision to act stemming from a disposition (*saṅkhāra*) or habit of mind that has been gradually developed. Macy regards *cetanā* as intention that arises from the mutual conditioning of cognitive processes and mental dispositions.

In this work it will be shown that though the Pāli texts do not regard *cetanā* as an autonomous controlling will, they do attribute to it the capacity to perform the following three functions: manifesting a purposive thought or intention, motivating action to implement that purpose, and directing purposive activity towards a chosen goal. *Cetanā* is conceived in Theravāda as a purposive impulse that arises within a specific state of mind (*citta*) and expresses the dominant cognitive perspectives and the emotional tensions that are present in the mind at the time of its arising. Coming into being as a purposive impulse or intention imbued with impetus, *cetanā* becomes the leading factor in the dynamic processes of the *saṅkhāras*. In this work, *saṅkhāras* are defined as the processes by which the required mental conditions are brought together in the continuum of consciousness to produce goal-oriented activities. *Cetanā* is conceived in Theravāda as a mental function that participates in both the cognitive and the dynamic dimensions of the continuum of consciousness. It is postulated that because *cetanā* is linked to the cognitive processes of the *citta* as well as to the motivational dynamism of the *saṅkhārakkhandha*, it is constituted of both purposive thought and motivating impetus. In the Theravāda view, *cetanā* becomes the linking function through which purpose becomes dynamic and motivation becomes purposive. Through the concept of *cetanā*, therefore, Theravāda avoids the notion of a rift between intention and action. Though unconditioned freedom of choice is not claimed in the *Suttas* and the *Abhidhamma*, Theravāda maintains that transformations in motivation and behaviour can be brought about through the mind's ability to observe its contents and become aware of the patterns of conditioning that operate in its processes.

Working Definitions of Key Terms

For purposes of clarification, I distinguish the two terms "intention" and "volition". In this work, the two terms "purposive thought" and "intention" are taken to be synonyms that signify the cognitive act of deciding to pursue a specific goal. Intention connotes purposive thought or aspiration; it indicates planning and an image of the future. Purposive thought implies the availability of alternatives and the focusing of attention on the chosen alternative. Emotional urges and discursive thought come together in an intention or purpose. However, an intention or purposive thought is not characterized by the impulse or impetus to initiate action; it can remain merely as an aspiration in the mind.

The term "volition" is used here to cover a much broader range of meaning than "intention" or "purpose". It connotes a complex function with three aspects: affirming a goal and intending to pursue it, initiating action for that purpose, and directing physical and mental activity towards that goal. Both "intention" and "volition" connote the orientation of the personality towards the future. Intention or purpose and volition cannot function without a goal and a "pull" that a mental picture of the future exerts on a person's present attitudes and behaviour. In addition to referring to a goal, the term "volition" indicates that the cognitive processes of purposive thought and conscious planning have the capacity to initiate goal-oriented action. "Volition" signifies that these cognitive functions of assessing possibilities and deciding on goals do not operate merely as subordinate aids of "drives" that are based on "needs", but have the dynamic energy to control and direct behaviour by reshaping attitudes, memories, and perspectives. Volition differs from intention or purposive thought in that it is endowed with the capacity to initiate action. In addition to the "pull" of a goal, volition is characterized by its own motivational impetus that "pushes" physical and mental processes towards that goal.

The distinction between "volition," "motivation," and "conation" is drawn in this work along the following lines. "Volition" indicates that cognitive processes, acting in conjunction with emotions, have a significant role in producing behaviour. The emphasis here is both on cognitive processes, such as appraisal of alternatives, choosing a purpose, and planning, as well as on the values that emotions place on objects. Volition occurs when physical and mental processes are directed towards a goal that is chosen through the interaction of cognitive and emotive processes. Volition, therefore, includes in its range of meaning both affirmation of a goal and the impetus to initiate action to attain that goal. I use the term "motivation" more narrowly to signify only the "push" to initiate action produced by the presence of specific factors in the mind. It will be shown in this work that Theravāda does not subscribe to the view that all motivation for action is ultimately based on a physiological or psychological "need". Mindfulness (*sati*), wise understanding (*paññā*) and systematic attention (*yoniso-manasikāra*) are described as motivating factors that become associated with the exertion of energy (*viriya*) and produce changes in behaviour. These factors of the Eightfold Path are described in the *Suttas* as motivating factors that ultimately bring about the assessment and renunciation of desires and psychological needs. I use the term "conation" in a general sense to indicate the basic capacity of conscious awareness to initiate action in the organism. "Conation" refers to mental activity without attributing ethical values to it.

I have not adopted a standard way of rendering *cetanā*. My purpose is to allow the connotations of the term to unfold from the texts. I have referred to *cetanā* as "goal-oriented impulse" or "purposive impulse", or "intention imbued with conative impetus" to show that Theravāda always links the functioning of *cetanā* both to the cognitive processes by which consciousness (*citta*) attends to objects, as well as to the impetus in consciousness to garner its resources and direct them towards goal-oriented activities (*saṅkhāra*).

ENDNOTES

[1] *sabbapāpassa akaraṇaṁ,*
kusalassa upasampadā,
sacittapariyodapanam,
etaṁ buddhāna sāsanam (Dhp. 183).

[2] In Pāli, the gerund usually signifies an action that precedes (*pubba kiriyā*) the action indicated by the main verb in the sentence (A.K.Warder, *Introduction to Pali,* 48). The second half of the Buddha's definition of *kamma,* therefore, may be translated as: "having intended, one performs action with body, speech, or mind". However, the rules of Saṁskṛt grammar specify that though the gerund more often connotes an action that precedes the action signified by the main verb, it can also convey an accompanying action (W.D.Whitney, *Sanskrit Grammar,* 354).

[3] K.R. Norman, *Pāli Literature,* 7-11.

[4] G. Erdorsy, "The Archaeology of Early Buddhism".

[5] O. von Hinüber, *A Handbook of Pāli Literature,* 25-26.

[6] K.R. Norman, *Pāli Literature,* 97.

[7] O. von Hinüber, *A Handbook of Pāli Literature,* 103.

[8] K.R. Norman, *Pāli Literature,* 122; O. von Hinüber, *A Handbook of Pāli Literature,* 102.

[9] O. von Hinüber, *A Handbook of Pāli Literature,* 104.

[10] K.R. Norman, *Pāli Literature,* 123-125; O. von Hinüber, *A Handbook of Pāli Literature,* 151.

[11] P. Olivelle, *Upaniṣads,* xxxvi-xxxvii.

[12] G. Feuerstein, *The Yoga-sūtra of Patañjali: An Exercise in the Methodology of Textual Analysis,* 26; I. Whicher, *The Integrity of the Yoga Darśana: A Reconsideration of Classical Yoga,* 320.

[13] W.J. Johnson, *Harmless Souls,* 46.

[14] A. Haldar, *Some Psychological Aspects of Early Buddhist Philosophy Based on Abhidharmakośa of Vasubandhu,* 9-14.

[15] A.K. Warder, *Indian Buddhism*, 220-223.

[16] C.A.F. Rhys Davids holds very strong opinions about what she calls "the Sakyan, or original 'Buddhist' teaching" (C.A.F. Rhys Davids, *The Birth of Indian Psychology and Its Development in Buddhism*, 43). She believes that the main teaching of the "original" Buddhism was the Way of Becoming (C.A.F. Rhys Davids, *Outlines of Buddhism : A Historical Sketch*, 18). According to her, whereas the *Upaniṣads* teach that the *ātman* is the eternal changeless Self, the Sakyan teaching is that the individual self is always growing into the "More" (*bhūyas*). She maintains that in the Buddha's teaching, the *Upaniṣadic* goal of eternal Being is replaced with the dynamic notion that the goal of living consists of becoming the "More" (Ibid., 21). She points out that the term *bhāvanā*, which signifies the cultivation of the mind through mindfulness and meditation, has the literal meaning of "making become".

C.A.F. Rhys Davids came to reject, as later additions made by the *Saṅgha*, those Buddhist doctrines that did not harmonize with her "original" Buddhism. She maintained that the concept of *anattā* and the analysis of the human being into five aggregates (*khandhas*) were later additions (C.A.F. Rhys Davids, *The Birth of Indian Psychology and Its Development in Buddhism*, 200-203). K.N. Jayatilleke voices the problems that critics have with the method of interpretation that they attribute to C.A.F. Rhys Davids (K.N. Jayatilleke, *Early Buddhist Theory of Knowledge*, 456). According to her critics, she makes certain assumptions about what she considers to be the "original" teachings of the Buddha, culls from the *Suttas* only what is in accordance with her assumptions, and rejects the rest as accretions resulting from the editing done by monks.

It is true that C.A.F. Rhys Davids is influenced by her theory of "original" Buddhism when she asserts that there is no concept of will in Theravāda. Nevertheless, her analysis of specific Pāli terms that carry psychological import, like *cetanā* and *saṅkappa*, is extensive and penetrating, and merits careful consideration. There are three aspects to her method of interpreting these terms. She places the terms in historical context by giving a detailed discussion of their occurrence in the *Upaniṣads*. She makes note of the Sāṁkhya and Yoga ideas in the *Upaniṣads* and discusses the impact of these ideas on terms like *citta*, *manas*, and *saṁkalpa*. In the introductory chapter of *The Birth of Indian Psychology and Its Development in Buddhism*, she points out the need for studies devoted to historical surveys of psychological concepts in the religious literature of India. The second aspect of her method is the discussion of some significant contexts in the Pāli texts where a specific psychological term occurs. Here, her vast knowledge of the *Sutta* and *Abhidhamma* literature gives weight to her interpretation. Finally, she looks for the etymological root of a word, to see if that throws light on its semantic range. She also refers to the meaning assigned to the term by other translators.

[17] C.A.F. Rhys Davids regards "desire" as a psychological term that signifies a blend of ideation and emotion, which is characterized by a persistent tension that compels the organism to act. Furthermore, she views desire as a mental function that can be directed either towards a morally good goal or towards a morally reprehensible one. For these reasons, she considers it appropriate to render *chanda* as "desire" (C.A.F. Rhys Davids, *The Birth of Indian Psychology and Its Development in Buddhism*, 278, 281).

[18] Her list of a number of Pāli terms translated as "desire" appears in *The Birth of Indian Psychology and Its Development in Buddhism* (p. 279) and in her article "On the Will in Buddhism". More recent interpreters of the Pāli tradition generally acknowledge the distinction between terms expressing basic conation and terms signifying volition with moral import. Rune Johansson, for example, classifies Pāli terms expressing moral values into three types: "negative terms" signifying unhealthy and morally bad motivations that lead to "bad" psychological and moral consequences; "positive terms" connoting psychologically healthy and morally "good" motivations; and "neutral terms" such as *saṅkappa*, *chanda*, and *icchā*, which he renders as "intention", "ambition", and "wish", respectively (R.E.A. Johansson, *The Dynamic Psychology of Early Buddhism*, 103-114). Neutral terms represent mental states that can be turned towards either morally good or morally blameworthy goals. The "neutral terms" in Johansson's classification coincide with what C.A.F. Rhys Davids calls terms indicating basic conation.

[19] C.A.F. Rhys Davids, *The Birth of Indian Psychology and Its Development in Buddhism*, 107, 278, 296.

[20] C.A.F. Rhys Davids, *Buddhism: Its Birth and Dispersal*, 85-86; C.A.F. Rhys Davids, *Outlines of Buddhism: A Historical Sketch*, 21.

[21] J.R. Carter, *Dhamma: Western Academic and Sinhalese Buddhist Interpretations*, 19-27, 172-173. The interpretation of *Dhamma* put forward by C.A.F. Rhys Davids is further developed by I. B. Horner. She maintains that *Dhamma* signifies "the will towards the highest, the right", in the teachings of the Buddha (I.B. Horner, *The Early Buddhist Theory of Man Perfected*, 48).

[22] C.A.F. Rhys Davids, *Outlines of Buddhism: A Historical Sketch*. 283, 297-298.

[23] The Theravāda position is that various physical and mental factors come together in accordance with the principle of *paṭicca samuppāda* (conditioned origination) and form the continuum that is designated as "individual personality". The human being is analyzed into five "groups" or "aggregates" (*khandhas*) of physical or mental processes: body (*rūpa*),

feelings (*vedanā*), perceptions and mental conceptions (*saññā*), constructive processes (*saṅkhāra*), and awareness leading to cognitive discernment (*viññāṇa*).

[24] H.V. Guenther, *Philosophy and Psychology in the Abhidharma*, 45-46.

[25] Theravāda teaches that craving (*taṇhā*) for physical and mental objects is the cause of sorrow (*dukkha*) and that craving can be overcome by cultivating the eight factors of the training that leads to liberation from sorrow. This Eightfold Path (*aṭṭhaṅgika-magga*) comprises right view (*sammā-diṭṭhi*), right resolve (*sammā-saṅkappa*), right speech (*sammā-vācā*), right bodily action (*sammā-kammanta*), right livelihood (*sammā-ājīva*), right effort (*sammā-vāyāma*), right mindfulness, (*sammā-sati*), and right concentration (*sammā-samādhi*). The first two aspects constitute wisdom (*paññā*), the next three comprise ethical discipline (*sīla*), and the final three bring about mental cultivation and concentration (*samādhi*).

[26] Johansson's interpretation of Theravāda revolves around two central themes that have aroused strong disagreement from other interpreters, for example, Peter Harvey (*The Selfless Mind: Personality, Consciousness and Nirvāṇa in Early Buddhism*, 81) and Sue Hamilton (*Identity and Experience: The Constitution of the Human Being According to Early Buddhism*, xxv-xxvi, 111). The first is his idea that Theravāda does not make a clear distinction between "material reality" and mental image. Johansson maintains that according to the Theravāda *Suttas*, the "objective world" is nothing but that which is experienced and "projected" by the mind in such a way that it is perceived as something external to the mind (R.E.A. Johansson, *The Dynamic Psychology of Early Byddhism*, 26-29, 85). Although Johansson emphasizes that "the Buddha was no idealist" (Ibid., 85), he seems to attribute to Theravāda an Idealist ontology, especially in his discussion of the Theravāda concept of *loka* (Ibid., 27-29). The second controversial theme is Johansson's interpretation of *citta* in the *Sutta* texts. He considers *citta* to be a profound dimension of consciousness that can separate itself from the aggregates and therefore can experience *nibbāna* (Ibid., 161-162). He also maintains that the *citta* of an *arahant* survives death (R.E.A. Johansson, *The Psychology of Nirvana*, 57-58).

Johansson's interpretation of motivation is influenced by his notion that Theravāda views the world as a "dynamic process" perpetually produced and purposefully "constructed" by our sensory perceptions, thought processes, and wishes. According to Johansson's interpretation, attraction (*rāga*) and aversion (*dvesa*) are the basis of motivational needs (R.E.A. Johansson, *The Dynamic Psychology of Early Buddhism*, 95-96, 104, 114-116). At the same time, motivational needs condition perception and the experiences through which a world (*loka*) is continually being constructed. With the growth of wisdom, motivations are reduced, the world-constructing activity ceases, and the *citta*, separating itself from the five aggregates, experiences *nibbāna*.

[27] Such enumerations of emotions and cognitive states that motivate a person, stage by stage, towards ethically good or ethically bad behaviour appear, for example, at A. IV. 353, V. 86-87, and D. III. 183.

[28] R.E.A. Johansson, *The Dynamic Psychology of Early Buddhism*, 208.

[29] Padmasiri de Silva's interpretation of Theravāda is set in the framework of Freudian psychology. His allegiance to Freud is most clearly seen in his explanation of *taṇhā*. He interprets *kāma-taṇhā*, *bhava-taṇhā*, and *vibhava-taṇhā* as craving for sensual pleasure, for self-preservation, and for annihilation. He takes these three forms of craving to be primary determinants of behaviour, comparable to the Freudian concept of drives. He correlates *kāma-taṇhā* with Freud's "pleasure" principle or libido, *bhava-taṇhā* with the instinct that strives for the preservation of the ego, and *vibhava-taṇhā* with the "death instinct" of Freud (*Buddhist and Freudian Psychology*, 172-178). In the case of *vibhava-taṇhā*, he says that though Theravāda does not posit a "death-wish", there are passages in the *Sutta* texts showing how aversion (*dosa*) and dormant hatred (*paṭighānusaya*) can exhibit as aggression towards oneself (*An Introduction to Buddhist Psychology*, 68-71). De Silva's Freudian bias is also seen in his interpretation of the concepts of *anusaya* and *āsava*. He sees in them evidence that Theravāda posits an unconscious dimension of the mind (P. de Silva, *Buddhist and Freudian Psychology*, 56-62; *An Introduction to Buddhist Psychology*, 72-75).

[30] P. de Silva, *An Introduction to Buddhist Psychology*, 18.

[31] Joanna Macy is well aware of the dangers of presenting Theravāda Buddhism as if it were an earlier form of general systems theory. She keeps in mind the vastly different cultural backgrounds of these two systems of thought, and she notes that their methods and goals are different. She seeks to develop a "reciprocal hermeneutic" by creating a dialogue between the perspectives of Theravāda Buddhism and general systems theory (J. Macy, *Mutual Causality in Buddhism and General Systems Theory: The Dharma of Natural Systems*, 19-20). Her aim is to utilize this reciprocal hermeneutic to enter more deeply into an analysis of the interdependence of causes and effects, which is the central subject of her study. She summarizes the "inherent characteristics" of a system as follows: any change in any part of the system will affect other parts of the system and the system as a whole; the system constantly stabilizes itself by reducing any deviation between goal and performance; the system will restructure itself by developing new patterns if it finds that previously established internal codes no longer function well; and the system is part of a larger whole with which it constantly interacts. Macy develops her reciprocal hermeneutic with reference to these four systemic features (Ibid., 76-77).

[32] The Theravāda theory of dependent origination (*paṭicca-samuppāda*) gives support to the idea that all physical and mental states are impermanent (*anicca*) and that they cannot claim a permanent essence or self. Dependent origination affirms that all physical and mental states arise through the coming together of the necessary causes and conditions. According to this causal theory, all the required conditions must come together to bring about the effect. No subset of conditions can claim to be sufficient; it is the coming together of all the conditions that produces the effect. Macy presents an impressive selection of references from the *Sutta* literature, the *Abhidhamma*, and the *Visuddhimagga* to substantiate her argument that *paṭicca-samuppāda* signifies the interdependence of cause and effect and not a temporal sequence of causes and effects (Ibid., 48-58). Perhaps the most important reference is to S. II. 113, where Sāriputta compares the relationship between *viññāṇa* as cause and *nāma-rūpa* as effect to two sheaves of reeds leaning on each other.

[33] Charles Tart explains the implications of a "systems approach" to the study of consciousness in his work *States of Consciousness.* A "systems approach" views consciousness, not as a conglomerate of disparate mental functions, but as a system of mutually dependent components. These components are regarded as interdependent factors that function together and constantly interact with constantly changing environments. For this reason, a systems approach emphasizes that any study of the components of consciousness is incomplete without a sense of the system as a whole engaging with the environment. Furthermore, the "systems approach" emphasizes that in order to understand consciousness as a systematic whole, it is necessary to give due regard to the environments in which it functions and the goals towards which it aspires.

[34] J. Macy, *Mutual Causality in Buddhism and General Systems Theory: The Dharma of Natural Systems,* 82-85, 93.

[35] Ibid., 136.

[36] R.E.A. Johansson, *The Dynamic Psychology of Early Buddhism,* 119, 136, 209, 211.

[37] C.A.F. Rhys Davids, *The Birth of Indian Psychology and Its Development in Buddhism,* 276.

[38] H.V. Guenther, *Philosophy and Psychology in the Abhidharma,* 41.

[39] P. de Silva, *Introduction to Buddhist Psychology,* 20, 78.

[40] In his *The Principles of Buddhist Psychology*, David Kalupahana argues that the Buddha was able to develop his thought in a radically different direction from the Indian traditions of his day because he made psychology the cornerstone of his philosophical enterprise. Kalupahana maintains that fruitful comparisons can be made between the radical empiricism of William James and the teachings of the Buddha. The thrust of his argument is that a psychological approach to philosophical reflections enabled the Buddha and William James to eschew not only substantialism and essentialism but also any theory of *a priori* forms and categories that resemble the "structures of knowledge" put forward by Immanuel Kant (D. Kalupahana, *The Principles of Buddhist Psychology*, 8-11).

The most significant problem that I see in Kalupahana's interpretation is his outright refusal to acknowledge that the cultural and religious setting into which the Buddha was born must have exerted some influence on his psychological views. The tone of Kalupahana's work gives the impression that he is casting the ancient teachings of the Buddha in the mould of modern radical empiricism.

[41] L. de La Vallée Poussin, *The Way to Nirvāṇa: Six Lectures on Ancient Buddhism as a Discipline of Salvation*, 70.

[42] S. Collins, *Selfless Persons: Imagery and Thought in Theravāda Buddhism*, 82, 201.

[43] J.P. McDermott, *Development in the Early Buddhist Concept of Kamma/Karma*, 27; W.L. King, *In the Hope of Nibbana: An Essay in Theravāda Buddhism*, 121; R.F. Gombrich, *Theravāda Buddhism*, 67.

[44] R.F. Gombrich. *Theravāda Buddhism*, 66-68.

Chapter I
Concept of Volition in the *Upaniṣads*

The *Sutta* literature portrays the region where the Buddha lived and taught as the rapidly developing homeland of a vibrant society shaped by several cultural trends. In many ways these cultural trends, such as the push to urbanization and the desire to preserve traditional agricultural societies, complemented and supported each other. However, they also became the source of rivalry and conflicts. The *Suttas* describe many world-views put forward by a variety of teachers and students, who came to be known as *śramaṇas* (Pāli: *samaṇa*). The Buddha and his followers formed one of the *samaṇa* communities. Though a distinction is made in the *Suttas* between the *brāhmaṇas* of the Vedic tradition and the *samaṇas* of the non-Vedic traditions, the *Upaniṣads*[1] and the *Sutta-piṭaka* were addressed to people who shared many ideas and ideals.

Both the *Upaniṣads* and the *Suttas* display a need to understand how the human personality is constituted and how the processes of the mind work. There are indications that terms connoting cognitive processes, emotions, and conative capacities are shared by both the Upanisadic and the Buddhist traditions, though the shades of meaning assigned to these terms are sometimes very different in the two traditions. In his article "Theravāda Buddhism and Bhahmanical Hinduism: Brahmanical Terms in a Buddhist Guise", K.R. Norman emphasises that many terms frequently used in the *Sutta-piṭaka* are related to the terminology of Brahmanical Hinduism. At the same time, he takes the position that the Buddha infuses these Brahmanical terms with new meaning by removing them from "a framework of ritualism" and giving them "a moral and ethical sense".[2] In the valuable introductory essays that precede some of the *Suttas* in *Dialogues of the Buddha,* T.W. Rhys Davids seeks to demonstrate that the Buddha adapted and reinterpreted some brahmanical teachings and practices in such a way as to fit in with his own ethical ideals.[3]

In this chapter the focus is on issues pertaining to the dynamics of volition that are of interest to both the Upaniṣadic and the Theravāda traditions. At the outset, it is important to note that both traditions affirm a holistic view of consciousness and perceive thought processes, emotional states, and motivational functions as experiences involving each other, rather than as separate strands within consciousness. In both traditions, *hṛd* (heart), *manas* (mind), and *citta* (continuum of consciousness) are terms that indicate consciousness developing as an organic whole. Both traditions set their ideas regarding the processes of volition in the context of *karma* and rebirth. It is sometimes contended that the Buddha "ethicized" the notion of *karma* by making the intention that motivates a specific act, rather than the act itself, the primary factor on which the moral quality of that act depends. This contention can be countered by showing that before the advent of the Buddha, the teachers of the *Upaniṣads* were profoundly concerned that their disciples should become aware of the moral quality of the diverse mental attitudes that generate intentions and instigate acts. These teachers stressed the relationship between mental attitude and action. Moreover, from a psychological perspective, both the Upaniṣadic and the Buddhist traditions display the need to distinguish between desire (*kāma, tṛṣṇā*), which they invariably look upon as a cause of sorrow, and intention or purposive thought that can serve either a morally good aim or a reprehensible one. In the Vedic tradition, *saṁkalpa* is a term that is developed and utilized to indicate resolute intention that can lead either to a morally good goal or to one that is blameworthy. *Kratu* is another term that signifies firmness of intention or strength of purpose. This chapter outlines the range of meaning of the two terms *saṁkalpa* and *kratu* and shows how they are distinguished from *kāma*.

The Possibility of Volitional Endeavour in the Realm of Ignorance and Rebirth

There are passages in the *Upaniṣads* that appear to deny freedom of choice to individuals caught up in day-to-day experiences. For example, the *Kauṣītaki Upaniṣad* declares that the Sovereign of the universe decides who will perform good acts that open up a blessed destiny and who will engage in evil that leads to suffering in a nether realm (Ks.U. III. 8). The *Maitrī Upaniṣad* compares a person bound by the deluded sense of an independent "I", who claims to be the possessor and controller of objects, to an ensnared bird (Mt.U. III. 2). Nevertheless, the main thrust of the Upaniṣadic teaching is that the human mind is capable of making morally good and beneficial choices and of exerting itself in seeking knowledge, precisely when it is still bound by ignorance and rebirth. The *Upaniṣads* state that without such volitional endeavour it is not possible to experience the *ātman* and to become freed from sorrow. For example, though Yājñavalkya defines the human being as "consisting of desires" (*kāmamaya*) in the *Bṛhadāraṇyaka Upaniṣad*, he urges his listeners to undertake the disciplines that will lead to knowledge of Brahman (B.U. IV. 4.22-23). The emphasis on the need to cultivate the disciplines of *yoga* is intensified in the *Kaṭha*, *Muṇḍaka*, *Śvetāśvatara*, and *Maitrī Upaniṣads*. It is clearly recognized in these *Upaniṣads* that the purification, quiescence and concentration of the mind require powerful and sustained application of one's volition. Yet, the call to make such volitional effort is addressed, not to adepts, but to disciples still struggling against the lure of earthly successes and heavenly rewards. Thus, the *Muṇḍaka Upaniṣad* stresses that austerity (*tapas*) and discipline are integral to the cultivation of *yoga* (M.U. I. 2.11), and it concludes that the goal can only be attained by one who strives (*yatate*) to cultivate the disciplines of *yoga*, not by one who is lacking in strength (M.U. III. 2.4). Similarly, the *Maitrī Upaniṣad* contains powerfully worded instructions for purifying and concentrating the mind (Mt.U. VI. 18-28).

The prevailing Upaniṣadic view, therefore, is that though the causal processes of *karma* apply universally, people still have the capacity, within the boundaries of *karma*, to reflect on the alternatives open to them, to choose their goals, and to initiate action to fulfil those goals. In order to communicate their practical teachings, the *Upaniṣads* utilize a range of terms that refer to diverse functions that they attribute to the mind. A basic feature of these terms is that they do not refer to mental functions as disparate factors or as clearly demarcated cognitive, emotive, and volitional faculties. Thoughts, emotions, perceptions, and motivational capacities are shown to be dynamic components unified in the mind.

The Dynamic Unity of the Mind and Its Components

In his work *The Origins of Indian Psychology*, Reat focuses on three terms that were utilized in the *Ṛgveda* to signify consciousness as a whole: *hṛd* (heart), *manas* (mind), and *citta* (thought, state of mind). These three terms are found also in the *Upaniṣads*, with *manas* occurring by far most frequently.[4] In the Pāli literature, *citta* becomes the preferred term to denote consciousness in a general sense, but *manas* frequently carries this meaning. The term "heart" (Pāli: *hadaya*), on the other hand, represents the originating and unifying centre of thoughts, of feelings, and especially, of powerful passions. The way these three terms are used attests to the fact that these early texts view consciousness as an undivided whole, despite their interest in distinguishing its various functions.

Hṛd (heart): the core of the personality

A passage in the *Aitareya Upaniṣad* reveals that the Upaniṣadic view follows the trend in the *Ṛgveda* to regard the "heart" as the centre of cognitive, conative, and emotive modes of experience, as well as of vitality (A.U. III. 1.2).[5] In this passage, *hṛd* and *manas* (mind) are regarded as synonymous, and the mind is said to be the home of cognitive functions ranging from basic conscious awareness and memory to inspired wisdom. The mind is also regarded as the basis of functions related to the voluntary initiation of action, which include impulse (*jūti*), intention (*saṁkalpa*), purpose (*kratu*), desire (*kāma*), and control (*vaśa*). *Saṁkalpa* and *kāma* have their parallels in the psychological vocabulary of Theravāda. The interesting term *kratu* is rarely seen outside the *Vedas* and *Upaniṣads*, but by straddling in its semantic range purposive thought and impetus to act, it points in the direction of *cetanā* in the *Suttas*. The rare term *jūti* is derived from a verb root that signifies "to press forward", "to impel", or "to incite", and it expresses excitation of the organism or application of energy (S.E.D. 424, col. 2). In her discussion of the *Aitareya* list of mental functions, C.A.F. Rhys Davids regards both *jūti* and *vaśa* as "purely volitional".[6] In the *Abhidhamma* system, *javana*, which is related to *jūti*, indicates a series of karmically active impulses that occur in cognitive processes. *Vaśa* signifies "will, wish, desire", as well as "authority, power, control, dominion" (S.E.D. 929, col. 2). It is rarely used in the *Upaniṣads* in the sense of exerting control over oneself. An exception is in a passage of the *Kaṭha Upaniṣad* (K.U. I. 3.4-6) where the faculties (*indriyāṇi*) of a person whose mind is unrestrained are said to be uncontrolled (*avaśyāni*), and the faculties of a person of sound understanding and restrained mind are described as *vaśyāni* (controlled).

Citta: the range of the mind

If the term *hṛd* indicates the inward centre of the mind in the Upaniṣadic view, *citta* refers to its spreading diameters. Reat explains that the verb root *cit-* and its derivatives in the *Ṛgveda* resemble the Buddhist concept of *citta* in that they both refer very broadly to consciousness as the home of all manner of mental functions.[7] Reat also observes that in the *Ṛgveda* the specific connotation of the verb root *cit-* depends on whether it is linked with the intellectual thought of the mind (*manas*), the emotions of the heart (*hṛd*), or with conative functions. In conjunction with *kratu*, the verb root *cit-* signifies purposive thought imbued with the impetus to initiate action.[8] The Vedic use of the term *citta* to signify mental activity in general is continued in the *Upaniṣads*. It is said in the *Kauṣītaki Upaniṣad* that when *citta* departs from the body of a dying person (*udakramīt cittam*), the senses begin to fail. The dying person does not hear, does not see, does not utter words, and does not think (Ks.U. III. 3).

The term *cetanā* occurs only a few times in the *Ṛgveda*.[9] According to Gonda's interpretation, in the *Ṛgveda*, the causative form of the verb root *cit-*, from which *cetanā* is formed, has the primary meaning of "to make visible". He shows that *cetanā* also embraces in its meaning both "to exhibit to the sight" as well as "to disclose" to the mind something previously unknown.[10] Both Gonda and Reat take *cetanā* in the *Ṛgveda* to be primarily indicative of cognitive processes of perceiving, knowing and thinking. Neither of them finds in the Vedic use of this term the sense of "volition" that it acquires in the *Tipiṭaka*.

In its rare occurrences in the *Upaniṣads*, *cetanā* enfolds in its range of meaning both the very basic sentience that empowers the body and mind to put forth their manifold functions as well as the power of knowledge that belongs only to Brahman. In the *Kaṭha Upaniṣad* Brahman is adored as the "Eternal One amidst ephemeral beings, the Conscious One among conscious beings, (*cetanaś cetanānām),* the One among the manifold" (K.U. II. 2.13). The significance of the phrase "the Conscious One among conscious beings" is further elucidated in the *Maitrī Upaniṣad* (Mt.U. II.3-6). Here, the body is compared to a cart that is devoid of sentience (*śakaṭamivācetanam idaṁ śarīram*). The *Upaniṣad* poses a rhetorical question regarding the identity of the powerful divine being by whom the insentient body has been made sentient.[11] The answer is given that *Prajāpati,* the Lord of Creatures, has the power to establish this body, which is devoid of conscious awareness (*acetanam*), as a being endowed with consciousness (*cetanavat*). In this context, *cetanā* probably signifies basic sentience that vitalizes the body and functions, not only as the mind's power to cognize objects, but also as the basic dynamism that impels a person to seek out and pursue goals.

Manas (mind): the controlling centre

Manas, the third Upaniṣadic term that signifies a holistic view of consciousness, differs from *hṛd* and *citta* in that it stresses the capacity of consciousness to regulate the sensory and motor functions of the individual. If *hṛd* signifies the inward centre from which conscious functions emanate, and if *citta* indicates the range of these functions, *manas* points to the capacity of consciousness to interpret sensory information and to coordinate cognition with motor responses.

Both Gonda and Reat emphasize two features of *manas* in the *Ṛgveda:* the wide range of *manas* as the agent and locus of thought, volition, and emotion, and the capacity of *manas* to "realize" itself in ideas and purposes. They designate this capacity of "realization" as the mind's "inventiveness" (Gonda) or its "creativity" (Reat). According to Gonda's interpretation, in the *Ṛgveda* the verb root *man-* expresses the capacity of the mind not only to form a clear conception or powerful mental image of an object, but to make that object something actual. The verb root *man-*, therefore, carries the affirmation that when the mind ardently concentrates on an object, then the object will be brought into effect by the mind. For example, Gonda says that the Vedic view holds that the mind of the poet not only fervently aspires for, but actually "produces", the poetic vision—or at the least becomes the point of origin of poetic illumination. When the mind of the poet is ardently concentrated on the aspiration to see, the power of the aspiration brings about the vision. One becomes a seer by the mind's aspiration to see, and the vision is "realized" by the mind.[12]

The *Upaniṣads* follow the *Ṛgveda* in assigning to the mind wide-ranging functions. They regard the mind as the agent and the home of cognitive, volitional, and emotional processes. The *Bṛhadāraṇyaka Upaniṣad* and the *Kauṣītaki Upaniṣad* seek to demonstrate that the mind's attention is essential for the functioning not only of the sense organs but also of the organs that govern motor activities. The point is made that none of these organs is able to perform its appointed task if the mind is "elsewhere" (*anyatra*), and the conclusion is then drawn that ultimately it is the mind that sees or smells (B.U. I. 5.3; Ks.U. III.7).[13] Similarly, in the *Majjhima-nikāya*, it is posited that whereas the five senses have diverse objects (*nānā-visayāni, nānā-gocarāni*), the mind (*manas*) functions as the resort (*paṭisaraṇam*) of the five senses and experiences (*paccanubhoti*) all their objects (M. I. 295). From the description of the mind's interaction with the senses and the organs of action in the *Kauṣītaki Upaniṣad* (Ks.U. III.7), it can be inferred that in the Upaniṣadic view, the mind coordinates incoming sensory information with outgoing voluntary responses. Furthermore, it is to be noted that in the *Bṛhadāraṇyaka Upaniṣad*, the mind is viewed not only as the agent of perception (B.U. I. 5.3), but also as the goal or "uniting place" (*ekāyana*) of conceptualizations (*saṁkalpa*) (B.U. II. 4.11, IV. 5.12).

The *Bṛhadāraṇyaka Upaniṣad* provides a list of faculties of perception and correlates each with the object that controls it. The mind (*manas*) is named as one of the faculties of perception (*graha*), and the object that exerts a controlling influence on the mind (*atigraha*) is designated as *kāma* (object of desire) (B.U. III. 2.1-9).[14] It is implied here that there is a reciprocal relationship between the mind and its object. The object, for its part, has features that cause the mind to be interested in it; the mind, for its part, is motivated to focus on that which grasps, holds, and controls its attention. The mind's function of becoming motivated to seek out that which attracts its attention is regarded as integral to the process of perception, and the cognitive capacity of the mind to receive information is held to be inseparable from its outgoing conative dynamism. The mind actively "reaches out" to grasp an object of interest. If the thing that comes within the purview of the mind is an object of desire (*kāma*), the chances are that the mind's attention will be drawn to that object and perception will occur. It is significant that both in Saṁskṛt and in Pāli, the term *kāma* comes to signify the mental state of desire as well as the object of desire (S.E.D. 271, col. 3; P.E.D. 203, col. 1). According to the Upaniṣadic view, therefore, perception is a dynamic interaction that affects both the object and the mind. For this reason, perception is regarded as a morally weighted process.

The *Maitrī Upaniṣad* gives its version of the reciprocity between the mind and its objects a specifically Sāṁkhya slant (Mt. U. VI.10).[15] In this passage, the world is compared to food (*anna*) with the three characteristics of pleasure (*sukha*), pain (*duḥkha*), and delusion (*moha*).[16] It is obvious that these three characteristics emerge only through the interaction between the mind and its objects. In this process of interaction, the mind is affected by the impact of objects. Simultaneously, the manner in which objects appear to the mind—characterized by pleasure, pain, or delusion—is influenced by the attitudes that dominate the mind that perceives them.

This Upaniṣadic idea that there is a reciprocal influence between one's state of mind and the objects that one perceives is taken up again in the *Sutta* literature. Furthermore, the *Suttas* echo the notion that one's desire (*kāma*) and intention (*saṅkappa*) stem from the impacts that objects have on the mind. The discipline the Buddha taught includes being vigilant so that the mind does not become entranced by the defining features of objects (*na nimittaggāhī hoti*) or by their detailed characteristics (*nānuvyañjanaggāhī*). The warning is given that covetousness (*abhijjhā*), dejection (*domanassa*), and other morally wrong, unwholesome (*akusala*) states of mind arise when a person is enthralled by the objects of the senses (D. I. 70; A. I. 113; A. II. 16). Moreover, contacts with objects are regarded as the sources of *cetanās* consisting of wholesome and unwholesome purposive impulses (D. II. 309, III. 244). Desire and passion for sensory experiences and mental stimulation are linked with yearning for the past, attachment to the present, and projection into the future (M. III. 197). From a psychological perspective, both the *Upaniṣads* and the *Suttas* view perception as the cause of morally good and evil purposes.

The Upaniṣadic view of the impact that this reciprocity between the mind and its objects has on the mind's function of volition is reflected in the well-known analogy of the chariot and its driver. In the version that occurs in the *Kaṭha Upaniṣad*, the *ātman* is likened to the owner of the chariot (*rathin*), the body to the chariot, the faculty of cognitive awareness and intellection (*buddhi*) to the driver of the chariot, the senses to the galloping horses, and the mind to the reins (*pragraha*) by which the horses are controlled (K.U. I. 3.3-6). The *Kaṭha Upaniṣad* maintains that the senses can only be kept in check (*vaśyāni*) by a controlled mind (*yuktena manasā*). Furthermore, this *Upaniṣad* says that only a person with understanding (*vijñānavān*) who is pure (*śuciḥ*) and mindful (*samanaskaḥ*) can reach the end of the journey. In this context, purity (*śuci*) signifies "unsullied, undefiled, innocent, honest, virtuous" (S.E.D. 1081, col. 1). Since the *Kaṭha Upaniṣad* insists not only on understanding but also on purity of purpose as conditions for the mind's control over the senses, it can be inferred that the type of control meant here includes refraining from both false perceptions and the harmful purposes that can follow from distorted perceptions. In other words, the empowered mind can regulate the senses when its cognitive functions are controlled by understanding and attention, and it can restrain the organs of action when its own motivational capacities are restrained by purity of purpose. The reciprocity of perception and purpose is implied in these verses of the *Kaṭha Upaniṣad.*

The theme of bondage to *karma* and ignorance that the *Maitrī Upaniṣad* so relentlessly emphasizes echoes throughout the *Upaniṣads*. Nevertheless, the main message of the *Upaniṣads* affirms that the mind can be trained and released from ignorance. From a psychological perspective, the argument can be made that this affirmation is based on a holistic view of consciousness. When consciousness is seen as an organic whole, it is implied that thoughts, emotions, and conative energies are interconnected in such a way that wholesome changes in one set of mental processes will set off a pattern of wholesome influences throughout the mind. A similarly holistic view of consciousness underlies an equally strong affirmation in the *Suttas* that the mind is responsive to training. The concept of the "protected state of mind" (*rakkhita-citta*) signifies that the interlinked processes of cognition, emotion, and conative dynamism are all equally guarded by the disciplines of the Eightfold Path. It is stated in the *Aṅguttara-nikāya* that the guarded mind entails the guarding of all acts of body, speech, and mind (A. I. 7; Dhp. 33-39).

Saṁkalpa (Conceptualization, Intention)

In the *Tipiṭaka*, the second factor of the Eightfold Path is *sammā-saṅkappa.* The firm determination or resolve of mind required in the Path is indicated by the term *saṅkappa.* Though the term *saṁkalpa* does not occur often in the *Upaniṣads*, it adds an important dimension to Upaniṣadic thought by forging a link between conceptualization and intention. The noun *saṁkalpa* includes in its frame of reference both the cognitive processes of conceptualization and purposive thought as well as the volitional factors of intention and resolve that aspire for action to fulfil those purposive thoughts (S.E.D. 1126, col. 2-3). The range of meaning of *saṁkalpa* becomes evident, for example, in Radhakrishnan's translation of the term in two identical passages of the *Bṛhadāraṇyaka Upaniṣad*, where *manas* (mind) is said to be the "uniting place" or goal (*ekāyana*) of all manifestations of *saṁkalpa*. In the first of these passages (B. U. II. 4.11), Radhakrishnan renders *saṁkalpa* as "determination". Here he is following Śaṁkara, who defines *saṁkalpa* as the process of cognitively determining the nature of a thing (*pratyupasthita-viṣaya-vikalpanaṁ*), for example, whether it is white or blue.[17] However, in the second passage (B.U. IV. 5.12), which is identical with the earlier one, Radhakrishnan translates *saṁkalpa* as "intention". The variation in translation shows that *saṁkalpa* includes both determining the nature of an object as well as deciding how to react to that object. Olivelle regards *saṁkalpa* in the *Upaniṣads* as a "very elusive concept" that connotes not only "intention, will, or purpose", but also, in a ritual setting, the announcement of one's resolve to perform a sacred ceremony. He adds that the verbal forms linked to *saṁkalpa* connote forming, designing, and producing something.[18]

The *Chāndogya Upaniṣad* (C.U. VII. 5.1) brings together *manas*, *saṁkalpa*, and *citta* in the following manner: when a person becomes engaged in thought (*cetayate*), then that person conceives a purpose (*atha saṁkalpayate*), applies the mind (*atha manasyati*), and utters speech (*atha vācam īrayati*). Here the faculty of thought (*citta*) is given a status more basic than the mind and its function of controlling the senses and organs of action. At the same time, the capacity to conceptualize and form intentions and purposes (*saṁkalpa*) is posited as the driving force behind the operations of the mind (*manas*). However, it is possible to conceive a purpose in the mind without implementing it in action. This passage of the *Chāndogya Upaniṣad* indicates that when a purpose has been conceived through the capacity of conceptualization (*saṁkalpa*), *manas* comes into play as the faculty that grasps the purpose and implements action in order to bring the purpose to fulfilment (*manasā manasyati*). The verb *manasyati*, therefore, signifies the fusion of conceptualization and conative energy in such a manner that the mind both reflects on a purpose and "realizes" it through action.

The moral dimension of *saṁkalpa* is demonstrated in another passage of the *Chāndogya Upaniṣad* (C.U. I. 2), where the teaching is set in the context of an episode in the story of the ongoing cosmic warfare between the gods and the titans (*asura*). The passage narrates how the *asuras* proceed to infect the sense faculties, speech, and mind with karmic demerit and moral evil (*pāpa*) so that each of these becomes twofold: it sometimes functions as it ought to function, and sometimes it functions inappropriately. The mind conceives both what it ought to conceive and what it ought not to conceive (*saṁkalpanīyaṁ cāsaṁkalpanīyaṁ ca*). The story of the gods and *asuras* shows that *saṁkalpa* can be interpreted in such a way as to include the mind's capacity to conceptualize as well as the ideas, imaginations, and purposes—both good and evil—into which these conceptualizations are shaped. The *Chāndogya* narrative of the warfare between the gods and the *asuras*, therefore, posits the interdependence between clear, undistorted thought and morally good behaviour. This interdependence of clarity of thought, purity of intention and a morally good way of life is illustrated in a similar story in the *Saṁyutta-nikāya* (S. IV. 201-202) that describes the defeat and bondage of the lord of the *asura* world, who is called Vepacitti in the *Sutta-piṭaka*. As Vepacitti stood as a prisoner in the assembly hall of the *devas*, when he correctly perceived the genuine goodness and righteousness of the *deva* world, his shackles fell away. However, when he falsely conceived of the *deva* world as evil and yearned for the unrighteous *asura* realm, his bondage returned. The real bondage of Vepacitti was his distorted conception of good and evil; his morally reprehensible intentions followed from his distorted cognitions.

It is significant that both in the *Upaniṣads* and in the *Suttas*, *saṁkalpa/saṅkappa* is a morally neutral term. The story of the *asuras* in the *Chāndogya Upaniṣad* emphasizes that the purposes and intentions that take shape in the mind can become either good or evil (C.U. I. 2.6.). Similarly, in the *Sutta* literature, intentions based on covetousness (*kāma-saṅkappa*), malevolence (*vyāpāda-saṅkappa*), and cruelty (*vihiṁsā-saṅkappa*) are regarded as the effects of perceptions that are influenced by correspondingly unwholesome emotions in the mind of the perceiver (M. II. 27-28). On the other hand, wholesome *saṅkappas* of renunciation, benevolence, and kindness are said to arise when wholesome emotions prevail in the mind of a person cognizing sensory and mental objects.

In the final analysis, both the *Upaniṣads* and the *Suttas* maintain that all intentions and purposes, both wholesome and unwholesome, inevitably bind a person to future goals and aspirations. For this reason, the *Maitrī Upaniṣad* (Mt.U. VI.19)[19] teaches that a person disciplined in *yoga* should become free of all *saṁkalpas* (*niḥsaṁkalpas tatas tiṣthet*). In the *Suttas*, goal-oriented impulses stemming from the mind (*mano-sañcetanās*) are regarded as a "nutrient" (*āhāra*) that motivates more and more wholesome and unwholesome acts in the processes of *kamma* and keeps a person bound to future rebirth (S. II. 98-99; D. III. 211; M. I. 48). In the *Saṁyutta-nikāya*, the story of Vepacitti is immediately followed with the teaching that when the deluded notion of an autonomous and permanent "I" (*ahaṁ*) dominates consciousness, a person experiences sorrow because of the multiplication of thoughts (*maññita*), the proliferation of concepts (*papañca*), and all manner of conceits (*māna*) formed in the mind. From a psychological perspective, the *Suttas* concur with the *Upaniṣads* in maintaining that the predilection to form future-oriented thoughts, purposes, and intentions ceases when one cultivates the disciplines that lead to liberation from sorrow.

"Ethicization" of the Idea of *Karma*

In his work *Theravāda Buddhism,* Gombrich claims that the Buddha's "great innovation" was to declare that the moral value of an act resides in the intention that supports the act.[20] Gombrich's position is in agreement with an earlier statement by E.J. Thomas, who strongly states his view that Buddhism "transformed the doctrine of karma" by making the moral value of a deed "dependant on motive" rather than solely upon the external action.[21] However, in the pre-Buddhist period, the *Bṛhadāraṇyaka Upaniṣad* put forward the view that the moral quality of an act depends, not solely on the act itself, nor on its consequences, but primarily on the mental attitudes that produce and shape the act (B.U. IV. 4.5-6). In this *Upaniṣad*, the sage Yājñavalkya presents two choices for the role of the governing principle in the rebirth process: *karma* (action) and *kāma* (desire).[22] He first presents the view of those who hold that what a person turns out to be—that is to say, how a person develops—depends on how that person acts (*yathākārī*) and habitually behaves (*yathācārī*). According to this view, a person who performs good actions will become good and garner merit (*puṇya*), while a person who does bad acts will become bad and accumulate demerit (*pāpa*). The second view links *kāma* (desire), *kratu* (purpose), and *karma* (action) in a causal series. Here it is held that a person consists of desires (*kāmamaya evāyam puruṣa*). Desire (*kāma*) is posited as the basic factor that gives rise to a person's purpose or resolve (*kratu*); this *kratu*,[23] in turn, is regarded as the cause of actions (*karma*); and finally, actions are said to determine what accrues to a person in the process of rebirth. In the Vedic hymns and in the *Upaniṣads*, the term *kratu* includes in its range of meaning both the cognitive functions of intelligence, understanding, and poetic inspiration as well as the action-producing functions of determination, desire, and will (S.E.D. 319, col. 1). With regard to the dynamics of volition, *kratu* covers both the purpose that arises in the mind as well as the capacity of the mind to initiate action to achieve that purpose.

There are statements in the *Upaniṣads* that define *karma* and rebirth in terms of strict moral retribution (C.U. V. 10.7; Ks.U. I.2). Without denying the idea of moral retribution, Yājñavalkya shifts the focus to the causal link between the way one acts and one's psychological make-up. He states that whether one is to be counted as a good person (*sāduḥ*) or as a bad person (*pāpaḥ*) depends not only on specific acts that one has performed (*yathākārī*), but also on one's accustomed modes of behaviour (*yathācārī*). Furthermore, Yājñavalkya does not view each action as an isolated event, but as the end product of a causal process that begins with motivating desire (*kāma*). It is significant that Yājñavalkya does not consider the motivating drive of desire to be the sole factor governing action. His view of *karma* provides for the intervention of cognitive processes of purposive deliberation signified by *kratu*. Because of the mental processes of "filtering" and "sorting" that occur in purposive deliberation, one can presume that not every motivating impetus of desire (*kāma*) becomes a firm purpose or intention (*kratu*). Similarly, not every intention becomes action. Thus, Yājñavalkya's interpretation of *karma* implies that motivating desires (*kāma*) produce related emotions and purposes (*kratu*) and that these purposes, which are constituted of purposive thought imbued with the capacity to initiate action, produce acts that carry moral values (*karma*). Purposes and resolves (*kratu*) are posited as the motivating causes that produce action. It can be argued that Yājñavalkya "ethicized" *karma* through his position that the moral value of an act (*karma*) is to be found in the link between the concretely manifest act and the chosen purpose (*kratu*) in the mind of the person who performs the act. Yājñavalkya's statement implies that whether the act is morally good or morally reprehensible depends on the moral quality of the purpose (*kratu*) on which it is based. Furthermore, since the act can be either morally good or morally bad, it can be inferred that in this context *kāma* signifies desire in the sense of a motivating impulse or stimulus that can direct action towards either a morally good and beneficial goal or towards moral evil.

Kāma, Saṁkalpa, and *Kratu* in the Process of Rebirth

The idea that desire provides both drive and direction in the course of rebirth is either overtly stated or implied throughout the Upaniṣadic tradition. Similarly, in the *Suttas*, craving (*taṇhā*) and ignorance (*avijjā*) are regarded as the fundamental factors that not only cause rebirth, but also chart the course of future lives. The descriptions of *kāma* in the *Upaniṣads* and *taṇhā* in the *Suttas* suggest that the two terms denote a drive that arises from a felt need, becomes manifest as emotional and physical tension, and retains its capacity to initiate action until the need is assuaged. Thus, *taṇhā* or *kāma* is to the emotions what appetite is to the body: desire impels action.

At the same time, the *Upaniṣads* and the *Tipiṭaka* balance their statements on the motivating power of desire with terms like *kratu*, *saṁkalpa/saṅkappa*, and *cetanā*. These terms point to a motivational capacity that arises primarily from cognitive processes such as goal-oriented thought, purpose, and intention. Though *kratu*, *saṁkalpa*, and *cetanā* are often conditioned by desire, their link with the cognitive processes of purposive thought differentiates them from the primarily emotion-driven functioning of *kāma* and *taṇhā*. Nevertheless, it is posited that purposive thoughts and intentions, like the motivational drive of desire, constantly produce new aspirations, projects, and plans, keeping the mind bound to the hope of fulfilment in the future. Since purposive thoughts, intentions, and resolves bind the mind to future goals, it is implied that there is a powerful interaction in the processes of the mind between the emotion-charged motivating drive towards objects, which desire (*kāma*) represents, and the cognitively based functions of *kratu* and *saṁkalpa*. It follows that both in the *Upaniṣadas* and in the *Suttas*, this mutual conditioning between the drive of desire (*kāma*) and the preoccupation of thought processes such as *kratu* and *saṁkalpa* with purposes and goals comes to be regarded as a fundamental cause of the perpetuation of sorrow and rebirth.

The *Praśna Upaniṣad* (P.U. III.10) says that the course of rebirth is determined by whatever attitude of mind a person experiences at the time of death (*yaccittaḥ*). This passage proceeds to reiterate that the transmigrating self moves on to whatever realm of rebirth the mind aspires for and resolves to attain (*yathā saṁkalpitaṁ lokaṁ nayati*). This heartfelt aspiration or strong resolve should be seen in a ritual context. It was believed that certain rituals performed with proper intent (*saṁkalpa*) would lead to a felicitous rebirth. The aspiration of a dying person would then be an echo of the aspiration and intention with which that person performed rituals and meditations in the course of life. The *Suttas* affirm the idea that one is reborn in the realm (*loka*) that one resolves to attain, especially at the hour of death. The *Saṅkhārupapatti-sutta* of the *Majjhima-nikāya* is based on the notion that rebirth in any of the lofty cosmic realms is attainable by a person who forms a firm resolve to be reborn there. It is postulated that when the mind concentrates unwaveringly on a firmly held resolve, then that resolve has the capacity to bring about its own realization. According to the traditional ideas regarding rebirth, in order to realize the aspiration to be reborn in an exalted cosmic realm, one must practise concentration of mind and ardently cultivate the purity and peace of the higher levels of meditation that match the luminous calm of the realm of rebirth towards which one's mind aspires (M. III. 99-103).

The *Bṛhadāraṇyaka Upaniṣad* (B.U. V. 15.3) and the *Īśā Upaniṣad* (I.U. 17) contain an ancient chant that invokes *Agni*, the god of the ritual fire, to guide a dying person along a good path that leads to rebirth in a realm of prosperity. The following is a verse of the chant:

Aum krato smara, kṛtaṁ smara, krato smara, kṛtaṁ smara
(*O Kratu*, remember, remember the deed.)

In this verse, *Kratu* is an epithet of *Agni*, the god of the sacrificial fire, who presides over human intelligence, from which all intentions and purposes proceed.[24] However, the verse also indicates the bond between the purposes (*kratu*) and the acts (*karma*) of the dying person. In order to see the significance of this ancient chant, it is necessary to keep in mind the connotations of *kratu*. This term includes in its range of connotations not only intention, resolve, or purpose, but also the intelligence or understanding that shapes the purpose, the ritual act that achieves the purpose, and the goal of inspiration or wisdom towards which the purpose is ultimately directed.

This chant resonates with the sage Śāṇḍilya's teaching in the *Chāndogya Upaniṣad* (C.U. III. 14.1). The crux of Śāṇḍilya's teaching is that a person is constituted of purpose (*kratumayaḥ puruṣaḥ*). Śāṇḍilya puts forward the view that what happens after death depends on the purpose (*kratu*) that a person affirms while living in this world and confirms at the hour of death.[25] He concludes with the admonition that one should make a purpose for oneself (*sa kratuṁ kurvīta*). Śāṇḍilya's statement about *kratu* occurs in the context of his teaching that one should meditate on Brahman as the ultimate cause of all that exists and as the indwelling presence in every being, the tiniest as well as the greatest. Śaṁkarācārya interprets *kratu* in this context as the ardent sense of purpose with which one should undertake meditation on Brahman in the manner taught by Śāṇḍilya, especially as death approaches.[26] Meditation and ritual are regarded as essential to facilitate a good rebirth. Nevertheless, it is significant that in Śāṇḍilya's teaching, it is the resolve or purpose (*kratu*) underlying the ritual and the meditation, rather than action (*karma*), that is declared to be the crucial factor in determining future consequences. Śaṁkara comments that the consequences to be experienced in the process of rebirth are commensurate with the purpose or aspiration that a person forms in the course of life (*kratvanurūpam phalam*).[27]

Since *kratu* occurs only a very few times in the *Upaniṣads*, it is not easy to arrive at a firm conclusion regarding its meaning in these texts. Śaṁkarācārya's commentary and the interpretation of modern scholars suggest that *kratu* signifies the coming together of a purpose that is held with conviction and the mental power to translate that purpose into action. The references to the concept of *kratu* in the *Upaniṣads* are significant, even though they are rare. They show that according to the Upaniṣadic view, the moral quality of an act and its karmic fruition depend not only on the act itself, but also on the purpose (*kratu*) that motivates the act. It was noted that Yājñavalkya defines a human person as *kāmamaya* (constituted of *kāma*). To get a complete picture of the Upaniṣadic view of a human person, however, Yājñavalkya's definition must be supplemented with Śāṇḍilya's definition in the *Chāndogya Upaniṣad* (C.U. III. 14.1). Here a human person is defined as *kratumaya* (constituted of *kratu*). This definition regards a human person as one who perpetually forms purposes that seek to become realized in acts. It can be argued that though the term *kratu* drops away and is seldom found in later discourses on *karma*, the idea that a person is "constituted of purpose" leaves its mark on the culture in which Hinduism, Jainism, and Buddhism develop their fundamental concepts. The "ethicization of *karma*" can be traced back to the notion of *kratu*. In the thought of Yājñavalkya, *kratu* (purpose, intention, resolve) is the bridge between *kāma* (desire that impels a person to act) and *karma* (action that brings commensurate consequences). In the definition of *kamma* that the Buddha puts forward, *cetanā* (purposive impulse) is the bridge between a specific state of mind (*citta*) and an act of body, speech, or mind in which the dominant thought and emotion in that state of mind become expressed (A. III. 415). In both cases, the emphasis is not solely on the drive to act (*kāma, taṇhā*) or on the act itself (*karma/kamma*). Intention, resolve, and purposive impulse (*kratu, cetanā*) are taken into account in explaining the moral significance of an act and its consequences.

Kratu and *Saṅkhāra*

K.N. Jayatilleke argues that the concept of *saṅkhāra* in Theravāda can be regarded as the "historical successor" of the Upaniṣadic concept of *kratu.*[28] Whereas there are only a very few occurrences of the term *kratu* in the *Upaniṣads*, *saṅkhāra* is a prolific term in the Pāli texts. Moreover, *kratu* is not defined in any of the contexts where it is found. On the other hand, there are definitions of *saṅkhāra* both in the *Suttas* and in the *Abhidhamma* that offer some guidance in translating this term, even though its semantic range continues to baffle interpreters. Jayatilleke's contention is that the Theravāda portrait of the "human person" as a mere bundle of *saṅkhāras* (*suddha-saṅkhāra-puñja*) resembles the Upaniṣadic view that the human person is constituted of *kratu* (*kratumaya*). The Theravāda idea of *saṅkhāra-puñja* (S. I. 135) is based on the notion that no being can claim to possess an autonomous and permanent "self" (*attā*). For example, in the *Theragāthā*, the *arahant* Adhimutta says that the notion of "I" does not invade his mind and that there is no fear for one who perceives only the continuity (*santati*) of *saṅkhāras* (Tha. 715-716). The Upaniṣadic use of the word *kratumaya* conveys that a human being is shaped and developed within the rounds of rebirth by the intentions that are formed in the mind. The meanings attributed to the term *kratumaya* are developed in a context where the idea of the *ātman* is affirmed. For this reason the Upaniṣadic concept of *kratumaya* differs from the Theravāda idea of *saṅkhāra-puñja.*

Both *saṅkhāra* and *kratu* indicate that the motivating power of purpose influences the functioning of consciousness as a dynamic unity and gives direction to the development of one's entire personality. However, whereas the term *kratu* can be appropriately used in referring to ritual acts or resolute meditation leading to knowledge of Brahman, the term *saṅkhāra* in the *Suttas* belongs to a world-view where the causal theory of conditioned origination is regarded as central. *Saṅkharas* are dynamic psychological processes where purposes are formed and habitual acts are put forth in accordance with conditioned origination.

Conclusion

To appreciate the Upaniṣadic approach to the dynamics of volition, it is necessary to seek out the criteria that differentiate two motivating factors: intention or purpose (*saṁkalpa*, *kratu*), which is regarded as a mental state that can be directed either towards mundane goals or towards liberation from ignorance and rebirth; and the motivational impetus of *kāma*, which is regarded as inevitably leading to sorrow and to rebirth. In the *Aitareya Upaniṣad*, for example, *saṁkalpa* and *kāma* appear separately in the list of mental states that are said to constitute the "heart" (A.U. III. 1.2). When Yājñavalkya states that *kāma* is the basis of *kratu*, and that *kratu* is the basis of *karma* (B.U. IV. 4.5), the term *kāma* does not signify a mental state that is necessarily morally reprehensible. In this context, *kāma* has the nature of a motivational impetus that might lead equally to deeds of merit or to deeds of demerit. In the same manner, the *Kaṭha Upaniṣad* speaks of two types of goals: the pleasant (*preyas*) and the good (*śreyas*) (K.U. I. 2.2). Here the pleasant includes the things of the earth that are beautiful and powerful. The *Kaṭha Upaniṣad* says that ignorant folk (*manda*) choose the pleasant, while the wise ones (*dhīra*) aspire for the good. In this context, desire turned towards pleasant goals is deemed foolish, but is not condemned as necessarily evil. In the *Bṛhadāraṇyaka Upaniṣad*, Yājñavalkya says that because all the people and things that one cherishes are caught up in processes of change, they ultimately desert (*parāduḥ*) a person who does not recognize the indwelling presence of the *ātman* in all things (B.U. IV. 5.7). Here also, loving attachment to the things and people of this transitory world is considered ultimately futile, but is not condemned as evil by its very nature.

In the *Upaniṣads*, *kāma* is condemned, not because it is necessarily ethically bad or because it always causes acts of demerit (*pāpa*), but because it inevitably leads to sorrow (*duḥkha*) and to bondage to the future. From a psychological perspective, *kāma* causes sorrow in two ways: by functioning as a motivating drive that binds a person to think primarily in terms of needs and their fulfilment; and by blocking purposive reflection and discernment. The pursuit of objects is perceived as futile because they are ephemeral by nature (*śvo-bhāva*) and subject to decay (K.U. I. 1.26-27). For this reason, the *Upaniṣads* do not teach that one group of objects is to be chosen over others, but that all the desires that dwell in the heart are to be renounced (B.U. IV. 4.7; K.U. II. 3.14). From a psychological perspective, the renunciation of the mental state of desire signifies liberation from the tunnel vision where one can think only in terms of setting up targets and attaining them. The blocking of purposive reflection and discernment that occurs when *kāma* dominates the mind is implied throughout the *Upaniṣads* and is most clearly spelt out in the *Maitrī Upaniṣad* (Mt.U. VI.30). Here a person whose life is motivated by desires is described as unsteady (*asthiraḥ*), wavering (*calaḥ*), confused (*lupyamānaḥ*), full of covetousness (*saspṛhaḥ*), and agitated (*vyagraḥ*). All these characteristics can be summed up in the term *moha* (delusion).

Though *kāma* is perceived as a powerful motivational drive in the *Upaniṣads*, it does not exclude other mental factors that initiate activity in the organism. The *Upaniṣads* unequivocally affirm another type of conative process where purposive deliberation or goal-oriented thought plays a more dominant role. In those Upaniṣadic passages where there is a reference to purposive deliberation and decision-making, it is taken for granted that these cognitive processes have the capacity to initiate action. The mind's capacity to form purposes and initiate action to realize those purposes is conveyed in the *Chāndogya Upaniṣad* (C.U. VII. 3.1) by the phrase *manasā manasyati,* which indicates a person engaging the mind as a whole in a process of purposive deliberation and decision-making. In this passage of the *Chāndogya Upaniṣad,* the use of direct speech sharpens the sense of governing oneself through one's own mind. One makes up one's mind: "I should learn the sacred verses", "I should perform the sacrificial rites", "I should desire children and cattle".[29] The teachers in the *Upaniṣads* constantly warn their disciples that desire (*kāma*) and its motivational drives have the power to confuse and infatuate the mind. Nevertheless, the mind is portrayed as capable of monitoring and renouncing needs in order to fulfil its purposes and express its decisions. Expressions of *saṁkalpa* can remain solely dominated by *kāma,* or they can be brought under the control of purposive thought. As the analogy of the chariot in the *Kaṭha Upaniṣad* (K.U. I. 3.4-9) indicates, the contrast is between the trained mind, which gradually becomes skilful in forming and realizing its purposes, and the untrained mind, which loses its capacity to distinguish between that which is good (*śreyas*) and that which is cherished because it gives pleasure (*preyas*).

In the *Upaniṣads,* volition is a mode of functioning of the *citta* as a whole. There is no evidence of an autonomous principle of volitional energy or "will" that governs the *citta.* Though *manas* is often featured as a centre of decision-making, *manasyati* connotes the entire *citta* operating in such a way as to form an intention and initiate action to achieve a chosen goal. It is significant that *manas* is perceived as the centre not only of intention but also of cognition and emotion. Moreover, there is no indication of a dichotomy between cognitive awareness and conative dynamism in the processes of the mind. Nowhere is it suggested that though the *manas* may form a decision, it is dependent on a separate dynamic principle (*śakti*) within consciousness to implement action and achieve its goal. The mind is not dependent on *kāma* to provide motivational impetus; on the contrary, processes of purposive reflection are perceived to have the capacity to control or re-direct *kāma.*

ENDNOTES

[1] This chapter is concerned only with the principal *Upaniṣads* that were composed probably in the period between the seventh century B.C.E. and the beginning of the common era (P. Olivelle, *Upaniṣads,* xxxvi-xxxvii). I have relied on the translations of these *Upaniṣads* by R.E. Hume, S. Radhakrishnan and, more recently, by P. Olivelle.

[2] K.R. Norman, "Theravāda Buddhism and Brahmanical Hinduism: Brahmanical Terms in a Buddhist Guise", 193.

[3] T.W. Rhys Davids, *Dialogues of the Buddha,* 1:63, 104-105, 141, 165, 206, 287.

[4] C.A.F. Rhys Davids, *The Birth of Indian Psychology and Its Development in Buddhism,* 21.

[5] At A.U. III. 1.2, *hṛd* is identified with *manas* (mind) and is said to possess the following mental functions: *saṁjñāna* (sentience), *ājñāna* (perception), *vijñāna* (distinguishing, discriminating objects), *prajñāna* (intelligence), *medhā* (mental vigour, wisdom), *dṛṣti* (insight), *dhṛti* (constancy, steadfastness), *mati* (thought), *manīṣā* (wisdom, inspiration), *jūti* (impetus, impulse), *smṛti* (memory), *saṁkalpa* (conceptualization, intention), *kratu* (purpose, resolve), *asu* (life), *kāma* (desire), and *vaśa* (control). Among the mental functions in the *Aitareya* list, *jūti, saṁkalpa, kratu* and *kāma* are linked in some way with intention and the capacity to initiate action.

[6] C.A.F. Rhys Davids, *The Birth of Indian Psychology and Its Development in Buddhism,,* 108.

[7] N.R. Reat, *The Origins of Indian Psychology,* 101.

[8] Reat cites the following verses from Griffith's translation of the *Ṛgveda* to show how the verb root *cit-* is used.

May he who knows [*vidvān*] distinguish [*vicinavat*] sense [*citti*] and folly [*acitti*] of men, like straight and crooked backs of horses. (Ṛg. IV. 2.11)

Ensign of sacrifice from of old, Agni well knoweth with his thought [*agnirdhiyā sa cetati*] to prosper this man's aim and hope. (Ṛg. III. 11.3)

That *Agni*, wise High-Priest, in every house takes thought for sacrifice and holy service, yea, takes thought, with mental power, for sacrifice. [*kratvā yajñasya cetati*]. (Ṛg. I. 128.4)

[9] Reat refers to two verses where the term *cetanā* is used in the *Ṛgveda* (Ṛg. VIII. 13.18; VIII. 92.21). In these verses, the poet says that *cetanā* is stirred, or literally "churned", by the fire ritual (*yajñamatnata*). Reat translates *cetanā* as "thought" in this verse, while Griffith prefers to render it as "mind" (N.R. Reat, *The Origins of Indian Psychology*, 102; R.T. Griffith, *The Hymns of the Ṛgveda*, 404).

Griffith translates:

At the Tṛkadrukas the Gods span sacrifice that stirred the mind: [*Trikadrukeṣu cetanaṁ devaso yajñamatnata*] (Ṛg. VIII. 13.18, repeated at Ṛg. VIII. 92.21)

[10] J. Gonda, *The Vision of the Vedic Poets*, 100.

[11] S. Radhakrishnan, *The Principal Upaniṣads*, 800.

[12] J. Gonda, *The Vision of the Vedic Poets*, 75, 146.

[13] *anyatra manā abhūvaṁ nādarśam, anyatra manā abhūvaṁ nāśrauṣam iti, manasā hy eva paśyati, manasā śṛṇoti* (B.U. I. 5.3).

[14] *mano vai grahaḥ sa kāmenātigrāheṇa gṛhītaḥ, manasā hi kāmān kāmayate* (B.U. III. 2.7).

The designation *graha* suggests that the sense organ "grasps" the objects. The designation *atigraha* as applied to the object is interesting since it conveys "surpassing" or "seizing" (S.E.D. 13, col. 3). The *Bṛhadāraṇyaka Upaniṣad* says that the sense organ (that which "grasps") "is grasped" (*gṛhīta*) by the object, suggesting control of the sense organ and mind by the object. The mind is said to be "grasped" by desire since the mind's attention is attracted by objects that are characterized by qualities that arouse desire.

[15] The *Maitrī Upaniṣad* upholds a Sāṁkhya cosmology. Accordingly, it is said here that the following elements evolve in order that the manifold world may be experienced: the psychological factors comprising the intellect (*buddhi*), ascertainment of objects and determined effort to achieve goals (*adhyavasāya*), intention (*saṁkalpa*), pride in the sense of individual selfhood (*abhimāna*), the five senses, and the organs of action (Mt.U. VI.10).

[16] The term *moha* signifies that the mind becomes so exclusively focused on one set of objects or persons that it remains ignorant of the others involved in any given situation. As a consequence it falls into a state of bewilderment and confusion. *Moha* expresses a constellation of unwholesome mental states that affect both cognition and volition. These include: infatuation, the bewilderment that follows, and the resultant tendency to fall into folly and error (S.E.D. 836, col. 1).

[17] S. Radhakrishnan, *The Principal Upaniṣads*, 175-176. C.A.F. Rhys Davids notes that translators of the *Upaniṣads* working in European languages were well aware of the range of meanings included in the term *saṁkalpa*. She produces a very interesting chart showing how six different scholars had translated *saṁkalpa* in nine different passages in the *Upaniṣads* (*The Birth of Indian Psychology and Its Development in Buddhism*, 121). The chart demonstrates that *saṁkalpa* had been translated as "conception", "imagination", "will", "wish", "determination", "resolve", "thought", and "intention".

[18] P. Olivelle, *Upaniṣads*, 352.

[19] Similarly, in the *Bhagavad-gītā* (Bhg. VI.2, 4, 24) the disciple of *yoga* is told that all desires that are born of *saṁkalpa* (*saṁkalpa-prabhavān-kāmān*) should be renounced.

[20] R.F. Gombrich, *Theravāda Buddhism*, 67.

[21] E.J. Thomas, *The History of Buddhist Thought*, 117.

[22] *Yathākārī yathācārī tathā bhavati, sādhukārī sādhur bhavati, pāpakārī pāpo bhavati; . . . athau khalv āhuḥ: kāmamaya evāyam puruṣa iti, sa yathākāmo bhavati, tat kratur bhavati, yat kratur bhavati, tat karma kurute, yat karma kurute, tat abhisampadyate* (B.U. IV. 4.5).

Radhakrishnan renders *kratu* as "will" in this context (S. Radhakrishnan, *The Principal Upaniṣads*, 270). Hume prefers "resolve"

(R.E. Hume, *The Thirteen Principal Upaniṣads*, 140). Olivelle also translates *kratu* as "resolve" (P. Olivelle, *Upaniṣads*, 65).

[23] Abel Bergaigne interprets *kratu* as an "intellectual or moral force" that is either present as a potential in a person's mind or becomes expressed as a resolve. He adds that *kratu* may be translated, according to the context, as "intelligence", or as "will" and "resolution", or more simply, as "desire" (A. Bergaigne, *Vedic Religion*, 3: 312). This statement by Bergaigne indicates that *kratu* includes in its meaning both the cognitive capacity of intelligence as well as the resolve to carry out the purposive thoughts put forth by intelligence.

Griffith says that *kratu* covers in its meaning both act (*karma*) and wisdom (*prajñā*) (R.T. Griffith, *The Hymns of the Ṛgveda*, 3, n.8). However, he translates *kratūyanti kratavo hṛtsu dhīyato* (Ṛg X. 64.2) as "The will and thoughts within my breast exert their power".

[24] Radhakrishnan translates *kratu* as "Intelligence", in the context of the chant at B.U. V. 15.3. Following the commentary of Śaṁkara, Radhakrishnan notes that this Intelligence (*kratu*) is *saṁkalpātmaka*, characterized by intentions and resolves (S. Radhakrishnan, *The Principal Upaniṣads*, 304). Śaṁkara's commentary explains that the dying person is praying to *Agni*, the God of the sacrificial fire, who presides over the mind of the dying person and is identified with the deliberations and purposes in the mind (Swami Mādhavānanda, *Bṛhadāraṇyaka Upaniṣad: With the Commentary of Śaṅkarācārya*, 862-864).

[25] . . . *yathā-kratur asminl loke puruṣo bhavati tathetaḥ pretya bhavati* (C.U. III. 14.1).

[26] G. Jha, *Chāndoygyopaniṣad*, 152.

[27] Cited in S. Radhakrishnan, *The Principal Upaniṣads*, 391.

[28] K. N. Jayatilleke, "Some Problems of Translation and Interpretation", (1): 220-224. Jayatilleke points out that both terms are derived from the verb root *kṛ-* (to do or to make), and he holds that while *kratu*, like *saṅkhāra*, connotes "a voluntary decision made in the pursuit of ends", there is a difference between the two terms, because *saṅkhāra* includes action as well as decision in its meaning. Furthermore, he says that the relationship between *kratu* and *karma* resembles the relationship between *saṅkhāra* and *kamma*. Jayatilleke argues that just as the Upaniṣadic tradition posits that the next birth will be commensurate with

the *kratu* that a person upholds in this life, so also the Theravāda view maintains that the *saṅkhāra* of a dying person determines the nature of consciousness (*viññāṇa*) in the next birth. In this context, he translates *saṅkhāra* as "habitual volitional activities" and *kratu* as "purpose". Jayatilleke also maintains that the Buddhist view that all expressions of *saṅkhāra* cease in *nibbāna* resonates with the Upaniṣadic view (S.U. III.20) that the *ātman* is free of *kratu* (*akratu*). Here he renders *saṅkhāra* as "purposive activities" and *kratu* as "purposive will".

[29] . . . *sa yadā manasā manasyati, mantrān adhīyīyeti, athādhīte, karmāṇi kurvīyeti, atha kurute, putrāṁśca paśuṁśceccheyeti, athecchate* (C.U. VII. 3.1).

Chapter II
Buddhist Debates With Early Jainas

The Buddhist *Suttas* contain several accounts of the Buddha's debates with the *samaṇa* community known as the Nigaṇṭhas (Saṁskṛt: Nirgrantha).* They are the forerunners of the Jainas, and their leader, called Nātaputta in the *Suttas*, is known in the Jaina tradition as the great teacher Vardhamāna Mahāvīra. It is difficult to assess to what extent one can rely on the Buddhist *Suttas* for an accurate account of early Jaina doctrines. The accepted practice in the Buddha's time of sharpening the debate by exaggerating and ridiculing the opponent's point of view undoubtedly accounts for some of the barbed statements against the Nigaṇṭhas. The debates between the Buddha and the Nigaṇṭhas focus on questions concerning volition: whether the mind can be controlled and purified by voluntarily accepting the pain of ascetic disciplines; whether intention or act carries greater moral significance; whether the theory of *kamma* leaves room for human initiative and moral responsibility; whether the concept of human initiative is viable if it is not supported by the idea of an autonomous self that is the source of the energy of volition; and what is to be included under the term "act" (*kamma*). These debates are of utmost importance in investigating the Buddha's approach to the

---

* In this chapter, I have used Pāli terms when discussing the Buddhist tradition and Saṁskṛt terms when discussing the Jaina tradition. When I address the concepts that pertain to both traditions, I have used Pāli terms.

dynamics of volition since he elaborates and clarifies his statements when he is further questioned—and sometimes ridiculed—by the Nigaṇṭhas.

Debate on the Efficacy of Ascetic Endeavour in Controlling the Mind

The *Cūḷadukkhakkhandha-sutta* records that Nātaputta (Mahāvīra) taught his disciples the following two methods of training: by practising severe austerities (*tapas*), they should annihilate (*nijjaretha*) the demerit of past evil *kamma* that they had accumulated; and by keeping body, speech, and mind well controlled (*saṁvuta*) they should prevent any new *kamma* from accumulating (M. I. 93).[1] It is implied that the Nigaṇṭhas believed that the voluntary acceptance of the severe pain suffered in practising austerities (*tapas*) would gradually wear away the demerit (*pāpa*) of past unwholesome *kamma* and prevent the arising of its painful consequences. At the same time, they evidently hoped to avoid the consequences of new acts (*nava-kamma*) in two ways: by restraining their actions of body, speech, and mind; and by abstaining from injuring any living being. Jacobi maintains that the *Cūḷadukkhakkhandha-sutta* gives an accurate statement of early Jaina teaching and quotes identical statements from the *Uttarādhyayana*, a Jaina canonical text (Prakṛt: *Uttarajjhayaṇa*).[2]

The *Cūḷadukkhakkhandha-sutta* describes how the Buddha demonstrates to the Nigaṇṭhas that they cannot be certain that a specific amount of suffering—which has accrued to them as the commensurate consequence of past morally wrong acts—has already been nullified by the practice of painful ascetic disciplines. The Buddha goes on to show them that they can neither verify the precise amount of painful karmic consequence (*kamma-vipāka*) that still remains to be annihilated by ascetic discipline nor assume that when a stipulated amount of karmic demerit is annihilated, all painful consequences of past *kamma* will be brought to an end. The crux of the Buddha's argument is that it is not possible to quantify *kamma* in such a way as to perfectly balance a sum of past actions with a projected sum of commensurate consequences. The second argument that the Buddha advances in the *Cūḷadukkhakkhandha-sutta* is based on his criticism of the Nigaṇṭha view that whenever pleasure is gained, it is always as a consequence of pain endured in the past for the sake of a good cause (M. I. 93). Basing their position on the dictum of "no pain no gain", the Nigaṇṭhas argue with the Buddha that the principle of *kamma* decrees that pleasure can never come as the consequence of pleasurable experiences (*na kho āvuso Gotama sukhena sukham adhigantabbam).*

In the *Mahāsaccaka-sutta* of the *Majjhima-nikāya,* the Nigaṇṭha Saccaka opens the debate by distinguishing between two groups of teachers: those who pursue the training of the body (*kāya-bhāvanā*) without simultaneously training the mind, and those who focus exclusively on nurturing the mind (*citta-bhāvanā*) while neglecting the development of the body (M. I. 237-238). He describes the former as those whose minds are totally overcome by anguish when they suffer physical illness. His verdict is that this mental breakdown occurs because they have neglected to train the mind and have allowed the body to hold total sway over the mind (*kāyanvayaṁ cittaṁ hoti, kāyassa vasena vattati*). Saccaka then contrasts those who focus on physical fitness with those who exclusively nurture their minds—only to find their bodies collapsing in situations of mental distress. According to Saccaka's diagnosis, the body breaks down under those conditions because it is dominated by the mind (*cittanvayo kāyo hoti, cittassa vasena vattati*). With this preamble, the Nigaṇṭha Saccaka proceeds to challenge the Buddha with the accusation that his disciples train the mind exclusively and neglect the training of the body.

When the Buddha asks the Nigaṇṭha for his definition of the training of the body (*kāyabhāvanā*), the latter refers to the method of some *samaṇa* teachers who practised the ascetic discipline of reducing their intake of food to an extremely small quantity. Evidently, the Nigaṇṭhas considered fasting to be a supreme form of controlling the mind and disciplining the body. The Buddha presents his case (M. I. 239-240). He describes the noble disciples (*ariyasāvaka*) possessing well trained bodies and minds (*bhāvita-kāya, bhāvita-citta*) as those who neither become enamoured of pleasure (*sukhasārāgī*) when they experience joy nor distraught and deluded when they are stricken by feelings of pain (*dukkha-vedanā*). The Buddha says that the mark of a person whose body is well trained is that pleasant feeling does not control and occupy the mind; and the mark of a person with a well cultivated mind is that painful feeling does not overpower thought processes and persist in the mind.[3]

The Buddha's reply to the Nigaṇṭha Saccaka's challenge is rich in nuances of meaning. The Nigaṇṭha makes no mention of pleasant feelings. His chief contention is that the mind is devastated by the experience of physical pain when the body becomes dominant, whereas the body is wrecked by mental grief when the mind becomes sovereign. The Buddha, on the other hand, emphasizes the role of pleasure (*sukha*) as well as of pain (*dukkha*) in his approach to training. With reference to the training of the body, the Buddha focuses, not on the ability to endure deprivation, but on the capacity to remain non-attached to pleasure and retain the mind's equilibrium. With reference to the cultivation of the mind, the Buddha emphasizes not only non-attachment to pleasure, but also true strength and equanimity in situations of pain. The emphasis is shifted from voluntary sensory deprivation and ascetic endurance of pain to non-attachment as a sustained mental attitude. The Buddha's concern in training is that neither pleasant nor painful feelings should envelop and take over the mind.

Furthermore, the Nigaṇṭha Saccaka posits a dichotomy between the body and the mind when he declares that the crux of the training is to ensure that neither the body nor the mind should wield control over the other. The Buddha, on the contrary, upholds the integral relationship of the body and the mind when he states that the body is well trained when pleasant bodily sensations do not obsess and subjugate the mind. The crucial point in the Buddha's argument is that it is only when a *brāhmaṇa* or *samaṇa* has the inner attitude of well cultivated renunciation (*suppahīno*) and genuine quiescence (*suppaṭippasaddho*) that he attains knowledge, insight, and full enlightenment, regardless of whether or not he experiences painful, severe, piercing feelings associated with asceticism (M. I. 242).

From the above statement, it can be concluded that the Nigaṇṭhas define the role of volition (especially with regard to the training that aims for the goal of liberation from rebirth) as the capacity of deliberately cultivating painful disciplines and renouncing pleasures. In his criticism of the Nigaṇṭha attitude to volition, the Buddha questions the notion that the power of volition consists of the capacity to endure pain voluntarily and remain unswerving in following a chosen discipline. In developing his argument, he focuses on cultivating the mind's ability to assess the consequences of a decision and to change course, if necessary, in order to reach one's ultimate spiritual goal. The Buddha maintains that there are circumstances in which ascetic disciplines become futile and should be abandoned, whereas wholesome pleasures that facilitate progress in the spiritual path ought to be pursued. The core of the Buddha's teaching is the cultivation of non-attachment and the development of the capacity to make choices without being governed solely by experiences of pleasure and pain. He also persuades his opponent to rethink the Nigaṇṭha view that the experience of pleasure is always opposed to the cultivation of moral goodness and spiritual wisdom.

In order to make his point, the Buddha describes the gruelling ascetic disciplines that he rigorously cultivated during his quest for enlightenment, and he explains why he abandoned such painful striving (M. I. 242-247). The Buddha tells the

Nigaṇṭha Saccaka that as he took on more and more severe ascetic disciplines, his thoughts remained serene and lucid, so that the painful physical feeling did not overwhelm his mind and establish a hold over it (*uppannā dukkhā vedanā cittaṁ na pariyādāya tiṭṭhati*). This statement, which the Buddha repeats as he recounts each stage of his own ascetic practice, signifies that however severe the physical pain, he firmly retained the ability to assess his progress and to evaluate the efficacy of ascetic endeavour as a method that claimed to lead to liberation.

The narrative has a tone of gentle simplicity and candour as the Buddha tells Saccaka that at the severest point of his asceticism, when he pondered whether there could be a path to liberation from ignorance other than ascetic endeavour, he remembered how, in his youth, he had spontaneously experienced the rapture of the first plane of meditation under the cool shelter of a rose-apple tree (M. I. 246). The Buddha explains that this recollection produced in him the conviction that the serene joy of meditation was indeed the way to enlightenment. He then says that the turning point in his quest came when he resolved that he would not fear (*na bhāyāmi*)[4] pleasure (*sukha*) that had nothing in common with sensual desire (*kāma*) and with unwholesome mental states (*akusalā dhammā*). Here the Buddha shows the Nigaṇṭha that the experience of pleasure does not necessarily entail a growing desire for pleasures or the unwholesome mental states of greed (*lobha*), aversion (*dosa*), and delusion (*moha*). Through this narrative, the Buddha takes the Nigaṇṭha to the crucial moment in his own lengthy quest when he experienced the firm conviction that pleasure neither invariably produces unwholesome mental states nor necessarily opposes spiritual striving (M. I. 247).

The Buddha continues his narration, explaining that as he moved towards his goal stage by stage, his mind was not unsettled by the pleasant feelings of meditation (*jhāna*) and the bliss of liberating knowledge (*ñāṇa*). Earlier in the narrative, as the Buddha describes each stage of his own ascetic striving, he repeats the statement that painful feelings did not invade his mind and dwell there. At the conclusion of the narrative, as the Buddha describes his experience of the stages leading to liberating knowledge, he adds the refrain that the newly arising pleasant feelings of each stage did not invade the mind and become established there (*uppannā sukhā vedanā cittaṁ na pariyādāya tiṭṭhati*) (M. I. 247-249).

Two very different concepts of how volitional effort is employed in the spiritual quest can be extrapolated from the *Mahāsaccaka-sutta.* In the Nigaṇṭha view, the spiritual path takes the form of a series of vows that must be fulfilled. As a consequence, the Nigaṇṭhas perceive the role of volition as the sustained effort to persist in a resolve, whatever obstacle may arise. The idea of steadfastly keeping a vow is not absent in the Theravāda tradition. In the *Kīṭāgiri-sutta* of the *Majjhima-nikāya,* it is said that those disciples whose training is motivated and guided by a heartfelt attitude of faith (*saddhānusārī*) should make a vow to follow the Buddha's way, even if the effort causes the blood to dry up and sinews to wither away (M. I. 481). The *Kīṭāgiri-sutta* teaches that energy (*viriya*) should be applied and maintained until whatever can be gained through human stamina (*purisatthāma*), human energy (*purisa-viriya*), and human endeavour (*purisa-parakkama*) has been gained. The concept of *viriya* in the *Kīṭāgiri-sutta* resembles the Jaina view, which conceives of volition as resolute application of energy. According to Schubring's interpretation, "will" is conveyed in the Jaina canonical texts by the synonyms "*uṭṭhāṇa kamma bala vīriya purisakkāra-parakkama*" (preparedness, action, energy, human vigour, valour).[5]

Whereas the *Kīṭāgiri-sutta* perceives volitional effort in the religious quest as the unswerving application of energy in the fulfilment of a heroic vow, the *Mahāsaccaka-sutta* puts the emphasis on the mind's capacity of purposive reflection and decision-making. In this *Sutta,* volitional effort does not involve subjugating the body at any cost or resolutely pursuing a single method in all circumstances. The focus, rather, is on coordinating the application of energy with the mind's capacity to judge whether or not progress is being made through the method chosen for attaining a goal. The voluntary endurance of pain is not put forward as the main criterion of progress in the *Mahāsaccaka-sutta*, and pleasant feelings that are not inimical to the spiritual endeavour are not rejected.

The debate between the Buddha and the Nigaṇṭhas concerning the relationship between pleasant feelings and moral values is further developed in the *Devadaha-sutta* (M. II. 223-225). The primary contrast, for the Nigaṇṭhas, is between ascetic discipline (*tapas)* and pleasure (*sukha*). The former they consider to be painful but always morally good and beneficial; the latter they regard as a harbinger of moral evil and sorrow. The Buddha distinguishes between fruitful (*saphala*) and fruitless (*aphala*) striving, and challenges the Nigaṇṭhas with the idea that within the methods of fruitful striving, there is a place for the type of pleasure that is in harmony with virtue (M. II. 225). Pleasure that accords with virtue is distinct from craving for sensory pleasures (*aññatr' eva kāmehi*) and from unwholesome mental states (*aññatra akusalehi dhammehi*) (M. I. 247). According to the Buddha's definition, in the fruitful way of striving one is not overwhelmed by pain and one does not overwhelm oneself with self-imposed pain. Moreover, in pursuing a fruitful method of training, one neither renounces pleasure that synchronizes with what is ethically good (*dhammikañ ca sukhaṁ na paricajjati*), nor does one unduly cling to wholesome and beneficial pleasures (*tasmiñ ca sukhe anadhimucchito hoti*) (M. II. 223).[6] Furthermore, the Buddha maintains that striving can be designated as fruitful only if the kind of effort put forth and the amount of energy expended are both appropriate for a specific situation. He points out that painful, disciplined striving is required when it serves to cleanse the mind of the type of unwholesome mental states (*akusalā dhammā*) that tend to multiply in pleasant circumstances (M. II. 225). However, the Buddha stresses that such painful striving becomes unnecessary after those unwholesome mental states diminish and wholesome states begin to flourish.[7] Here the Buddha gives a fine analogy: an arrowsmith heats an arrow to straighten it, and when he has achieved his purpose he ceases to apply heat. A skilled craftsman and a skilled *samaṇa* know when to stop.

Debate on the Moral Significance of Intention and Act

Perhaps the best known of the debates between the Buddha and the Nigaṇṭhas occurs in the *Upāli-sutta* of the *Majjhima-nikāya* (M. I. 376-380). Here the lay disciple Upāli puts forward the view of his Nigaṇṭha teacher, Nātaputta (Vardhamāna Mahāvīra). According to Upāli, Nātaputta teaches that in the matter of the perpetration of morally wrong action a misdeed of the body is to be judged as more blameworthy (*mahāsāvajjatara*) than a misdeed of speech or thought. In other words, the Nigaṇṭha position, as presented in the *Upāli-sutta*, is that what is actually done carries greater moral significance than what is said or contemplated in thought. The Buddha's position is that moral responsibility has its basis in acts of the mind (*mano-kamma*) (M. I. 373).[8] Although the Buddha does not use a term that directly conveys "purpose" or "intention", it is obvious that *mano-kamma* includes these connotations. The Buddha's statement, therefore, can be rephrased to signify that moral value resides in the mental function of forming an intention, rather than in an act of body or speech.

In the course of the debate with Upāli, the Buddha demonstrates that in actual practice, the Nigaṇṭhas themselves give greater moral weight to mental functions than to verbal expressions (*vacī-kamma*) or physical actions (*kāya-kamma*). The Buddha drives home his argument with concrete examples, of which the following one is the most telling. The Buddha puts forward the hypothetical case of a Nigaṇṭha who adheres strictly to the prescribed ethical restraints, but cannot avoid destroying innumerable minute living beings by stepping on them while walking (M. I. 377). The Buddha asks his opponent Upāli what karmic consequences the Nigaṇṭha teacher Nātaputta (Mahāvīra) foresees for that particular harmful act. Upāli replies that Nātaputta does not consider an act that is done without prior intention (*asañcetanika*) to carry much moral blame. The Buddha then asks how Nātaputta would judge the case if a Nigaṇṭha were to intend (*sace pana . . . ceteti*) to kill those tiny living beings while walking. Upāli concedes that the harmful act would certainly be judged as greatly reprehensible (*mahāsāvajja*) if it is intended. The Buddha then asks under what category of acts Nātaputta would classify intention (*cetanaṁ . . . Nigaṇṭho Nātaputto kismiṁ paññāpeti*). Upāli has to admit that Nātaputta would classify *cetanā* under the category of mental acts. In this way, the Buddha makes the Nigaṇṭha householder Upāli see for himself that in concrete situations the Nigaṇṭha teacher Nātaputta assigns greater moral significance to the mental act (*mano-kamma*) of intention (*cetanā*) than to physical acts (*kāya-kamma*) such as inadvertently stepping on minute living beings while walking. The narrative context of the *Upāli-sutta* is very helpful in clarifying the meaning of *cetanā*. Although the term is not defined, the context indicates that it connotes intention, purpose, or goal-oriented thought in contrast to an act of body or speech. The *Upāli-sutta* is also important because of the issues it raises concerning the Jaina view of intention.

One of the issues in interpreting the central concepts of Jainism is how much of a divergence there is between early Jainism,[9] especially as taught in the Jaina canon and described in the Buddhist *Suttas*, and Jainism as represented in the philosophical texts of a later period, starting with the *Tattvārtha-sūtra* of Umāsvāti. There is still much controversy regarding the date of the *Tattvārtha-sūtra*. According to W.J. Johnson, this text was composed between 150 C.E. and 350 C.E.[10] P.S. Jaini maintains that the main tenor of the Jaina tradition remains unchanged through the ages. Johnson, however, argues in his *Harmless Souls*[11] that there is a considerable difference between the essentially ascetic teaching of the Jaina canon and the reinterpretation of the teaching by Umāsvāti, who gives due weight to the legitimate concerns of lay followers. According to Johnson's interpretation, whereas in early Jainism, injury (*hiṁsā*) to living beings is viewed as invariably evil and karmically binding, regardless of the intention and mental attitude of the agent, in the *Tattvārtha-sūtra* of Umāsvāti, the moral quality of an act is judged on the basis of whether or not it is imbued with injurious passions (*kaṣāya*) and whether or not it is intended.

According to Jacobi, the *Sūtrakṛtāṅga* (*Sūyagaḍaṁga*) corroborates the statement in the *Upāli-sutta* that the Nigaṇṭhas regarded, not what was said (*vacī-kamma*) or contemplated in the mind (*mano-kamma*), but the actual physical act (*kāya-kamma*) as the basis of moral responsibility and the occasion for karmic bondage to occur.[12] To demonstrate that early Jainism bases moral responsibility not on the intention but on the act as such, Jacobi calls attention to the caricature of the Buddhist position in the *Sūtrakṛtāṅga*.[13] The Buddhists are ridiculed as maintaining that if a person thrusts a spit through a man, mistaking him for a granary that is vaguely shaped like a human form, or barbecues a baby, mistaking the baby's figure for a large gourd, that person should not be judged as guilty of murder since the act is unintended. Johnson refers to the same passage and concludes that by mocking the Buddhists, the Jainas emphasize their own view that moral responsibility is based, not on intention or lack of it, but on whether or not the act involves injury to a living being.[14]

It could be argued, however, that Jacobi and Johnson tend to overemphasize the moral significance that the Nigaṇṭhas place on the physical act and underestimate those Jaina canonical passages that give much importance to attitudes and the passions of the heart. Though Johnson does not alter his view regarding early Jainism, he does refer to statements in the Jaina canonical texts that strongly instruct a monk to cultivate a wholesome inner attitude that will save him from physical misdeeds. A typical passage in the *Sūtrakṛtāṅga* (II. 2. 51) teaches a monk not to be enticed by stimulations of the senses. Further instructions admonish him not to give way to wrath, pride, deceit, and greed. He is warned not to engage in quarrelling or telling lies and not to commit himself to wrong belief. The *Sūtrakṛtāṅga* explains that a monk avoids misconduct and ceases to acquire *karma* by following these instructions.[15] The "passions" consisting of wrath, pride, deceit, and greed, which produce unwholesome intentions, are mentioned in the scriptural texts.[16] Although early Jainism maintains that it is not the intention but solely the act that generates *kamma*, it is significant that the canonical texts emphasize that acts are motivated by corresponding emotions and cognitive processes.

Though the Buddha and the Nigaṇṭhas differ greatly in their view of the relative moral significance to be assigned to acts of the mind (*mano-kamma*) and to concrete physical deeds (*kāya-kamma*), nevertheless both parties agree that neither moral goodness nor spiritual insight can be attained without cultivating a mind that is free of dangerous passions, intentions of causing harm (*hiṁsā*), and carelessness or negligence (*pramāda*). It follows that both agree that behaviour cannot be changed unless there are corresponding changes in mental attitude. In Theravāda, avoiding laxity and inattention with regard to all the details of daily life becomes an important aspect of the discipline of mindfulness (*satipaṭṭhāna*). Though the Buddha accords primacy to intention, he insists on thoughtful vigilance directed to one's words and actions; though the Nigaṇṭhas give greater significance to the physical deed, they emphasize the need for a watchful mental attitude that seeks to be free of unwholesome passions.

Whereas the actual process by which bondage to *karma* occurs is left unspecified in the Jaina canonical texts, the *Tattvārtha-sūtra* (VI. 1-4) takes the position that it is the presence of the passions in the soul that produces bondage. P.S. Jaini explains that unlike any other school of thought in India, the Jaina tradition defines *karma* as a form of fine matter and maintains that bondage (*bandha*) to *karma* occurs when there is an influx (*āsrava*) of particles of karmic matter into the non-material soul (*jīva*).[17] In his *Early Jainism*, K.K. Dixit maintains that the earliest canonical texts give little indication about the precise cause—whether physical or mental—that produces the influx of fine matter into the soul.[18] The later philosophical manual, the *Tattvārtha-sūtra*, clarifies this issue by maintaining that while acts of body, speech, and mind provide the occasion for karmic matter to enter the soul, it is the inner attitude and intentions caused by the passions that make it possible for karmic matter to adhere to the soul.

Two types of actions are distinguished in the *Tattvārtha-sūtra*.[19] Acts that are motivated by the passions of anger, pride, deceit, and greed (*krodha, māna, māyā, lobha*) are designated as "rebirth-causing" (*sāmparāyika*). They are said to produce merit (*puṇya*) or demerit (*pāpa*) and bring about different types of rebirth. In the *Tattvārtha-sūtra* (VI. 4), these four passions that cause bondage to *kamma* are collectively designated as *kaṣāyas*. On the other hand, actions that are free of the *kaṣāyas* are known as "transient" or "fleeting"(*īryāpatha karma*). The *Tattvārtha-sūtra* holds that their effect is short-lived and does not extend beyond the present life; they do not influence the course of rebirth.[20]

Vīrya and Volition in Jainism

When the question regarding the ultimate source of volitional energy is raised, the Jaina view is that volition is rooted in the property of energy (*vīrya*) that is inherent in the soul. It is a fundamental affirmation of the Jaina tradition that together with consciousness (*caitanya, cetanā*) and bliss (*sukha*), energy (*vīrya*) is present as an inviolable quality of the soul. This energy is regarded as an autonomous quality in the soul, neither dependent on nor derived from consciousness and bliss. According to P.S. Jaini's interpretation, the soul's fundamental energy (*vīrya*) is the ultimate source not only of all manifestations of conative dynamism in daily life, but also of all expressions of knowledge, from basic conscious awareness to ultimate wisdom. He explains that *vīrya* is regarded in Jainism as "a sort of meta-quality, an abstract force" that empowers the cognitive features of the individual and makes it possible for cognition to occur.[21] Mehta gives a similar elucidation of the concept of *vīrya* in his *Jaina Psychology*. He explains that in the Jaina tradition, *vīrya* is affirmed to be an inherent capacity of the soul and that all cognitions, emotions, and initiatives to act are looked upon as expressions of this fountainhead of energy.[22]

P.S. Jaini's interpretation of *vīrya* in Jainism resembles what C.A.F. Rhys Davids means by "will". For her, the will is essentially autonomous or "self-directing", and she maintains that it would be meaningless to posit a self-directing capacity unless it is grounded in a self, "the willer". The concept of *vīrya* signifies that Jainism regards volitional energy as a quality that defines the very nature of the self (*jīva*). In P.S. Jaini's interpretation, the Jaina concept of *vīrya* represents the capacity that expresses what a person is and seeks to become. The Jaina tradition holds that the tragedy of being human is that *vīrya* can never be fully expressed as long as karmic matter obscures and hinders the soul's innate capacities. It is worth noting that in the principal *Upaniṣads*,[23] in the *Yoga-sūtra* (I. 20, II. 38), and in the Pāli *Suttas*, *vīrya/viriya* does not signify a "meta-quality" representing the ultimate source of psychic energy in a person, but refers only to specific applications of volitional energy.

Debate on Whether the Processes of *Kamma* Negate Human Initiative

The *Devadaha-sutta* maintains that the Nigaṇṭhas uphold the view that human volition and effort can do nothing to alter the processes by which *kamma* brings forth its consequences (M. II. 220-221). In the course of their debate with the Buddha, the Nigaṇṭhas are put in the position of admitting that their gruelling ascetic practices cannot prevent the fruition of past *kamma* nor alter the circumstances in which its consequences will be experienced.

In the *Devadaha-sutta*, the Nigaṇṭhas specify various circumstances that have a bearing on the processes of *karma*, and they maintain that the consequences of past deeds cannot be changed by striving or effort (*upakkamena vā padhānena vā*). Their arguments nclude the following concepts regarding the inflexible nature of the processes of *karma*: the painful or pleasant karmic consequences that accrue to a person cannot be altered; the time when the effect of a specific deed is to be experienced remains fixed and cannot be made earlier or later; the amount and intensity of painful and pleasant consequences cannot be lessened or magnified; and a deed whose effects must necessarily be experienced (*vedanīyam*) cannot be changed into a deed that does not come to fruition and whose effects need not be experienced (*avedanīyam*). The technical terms used in the *Devadaha-sutta* suggest that debates regarding whether the consequences of *karma* are predetermined were common among the *samaṇa* communities.

In the *Suttas*, the rigid stance of the Nigaṇṭhas is contrasted with the Buddha's flexible interpretation of *kamma*. McDermott argues in *Development in the Early Buddhist Concept of Kamma/Karma* that the Buddha regarded the "moral character" manifested by a person throughout the course of life to be the crucial determining factor with regard to how the effects of past *kamma* would come to fruition and be experienced by that person.[24] In this context, McDermott refers to the *Aṅguttara-nikāya* (A. I. 250), where it is said that the wrong-doing committed by a person whose moral character is generally good entails only minimum of unhappy consequences that do not extend beyond the present life. However, a similar wrong-doing committed by a person whose moral character is generally evil is conceived as *kamma* that produces extensive and acutely painful consequences—even rebirth in *Niraya* hell. The following analogy in this passage of the *Aṅguttara-nikāya* illustrates the point: a small amount of salt can make a glass of water undrinkable, but cannot alter the taste of the waters of the River Gaṅgā.

The *Mahākammavibhaṅga-sutta* (M. III. 210-215) provides the main textual basis for McDermott's argument. Here the Buddha distinguishes the following four possibilities with regard to the fruition of *kamma* in order to demonstrate that the course of *kamma* is not rigidly determined. A person commits evil deeds and experiences a sorrowful rebirth. This is a case of *kamma* that is incapable of producing happy results and shows itself to be incapable of doing so. Another person, in spite of committing evil deeds, still enjoys a happy rebirth. In this case, *kamma* that is incapable of producing happy results appears to be capable of doing so. A third person, whose life is replete with good deeds, enjoys a happy rebirth. The Buddha says that this third example is a case where *kamma* that has the capacity to produce happy results shows itself to be capable of achieving such results. Finally, in spite of abstaining from evil and doing good deeds, a person experiences an unhappy rebirth. This is a case of *kamma* that has the capacity to produce happy results but gives the appearance of being incapable of doing so. The Buddha maintains that though the four cases presented above do occur, none of them should be made the basis of general statements regarding the relationship between *kamma* and its mode of fruition. According to the Buddha's teaching, it would be invalid if a person were to witness any one of the above cases and on that basis conclude: "This alone is true; anything else is false" (*idam eva saccaṁ mogham aññam*) (M. III. 210-213). It is implied here that those who maintain that good acts invariably lead to happy consequences and evil acts always bring unhappy results uphold a rigidly deterministic view of *kamma*. At the same time, those who deny any correlation between the moral quality of an act and its consequences are regarded as adherents of a theory of pure chance.

The Buddha proceeds to point out that during the interval of time between the performance of a specific deed and its fruition, other acts can occur that could either transform the character of the person who performed the deed or affect the manner in which that particular deed reaches karmic fruition and puts forth its consequences (M. III. 214-215). According to the Buddha's argument, in the case of a happy rebirth occurring in spite of evil deeds, either those evil deeds were offset by good deeds that preceded or followed them in time, or the person was able to make a commitment to the right view (*sammā-diṭṭi*) at the hour of death. Likewise, if a person whose deeds are good experiences a sorrowful rebirth, either evil deeds (*pāpa-kamma*) were done before or after the good deeds, or the person turned away from the right view and became drawn to a wrong view (*micchā-diṭṭhi*) close to the time of death. Both *brāhmaṇas* and *samaṇas* regarded a person's attitude of mind at the time of death to be a crucial factor in determining the course of *kamma*.

The commentary to the *Majjhima-nikāya* (MA. V. 20) gives the following explanation regarding the question of why the consequences of *kamma* sometimes appear to be incompatible with the moral quality of the deed. When a great amount of unwholesome *kamma* has already been accumulated, a comparatively strong unwholesome deed can temporarily block the consequences of any wholesome *kamma* from taking effect and put forth its own unhappy consequences. If a person who has done many unwholesome deeds experiences a change of heart and does a strong good deed when death is approaching, then that person may enjoy a happy rebirth and the unwholesome deeds may be temporarily prevented from attaining fruition. In the same way, when a person has already accumulated much wholesome *kamma*, a strong wholesome deed could temporarily block an unwholesome deed from putting forth painful consequences. Finally, a powerful morally wrong deed performed when death is close at hand may supersede the good consequences of previous wholesome *kamma* and bring about a sorrowful rebirth.

The *Mahākammavibhaṅga-sutta* itself offers no comment on the Buddha's analysis of *kamma*. However, the Buddha's stance implies that whenever there appears to be a disparity between a deed and how its consequences are experienced, a better understanding can be reached by seeing the deed in question, not in isolation, but in relation to the agent's other deeds. Moreover, the Buddha indicates that the attitudes and views that accompany deeds are crucial factors in determining the course of rebirth. In other words, the Buddha maintains that the consequences of acts come into effect, not as separate incidents, but through processes of mutual conditioning. According to McDermott's interpretation, the Buddha's view is that the mode of fruition of any *kamma* is conditioned by the "moral character" of the agent.[25] The *Mahākammavibhaṅga-sutta* shows, however, that in the Buddha's view, the fruition of *kamma* is dependent also on the influences that a person's wholesome and unwholesome deeds have on each other and on the interaction between views and acts in a person's life. From a practical perspective, the Buddha's analysis of *kamma* in the *Mahākammavibhaṅga-sutta* demonstrates that since the mode of fruition of any *kamma* is not unalterably fixed, the manner in which the consequences of that *kamma* will arise and be experienced can be altered by paying attention to one's views and attitudes and by fruitful effort and striving (*saphala upakkama, saphalaṁ padhānaṁ*).

Whereas the *Devadaha-sutta* (M. II. 220-221) ascribes a rigid and deterministic view of the fruition of *kamma* to the Nigaṇṭhas, modern interpreters emphasize that the hallmark of later Jainism is an "emotional commitment to self-reliance".[26] P.S. Jaini explains that in the Jaina theory of *karma*, the exact amount (*pradeśa*) of karmic matter that enters the soul depends on the "degree of volition" that drives the act.[27] At the same time, according to Jaini's elucidation, the Jaina tradition postulates that the length of time that karmic matter adheres to the soul (*sthiti*) and the specific result (*anubhava*) of any given act depend on the strength or weakness of the passions that motivated the act.[28] Jaini's interpretation agrees with that of von Glasenapp, who explains that in the Jaina view, the duration of time that a specific *karma* remains latent in the soul and the intensity of its effect depend on the "state of mind (*adhyavasāya*)" of the agent at the time when the act was done.[29] Jaini's interpretation also focuses on the wide-ranging powers that the later Jaina tradition ascribes to the volitional energy (*vīrya*) of the soul with regard to the fruition of *karma*. The Jaina tradition that developed after the *Tattvārtha-sūtra* posits that the soul's volitional energy can either hasten or postpone the moment of fruition, either sharpen or diminish the intensity of the effect of a specific *karma*, and even render *karma* incapable of having any impact whatsoever.[30]

Debates Regarding the Nature and Ultimate Basis of the Capacity to Initiate Action

Though the Buddha and the Nigaṇṭhas disagreed with each other regarding the source of motivational energy in a human being, both rejected the deterministic view of the Ājīvakas. The Ājīvaka teacher Makkhali Gosāla put forward the view that "human volition" and "moral choice" are meaningless concepts because the life of every being is totally controlled by a principle of fate or destiny (*niyati*). In the Buddhist *Suttas*, the determinism of the Ājīvakas is called *ahetukavāda* (the doctrine of non-causality) because of its central tenet that human effort cannot prevail against all-controlling destiny and cannot produce any results (M. I. 407, 516-517; D. I. 54). The Buddha does not give a theoretical refutation of *ahetukavāda*, but he focuses on the practical implications of believing that one's entire life is governed by unalterable fate (*niyati*). Makkhali Gosāla's view is rejected because it teaches that all beings are totally lacking in control, strength, and energy (*sabbe jīvā avasā abalā aviriyā*) (M. I. 407; D. I. 53). The Buddha maintains that commitment to the deterministic view of the Ājīvakas deprives people of all inducement for moral endeavour and spiritual discipline. He points out that from the perspective of *kamma*, determinism entails that the yogic practices of austerities (*tapas*) and purity of life based on sexual restraint (*brahmacariya*) are of no avail since one cannot, through voluntary effort, alter the effects of past deeds (D. I. 54). The Nigaṇṭhas, like the Buddha, disagreed with the Ājīvakas, and they taught that it is possible to prevent a sorrowful future by voluntarily choosing a life of ascetic discipline.

In the *Suttas* the Nigaṇṭhas characterize their teaching as the very essence of *kiriyavāda* (doctrine of action) and ridiculed the Buddha's view as a form of *akiriyavāda* (doctrine of non-action). In the introduction to his work *Jaina Sutras*, Jacobi explains *kriyāvāda* as the doctrine that the soul is both the agent of action and the recipient of the consequences of action. *Akriyāvāda*, on the other hand, is interpreted by Jacobi as a term that can refer to either of two views: it can refer to the doctrine that a soul does not exist or to the teaching that whereas the soul does exist, it neither acts nor is affected by actions.[31] Folkert agrees with Jacobi's explanation of the term *kriyāvāda* in the Jaina texts, and he adds that *kriyāvāda* includes the following tenets: the self exists; it becomes the agent of action and bears responsibility for its deeds; and it experiences *karma* and rebirth because of carelessness (*pramāda*) in its activities. Folkert maintains, however, that the term *kriyāvāda* only gradually acquired the meaning ascribed to it by Jacobi. According to Folkert's analysis, *Sūtrakṛtāṅga* I.12, where the principles of *kriyāvāda* are delineated, belongs to a later stratum of the Jaina canon.[32]

The *Sūtrakṛtāṅga* explains *kriyāvāda* as the teaching which maintains that sorrowful consequences are caused by one's own acts.[33] The *akriyāvādin* is defined as one who does not accept that *karma* has the power to produce results that can come into effect in a future period of time. Jacobi explains that this definition of an *akriyāvādin* is a reference to the Buddhists, who maintain that what exists in the present does not continue into the future.[34]

Furthermore, the Buddhists reject the Jaina idea that the capacity of the mind to initiate bodily action is ultimately based in a power of volition (*vīrya*) that is an inherent property of an autonomous soul (*jīva*). The Buddha is branded as an *akiriyavādin* by Nātaputta in the story of Sīha, the householder disciple of the Niganṭhas (A. IV. 180-181).

In the Buddhist *Suttas*, the teaching of the Buddha is called *kiriyavāda*, and the designation *akiriyavāda* is reserved for the view of the *samaṇa* teacher Pūraṇa Kassapa, who holds that moral distinctions are meaningless and invalid and that acts that are classified as good and bad do not, in fact, lead to the accumulation of merit (*puñña*) and demerit (*pāpa*) (M. I. 406, 516-517; D. I. 52-53). The Buddha's opposition to Pūraṇa Kassapa's view makes it clear that in Buddhist usage *kiriyavāda* represents the doctrine that not only upholds the idea of *kamma*, but also maintains that the individual has the capacity to initiate actions and bears responsibility for those actions. Since the Buddha does not accept the Niganṭha view that the soul exists and is involved in action, his definition of *kiriyavāda* differs from the definition in the *Sūtrakṛtāṅga*. As in the case of the Ājīvkas teaching of non-causality, in opposing Kassapa's teaching of non-action, the Buddha focuses, not on the theoretical premises of the doctrine, but on its practical implications (M. I. 405-409). The Buddha maintains that those who accept *ahetukavāda* or *akiriyavāda* cannot uphold wholesome (*kusala*) states of good behaviour (*sucarita*) since they do not acknowledge that individuals have the capacity to initiate acts that will make an impact on the future course of their lives. In the *Aṅguttara-nikāya*, while condemning the deterministic *ahetukavāda* of the Ājīvakas, the Buddha declares that the teaching of all the *arahants* and Buddhas of the past and his own teaching as a fully awakened being is *kammavāda, kiriyavāda, viriyavāda* (A. I. 286-287). In this context, *viriya* signifies the energy to initiate and pursue goal-oriented action, *kiriya* connotes action that proceeds from the motivating energy (*viriya*) of an individual who is responsible for that action, and *kamma* indicates that such action (*kiriya*) arises from causes and conditions, has moral value, and produces commensurate consequences. *Akiriyavāda* is a denial of *kamma*, *kiriya* and *viriya*.

The above definition points to important differences in the way the basic mental capacity of initiating action is conceived by three *samaṇa* groups: the Ājīvakas, the Jainas, and the Buddhists. The Ājīvakas maintain that in the final analysis human beings do not have the capacity to initiate any type of action since all physical and mental processes are predetermined by an inexorable fate (*niyati*). According to the Jainas, the idea that human beings have the capacity to initiate action is meaningless and baseless unless this capacity is shown to be a manifestation of a volitional power (*vīrya*) that is grounded in the very nature of an autonomous soul (*jīva*). The Buddhists hold that both the capacity of the mind to initiate acts (*ārambha-dhātu*) and the energy (*viriya*) that is applied in carrying out an intention are observable mental factors that come into existence when appropriate causal conditions are present in the body and in the consciousness continuum. In the Buddhist view, these mental factors of motivational energy and the capacity to initiate action are not rooted in a permanent self. The capacity of these motivational factors to initiate action is regarded as a function that is derived from the same causal conditions through which they come into being in the continuum of consciousness.

Comprehensive Definition of Action in Early Jainism and in the *Suttas*

Both in the early Jaina tradition and in the *Suttas*, acts that carry moral values and bring about karmic consequences are said to be of three types: physical, verbal, and mental. In the *Upāli-sutta*, the Nigaṇṭha Tapassī says that their teacher, Nātaputta, classifies acts in terms of three types of *daṇḍa*[35] (literally, "rod of punishment"): physical, verbal, and mental (M. I. 371-372). The term *daṇḍa* refers to the Nigaṇṭha view of the painful consequences of action. The Buddha replies that whereas he prefers the term *kamma* to *daṇḍa*, he also classifies acts in the same way. Moreover, both traditions hold that these acts of body, speech, and mind can be performed in three ways: one can commit the act oneself, or instigate another to do so, or approve of the act when it is committed by someone else. In *Early Jainism*, Dixit maintains that the earliest "Jaina treatment of ethical problems" was to say of a wrong-doing that it was either committed by oneself, or that one verbally instigated another to commit it, or that one mentally approved of it when it was done by another person.[36] One of the oldest Jaina texts, the *Sūtrakṛtāṅga*, says that if one kills living beings, or causes others to kill, or approves of the killing of living beings, then one's evil *karma* will keep on increasing.[37]

As in the Jaina tradition, in the *Aṅguttara-nikāya* also unwholesome acts of body, speech, and mind are further classified as acts done by oneself (*attanā*), acts that one causes to be done by another (*parañ ca samādapeti*), and acts of which one approves (*samanuñño hoti*) (A. V. 305-307). The *Aṅguttara-nikāya* adds a fourth type, which comprises acts that one praises and implicitly recommends (*vaṇṇaṁ bhāsati*). According to the *Aṅguttara-nikāya*, each unwholesome act of body, speech, and mind becomes fourfold: one can do it oneself, instigate another to do it, give it one's seal of approval, or recommend it through high praise (A. V. 307-308). Since these acts are designated as morally wrong or "unwholesome" (*akusala*), it is evident that they are regarded as intentional acts that carry karmic consequences. Though this passage in the *Aṅguttara-nikāya* refers to unwholesome acts as fourfold, this description obviously applies also to wholesome acts. Moreover, since Theravāda defines *kamma* as the concrete realization of intention or purposive thought, it follows that intentions also can be regarded as fourfold. Intention can be interpreted to include expressing approval of a deed (*anumodana*) or describing it as something splendid, with the purpose of instigating someone to perform that deed.

Examples from the *Vinaya-piṭaka* demonstrate that both the term *sañcetanika-kamma* (intentional act, purposive act) and the notion of a deliberate act performed on the basis of intention or prior purpose (*sañcicca*) are interpreted comprehensively so that they include a range of meanings. Intentional murder, for example, is interpreted in such a way as to include the following cases: deliberately depriving a human being of life; prompting or instigating another to kill by expressing a determination, resolve, or wish to cause death; inciting a person to commit suicide; and praising death as something glorious, with the intention of persuading a person to find a way to die (Vin. III. 73-76).

Primacy of Intention Upheld in the *Vinaya-piṭaka* and the *Kathāvatthu*

The *Vinaya-piṭaka* takes the position that moral value resides primarily in the intention that becomes expressed in an act, rather than in the act as such. An offence against the monastic community is defined as the intentional breaking of a monastic rule (Vin. III. 12, 73, 112, IV. 90). Intentional offence (*sañcetanika-vītikkama*) is defined as a wrong action that is done by a person who acts knowingly (*jānanto*) and with conscious awareness (*sañjānanto*) after purposefully thinking (*cecca*) and deliberating over it (*abhivitaritvā*) (Vin. IV. 290). If a rule is broken unintentionally, it is not regarded as a serious offence against the monastic community. "Unintentionally" (*asancicca*) is explained as an act that is done "without thinking" (*assatiyā*) by a person who does not know (*ajānantassa*), or is ill (*gilānassa*), or is mentally unstable (*ummattakassa*). The unintentional act is also regarded as not planned by oneself and not intentionally instigated by another person.

The term that is most difficult to interpret in the *Vinaya* definition of *asañcicca* (without intending, not having intended) is *assatiyā*. The term *asati* signifies not being attentive, not keeping in mind, and *asatiyā*, the instrumental case, indicates "through forgetfulness", or "not intending" (P.E.D. 672, col. 2). *Assatiyā* does not occur frequently, and is mainly found in the *Vinaya-piṭaka*. Horner translates *assatiyā* as "without thinking".[38] *Sati* signifies not only recollection of the past, but also being attentive to what is happening in the present. It follows that in the definition of *asañcicca*, *assatiyā* indicates that an act is "unintentionally done" by a person whose mind is not attentive to what is happening in that situation. The unintentional act is done without alertness and attention, and therefore is not deliberately planned with a goal in view. *Ajānanta* indicates a person who either does not know the circumstances that surround the act or does not comprehend the consequences that the act entails. Whereas *assatiyā* signifies lack of attention, *ajānanta* indicates lack of knowledge.

The following are two examples of unintentional acts described in the *Vinaya-piṭaka*. When the monks of Āḷavī were preparing a site for a monastery, a "badly held stone" slipped from the hand of a monk working at an upper level and fell on a monk standing below, causing his death.[39] Horner's translation suggests that the monks did not have sufficient knowledge of construction work and that the tragic consequence was an accident. Another example is of a group of monks unknowingly administering an incorrect medical treatment to a sick monk and causing his death. Here again, the death is seen as the result of lack of sufficient knowledge on the part of those who committed the unintentional act. The emphasis in these two examples is on the term *ajānanto* (one who does not know) in the definition of an unintentional act that does not constitute an offence against the monastic life. In these examples, the act is classified as unintentional primarily because the agent is beset by lack of knowledge (*ajānanto*) rather than because he performed the act without paying attention to what he was doing (*assatiyā*).

The *Kathāvatthu* (Kvu. 593-595) records further debates on the controversial point of whether moral value resides in the act itself or in the intention underlying the act. In the debate, the opponents of the Theravādins maintain that there are five crimes so totally reprehensible that they lead immediately to retribution in the form of excruciatingly painful rebirth. These five crimes comprise killing one's mother, or father, or an *arahant*, shedding the blood of a Buddha, and causing a schism in the *Saṅgha.* The Theravādins maintain that even in these five cases, the act must be judged on the basis of the intention of the person who commits the act. They insist that the distinction that is made in the *Vinaya* between deliberate murder and causing accidental death extends also to these five crimes. In this context, the Theravādins cite a passage in the *Vinaya* that distinguishes between those who intend to cause a schism in the *Saṅgha* and those who are mistaken with regard to the teaching of the Buddha and unintentionally cause a schism.[40] The fact that this section of the *Kathāvatthu* is entitled *Asañcicca-kathā* leaves no doubt that the focus of the debate is not on retributive justice for the five acts that were regarded as the most reprehensible, but on the question of whether unintentional wrongdoings should be treated as punishable crimes. McDermott points out that the Theravādins insist that primacy must be given to the "intentional impulse" (*cetanā*) in judging all acts, including the five most evil crimes.[41]

Although the Buddhist tradition considers intention to be primary in judging the moral significance of an act, like the Jainas, Buddhists also maintain that careful attention (*appamāda*) to all the concrete details of daily life is the basic discipline in the spiritual path. For example, in the *Cūḷagosiṅga-sutta*, when the monks report to the Buddha that they are living a life guided by *appamāda* (watchful alertness, careful attention), he is interested in such details as whether they are keeping the dining room clean, filling the water jars regularly, and emptying out the garbage carefully without causing harm to plants and living beings (M. I. 207). In the *Cūḷagosiṅga-sutta*, this discipline of careful attention is seen as the basis for cultivating serenity and the planes of meditation (*jhāna*). Similarly, the *Mahāsatipaṭṭhāna-sutta* explains mindfulness as the practice of maintaining clarity of mind and uninterrupted awareness with regard to both one's own mental states as well as the physical details that fill the day (D. II. 92). It follows, therefore, that though the Buddhist tradition maintains that moral value rests in the intention that instigates the act, and not solely in the act, the *Suttas* and the *Vinaya-piṭaka* insist on the need not only for attention and scrupulous care in actually performing the deed, but also for thought and understanding with regard to the circumstances surrounding the act and the consequences that it entails.

Conclusion

When the Jainas call Buddhism a doctrine of non-action (*akriyāvāda*) they are pointing to a crucial difference between their view of volition and the Buddhist view. The Jainas maintain that the ultimate source of human volition and activity is the property of energy (*vīrya*) that is inherent in the soul (*jīva*). From the Jaina point of view, Buddhism is a doctrine of non-action because it does not accept the idea of a soul that is the source of energy (*vīrya*), consciousness (*caitanya/cetanā*),[42] and bliss (*sukha*). According to the Buddhists, since all intentions, all applications of energy (*viriya*), and all acts of body, speech, and mind arise through causes and conditions, none of these factors can claim to be autonomous or sovereign.

In the *Suttas*, the Buddha's concept of fruitful effort and striving (*saphala upakkama, saphalam padhānam*) distinguishes his view of volition and effort from that of the Niganṭhas. According to Buddhist accounts, the Niganṭhas conceive of strong volitional effort as unswerving application of energy for the fulfilment of intentions, decisions, resolves, and vows. Moreover, according to the *Suttas*, the Niganṭhas maintain that voluntary effort in enduring the physical pain resulting from austerities and ascetic practices is the surest way to develop mental strength and resolve. The Buddha, on the other hand, gives a greater role to the cognitive processes of assessing both pain and progress in any volitional effort. "Fruitful striving" signifies matching the volitional effort to the chosen goal. In the Buddha's teaching, fruitful striving involves two methods of acting: renouncing painful disciplines when they are not effective in reaching the goal; and embracing joy, when it is not associated with sensual desire or with unwholesome mental states, as a most effective aid in the path that leads to freedom from ignorance. The Buddha's interpretation of the concept of fruitful striving implies that volitional effort has a cognitive component that formulates wholesome purposes and assesses the appropriateness of the methods with regard to the goal.

The *Suttas*, the *Vinaya-piṭaka*, and the *Kathāvatthu* agree that Theravāda upholds the view that moral value resides primarily in the intention that instigates an act. However, Theravādins do not maintain that moral value resides solely in the intention and that the physical or verbal act has no moral significance. In the *Suttas* and in the *Abhidhamma* texts, wholesome and unwholesome intentional acts (*sañcetanika kamma*) are conceived as acts involving the integration of purposive thought with concrete activity of body, speech, and mind. *Kamma* is defined as a purposive impulse (*cetanā*) becoming concretely realized in an act of body, speech, or mind (A. III. 415). The purposive impulse and the act in which it becomes expressed are conceived as a single whole. It is this configuration of purposive impulse and act that is assessed as wholesome or unwholesome.

ENDNOTES

[1] Nātaputta, the Nigaṇṭha teacher, maintains that the annihilation of the demerit (*pāpa*) of past *kamma* can be achieved through the sharp pain (*kaṭuka*) of arduous austerities (*dukkara-kārikā*). The Nigaṇṭha teaching is that restraint (*saṁvuta*) of body, speech, and mind amounts to non-performance (*akaraṇam*) of acts of demerit with painful future consequences. This restraint signifies living according to the rules of asceticism and non-violence. The cessation (*byantibhāva*) of past *kamma* is attained through austerities (*tapas*), and the removal of future karmic consequences (*āyatim anavassava*) is attained through the non-performance of new *kamma* (*nava-kamma*). Non-performance of *kamma* leads to cessation of sorrow (*dukkhakkhaya*) (M. I. 93).

[2] H. Jacobi, *Jaina Sutras*, 2:xv-xvi.

[3] The phrase *cittaṁ na pariyādāya tiṭṭhati* (M. I. 239) signifies that the pleasant or unpleasant feeling does not completely exhaust or overpower the mind and continue to prevail over it.

[4] The term *bhaya* includes both the emotion of fear and the fearsome situation. Lists of physical and mental perils are included in the *Aṅguttara-nikāya* (A. II. 121-123).

[5] W. Schubring, *The Doctrine of the Jainas*, 172.

[6] Bhikkhu Bodhi points out that M. II. 223 refers to the Middle Way (Bhikkhu Bodhi, *The Middle Length Discourses of the Buddha*, 1302). In the fruitful way of striving (*saphalaṁ padhānam*), one does not urge oneself obsessively to practise painful disciplines. Thus, one does not "soil" oneself with suffering (*na . . . attānam dukkhena addhabhāveti*), nor does one indulge (*sukhe anadhimucchito hoti*) in objects of pleasure. *Addhabhāva* has the literal meaning of being soiled or wet and the figurative meaning of being attached to, or intoxicated by, some object (P.E.D. 26. col.1).

[7] In the *Devadaha-sutta*, the Buddha teaches the balanced cultivation of both determined effort (*saṅkhārappadhāna*) and equanimity (*upekha-bhāvanā*) (M. II. 224). Determined effort causes a person to no longer feel passion towards the object that causes sorrow (*virāgo hoti*); and training in equanimity causes the sorrow to fade away (*dukkhaṁ nijjiṇṇaṁ hoti*). The commentary designates this balance of striving and equanimity as the "pleasant path that soon leads to direct knowledge" (*sukhā paṭipadā khippābhiññā*) (MA. IV. 15).

[8] *Imesaṁ . . . tiṇṇaṁ kammānaṁ . . . manokammaṁ mahāsāvajjataraṁ paññāpemi pāpassa kammassa kiriyāya pāpassa kammassa pavattiyā, no tathā kāya-kammaṁ no tathā vacī-kammam* (M. I. 373).

[9] W.J. Johnson, *Harmless* Souls, 4. Johnson takes the following to be the earliest texts of the Jaina canon: (1) *Ācārāṅga-sūtra* (*Āyāraṁga*), (2) *Sūtrakṛtāṅga* (*Sūyagaḍaṁga*), (3) *Daśavaikālika* (*Dasaveyāliya*), and (4) *Uttarādhyayana* (*Uttarajjhayaṇa*). He designates the teaching that is given in these texts as "early Jainism". Whereas precise dating of these texts is not possible, Jacobi suggests that the collecting of the Jaina canon must have taken place sometime during the end of the fourth or the beginning of the third century B.C.E. (H. Jacobi, *Jaina Sutras*, 1: xliii)

[10] W.J. Johnson, *Harmless Souls*, 46.

[11] W.J. Johnson, *Harmless Souls*, 4-40.

[12] H. Jacobi, *Jaina Sutras*, 2:xvii.

[13] Ibid., 2:414-415.

[14] W.J. Johnson, *Harmless Souls*, 19.

[15] H. Jacobi, *Jaina Sutras*, 2:352.

[16] For example, Ibid., 1:248, 302. The term *kaṣāya* has the literal meaning of a distillation from plants that is astringent in taste, or a paste of reddish yellow colour used for painting walls (P.E.D. 201. col.1). It carries the figurative meaning of a stain or flaw in the mind. The Pāli equivalent, *kasāya*, signifies the three fundamental unwholesome motivations: *lobha* (greed), *dosa* (aversion), and *moha* (delusion) (Vbh. 368).

[17] P.S. Jaini, *The Jaina Path of Purification*, 112.

[18] K.K. Dixit, *Early Jainism*, 9.

[19] The *Tattvārtha-sūtra* (VI.1-4) states that activities of body, speech, and mind provide the occasions for the influx (*āsrava*) of fine karmic matter into the soul (*jīva*). The Pāli term *āsava* refers exclusively to mental states that corrupt the mind. The *Tattvārtha-sūtra* (IV. 3) explains that *āsrava* is of two kinds: good (*śubha*), which is the influx of

meritorious (*puṇya*) *karma;* and bad (*aśubha*), which is the inflow of *karma* characterized by demerit (*pāpa*).

[20] W.J. Johnson, *Harmless Souls,* 48-50; J.L. Jaini, *Tattvarthadhigama Sutra,* 125.

[21] P.S. Jaini, *The Jaina Path of Purification,* 105.

[22] M.L. Mehta, *Jaina Psychology,* 141.

[23] The term *vīrya* seldom appears in those passages in the *Upaniṣads* that give instruction in *yoga.* One significant reference to *vīrya* is at B.U. I. 2.6, where it signifies vigour or life-energy connected with the vital breaths.

There are two references to *vīrya* in the *Yoga-sūtra* (YS. I.20, II.38). In the first of these, *vīrya* is one of a pentad of qualities: *śraddhā* (faith), *vīrya* (energy), *smṛti* (recollection), *samādhi* (concentration) and *prajñā* (understanding). These qualities are known as the "five faculties" in Buddhism. In the second reference, *vīrya* connotes vigour or energy. Here the *Yoga-sūtra* says that *vīrya* can be attained through the practice of *brahmacarya* (sexual restraint and purity of mind).

[24] J.P. McDermott, *Development in the Early Buddhist Concept of Kamma/Karma,* 20.

[25] Ibid., 21.

[26] P.S. Jaini, *The Jaina Path of Purification,* 138.

[27] In this context, P.S. Jaini (Ibid., 113, n.19) cites the following statement from the *Tattvārtha-sūtra: Tīvra-manda-jñātājñāta-bhāvādhikaraṇa-vīrya-viśeṣebhyas tad viśeṣaḥ* (VI.6). The import of this aphorism is that there can be differences in the influx (*āsrava*) of karmic matter when the same deed is done by different persons. According to P.S. Jaini's interpretation, the *Tattvārtha-sūtra* says here that the exact amount (*pradeśa*) of karmic matter that enters the *jīva* depends on "the *degree of volition*" with which the act is undertaken. The aphorism states that the differences (*viśeṣa*) in the influx of karmic matter are caused by differences (*viśeṣebhyaḥ*) in the actions of people, based on the following factors: intensity (*tīvra-bhāva*) or mildness (*manda-bhāva*) of desire or purpose, knowledge (*jñāta-bhāva*) or lack of knowledge (*ajñāta-bhāva*), and the energy of volition (*vīrya*) put forth by the agent.

[28] P.S. Jaini, *The Jaina Path of Purification,* 113.

[29] H. von Glasenapp, *The Doctrine of Karman in Jain Philosophy*, 3.

[30] P.S. Jaini, *The Jaina Path of Purification*, 139.

[31] H. Jacobi, *Jaina Sutras*, 2: xxv.

[32] K.W. Folkert, *Scripture and Community: Collected Essays on the Jains*, 263, 269-270.

[33] H. Jacobi, *Jaina Sutras*, 2: 317.

[34] Ibid., 2:316, n. 3.

[35] Johnson suggests that according to the Nigaṇṭhas, all activity involves the danger of harming living beings, and as a consequence, they taught that all acts of. body, speech, and mind can produce painful karmic consequences. In this sense, all acts are "punishing rods" (*daṇḍas*) (W.J. Johnson, *Harmless Souls*, 12). Jacobi (*Jaina Sutras*, 2: xvii), however, points out that both terms, *kamma* and *daṇḍa*, occur with almost equal frequency in the Jaina canonical texts.

[36] K.K. Dixit, *Early Jainism*, 88.

[37] H. Jacobi, *Jaina Sutras*, 2: 236.

[38] I.B. Horner, *The Book of the Discipline*, 3:186.

[39] Ibid., 1:140.

[40] Ibid., 5:287.

[41] J.P. McDermott, *Development in the Early Buddhist Concept of Kamma/Karma*, 94.

[42] In the Jaina tradition, *caitanya* or *cetanā* is defined as that quality that enables the soul to become a knower (P.S. Jaini, *The Jaina Path of Purification*, 104). The Jaina tradition does not ascribe to *cetanā* the function of intention, purpose, or volition.

Chapter III

Conditioned Origination and *Cetanā*

The causal theory of conditioned origination (*paṭicca-samuppāda*) is the hub around which the psychological and ethical concepts as well as the practical disciplines of Theravāda revolve. Furthermore, in Theravāda, the entire range of the dynamics of volition is seen to be defined by the conditioned arising and the interdependent functioning of all physical and mental states. It follows, then, that whatever role *cetanā* may fulfil in purposive deliberation, choice of goal, and initiation of goal-oriented action, all of these functions are to be regarded as mutually supporting processes that can only arise through causes and conditions.

In the *Sutta* and *Abhidhamma* literature, the nature and functions of *cetanā* are described and analyzed in relation to either the continuum of states of consciousness (*cittas*) or the mind's capacity to assemble its resources and "construct" goal-oriented activities (*saṅkhāras*). Moreover, it is posited that both the processes of purposive deliberation that occur in the series of states of consciousness and the processes of goal-oriented action that are manifested in the mind's constructive activities have to deal with persistent unwholesome tendencies (*anusayas*) that afflict the mind. The notion of *cetanā* is framed by the concepts of *citta*, *saṅkhāra*, and *anusaya*, and these three concepts, which are basic to the psychological and ethical views of Theravāda, acquire their specific nuances of meaning through their relationship to the causal theory of conditioned origination. Especially with regard to the concept of *anusaya*, great care is taken in the *Kathāvatthu*, the *Visuddhimagga*, and in the commentarial literature to stress that conditioned origination abrogates the notion that tendencies and dispositions subsist unchanged in the mind.

Whereas the Pāli *Suttas* consider *cetanā* to be a purposive impulse characterized by the capacity to initiate goal-oriented action, the Upaniṣadic, Yoga, and early Jaina traditions view *cetanā* as basic cognitive awareness. In the *Upaniṣads*, *cetanā* signifies conscious awareness in a general sense (K.U. II. 2.13; S.U. VI. 13), or more specifically, the basic sentience that vitalizes and moves the body (Mt.U. II. 6). In the *Yoga-sūtra*, *cetanā* occurs only once in the compound *pratyak-cetanā* (YS. I.29). Here *cetanā* signifies a specific state of consciousness where there is direct awareness of the soul (*puruṣa*). In the Sāṁkhya tradition, *cetanā* refers to the inviolable consciousness of the soul. Similarly, in the Jaina tradition *cetanā* refers to the innate capacity of the soul (*jīva*) to function as a knower.[1] However, the Jaina tradition holds that the soul's inherent capacity to know cannot be fully manifested as long as a person is bound to the course of rebirth. According to the Jaina view, in the course of rebirth, consciousness pervaded by ignorance (*ajñāna-cetanā*) manifests as twofold: consciousness obsessed with the sense of functioning as the agent of action (*karma-cetanā*), and consciousness concentrated on acquiring the consequences of acts (*karma-phala-cetanā*). When consciousness attains a vision of the innate qualities of the soul, it is said to be pervaded by knowledge (*jñāna-cetanā*).[2] In the Upaniṣadic, Sāṁkhya, Yoga and Jaina traditions, therefore, *cetanā* signifies either a state of consciousness or a specific way in which consciousness functions.

What distinguishes *cetanā* in Theravāda is that it becomes associated with the dynamism of *saṅkhāra* and is endowed with the capacity to initiate intentional acts of body, speech, and mind. Whereas one might expect the action-producing capacities of *saṅkhāras* to be constituted of modalities of energy such as *viriya* (effort, vigour) or *chanda* (impetus to act), the *Suttas* and the *Abhidhamma* texts posit that *saṅkhāras* are formed of different classes of *cetanās*. The association of *cetanās* with the *saṅkhārakkhandha* clearly indicates that *cetanās* are regarded as dynamic motivational factors. Further evidence of the shift in the meaning of *cetanā* from basic sentience and conscious awareness in the *Upaniṣads* to action-producing impulse in Theravāda is that *kamma* is defined, not in terms of *saṅkhāras* and their power to initiate goal-oriented acts, as one might expect, but in terms of *cetanā* (A. III. 415). In this definition, *cetanā* is regarded as synonymous with *kamma*.

Cetanā in the Holistic View of Consciousness Represented by *Citta*

Theravāda resembles the Yoga tradition in its use of *citta* as an "umbrella term" to include all processes of individual consciousness and to indicate their dynamic unity. The distinctive feature of Theravāda, however, is that this holistic view of consciousness shared with the Yoga tradition is transformed into the picture of a continually changing continuum that holds together networks of mutually dependent mental states. The continuum shows itself to be a dynamic unity of mental factors (*cetasikas*) coming into being and passing away in accordance with conditioned origination.

In the *Suttas* and *Abhidhamma* literature, *citta*, *manas*, and *viññāṇa* are regarded as synonymous terms that denote the continuum of consciousness (S. II. 94-95; Dhs. 10; Vbh. 87). However, since these three terms indicate three different ways in which the continuum of consciousness functions and manifests itself, they do have specific meanings. *Manas* indicates the process of conscious awareness acting both as the coordinator of the data of the five senses and as the perceiver of *dhammas* (mental objects) such as concepts and mental images. *Manas* also represents thinking in a general and all-inclusive sense. *Viññāṇa* signifies the continuity of conscious awareness and the capacity of consciousness to interact with the environment, thereby making all experience possible. The continuity is said to be preserved not only during a single life span, but also in the vast course of innumerable rebirths. However, Theravāda maintains that conscious awareness (*viññāṇa*) is not self-generating, but arises in every instance through sensory or mental stimulation, and ceases when the stimulation has run its course. Continuity between past and present conscious awareness is explained, therefore, not by positing a foundation of changeless stability, but in terms of the conditioning of every mental factor by causal influences from the past. Thus, continuity and conditioning are viewed as interdependent factors. Conditioning produces continuity, but conditioning cannot occur without continuity in the production of causes and effects.

If *viññāṇa* represents continuity of conscious awareness, *citta* indicates a cross-section, as it were, of the continuum of consciousness at any given time. The cross-section shows conscious awareness (*viññāṇa*) arising at any given time, conditioned by feeling, perception, emotion, and goal-oriented activity. These mental factors that arise together with *viññāṇa* influence each other in such a way as to manifest a specific state of mind or poise of consciousness (*citta*). These states of mind (*cittas*) form a series and constitute the continuum of individual experience. *Citta*, as a transitory state of mind, is a configuration of mental factors—such as energy, attention, thoughts, and emotions—conditioning each other as well as conscious awareness itself. No such configuration of mental states can arise unless there is "contact" (*phassa*) between conscious awareness (*viññāṇa*) and an object. In order to avoid confusion, it should be noted at the outset that the term *citta* is utilized in two ways in the *Abhidhamma* system of classification. On the one hand, *citta* signifies a specific state of mind formed by a configuration of mental factors that comes into being and passes away. On the other hand, *citta* also signifies a series of states of mind forming an individual mental continuum. In this second sense, the term *citta* is utilized to indicate a continuum of *cittas*, each *citta* followed by the next in a series (*citta-santati*) that constitutes what is conventionally known as the "individual" (Kvu. 458).

In the *Abhidhamma* system of classification, *cetasikas* are the cognitive, emotive, and action-producing mental factors that arise together and form a state of mind (*citta*) at any given moment of time. It follows that *citta* is not conceived as bare conscious awareness that can somehow be separated from mental coefficients, properties, and functions. On the contrary, *citta* signifies a transitory constellation of cooperating mental factors (*cetasikas*) interacting with each other and with the continuum of conscious awareness (*viññāṇa*).[3] In this system of classification, *cetanā* is regarded as one of the *cetasikas* that is present in every state of mind.

The term *citta* occurs in passages in the *Suttas* that describe the entire consciousness (*citta*) of an individual becoming pervaded by a strong emotion or motivational impulse. In different contexts the *citta* as a whole is said to be *pariyādinna* (overpowered), *khitta* (upset, unbalanced), *upakkiliṭṭha* (defiled), *kilanta* (weary), *santa* (peaceful), *alīna* (sincere, unstained), *pasanna* (clear, full of faith), *vasībhūta* (mastering, controlling), or *vimutta* (liberated).[4] In *Philosophy and Psychology in the Abhidharma*, Guenther regards every transitory constellation of mental factors designated as *citta* to be an "attitude" of mind. According to Guenther's interpretation of the *Abhidhamma*, an attitude of mind (*citta*) comes into existence through the interaction of the cognitive, emotive and motivational features displayed by a set of mental factors that arise together and form a dynamic unity. In this interaction, certain mental features become dominant, giving the attitude of mind (*citta*) its distinctive quality. Guenther maintains that the concept of changing attitudes can explain why a person is strongly affected by certain stimuli on some occasions while remaining unaffected at other times. Guenther explains that a person who experiences a certain attitude of mind (*citta*) is "ready for something", and that this "readiness" results from a "certain subjective group-pattern" [5]. Every *citta* configuration brings together certain components that harmonize with its principal characteristics, while leaving out factors that are not compatible. Out of this network or "group pattern" of cognitive, emotive and motivational features issues an "attitude" of mind that is "ready" to function in a certain way in relation to the environment.

In *The Path of Purification*, Bhikkhu Ñāṇamoli explains that the *Abhidhamma* system interprets *citta* to be a "momentary type-situation" arising through the interplay of conscious awareness (*viññāṇa*) with the "tone"—that is to say, the distinctive quality—belonging to concomitant mental factors.[6] A *citta* is defined by Bhikkhu Ñāṇamoli as the momentary display of a typical "manner of consciousness". When Buddhaghosa was writing, the theory of momentariness was well established in the *Abhidhamma* system. By describing a *citta* as a momentary type-situation, Bhikkhu Ñāṇamoli indicates that the *Visuddhimagga* regards each *citta* as a momentary state of mind that displays a typical set of dominant characteristics. Every *citta* is rendered easily recognizable and classifiable through its dominant characteristics. Thus, because of the presence of certain types of governing qualities, *cittas* are classified into the three types: wholesome, unwholesome and morally indeterminate. The definition of *citta* given in the *Atthasālinī* validates the interpretations of Guenther and Ñāṇamoli, who concur in regarding the *citta* as an "attitude" or typical frame of mind (Asl. 63-65).

The definition in the *Atthasālinī* begins by saying that *citta* is that which thinks about (*cinteti*) or discerns (*vijānāti*) an object.[7] But the definition soon demonstrates that *citta* is a far richer term than its derivation from the verb *cinteti* would warrant. According to the *Atthasālinī*, the term *citta* is associated with the verb *cināti/cinoti* which connotes "to heap up, to collect, to accumulate" (P.E.D. 268, col. 2). Furthermore, as a pun, the *Atthasālinī* associates the psychological term *citta* with the commonly used term *citta* (Saṁskṛt: *citra*) meaning "that which is variegated" or, more simply, "a picture". These associations of *citta* with *cināti* and *citra* are not etymological; they serve as didactic devices and are for purposes of exegesis. The definition in the *Atthasālinī* states that the *citta* builds itself up as a series (*attano santānaṁ cinoti*) through the cognitive processes of perception and thought. From another perspective, the *citta* is said to be "built up" (*cita*) or perpetuated through the influence of the unwholesome mental states (*kilesas*) that cause the mind to crave future goals and the fruition (*vipāka*) of *kamma*.[8] The *Atthasālinī* goes on to point out that *citta* is a generic term that represents a multitude of attitudes of mind that are variegated with regard to their contents and the circumstances in which they occur. Reading between the sentences of the *Atthasālinī*, one gets a sense of the splendour and wondrous quality of the *citta*. The Saṁskṛt term *citra* conveys "bright", "strange", and "wonderful", as well as "variegated" (S.E.D. 396, col. 1). It is called *citta* because it produces variations,[9] painting an endless variety of mental pictures.

The *Atthasālinī* says that the series of *cittas* that form the continuum of consciousness display a vast variety of characteristics by varying the patterns of the mental factors (*cetasikas*) that arise within the continuum, just as a master artist (*citta-kāra*) creates masterpieces with rich variations of colour and design (Asl. 64). Attitudes of greed, aversion, and delusion, attitudes of generosity, friendship, and understanding, attitudes characteristic of the realm of sensory experience, and states of mind that prevail at various planes of meditation are compared to variegated pictures painted by the mind. In this analogy of painting, the *citta* is both the creative painter and the many-coloured pictures. As the artist creates many scenes, the *citta* creates its experiences in the many realms of rebirth and is itself constantly re-created through these experiences. In this context, the *Atthasālinī* refers to a passage of the *Saṁyutta-nikāya* where the Buddha puns on the word *citta*, declaring the mind to be more variegated (*cittataram*) than the paintings of the various realms of rebirth used by teachers to make their teachings about *kamma* vivid and unforgettable (S. III. 151-152). The *Atthasālinī* explains that the diversity of experiences in the diverse realms of rebirth is due to *kamma*, and it attributes the vast variations in the acts that have karmic consequences to the endless creative activity of the *citta*. Furthermore, the *Atthasālinī* (Asl. 64) insists that wholesome and unwholesome physical acts with karmic consequences—such as giving gifts, good conduct, injuring others, and behaving deceitfully—are performed, in the final analysis, just by the *citta* (*citta-katam eva*). The purport of this statement is that various attitudes of mind displayed in the continuum of *cittas* are the basis of corresponding physical and verbal acts. Attitudes of mind produce acts.

The verb *ceteti* can now be interpreted in relation to *citta*. *The Pali-English Dictionary* gives the meaning of *ceteti* as "to think, to reflect, to be of opinion". In special contexts where *ceteti* is used with the dative case, it connotes "to set one's heart on, to think upon, strive after, desire" (P.E.D. 269, col. 1). For example, *Vakkali . . . vimokkhāya ceteti* signifies "Vakkali has set his mind on liberation" (S. III. 121). The following examples further illustrate the meaning of *ceteti*. On one occasion, the Buddha is told that one of his disciples, tormented by pain and wishing to die, has set his mind on death (*maraṇaṁ cetayati*) (S. I. 121).[10] In this context, the verb *cetayati*, which is another form of *ceteti*, can be interpreted as "to intend" since it is linked with *ākaṅkhati*, which signifies "to wish for, think of, desire; intend, plan, design" (P.E.D. 93, col. 1). The relation between the mental function indicated by *ceteti* and a specific attitude of mind (*citta*) is conveyed well in the following statement made by the Buddha. Explaining the harmful nature of unwholesome mental states, the Buddha says that when one is beset by greed (*ratto*) or by ill will (*duṭṭho*) or by delusion (*mūḷho*), then one is intent on (*ceteti*) harming oneself, or others, or both oneself and others. The Buddha goes on to say that when greed, ill will, and delusion are eliminated, then one no longer has the purpose of causing harm (S. IV. 339-340; A. I. 156-157).[11] The person who "intends" or "is occupied with" (*ceteti*) causing harm is described as "overcome" (*abhibhūto*) by greed, ill will, or delusion. The *citta* of such a person is considered to be overpowered or subjugated by the harmful emotion (*pariyādinna-citto*). It should be noted that *ceteti* signifies forming a purpose, rather than the application of energy to fulfil that purpose. Nevertheless, cognition and the capacity to initiate action are not seen as disparate faculties in the *Suttas* and in the *Abhidhamma.* Thought and motivational energy are regarded as processes that mutually condition each other and manifest a certain attitude or frame of mind.

Conflict and Control in the *Citta*

The verses in the *Theragāthā,* the *Therīgāthā,* the *Dhammapada,* and the *Sutta-nipāta* offer personal descriptions of how the transformation of the *citta* was experienced by those who devoted themselves to the disciplines of the Eightfold Path in the early period of Buddhism.[12] Some of these verses are poignant and profoundly moving. It should be possible to extrapolate from the personal accounts in the *Theragāthā* and the *Therīgāthā* a more intimate view of the concepts of *citta* and *cetanā* that can supplement the more formal statements in the *Suttas.* A recurrent theme in these verses is how to control the *citta.* Of special interest in this regard is the remarkable poem attributed to the *thera* named Tāḷapuṭa (Tha. 1091-1145). Addressing his own wayward *citta,* Tāḷapuṭa longingly asks when he will be able to overcome inclinations to desire, hatred, and delusion. He yearns to quieten his mind with mindfulness, attain the freedom of the sages, and feel the beauty of the woodlands. He reminds his *citta* that he did not leave his family and circle of friends because of ill-fortune, banishment, or lack of a livelihood, but because his *citta* had persistently urged him to consider the sorrow in impermanence, the emptiness of the self, and the misery of rebirth. He tells his *citta* that formerly he had followed its bidding when it had led him through countless rebirths. He chides his *citta* for straying from the discipline taught by the Buddha and resolves to tame and control it by meditation and the practice of mindfulness.

In other verses of the *Theragāthā* (Tha. 214, 356), the *citta* is called a "witch" and a "deceiver" (*cittakali, cittadubbhaka*). Controlling the *citta* is compared to taming an untamed elephant (Thi. 49) or to restraining an elephant with a hook and tying it firmly to a post (Tha. 77, 1130). In the *Therīgāthā* (Thi. 42), Uttamā laments that she lacks control over her *citta* (*citte avasavattinī*). Another *therī* attributes her inability to subdue her *citta* to her lack of systematic attention to objects (*ayoniso-manasikāra*), her passion for sensual pleasure (*kāma-rāga*), and her pride (Thi. 77).[13] Guttā warns herself not to fall under the sway of the *citta* (Thi. 163),[14] and another *therī* quietly declares that she has attained control over her own *citta* (Thi. 233).[15]

There is no word in these early texts that indicates an overriding "will" with the sovereign ability to control the *citta* and bring about a change of behaviour. The term *cetanā* does not fulfil that role in these verses. The term *saṅkappa* occurs in a few of the verses with the meaning of "intention" or "aspiration". One *thera* says that the intentions (*saṅkappas*) with which he entered his meditation hut have been carried out successfully (Tha. 60);[16] another tells how the Buddha, understanding his intentions (*saṅkappamaññāya*), exhorted him to enter the training of the *Saṅgha* (Tha. 376);[17] and a third *thera* declares with confidence that his intentions are fulfilled, like the moon attaining its fullness (Tha. 546).[18] In these verses, the term *saṅkappa* conveys an "aspiration", "resolve", "purpose", or "intention" formed in the mind. However, the connotations of *saṅkappa* in these verses emphasize the cognitive processes of purposive thought rather than the motivational processes of initiating action in fulfilment of that purpose. Though the need to exert great energy (*viriya*) in order to pursue the Eightfold Path is emphasized in the *Theragāthā* (Tha. 148, 167, 515),[19] the meaning of *viriya* does not include purposive deliberation and the intention to pursue a chosen goal. *Viriya* is not perceived here as the function of purposive thought that decides on a goal, but as the process of applying energy once the resolve to fulfil a purpose has arisen in the *citta.* Neither *saṅkappa* nor *viriya* connotes "will" in the sense of a controlling function that both chooses a goal and implements goal-oriented action.

In the *Dhammapada,* the mind (*manas*) is said to be the forerunner and the leader with regard to both wholesome and unwholesome mental states (Dhp. 1-2).[20] Here the term *manas* can be taken as a synonym of *citta,* and these verses can be interpreted to mean that it is one's mind-set or attitude of mind that determines whether one's thoughts, emotions, purposes, and behaviour will be either wholesome or unwholesome. The *Dhammapada* commences its set of verses on the *citta* by focusing on how immensely difficult it is to subdue the swiftly changing *citta* (Dhp. 33-36).[21] At the conclusion of its description of the *citta,* the *Dhammapada* declares that whereas an ill directed *citta* (*micchā-paṇihitaṁ cittam*) is one's worst enemy, a well directed *citta* (*sammā-paṇihitaṁ cittam*) becomes one's truest friend (Dhp. 42-43). This description of the *citta* in the *Dhammapada* evokes questions about how the change from "ill directed" to "well directed" occurs. In the *Therīgāthā,* the women attribute the redirection of the *citta* and the motivation to enter the Eightfold Path to the personal tragedies they had lived through.[22] In the *Theragāthā,* it is more often a direct encounter with the Buddha or with a competent teacher that is declared to be the cause of the fundamental reorientation of the *citta.*[23] In both cases, it is the awareness of the transient nature of all things and the pain of attachment to things that decay and people who change that bring about the resolve to enter the Path of the Buddha. In these verses of the *Theragāthā* and *Therīgāthā,* the awareness that all beings change, decay and die is not merely a concept that engages one's thoughts and ideas, but an immediate experience that strikes at the very core of one's being, causing a redirection of the *citta* towards different goals. This radical change in the *citta*, however, is neither regarded as an experience that happens without a cause, nor is it attributed to the act of an autonomous will. Transformations are shown to be conditioned by the emotional reactions and habit patterns in the *citta* of the person who comes to feel the ephemerality of all life.

In the *Theragāthā*, *Therīgāthā*, *Sutta-nipāta*, and *Udāna*, the "I" (*aham*) sometimes plays the role of the controller of the *citta*. For example, Uppalavaṇṇā claims, "I have control over my mind" (*cittaṁhi vasībhūtāham*), and Tāḷapuṭa goes so far as to tell his *citta* that it will surely perish (*citta parābhavissasi*), while he himself, freed from ignorance and sorrow, will roam on delightful mountaintops that are crowned with clouds (Thi. 233; Tha. 1144). Even where the pronoun *aham* does not occur, the form of the verb indicates the first person singular in verses that suggest the control of the *citta* by the self (Tha. 355, 357, 358; Thi. 50). However, the presence of the pronoun "I" should be taken, in these cases, merely as a convention of speech, not as the affirmation of a controlling self who is the agent of willing. Collins emphasizes in *Selfless Persons: Imagery and Thought in Theravāda Buddhism* that when the terms *aham*, *attā* (self), and *attānam* (oneself) are used to describe or express those aspects of Buddhist training where the mind examines its own contents, this usage is "simply a fact of Indo-Aryan syntax structure". He points out that the use of these terms neither opposes nor calls into question the Theravāda teaching of *anattā*.[24] Nowhere in these early Buddhist texts do we find the injunction to cultivate the sense of self in order to gain mastery over the *citta*. On the contrary, the idea of a permanent and separate self that owns the *citta* is seen as the product of a persistent tendency towards conceit (*mānānusaya*).[25] There are several references to the problems caused by conceit (Tha. 102, 427-428) and lack of vigilance (Thi. 36, 38; Dhp. 21-32). In a verse of the *Theragāthā*, the *thera* Adhimutta rejoices that the thoughts "I have been" and "I shall become" are no longer present in his mind (Tha. 715).

In the *Udāna*, removal of deceit and conceit (*māna*), cessation of greed, quiescence of longing, and freedom from the feeling of "mine" (*amama*) are counted as the qualities of one deserving of the appellation *brāhmaṇa*, *samaṇa*, or *bhikkhu* (Ud. 29). The *Udāna* includes speculative theories and debates arising from the thought that "I" or "other" exists as an autonomous agent among the causes of bondage to sorrow and rebirth. The wise are said to be free of the thoughts "I do" and "another person does" (Ud. 70).[26] These statements make it clear that these texts do not support the practice of developing the idea of the self as the guardian and guide of the mind.

The answer to the question regarding the identity of the "controller of the *citta*" is that the *citta* as a whole, responding to external influences and internal impulsions, undergoes changes of attitude, thereby assessing, redirecting, and transforming its own contents. To remain consistent with the principle of conditioned origination, it is necessary to preclude any suggestion that the continuum of consciousness (*citta*) is other than, or separable from, its constituents. For this reason, the capacity for internal redirection and transformation cannot be regarded as an autonomous mental factor, but must be viewed as a function that emerges within the continuum of consciousness through the mutual conditioning of its constituents. The concept of *anattā* entails that the internal dialogues, so dramatically presented in the *Theragāthā* and *Therīgāthā*, are to be seen as portrayals of the tensions and adjustments in the conditioned series of configurations of mental factors that are experienced as diverse "attitudes" of mind.

The Mind's Capacity to Know Itself

Theravāda affirms the capacity of the *citta* to become aware of itself and to know its own contents.[27] With reference to the disciplines of the Eightfold Path, the ability of the *citta* to mindfully observe the mental factors (*cetasikas*) that constitute it as an "attitude of mind" is conveyed by the term *paccavekkhaṇa*. Generally, *paccavekkhaṇa* signifies "looking at, consideration, regard, attention, reflection, contemplation, reviewing" (P.E.D. 384, col. 2). *Paccavekkhaṇa*, therefore, represents observation that deepens into insight, and it includes both paying attention to objects as well as contemplation of one's own mind. In the instructions for mindfulness of the body given in the *Visuddhimagga*, Buddhaghosa points to the difference between the self-aware mind and components of the body, which do not have the capacity of becoming aware of their mutual relationships (Vsm. XI. 48-80). For example, he remarks that finger nails cannot know that they grow on finger tips, and finger tips do not know that nails grow on them. Lacking basic conscious awareness (*acetana*), parts of the body are seen to be incapable of experiencing and observing each other (*aññamaññam ābhoga-paccavekkhaṇa-rahita*).

The role of *paccavekkhaṇa* in the practice of mindfulness is explained in the teaching that the Buddha gives to Rāhula (M. I. 415-417). The Buddha tells Rāhula that before, during, and after any act of body, speech, or mind, he should engage in repeated reflection[28] on whether the act is wholesome or unwholesome, and whether it can cause harm to oneself, to another being, or to both parties. Furthermore, the Buddha's instruction to Rāhula implies that the mind's awareness of a mental function can be simultaneous with that function. For this reason, the Buddha compares the mind to a reflecting mirror (M. I. 415).[29] The crux of the argument is that this capacity of reflexive awareness makes it possible for the mind to bring about internal adjustments and transformations. The Buddha concludes by telling Rāhula that *paccavekkhaṇa* will lead to wholesome behaviour. The whole discourse bears witness to the view that the mind is a self-assessing, self-adjusting system where the organic whole and its dynamic components are in constant dialogue, as it were.

This analysis of mental processes has affinities to Joanna Macy's interpretation of the *citta*. She describes the *citta* as a system of mutually conditioning constituents that has the capacity not only to observe its own contents, but also to make adjustments to its own processes in response to external impacts or internal tensions. The ability to vary its response to changing circumstances by becoming flexible (*mudu*) and adaptable (*kammañña*), like a master artist at work (A. I. 9; Asl. 64-65), and the ability to observe its own contents (*paccavekkhaṇa*), can be perceived as the twin capacities by virtue of which the *citta* becomes a self-adjusting, self-transforming system. References to the "I" controlling the *citta* can be interpreted as the aptitude of the *citta* to become trained (*bhāvita*), tamed (*danta*), guarded (*gutta*), protected (*rakkhita*), and restrained (*saṁvuta*) through the function of observing its own processes (A. I. 5-7). This self-monitoring capacity of the *citta* cannot be interpreted as a function that overrides the principle of conditioned origination. However, it can be posited that though the mind's self-reflective awareness is itself a conditioned process, it does make the mind directly aware of how conditioning works in its own processes. Awareness of how processes of conditioning work upon the mind can gradually become a primary influence that shapes the future development of the mind and the choices that the mind makes.

Thought and Volition as Functions of *Manas*

Both in the *Upaniṣads* and in Theravāda, the term *manas*, like the term *citta*, refers to the mind as an organic whole constituted of interrelated functions. It was shown in Chapter I that *manas* indicates the capacity of consciousness to coordinate and direct the sensory and motor functions of the individual (B.U. I. 5.3; Ks.U. III. 7). *Manas* also signifies the centre of discursive thought and represents agency with regard to desires (*kāma*) (B.U. III. 2.7) and intentions (*saṁkalpas*) (B.U. II. 4.11, IV. 5.12). There are passages in the *Upaniṣads* where *manas* connotes volition. In the *Chāndogya Upaniṣad*, for example, *manasā manasyati* connotes, not only purposive deliberation leading to the choice of a goal, but also the capacity to initiate action to achieve that goal (C.U. VII. 3.1).

Manas is viewed both as the home of emotions and as the source of discursive thought. In the following examples taken from the *Sutta* literature, *manas* refers to the mind regarded as an internally coherent whole. The holistic significance of *manas* is perhaps best illustrated in the terms *somanassa* (pleasant or happy state pervading the whole mind) and *domanassa* (uneasy or troubled state of the entire mind). Similarly, *pītimana* signifies a glad or joyful state of mind (Sn. 766), *manopadosa* conveys anger or ill will affecting the whole mind (D. III. 72; M. I. 377; Sn. 702), and *manopakopa* indicates anger filling the mind (Dhp. 233). In these examples, *manas* is seen as the centre from where emotions originate and spread their influence.

Moreover, both intention to pursue a goal and the capacity to initiate action towards that end fall within the range of *manas*. The capacity of *manas* to initiate action becomes apparent in the use of the instrumental case of *manas* (*manasā*) to indicate an action performed by the mind as a whole. In the contexts where the instrumental case of *manas* occurs, it becomes almost impossible to delineate a distinction between "thought about an object" and "intention towards that object". For example, the distinction between cognizing an object and intending to obtain it is hardly recognizable in the following statement in the *Diṭṭhi-saṁyuttam*. Here it is said that various views regarding the self and the world arise because of attachment to ephemeral objects that are "cognized, attained, searched for, and pondered over by the mind (*manasā*)" (S. III. 204-216).[30] The mutual conditioning of cognition, emotion, and the capacity to initiate action becomes further evident in the following three functions of *manas*: production of sentiments such as goodwill (*avyāpāda*) and ill will (*vyāpāda*) that carry karmic consequences and are designated as "mental deeds" (*mano-kamma*); the mind's attention to objects (*manasikāra*); and application of the mind in processes of thought (*vitakka*). *Mano-kamma, manasikāra,* and *vitakka* are described as occasions when *manas* exhibits its capacity not only to determine the characteristics of specific objects, but also to express its interest in those objects and its intentions towards them.

Mano-kamma: mental activity expressive of the entire mind

Detailed accounts of *kamma* in the *Majjhima-nikāya* (M. III. 209-210) and the *Aṅguttara-nikāya* (A. V. 292-299) classify unwholesome *kamma* as follows: the three physical acts, consisting of taking life (*pāṇātipāta*), stealing (*adinnādāna*), and sexual misconduct (*kāmesu micchācāra*); the four verbal acts consisting of lying (*musā-vāda*), malicious speech (*pisuṇā-vācā*), harsh, hurtful speech (*pharusā-vācā*), and ignorant, frivolous speech (*samphappalāpa*); and the three mental acts, namely, covetousness (*abhijjhā*), ill will, or malevolence (*vyāpāda*), and wrong view (*micchā-diṭṭhi*). Types of action that are specifically opposed to these unwholesome acts constitute the ten wholesome acts. It becomes immediately obvious that a "mental act" (*mano-kamma*) is not conceived of as a cognitive function that is performed solely for the purpose of gaining knowledge. A wholesome or unwholesome mental act (*mano-kamma*) represents cognitive processes that affect the whole mind through their relationship to emotionally charged mental states such as ill will or goodwill. In every *mano-kamma,* knowledge of an object becomes an emotionally conditioned intention that carries moral values and entails commensurate consequences The concept of *mano-kamma* shows that *manas* is understood as a system of mutually conditioning thoughts, emotions, and action-producing purposive impulses. This holistic view of the mind is based on the concept of conditioned origination.

In the Theravāda view of *manas*, right and wrong views are regarded not as merely theoretical enterprises of reason, but as *kamma* performed by the mind. The *Sabbāsava-sutta*, for example, seeks to demonstrate that philosophical theories, views, and opinions have a bearing, not only on whether or not one's concepts are intellectually sound, but also on whether or not one's emotions and choices of goals are morally wholesome (M.I. 8-9). In *Selfless Persons: Imagery and Thought in Theravāda Buddhism*, Collins emphasizes the Buddhist position that views and theories regarding the self and the world are rooted in emotional investments of the mind and put forth patterns of conditioning that affect all aspects of consciousness. Consequently, views generate *mano-kamma* expressive of desire to appropriate objects and to magnify the self.[31]

Manasikāra: the influence of attention on emotion and on motivation to act

In the *Suttas* the cognitive process of vigilant and systematic attention (*yoniso-manāsikāra*) is regarded as a powerful mental factor that both clarifies one's thoughts and purifies one's emotions. It is posited that systematic attention cleanses the mind of the predilection for speculative views, eradicates the emotional roots of views, and changes the behaviour patterns in which views seek to become manifest. In the *Aṅguttara-nikāya*, systematic application of alertness and attention is taught as a potent method in overcoming the three basic unwholesome motives of action, namely sensual passion (*rāga*), hatred (*dosa*), and delusion (*moha*) (A. I. 200). This passage emphasizes that when systematic attention is absent, the beauty in objects can arouse sensual passion and their unattractive features can cause the mind to react with hatred. In the *Therīgāthā* (Thi. 77), the *therī* Sīhā laments that she has fallen prey to pride and passion and lacks control over her mind because of neglecting the cultivation of systematic attention.

Because *manas* is regarded as a system of mutually conditioning factors, the cognitive processes of systematic attention are perceived to be capable of influencing emotional responses, conditioning motivational impulses, and changing patterns of behaviour. The Theravāda view of *manas* does not posit rifts between thought and emotion or between thought and motivation to act. Consequently, much importance is given to the therapeutic value of wise and systematic attention in the practice of the Eightfold Path.

Vitakka: the capacity of thought to motivate action

The connotations of *vitakka* in the *Suttas* include the initial application of the mind to an object, reasoning, and thinking in general. However, the classification of *vitakkas* into wholesome and unwholesome types in the *Saṅgīti-sutta* (D. III. 215) demonstrates that *vitakkas* are not regarded merely as processes of discursive thought. They are considered to be complex mental states that are conditioned by emotions and carry moral values. Unwholesome and morally reprehensible (*akusala*) applications of thought (*vitakkas*) are reckoned as threefold: sensual desire (*kāma*), ill will or malevolence (*vyāpāda*), and cruelty (*vihiṁsā*). Wholesome (*kusala*) *vitakkas* are classified as dispassion or renunciation (*nekkhamma*), absence of ill will (*avyāpāda*), and non-cruelty (*avihiṁsā*). Wholesome and unwholesome *vitakkas*, therefore, are constituted of thought that is blended with emotion and is capable of producing intentions and influencing behaviour. The complex nature of *vitakkas* once again demonstrates that Theravāda conceives of the mind as an organic whole of mutually conditioning thoughts, emotions and motivational energies. It is noteworthy that wholesome perception (*saññā*), wholesome applications of thought (*vitakkas*) and wholesome intentions (*saṅkappas*) are classified similarly. They are considered to be marked by either dispassion, absence of ill will, or absence of cruelty. Unwholesome perceptions, thoughts and intentions are regarded as expressions of either sensual desire, malevolence, or cruelty (D. III. 215). It becomes evident that in Theravāda, *saññā*, *vitakka*, and *saṅkappa* are complex mental states shaped by the interpenetration of thought, emotion and motivation. They bear witness to the Theravāda view of the mind as an integral whole constituted of mutually conditioning processes.

Conditioned Origination and Interpretation of *Saṅkhāra*

The *Saṁyutta-nikāya* briefly states that the six classes of *cetanās*, which arise when the five senses and the mind contact their respective objects, are the factors that constitute the *saṅkhāras* (S. III. 60). Precisely how *cetanās* function as constituents of *saṅkhāras* is not made clear in the *Suttas*, and *saṅkhāra* remains a complex and elusive concept. However, in seeking to understand what *saṅkhāras* are and how they function, it is helpful to remember at the outset that the verb *karoti*, to which the noun *saṅkhāra* is linked, includes in its meaning both "to do" as well as "to make". *Saṅkhāras* are active mental factors that motivate further physical and mental doings; at the same time, *saṅkhāras* "construct", "compose" or "put together". In the case of *saṅkhāras*, to act is to make, and it is by virtue of making or putting together that *saṅkhāras* become active. In *Selfless Persons: Imagery and Thought in Theravāda Buddhism*, Collins refers to Frauwallner, who renders *saṅkhāra* as *Gestaltung* (formation) and interprets the term to include also a reference to *gestaltet* (the formed).[32] *Saṅkhāras* both make and are made. The term *saṅkhāra* includes in its meaning both effective action and the effects of action. Frauwallner maintains that the meaning of *saṅkhāra* developed from the idea of "formation" to the concept of willed constructive activity. He points out that the verb root *kṛ-* includes in its meaning "to prepare", "to get ready", and he holds that *saṅkhāra* came to connote that something is put in a state of "readiness", so that this condition of preparedness continues to give impetus and to produce effects.[33] He suggests that the development in the meaning of *saṅkhāra* from "formation" to "willed activity" was influenced by the use of the term in "living speech". As evidence, he shows that the term *saṁskāra* is used in the *Sāṁkhya-kārikā* to signify the state of the wheel which the potter has rotated in such a way that it is ready to keep on revolving when he removes his hand (Sk. 67). Similarly, in the *Rathakāra-vagga* of the *Aṅguttara-nikāya* (A. I. 112), the term *abhisaṅkhāra* refers to the impetus or propulsion that sets the wheel of a chariot in motion and keeps it moving until the range that the force of the impetus is able to cover has been covered (*yāvatikā-abhisaṅkhārassa gati*).

In the two examples of the potter's wheel and the chariot wheel given above, the terms *saṅkhāra* and *abhisaṅkhāra* refer, not to the motivating power of volition, but to the initiation of movement in the physical realm. However, Frauwallner's thesis is that *saṅkhāra* came to designate "an exertion of a mental influence or readiness", especially in the *Tipiṭaka*. "Mental readiness" signifies being poised and set for a specific type of exertion. According to Frauwallner's interpretation, the state of "mental readiness" that is shown when a person decides upon a course of action is what is meant by *saṅkhāra*. Frauwallner holds that the six classes of *cetanās* that are said to constitute *saṅkhāras* (S. III. 60) are the "attitudes of the will" or "impulses of will" that direct the five sense organs and the *manas* to their respective objects.[34]

Collins bases his interpretation of *saṅkhāra* not only on the work of Frauwallner, but more significantly on Lilian Silburn's theories about how time and ritual were conceived in the Vedic tradition. In her *Instant et Cause: Le Discontinu dans la Pensée Philosophique de l'Inde*, she maintains that time is described in the Vedic tradition, not as a primordial medium in which all things occur, but as something to be regularly produced and prolonged through the "constructive activity" of the Vedic ritual.[35] The view of *saṅkhāra* put forward by Collins follows from the theory that the Vedic tradition viewed the fire ritual (*yajña*) as the "constructive activity" by virtue of which both those who performed the ritual and the cosmos itself were regenerated. According to this interpretation of the Vedic ritual, those who regularly performed the ritual believed that through the fire ritual a future time was ensured, wherein they could enjoy the fruition of merit that had accrued from the ritual.

Collins maintains that the Buddhist concept of *saṅkhāra* is developed from the Vedic idea that after death occurs, a person who has acquired a store of merit by performing the Vedic rituals is reborn into a happy "world" (*loka*) with a body that is "constructed" (*saṁskrīyate*), part by part, as a result of the verses chanted by the priest.[36] According to this interpretation, *saṅkhāras* in Theravāda are mentally planned or "constructed" activities that bring about the prolongation of time, like the Vedic *yajña*, by being oriented towards future goals. *Saṅkhāras* are defined as acts of merit and demerit that entail karmic effects. Such acts require the lengthening of time by means of rebirth in order to reach proper fruition (*kamma-vipāka*) and put forth their effects. The crux of the argument put forward by Collins is that Buddhism "drew on" Vedic notions of regenerating life and lengthening time by means of ritual activity to develop its own notion of producing rebirth and lengthening time by means of constructive mental activity. According to this argument, Theravāda conceives of *saṅkharas* as intentional acts that produce temporal continuity by entailing karmic consequences, just as the Vedic fire ritual revitalizes the cosmos and produces the prolongation of time.[37] Every time they are performed, both the exalted Vedic fire ritual and the *saṅkhāras* of everyday life construct and produce the future. Silburn holds that in the *Suttas* the terms *saṅkhāra* and *abhisaṅkhāra* convey the convergence of voluntary motivations and "unconscious tendencies" in such a way that they are poised or "prepared" to achieve a more or less consciously desired goal. According to her interpretation, *saṅkhāra* always implies interest in achieving a goal, and she views this goal-oriented intention of *saṅkhāra* as a passage from the present to the future.[38]

With regard to the relationship between *cetanā* and *saṅkhāra*, Collins offers both "volition" and "intention" as translations of *cetanā*. Furthermore, he maintains that the sustained emphasis given in the Buddhist scriptures to the intention underlying an act that produces karmic consequences marks "a very thorough ethicisation of the idea of *karma*" in the Buddhist tradition.[39] Collins gives a coherent and plausible interpretation of how the Buddhists may have been influenced by Vedic notions of ritual in developing their own concept of *saṅkhāra*. Nevertheless, the fact remains that ideas regarding the origin of *karma*, the Vedic view of time, and the purpose of the Vedic ritual continue to be matters for speculation.

In this work, I take a different approach by investigating, not the origins of the concept of *saṅkhāra*, but the differences in the connotations of *saṁskāra/saṅkhāra* as a psychological term in the *Yoga-sūtra* and the *Vyāsa-bhāṣya* on the one hand, and the *Suttas* and *Abhidhamma* on the other. The concept of *saṁskāra* in the Yoga tradition and the concept of *saṅkhāra* in Theravāda are aligned to two very different theories of causality. Whereas the Yoga tradition upholds the idea that the cause already contains the effect in a potential state (*satkāryavāda*), Theravāda maintains that the effect comes into being through the convergence of the necessary conditions (*paṭicca-samuppāda*). In the Yoga tradition, a *saṁskāra* is looked upon as a subliminal impression that subsists in the mind. In Theravāda, a *saṅkhara*, by definition, is a configuration of mental factors that comes into being and passes away in accordance with conditioned origination.

Saṅkhāras as Processes of "Combining" and "Constructing"

In the *Saṁyutta-nikāya*, the Buddha illustrates conditioned origination as it is manifested in the process of rebirth with two telling analogies (S. II. 86, 88). The first focuses on the fact that an oil lamp burns only when the supply of oil remains constant and the wick is continually adjusted. The second points out that fertile soil cleared of weeds, sufficient water, light, and room for roots to expand are necessary conditions for the growth of a tender sapling. These analogies show that the causal theory of conditioned origination implies that the term "cause" (*paccaya*) refers to a set of conditions, all of which are necessary to produce the effect, but none of which can claim to be sufficient on its own. According to this causal theory, it is the convergence and compounding of these factors that produces the effect. Thus, conditioned origination differs radically from the Sāṁkhya and Yoga theory of *satkāryavāda*, where the cause is defined as that which already contains the effect in potential form. Furthermore, according to *satkāryavāda*, the cause has the inherent capacity to produce the effect; other conditions only "assist" by removing obstructions (YS. IV.3).

Kalupahana explains in *Causality: The Central Philosophy of Buddhism* that the theory of conditioned origination maintains that all the necessary factors "constitute one system or event" and therefore can be referred to as a single cause. The effect will not be produced unless the cause includes all the necessary factors. No single factor or subset of factors within the cause can bring about the effect.[40] This view of the cause as "a set of jointly sufficient conditions" is fully developed in the *Visuddhimagga* (XVII. 16-20). Buddhaghosa begins his exposition by saying that *samuppāda* indicates that the effect arises "in coordination with" (*saha*) and "rightly" (*sammā*), not singly (*na ekekato*) and not without a cause (*nāpi ahetuto*) (Vsm. XVII. 16).[41] Buddhaghosa goes on to explain that "in coordination with" signifies that the effect arises by depending on a combination of conditions, never regardless of them. Next, he says that *samuppāda* refers to the idea that the causal factors form a combination (*hetu-samūha*) because they operate interdependently (*aññamaññena*), both in the sense of producing a result to which they all contribute and in the sense of not exhibiting any deficiency or lack of capacity when they all function jointly (Vsm. XVII. 17, 18). Finally, Buddhaghosa says that *samuppāda* signifies that the conditions forming the cause act "equally" (*samam*) and jointly (*saha*), not piece by piece nor one after another, in producing the resultant states (Vsm. XVII. 20).[42]

In the causal theory of conditioned origination, it is the coming together of all the necessary causal factors that becomes the sufficient condition for the arising of the effect. *Paṭicca-samuppāda* does not posit any source of causal energy operating over and above the convergence of the causal conditions. In the *Atthasālinī* the term *samaya*, interpreted as *samavāya* (coming together, combination), signifies the concurrence of the causal conditions (*paccayānaṁ sāmaggī*) and their interrelated functioning in the production of the effect (Asl. 58-59).[43] The *Atthasālinī* points out that the notion of a configuration of causes precludes the view that a single cause is sufficient to produce an effect (Asl. 59).[44] The idea that the capacity to produce an effect resides in the concurrence and combining of antecedent conditions is the basis of Stcherbatsky's interpretation of *saṅkhāra*. According to him, *saṅkhāra* connotes a "co-factor" that combines with other factors in producing the effect.[45] Furthermore, he argues that "dependent origination" becomes synonymous with "combined origination", since it is the combining of antecedent factors that makes for the dependent arising of the effect (*saṁskṛtatvam* = *pratītya-samutpannatvam*).[46]

Stcherbatsky also stresses that Buddhists of all schools regard physical and mental factors, not as static substances, but as burgeoning energies. He argues that *saṅkhāra* is a "co-operator" functioning as a "synergy" that combines with other energies to produce the effect. Stcherbatsky explains that the designations "synergies" and "co-operators" indicate that the energies invariably function "in mutual interdependence according to causal laws".[47] Before proceeding further, it should be noted that Stcherbatsky's interpretation is based on texts of the Sarvāstivāda School of Buddhism. According to his interpretation, the "central conception" of Buddhism is the idea that all physical and mental factors are constituted of irreducible and distinct elements known as *dharmas* that are fleeting energies manifesting only for a moment (*kṣaṇa*). Stcherbatsky stresses that the very nature of each *dharma* is causal energy (*kriyā*). He maintains that each *dharma* functions as a cause in the "point-instant" that is its duration, and he concludes that "the Buddhist theory of Causation is a direct consequence of the theory of Universal Momentariness".[48] Stcherbatsky has been faulted for extending the theory of momentariness (*kṣaṇikavāda*) to all schools and periods of Buddhism. Kalupahana argues that, whereas change is the basic factor of conditioned origination, the theory of momentariness does not appear in Theravāda before the time of Buddhaghosa.[49] According to Kalupahana's interpretation, in the *Suttas* impermanence (*anicca*) signifies, not momentariness, but coming into being and ceasing to be, birth and destruction.[50] However, Kalupahana does not present sufficient support for his position that the theory of momentariness is a later development in Theravāda, emerging during the time of Buddhaghosa. An extensive and detailed theory of distinct *dhammas* is already present in the *Dhammasaṅgaṇi*. It is possible that the idea of momentary *dhammas* was developed well before the time of Buddhaghosa.

It is possible to reject Stcherbatsky's view that the theory of momentariness is a feature of all periods of Buddhism while affirming his statement that "combined origination" is a synonym of "conditioned origination". When the Theravāda concept of *saṅkhāra* is set within the context of conditioned origination, it becomes clear why the two meanings—"combination" and "causal dynamism"—cohere in this term. When *saṅkhāra* is viewed in relation to *paṭicca-samuppāda*, it becomes clear that the term refers both to configurations of mutually dependent conditions that produce changes and to the effects produced just by the concurrence and combination of these conditions. In this work, when I refer to *saṅkhāras* as the mind's "constructive activities" or "goal-oriented activities", the term "activity" includes both the process of conditioning by which a karmically operative act is produced as well as the act itself.

"Subliminal Impression" in the Yoga Tradition and "Mental Formation" in Theravāda

In *A History of Indian Philosophy*, Dasgupta maintains that there is a crucial difference between *saṁskāra* in the Yoga tradition and *saṅkhāra* in Theravāda.[51] After reviewing the different meanings of *saṁskāra* put forward by the grammarian Pāṇini, Dasgupta maintains that *saṅkhāra* indicates "aggregation" (*samavāya*), which is one of the meanings suggested by Pāṇini. Dasgupta explains that in the Hindu schools of thought, *saṁskāra* signifies a residual "impression" of a cognitive, emotive, or motivational experience, which remains in the mind after the experience has ended.[52] C.A.F. Rhys Davids makes the same point in a note in *The Book of Kindred Sayings*.[53] She comments that she has not traced in Theravāda Buddhism any evidence that *saṅkhāra* carries the meaning of "predisposition" in the Yoga sense of a subliminal tendency (*vāsanā*) that can remain in the mind for a long period of time. Similarly, Nyanatiloka maintains that it would be inappropriate to conceive of *saṅkhāras* as tendencies residing latently in a "subconscious" level of the mind. He goes on to say that the notion of "subconscious tendencies" is "entirely inapplicable" to what *saṅkhāra* signifies in Theravāda.[54]

Although the *Suttas* put forward the view that *saṅkhāras* arise and produce effects in accordance with conditioned origination, there is no description of the stages by which a *saṅkhāra* is shaped and formed. A clearer picture emerges when *saṅkhāra* in the *Suttas* and the *Abhidhamma* is contrasted with *saṁskāra* in the *Vyāsa-bhāṣya*. The Yoga view of *saṁskāra* is based on the causal theory that whatever arises as an effect is previously present in a latent form in the cause. The *Vyāsa-bhāṣya* describes a *saṁskāra* as the residual impression that is left on the mind as the result of a past experience. The *saṁskāra* itself and the memory (*smṛti*) that it puts forth as its effect under appropriate conditions are said to have the same characteristics as the experience that initially produced the *saṁskāra* (VB. I.11). This idea of *saṁskāras*—according to which subliminal impressions "store" information from past experiences and produce memories in which that information is "retrieved"—is supported by the causal theory of *satkāryavāda*. With regard to the Yoga view of the formation of *saṁskāras*, the causal theory that the effect is latently present in the cause has the following implications: the subliminal impression that is to be left on the mind is already a latent factor in the experience; the memory of the experience is contained in the subliminal impression as a potential component awaiting retrieval; and the overt behaviour instigated by the memory is concealed within the memory in embryonic form. The Yoga tradition conceives of the *citta* as the substratum from which subliminal impressions (*saṁskāras*) manifest their effects. According to the interpretation given in the *Vyāsa-bhāṣya*, when these subliminal impressions lie dormant in the *citta* of an individual for a vast period of time, they function as deep-seated latent tendencies (*vāsanās*). The entire *citta* is said to be pervaded by the latent tendencies, like a fisherman's net that is covered all over with knots (VB. II.13). Because of the presence of these *vāsanās* or latent tendencies, the memory of an experience can remain in the *citta*, like a lingering perfume, for a vast period of time in the process of *karma* and rebirth. When the time is appropriate, a latent tendency produces a new experience that harkens back to an experience in the past that caused the latent tendency to take shape and remain indelibly in the mind. The Yoga tradition maintains that the presence of these latent tendencies remains unknown to the conscious mind. In this sense, they are conceived of as "unconscious tendencies".

The concept of a subliminal impression that persists through time in the mind cannot fit into the causal theory of conditioned origination. It would not be valid to conceive of *saṅkhāras* as "structures", "dispositions", or "tendencies" that are somehow fixed in the mind so that they are capable of producing repeated patterns of behaviour. In *Selfless Persons: Imagery and Thought in Theravāda Buddhism*, Collins alludes to passages in the *Milindapañha* where the discussion focuses on how continuity can be maintained between a deed and its consequences, when all physical and mental factors are impermanent and there is no enduring self.[55] The answer is given that it is not possible to specify a "place" where deeds are "stored" until they produce their effects, just as one cannot point to the fruit of a tree that has not yet yielded fruit (Mil. 72).[56] This statement implies that though *saṅkhāras* are the medium through which the processes of *kamma* operate, they are not to be understood as subliminal impressions or latent tendencies that remain unchanged in the mind and contain the consequences of *kamma* in a potential form.

In the *Suttas*, the term *saṅkhāra* carries multiple meanings, some of which are not easy to unravel. However, there is no ambiguity in the statements where *saṅkhāras* denote acts that have karmic consequences. In the *Majjhima-nikāya*, *saṅkhāras* are classified as *saṅkhāras* of body, speech, and mind (M. I. 54), and in other passages three types of *saṅkhāras* are specified: *saṅkhāras* of merit, *saṅkhāras* of demerit, and *āneñja-saṅkhāras* (D. III. 217; S. II. 82). It was believed that the third type would lead to rebirth in realms that have the same peaceful, immutable features as the higher levels of meditation. Clearly, in these passages *saṅkhāras* are acts conditioned by past experience that carry moral values of "wholesome" or "unwholesome" and produce commensurate consequences. These same acts are also designated as intentional (*sañcetanika*) acts of body, speech, and mind (M. III. 209; A. V. 292-297). This designation affirms the bond between *saṅkhāra* and *cetanā* and shows that these acts are considered to be instigated by the goal-oriented thoughts and impulses that constitute *cetanās*. It should be noted that in these passages where *saṅkhāras* are classified, the term *saṅkhāra* includes in its connotations both the motivational conditions that produce the act as well as the act itself. *Cetanā* as purposive impulse is the leading condition in the production of *saṅkhāras* of body, speech, and mind.

To interpret *saṅkhāras* as conditioned processes of body, speech, and mind is to place them in the context of the Middle Way. If the effect is already present in the *saṅkhāra* in a latent state, as the Yoga tradition maintains, then the nature of the effect is already determined and predictable. On the other hand, when conditioned origination is accepted, every act of body, speech, or mind is viewed as the product of a set of dynamic conditions that are placed within a network of mutually conditioning personality factors and external influences. The Buddha's argument in the *Mahākammavibhaṅga-sutta* is based on similar premises (M. III. 210-215). Conditioned origination opens the way for a wide range of possible consequences arising from mutually dependent conditions that are continually subject to change. Nevertheless, morally weighted goal-oriented activities (*saṅkhāras*) do not arise as novel experiences. They arise through configurations of causal conditions that follow one another, not in a random fashion, but according to causal order. Similar patterns of conditioning, therefore, begin to emerge in the dynamic process producing repetitions of similar types of acts. In psychological terms, these patterns of similarity are experienced as habits of body, speech and mind. For example, when non-greed, non-hatred, and non-delusion are listed as the three "wholesome roots" (*kusala-mūla*), it is implied that they occur repeatedly as conditions in the continuum of consciousness and produce wholesome habitual behaviour. In order to produce these wholesome roots, the disciplines of the Eightfold Path ensure that repeated patterns of wholesome conditions are set up in the mind of the disciple. As a consequence, repeated wholesome *saṅkhāra* processes that are experienced as wholesome habits arise in the disciple's mind. Conditioning implies that the effect is commensurate—or at least compatible—with the cause. Similar conditions produce similar effects; consequently, repeated patterns tend to appear in a process governed by conditioned origination.

Since conditioned origination implies impermanence (*anicca*) and rejects the notion of an autonomous entity, patterns of conditions cannot be viewed as "predispositions" embedded in the mind or as lasting "structures" superimposed on concrete processes. For purposes of conceptual analysis, the patterns of conditioning can be looked upon as separate from physical and mental processes, but they do not exist apart from the concrete processes that they condition. When certain configurations of mental conditions prevail over concomitant mental conditions, they cause similar patterns of mental conditions to occur repeatedly in the continuum of consciousness. When conditioned origination is affirmed, it follows that these patterns have no existence apart from the concrete mental conditions, such as thoughts, emotions and motivations, that come into being and pass away. *Saṅkhāras* include in their function both the forming of the repeated configurations of similar conditions and the repeated production of similar acts that can be conceptualized as habits. *Saṅkhāra* processes exhibiting as habits, therefore, are comparable to currents in a river. They participate in the flow and are affected by the conditions of the river, but they also direct its flow.

Since *saṅkhāras* are said to be constituted of different types of *cetanās* (S. III. 60), it follows that *cetanās* must be regarded as participants in the habit-forming and habit-manifesting functions of *saṅkhāra* processes. Since *cetanās* function within *saṅkhāra* processes as intentions imbued with motivational impetus, the cognitive content of the intentions as well as their capacity to initiate action become conditioned by the habit patterns that *saṅkhāra* processes exhibit. As constituents of *saṅkhāras*, *cetanās* often—but not invariably—arise as purposes that express the motivating power of habits. For example, in the context of the Eightfold Path, *cetanās* arise as wholesome purposive impulses, displaying the conditioning influence of wholesome habits that have been formed through *saṅkhāra* processes.

Saṅkhāra as Intentional Act

There are passages in the *Suttas* where the term *saṅkhāra* clearly carries the meaning of an intention or determined effort. The following are examples of intentional acts that are motivated by *saṅkhāras*: acts that are instigated by means of special applications of energy (*sasaṅkhāra*); "prior resolve" (*pubbe abhisaṅkhāra*) that sustains an activity for an intended period; resolute effort (*saṅkhārappadhāna*) in striving to overcome unwholesome mental states; and determined striving in concentrating the mind for the purpose of attaining a special yogic power (*padhāna-saṅkhāra-samannāgata iddhipāda*). These examples demonstrate the necessary mental conditions coming together around a strong intention or powerful purpose that functions as the core condition in producing the intended effect.

Sasaṅkhāra: saṅkhāra as application of effort

According to the commentarial literature, *saṅkhāra* has the meaning of "effort" or "exertion" in the compounds *sasaṅkhāra* (with *saṅkhāra*) and *asaṅkhāra* (without *saṅkhāra*). In several passages of the *Sutta* literature, the terms *sasaṅkhāra* and *asaṅkhāra* occur in descriptions of one who attains complete freedom from the process of rebirth (*parinibbāyin*). The *Aṅguttara-nikāya* gives the title of *sasaṅkhāra-parinibbāyī* to one who attains *parinibbāna* by virtue of difficult disciplines such as meditations focused on impermanence, death, and the unlovely factors present in the body (A. II. 155). The person who attains *parinibbāna* by cultivating the bliss of the first four levels of meditation is said to be one who reaches this goal without strenuous effort (*asaṅkhāra-parinibbāyin*). The commentary to the *Aṅguttara-nikāya* explains *sasaṅkhārena* as *sappayogena* (AA. III. 142). The term *payoga* connotes "means" as well as "exertion" and "preparation" (P.E.D. 418, col. 1). In this context, therefore, *sappayoga* has the meaning of "with efficacious effort". The commentary to the *Dīgha-nikāya* explains *sasaṅkhāra-parinibbāyī* as "one who has attained with difficulty, being fatigued with effort" (*sappayogena kilamanto dukkhena patto*) (DA. III. 1030). *Asaṅkhāra-parinibbāyī* indicates one who has attained *parinibbāna* with ease, without being exhausted by exertion (*appayogena akilamanto sukhena patto*).

In the *Atthasālinī*, *sasaṅkhāra* conveys both "with effort" and "with instigation" (Asl. 156). The author of the *Atthasālinī* regards *sasaṅkhārena* to be a term not commented upon previously (*apubbaṁ*), and he explains it as *sa-ussāhena* (with energy), *sappayogena* (with exertion), *sa-upāyena* (with expedient means), and *sapaccaya-gahaṇena* (by grasping the cause). The concrete examples that are given to elucidate *sasaṅkhāra*, however, bring the meaning of the term closer to "with instigation" or "with prompting". The *Atthasālinī* presents the case of a young monk who thinks of many excuses to avoid his duties of sweeping the courtyard of the shrine, serving an older monk, or listening to an exposition of the *Dhamma* (Asl. 156). However, he admonishes himself and sets about his duties, or he is counselled by another person who points out the benefits of doing the tasks allotted to him, or he is simply ordered to carry out his responsibilities. In these three cases, a wholesome attitude of mind (*kusala-citta*) is produced either through self-instigation or instigation by another.

Pubbe abhisaṅkhara: saṅkhara as resolve

Another instance where *saṅkhāra* signifies firm resolve correlated with effort is in the *Visuddhimagga* (Vsm. XXIII. 12).[57] Here the *Visuddhimagga* refers to instructions given in the

Majjhima-nikāya for attaining the level of meditation called "signless release of the mind" (M. I. 296-297). In this context, *saṅkhāra* indicates the prior commitment that a monk makes, which enables him to maintain a particular level of meditation for a specific period of time. The commentary to the *Visuddhimagga* explains *pubbe abhisaṅkhāra* (prior resolve) as *cittassa abhisaṅkharaṇa* (an act of mental determination). By making a prior pledge, the monk commits himself to remain in meditation for a certain period of time. He does so with the thought, "I shall get up when the moon or the sun has moved so far in the sky" (VsmA. 3:1662).

Recalling Frauwallner's interpretation of *saṅkhāra* as putting something in a "state of readiness" that will continue to bring forth effects in the future, *pubbe abhisaṅkhāra* can be interpreted as a resolve that puts the mind in a state of readiness for goal-oriented action. The power of the resolve and the state of preparedness that ensues from it determine the time period during which the impetus of that resolve will continue to be operative in the mind of the monk. A comparison can be made between the concept of *pubbe abhisaṅkhāra* and the reference in the *Aṅguttara-nikāya* to a chariot wheel which will travel the distance that is determined by the force of the impulse that sets it in motion (*yāvatikā abhisaṅkhārassa gati*) (A. I. 111). The mental resolve and the act of setting the wheel in motion are both designated as *abhisaṅkhāra* because they refer to a "state of readiness". "Ready" implies ready to pursue a goal, and the state of readiness both provides an impetus and also determines to what extent that impetus will remain operative. The commentary to the passage that describes the chariot wheel explains *abhisaṅkhārassa gati* as *payogassa gamanam* (AA. II. 181). Since *payoga* includes in its connotation "means", "preparation", and "exertion", in this context *payogassa gamanam* indicates that the push given by the driver puts the wheel in a state of preparedness for a specific span of movement. Similarly, the resolve that the monk makes is the "push" that makes his mind ready for exertion of effort, and the extent to which the exertion will continue to be effective depends on the strength and content of the resolve.

Saṅkhārappadhāna: resolute effort in striving towards a goal

Another instance where *saṅkhāra* connotes resolute effort in the fulfilment of a goal is found in the term *saṅkhārappadhāna*, which occurs, for example, in a passage where the Buddha explains his method of fruitful striving to the Niganṭhas. (M. II. 223). Here the Buddha gives the example of a man who is overcome with sorrow because of his love for a woman who does not feel the same way about him. He puts forth energetic effort (*saṅkhārappadhāna*) to root out the source of his sorrow. As the cause of his sorrow begins to fade, he realizes that in order to make his striving truly fruitful, he must balance effort with equanimity. He cultivates serene equanimity (*upekkhā*) to remove the final traces of his pain. The commentary to the *Majjhima-nikāya* (MA. IV. 11) explains *saṅkhāra* in the phrase *saṅkhāraṁ padahato* as "with efficacious effort" (*sampayoga*). However, the context suggests that in the compound term *saṅkhārappadhāna*, *saṅkhāra* signifies, not bare effort, but effort that is shaped by resolve or determination.

The phrase *padhāna-saṅkhāra* (striving with determination) is found also in instructions for the cultivation of the four types of intense mental concentration (*samādhi*) that can lead to the attainment of supernormal power (D. II. 213; M. I. 103; A. I. 39, 217). The person who desires supernormal powers is taught to concentrate the mind with resolute effort, taking one of the following four factors as the focus of meditation: the mental function of impetus to act (*chanda*), or the mental function of energy (*viriya*), or consciousness itself (*citta*), or the mental function of analytic investigation (*vīmāṁsā*). A supernormal power (*iddhi*) that is based on energy, for example, is said to be characterized by resolute striving applied to focusing the mind on energy (*viriya-samādhi-padhāna-saṅkhāra*) (S. V. 264; A. II. 256, III. 82). In his translation of the *Visuddhimagga*, Bhikkhu Ñāṇamoli renders *padhāna-saṅkhāra* as "will to strive" (Vsm. XII. 50, 51). The term *padhāna-saṅkhāra* indicates that in this case, the configuration of mental conditions (*saṅkhāra*) takes the form of a strong resolve or determination that effectuates striving (*padhāna*).

The examples of *saṅkhāra* given above include the "prior resolve" of a person preparing to sit in meditation, the impulse that sets a wheel in motion, and the putting forth of resolute effort to overcome an unwholesome (*akusala*) habit of mind or to attain a supernormal power. What these disparate examples have in common is that the term *saṅkhāra* signifies, in every case, the application of energy to achieve a specific purpose. In the examples where the reference is to psychic energy, *saṅkhāra* also connotes firm intention or resolve. Thus, these examples demonstrate that *saṅkhāras* are not to be conceived merely as motivational drives or stimuli based on physical needs and emotional tensions. Since the motivational energy of *saṅkhāras* is imbued with purpose, intention, aspiration, or resolve, it follows that *saṅkhāras* are integrally linked with cognitive processes of purposive thought. In the chapters that follow, it will be shown that *cetanās* provide the medium through which the cognitive functions that arise in the *cittas* become fused with the motivational capacities of *saṅkhāras*.

The Influence of *Āsavas* and *Anusayas* on the Dynamics of Motivation

Whereas *saṅkhāras* include both wholesome and unwholesome mental activities, there is frequent mention in the *Suttas* of *āsavas* and *anusyas*, both of which are regarded as exclusively unwholesome motivating forces. *Āsavas* are viewed as addictive unwholesome habits that corrupt the mind with such potency that they are not completely overcome till wisdom is fully established and enlightenment is attained. *Anusayas* are regarded as persistent tendencies that gradually lose their power as a person cultivates the disciplines of the Eightfold Path.

Four *āsavas* are mentioned in the *Suttas*:[58] the desire for objects that please the senses and the mind (*kāmāsava*); the desire to prolong existence (*bhavāsava*); the predilection for speculative views (*diṭṭhāsava*); and ignorance (*avijjāsava*).[59] The Pāli term *āsava* is related to the Jaina term *āsrava,* which signifies the "influx" of fine karmic matter into the individual self. *Āsava* carries meanings of both "inflow" and "outflow". According to the *Visuddhimagga,* the term *āsava* signifies the "oozing out" of sensual desire, attachment to life, speculative views, and ignorance from the unrestrained senses of an ordinary person, like water out of a cracked pot (Vsm. XXII. 56). *Āsavas* in Theravāda, therefore, bear a resemblance to the Jaina notion of the four *kaṣāyas* (anger, pride, deceit, and greed) that cause karmic matter to cling to the soul. A better understanding of the *āsavas* can be gained, however, by comparing them to the mental afflictions (*kleśas*) in the Yoga tradition. It is a basic postulate of the Sāṁkhya and Yoga traditions that the entirety of empirical life is based on a radical state of ignorance. In the Yoga tradition, this fundamental obscuration (*avidyā*) is defined as a mistaken cognition (*khyāti*) whereby the products of nature (*prakṛti*), which are transient, impure, afflicted by sorrow, and essentially different from the soul (*puruṣa*), are erroneously cognized as eternal, pure, pleasurable, and identical with the soul (YS. II.5). *Avidyā* (ignorance) is considered to be fundamental because it constitutes empirical consciousness and the very experience of being an individual person. *Avidyā* establishes empirical consciousness by becoming the matrix of the other four mental afflictions, namely, the affirmation of individual selfhood (literally, "I-am-ness") (*asmitā*), attachment (*rāga*), aversion (*dveṣa*), and tenacity in holding on to life (*abhiniveśa*).[60]

In the Yoga tradition, *kleśas* are regarded as the prime obstructions to liberating knowledge (*kaivalya*). Nevertheless, from the perspective of everyday life in time and space, these very mental afflictions instigate and produce individual activity by providing the basic motivations that sustain both individual experience and community life. In the final analysis, all history and culture, all art and science, are outgrowths of the *kleśas*. Feuerstein explains that the *kleśas* endow the body and mind with dynamic features that support phenomenal consciousness. *Kleśas* "urge the organism to burst into activity" and to experience emotions, ideas, hopes, and aspiration for goals.[61] Likewise, in Theravāda the *āsavas* function as the fundamental factors that cause individuals to cling to life and crave the expansion and enhancement of sensory and rational experience. *Āsavas* and *anusayas*, therefore, mark individual life with a paradox at its very core. They impel the senses and the mind to grow, to create, to explore, and to seek out new adventures on earth and in space. At the same time, they prevent individuals and societies from really seeing the transitory and conditioned nature of all beings, and they inevitably lead to profound sorrow. They constitute the dynamics of individual life within the realm of rebirth.

The *Atthasālinī*[62] says that the *āsavas* are so named because they flow (*savanti*) and move forward (*pavattanti*) through the senses and the mind, spreading their unwholesome influence (Asl. 48). Moreover, the *Atthasālinī* notes that the term *āsava* also refers to liquor that has been fermenting for a long time, and compares the four *āsavas* to potent, addictive intoxicants. From the point of view of conditioned origination, *āsavas* are unwholesome mental factors that powerfully condition mental processes and produce persistent habits of body, speech, and mind. They infatuate the mind and cause it to ignore whatever contradicts the world-view that they project. The *Atthasālinī* stresses that the dangerous power of the *āsavas* circulates to the loftiest levels of the realms of rebirth (Asl. 48). In another passage, the *Atthasālinī* explains that the *āsavas* can only be removed gradually in the four stages of the Path of liberation (Asl. 372).[63] Only the fully enlightened *arahant* is deemed worthy of the appellation *anāsavo* (one who has no *āsavas*).[64]

The description of the *āsavas* in the *Suttas*, the *Visuddhimagga*, and the *Atthasālinī* powerfully demonstrates that because of these "intoxicants", even when conditioned origination is affirmed by one's reasoning intellect, one does not experience the world in terms of transitoriness (*anicca*) and absence of a permanent self (*anattā*). The *Aṅguttara-nikāya* (A. II. 52) specifies four distortions (*vipallāsas*) that affect a person's perception (*saññā*), thought (*citta*), and view (*diṭṭhi*). Because of these distortions, a person sees the impermanent (*anicca*) as permanent, that which is not self (*anattā*) as self, the painful (*dukkha*) as pleasant, and the unlovely (*asubha*) as lovely. The *Visuddhimagga* correlates the four *āsavas* with the four "distortions" that are described as constituting the everyday experiences of unenlightened ordinary people (*puthujjana*) (Vsm. XIV. 226-230). The *āsava* of ignorance, which is regarded as the basis of the other *āsavas* (A. III. 414), is correlated with the distorted perception by which the impermanent is experienced as the permanent (Vsm. XIV. 229). This distortion entails that *paṭicca-samuppāda* is ignored by ordinary people who structure their experience in such a way that they perceive a universe of stable objects demarcated by recognizable identifying features. The *āsava* of attachment to life (*bhavāsava*) is correlated with the distorted view of perceiving pleasure in objects that are conditions for the arising of sorrow (Vsm. XIV. 227). This *āsava* causes people to value their own lives supremely and to resist anything that obstructs the perpetuation and enhancement of the self. The *āsava* of passion for objects of sensory pleasure (*kāmāsava*) is correlated with the distorted vision that sees loveliness (*subha*) in objects that have basic unlovely features that are liable to lead to sorrow (Vsm. XIV. 226). It is obvious that this *āsava* causes the average person to seek out more and more sensory experience and to dread sensory deprivation.

In explaining the *āsava* of predilection for views (*diṭṭhāsava*), the *Visuddhimagga* (Vsm. XVII. 277) refers to a passage of the *Saṁyutta-nikāya* (S. III. 3) where Sāriputta explains that sorrow arises when a person experiences any one of the five aggregates (*khandhas*) with the idea of identifying with that aggregate and seeking to posses it. It is stated in this *Sutta* that the sense of "I" and the experience of "mine" are developed by identifying the "individual self" with the body, feelings, perceptions, and the mind's constructive activities. Through this *āsava* of attachment to views, experience becomes uniquely personal and one's relationship to objects comes to be defined in terms of a firmly held world-view (*diṭṭhi*) based on the concept of the self as the agent of action and recipient of the consequences of action. If the *āsavas* did not operate, the average person would not ignore conditioned origination, and experience would not take the form of unique individual subjects personally relating to a stable world of clearly demarcated objects. Nor would there be a desperate urgency to multiply, preserve, and perpetuate this form of experience. Such is the power of the *āsavas* that they become associated in the *Suttas* with ignorance and desire, the primary causes of rebirth that persist through countless lives. Nevertheless, throughout the *Suttas* there is the clear affirmation that *āsavas* can be overcome, and vigilant systematic attention (*yoniso-manasikāra*) is prescribed as the simple, most effective antidote against the intoxicating influence of the *āsavas* (M. I. 9).

The Arising of Uncorrupted Mental States

Since it is posited in the *Suttas* that *āsavas* and *anusayas* persistently arise in the mind, an important question is how wholesome purposive impulses (*cetanās*) can come into existence without being blocked by these unwholesome motivational impulses. The *Suttas* strongly affirm that wholesome states arise in the minds of those who are not free of the *āsavas*. The term *anāsava* is sometimes employed to refer to factors of the Path of liberation cultivated by those who are not free of the *āsavas*. The two terms *sāsava* (conditioned by the *āsavas*) and *anāsava* (free of the *āsavas*) are dramatically opposed in a passage of the *Majjhima-nikāya* (M. III. 72-73). Here it is said that five of the eight factors of the Eightfold Path, namely, right view, right intention, right speech, right action, and right livelihood, can be cultivated in either of two modes: *sāsava* or *anāsava*. For example, when right intention (*sammā-saṅkappa*), which consists of purposes and aspirations based on renunciation (*nekkhamma*), non-hatred (*avyāpāda*), and non-violence (*avihiṁsā*), is cultivated by a person who desires karmic merit and a felicitous rebirth, then right intention becomes conditioned by the *āsavas* (*sāsava*).[65] The consequence of *āsava*-laden right intention is described as attachment to the things of this world, which perpetuates rebirth (*upadhi-vepakka*) and ultimately causes sorrow. It is emphasized in this passage that when right view, right intention, right speech, right action, and right livelihood are cultivated in the framework of the *āsavas*, though they may bring rich benefits within the realm of rebirth (*puññābhāgiya*), they still contain the danger of subtly arousing the longing for personal merit and future rewards, thereby prolonging greed, sorrow, and rebirth.

According to the vivid imagery of the text, right view, right effort, and right mindfulness "run around" (*anuparidhāvanti*) and protectively encircle the five factors named above and gradually release them from the motivating power of the *āsavas*. When right view, right intention, right speech, right action, and right livelihood are no longer motivated by the *āsavas*, they are characterized as "supramundane" (*lokuttara*). The term *lokuttara* signifies that these virtuous acts do not partake of karmic merit and do not belong to the mundane sphere of *karma* and rebirth; they partake of wisdom and become aspects of the Eightfold Path (*maggaṅga*) that leads to liberation from rebirth. The passage goes on to say that when right intention is cultivated by a person whose mind is noble and free of the *āsavas* (*ariya-cittassa anāsava-cittassa . . . sammā-saṅkappo*), then the right intention is to be regarded as supramundane and free of the *āsavas*. Although the mind of the person who cultivates right intention as a factor of the supramundane Path is said to be free of the *āsavas*, the fact that this person is still following the Path indicates that the perfect freedom and wisdom of an *arahant* has not yet been attained.

The *Visuddhimagga* also distinguishes between mundane (*lokiya*) and supramundane (*lokuttara*) practice of virtue (*sīla*), and specifies that only the supramundane is *anāsava* (Vsm. I. 32). It is significant that like the *Majjhima-nikāya* passage (M. III. 72-73), the *Visuddhimagga* does not limit the term *anāsava* to the perfect liberation from *āsavas* experienced by the *arahant*. Both texts include the stages of the Path of liberation in the connotations of *anāsava*, provided these stages are cultivated without attachment and aspiration for karmic merit.[66] The term *anāsava*, therefore, is found in two different contexts. When the reference is to an *arahant*, *anāsava* signifies total freedom from the *āsavas*. On the other hand, when the stages of the Path are characterized as *anāsava*, the term connotes, not "without *āsavas*", but "leading to complete cessation of the *āsavas*". The stages of the Path are called *lokuttara* (supramundane) because they do not lead to further accumulation of *kamma* but bring about the cessation of *kamma*. The brief description of mundane (*lokiya*) virtue in the *Visuddhimagga* points to a tension in the motivations of those who ardently practise virtue (*sīla*), even though they are not free of the influence of the *āsavas* (Vsm. I. 32). According to the *Visuddhimagga*, these actions of mundane virtue have a double consequence. On the one hand, since mundane virtue still functions within the processes of rebirth, it brings about not only earthly benefits but also karmic merit and an excellent future rebirth (*bhava-visesāvaha*). On the other hand, by cleansing and gladdening the mind of a person who cultivates the Eightfold Path, mundane virtue simultaneously prepares the way for the renunciation of future goals and future lives (*bhava-nissaraṇassa ca sambhāra*). The *Visuddhimagga* does not expand on this important statement, but it does provide, as an example of mundane virtue that is not exempt from *āsavas*, a standard account of the process by which a person cultivates the virtues and the mental disciplines that lead, step by step, to the freeing of the mind from attachment to existence in the wheel of rebirth. The implication is that mundane virtue and mindfulness, though *āsava*-ridden, prepare the way for the removal of the *āsavas* and the development of supramundane virtue. Mindful dedication to virtuous acts leads a person to experience the conditioned nature of all things, including mundane virtue, and wise awareness of conditioning gradually leads to the supramundane goal. It can be inferred that by gradually deepening a person's understanding of conditioned origination, acts of mundane virtue lead to a gradual removal of the distorted perceptions spawned by the *āsavas*. In this way, the mundane bring about the supramundane.

These passages in the *Majjhima-nikāya* (M. III 72-73) and *Visuddhimagga* (Vsm. I. 32) profoundly affect the practice of ethics in Theravāda. It is to be noted that these passages deliberately avoid a dichotomy between the mundane practice of virtue (*sīla*), which is not free of the defilements (*āsavas*) of the sphere of *kamma*, and the supramundane purity (*anāsava*) of *nibbāna*. The disciplines of the Eightfold Path prepare the way for *nibbāna* when they are cultivated with wise understanding and without aspiration for karmic merit. For this reason, they are designated as supramundane. At the same time, *nibbāna* as the supramundane goal influences and directs the Eightfold Path and draws it into the sphere of supramundane wisdom.

Furthermore, since the aggregates are said to be drenched with the polluting flow of the *āsavas*, it becomes necessary to ask how the wholesome "roots" (non-greed, non-aversion, and non-delusion) can sprout in the aggregates, and how the factors of the Eightfold Path can be cultivated. The answer to this question must be found within conditioned origination. The *āsavas* are neither primordial nor self-sustaining: they come into being through causes and conditions, and they function only as long as conditions are conducive for their perpetuation. Although there is no sustained discussion in the *Suttas* about how *āsavas* are actually formed, it would not be incorrect to think of them as unwholesome *saṅkhara* formations that have become intractable and addictive habits through repetition. The *Sabbāsava-sutta* maintains that unsystematic, distracted attention (*ayoniso-manasikāra*) produces the environment in which the *āsavas* come into existence and thrive (M. I. 7).[67] Whereas unsystematic attention is described as the ceaseless preoccupation with the nature of the "I" and the mode of its existence in the past, present, and future (M. I. 8),[68] systematic attention (*yoniso manasikāra*) is shown to be just thoughtful, thorough reflection on the nature of sorrow and the Four Noble Truths (M. I. 9).

The *Sabbāsava-sutta* does not explain either why *yoniso-manasikāra* has the capacity to combat the powerful motivating energy of the *āsavas* or how it is to be cultivated. *Yoniso-manasikāra* represents the cognitive process of focusing the mind and giving proper attention. It has the aim of knowing objects thoroughly. That *manasikāra* is regarded as a cognitive process, rather than as a conative factor, becomes clear when the injunction to pay attention (*manasikarotha*) is coupled with the injunction to reason well (*vitakketha*) (A. I. 171; D. I. 214). *Manasikāra* is not classified either in the *Suttas* or in the *Abhidhamma* system with factors like energy (*viriya*) and effort (*vāyāma, padhāna*) that have the ability to initiate action to cleanse the mind of unwholesome mental states. It becomes necessary, therefore, to further investigate the power to combat obdurate mental corruptions that is assigned to the mind's capacity of systematic attention. In the commentary to the *Sabbāsava-sutta*, *ayoniso-manasikāra* is explained as attention that is the wrong means (*anupāya*) and the wrong way (*uppatha*) (MA. I. 64). This type of attention is declared to be unsystematic because it perceives the permanent in the impermanent, pleasure in the painful, the self in what is not a self, and beauty in that which is not fully beautiful. The commentary, therefore, regards unsystematic attention to be the wrong means because it causes these four distortions (*vipallāsas*) of perception that constitute the *āsava* of ignorance. The conclusion can be drawn that *yoniso-manasikāra* functions as vigilant, sustained, and systematic attention focused on the conditioned origination of objects.

The distortions are regarded not only as erroneous cognitions but also as unwholesome motivations leading to unwholesome goal-directed activities (*saṅkhāras*). By leading a person to perceive things as they actually are (*yathā-bhūtam*) in relation to conditioned origination, systematic attention opens the way to wholesome intentions towards objects. The cognitive capacity of alert, systematic attention gradually prevails over the emotive and motivational power of the *āsavas* by becoming a leading condition that works together with other wholesome conditions for the arising of wholesome emotions and intentions. If the *Sabbāsava-sutta* regards the cognitive function of giving methodical attention to objects to be the most effective antidote to the unwholesome motivations of the *āsavas*, this is because, in the Theravāda tradition, cognition, emotion, and motivating energy are seen as mutually dependent functions in the holistic view of the mind. Careful systematic attention prepares the way for wise understanding (*paññā*).

Anusayas as Factors of Motivation Within Conditioned Origination

The term *anusaya* (proclivity, inclination, tendency) is related to the verb *anuseti*, which literally means "to lie down with" or "to be attached" to something. According to the *Pali-English Dictionary*, *anuseti* connotes the tendency to obsess the mind over a period of time and to remain latent in the mind as the cause of habitually arising unwholesome mental states (P.E.D. 44, col. 2). Several passages in the *Sutta* literature list the following seven *anusayas*: sensual passion (*kāma-rāga*), ill will (*paṭigha*), predilection for speculative views (*diṭṭhi*), sceptical doubt (*vicikicchā*), conceit (*māna*) that produces the sense of a separate self, desire for continued existence (*bhava-rāga*), and ignorance (*avijjā*) (D. III. 254, 282; S. V. 60; A. IV. 9).

Though *anusaya* is sometimes interpreted as a latent, not yet activated, state of existence, any such interpretation goes against the basic Theravāda tenet that conditioned origination precludes the notion that any physical or mental factor can remain unchanged. In this regard, it is worth noting that the Yoga concept of *vāsanās* as residual potencies that reside in the subtle matter of the *citta* for vast periods of time has no equivalent in the *Sutta* and *Abhidhamma* literature. There is no description in the *Suttas* of *anusayas* in a latent and unexpressed state, though the notion of latency seems to be implied when *anusayas* and *āsavas* are mentioned. For example, although the *Mahāmāluṅkya-sutta* of the *Majjhima-nikāya* maintains that the *anusayas* are present in the mind even of a small child (M. I. 433-434), there is no description of the form that *anasuyas* take when they are not openly manifested, and no account of how they persist in the changing processes of the personality.

The *Mahāmāluṅkya-sutta* opens with a discussion of how the unwholesome mental states that constitute "the five lower fetters" arise. These five lower fetters (*saṁyojanas*), which resemble the *anusayas*, are the following: the speculative view that upholds the idea of "oneself", doubt that takes the form of wavering, obsessive adherence to rules and observances, desire for sensual pleasure, and ill will. The Buddha explains to Māluṅkyaputta that the lower fetters are not present in an infant since the infant does not have the maturity to experience the ideas and emotions that constitute these afflictive mental states. For example, the Buddha points out that a child who has no notion of its own self as agent of action could hardly be fettered with the consciously held view of individual selfhood. However, the Buddha maintains that the *anusayas* that correspond to the fetters exist in the infant. Thus, the Buddha states that the tendency towards the view of "oneself" (*sakkāya-*

diṭṭhānusaya), for example, "lies within" (*anuseti*) the infant. It is implied here that since the *anusayas* are present in a hidden manner within the mind of a child, there is the possibility for the clearly evident unwholesome mental states that constitute the fetters to arise from the *anusayas* and become effective as the child grows. However, the Buddha does not explain precisely how the fetters are related to the *anusayas*. He does not say that the fetters are contained in the *anusayas* in a potential form.

With the acceptance of the theory of momentariness in the *Abhidhamma* system of classification, the problem of explaining how the *āsavas* persist in the continuum of consciousness becomes more difficult.[69] Jaini points out that momentariness was interpreted to signify that only one state of mind (*citta*)—wholesome, unwholesome, or ethically indeterminate—could come into existence and be experienced at any given moment. Since *anusayas* are counted as unwholesome, their latent presence in the mind would entail that no wholesome mental state could come into being. Jaini explains that in order to steer clear of the notion that the latent presence of *anusayas* in the mind precludes the arising of wholesome mental states, Buddhaghosa avoids the notion of latency in his definition of the *anusayas*.[70] Furthermore, in the commentaries to the *Suttas* and in the *Visuddhimagga*, Buddhaghosa seems to deliberately keep away from the idea that the obsessive emotions (*pariyuṭṭhāna*) that become openly manifest and fetter the mind are present in the *anusayas* in a latent state. Buddhaghosa holds that the same unwholesome mental state—for example, adherence to views (*diṭṭhi*)—is called an *anusaya* because it has not been renounced (*appahīnaṭṭhena anusayo*) through the disciplines of the Eightfold Path, and is designated as a "fetter" because it binds the mind to the process of rebirth (*bandhanaṭṭhena saṁyojanaṁ*) (MA. III. 145).[71] In other words, Buddhaghosa maintains that though the two terms *anusaya* and *saṁyojana* have different connotations, they both denote a consciously experienced mental state. In the *Visuddhimagga*, Buddhaghosa defines *anusayas*, not as latent tendencies that lie dormant in the mind, but as inveterate mental states that have two features: first, the capacity to stand their ground (*thāmagata*) against counteractive conditions; and second, the capacity to function as conditions for the arising (*uppatti-hetu-bhāva*), again and again (*punappunam*), of sensual desire and other mental fetters (Vsm. XXII. 60). Here Buddhaghosa interprets the verb *anusenti* to signify "persisting" in the sense of repeatedly occurring as dominant afflictive mental conditions in the continuum of configurations of conditions (*saṅkharas*) that continually produce conditioned acts of body, speech, and mind.

The commentaries to the first four *Nikāyas* state that impure states of mind (*kilesas*) occur in three stages: in the *anusaya* stage they are tendencies that are not yet activated; in the *pariyuṭṭhāna* stage they become openly active and are experienced as unwholesome mental states that fetter the mind; and in the *vītikkama* stage they motivate reprehensible acts of body, speech, and mind.[72] It is in the third stage that *anusayas* can be seen as giving rise to corresponding *cetanās* that instigate unwholesome acts (*kamma*). However, the *anusaya* stage is not explained in the commentaries as a period when a residual impression resulting from an impure act remains inactive and latent in the mind, waiting for an opportunity to become manifest as an act of body, speech, or mind. On the contrary, *anusaya* is described as a stage when an ethically unwholesome mental disposition or habit becomes intractable (*thāmagata*) because the mind resorts to it again and again, without being able to abandon it (MA. I. 182; SA. III. 137).

Despite the fact that the *Visuddhimagga* and these commentaries turn away from the idea of latency in their interpretation of *anusaya*, it does appear that in the *Suttas*—for example, in the *Mahāmāluṅkya-sutta*—*anusaya* stands for a latent tendency that becomes expressed in outward behaviour when circumstances are appropriate. However, it is made clear in the *Suttas* that persistent tendencies are formed through causes and conditions and that they become expressed in acts of body, speech or mind only when the necessary conditions are present. It is emphasized in the *Suttas* that the presence of *anusayas* in the mind does not predetermine behaviour and that *anusayas* do not become activated if counteractive conditions are cultivated.

The Conditioned Arising of *Anusayas*

In the *Suttas*, the verb *anuseti* is sometimes associated with objects of sensory experience and sometimes with the persons who experience these objects. When *anuseti* is associated with objects, the emphasis is on how feelings (*vedanā*) resulting from sensory stimulation repeatedly become causal conditions for the activation of tendencies, proclivities, or dispositions. When *anuseti* is associated with the experiencing subject, the verb connotes obsessive attachments to certain experiences. In both cases, *anusayas* are viewed as powerful motivating factors that produce purposive impulses (*cetanā*) and goal-oriented activities (*saṅkhāras*) of body, speech, and mind.

In the *Cūḷa-vedalla-sutta*, the *bhikkhunī* Dhammadinnā explains that when pleasure, pain, and neutral feelings characterized neither by pleasure nor by pain arise from contact with objects, these feelings produce, respectively, *anusayas* of sensual passion (*kāma-rāga*), aversion (*paṭigha*), and ignorance (*avijjā*) (M. I. 303-305). The thrust of her argument, however, is that pleasure, pain, and neutral feelings do not invariably entail the activation of *anusayas* and their motivating capacities.[73] An analysis of Dhammadinnā's argument shows that in the first part she stresses that far from being primordial factors in the personality, *anusayas* acquire their ability to function as tendencies that motivate habitual unwholesome responses through causes and conditions. She points out that the *anusayas* of sensual passion, aversion, and ignorance would not acquire the capacity of functioning as persistent proclivities without the facilitating conditions provided, respectively, by pleasant, painful, and neutral feelings. In the second part of her analysis, she argues that sensual passion, aversion, and ignorance do not necessarily function as unwholesome tendencies whenever pleasurable, painful, and neutral sensations are experienced. She demonstrates that it is possible to establish counteractive conditions to prevent the activation of *anusaya*s when feelings are experienced.

The verb *anuseti* is often associated with the person who experiences objects rather than with the objects experienced. In these contexts, *anuseti* conveys "to obsess", "to fill the mind persistently", "to be continually cropping up" (P.E.D. 44, col. 2). A passage in the *Majjhima-nikāya* indicates that *anusaya*s are activated not solely because objects are capable of causing pleasure, pain, or neutral feeling, but because of the way a person reacts to sensory experience (M. III. 285). If a person is delighted by a pleasant sensation, welcomes it, and covets it, then the tendency towards sensual passion is compulsively present in that person (*tassa rāgānusayo anuseti*). When a painful sensation arises, if a person grieves, mourns, laments, weeps with anguish, and feels distraught, then the tendency to aversion persists in that person (*tassa paṭighānusayo anuseti*). When a neutral feeling of neither pleasure nor pain arises, if one does not clearly see the origin, cessation, and future effect of that feeling, then the tendency to ignorance obsesses that person (*tassa avijjānusayo anuseti*) in the form of delusion or confusion. It is not clear from the context whether the tendency causes the person's emotional reaction to a specific sensory experience, or whether the repeated emotional experiences (*pariyuṭṭhāna*) cause a corresponding tendency somehow to be formed in the mind. It is plausible that *anuseti* here signifies both that the activation of a habitual tendency produces the emotional reaction and that the openly expressed emotions strengthen the inward capacity of the tendency or proclivity to somehow remain in the mind and to persistently obsess a person.

In another context (S. III. 131), the wise and elderly *thera* named Khemaka illustrates the obduracy of *anusayas* with the analogy of a dirty cloth that retains a faint odour of detergent even after it has been washed clean. Through this analogy, Khemaka explains how the subtle conceit of "I am", the desire expressed as "I am", and the persistent tendency to feel "I am" (*asmīti anusaya*) remain in the mind of a *bhikkhu*, even though he has achieved release from the five "lower fetters". Khemaka concludes by saying that just as the unpleasant odour will leave the cloth if it is kept in a sweet-scented chest, so the subtle proclivity to posit a self as the agent who acts and experiences objects will leave the mind of a *bhikkhu* if he continues to contemplate "arising and passing away" in relation to the five aggregates that form the "personality". These examples show that there is sufficient evidence to draw the conclusion that in the *Suttas*, *anusayas* represent causal conditions that somehow persist in the mind even when they do not become overtly expressed as obsessive mental states (*pariyuṭṭhānas*). The phrase *dīgharatta-anusayita* (Tha. 768, 1275; Sn. 355, 649) suggests that *anusaya* signifies the presence of certain unwholesome conditions in the mind over a long period of time.

Buddhaghosa's explanation, which seeks to avoid the notion of latency, can be interpreted to mean that *anusayas* are just the repeated convergence of unwholesome causal conditions in the continuum of consciousness (Vsm. XXII. 60). It is evident that his interpretation of *anusaya* proceeds from the Theravāda teaching of conditioned origination. This theory of causality postulates that when the necessary causal factors converge, the effect will follow in due course, without the need for a connecting factor to act as a link between cause and effect. Given conditioned origination, it is not necessary to posit *anusaya* as a latent factor that exists through time and links unwholesome experiences of the past with resultant obsessive patterns of unwholesome behaviour (*pariyuṭṭhāna*) in the present and the future. For example, Buddhaghosa's interpretation implies that *rāgānusaya* is not to be conceived as a subliminal mental impression or fixed mental structure that links past excitement and pleasure in contacting an object with the manifest passion that is experienced whenever that same object is encountered at a later time. No such link is deemed necessary when conditioned origination is affirmed; the convergence of the necessary causal conditions is regarded as sufficient for the effect to follow in due course.

The definition of *anusaya* in the *Visuddhimagga* implies that according to Buddhaghosa, the strength and obduracy of *anusayas* is to be explained, not in terms of their latency, but in terms of their capacity for repetition. It is posited that *anusayas* grow in strength as they occur again and again as unwholesome mental conditions that become expressed repeatedly in analogous patterns of unwholesome behaviour. In the *Kathāvatthu* (Kvu. 405-408) there is a similar explanation of *anusayas*, again based on the Theravāda teaching of conditioned origination. In their debate with their opponents, the Theravādins maintained that *anusayas* are conditioned and conditioning factors that are to be included in the category of *saṅkhāra*. According to the explanation given in the commentary to the *Kathāvatthu*, the opponents held that *anusayas* are latent factors that are ethically indeterminate (*avyākata*) and exist without a cause (*ahetuka*) (KvuA. 116). In the debate, the Theravādins defined *anusayas* as constituents of the *saṅkharakkhandha* and maintained that the necessary causal conditions for the arising of *anusayas* occur when the sense organs and the mind make contact with their respective objects.

Anusaya and *Cetanā*

The verbs *ceteti* (to intend, to think purposefully), *pakappeti* (to plan, to arrange) and *anuseti* (to function as a persistent tendency) are found together in three short sections of the *Saṁyutta-nikāya* (S. II. 65-67).[74] Each of these sections is entitled *Cetanā*. These passages begin with the statement that what one intends, plans, and has a tendency towards becomes an object (*ārammaṇam*) for the mind. The object is said to provide for the maintenance and continuance (*ṭhiti*) of consciousness (*viññāṇa*) by causing it to develop towards future rebirth. This statement, however, is emended. The passage goes on to declare that even if a person does not actually intend (*ceteti*) or plan (*pakappeti*), but only habitually tends (*anuseti*) towards pursuing an object, this tendency is sufficient to provide a support for consciousness and to direct it towards rebirth. These statements in the *Saṁyutta-nikāya* are based on a fundamental Theravāda teaching which maintains that conscious awareness (*viññāṇa*) is neither self-sufficient nor permanent, but is dependent on active engagement with sensory and mental objects for its perpetuation (M. I. 258-259). The *Saṁyutta-nikāya* maintains that whereas consciousness is usually provided with objects through the functions of intending and planning, the mere presence in the mind of *anusayas* that cause inclinations towards specific objects is sufficient to ensure not only the perpetuation of consciousness, but also its fecundity.

The commentary explains that the unwholesome goal-directed thoughts and impulses that constitute unwholesome *cetanās* are conditioned by the unwholesome habits and tendencies that *anusayas* represent (SA. II. 70). *Anuseti* is explained in the commentary with the statement that *anusayas* support unwholesome *cetanās* based on greed (*lobha*) and on speculative views (*diṭṭhi*) in the two following ways. As "conascent conditions" (*sahajāta-paccaya*), *anusayas* arise simultaneously with *cetanās* and support them through a relationship of mutuality and interdependence. As "support conditions" (*upanissaya-paccaya*), *anusayas* provide antecedent conditions in the consciousness continuum for the arising of unwholesome *cetanās*. The commentary is obviously referring to the way persistent tendencies instigate, condition, and support unwholesome goal-oriented impulses (*cetanās*). *Anusayas* are not defined here in terms of latency or dormancy, and it is not implied that *anusayas* cause the arising of *cetanās* while remaining latent and unknown to the conscious mind. The point here is that *anusayas*, repeatedly occurring in the form of unwholesome conditions in the continuum of consciousness, produce unwholesome purposive impulses (*cetanās*).

The commentary (SA. II. 72) goes on to say that when a person intends (*ceteti*), plans (*pakappeti*), and is obsessively inclined (*anuseti*) to seek certain objects, then consciousness is supported and perpetuated by these functions in such a way that it "grows abundantly" (*viññāṇe virūḷhe*) and develops a "bent" (*nati*) towards future goals and rebirth. The commentary gives craving (*taṇhā*) as the synonym of *nati* and explains that *nati* signifies the "bending" of the mind towards objects that bring delight. In other contexts, it is said that when a person relies on objects, restlessness, lack of tranquillity, further inclination (*nati*) towards objects, and rebirth follow one after the other as consequences (S. IV. 59; M. III. 266). *Anusayas*, therefore, can be interpreted as mental factors that cause the mind to incline towards, or to crave for, certain goals, while they gain strength as the mind repeatedly ponders over those goals.

On the basis of these passages, a circular relationship can be posited between *anusayas* and the goal-directed thoughts and purposes of *cetanā*. *Anusayas*, functioning as tendencies, condition the arising of the unwholesome purposes and goal-oriented impulses that constitute unwholesome *cetanās*. At the same time, these unwholesome purposive impulses become the vehicles through which the unwholesome habits and tendencies produced by *anusayas* find expression. Tendencies become very strong and obdurate when they are repeatedly expressed as unwholesome purposive impulses. When *anusayas* and *cetanās* increase and intensify, they produce a bent of mind expressive of craving, which further strengthens the *cetanās* and renders the *anusayas* more intransigent (*thāmagata*). However, whereas *anusayas* are always regarded as unwholesome in their manner of functioning, *cetanās* can be either wholesome or unwholesome.

Anusayas and the Question of "Unconscious" Motivation

In *The Dynamic Psychology of Early Buddhism*, Rune Johansson argues that there are no passages in the *Suttas* that unequivocally spell out a theory of "unconscious motivation".[75] In this context, Johansson refers to the *Mahāmāluṅkya-sutta* where the Buddha affirms that the *anusayas* are present in the mind of an infant (M. I. 432-433). According to Johansson's argument, the import of this passage is that though underlying tendencies are present in an innocent child, they neither become activated nor motivate reprehensible behaviour until the child matures and conditions are appropriate for their activation. Johansson concludes that this passage proves that in the *Suttas*, *anusayas* may be conceived as factors whose presence is not known to the conscious mind, but they are not described as factors that influence behaviour when they are in that latent state. In other words, Johansson maintains that in the *Suttas*, *anusayas* are not described as factors of unconscious motivation. Johansson also refers to the passage where the *thera* Khemaka explains to the *bhikkhus* that though a person has made progress in the Eightfold Path, subtle traces of the tendency to feel "I am" (*asmīti anusaya*) may remain in the mind (S. III. 131). Here again, Johansson stresses that the passage gives no indication that this tendency to perceive the self mistakenly as autonomous and permanent may influence the mind while the mind remains unaware of the tendency and its influence. In fact, in this passage Khemaka clearly states that he is well aware of the lingering presence in his mind of the tendency to affirm an autonomous self through the notion "I am", though he no longer ignorantly identifies any of the five aggregates as the self. Johansson argues that the Buddha did not develop a theory about "repressed drives" and "forgotten memories" that influence the conscious mind. He concludes that whereas the *Sutta* passages he has examined show that *anusayas* may be latent in the mind, these passages do not demonstrate that *anusayas* "can be active and influence activity" while they are in a latent state.

In a later article entitled "Defence Mechanisms According to Psychoanalysis and the Pāli Nikāyas", Johansson changes his position somewhat. Here he argues that the *Suttas* contain passages where motivation and behaviour are analyzed in such a way as to suggest that people often adopt measures, consciously or unconsciously, to defend the ego (*aham*). According to Johansson, the thrust of these passages is that when *āsavas* and *anusayas* become manifest in acts of body and speech, they show themselves as addictive habits and persistent proclivities that can be interpreted in terms of defence mechanisms and ego inflations. However, he maintains that these passages do not show conclusively that the Buddha and his followers viewed *anusayas* and *āsavas* as factors that act on the mind in such a way that the mind is unaware of their motivating influence. To illustrate his point, Johansson refers to a passage in the *Aṅguttara-nikāya* (A. IV. 192-195) that describes the different reactions of monks when they are reproved for unwholesome behaviour. He argues that the reactions of the monks could be interpreted in Freudian terms as behaviour based on repression, aggression, projection, regression, and compensation. However, he stresses that there is no attempt in the text itself to explain their behaviour in terms of motivation arising from an "unconscious" level of the mind.

Padmasiri de Silva, on the other hand, quite emphatically endorses the view of Jayatilleke, who argues that there are passages in the *Suttas* containing unambiguous references to an "unconscious component" in the mind.[76] De Silva maintains that these passages affirm the presence of dormant *anusayas* in the mind and substantiate the notion that the activation of *anusayas* "can occur without conscious awareness". He argues that this psychological process by which latent *anusayas* become active without the knowledge of the conscious mind can be regarded as "unconscious motivation". According to de Silva's analysis, "unconscious motivation" is posited in the following three contexts: in the *Dīgha-nikāya* (D. III. 105) where reference is made to the "stream of consciousness" (*viññāṇa-sota*); in a passage of the *Aṅguttara-nikāya* where the yogic power of directly knowing the mind of another person is mentioned (A. I. 171); and, more significantly, in the notion of a mental act performed by a person who acts without deliberation and proper attention (*asampajāno*).

The reference to the "stream of consciousness" (*viññāṇa-sota*) is in a passage that focuses on the "four attainments of vision" (*dassana-samāpatti*). It is stated here that a person who has reached "the third attainment" through mental concentration has gained the ability to directly perceive another person's "stream of consciousness". The claim is made that it is possible to directly know the stream of consciousness of another person through yogic power and to perceive that though consciousness is established both in "this world" and in the "world beyond", it retains its single flow and remains "unbroken" in both of these aspects (*ubhayato abbocchinnam*). The idea of being "stationed" in the next world (*paraloke patiṭṭhitam*) is interpreted in the commentary to the *Dīgha-nikāya* as a reference to factors present within the consciousness continuum that already act as causal conditions for future rebirth. It is a central concept in Theravāda that consciousness is not self-perpetuating but needs to be continually maintained through engagement with objects. Consciousness is viewed as being "stationed" or situated in physical and mental objects that provide the supporting conditions for its maintenance and perpetuation. The commentary says that the stream of consciousness becomes stationed in this world through the supporting conditions of desire and passion (*chanda-rāga-vasena*). The same stream of consciousness of the present life is vividly described as "pulling along" the supporting conditions that perpetuate consciousness and ensure rebirth in accordance with *kamma* (*kamma-bhavam*), so that consciousness becomes established in the "next world" even while the present life is still continuing (DA. III. 888). According to Jayatilleke's interpretation, that part of the stream of consciousness which is already established in the next world consists of "dynamic *saṅkhāras*" that continue "in a state of flux in the Unconscious".[77] Jayatilleke regards this stream of *saṅkhāras* operating within the conscious continuum in the present life to be a powerful unconscious process that motivates future behaviour and causes future rebirth. In his view, the conscious mind is not aware of this dynamic flow of *saṅkhāras*, but a person who is trained in meditation can directly perceive this hidden dimension of another person's stream of consciousness. De Silva follows Jayatilleke's interpretation.[78]

According to Jayatilleke's explanation, the reference to an aspect of the stream of consciousness that is directed towards a future existence, even while the present life is still in progress, implies that the stream of consciousness is filled with subliminal tendencies "of which the person is not aware". He interprets these dynamic *saṅkhāras* to be residual "impressions" of one's "volitional activities" that persist in the Unconscious as karmic conditions for future rebirth. Jayatilleke's argument is not convincing. The term *kamma-bhava* in the commentary, indeed, is a reference to wholesome and unwholesome constructive activities (*saṅkhāras*) in the mind that condition consciousness in such a way that it is already poised for future rebirth. However, neither this *Sutta* passage nor its commentary describes *saṅkhāras* as subliminal impressions. Neither suggests that *saṅkhāras* persist in the mind in the form of latent dispositions that act upon the mind while the mind remains unaware of their potent influence.

The second passage says that a person who attains a certain plane of calm concentration (*jhāna*) acquires the telepathic power, both to know directly how configurations of goal-oriented mental conditions (*mano-saṅkhāras*) are arranged in the mind of another person, and to predict what thoughts that other person will think in the future (A. I. 171). Jayatilleke holds that the term *mano-saṅkhāra* in this passage refers to a flux of subliminal impressions of past "purposive actions" that "in some sense survive" their actual occurrence, remaining in the mind as a powerful influence on future thoughts and behaviour. According to Jayatilleke's interpretation, a person does not consciously experience this flux of dynamic *saṅkhāras*, though it is very clearly seen by a person with telepathic powers. Jayatilleke, therefore, concludes that this passage contains "perhaps the earliest historical mention of unconscious mental processes". Again de Silva affirms Jayatilleke's interpretation. However, this passage does not say that the mental *saṅkhāras* are latent processes of which the subject is not aware. In other contexts (for example, M. I. 390-391; A. I. 122; II. 158, 231) the term *mano-saṅkhāra* conveys a configuration of mental factors leading to purposive mental activity. This passage can be interpreted to mean that a person with telepathic powers observes exactly how the patterns of mental factors are organized in another person's mind (*yathā imassa bhoto mano-saṅkhare paṇihitā*). On the basis of this observation, he is able to predict what specific thought the person will subsequently think (*amun nāma vitakkam vitakkissati*). The commentary does not state that the person is unaware of the internal patterns of thought (*mano-saṅkhāra*) that become known to another through telepathy (AA. II. 270).

The third passage on which de Silva bases his argument makes the point that intentional acts of body, speech, and mind that are instigated by purposive impulses (*cetanā*) lead to commensurate consequences of personal pleasure and pain (A. II. 157-158 = S. II. 39-40). This passage is important for an understanding of *cetanā*, and I will return to it in the next chapter. Here, the focus is on one class of acts, namely "undeliberate" acts. These are reckoned among the classes of morally weighted acts that are motivated by *cetanā* and lead to karmic consequences. *Asampajāno*, in this passage, conveys that the acts are not premeditated and are done by a person who acts without consideration or without attention (for example, *asampajāno . . . kayasaṅkhāram abhisaṅkharoti*). Bodhi translates *asampajāno* as one who acts "undeliberately",[79] while C.A.F. Rhys Davids, in her translation of the *Saṁyutta-nikāya*, prefers "unwittingly".[80] The commentary explains *asampajāno* as a person acting without knowledge of the consequences of the act and gives the example of children who imitate their parents in performing the rituals at a shrine without knowing the karmic consequence of their acts (SA. II. 58). De Silva, however, interprets *asampajāna mano-saṅkhāra* as a mental disposition or train of thought, which is motivated by "unconscious tendencies".[81] He therefore regards the *anusayas* as unwholesome tendencies that motivate acts of body, speech, and mind, without the mind being consciously aware of their subliminal presence.

It is to be noted that the passage in which the term *asampajāno* (a person who acts unknowingly) occurs deals with karmically operative acts that are caused by intentions (*sañcetanās*) pertaining to body, speech, and mind and lead to commensurate consequences. De Silva's argument can be interpreted to mean that when a person acts "unknowingly", the mind is aware of arriving at an intention, but is unaware of the persistent tendency (*anusaya*) through which such an intention arises in the mind. However, this is not the way *anusayas* are described. For example, a person who is acting under the influence of the *anusaya* of conceit or the *anusaya* of repulsion is said to be aware of the persistent sense of self-pride or the incessant feeling of dislike as well as the intention it instigates. We have the case of Khemaka, who is aware that the *anusaya* that causes the sense of "I" operates in his mind, even though he has attained a certain level of wisdom (S. III. 131). In other contexts, a person who acts deliberately and with proper attention and mindfulness is designated as *sampajānakārin* (D. I. 70, II. 95). *Asampajāno* can be interpreted, in accordance with the commentary (SA. II. 58), to signify a person who acts with intention, but lacks either proper attention to the act or sufficient knowledge of the circumstances in which the act is done and proper consideration of the consequences that might follow. Though *āsavas* and *anusayas* are described as powerful, they are not regarded as inherent to the mind or as self-sustaining. Johansson has argued convincingly that in the *Suttas*, there is no description of *anusayas* and *āsavas* motivating the mind while the mind remains unaware of their presence.

Since *anusayas* and *āsavas* are regarded as factors governed by conditioned origination, it is affirmed that they will cease when the conditions that perpetuate them are removed. The *Visuddhimagga* (Vsm. I. 13) says that whereas the processes by which mental obsessions (*pariyuṭṭhānas*) give rise to unethical acts can be forestalled by calming meditation (*samādhi*), the processes by which mental obsessions arise from persistent tendencies (*anusayas*) can only be obliterated by sustained practice of mindfulness leading to wisdom (*paññā*). There are several passages in the *Suttas* where instructions are given for the cultivation of mindfulness in order to remove *anusayas* (S. II. 252-253; III. 130; IV. 209-210, 212). It is to be noted that mindfulness is the practice of focusing on what is directly present to the senses and the mind. In passages where instructions are given for the practice of mindfulness, there is no reference to motivations that may be experienced without the mind being aware of the sources of those motivations and the mode of their arising. In the *Suttas* the practice of mindfully observing the continuum of consciousness (*cittānupassanā*) is never described as a process of delving into the Unconscious or of bringing into awareness latent mental states that act upon the mind without the mind being aware of their presence and influence.

Conclusion

All psychological processes of the *citta*, of *saṅkhāras*, and of *anusayas* are explained in Theravāda through its central principle of conditioned origination. According to Theravāda, whenever *cetanās* emerge as purposive impulses from attitudes of mind (*cittas*), or constitute the constructive activities of the mind (*saṅkhāras*), or interact with the tendencies and obdurate habits that *anusayas* and *āsavas* represent, they are governed by causal processes. Theravāda does not posit an overriding "will" or sovereign reason to explain how mental conflicts are resolved or how processes that constitute the continuum of consciousness are controlled. Consciousness is viewed as an organic system where the vibrantly creative whole and its dynamic constituents mutually condition each other. References to an "I" that acts as a controlling agent must be interpreted to signify that the mind can function as a self-evaluating integral whole that exerts its conditioning influence on the processes that constitute consciousness.

Upholding the principle of conditioned origination, Theravāda avoids defining *saṅkhāras* as subliminal impressions of past experiences that already contain future effects in a latent state. In the *Sutta* and *Abhidhamma* literature, the constituents of the *saṅkhārakkhandha* are regarded as dynamic processes that put into action the mind's capacity to bring together causal conditions in such a way as to produce further effects. These effects are configurations of factors that manifest both as habitual acts of body, speech, and mind and as the aggregates (*khandhas*) of physical and mental states that make up the individual "person". *Saṅkhāras*, therefore, have a major role in forming the "person" who is conceived as the agent of action. *Saṅkhāras* also produce the purposive acts of body, speech and mind through which the person develops and finds self-expression within the processes of *kamma* and rebirth. By arousing the mind to engage with objects and by producing goal-oriented acts, *saṅkhāras* bring about further developments in the consciousness continuum and keep it always oriented towards the future.

Cetanās are conceived as purposive impulses that arise from sensory and mental contact with objects and take the primary motivating role in the constructive activity by which *saṅkhāras* assemble mental functions and compose further intentional acts of body, speech and mind. In keeping with conditioned origination, it is posited that *saṅkhāras* serve as the link between past experiences and future goals. They preserve the continuity with past conditions, although this continuity is not simple and straightforward, but is marked by complex relationships between networks of causes and conditions. Innovations are produced through the cessation of some conditions in the continuum of consciousness and the grouping of other conditions in new ways. The important conclusion to be drawn is that *saṅkhāras* in Theravāda perform the same function of linking the past with the present and the present with the future that *saṁskāras* perform in the Yoga tradition, even though *saṅkhāras* are not conceived as lasting imprints on the mind. The *Vyāsa-bhāṣya* (VB. IV.9) vividly illustrates the role of *saṁskāras* and *vāsanās* by explaining that the habits of a cat, for instance are preserved in the deep structures of the mind by subliminal impressions (*saṁskāras*) and latent tendencies (*vāsanās*) over long periods of time. According to the Yoga tradition, because *saṁskāras* and *vāsanās* preserve the past, the habits of a cat are easily resumed when rebirth as a cat occurs. In Theravāda, *saṅkhāras* ensure continuity by continually gathering up the dominant features of the continuum of consciousness and forming causal conditions into dynamic configurations that not only follow one another in an ongoing ordered series, but also form networks through the processes of mutual conditioning. Birth as a cat influences consciousness in a specific manner, and it also introduces into the continuum of consciousness conditions for rebirth as a cat to occur when the necessary mental factors are brought together through the constructive activity of *saṅkhāra* processes.

The conditioning and conditioned processes that constitute *saṅkhāras* are also "carriers" of karmic merit and demerit: through them complex networks of causes are formed, linking the time when an act is performed and the time when the consequences of the act are experienced. However, Theravāda strongly emphasizes that all the constituents that form *saṅkhāra* processes come into being and pass away. It will be shown in Chapter VII that according to the explanation given in the *Visuddhimagga* (XVII.173-174), conditioned origination implies that when a purposive act is performed, the consequences follow in due course. It is postulated that there is no need for a third factor that somehow remains unchanged and acts as a link between a specific past act and its future consequence. For this reason, in the *Abhidhamma* system, *saṅkhāras* are not conceived as residual impressions of purposive acts that somehow survive in the "unconscious" level of the mind.

The *Kathāvatthu* (Kvu. 405-408) records a debate where the Theravādins strongly uphold their position that *anusayas*, like other mental states, are conditioned by mental objects. The conclusion is drawn that *anusayas* are to be classified as *saṅkhāras*. Nevertheless, the descriptions in the *Suttas* suggest that there is a difference between *saṅkhāras* and *anusayas*: whereas *saṅkhāras* are motivational processes producing purposive acts of body, speech, and mind, *anusayas* are conditions that operate within the dynamic processes of the *saṅkhārakkhandha* in a specific manner marked by repetition and persistence. *Anusayas* can be interpreted as configurations of specific unwholesome mental factors (for example, the feeling of "I" and "mine", passion for objects that give pleasure, and repulsion towards objects that cause pain) that tend to produce conditions similar to themselves, with the result that the similarities keeps recurring in the continuum of consciousness. Whereas goal-oriented acts produced by *saṅkhāra* processes come into being and pass away, the repetition of afflictive factors that constitute an unwholesome *anusaya* continues through many life spans, until the tendency for addictive repetition is removed by cultivating the disciplines of the Eightfold Path. Although in certain *Sutta* passages the concept of *anusaya* seems to imply the notion of latency, it is noteworthy that the *Visuddhimagga* and the commentaries to the first four *Nikāyas* avoid defining *anusayas* as mental factors that remain latent in the mind. There are passages in the *Suttas* where *anusayas* and *cetanās* are regarded as factors that produce the intentional acts through which the continuum of consciousness develops its desire for future goals, for prolongation of life and for rebirth (S. II. 65-67). These passages can be interpreted to signify that *anusayas* condition purposive impulses and motivating intentions in such a way as to perpetuate persistent unwholesome habits that become mental "fetters". Under the influence of *anusayas*, *cetanas* produce purposive acts that function as the medium through which *anusayas* become overtly expressed in obsessive mental states (*pariyuṭṭhānas*) and compulsive behaviour.

ENDNOTES

[1] W.J. Johnson, *Harmless Souls*, 125-126.

[2] P.S. Jaini, *The Jaina Path of Purification*, 147-148, n. 25.

[3] H.V. Guenther, *Philosophy and Psychology in the Abhidharma*, 47.

Guenther maintains that the author of the *Atthasālinī* favours a theory of the mind that resembles Yogācāra. According to Guenther, the *Atthasālinī* posits that the *citta* maintains its own identity and is not dependent on the *cetasikas*. To support his interpretation, he quotes the following passage from the *Atthasālinī*:

> *Yathā hi rūpādīni upādāya paññattā suriyādayo na atthato rūpādīhi aññe honti ten' eva yasmiṁ samaye suriyo udeti tasmiṁ samaye tassa teja-saṅkhātaṁ rūpaṁ pīti evam vuccamāne pi na rūpādīhi añño suriyo nāma atthi. Tathā cittaṁ phassādayo dhamme upādāya paññāpiyati. Atthato pan' ettha tehi aññaṁ eva.* (Asl. 113)

The *Atthasālinī* begins by saying that the sun and other phenomena come to be known through their physical form and other qualities and that they are not different from their qualities (*na aññe honti*). Though it can be said that when the sun rises, at that time its qualities such as its physical form also come into existence, nevertheless, the sun is not different from its qualities. The *Atthasālinī* maintains that the *citta* is not analogous to the sun in this matter. The passage quoted above says that though the *citta* also is known from mental factors (*dhammas*) such as sensory contact, in actual fact the *citta* is different from these mental factors (*tehi aññaṁ eva*).

The edition to which Guenther refers is different from the Pali Text Society edition (quoted above) at a crucial point. He renders the text as follows: *na tatha cittam; passādayo dhamme upādeya paññāpiyati; atthato pan' etam tehi aññam eva* (H.V. Guenther, *Philosophy and Psychology in the Abhidharma*, 47, n. 3). According to this edition, whereas the sun is known through its radiance and other qualities, the case of the *citta* is different (*na tatha cittam*). Guenther's translation of this passage implies that the *citta* is not known through its factors in the same way that the sun is known through its qualities. The most difficult problem for anyone interpreting this passage, however, arises with the very last part, where the *Atthasālinī* says that *citta* is different (*aññam*) from its components. If the word "different" is taken to mean that consciousness is somehow autonomous and independent of its properties (*cetasikas*), as Guenther's interpretation would suggest, this would go against the Theravāda tenet of conditioned origination. In fact, the *Atthasālinī* offers a clarification of its declaration that the *citta* is different from its components (Asl. 114). The *Atthasālinī* explains states that arise together with it. On the other hand, the term *citta* can be used in an exclusive sense in order to differentiate the *citta* from the *cetasikas* in such a manner as to distinguish the specific quality of each *cetasika* (*sārūpena pabhedato*). The *citta* is distinguished from the *cetasikas* so as to indicate that every component of the totality, for example, sensory contact (*phassa*), exhibits distinct characteristics and functions. This explanation signifies that although consciousness cannot originate autonomously or function independently of its constituents, nevertheless, for purposes of analysis and classification, it can be distinguished from them. The *Dhammasaṅgaṇi* specifies that the *vedanākkhandha*, *saññākkhandha*, and *saṅkhārakkhandha* constitute the *cetasikas* (Dhs. 209). The *citta* neither arises nor functions apart from these *khandhas*.

[4] The following descriptions of the *citta* occur in various contexts: *pariyādāya ṭhassati, pariyādinna-citto, pariyādāya tiṭṭhati* (S. II. 226, 228; A. IV. 160; D. III. 249), *khitta* (A. II. 52), *upakkiliṭṭha, saṅkiliṭṭha* (S. I. 179, III. 151), *kilanta* (D. I. 20, III. 32), *santa, upasanta* (D. III. 49, S. I. 141, Sn. 746), *alīna* (A. V. 149, Sn. 68, 717), *pasanna* (Sn. 316, 403, 690), *vasībhūta* (S. I. 132; A. I. 165), *vimutta* (S. I. 28, 29, 46; A. III. 245, V. 29; Sn. 23).

[5] H.V. Guenther, *Philosophy and Psychology in the Abhidharma*, 12.

[6] Bhikkhu Ñāṇamoli, *The Path of Purification*, 507, n. 35.

[7] *Cittan ti ārammaṇaṁ cintetī ti cittaṁ vijānātī ti attho* (Asl. 63).

[8] . . . *javana-vīthivasena attano santānaṁ cinotī ti cittaṁ. Vipākaṁ kammakilesehi citam ti cittam* (Asl. 63). I follow Pe Maung Tin's translation in *The Expositor*, 85.

[9] . . . *cittakaraṇatāya cittan ti evaṁ p' ettha attho veditabbo* (Asl. 63).

[10] *Sāvako te mahāvīra maraṇaṁ maraṇābhibhū*
ākaṅkhati cetayati taṁ nisedha jutindhara (S. I. 121).

[11] *Ratto kho brāhmaṇa rāgena abhibhūto pariyādinnacitto atta-vyābādhāya pi ceteti para-vyābādhāya pi ceteti ubhaya-vyābādhāya pi ceteti cetasikaṁ pi dukkhaṁ domanassaṁ paṭisaṁvedeti. Rāge pahīne n'eva atta-vyābādhāya pi ceteti . . . na cetasikaṁ dukkhaṁ domanassaṁ paṭisaṁvedeti* (A. I. 156-157). Similar statements are made regarding *dosa* and *moha*.

[12] K.R. Norman concludes that the verses compiled in the *Theragāthā* and the *Therīgāthā* were composed from the period when the *Saṅgha* was first formed until the middle of the third century B.C.E. (K.R. Norman, *The Elders' Verses I. Theragāthā*, xxix; *The Elders' Verses II. Therīgāthā*, xxxi). Von Hinüber draws attention to the beauty of these verses and points out that they "allow a unique glimpse at very early Indian poetry otherwise completely lost" (O. von Hinüber, *A Handbook of Pāli Literature*, 53). The *Sutta-nipāta* is said to contain some of "the oldest Buddhist poetry known to us", perhaps going back to the time of the Buddha (K.R. Norman, *Pāli Literature*, 63). The *Dhammapada* is an interesting text because some of its verses are found also in Jaina or brahmanical texts. Norman suggests that the verses in the *Dhammapada* were culled from the popular collections of "floating verses" that existed in North India "in early times". These verses belonged to no particular group or sect. It is possible that the verses from the *Dhammapada* on the nature of the mind quoted in this chapter reflect ideas that belonged to Indian culture in general, rather than to Buddhism in particular.

[13] *Ayoniso-manasikārā kāma-rāgena additā*
ahosiṁ uddhatā pubbe citte avasavattinī (Thi. 77).

[14] . . . *mā cittassa vasaṁ gami* (Thi. 163).

[15] . . . *cittamhi vasībhūtāham* (Thi. 233).

[16] *Te me ijjhiṁsu saṅkappā yadattho pāvisiṁ kuṭim* (Tha. 60).

[17] *Mama saṅkappam aññāya codesi narasārathi* (Tha. 376).

[18] *So'haṁ paripuṇṇasaṅkappo cando pannaraso yathā* (Tha. 546).

[19] . . . *niccam āraddha-viriyehi paṇḍitehi sahāvase'ti* (Tha. 148).
. . . *nāvarajjhissaṁ, passa viriya-parakkamam* (Tha. 167, 515).

[20] *Manopubbaṅgamā dhammā manoseṭṭhā manomayā* (Dhp. 1, 2).

[21] *Phandanaṁ capalaṁ cittaṁ dūrakkhaṁ dunnivārayam*
ujuṁ karoti medhāvī usukāro va tejanam (Dhp. 33)
Dunniggahassa lahuno yatthakāmanipātino
cittassa damatho sādhu, cittaṁ dantaṁ sukhāvaham (Dhp. 35).

[22] The *therī* Ubbirī tells of her unbearable sorrow at the death of her daughter Jīvā (Thi. 51-53); Candā relates the daily pain of living as a widow without children (Thi. 122-123); Pañcasatā Paṭācārā and Vāsiṭṭhī recall the grief of cremating a beloved son (Thi. 127, 133-134); Kisāgotamī and Uppalavaṇṇā speak of the torment of a young wife in an extended family that takes advantage of her weakness (Thi. 213-223, 224-225).

[23] For example, Senaka recalls how he saw the Buddha teaching at the spring festival in Gayā (Tha. 287-290). Uruveḷakassapa says that he was a *samaṇa* with matted hair when he first met the Buddha. Proud of his own supernormal powers, at first he did not pay homage to the Buddha. Later, he became a disciple (Tha. 375-380). Jenta, the handsome son of a wealthy priest says that he was intoxicated with egoistic pride until one day he met the Buddha (Tha. 423-428). Cūḷapanthaka tells the moving story of how his fellow monks, despising him for his slow progress, told him to go back home. As he lingered despondently at the gate of the monastery, longing for the teaching, the Buddha came there, took him by the arm, led him back to the monastery, and gave him a towel to wipe his feet (Tha. 557-566).

[24] S. Collins, *Selfless Persons: Imagery and Thought in Theravāda Buddhism*, 75-76.

[25] . . . *vijjā vimuttiṁ paccessaṁ mānānusayam ujjahan ti* (Tha. 60).
. . . *animittañ ca bhāvehi mānānusayam ujjaha* (Thi.20).

[26] . . . *ahaṁ karomī ti na tassa hoti, paro karotī ti na tassa hoti* (Ud. 70).

[27] How this reflexive awareness originates and functions in the *citta* is not discussed at any length in the *Suttas*. There are passages that refer to the "luminosity" of the mind (D. I. 223, III. 223; A. I. 10). This idea of the natural

radiance (*pabhassara*) of the *citta* has been the subject of much debate. What is relevant here is that, in the Buddhist tradition, the mind's capacity to become aware of objects and to know itself are always regarded as basic connotations of the metaphor of light when it is applied to the mind. For further discussion of the luminous quality of the *citta* see S. Hamilton, *Identity and Experience: The Constitution of the Human Being According to Early Buddhism*, 98-101, 113-114; Bhikkhu Ñāṇananda, *Concept and Reality in Early Buddhist Thought*, 59-64.

[28] *Yad-eva tvaṁ Rāhula kāyena kammaṁ kattukāmo hosi tad-eva te kāya-kammaṁ paccavekkhitabbaṁ. . . . Karontena pi te Rāhula kāyena kammaṁ tad-eva te kāya-kammaṁ paccavekkhitabbaṁ. . . . Katvā pi te Rāhula kāyena kammaṁ tad-eva te kāyakammaṁ paccavekkhitabbaṁ* (M. I. 415-416).
The same is said for verbal and mental acts.

[29] *Taṁ kim-maññasi Rahūla: kimatthiyo ādāso ti.—Paccavekkhanattho bhante ti.—Evam-eva kho Rāhula paccavekkhitvā paccavekkhitvā kāyena kammaṁ kattabbam* (M. I. 415).
The same statement is made about acts of speech and mind.

[30] *Yaṁ pidaṁ diṭṭhaṁ sutaṁ mutaṁ viññātaṁ pattaṁ pariyesitam anuvicaritam manasā tam pi niccaṁ vā aniccaṁ vā ti* (S. III. 203, 206, 208, 209).

[31] S. Collins, *Selfless Persons: Imagery and Thought in Theravāda Buddhism*, 119.

[32] Ibid., 202.

[33] E. Frauwallner, *History of Indian Philosophy*, 1: 159.

[34] Ibid., 1:159-160.

[35] L. Silburn, *Instant et Cause: Le Discontinu dans la Pensée Philosophique de l'Inde*, 41-48, 76-80.

[36] S. Collins, *Selfless Persons: Imagery and Thought in Theravāda Buddhism.*, 55.

[37] Ibid., 54-56, 223.

[38] L. Silburn, *Instant et Cause: Le Discontinu dans la Pensée Philosophique de l'Inde*, 201.

[39] S. Collins, *Selfless Persons: Imagery and Thought in Theravāda Buddhism*,, 56, 82, 201.

[40] D.J. Kalupahana, *Causality: The Central Philosophy of Buddhism*, 59.

[41] *Uppajjamāno ca, saha sammā ca uppajjati, na ekekato, nāpi ahetuto ti samuppādo* (Vsm. XVII. 16).

[42] *Tasmā paṭicca samaṁ saha ca, na ekekadesaṁ, nāpi pubbāpara-bhāvena ayaṁ paccayatā dhamme uppādeti* (Vsm. XVII. 20).

[43] *Samavāyo ca nāma sādhāraṇa-phala-nipphādane aññamaññāpekkho hoti* (Asl. 59).

[44] *Etesu hi samavāya-saṅkhāto samayo anekahetuto vuttiṁ dīpeti tena ekakāraṇavādo paṭisedhito hoti* (Asl. 59).

[45] T. Stcherbatsky, *Buddhist Logic*, 1:127.

[46] Ibid., 1:127, n. 6.

[47] Ibid., 1:5.

[48] Ibid., 1:119.

[49] D.J. Kalupahana, *Causality: The Central Philosophy of Buddhism*, 148.

[50] Ibid., 84.

[51] S. Dasgupta, *A History of Indian Philosophy*, 1:263, n. 1.

[52] Ibid.

[53] C.A.F. Rhys Davids and F.L. Woodward, *The Book of Kindred Sayings*, 1:158, n. 4.

[54] Nyanatiloka, *Buddhist Dictionary: Manual of Buddhist Terms and Doctrines*, 191-192.

Despite the comments of C.A.F. Rhys Davids and Nyanatiloka, in the Pāli texts the term *vāsanā* does occasionally bear the meaning of a subsisting influence that may manifest its effects in the future course of rebirth. For example, the commentaries to the *Suttas* present instances where the teaching of the Buddha remains as a *vāsanā* in the mind, though a person is not able to pursue the Eightfold Path in the present lifetime (MA. II. 283 and DA. III. 831).

The phrase *pubbe vāsita-vāsanā* is found in the *Milindapañha* (Mil. 263). In the *Sutta-nipāta* (Sn. 1009) we find *pubba-vāsana-vāsita*, and in the *Visuddhimagga* (Vsm. VI. 43) there is the phrase *vāsita-vāsano*. In these passages the reference is to people who carry the influence of morally good acts from past lives. Norman translates the phrase *pubba-vāsana-vāsita* in the *Sutta-nipāta* as "impregnated with their former (good) impressions" (K.R. Norman, *The Rhinoceros Horn*, 161).

In the *Nettippakaraṇa* (Net. 159), *vāsanā* is used in the very specific sense of "bright deeds with bright consequences" (*kammaṁ sukkaṁ sukkavipāṁ*), mentioned, for example, at A. II. 230-233. It is significant that both in the *Visuddhimagga* and in the *Nettippakaraṇa*, *vāsanā* has come to connote the felicitous fruition of wholesome, "bright" acts. Bhikkhu Ñāṇamoli translates *vāsanā-bhāgiyaṁ suttam* as "thread dealing with morality" (Bhikkhu Ñāṇamoli, *The Guide*, 212). None of these passages explains why the phrase *vāsita-vāsanā* does not include persons who carry the influence of karmic demerit (*pāpa*) from past lives.

Although, in the passages mentioned above, *vāsanā* carries the meaning of a residual influence from a past deed, the concept of *vāsanā* does not have the central role in Theravāda that it does in the Yoga tradition. In the *Abhidhamma* the *citta* is described in terms of co-present mental states that arise and pass away, not as the repository of subliminal impressions (*vāsanās*). Theravāda does not develop a theory whereby present mental states are regarded as manifestations of residual potencies.

[55] S. Collins, *Selfless Persons: Imagery and Thought in Theravāda Buddhism*, 187.

[56] *Tam kiṁ maññasi maharaja: yan' imāni rukkhāni anibbatta-phalāni sakkā tesaṁ phalāni dassetum. . . . Evam-eva kho mahārāja abbocchinnāya santatiyā na sakkā tāni kammāni dassetum. . . .* (Mil. 72).

Here Nāgasena tells King Milinda that just as one cannot show the fruit of a tree that has not yet produced fruit, so also, as long as the continuum of the present life has not been cut off by death, one cannot point to the fruition of *kamma* in a future life.

[57] The *Visuddhimagga* (Vsm. XXIII. 12) refers to instructions that the *Majjhima-nikāya* (M. I. 296-297) gives for attaining the level of meditation called "signless release of the mind". Among the requirements for attaining that level of meditation is *pubbe abhisaṅkhāra.*

[58] For example, at D. II. 81, 84, 91, 98, 126.

[59] A set of three *āsavas*, where *diṭṭhi* is omitted, is considered older (P.E.D. 115, col.1). *Kāmāsava, bhavāsava,* and *avijjāsava* are grouped together at M. I. 55; A. I. 165, III. 414; S. IV. 256.

[60] There is an obvious resemblance between *kleśas* in the Yoga tradition and *āsavas* in Theravāda. However, Theravāda gives a psychological explanation of the nature of *avijjā*, whereas in the *Upaniṣads* and in the Yoga tradition, the concept of ignorance is based on ontological ideas. These traditions affirm a soul that is constituted of pure, unchanging consciousness. The *Sabbāsava-sutta* (M. I. 8-9) states that ignorance arises because a person does not pay systematic attention (*ayoniso-manasikāra*) to the conditioned origination of all things and does not exercise restraint in experiencing sensory objects.

[61] G. Feuerstein, *The Philosophy of Classical Yoga*, 65.

[62] *Chakkhuno pi . . . pe . . . manato pi sandanti pavattantī ti vuttaṁ hoti. . . . Cirapārivāsiyaṭṭhenamadirādayo āsavā viyā ti pi āsavā* (Asl. 48).

The *Atthasālinī* emphasizes two characteristics of *āsavas*. They "flow" (*sandanti*) or "move forward" (*pavattanti*), both in the sense of spreading their influence in various sensory and thought processes, and in the sense of affecting future experiences and acts. Moreover, *āsavas* have an addictive power that they acquire by persisting as repetitive habits over a length of time. The *Atthasālinī* compares the action of *āsavas* to the persistence and intoxicating power of *madira* liquor that has fermented for a long time (*cira-pārivāsika*).

[63] The four stages of the gradual process of liberation are described as a gradual removal of mental factors that afflict and sully the psyche. The "stream-winner" (*sotāpanna*) is no longer a worldly person (*puthujjana*), but is regarded as a noble disciple (*ariya*). On reaching this first stage of the Noble Path, the first three fetters (*saṁyojanas*) that bind a person to rebirth are removed. These three are: the view that upholds the notion of a permanent self (*sakkāya-diṭṭhi*), doubt (*vicikicchā*), and attachment to rituals and ceremonies (*sīlabbata-parāmāsa*). In the second stage of the Path, the noble disciple is called the "once-returner" (*sakadāgāmī*). This stage is characterized by the attenuation of

two of the remaining fetters, namely, sensual passion (*kāmacchanda*) and ill will (*vyāpāda*). The third stage, that of the "non-returner" (*anāgāmī*), is distinguished by the total eradication of sensual passion and ill will. The stage of the *arahant* is marked by the removal of the remaining five fetters: attachment to the realm of form (*rūpa-rāga*), attachment to the formless realm (*arūpa-rāga*), pride (*māna*), restlessness (*uddhacca*), and ignorance (*avijjā*). When all these fetters and *āsavas* are removed, enlightenment is finally attained (Mahāthera Nārada, *Manual of Abhidhamma*, 430-432).

It is said in the *Atthasālinī* that the *āsava* of speculative views is removed in the first stage (*sotāpatti*). The *āsava* of sensual desire can be decreased in the second stage and renounced in the third stage (*anāgāmī*). The *āsavas* of attachment to life and ignorance are considered to be capable of retaining their hold until the final stage (*arahatta*) is attained (Asl. 371-372).

[64] For example, Dhp. 126, 386; Sn. 1133.

[65] *Sammā-saṅkappaṁ p' ahaṁ bhikkhave, dvayaṁ vadāmi. Atthi, bhikkhave, sammā-saṅkappo sāsavo puññābhāgiyo upadhi-vepakkho; atthi, bhikkhave, sammā-saṅkappo ariyo anāsavo lokuttaro maggaṅgo* (M. III. 73).

[66] Vsm. XIV. 9-10 identifies *lokiya* with *sāsava* and *lokuttara* with *anāsava*. At Vsm. XIV. 83-88, the mundane (*lokiya*) is defined as comprising the different modalities of consciousness ordinarily experienced through the senses and the mind as well as the types of consciousness experienced through calm concentration. The supramundane is defined as consciousness operating in the four paths: "stream entry", "once returning", "never returning", and the "path of the *arahant*". At Vsm XVII.115, the realm of rebirth is defined as the continuous coming into being of the aggregates (*khandhānam paṭipāṭi*); and at Vsm. XVII. 121, the modes of consciousness that pertain to the realm of rebirth are said to originate in *saṅkhāras* that provide the conditions for the formation of *kamma* and the fruition of *kamma*. At Vsm. XVII. 120, the supramundane— consisting of the four paths leading to liberation—is shown to be excluded from the round (*vaṭṭam*) of *kamma* and rebirth.

[67] *Ayoniso bhikkhave manasikaroto anuppannā c' eva āsavā uppajjanti uppannā ca āsavā pavaḍḍhanti* (M. I. 7).

[68] The person who lacks systematic attention wonders: "Did I or did I not exist in the past? What (*kim*) was I in the past? How (*katham*) was I in the past? Having existed as what kind of being, what further did I become in the

past?" The same questions are said to preoccupy this person with regard to the present and the future (M. I. 8).

[69] From what is said in the *Kathāvatthu* (Kvu. 405-408) regarding *anusaya*, it is apparent that much controversy surrounded this subject among early Buddhist sects. The *Kathāvatthu* holds that *anusayas* are to be included under the *saṅkhārakkhandha* and that they always function in relation to objects. In this way, the Theravādins maintain that *anusayas* are not self-perpetuating, but arise through causes and conditions.

[70] P.S. Jaini, "Sautrāntika Theory of *bīja*", 240.

[71] *Anusetī ti appahīnatāya anuseti anusayamāno saṁyojanaṁ nāma hoti* (MA. III. 144). *Evaṁ laddhikattā ti vitthāritaṁ tasmā so yeva kileso bandhanaṭṭhena saṁyojanam appahīnaṭṭhena anusayo ti idam atthaṁ sandhāya* (MA. III. 145).

It is said here that the very same mental affliction (*kilesa*)—for example, speculative view (*diṭṭhi*)—is designated as "fetter" (*samyojana*) because it causes bondage to the mind, and as *anusaya* because it has not been renounced.

[72] For example, DA. I. 19-20.

[73] *Na kho . . . sabbāya sukhāya vedanāya rāgānusayo anuseti, na sabbāya dukkhāya vedanāya paṭighānusayo anuseti, na sabbāya adukkhamasukhāya vedanāya avijjānusayo anuseti* (M. I. 303).

With fine precision, Dhammadinnā points out that the tendency to sensual passion does not lie latent in the serene pleasant feeling of the first level of meditation, the impulsion of aversion does not lie latent in the pain of yearning for enlightenment that is characteristic of the second level of meditation, and the deluding dullness of ignorance does not lie latent in the tranquil feeling of neither pleasure nor pain that pervades the fourth level of meditation (M. I. 303-304).

[74] *Yañca kho bhikkhave ceteti yañ ca pakappeti yañca anuseti ārammaṇam etaṁ hoti viññāṇassa ṭhitiyā. Ārammaṇe sati patiṭṭhā viññāṇassa hoti. Tasmiṁ patiṭṭhite viññāṇe virūḷhe āyatim punabbhavābhinibbatti hoti* (S. II. 65).

[75] R.E.A. Johansson, *The Dynamic Psychology of Early Buddhism*, 107-110.

[76] P. de Silva, *Buddhist and Freudian Psychology*, 51-61; *An Introduction to Buddhist Psychology*, 72-77.

[77] K.N. Jayatilleke, "Some Problems of Translation and Interpretation", I: 216.

[78] P. de Silva, *Buddhist and Freudian Psychology*, 54, n. 42.

[79] Bhikkhu Bodhi, *The Connected Discourses of the Buddha: A New Translation of the Saṁyutta Nikāya*, 1:561.

[80] C.A.F. Rhys Davids and F.L. Woodward, *Kindred Sayings*, 2:31.

[81] P. de Silva, *Buddhist and Freudian Psychology*, 56.

Chapter IV
Cetanā in the *Sutta* Literature

Although the *Suttas* are the focus of Chapters IV and V and later chapters have selected *Abhidhamma* texts as their basis, this division does not imply that *saṅkhāra* and *cetanā* are conceived differently in the earlier and later groups of texts. The *Sutta-piṭaka*, the *Abhidhamma-piṭaka*, and the commentarial literature can be viewed as a single integral whole since they fall within a unified scholarly tradition that came to be known as Theravāda. This chapter and the next are based on the premise that Theravāda seeks to preserve its own coherence and consistency throughout the various texts in which these two multifaceted terms, *saṅkhāra* and *cetanā*, are utilized and interpreted. I will, therefore, refer to *Abhidhamma* texts and to the commentarial literature[1] when they shed light on passages in the *Suttas* where *saṅkhāra* and *cetanā* occur.

The challenge in interpreting the concept of *cetanā* in the *Sutta* literature comes from the paucity of references to this term, despite its obvious importance for understanding the Theravāda approach both to *kamma* and to the Eightfold Path. The nuances of meaning in *cetanā* have to be extrapolated from passages in which other concepts, especially *saṅkhāra, kamma,* and rebirth, are elucidated. Although *cetanā*, like *citta*, is grammatically associated with the verb *ceteti*, it is difficult to find passages in the first four *Nikāyas* that overtly link *cetanā* to the cognitive functions of intellection and purposive thought that are conveyed by *ceteti*. It is not easy to find in the first four *Nikāyas* a passage where *cetanā* is described as the function of forming a purpose, or reflecting on possibilities, or choosing a goal. The closest that we get to such an understanding of *cetanā* is in the final section of the *Aṅguttara-nikāya* (A. V. 292-303). From the description of wholesome and unwholesome acts given in the discourses that form this section, the inference can be drawn that an act (*kamma*) characterized by intention or purpose (*sañcetanā*) emerges from, and expresses, a specific attitude of mind (*citta*). It is not surprising that the *Atthasālinī* (Asl. 84-102) bases its lengthy explanation of the relationship between *cetanā* and *kamma* on this section of the *Aṅguttara-nikāya*. Just as the relationship of *cetanā* to *citta* requires clarification, so also the precise function that *cetanā* serves as a constituent of *saṅkhāra* is not fully explained in the *Suttas*.

In this chapter, four functions of *cetanā* are distinguished. In the first and most basic of these functions, *cetanā* becomes associated with other fundamental mental factors, such as attention and feeling, which constitute rudimentary sentient awareness. A second function is the role of *cetanā* as purposive impetus. In this context, the connection that *cetanā* has with *patthanā* (aspiration towards a specific goal) and *paṇidhi* (resolve) is emphasized. A third function is based on the relationship of *cetanā* to *kamma*. Before elaborating on this function of *cetanā*, however, it is necessary to examine the mutual relationship between *saṅkhāra*, *cetanā*, and *kamma*. In order to demonstrate that *cetanā* functions as a purposive impulse or motivational impetus in the process of putting forth *kamma*, the two terms *abhisaṅkhāra* and *sañcetanā* are explored at some length. This is followed by an investigation of the function of *cetanā* as one of the "nutriments" that feeds the processes of *kamma* and perpetuates rebirth. This exploration of the role of *cetanā* in relation to *kamma* closes with an analysis of the detailed definition of *cetanā* that occurs in the *Milindapañha*. In this definition, *cetanā* is regarded as the vehicle of *kamma*. Though the term *cetanā* occurs only rarely in relation to the Eightfold Path, there are a few passages where the Buddha speaks of a type of *cetanā* that renounces *kamma* and prepares the mind to follow to the Eightfold Path. This specific relationship to the Eightfold Path is the fourth function of *cetanā* explored in this chapter.

Cetanā as Basic Sentience

Whereas there are several references in the *Suttas* to the quietening (*samatha*)[2] and the final cessation (*nirodha*)[3] of the constructive activities (*saṅkhāras*) by which the mind gathers its resources and puts forth goal-oriented acts, the cessation of *cetanā* is never posited as a condition for the attainment of *nibbāna*. This is because *cetanā* is regarded as a basic and necessary factor for the maintenance of sentience. A poem in the *Saṁyutta-nikāya* (S. III. 143) describes death as a state where life (*āyu*), heat (*usmā*), and conscious awareness (*viññāṇa*) depart from the body, leaving it to be cast away as a thing devoid of *cetanā* (*acetana*).[4] Bodhi translates *acetana* in this context as "without volition",[5] but Woodward paraphrases the term as "senseless thing" in *The Book of Kindred Sayings*.[6] In his note to this poem, Woodward refers to the *Dhammapada* where the dead body is compared to a useless, burnt log of wood (Dhp. 41). In the *Majjhima-nikāya* (M. I. 296), a dead body is likened to a block of wood, which has no *cetanā* (*yathā kaṭṭham acetanam*). In these contexts *acetana* refers to an insentient thing that lacks the basic conscious awareness that makes any form of cognition, emotion, or volition possible. It is to be noted that this is the meaning that *acetana* conveys in the *Maitrī Upaniṣad*. In this *Upaniṣad*, the physical body is compared to a cart that cannot drive itself since it is not endowed with conscious awareness (*cetanā*) (Mt.U. II.4). The fact that both in the *Upaniṣads* and the *Suttas*, *acetana* refers to something that lacks basic conscious awareness or sentience should not be taken as an indication that the concept of *cetanā* in the *Suttas* developed out of the Upaniṣadic tradition. Rudimentary awareness correlated with vitality is only one of the meanings assigned to *cetanā* in the *Suttas*. Furthermore, in the *Upaniṣads*, *cetanā* does not carry the specific meaning of purposive impulse imbued with the capacity to initiate goal-oriented action that has karmic consequences.

The mind-body organism is sometimes referred to in the *Suttas* as *nāma-rūpa*. The standard definition of *nāma-rūpa* identifies *rūpa* as the physical aggregate (*rūpakkhandha*). *Nāma* is said to be constituted of the four non-physical aggregates: feelings (*vedanākkhandha*), perceptions (*saññākkhandha*), the mind's constructive activities (*saṅkhārakkhandha*), and conscious awareness (*viññāṇakkhandha*) (Vsm. XIV. 11). However, an unusual definition of *nāma* occurs in a passage of the *Saṁyutta-nikāya*, where *vedanā* (feeling), *saññā* (perception), *cetanā* (purposive impulse), *phassa* (contact of the senses and the mind with their objects), and *manasikāra* (attention) are named as its constituents (S. II. 3-4). These factors are regarded as the basic requirements for any cognitive, emotive, or action-oriented experience in the continuum of consciousness (*citta*).

As a factor of basic sentience (*nāma*), *cetanā* can be regarded as the preliminary stirring of conative energy that vitalizes the organism and moves the body and mind towards an object of interest. As a primary factor present in all states of consciousness, *cetanā* can be viewed as the impulse that directs attention to objects and causes conscious awareness (*viññāṇa*) to be motivated by things in its environment. A significant passage of the *Majjhima-nikāya* (M. I. 259) declares that consciousness is not self-perpetuating, but always arises dependently through the contact (*phassa*) that the consciousness continuum and the appropriate sensory faculty make with an object. Through its qualities, the object plays its part by capturing the attention of the mind. The mind, for its part, is conditioned by past experience to turn towards certain objects and to avoid others. *Cetanā* and the other basic mental factors direct the mind's attention to objects. It follows, then, that the function of *cetanā* is never totally devoid of orientation towards a goal, though it does not have the character of a fully developed purposive impulse or of an intention imbued with motivational impulse in the rudimentary stages of perception. The concept of *nāma* implies that even when *cetanā* functions only as a rudimentary mental factor that stirs the psychophysical organism, it coordinates co-present physical and mental factors in such a way that they are directed towards objects that are of interest to the organism. In this sense, the function of *cetanā* is conceived to be goal-oriented even when it functions as a basic factor of sentience.

In several passages in the *Suttas*, *cetanās* are named among the mental states that are generated in the matrix of sensory and mental stimulation when there is contact (*phassa*) between the sense organs and their respective objects. The mind (*manas*) is counted as one of the senses, and mental factors such as concepts, sensory data, and mental images are included among "mental objects" (*dhammas*). The *manas* is also described as the organ that coordinates and synthesizes the sensory data of the five senses. The mind, therefore, is said to experience (*paccanubhoti*) and comprehend the sensory range of the other senses (M. I. 295; S. V. 218). In the *Saṅgīti-sutta* of the *Dīgha-nikāya* (D. III. 243-244), the mental factors that arise in a situation of sensory or mental contact with an object are enumerated in the following order: six types of feeling (*vedanā*), six types of perception (*saññā*), six types of purposive impulse (*sañcetanā*), and six types of craving (*taṇhā*). Each of the six types of feeling is named by relating it to the sense organ through which the feeling is produced. For example, a feeling that arises through seeing an object is designated as "*vedanā* born of eye-contact".[7] The six types of perception (*saññā*), intention (*sañcetanā*), and desire (*taṇhā*), however, are classified in terms of the respective objects to which they are related.[8] For example, a purposive impulse that arises through hearing a sound is called "*sañcetanā* born of sound". These lists suggest that the subjective pole of experience is regarded as the primary cause in the arising of pleasure, pain, and neutral feelings (*vedanā*), whereas sensory and mental objects are viewed as the controlling factors in arising of perceptions, purposive impulses, and desires. The order in which these mental states that arise through sensory contact are listed also signals that every purposive impulse is conditioned by one of the six types of sensory contacts, feelings, and perceptions. In the same manner, the sequence of the mental factors generated by contact with objects in the *Saṅgīti-sutta* list (*phassa, vedanā, cetanā, taṇhā*) posits that contact with an object that arouses a feeling of pleasure does not arouse desire for the object, unless there is the intervention of some motivating interest or purposive impulse (*sañcetanā*) with regard to the object.

The *Mahāsatipaṭṭhāna-sutta* (D. II. 308-309) also provides a list of mental factors generated when the five senses and the mind make contact with their respective objects. The mental factors included in the list are similarly divided into two classes: the six types of cognitive awareness (*viññāṇa*), feeling (*vedanā*), and perception (*saññā*) are classified in terms of their relationship to the sensory or mental organ where contact with the object occurs; and the six types of purposive impulse (*sañcetanā*), craving (*taṇhā*), application of thought (*vitakka*), and reflection (*vicāra*) are classified in terms of their relationship to the objects of the five senses and the mind. Each mental factor of this class, for example *sañcetanā*, becomes sixfold because it arises through five types of sensory objects as well as through mental objects. The order in which the mental factors are arranged in this list implies that each factor functions as a causal condition in the arising of those that follow it. Thus the arising of craving, thought, and reflection in relation to an object is motivated and conditioned by one's purposive impulse (*sañcetanā*) towards the object. In certain contexts, *vitakka* signifies, not discursive thinking, but wholesome or unwholesome sentiments such as goodwill (*avyāpāda*) or ill will (*vyāpāda*) that can powerfully affect, and be affected by, motivating intentions and purposive impulses (*cetanās/sañcetanās*) (M. I. 114; D. III. 215).

The lists are important because they show that in the *Suttas*, cognitive processes such as basic cognitive awareness (*viññāṇa*), perception (*saññā*), and thought (*vitakka*), as well as action-producing factors, such as purposive impulse (*cetanā*) and craving (*taṇhā*), are regarded as arising from a common source, namely sensory and mental stimulation. In the *Suttas*, cognitive factors such as thought, reflection, systematic attention (*yoniso-manasikāra*), and wisdom (*paññā*) are regarded as having the motivational capacity to initiate action. At the same time, motivational factors such as purposive impulse and desire are viewed not just as drives based on physical needs and emotional tensions, but as mental factors that have some relationship to cognitive processes through which objects are evaluated and purposes are formed. In these lists of mental factors, the interweaving and mutual conditioning that is posited between motivational and cognitive processes is traced to their common origination in the matrix of sensory and mental contact (*phassa*) with objects

Cetanā as Intention Imbued with Impetus to Act

Among the texts of the *Abhidhamma* genre, the *Atthasālinī* is distinguished by its detailed exposition of psychological concepts. In this chapter, I focus on the *Sutta* passages to which the *Atthasālinī* refers to substantiate its interpretation of *cetanā*. Moving beyond analogies and cryptic definitions, the *Atthasālinī* gives a full account of how *cetanā* functions as the bridge between the cognitive function of purposive deliberation through which the goal is determined and the conative function of initiating action to achieve that goal. This detailed analysis of the relationship between purposive impulses (*cetanā*) and acts with karmic consequences in the *Atthasālinī* can be read as a commentary to the chapter of the *Aṅguttara-nikāya* (A. V. 283-303) entitled, The Body Generated by Deeds (*Karajakāya-vagga*). In the *Karajakāya-vagga*, an act that carries karmic merit or demerit is shown to be an act that expresses an intention or purpose (*sañcetanika-kamma*). Furthermore, the *Atthasālinī* quite unambiguously identifies an act (*kamma*) that can be evaluated as morally good or bad with the purposive impulse (*cetanā*) that motivates it. In other words, the *Atthasālinī* maintains that an act with karmic consequences is the very manifestation of an intention imbued with motivational impetus (*cetanā*). In support of its position, the *Atthasālinī* cites the following passages: the definition of *kamma* (A. III. 415) where the Buddha says that it is *cetanā* that he regards as *kamma*; the description of intention in relation to four types of karmically operative acts given at S. II. 39-40 and repeated at A. II. 157-158; and the statement on *kamma* at M. III. 208-209 where ten types of acts of body, speech, and mind that entail karmic consequences are enumerated and designated as acts motivated by purposive impulses (*sañcetanika-kamma*). These passages are significant, because the Theravāda tradition, especially in its commentarial literature, finds in them support for defining *cetanā* as a morally wholesome or unwholesome purposive impulse that becomes concretely realized in a corresponding act (*kamma*) of body, speech or mind.

Intention in relation to "instigated" and "undeliberate" acts

In a passage of the *Saṁyutta-nikāya* (S. II. 39-40), deeds entailing karmic consequences are said to be fourfold with reference to the manner in which action is initiated. These four types of deeds are described as deeds based on one's own initiative (*sāmam*); deeds caused by the action of others (*pare*); acts that are done deliberately (*sampajāna*); and acts that are "undeliberate" (*asampajāna*).[9] It is clearly stated in this passage that all four categories of deeds are based on motivating intentions or purposive impulses that arise in relation to the body (*kāya-sañcetanā*) or to speech (*vacī-sañcetanā*) or to the mind (*mano-sañcetanā*). Thus these purposive impulses are regarded as the causes (*hetu*) of acts of body, speech, and mind that fall into the above four categories. The category of "undeliberate action" was discussed in Chapter III in connection with Padmasiri de Silva's contention that *asampajāna* refers to an action influenced by "unconscious motivation".

An act that is caused by others (*pare*) is defined in the commentary (SA. II. 58) as an act that is prompted or instigated (*sasaṅkhāra*).[10] It was noted in Chapter III that when *saṅkhāra* occurs within the compound term *sasaṅkhāra*, it connotes either the application of extra energy on one's own part or instigation by another. The *Atthasālinī* gives the example of a novice who carries out his duties when another person prompts him to do so (Asl. 156). An act that is instigated by another can be regarded as motivated by an intention or a purposive impulse (*sañcetanika*) when it includes the acquiescence of the person who actually performs the deed.

The term *asaṁpajāno* is explained in the commentary as a person who knows how to perform an act but has no understanding of its consequences.[11] The example is given of children who imitate their parents in performing rituals at a shrine but have no understanding of the karmic consequences (*vipāka*) of such acts. However, when applied to an act with karmic consequences, the explanation given in the commentary seems limited. The term *asampajāna* has other connotations that can be better understood by studying the meaning of its opposite, *sampajāna.* For example, in a passage of the *Dīgha-nikāya* (D. III. 45) where we have the description of a false ascetic (*tapassī*) who deliberately engages in deception, the term *sampajāna-musāvāda* signifies a deliberate lie. He is described as a person who maintains that he approves of something when he does not and insists that he disapproves of something when he actually approves of it. In this context *sampajāna-musāvāda* signifies a lie that is deliberate in the sense that it is premeditated and spoken with full awareness. The *Aṅguttara-nikāya* provides the example of a person who knowingly speaks a lie (*sampajāna-musā*) by giving false witness at a court (A. I. 128, V. 265).

Since the term *sampajāna* carries the meaning of premeditated and deliberate when applied to an act, it follows that *asampajāno* refers to a person who acts with intention but without prior reflection or without an understanding of the implications and consequences of the act.

In spite of the explanation given above, the term *asampajāno* continues to pose problems of interpretation. The term *sampajānakārin*[12] refers to one who acts thoughtfully and with attention. Since *sampajāno* refers to a person who is mindful and attentive, *asampajāno* can indicate a person who acts negligently, without proper care and attention. It is difficult to see how a person can be lacking in attention and yet act with intention (*sañcetanā*). One solution would be to take note that both deliberate acts and acts done without proper attention can be based on habits. Responsibility for one's intentions must include responsibility for the attitudes of mind and the habits that condition and give rise to those intentions. Both *sampajāno* (a person who is acting with deliberation, attentiveness, continual mindfulness) and *asampajāno* (a person lacking in understanding and attention) can be acting on the basis of habits of mind cultivated over a period of time through past intentional deeds. As a matter of fact, in the *Suttas* acts are evaluated as wholesome or unwholesome even when they are done out of sheer habit, without proper attention. One is held responsible, for example, for mental habits of negligent carelessness (*pamāda*), laziness and lethargy (*thīna-middha*), or obsessive worry (*vicikicchā*), which may lead to acts done inattentively, without due deliberation. Thus, the connotations of the terms "intention" and "purpose" could be expanded to include the habits of thought and the way of life from which they arise. A deed done inattentively and out of sheer habit could be called an intentional act (*sañcetanika-kamma*) in this sense.

Another passage that presents a set of acts based on intention or purposive impulse (*sañcetanā*) is found in the *Aṅguttara-nikāya* (A. II. 159). This passage states that when rebirth follows death, a new personality (*attabhāva*) is obtained in one of the four following ways: through one's own intention (*sañcetanā*) coming to karmic fruition; through another person's intention producing karmic effects; as the combined consequence of one's own and another person's intentions; or without either one's own intention or another person's intention producing a karmic consequence.[13] The short section of the *Aṅguttara-nikāya* where this passage occurs is entitled *Sañcetanika-vagga.* The same four ways of obtaining a new personality as a result of death and rebirth are listed in the *Saṅgīti-sutta* (D. III. 231).

To explain how the acquiring of a new personality can be due to one's own *sañcetanā*, the commentary gives the example of a certain class of gods who pursue sensual pleasure for aeons until they become tired (AA. III. 147). Wearied by pleasure, they stop eating and die. Death caused by another is illustrated in the commentary by the case of another group of gods who quarrel until they finally turn violently on each other. In his translation of the *Dīgha-nikāya*, T. W. Rhys Davids says in a note that death due to the intention of another (*para-sañcetanā*) is illustrated by a butcher slaughtering an animal.[14] However, Rhys Davids does not discuss the problem posed by the notion that though the reprehensible intentional act is performed by the butcher, the consequence is borne by the animal. This goes against the principle that one inherits the consequences of one's own intentional acts. One way around this problem would be to perceive the painful death as the karmic consequence of an act intentionally done sometime in the past by a person who was subsequently reborn as this unfortunate animal.

The commentary suggests that in the cases of suicide and murder, both the intentions of the person who suffers death and the intentions of another have a role in bringing about the ending of one life and the acquiring of another personality (AA. III. 148). The passage in the *Aṅguttara-nikāya* goes on to explain that in the case of a person who continually cultivates the higher levels of meditation, a new personality is attained through neither one's own intention nor the intention of another (A. II. 160). The Buddha tells Sāriputta that if a person attains the state of meditation called "neither-perception-nor-non-perception" and dwells in the peace and equanimity of that state, that person will be reborn in a beautiful cosmic realm corresponding to that state of meditation. Since there are no conceptualizations whatsoever in the mind of a person who abides in the *jhāna* level of "neither-perception-nor-non-perception", it follows that in the case of those who are reborn in cosmic levels of immutable peace, rebirth is not the result of any form of intentional activity.

Unfortunately, there is no definition of *sañcetanā* either in the passage from the *Sañcetanika-vagga*, where four ways of acquiring a new personality are described (A. II. 159-160), nor in the passage of the *Saṁyutta-nikāya* (S. II. 40), where acts initiated by oneself, acts initiated by another, deliberate acts, and "undeliberate" acts are distinguished. It is not clear whether *sañcetanā* is the cognitive function of deliberating and choosing between goals, or the conative function of initiating action to achieve a goal, or a combination of both functions. However, in both passages the context implies that *sañcetanā* is a purposive impulse, that is to say, an intention carrying the impetus to initiate action. In both passages it is implied that the act itself is the concrete expression of an intention or purposive thought (*sañcetanā*). In this sense, *kamma* is identified with *sañcetanā*.

The fusing of purposive impulse or motivating intention and act (*kamma*) in which it becomes concretely manifest is seen in a passage of the *Aṅguttara-nikāya* (A. II. 157-158), which contains the statement: "Given the presence of a body (*kaye . . . sati*), because of a purposive impulse related to the body (*kaya-sañcetanā-hetu*), joy and sorrow arise inwardly (*uppajjati ajjhattaṁ sukha-dukkhaṁ*)". The same statement is made with regard to purposive impulses that are related to speech (*vacī-sañcetanā*) and to the mind (*mano-sañcetanā*). It is noteworthy that there is no separate mention of an act (*kamma*) of body, speech, or mind in this statement, as distinct from a mere purposive impulse or motivating intention in the mind (*sañcetanā*). The passage maintains that purposive impulses (*sañcetanā*) are the cause (*hetu*) of joy or sorrow in a future birth. Nevertheless, it is implied that in every case the purposive impulse becomes expressed in a corresponding act of body, speech, or mind, and that joy or sorrow arise because of an intended act (*sañcetanikā-kamma*).

Intention, aspiration, and resolve

In passages where it is combined with *patthanā* (aspiration) and *panidhi* (resolve), the context indicates that *cetanā* carries the meaning of "motivating intention" or purpose.[15] Both *patthanā* and *paṇidhi* express an emotionally fervent affirmation of a fully formed intention, rather than the actual process of forming an intention by deciding on a goal. Furthermore, neither term connotes the application of energy to initiate goal-oriented action. The central meaning of both terms, *patthanā* and *paṇidhi*, is "aspiration", "request", "yearning", or "prayer". For example, the notion of wish or aspiration is dominant when the three terms (*cetanā*, *patthanā*, and *paṇidhi*) occur together in the imagery that illustrates how intentions provide "nutriments" for the mind. It is posited in the *Suttas* that purposive impulses arising in the mind bind a person to the sorrow of rebirth by feeding the mind's hunger for plans and goals (S. II. 99). The imagery portrays a man whose *cetanā* (intention), *patthanā* (yearning), and *paṇidhi* (wish) is to flee as far away as possible, even as he is being relentlessly drawn to a fiery pit of rebirth. The text speaks of the man's *ārakāvassa cetanā* (intention to get far away), *ārakā patthanā* (yearning to get far away), *ārakā paṇidhi* (wish to get far away). The man has a desperate wish to be released, even though he knows that he cannot initiate action to achieve his wish. The narrative indicates that in this context, *cetanā* has the meaning of intention or purposive thought.

In the commentarial literature, these three terms are interpreted as stages of a single process of forming and implementing an intention (AA. V. 69). *Cetanā* is distinguished from *patthanā* and *paṇidhi* by attributing to it the capacity to initiate action with the purpose of carrying out an intention. *Patthanā* is explained in the commentary to the *Aṅguttara-nikāya* as the preliminary process of focusing the mind on a general aspiration for future felicity: "May such and such an event actually come about". And *paṇidhi* is explained as the subsequent specific wish, such as, "May I be reborn as this or that god".[16] Unlike *patthanā* and *paṇidhi*, *cetanā* is explained in the commentary in terms of its capacity to initiate action in body, speech, and mind (*tīsu dvāresu nibattita-cetanā va gahitā*). The three terms also occur together in the *Kathāvatthu* (Kvu. 380-381). The commentary to the *Kathāvatthu* takes *patthanā* and *paṇidhi* to be equivalents of *cetanā* (KvuA. 110). *Patthanā* is said to represent *cetanā* in its preliminary stage of forming a purpose, while *paṇidhi* points to *cetanā* in its subsequent stage of persistence in that purpose.[17] The conclusion can be drawn that in the *Suttas*, *patthanā* and *paṇidhi* convey strong wish or aspiration, but do not include in their connotation the conative capacity to initiate goal-oriented action. When *cetanā*, *patthanā*, and *paṇidhi* occur together in the *Suttas*, the context indicates that *cetanā* signifies an intention or purpose in which an aspiration or wish is expressed, but the context does not warrant the conclusion that *cetanā* is endowed with the capacity to initiate action that could fulfil the aspiration. Unlike the commentary to the *Aṅguttara-nikāya*, the *Sutta* passages do not explicitly say that *cetanā* has the capacity to translate aspiration into action.

There are two passages (each entitled *Cetanā*) in the *Saṁyutta-nikāya*, in which the verb *ceteti* can be taken to mean "to form a purpose", or "to intend" (S. II. 66-67). In these passages, *ceteti* is associated with two other verbs, *pakappeti* and *anuseti*. *Pakappeti* signifies forming, arranging, designing, or planning in the mind with a view to implementing the plan (P.E.D. 379, col. 2).

Anuseti signifies having a persistent tendency or inclination. The passages say that when a person intends (*ceteti*), plans (*pakappeti*), or sustains inclination towards something, that thing becomes an object (*ārammaṇam*) that engages the mind. The passages go on to say that the object becomes a basis for the development and furtherance of the processes of conscious awareness and cognitive discernment (*viññāṇa*). This mode of developing conscious processes through persisting tendencies, intentions, and plans brings about the conditions that lead to bondage to the consequences of *kamma* and rebirth. The association of *ceteti* with *pakappeti* and the thrust of the whole passage imply that *ceteti* indicates, not only forming intentions and purposes in the mind, but also aiming or aspiring for action to implement those purposes. However, the verb *ceteti* indicates the cognitive functions of thinking and intending, and does not include in its meaning the actual dynamic function initiating action in the organism.

Attitude and habit as sources of purposive impulses

A more precise understanding of the sense in which *cetanā* connotes purposive impulse or intention endowed with impetus to act can be obtained from the descriptions of wholesome and unwholesome *kamma* found in the *Karajakāya-vagga* of the *Aṅguttara-nikāya* (A. V. 292-301). The vivid descriptions of specific wholesome and unwholesome acts given in the *Karajakāya-vagga* imply that in every case, the intention to act arises from a specific attitude of mind. For example, the intentional act of abstaining from injuring animals is considered to be rooted in an attitude of compassion. Furthermore, the wholesome and unwholesome *kammas* listed in the *Karajakāya-vagga* are habits of body, speech, and mind that can be viewed as manifestations of the conditioning activity of *saṅkhāras*. It can be inferred from the *Karajakāya-vagga*, then, that the intentions (*sañcetanās*) that precede and instigate acts with karmic consequences exhibit a twofold conditioning: they are influenced by the dominating factors (such as greed or non-greed) in the attitudes of mind (*cittas*) from which they arise; and they are conditioned by the habit patterns that are proliferated by the mind's goal-oriented activities (*saṅkhāras*).

In the *Karajakāya-vagga*, *sañcetanika-kamma* indicates those acts that are instigated by intentions, carry moral values of wholesome (*kusala*) or unwholesome (*akusala*), and lead to karmic consequences. It was shown in Chapter II that *sañcetanā* is implicitly linked with purposive thought in a passage of the *Upāli-sutta* (M. I. 377) stating that the Nigaṇṭha teacher Nātaputta does not judge the unintentional (*asañcetanikam*) act of harming minute living beings while walking to be greatly blameworthy. Here *asañcetanika* conveys an act that is not planned or deliberately chosen. These two passages can be contrasted with the *Mahākammavibhaṅga-sutta* (M. III. 209), where the term *sañcetanika-kamma* is used in passages that focus attention on the karmic consequences of intentional acts rather than on the attitudes and habits of mind that are the sources of the intentions.

The Formative Role of *Saṅkhāras* in the Processes of *Kamma*

In the *Sutta* literature, *saṅkhāra* is regarded as the mental function that works within the continuum of consciousness to bring together various mental factors and "form" them into mental configurations or "formations" that both serve a purpose and put forth consequences. The way *saṅkhāras* operate in composing fresh effects by bringing together causal conditions is indicated by the verb *abhisaṅkharoti*, and the configurations are designated as *saṅkhāras* or *abhisaṅkhāras*. These configurations are of two types. They make up the five aggregates—physical factors, feelings arising from sensory and mental stimulation, perceptions, the mind's constructive activities, and the continuum of conscious awareness—that constitute the "individual personality".

They also constitute intentional acts of body, speech, and mind that carry moral values and produce karmic consequences. *Saṅkhāras* construct the "personality" continuum as a series of configurations, and they also construct, as a dynamic series, the goal-oriented activities through which a person finds enhancement and self-expression. *Saṅkhāras*, therefore, have the capacity to produce not only the constructive processes within which *cetanās* arise as intentions and purposive impulses, but also the acts through which those purposes are implemented.

Both *saṅkhāra* and *abhisaṅkhāra* refer to acts that have karmic consequences (for example, S. II. 82; D. III. 217) However, the term *saṅkhāra* can also indicate, more generally, anything physical or mental that is temporary and conditioned (S. II. 190-192; Dhp. 277, 278). The term *abhisaṅkhāra* is not used in this general sense. The term *sankhārakkhandha* refers to the dynamic dimension of the continuum of consciousness that comprises the constructive activities by which mental factors are assembled in such a way as to produce goal-oriented acts.

Saṅkhāras and the formation of the individual personality

The *Khandha-saṁyutta* defines the *saṅkhārakkhandha* by stating that *saṅkhāras* are constituted of the six classes of *cetanās* that arise from sensory and mental stimulation (S. III. 63). It is interesting to note that basically the same definition of *saṅkhārakkhandha* occurs in one of the *Abhidhamma* texts, the *Vibhaṅga* (Vbh. 7-8), though this text was composed at a later period (*cakkhusamphassajā cetanā . . . pe . . . manosamphassajā cetanā—ime vuccanti saṅkharā paccuppannā*). It is possible to interpret this definition to signify that the function by which *saṅkhāras* bring together mental factors to form acts of body, speech, and mind is instigated by *cetanās*. Unfortunately, neither the *Khanda-saṁyutta* nor the *Vibhaṅga* clarify precisely how *cetanās* constitute the constructive activity of the *saṅkhāras*.

The *Saṁyutta-nikāya* (S. III. 87) succinctly defines the function of *saṅkhāra* as "forming (*abhisaṅkharoti*) something that is formed (*saṅkhatam*)".[18] The passage goes on to say that *saṅkhāras* form or compose each of the five aggregates. According to the commentary, each of the aggregates, distinguished by its specific nature (*bhāva*), is made in the same way that rice gruel is cooked for the purpose of making rice gruel, or a cake is baked for the purpose of producing a cake (SA. II. 292).[19] The commentary goes on to say that the aggregate of physical form (the body) is designated as "compounded" or "composed" (*saṅkhatam*), because it is produced by the assembling of antecedent conditions (*paccayehi samāgantvā kata-bhāvena saṅkhataṁ ti laddha nāmaṁ rūpam*). Furthermore, the commentary says that the specific nature of *rūpa* is produced through this act of composition: it becomes physical form (*rūpa*) because it has been "composed" in such a way as to produce its nature of "physicality" (*rūpa-bhāvāya abhisaṅkhatam*). Here *saṅkhatam* and *abhisaṅkhatam* do not differ in meaning. The arising of the specific nature of the other aggregates is similarly explained.

Every *saṅkhāra* is an "assembly" of causal factors, which assemble in such a way that they become the conditions for the production of another assembly of factors, just as the assembling of all the conditions for the baking of a cake produces a baked cake. The commentary (SA. II. 292) explains *abhisaṅkharoti* with three synonyms: *āyūhati* (to strive, to accumulate), *saṁpiṇḍeti* (to combine), and *nipphādeti* (to produce).[20] In the *Suttas*, *āyūhati* conveys "to endeavour, strain, exert oneself" (P.E.D. 106, col. 2), but in the commentarial literature *kammāyūhana* signifies producing and accumulating wholesome and unwholesome *kamma*.[21] *Saṁpiṇḍeti* connotes accumulating or amassing. The term means, literally, "kneading together" to form a ball (P.E.D. 692, col. 2). However, the analogies of cooking rice gruel and baking a cake demonstrate that *abhisaṇkharoti* signifies, not the mere accumulation of factors, but a synthesis that results in a new product with distinctive characteristics. For this reason, the commentary offers the third synonym *nipphādeti*, which signifies "to bring forth, produce accomplish" (P.E.D. 361, col. 1).

Saṅkhāras and the forming of intentional acts

A passage of the *Aṅguttara-nikāya* (A. I. 122) explains that a person forms (*abhisaṅkharoti*) three types of *kamma*: harmful *kamma* (*savyāpajjham*), *kamma* that is not harmful (*avyāpajjham*), and *kamma* that is both harmful and not harmful. The commentary explains *abhisaṅkharoti* as the amassing of such *kamma* (AA. II. 192). The synonyms of *abhisaṅkharoti* given here are *āyūhati* (strives, accumulates *kamma*), *rāsiṁ karoti* (forms a heap, amasses), and *piṇḍeti* (combines, blends together). Both *saṅkhāra* and *cetanā* are terms whose meaning cannot be fully understood outside the context of *kamma*. Within the continuum of consciousness, *saṅkhāras* perform a twofold function. From a psychological perspective, they are vehicles of the patterns of conditioning which form not only "individual personalities", but also the manifold thought processes, sentiments, acts, habits, and tendencies through which the personalities find self-expression. From the perspective of *kamma*, they are the bearers of karmic merit and demerit. *Saṅkhāra* processes are karmic processes in the sense that they constitute the series of acts of body, speech, and mind in which wholesome (*kusala*) and unwholesome (*akusala*) conditions are produced over and over again in seemingly endless variations, through many rebirths. In this way, wholesome and unwholesome conditions are "carried forward", as it were, in time.

From the perspective of *kamma*, *saṅkhāras* are classified in two ways. With reference to the "door of action", *saṅkhāras* are classified as acts of body, speech, and mind (*kāya-saṅkhāra*, *vacī-saṅkhāra citta-saṅkhāra*) (M. I. 54). In discourses related to the moral value of acts (S. II. 82), *saṅkhāras* are classified as threefold: acts of merit (*puñña-saṅkhāra*), acts of demerit (*apuñña-saṅkhāra*), and mental acts of "imperturbable" nature (*āneñja-saṅkhāra*). Similarly, with reference to the fruition of *kamma* (*kamma-vipāka*), *abhisaṅkhāras* are classified as characterized by merit and producing happy consequences (*puññābhisaṅkhāra*), characterized by demerit and producing painful consequences (*apuññābhisaṅkhāra*), and "imperturbable" (*āneñjābhisaṅkhāra*) (D. III. 217; S. II. 82, 83). The term *āneñjābhisaṅkhāra* refers to the configurations of imperturbable mental states experienced in the "formless" (*arūpa*) meditative planes that are marked by serene lucidity. It is postulated that when these meditative states are cultivated by those who are not totally free of ignorance (*avijjā*) and craving, they produce karmic consequences consisting of rebirth in cosmic realms that correspond in their tranquil characteristics to those higher states of meditation (M. II. 262-265).

It is implied in the *Nidāna-saṁyutta* that eagerness to enjoy a wide range of experiences and to prolong them are the reasons why a person "puts together" (*abhisaṅkharoti*) the mind's resources and produces goal-oriented acts (*saṅkhāras*) (S. II. 82-83). This passage goes on to explain that when a person, ignoring conditioned origination and the sorrow of *kamma*, produces acts of merit, acts of demerit, or acts pertaining to the imperturbable levels of consciousness, then, in the course of rebirth, that person's consciousness (*viññāṇa*) "proceeds" in the same direction as the goal-oriented acts.[22] From the perspective of *kamma*, this statement signifies that the moral quality of goal-oriented acts (*saṅkhāras*) conditions the course of a person's rebirth. From the perspective of psychological developments in the continuum of consciousness, this passage points to the mutual dependence of cognitive processes (*viññāṇa*) and the mind's capacity to form (*abhisaṅkharoti*) purposive acts (*saṅkhāras*). Goal-oriented acts are conditioned by the way consciousness discerns and experiences the world, and these acts give consciousness "a sense of direction" by endowing it with its perspectives and standpoints. A person whose mind is no longer beset by ignorance is described as one who neither cleaves to pleasant, unpleasant, or neutral states of mind, nor rejoices in the excitations and motivating capacities of feelings.[23]

The *Nidāna-saṁyutta* passage (S. II. 82-83) goes on to say that when a person is no longer preoccupied with bringing together the mental conditions and purposive impulses required for producing wholesome or unwholesome goal-oriented acts (*anabhisaṅkharonto, anabhisañcetayanto*), then there is release from bondage to the future and the pain of rebirth. It is posited that when the mind is released from its adherence to worldly objects and goals and from the excitement and worry caused by them (*na paritassati*), then a person directly experiences freedom from rebirth (S. II. 82).[24] In another passage of the *Saṁyutta-nikāya* (S. V. 449),[25] the urge to "form" (*abhisaṅkharonti*) purposive acts (*saṅkhāras*) with inevitable karmic consequences is associated with people who find excitement and delight (*abhiramanti*) in such acts. It can be inferred that in the *Suttas*, *saṅkhāra/sañcetanika-kamma* is regarded as an act generated by a mind that enjoys preparing and putting together intentions, projects, and resolves that strain towards the future. All these activities are interpreted to be the vital forces that keep alive the mind's delight (*abhinandana*) in new modes of experience and new goals.

Cetanā Made Concrete in *Kamma*

The Buddha's definition of *kamma*—where he maintains that *cetanā* and *kamma* are synonymous—is elucidated by passages in the *Suttas* where the terms *sañcetanā* and *sañcetanika* are associated with acts that have karmic consequences. In these passages, *sañcetanā* conveys a purposive impulse or motivating intention. I have already referred to the *Sañcetanika-vagga*, (A. II. 157-158 = S. II. 39-40), where it is stated that because of purposive impulses pertaining to the body, to speech, and to the mind (*sañcetanā-hetu*), joy and sorrow come into effect. In the *Sañcetanika-vagga*, the acts that are produced on the basis of purposive impulses (*sañcetanā-hetu*) are designated as *saṅkhāras* of body, speech, and mind, thereby indicating that each of these purposive acts is composed as a configuration of physical and mental factors. Acts of body, speech, and mind that are concrete expressions of purposive impulses (*sañcetanās*) are also designated as *sañcetanika-kamma* (M. III. 208-209; A.V. 293-295). The three terms *sañcetanika-kamma*, *saṅkhāra*, and *abhisaṅkhāra* denote a goal-oriented act that is conditioned by the past, is reckoned as "meritorious", "non-meritorious", or "imperturbable" on the basis of its moral value, and is capable of producing commensurate karmic consequences. The same act is described as *sañcetanā* because it gives concrete expression to motivating intention or purposive impulse, and as *saṅkhāra* or *abhisaṅkhāra* because it is formed of a set of conditioned processes.

According to a statement in the *Mahākammavibhaṅga-sutta* (M. III. 208-209), having performed an intentional act (*sañcetanikaṁ kammaṁ katvā*) through body, speech, or mind, a person experiences karmic consequences that are marked by feelings of pleasure, pain, or by neutral feelings characterized as "neither pleasure nor pain". There are parallel passages in the *Suttas* which declare that having "formed" or composed "formations" (*saṅkhāram abhisaṅkharitvā*) that manifest as deeds of body, speech, and mind, one experiences results that match the deeds. In a passage of the *Aṅguttara-nikāya* (A. I. 122), it is said that having "formed" or "composed" a harmful "physical formation" (*savyāpajjham kayasaṅkhāram abhisaṅkaritvā*), one is reborn in a harmful situation. Here the "physical formation" is a bodily deed which is motivated by a purposive impulse and shaped by a configuration of bodily factors. Corresponding statements are made with regard to "formations of speech" (*vacī-saṅkhāras*) and "mental formations" (*mano-saṅkhāras*).

Likewise, a passage in the *Saṁyutta-nikāya* (S. V. 449-450) describes the plight of those who take delight in "formations" (*saṅkhāresu abhiratā*). The reference is to those who enjoy "putting together" the ingredients for goal-oriented acts of body, speech, and mind. It is said here that "having formed formations" (*saṅkhāre abhisaṅkharitvā*), they experience aging, death, rebirth, and sorrow in all its variations. Though *sañcetanika-kamma*, like *saṅkhāra* and *abhisaṅkhāra*, denotes an act that has moral value and puts forth karmic consequences, the emphasis is on the notion that the act arises on the basis of a motivating intention or a purposive impulse (*sañcetanā*).

Intentional acts and the making of the body

In the *Saṁyutta-nikāya*, the Buddha teaches that the body belongs neither to oneself nor to another (S. II. 64-65).[26] The point here is that since there is no "self" (*attā*), the body cannot be regarded as belonging to any self. The passage goes on to define the body as "old *kamma*" or "past *kamma*" (*purāṇa-kamma*). Here, two other qualifying terms, namely *abhisaṅkhata* (composed or "formed") and *abhisañcetayita* (intended), are appended to the definition *purāṇa-kamma*.

In another passage of the *Saṁyutta-nikāya* (S. IV. 132), this definition that links the body with past *kamma* (S. II. 64-65) is applied to the senses and the mind.[27] Like the body, the senses and the mind also are designated as past *kamma* (*purāṇa-kamma*) and are described as *abhisaṅkhata, abhisañcetayita*. The Buddha says that he teaches old *kamma*, new *kamma*, the cessation of *kamma*, and the way leading to the cessation of *kamma* (S. IV. 132). Current acts of body, speech, and mind are described as new *kamma*. The attainment of liberation through the cessation of goal-oriented acts and their karmic consequences is designated as cessation of *kamma*, and the noble Eightfold Path is declared to be the way leading to the cessation of *kamma*. The idea that the present body is past *kamma* can be interpreted to mean that it is the end product of a vast chain of causes and conditions that extends into an immeasurable past. The Theravāda position, which holds that the five aggregates of the personality are interdependent, implies that physical and mental factors continually condition each other in the processes of living, dying, and being reborn. The goal-oriented thoughts and impulses, by which *cetanā* produces *kamma*, influence not only the mind but also the body. Thus, the body, no less than consciousness, bears witness to continuity and change. When the body and senses are called "old *kamma*", this signifies that they are the recapitulation, the living testimony, of all the past intentions and purposes that have been articulated in the continuum (*santati*) of *saṅkhāra* formations. Just as the trunk of a tree has its rings, in the body are the marks of an ancient past. Furthermore, the "new *kamma*" formed by present acts already anticipates future consequences. The future body is already in the making. By designating the body as "old *kamma*", the Buddha signals that the body is as much a vehicle of karmic continuity as consciousness (*viññāṇa*) is declared to be. Functioning as purposive impulses and motivating intentions, *cetanās* mould, not only the mind, but also the body.

Both the passage that describes the body as past *kamma* (S. II. 64-65) and the passage that describes the senses and the *manas* as past *kamma* (S. IV. 132) leave *abhisañcetanā* undefined. The commentary, however, distinguishes between *abhisaṅkhatam* and *abhisañcetayitam* by defining the former as "that which has been made (*katam*) by causal conditions (*paccayehi*) when they have assembled together (*abhisamāgantvā*)", and the latter as "that which is designed or planned (*pakappitam*) by a motivating intention or purposive impulse (*cetanā*)" (SA. II. 402).[28] *Pakappitam*, derived from the verb *pakappeti*, has the basic meaning of "to form" or "to arrange". However, the term also conveys "prepare, determine, plan" (P.E.D. 379, col. 2). It follows, then, that by glossing *abhisañcetayitam* as *cetanāya pakappitam* (formed or designed by *cetanā*), the commentary confers on *abhisañcetayitam* a cognitive content and the sense that the act has been planned through a goal-directed impetus or designed through a purposive impulse. These cognitive features distinguish *pakappitam* from *katam*, the term which the commentary associates with *abhisaṅkhatam*. Including in its meaning both "to make" and "to do", *katam* tends to convey that which is brought into existence (*uppāditam*) through the convergence of the necessary conditions (AA.V.84). Unlike *pakappitam*, *katam* does not necessarily include in its meaning the cognitive processes of planning, designing, or determining. The emphasis here is on the motivating capacity to initiate action in the organism.

The two terms *abhisaṅkharoti* and *abhisañcetayati* are distinguished in a similar manner in other passages of the commentarial literature. For example, in the commentary to the *Majjhima-nikāya* (MA. V. 57), *abhisaṅkharoti* is explained as an act by which the mind gathers its resources and brings together (*rāsiṁ karoti*) the necessary mental conditions, in the course of straining to put forth (*āyūhati*) *kamma*. *Abhisañcetayati* is explained as "to form" or "to design through thought" (*kappeti*). Similarly, in the commentary to the *Aṅguttara-nikāya* (AA. V. 84), *abhisañcetayitam* is glossed with the two terms: *cetitam* (intended) and *kappitam* (designed, planned). The Saṁskṛt term *kalpita* includes in its connotations "composed" and "invented" (S.E.D. 263, col. 1).

Intentional acts as bearers of moral value

In the *Karajakāya-vagga*[29] of the *Aṅguttara-nikāya* (A. V. 285-303), the term *sañcetanā* indicates a complex mental function that includes the following aspects: intending to pursue a specific goal, initiating action in the body and mind to fulfil that intention, and directing energy and action towards the goal. The *Karajakāya-vagga* shows that when *kamma* is defined in terms of *cetanā* (A. III.415), this does not mean that the purposive impulse by itself constitutes wholesome or unwholsome *kamma*. A *sañcetanika-kamma* is a *saṅkhāra/abhisaṅkhāra*—that is to say, not merely an intention in the mind, but a purposive act endowed with moral value that puts forth karmic consequences. *Kamma* is *cetanā* expressed in action, motivating intention made concretely manifest. Furthermore, the *Karajakāya-vagga* shows that in the classification of *kamma* as wholesome and unwholesome, the criterion is not solely whether the purposive impulse is wholesome. On the contrary, motivating intention or purposive impulse (*cetanā*) and the act (*saṅkhāra*) that expresses it are taken as an integral whole, so that a morally good bodily act, for example, signifies that both the intention and the bodily act are morally blameless. However, when conditioned origination is affirmed, it is implied that when the *cetanā* is morally good, the act that ensues from it will also be good.

The *Karajakāya-vagga* and the *Sāleyyaka-sutta* (M. I. 286-289) are helpful in assessing the significance of *sañcetanika-kamma* in the *Sutta* literature since they provide concrete examples of the standard list of ten wholesome and ten unwholesome acts of body, speech, and mind. These became the commonly cited examples of such acts in the commentarial and *Abhidhamma* literature. In the *Karajakāya-vagga* (A. V. 292), the three morally unwholesome (*akusala*) acts of the body (injury to living beings, theft, and sexual misconduct) and the four types of unwholesome acts of speech (false, malicious, harsh, and idle speech) are said to be characterized by unwholesome *sañcetanās* (*akusala-sañcetanikā*).[30] The physical acts and speech of a person who abstains (*paṭivirato hoti*) from these unwholesome acts are regarded as wholesome (*kusala*). The descriptions of wholesome acts show that "wholesome" signifies both abstaining from unwholesome behaviour and actively opposing it by manifesting morally good characteristics. The three unwholesome mental *kammas* (covetousness, ill will, and wrong view) and the three wholesome mental *kamma* (non-covetousness, goodwill, and right view) are shown to be complex mental states fuelled by emotions that become the basis of corresponding thoughts, aspirations and desires. For example, a person beset with covetousness is greedy for what others enjoy, and a person of ill will is described as having a malevolent mind-set (*vyāpanna-citto*). The intentions of a person of ill will are said to arise from a malignant frame of mind (*paduṭṭha-mana-saṅkappo*).

The term *sancetanā* is not defined either in the *Karajakāya-vagga* (A. V. 285-303) or in the *Sāleyyaka-sutta* (M. I. 286-289). From the descriptions of acts characterized by *sañcetanā* (*sañcetanika-kamma*) in these sections of the *Sutta* literature, the following inferences can be drawn: *sañcetanā* is conceived as purposive impulse or goal-oriented impetus that emerges from a specific attitude of mind; *sañcetanās* are perceived to be often conditioned by attitudes of mind that tend to be habitual; and it is assumed that *sañcetanās* function as conative impulses that have the capacity to initiate action. The examples given in the *Karajakāya-vagga* demonstrate that *sañcetanās* are not merely purposive thoughts, but purposive impulses charged with the motivating power to initiate action. The relationship between attitude of mind, intention, and act is demonstrated, for example, in the description of unwholesome acts of speech. The *Karajakāya-vagga* describes concrete instances of dishonest speech, slander, harsh speech, and frivolous chatter. In the description of a person who gives false witness before a council that seeks to uphold the law, the text strongly suggests that the person is a habitual liar. Motives are presented: we are told that the lie is spoken for the sake of either personal benefit, or the benefit of another, or for some material gain. It is made clear that the lie is told intentionally or knowingly (*sampajāna-musā bhāsitā hoti*) (A.V. 293). The reader can infer that the motives given above and the person's habits of mind led to the intention to lie.

Further examples of *sañcetanika-kamma* demonstrate that in the holistic view of consciousness espoused by Theravāda, purposive acts are seen to be conditioned aspects of a larger frame of mind (A. V. 289, 290, 293, 296). According to the *Karajakāya-vagga*, a person purposely injures a living being because of not having a compassionate heart towards all living beings (*adayāpanno sabba-pāṇabhūtesu*). A person who refrains from taking life is described as one who would be ashamed (*lajjī*) of doing wrong, who is compassionate (*dayāpanno*) and behaves with constant friendliness and compassion for all beings (*sabba-pāṇabhūta-hitānukampī viharati*). A person who engages in the unwholesome verbal *kamma* of slandering others is described as one who finds delight, joy, and merriment in discord (*vaggārāmo, vagga-rato, vagga-nandī*), and a person who abstains from slander is said to rejoice in harmony (*samagga*). These examples of wholesome and unwholesome *kamma* show that the intention to act is regarded as arising, not from an overriding "will", an overwhelming emotion, or a sovereign reason, but from an attitude of mind (such as compassion and friendliness or malicious delight in causing disharmony) in which cognitive, emotive, and conative factors are mutually dependent. The commentary to the *Aṅguttara-nikāya* goes further than the text does in interpreting the relationship of *cetanā* to the attitudes of mind from which they arise and to the deeds that they initiate (AA. V. 76). *Sañcetanika-kamma* is explained in the commentary as that which is done after intending and planning (*cetetvā pakappetvā katam*). The use of the gerunds *cetetvā* and *pakappetvā* shows that the intending and planning precedes and motivates the action that is designated as *sañcetanika-kamma*.[31]

The description of wholesome and unwholesome intentional acts (*sañcetaṇika-kamma*) in the *Karajakāya-vagga* (A. V. 299-301) is followed, appropriately, by instructions for the cultivation of the four "immeasurable" (*appamāṇa*) virtues: immeasurable friendship, compassion, joy in the success of others, and equanimity. The text holds that a person who cultivates friendliness (*mettā*) is liberated from covetousness, ill will, and delusion (*vigatābhijjho, vigata-vyāpādo, asammūḷho*). It is affirmed as a matter of complete certainty that a person who cultivates meditation on the four boundless virtues from a tender age will not engage in reprehensible acts of body, speech, and mind. In the same manner, another passage of the *Aṅguttara-nikāya* states that while a well-guarded state of mind (*citta*) will produce well-guarded, wholesome acts of body, speech, and mind, an ill-guarded *citta*, like a leaking roof, will produce acts dripping (*avassuta*) with greed (A. I. 261). To understand the full significance of this statement, one should keep in mind that the term *avassuta* is grammatically related to the term *āsava* (mental stain). The emphasis, in this passage and in the *Karajakāya-vagga*, is on the cultivation of wholesome attitudes of mind, so that wholesome intentional acts (*sañcetanika-kamma*) will freely flow from wholesome attitudes, in accordance with conditioned origination.

Debates on the relationship between intention, act, and the results of action

McDermott draws attention to the difference between the Theravāda position and the viewpoint expressed in the *Abhidharmakośa-bhāṣya* with regard to the precise nature of the relationship between *cetanā* and *kamma*.[32] He stresses that for the Theravādins, *cetanā* is *kamma*; that is to say, the purposive impulse is the act. According to Theravāda, goal-oriented acts of body, speech, and mind are nothing other than purposive impulses (*cetanās*) becoming actualized by setting in motion physical, vocal, and mental processes. Theravādins, therefore, maintain that purposive impulse and purposive act (*sañcetanā* and *sañcetanika-kamma*) are identical and inseparable, though they can be distinguished for purposes of conceptual analysis. McDermott points out that the *Abhidharmakośa-bhāṣya*, on the contrary, defines *cetanā* as mental *kamma* (*cetanā mānasam karma*) and distinguishes *cetanā* from physical and verbal acts on the grounds that these acts are born from *cetanā* (*tajjam vākkāya-karmaṇī*) (Abhk. IV.1). This statement in the *Abhidharmakośa-*

bhāṣya can be interpreted to mean that acts of body and speech differ from intention (*cetanā*) in two ways: they contain physical and vocal elements not present in the intention, and they are subsequent to the intention.

Although the distinction that McDermott makes between the Theravāda and the *Abhidharmakośa-bhāṣya* views of *kamma* is helpful, it would not be correct to say that Theravāda views *kamma* as nothing else but *cetanā*. It would be a fairer assessment to hold that in the definition given at A. III. 415 and in the *Atthasālinī* (Asl. 84, 87, 88) *kamma* is viewed as a complex whole where *cetanā*, on the one hand, and the physical, vocal, or mental processes, on the other, are distinguishable but integrated. Purposive impulses alone do not make purposive acts. *Cetanā* is identified with *kamma* by virtue of becoming expressed in concrete acts of body, speech, and mind. It will be shown in Chapters VI and VII that the *Visuddhimagga*, the *Atthasālinī*, and the commentaries to the first four *Nikāyas* throw further light on this issue by emphasizing the dynamic nature and the motivating function of *cetanā*. In these texts, *cetanā* is consistently regarded as a purposive impulse which, by its very nature, becomes expressed in corresponding acts. This characteristic function of initiating action, therefore, distinguishes *cetanā* from other mental factors such as wish (*icchā*), intention (*saṅkappa*), aspiration (*patthanā*), and even resolve (*paṇidhi*), which can remain as mental experiences without necessarily initiating action.

Another debate on the subject of *kamma* concerned the process by which an intentional act puts forth karmic effects. Proponents of *kamma* maintained that there must be a process of "accumulation" (*upacaya*) by which the deed is integrated into the consciousness continuum of the doer and "stored" or "accumulated" there until the time is right for the karmic effects (*kamma-vipāka*) to be produced. The *Karajakāya-vagga* declares that an intentional act (*sañcetanika-kamma*), accomplished and "accumulated" (*upacita*), cannot be annihilated without its consequence being experienced in this very life or in a future rebirth (A. V. 292, 294, 297, 298, 299). In a debate recorded in the *Kathāvatthu*, the Theravādins argue that just the performing of an act instigated by a purposive impulse (*cetanā*) ensures that the deed will produce effects at the appropriate time (Kvu. 520-522). In other words, the Theravādins maintain that the capacity of an intentional act (*sañcetanika-kamma*) to put forth karmic effects is an inseparable component of the act. The opponents of Theravāda uphold the view that since the act and its effect are set apart by a period of time, there must be a connecting factor that survives the act and persists until the effect is produced. For this reason, they posit "accumulation" (*upacaya*) as the factor that links the act that has passed away and the effect that has not yet come to be. Dube, in his *Cross Currents in Early Buddhism*,[33] explains that since the followers of Theravāda hold that conditioned origination requires no intervening principle to connect cause and effect, they do not find it necessary to interpret "accumulation" as a factor that persists after the intentional act and functions as a link with its outcome.[34]

The relationship between *kamma* and *upacaya* continued to be debated in the Buddhist schools. The *Abhidharmakośa-bhāṣya* makes a distinction between *kamma* and *upacaya*, and posits intention (*cetanā*) as one of the conditions for the arising of *upacaya* (Abhk. IV.120). According to the *Abhidharmakośa-bhāṣya*, the necessary conditions for the integration of a deed into the karmic process of an individual include the association of an intention with the deed (*saṁcetana*), the completion of the deed (*samāpti*), the absence of remorse (*niṣkaukṛtya*) or any counteractive factor such as confession or repentance, the presence of factors that are the necessary accompaniments of the deed (*parivāra*), and the fruition (*vipāka*) of the deed in the form of pleasant and unpleasant consequences.[35] In this context, the *Abhidharmakośa-bhāṣya* states that an act motivated by *cetanā* is performed after purposive deliberation (*saṁcintya kṛtam*) and is not done unknowingly or hastily, without prior intelligent assessment (*nābuddhipūrvam na sahasā kṛtam*).[36] Both the terms *saṁcintya* and *buddhipūrvam* indicate that cognitive processes of reflection, directed thought, decision-making, and choice of goal precede the act.

The *Abhidharamakośa-bhāṣya* separates the act and its consequences and posits a special factor of "accumulation" to ensure the preservation of the potency of the act until the consequences are produced. Theravāda, on the other hand, does not separate an intentional act (*sañcetanika-kamma*) from its capacity to put forth commensurate consequences (*kamma-vipāka*), just as it does not separate a purposive impulse and the act that the purpose motivates. According to Theravāda, the very fact that a wholesome or unwholesome intentional act is performed entails consequences in the consciousness continuum of the doer. No further factor, such as "accumulation", is deemed necessary to ensure that the consequences of the act come into effect.

Intention as "nutriment" for rebirth

The powerful notion of "food" (*āhāra*) in the *Sutta* literature stresses that all living beings are vulnerable and will perish unless body and consciousness are constantly nourished and revitalized. "All beings subsist by nutriment (*āhāraṭṭhitikā*), all subsist through processes of conditioning (*saṅkhāraṭṭhitikā*)", says the *Dīgha-nikāya* (D. III. 211). Four "nutriments" are specified as necessary conditions for the perpetuation of life and rebirth: food that is eaten preserves the body; contact with objects engenders pleasant, unpleasant, and neutral feelings (*vedanā*) that motivate further acts; purposive impulses in the mind (*mano-sañcetanā*) produce the acts (*kamma*) that lead to different types of existence and experience; and consciousness becomes the condition for the arising of the psychophysical organism (*nāma-rūpa*) at the time of rebirth (SA. II. 25). *Mano-sañcetanā* is interpreted to be the impetus that drives the mind to seek out one goal after another in the pursuit of what is regarded as advantageous for oneself and for society.

Engaging in a play on words, the commentary to the *Saṁyutta-nikāya* (SA. II. 22) interprets nutriments (*āhārā*) as causal conditions (*paccayā*) and explains that conditions are designated as *āhārā* because they "bring" (*āharanti*) their own results. The commentary goes on to explain that although there are other conditions through which beings are born and are sustained, just these four are called nutriments because they serve as the distinctive conditions (*visesa-paccayā*) through which a continuum of personal consciousness (*ajjhattika-santati*) is maintained.[37] In the *Nidāna-saṁyutta* (S. II. 12) where the links of the chain of rebirth are delineated, the nutriments are said to have craving as their cause (*taṇhā-nidānā*). The *Majjhima-nikāya* also explains that an inseparable link is forged between craving and nutriment because the four nutriments arise when craving arises and cease when craving ceases (M. I. 48, 261). It is implied here that the four nutriments and craving exist and have meaning only in relation to each other. Food of every type is a danger because, just by nourishing, it sets up the conditions for further hunger. Paradoxically, food that satisfies becomes synonymous with insatiability. The idea that food is the basis of all life can be traced back to the Vedic tradition. The *Taittirīya Upaniṣad* celebrates food in a verse which says that all the beings that inhabit this earth are born from food, live by food, and pass into food when life ends (T.U. II. 2.1).[38]

The *Saṁyutta-nikāya* supplies terrifyingly vivid analogies to illustrate the danger in each of the nutriments (S. II. 98-99). *Mano-sañcetanā* is described as a fiery pit towards which two strong men are dragging a helpless person. According to the explanation given in the commentary, the fiery pit is the course or rebirth, the victim is the ignorant person infatuated by the gains of the realm of rebirth, the two strong men who drag the victim to the fire are wholesome and unwholesome *kamma*, and the time it takes for the men to haul their victim represents the time when *kamma* is performed and accumulated (*kammāyūhana-kālo*) (SA. II. 112-113). This analogy is considered apt because it portrays how continually accumulating *kamma* pulls along in its wake a chain of inescapable consequences. *Mano-sañcetanā* is dangerous because every act that it instigates produces a craving for more aspirations, plans, and goal-oriented activities. The purposive impulses in the mind that *mano-sañcetanā* represents can be either wholesome or unwholesome, depending on the moral quality of both the attitude of mind (*citta*) from which they arise and the acts (*kamma*) that they produce. However, wholesome intentions, like unwholesome intentions, are regarded as dangerous because they too can cause the mind to succumb to the lure of living for future goals.

Such renderings as "intention" and "purposive impulse" do not even begin to convey the Theravāda view of the powerfully creative, and ultimately tragic, influence of *mano-sañcetanā* as motivating energy in the lives of individuals and societies. Nyanaponika Thera explains that *mano-sañcetanā* manifests itself in the "incessant urge" in the human mind to invent, create, plan, and build, as well as to injure and destroy.[39] *Mano-sañcetanā* makes the world both a nurturing place, where faith in good relationships and the hope of prosperity for all are continually revived, as well as a dangerous arena for power-play and conquest. Hope and despair follow each other in the mind's ability to endlessly perpetuate goal-oriented impulses. *Mano-sañcetanā* destroys at the same time that it nourishes.

In Theravāda, *mano-sañcetanās* are viewed as the motivating impulses that transform the continuum of consciousness (*citta*) into a dynamic "personal series" (*ajjhattika-santati*). Impelled by the purposive impulses of *mano-sañcetanā*, the *citta* becomes a creative artist (*citta-kāra*) aspiring for self-expression. At the same time, the aspirations become vitiated by ignorant craving, with the result that consciousness suffers bondage to purposive impulses, hopes, and resolves that keep the mind relentlessly oriented towards the future. Consciousness itself becomes food (*āhāra*) for the perpetuation of rebirth when thought processes and emotions are conditioned by the mind's ability to perpetuate goal-directed impulses (*mano-sañcetanā*). Nyanaponika Thera quotes the sub-commentary to S. II. 12-14 where *viññāṇa* as *āhāra* is equated with *abhisaṅkhāra-viññāṇa*.[40] The commmentarial term *abhisaṅkhāra-viññāṇa* represents consciousness (*viññāṇa*) that is conditioned by the action-initiating, future-oriented processes of *saṅkhāra* and is poised for the prolongation of life and the furtherance of rebirth. C.A.F. Rhys Davids translates *abhisaṅkhāra-viññāṇa* as "constructing, storing consciousness" in *A Buddhist Manual of Psychological Ethics*.[41] Nyanaponika Thera renders the term as "*kamma*-forming consciousness".[42]

A passage in the *Aṅguttara-nikāya*, compares *kamma* to a farmer's field, consciousness (*viññāṇa*) ready for rebirth to a seed ready to sprout, and craving for the enjoyment of objects and the prolongation of life to the moisture that nourishes the seed (A. I. 224). The passage goes on to say that consciousness becomes established (*patiṭṭitam*) in a realm of rebirth that is commensurate with the *kamma* that it has accumulated. The commentary says that this analogy of a seed ready to germinate illustrates the process by which consciousness (*viññāṇa*) becomes a vehicle for action-producing purposive impulses (*abhisaṅkhāra-viññāṇa*) and reaches a state of "maturation" (*virūhana*) that makes it ready for rebirth (AA. II. 334).[43] From the perspective of *kamma* and rebirth, the "germinating process" illustrates wholesome and unwholesome purposive activities (*abhisaṅkhāras*) urging consciousness towards rebirth and renewal of *kamma*-forming activities. From a psychological perspective, the germinating process is a picture of the impetus and urgency in purposes and plans to "mature" and to become manifest in activities that enhance the individual personality and enrich the world in which it is situated (*patiṭṭitam*).

It is significant that the *Aṅguttara-nikāya* considers not only consciousness as a whole, but more specifically *cetanā* and *patthanā* (aspiration) to be "stationed" (*patiṭṭhitam*) in a realm of rebirth (A. I. 224).[44] This statement brings into focus the Theravāda view that the purposive impulses constituting *cetanās* cannot survive or be perpetuated unless they are "stationed" in a supporting realm of objects to which they are attuned. Intentions and purposes are regarded as meaningless unless they are positioned in a realm of objects and goals. At the same time, it is posited that objects are coordinated and form a coherent realm of experience by becoming the goals towards which the purposive impulses are directed. The *Aṅguttara-nikāya* says that purposive impulses (*cetanā*) and aspirations (*patthanā*) become established in the "lower realm", the "intermediate realm", or the "most excellent realm". The commentary (AA. II. 334) explains these three realms, respectively, as the world of sense-desire, the "realm of form", and the "formless realm". In the present life these three realms correspond to three modes of experience: ordinary sensory and mental processes; lower planes of meditation, where the mind concentrates on forms (*rūpajjhāna*); and the higher planes of "formless" meditation (*arūpajjhāna*). The commentary designates the purposive impulse and aspiration that becomes established (*patiṭṭhitā*), persist, and bring forth goal-oriented acts in a specific realm of experience as *kamma-cetanā* and *kamma-patthanā* (AA. II. 334). Nyanatiloka renders *kamma-cetanā* as "karmic volition" and explains it as the purposive impulse that produces an act entailing karmic merit or demerit.[45] Such *kamma*-forming purposive impulses are the causes of the prolongation of the consciousness continuum and the experience of rebirth.

Cetanā Defined as *Kamma* in the *Milindapañha*

Detailed definitions of *cetanā* are found in the *Milindapañha* (Mil. 61-62),[46] the *Visuddhimagga*, and the *Atthasālinī* (Vsm. XIV. 135; Asl. 111-112). Of these, the *Milindapañha* definition is analyzed here and the other two are reserved for Chapter VIII. The significant question with regard to these definitions is whether they view *cetanā* primarily as the cognitive function of assessing possibilities and determining a goal, or as the conative function of initiating action in the organism. Since large parts of the *Sutta* literature were composed before the *Milindapañha*, the definition of *cetanā* in this text shows what had come to be accepted as the meaning of this term when the earliest section of the *Milindapañha* was composed between 100 B.C.E. and 200 C.E.

At the core of the definition of *cetanā* in the *Milindapañha* is the statement that *cetanā* has two defining characteristics: *cetayita lakkhaṇa* and *abhisaṅkharaṇa lakkhaṇa* (Mil. 61-62). The term *cetayita* is related to the verb *ceteti* (to think, plan, intend, or purposefully conceive). The other defining characteristic, *abhisaṅkharaṇa*, associates *cetanā* with the action-producing constructive activity of the *saṅkhārakkhandha*. *Abhisaṅkharaṇa* refers to the constructive processes by which causal conditions in the continuum of consciousness come together under the influence of a motivating factor and "compose" goal-directed acts of body, speech, and mind. It was noted earlier in this chapter that the *Abhidharmakośa-bhāṣya* (Abhk. IV. 120) maintains that an act brought about by *cetanā* is performed, not hastily and not without exercising the intellect (*nābuddhipūrvam*), but after due thought and consideration (*saṁcintya*). This statement clearly connects *cetanā* with the verb-root *cint-* ("to think about", "to reflect upon", or "to consider"). Furthermore, by employing the term *buddhi* in this context, the *Abhidharmakośa-bhāṣya* leaves no doubt that it links *cetanā* with the processes of discernment, assessment, and judgment. Although the definition of *cetanā* that the *Milindapañha* offers does include the phrase *cetanāya cetayitvā*, this definition does not associate *cetanā* as explicitly and strongly with processes of intellection and purposive thought as the *Abhidharmakośa-bhāṣya* does.

In the *Milindapañha*, the function of *cetanā* in the process of *kamma* is illustrated with the following analogy:

> It is analogous to the case of a man who, having prepared poison (*visam abhisaṅkharitvā*), may drink it himself and cause others to drink it. He would experience pain and so would they. In the same way, a certain person, having purposefully contemplated an unwholesome act (*akusalaṁ kammaṁ cetanāya cetayitvā*), would fall into a sorrowful state and be reborn in *Niraya*-hell, and so would those who followed his instruction (Mil. 61).

The phrase *cetanāya cetayitvā* signifies applying *cetanā* in the processes of thought. The phrase could be rendered as "having intended", "having contemplated", or "having purposefully thought out". The *Milindapañha* goes on to say that when a person exercises *cetanā* in performing a wholesome act, then that person enters a happy destiny and reaches a celestial abode. The analogy is given of a person who prepares a healthy drink by bringing together (*ekajjham abhisaṅkharitvā*) wholesome and delicious ingredients, drinks of it, and gives it to others. The one who prepares the drink and those who share it would experience pleasure.

The problem in interpreting this passage is that whereas one of the key terms, *abhisaṅkharitvā*, is connected only with the analogies, the other key term, *cetayitvā*, is associated only with the wholesome and unwholesome deeds that the analogies are meant to elucidate. What is not clear is the precise relationship between *abhisaṅkharitvā* and *cetayitvā*, and precisely how the analogies apply to the term *cetayitvā*. It cannot escape the reader's notice that the analogies focus on assembling the necessary means to produce a result rather than on the decision-making function of choosing a goal. Nothing is said about the intention of the person who prepares the poisonous drink. In the case of the nourishing drink, the choice ingredients are actually named, and the emphasis seems to be not so much on why the drink is prepared as on how it is blended. In fact, the purpose it serves seems to follow as a matter of course from the nature of the drink. *Abhisaṅkharaṇa*, which is given as the second defining characteristic of *cetanā*, is associated with the preparation of the drink, and the first defining characteristic, *cetayita*, is connected with performing an act that is capable of producing karmic consequences. If producing the drink is analogous to producing a deed that entails karmic fruition, then the meaning of *cetayita* becomes indistinguishable from the meaning of *abhisaṅkharaṇa*. On the basis of the analogy, it would be possible to interpret *cetāyita* as the conative function of motivating action, not as the cognitive function of assessing possibilities and forming a purpose. It is important to note, however, that assembling mental states and motivating purposive acts is regarded as the function of the *saṅkhārakkhandha*. These actions are not usually included in the meaning of the verb *ceteti*.

It is puzzling that the definition in the *Milindapañha* does not elucidate the phrase *cetanāya cetayitvā* and the important connotations of "purposive reflection" and "intention" that can be attributed to *cetanā* on the basis of its connection with the verb *ceteti*. An answer to this puzzle begins to emerge when the definition of *cetanā* in the *Milindapañha* is compared with the definitions in the *Atthasālinī* and the *Visuddhimagga* (Asl. 111-112; Vsm. XIV. 135). Only *cetayita* is given as the characteristic (*lakkhaṇa*) of *cetanā* in these two texts, and the *Atthasālinī* holds that all *cetanās* without exception have *cetayita* as their defining quality. Earlier in this chapter it was shown that *cetanā* is a necessary factor for consciousness to function even in a rudimentary manner. When *cetanā* occurs in the rudimentary stages of perception, it does not take the form of a fully developed purposive impulse and does not produce wholesome and unwholesome deeds. Since *cetanā* does not invariably arise as a fully developed intention or purpose, the *Atthasālinī* does not explain the meaning of *cetanā* by associating it with cognitive processes of intention and decision-making. On the contrary, the *Atthasālinī* interprets *cetayita* as the distinctive function by which *cetanā* coordinates mental states and directs them towards an object of interest. Even in the most basic states of consciousness, *cetanā* performs the function of causing the mind and its functions to attend to an object. The *Atthasālinī* is a later text than the *Milindapañha*, and the definition of *cetanā* in the *Atthasālinī* is more coherent and shows more thorough analysis than the definition in the *Milindapañha*. According to the explanation given in the *Atthasālinī*, it is only in cases where a *sañcetanika-kamma* (purposive act) is produced that *cetanā* connotes intention or purposive impulse supported by cognitive processes of assessment and decision.

The definition of *cetanā* that the *Milindapañha* presents is confusing because, of the two characteristics that it attributes to *cetanā*, *abhisaṅkharaṇa*, in fact, is restricted in the first four *Nikāyas* to cases where *cetanā* manifests as a purposive impulse or motivating intention that brings together causal conditions and produces (*abhisaṅkharoti*) an act with karmic consequences. The other characteristic, *cetayita*, can apply to all cases where *cetanā* arises only if it (*cetayita*) is defined, not as purposive impulse or intention, but as a factor of basic conscious awareness that directs the mind to objects of interest even in the preliminary stages of perception.

Cetanā and the Eightfold Path

The term *cetanā* does not have a prominent role in those passages of the *Sutta* literature that describe the disciplines of the Eightfold Path. *Viriya* (energy), *chanda* (impetus to act), and *padhāna* (effort) are the terms that most frequently convey the ardent effort that characterizes the Eightfold Path, and *saṅkappa* is the term that expresses a firm intention to pursue the Path. *Cetanā* is conspicuously absent. However, there are two passages that comment on the role of *cetanā* in directing the mind towards liberation. The first of these is set in the context of *kamma* and refers to a special *cetanā* directed towards renunciation (*kammaṁ pahanāya cetanā*). It turns away from *kamma* and opens up the Path that leads towards liberation. The second passage is significant because it declares that special interventions of *cetanā* are not necessary (*na cetanāya karaṇīyaṁ*) in the course of the Eightfold Path since each stage, when properly cultivated, "naturally" leads to the next, drawing closer to liberation from sorrow.

Cetanā as purposive impulse that renounces kamma

In the *Sutta* literature *kamma* is said to be of four types: "dark" *kamma* with "dark" consequences; "bright" *kamma* with a "bright" outcome; "dark and bright" *kamma* with mixed "dark and bright" consequences; and finally, *kamma* that is "neither dark nor bright" and leads to consequences that are "neither dark nor bright" (A. II. 230-231; D. III. 230; M. I. 389-391). "Dark" acts are defined as harmful, injurious (*savyāpajjham*) acts that cause rebirth in a realm where one endures extreme pain. "Bright" acts are said to be free of harm or injury. Deeds that are "both dark and bright" are described as acts that are both injurious and non-injurious, depending on the perspective from which they are assessed. They produce results that are both pleasant and painful. The phrase *saṅkhāram abhisaṅkharoti*, which occurs in relation to these three categories of deeds, signifies the assembling of mental factors that function together to produce an act that has karmic consequences.

The fourth type is described as *kamma* that conduces to the waning away of *kamma* (*kammakkhayāya saṁvattati*). The omission of the phrase *saṅkhāram abhisaṅkharoti* in relation to the fourth type of *kamma* signifies that the act is not motivated by the desire for present benefits or future goals that fall within the processes of *kamma.* Since the definition of *kamma* that the Buddha gives (A. III. 415) states that in all cases, without exception, *kamma* is motivated by *cetanā*, this fourth category of *kamma* also is explained in relation to *cetanā.* However the *cetanā* that motivates the fourth type of *kamma* is distinguished by its purpose of renouncing (*pahānāya*) the first three types of *kamma* and the effects they produce. The commentary to the *Majjhima-nikāya* defines these four categories of *kamma* by correlating them with corresponding types of *cetanās* (MA. III. 103-105), even though in the *Majjhima-nikāya* itself (M. I. 389-391) the word *cetanā* does not appear in relation to the first three types of *kamma.* The commentaries to the *Majjhima-nikāya* and the *Aṅguttara-nikāya* define "dark" *kamma* as unwholesome *cetanā,* "bright" *kamma* as wholesome *cetanā*, and *kamma* that is "neither dark nor bright" as *cetanā* that pertains to the path of liberation (*magga-cetanā*).[47]

The *Aṅguttara-nikāya* goes on to state that *kamma* that is "neither dark nor bright" comprises the eight factors of the Eightfold Path as well as the seven "factors of wisdom" (*bojjhaṅgas*), namely, mindfulness (*sati*), investigation of *dhammas* (*dhamma-vicaya*), energy (*viriya*), rapture (*pīti*) that is experienced in states of meditation, tranquillity (*passaddhi*), concentration (*samādhi*), and equanimity(*upekkhā*) (A. II. 236-237). This fourth type of *cetanā*, like other *cetanās*, cannot arise outside the conditioning influence of a specific frame of mind. The disciplines of ethical virtue, mindfulness, meditation, and wisdom can be described as formations of wholesome behaviour patterns (*saṅkhāras*) that are distinctive to the Eightfold Path. In this sense, the *cetanās* of the Path (*magga-cetanā*) are conditioned by the cognitive features of the Eightfold path (such as right view and wise understanding) and by *saṅkhāras* that are the vehicles through which the disciplines are cultivated and conserved.

Purposive impulse and the way of nature

There is a remarkable passage in the *Aṅguttara-nikāya* where yet another dimension of *cetanā* is revealed (A. V. 2-4). It is stated here that a disciple steadfastly following the Path of liberation does not need to bring into effect the purposive impetus of *cetanā* at every stage. With utmost simplicity, the *Aṅguttara-nikāya* states that the motivating dynamism of *cetanā* is not required since each stage leads naturally and in due order to the next, in accordance with the principle of conditioned origination. This passage in the *Aṅguttara-nikāya*[48] begins with the statement that a person who is virtuous (*sīlavant*) need not exercise *cetanā* (*na cetanāya karaṇīyam*) to produce the goal-oriented thought, "May freedom from regret (*avippaṭisāra*) arise in me", since it is only natural (*dhammatā esā*) that freedom from regret will develop in a person who renounces what is unwholesome and cultivates virtue. The progress from each stage of the training to the next is described similarly.

In an article entitled "Wrong Notions of *Dhammatā* (*Dharmatā*)", Walpola Rahula explains that *dhammatā* means "it is so", "it happens that way", "it is natural".[49] Rahula points out that *dhammatā* corresponds to two other terms, *dhammaṭṭhitatā* and *dhamma-niyāmatā*, which he renders as "stability of nature" and "way of nature". These two terms are found in the *Nidāna-saṁyutta* in a statement that celebrates the central importance of the principle of conditioned origination for Theravāda (S. II. 25). It is affirmed here that the conditioned arising of things continues uninterruptedly, whether or not Buddhas are born into our world. It follows that "it is natural" (*dhammatā*) means "it is in accordance with conditioned origination". In the *Aṅguttara-nikāya* (A. V. 2-4), each stage in the cultivation of the mind (*bhāvanā*) is shown to be a natural consequence of the conditions set up in the previous stages (Chart 1). As each stage is named, the refrain is repeated that there is no need to put forth a purposive impulse (*na cetanāya karaṇīyam*) since it is natural (*dhammatā esā*) that the next stage should follow. The passage concludes with the statement that each stage entails (*abhisandeti*) the next, each stage fulfils (*paripūreti*) the next, so that one may go from "here" (*apara*) to "the farther shore" (*pāram*).[50] The commentary explains "here" as circling in the realms of rebirth and "the farther shore" as *nibbāna* (AA. V. 2). According to the commentary (AA. V. 1), *na cetanāya karaṇīyam* signifies that the next stage is "not to be brought about (*na . . . kātabbam*) through intention or purposive thinking (*cetetvā*), conceptualizing (*kappetvā*), or planning (*pakappetvā*)".[51] *Dhammatā* is explained as the "principle of nature" (*dhamma-sabhāva*) and as "causal order" (*kāraṇa-niyama*) (AA. V. 1).

This statement of firm confidence that the stages of the Eightfold Path develop naturally, each preparing the conditions for the emergence of the next, elucidates what the term *bhāvanā* comes to mean in the *Suttas*. *Bhāvanā* conveys causing the mind to gradually develop quiet concentration (*jhāna*) and lucid mindfulness (*sati*) by providing the conditions for such development. By saying that special interventions of purposive impulse are redundant, the *Aṅguttara-nikaya* expresses the idea that when the disciplines are followed faithfully, the mind develops naturally, according to its own processes of growth. Behind this statement in the *Aṅguttara-nikaya* is the central Theravāda affirmation that the mind, like everything else in the universe, develops naturally, in accordance with conditioned origination. The direction that the growth will take depends on the conditions provided. There is no guarantee that the mind, of its own accord, will develop in a particular way, nor can *cetanā* act as a governing will that directs the development. There is only the guarantee that the development will be in accordance with the causal conditions (*paccayas*).

Though there are many passages in the *Suttas* that stress the need for strenuous effort in cultivating the disciplines of the Eightfold Path, in this passage of the *Aṅguttara-nikāya*, the purposive impetus of *cetanā* is shown withdrawing, as it were, in order to allow the mind's development (*bhāvanā*) to proceed according to its own inner impulse. The commentary to the *Dīgha-nikāya* (DA. II. 432) explains *dhammatā* as "order" or "causal uniformity" (*niyāma*) and specifies the following five types of *niyāma*: "the order of *kamma*" (*kamma-niyāma*) manifested in the causal processes in which wholesome and unwholesome acts produce commensurate results; "the order of the seasons" (*utu-niyāma*); "the order of seeds" (*bīja-niyāma*) whereby each seed produces a plant that is of the same species as itself; "the order of consciousness" (*citta-niyāma*),[52] shown in the orderly procedure whereby each mental state causes the arising of the next; and "the order of *dhamma*" (*dhamma-niyāma*) manifested in the ordered sequence of events from birth to *parinibbāna* that takes place in the lives of all the Buddhas. Although *citta-niyāma* is a term that belongs to the commentarial literature, the notion that mental processes develop in accordance with conditioned origination is taken for granted in the *Suttas*.

The following *Sutta* passages echo the notion that when the cultivation (*bhāvanā*) of the mind proceeds stage by stage there is no need for the involvement of the motivating impetus of *cetanā*. In the *Cūḷavedalla-sutta*, Dhammadinnā is asked how the level of meditation that is characterized by the cessation of the processes of perception and feeling (*saññā-vedayita-nirodha*) is attained (M. I. 301-302). This level of meditation is regarded in the *Suttas* as the culmination of calm concentration, attained only after a person has cultivated the four levels of "meditation with form" (*rūpajjhāna*) and the four "formless meditations" (*arūpajjhāna*). Dhammadinnā points out that a person who attains this exalted level of meditation does not think, "I shall attain", or "I am attaining", or "I have attained". She goes on to explain that the mind (*citta*) has been so developed (*bhāvitam*) that it proceeds towards that culminating level of perfect quiescence.[53] The gist of her statement is that the attainment follows from the training, and is not dependent on intentions to attain that are focused on the idea of the self as the "attainer". Though the term *cetanā* does not occur in Dhammadinnā's discourse, goal-oriented reflection or purpose is indicated in the deluded thought that the self as agent strives towards attaining a certain plane of meditation.[54]

Similarly, a passage of the *Saṁyutta-nikaya* (S. III. 153-154) declares that though a *bhikkhu* who devotes himself to the cultivation of the mind (*bhāvanā*) might not experience the wish (*icchā*), "May my mind be released from the *āsavas*", in fact, by virtue of the gradual and cumulative training, his mind is released from the *āsavas*.[55] The same passage emphasizes that when a person does not train and develop the mind, mere wishing will not bring liberation from the *āsavas*. The term *cetanā* does not appear in this passage either, but the term *icchā* signifies a wish that could develop into an intention or resolve. The thrust of this passage is clearly that the purposive impetus to attain a goal is fruitless without practice, and when practice is well established, purposive impetus becomes superfluous. Three analogies are included in this passage.[56] The first is of a hen that hatches her eight, ten, or dozen eggs by sitting over them properly, providing proper warmth, and caring for them. Even though the hen may not have the thought, "May my chickens hatch safely", when the time is right, the chickens do hatch safely because the hen has done her work properly. The second is of a carpenter who knows that the handle of his axe is wearing away. Although he may not note how much of the handle is worn down each day, he clearly knows it when the handle has completely worn away. Likewise, a *bhikkhu* who devotes himself to the cultivation of the mind (*bhāvanā*) may not know to what extent the *āsavas* that bind him are removed each day, but he experiences his freedom with certainty when he is totally released from bondage. In the third analogy the gradual wearing away of mental fetters through unwavering mental training is compared to the gradual breaking down of the riggings of an abandoned ship.

Similarly, the analogy of the relay of chariots in the *Rathavinīta-sutta* (M. I. 146-151) compares the way to *nibbāna* to a king's urgent expedition, where each stage of travel prepares the conditions for the smooth attainment of the next.[57] To facilitate the king's journey, seven chariots are kept ready for him. At each stage he dismounts from one chariot and enters the next, so that the seventh chariot finally races to the goal. None of the seven chariots can claim total credit for bringing the king to his destination, yet the king would not have reached the end of his journey without the service provided by each single one of the seven chariots. The *Rathavinīta-sutta* explains that as each stage of the path to *nibbāna* is being cultivated, it provides the conditions for entry into the next. If the conditions are present, further goal-oriented impulses are not required to ensure progress; arrival at the next stage is guaranteed by the simple fact that all the steps towards it have been traversed (M. I. 150-151).

Furthermore, the analogy of the relay of chariots can be interpreted to show that the mind of each charioteer is concentrated only on the stretch of the journey for which he is responsible. Just as each chariot completes its part of the journey and allows the next to take over, similarly, each stage of the Path of liberation becomes fulfilled by making way for the next. Like the eyes of the charioteer that are focused on the stretch of the road that the wheels are covering, the mind of the disciple is concentrated on the specific discipline that is being mindfully developed. *Cetanā*, as a factor of *kamma*, is defined as a forward-looking goal-oriented function. In this sense, every purposive impulse that is not *magga-cetanā* and does not fall within the Eightfold Path can be regarded as bondage to the future. At every stage of cultivating the mind, when one discovers that there is no need for the intervention of a goal-oriented purpose, to that extent one is released from the bondage to the future that *mano-sañcetanā* as "nutriment" represents. *Bhāvanā* signifies that when each step of the journey is mindfully traversed, then the journey's end comes about through the natural course of events (*dhammatā esā*). *Nibbāna* is experienced, not as a goal to be grasped, but as the point where the goal-oriented impulse of *cetanā* comes to rest and the steps of the Path reach their final home.

Conclusion

The concept of *cetanā* in the *Sutta* literature follows from a consistently held holistic view of the mind and a commitment to the idea of conditioned origination. This chapter shows that in the *Suttas*, *cetanā* is conceived as a purposive impulse that carries the impetus to initiate action aimed at achieving that purpose. *Cetanā* can be designated as "volition" in the sense that it fulfils three functions: intending to achieve a goal, initiating bodily and mental action, and directing that action towards the goal. However, according to the *Sutta* literature, *cetanā* never functions independently but is conditioned by processes of perception (*saññā*) and discernment (*viññāṇa*) as well as by the mind's capacity to bring together mental factors and produce goal-oriented acts (*saṅkhāra*).

It is affirmed in the *Suttas* that the function of *cetanā* is complex and multifaceted. *Cetanā* is included among the factors that are considered to be necessary for the most rudimentary functioning of conscious awareness and vitality (S. II. 3-4). In the incipient stages of perception, *cetanā* directs concomitant mental states towards an object, but does not have the function of a fully developed intention. When *cetanā* functions as a motivating intention, or in other words, as a purposive impulse, it serves as the link between thought and action by rendering thought into purposive reflection and instigating action to achieve that purpose. The acts that *cetanā* produces in this way are regarded as wholesome or unwholesome intentional acts (*sañcetanika-kamma*) that entail karmic consequences.

There are no passages in the first four *Nikāyas* where *cetanā* is explicitly defined as the cognitive function of choosing between alternatives and deciding on a goal. The definition of *cetanā* given in the *Milindapañha* (Mil. 61-62) stresses the motivating function of assembling (*abhisaṅkharaṇa*) concomitant mental factors to initiate wholesome and unwholesome acts. Though this definition also attributes to *cetanā* the characteristic of purposive thought (*cetayita*), no explanation is given of precisely how the cognitive processes of purposive thought acquire the capacity to motivate and direct action. However, it is possible to extrapolate from the *Karajakāya-vagga* the idea that *cetanā/sañcetanā* functions as a motivating impulse that links intention or purposive thought with the mind's capacity to produce wholesome and unwholesome purposive acts (A.V. 288-303). The examples of acts of body, speech, and mind given in the *Karajakāya-vagga* demonstrate that the purposive impulse (*sañcetanā*) that instigates an act with karmic consequences is always supported by a specific wholesome or unwholesome attitude of mind within which purposes are formed and decisions are made.

The definition of *kamma* that the Buddha gives (A. III. 415) can be analyzed into two parts. In the first part, where the Buddha declares that he regards *cetanā* as *kamma*, no difference whatsoever is posited between *kamma* and *cetanā*. The second part, where the Buddha says that a person performs *kamma* after exercising *cetanā* (*cetayitvā*), can be taken to mean that *cetanā*, in the form of a purposive impulse, precedes and instigates acts of body, speech, and mind. Such an interpretation of the Buddhas definition of *kamma* separates *cetanā* from *kamma* and makes the purposive act the direct consequence of a purposive impulse or motivating intention. On the other hand, when acts that have commensurate consequences in the processes of *kamma* are designated as *sañcetanika kamma*, this designation can be interpreted to mean that these acts concretely express purposive impulses in such a manner that *cetanā* and *kamma* imply each other (A. V. 292-299; M. III. 209). Without *cetanā*, *kamma* would not be put forth; without *kamma*, *cetanā* would not be shown forth. In the concept of *sañcetanika-kamma*, *cetanā* and *kamma* are viewed as an integral whole.

The two terms *sañcetanika-kamma* and *saṅkhāra* equally denote a goal-oriented purposive act of body, speech, or mind that has moral value and produces karmic consequences. At the same time, these two designations differ in connotation. *Sañcetanika-kamma* signifies that the act is an expression of purposive impulse or intention. *Saṅkhāra/abhisaṅkhāra* signifies that the act is produced by a configuration of causal conditions and that the act itself, as a product, is a configuration of many physical and mental factors. This linking of *cetanā* with *saṅkhāra* entails that purposive impulses and motivating intentions (*cetanās*) are conditioned by the habit-forming tendency of *saṅkhāras*. Intentions often arise from bodily and mental habits.

The powerful effect that purposive impulses produce in the processes of *kamma* is most vividly portrayed in the notion that *mano-sañcetanā* is one of the "nutriments" in the processes of *kamma*. The concept of "nutriment" signifies that though purposive impulses impel the mind to strive for all forms of individual development and social enhancement, they also cause suffering by keeping the mind bound to future goals and aspirations. When consciousness (*viññāṇa*) is profoundly influenced by the future-oriented propulsions of *mano-sañcetanā*, it yearns to perpetuate itself and becomes a "nutriment" for rebirth.

Two sets of passages that link *cetanā* to the Eightfold Path present two different perspectives on how *cetanā* functions in relation to the continuum of consciousness (*citta*). There are passages that refer to a certain type of *cetanā*, called *magga-cetanā* in the commentaries, which actively participates in the Eightfold Path by renouncing the processes of *kamma* and turning the mind towards enlightenment. In these passages, *cetanās* are seen as factors that facilitate firm resolve and rigorous practice. The wholesome attitudes that arise in the cultivation of mindfulness and wisdom put forth purposive impulses that motivate steadfast dedication to the Eightfold Path.

Another perspective on the relationship between purposive impulses (*cetanās*) and the Eightfold Path is presented in a passage of the *Anguttara-nikāya* (A. V. 2-5). Here the motivating impetus of *cetanās* is regarded as redundant when the disciplines of the Path are cultivated step by step. The central message of this passage is that the causal conditions that are present in a certain stage of the Eightfold Path bring about entry into the next stage, whether or not there is the intervention of a motivating intention. It is posited that attitudes of mind appropriate to the Eightfold Path will follow one another when the necessary conditions come together through a firm commitment to the training, whether or not there is the intention to facilitate the arising of these attitudes. Similarly, sorrow-producing attitudes will follow one another when unwholesome mental conditions come together in the deluded and untrained continuum of consciousness, whether or not one has the intention to produce these sad and harmful states of mind. These two perspectives on *cetanā*—one that stresses the effectiveness of purposive impulses in motivating both sorrow-producing and liberating attitudes of mind, and one that stresses that wholesome and unwholesome states of mind arise in accordance with conditioned origination regardless of intentions and purposes—are interwoven throughout the *Suttas* and the *Abhidhamma* literature.

ENDNOTES

[1] Both the Theravāda tradition and modern scholarship agree that the commentaries to the first four *Nikāyas*, which were composed by Buddhaghosa in Sri Lanka during the early part of the fifth century C.E., are based on ancient commentaries that were brought from India and translated into Sīhaḷa-bhāsā. Additions to these old commentaries were made until the first century C.E. by individual teachers, whose names and exegetical opinions were preserved in the old commentaries. By summarizing and translating this old commentarial

literature, Buddhaghosa produced a commentary in Pāli for each of the first four *Nikāyas*: the *Dīgha*, the *Majjhima*, the *Saṁyutta*, and the *Aṅguttara* (A.K. Warder, *Indian Buddhism*, 322; K.R. Norman, *Pāli Literature*, 118-122; O.von Hinüber, *A Handbook of Pāli Literature*, 100-103). Although the commentaries to the first four *Nikāyas* are based on ancient sources, they show the influence of the theory of momentary *dhammas* and the *Abhidhamma* classification of physical and mental states. In some passages of the commentaries (SA. II. 78; MA. III. 104-105; AA. II. 274), *cetanā* is classified as wholesome or unwholesome exactly in accordance with the enumeration of wholesome and unwholesome *cittas* in the *Atthasālinī* and the *Visuddhimagga*. Therefore, in referring to the commentarial explanations of *Sutta* passages, one should keep in mind that the commentaries contain the influence of later theories developed in the *Abhidhamma* system.

[2] For example, it is stated that the *Tathāgata* teaches the *Dhamma* for the removal of all sorrow-producing views (*diṭṭhi*) and underlying tendencies (*anusaya*), as well as for the stilling of all *saṅkhāras* (*sabba-saṅkhāra-samathāya*) (M. I. 136). The phrase *sabba-saṅkhāra-samatho* is found at M. I. 167 and M. I. 436.

[3] For example, *saṅkhārānaṁ nirodhena n' atthi dukkhassa sambhavo* (Sn. 731).

[4] *Āyu usmāca viññāṇaṁ yadā kāyaṁ jahantimaṁ*
apaviddho tadā seti parabhattam acetanaṁ (S. III. 143).

[5] Bhikkhu Bodhi, *The Connected Discourses of the Buddha: A New Translation of the Majjhima-nikāya*, 1:953.

[6] C.A.F. Rhys Davids and F.L. Woodward, *The Book of the Kindred Sayings*, 3:121.

[7] *Cha vedanā-kāyā. Chakkhu-samphassajā vedanā, sota-samphassajā vedanā, ghāna-samphassajā vedanā, jivhā-sampassajā vedanā, kāya-samphassajā vedanā, mano-samphassajā vedanā* (D. III. 243-244).

[8] For example, *Cha sañcetanā-kāyā. Rūpa-sañcetanā, sadda-sañcetanā, gandha-sañcetanā, rasa-sañcetanā, poṭṭhabba-sañcetanā, dhamma-sañcetanā* (D. III. 244).

[9] *Avijjāpaccayā va sāmaṁ vā tam Ānanda kāya-saṅkhāram abhisaṅkharoti yaṁ paccayāssa tam uppajjati ajjhattaṁ sukha-dukkham. Pare vāssa tam Ānanda kāya-saṅkhāram abhisaṅkharonti. . . . Sampajāno vā tam Ānanda kāya-saṅkhāram abhisaṅkharoti. . . .*

Asampajāno vā tam Ānanda kāya-saṅkhāram abhisaṅkharoti. . . . (S. II. 40).

The same statement is made with regard to *vacī-saṅkhāram* and *mano-saṅkhāram.*

[10] . . . *parehi anussāhito sāmam asaṅkhārika-cittena karoti, parehi kariyamāno sasaṅkhārika-cittenā pi karoti* (SA. II. 58).

The commentary distinguishes between two cases of instigation. In one case, a person is instructed by another, but later takes the initiative and acts without being instigated. In another case, a person is caused to act by another and performs an act when prompted to do so.

[11] . . . *mātāpitusu cetiya-vandanādīni karontesu anukarontā dārakā viya kevalaṁ kammam eva jānanto imassa pana kammassa ayaṁ vipāko ti ajānanto pi karoti* (SA. II. 58).

The commentary explains *asampajāno* as a person who acts with knowledge (*jānanto*) of the deed itself but with no knowledge (*ajānanto*) of its consequences.

[12] For example, A.V. 206, A. II. 210; D. I. 70, II. 95. In all these examples *sampajānakārin* refers to a monk who guards the senses and continually remains attentive and mindful, whatever he is doing. By contrast, *asampajāno* would refer to a person who acts without paying attention, perhaps from force of habit.

[13] *Atthi bhikkhave atta-bhāva-paṭilābho yasmin atta-bhāva-paṭilābhe atta-sañcetanā kamati no parasañcetanā. . . . parasañcetanā kamati no atta-sañcetanā. . . . attasañcetanā ca kamati para-sañcetanā ca. . . . n' ev' attsañcetanā kamati no para-sañcetanā* (A. II. 159).

[14] T.W. Rhys Davids and C.A.F. Rhys Davids, *Dialogues of the Buddha,* 3:222, n. 4.

[15] A. I. 32, 224, V. 212; S. II. 99,154.

[16] *Cetanā ti tīsu dvāresu nibbattita-cetanā va gahitā. Patthanā ti 'evarūpo siyan' ti evaṁ sati patthanā. Paṇidhī ti 'devo vā bhavissāmi devaññataro vā' ti cittaṭṭhapanā* (AA. V. 69-70).

[17] *Kusalena cittena samuṭṭhitan ti. . . . Tattha patthanā paṇidhī ti cetanāy' ev' etaṁ vevacanaṁ. Kusalacetanāy' eva hi pakappayamānā patthanā ti pakappana-vasena ṭhitattā paṇidhīti ca vuccati* (Kvu.A. 110).

[18] *Kiñca bhikkhave saṅkhāre vadetha? Saṅkhatam abhisaṅkharontīti bhikkhave tasmā saṅkhārā ti vuccanti. Kiñca saṅkhatam abhisaṅkharonti? Rūpaṁ rūpattāya saṅkhatam abhisaṅkharonti, vedanaṁ vedanattāya saṅkhatam abhisaṅkharonti, saññaṁ saññattāya saṅkhatam abhisaṅkharonti, saṅkhāre saṅkhārattāya saṅkhatam abhisaṅkharonti, viññāṇaṁ viññāṇatthāya saṅkhatam abhisaṅkharonti* (S. III. 87).

[19] *. . . yathā yāgum eva yāgu' tthāya pūvam eva pūv' atthāya pacati nāma, evaṁ paccayehi samāgantvākata-bhāvena saṅkhatan ti laddha-nāmaṁ rūpam eva rūp' atthāya yathā abhisaṅkhataṁ rūpaṁ nāma hoti* (SA. II. 292).

[20] *Tathā tad-atthāya rūpa-bhāvāya abhisaṅkharoti, āyūhati, sampiṇḍeti nipphādetī ti attho* (SA. II. 292).

[21] *Ayūhati* includes in its range of meaning performing and amassing intentional acts that have karmic consequences. For example, in the *Milindapañha* (Mil. 214) it is stated that Devadatta accumulated for himself *kamma* that would endure for an aeon (*kappaṭṭhiyaṁ kammam āyūhi*). *Āyūhati* has the meaning of "to strain, to strive" in the following contexts. The *Majjhima-nikāya* (M. I. 116) says that the Buddha, when he was still a Bodhisatta practising meditation, came to the realization that excessive thought and reflection tire the body, with the result that the mind becomes strained (*kāye kilante cittaṁ ūhaññeyya*). He also realized that a straining mind is far from genuine concentration of mind (*ūhate citte ārā cittaṁ samādhimhā ti*). In the *Milindapañha* (Mil. 326), *āyūhati* appears in a sentence that describes a person striving in the path of liberation (*so appavattāya maggam āyūhati*). In the *Saṁyutta-nikāya* (S. I. 48), the Buddha says that a wise *brāhmaṇa* who has attained the end of rebirth does not strain any further (*nāyūhati pāragato hi so ti*).

[22] *Avijjāgato yaṁ bhikkhave purisapuggalo puññaṁ ce saṅkhāram abhisaṅkharoti, puññūpagaṁ hoti viññāṇam. Apuññaṁ ce saṅkhāram abhisaṅkharoti, apuññūpagaṁ hoti viññāṇam. Āneñjaṁ ce saṅkhāram abhisaṅkharoti, āneñjūpagaṁ hoti viññāṇam* (S. II. 82).

[23] *So sukhaṁ ce vedanaṁ vedayati. Sā aniccāti pajānāti, anajjhositāti pajānāti, anabhinanditāti pajānāti.*

The same statement is made with regard to a painful mental state and a mental state that is neither painful nor pleasant (S. II. 82).

[24] *Anabhisaṁkharonto anabhisañcetayanto na kiñci loke upādiyati. Anupādiyaṁ na paritassati. Aparitassaṁ paccattaññeva parinibbāyati* (S. II. 82).

[25] *Te jātisaṁvattanikesu saṅkhāresu abhiratā . . . soka-parideva-dukkha-domanassupāyāsa-saṁvattanike pi saṅkhāre abhisaṅkharonti* (S. V. 449).

[26] *Nāyaṁ bhikkhave kāyo tumhākaṁ na pi aññesam. Purāṇam idam bhikkhave kammam abhisaṅkhatam abhisañcetayitaṁ vedaniyaṁ daṭṭhabbam* (S. II. 64-65).

[27] *Cakkhuṁ bhikkhave purāṇakammam abhisaṅkhatam abhisañcetayitaṁ vedaniyaṁ daṭṭhabbam* (S. IV. 132).
The other senses are described similarly.

[28] *Abhisaṅkhatan ti paccayehi abhisamāgantvā katam: abhisañcetayitam ti cetanāya pakappitam* (SA. II. 402).

[29] The term *kara-ja* signifies "born of deeds". The epithet *karaja-kāya* refers to the body as that which is generated from past *kamma.* Always used as a pejorative expression, *karaja-kāya* refers to the idea that the body is "impure" or "unlovely"(*asubha*) (P.E.D. 195, col.2).

[30] Three unwholesome physical acts are enumerated in the *Suttas* and in the *Abhidhamma* method of classification. The *Karajakāya-vagga* describes these as deeds characterized by unwholesome intentions (*akusala-sañcetanika*). These deeds cause pain and result in pain (A. V. 292). Corresponding statements are made about the four unwholesome acts of speech and the three unwholesome mental acts.

[31] It is interesting to note that the commentarial literature prefers *pakappeti* to *saṅkappeti* in explaining *cetanā* and *ceteti.* There is a subtle difference between the two terms *pakappa* and *saṅkappa,* though there is a significant overlap in their range of meanings. In the meaning of *saṅkappa* the cognitive aspects of coming to a decision and expressing a firm intention or strong resolve is predominant. In the meaning assigned to *pakappa,* the planning of action to actualize the purpose that is formed in the mind comes to the fore. *Pakappa* is closer than *saṅkappa* to the idea of gathering, arranging, and preparing one's resources and moving them towards a goal. *Ceteti, pakappeti,* and *anuseti* appear together at S. II. 65-67.

[32] J.P. McDermott, *Developments in the Early Buddhist Concept of Kamma/Karma*, 132-133.

[33] S.N. Dube, *Cross Currents in Early Buddhism*, 336.

[34] In the *Points of Controversy*, the translators S.Z. Aung and C.A.F. Rhys Davids render *upacaya* as "conservation of karmic energy" (301). Guenther interprets *kammūpacaya* as the "heaping up" of potential energy and *kamma-vipāka* as the development of this potential energy towards the putting forth of commensurate consequences of pleasure and pain (H.V. Guenther, *Philosophy and Psychology in the Abhidharma*, 19-20). The *Points of Controversy* clarifies the central issue in the debate. The Theravādins maintain that the position of the opponents is untenable for the following reason. The opponents agree with the Theravādins that both *kamma* and the fruition of *kamma* are coexistent with consciousness (*citta*) and are dependent on a mental object in order to come into effect. However, they then proceed to hold that *upacaya* is dissociated (*vippayutta*) from consciousness, does not arise in relation to an object (*anārammaṇa*), and functions by its own energy (Kvu. 158). The Theravādins conclude that there is no difference between *kamma* and the accumulation of *kamma*. *Tena hi na vattabbaṁ "Aññaṁ kammaṁ añño kammūpacayo ti"* (Kvu. 522).

[35] *Saṁcetanasamāptibhyām niṣkaukṛtya vipakṣataḥ*
Parivārādvipākācca karmopacitamucyate. (Abhk. IV.120)

[36] *katham saṁcetanaḥ? saṁcintya kṛtam bhavati nābuddhipūrvam, na sahasā kṛtam* (Abhk. IV.120).

The verb *saṁcintayati* signifies "to think about, think over, consider carefully, reflect about", as well as "to design, intend" (S.E.D. 1132, col. 2). *Nābuddhipūrvam* conveys that the act is not done hastily (*na sahasā kṛtam*), without prior thought. The term *buddhi* indicates intelligence and rational thinking.

[37] . . . *kasmā aññesu pi sattānaṁ paccayesu vijjamānesu ime yeva cattāro vuttā ti? Vuccate: Ajjhattika-santatiyā visesa paccayattā* (SA. II. 25).

[38] *annād vai prajāḥ prajāyante, yāḥ kāś ca pṛthivīm śritāḥ, atho' nnenaiva jīvanti, athainadapi yanty antataḥ* (T.U. II. 2.1).

[39] Thera Nyanaponika, *The Four Nutriments of Life*, 12-13.

[40] Ibid., 49, n.8.

[41] C.A.F. Rhys Davids, *A Buddhist Manual of Psychological Ethics*, 241, n. 1.

[42] Thera Nyanaponika, *The Four Nutriments of Life*, 49, n.8. In the *Visuddhimagga* (Vsm. XVII. 296), existence (*bhava*) is divided into two aspects: the *kamma*-forming process (*kamma-bhava*) and the *kamma*-formed rebirth process (*upapatti-bhava*) (Chart 14). The *kamma*-forming process is the cause, and the *karma*-formed process is the effect. Acts of body, mind and speech characterized by merit and demerit are performed in the *kamma*-forming process, resulting in the accumulation of *kamma*. When consciousness is conditioned by *mano-sañcetanā* and functions as nutriment, it can be regarded as the factor that takes the leading role in the *kamma*-forming process.

[43] *Kammaṁ khettan ti kusalākusala-kammaṁ virūhanaṭṭhānaṭṭhena khettaṁ. . . . Viññāṇaṁ bījan ti sahajātam abhisaṅkhāra-viññāṇaṁ virūhanaṭṭhena bījam. . . . Viññāṇaṁ patiṭṭhitan ti abhisaṅkhāra-viññāṇaṁ patiṭṭhitam* (AA. II. 334).

The notion of *abhisaṅkhāra-viññāṇa* shows that Theravāda does not perceive consciousness to be self-supporting and self-perpetuating, but regards it as a process that invariably requires an object or "basis" (*ārammaṇam*) that supports it and guarantees its perpetuation. Consciousness is always in the making, and intentions and purposes arising in the mind (*mano-sañcetanā*) guarantee its continuance by providing it with objects of interest and goals to be pursued. The term *patiṭṭhitam* (supported, established) is not only related to *ṭithi* but also to *patiṭṭhā*. The former term conveys "continuity" or "persistence", and the latter term indicates "support, resting place, stay, ground, help" (P.E.D. p. 405, col. 2). *Patiṭṭhitam* conveys the sense of continuing to exist by being supported.

[44] *Iti kho Ānanda kammaṁ khettaṁ viññāṇaṁ bījaṁ taṇhā sineho avijjā-nīvaraṇānaṁ sattānaṁ taṇhā-saṁyojanānaṁ hīnāya dhātuyā cetanā patiṭṭhitā patthanā patiṭṭhitā. Evam āyatiṁ punabbavābhinibbatti hoti* (A. I. 224).

The same statement is repeated with *majjhimā dhātu* and *paṇītā dhātu*.

[45] Nyanatiloka, *Buddhist Dictionary: Manual of Buddhist Terms and Doctrines*, 34, 157.

[46] The *Milindapañha* was probably shorter in its original form and was composed, not in Pāli, but perhaps in Gāndhārī (O.von Hinüber, *A Handbook of Pāli Literature*, 83). It is usually held that the *Milindapañha* is a composite text,

of which the earliest part was compiled between 100 B.C.E. and 200 C.E. (Ibid., 85), while the latest part must have been completed by the fifth century since it is quoted by Buddhaghosa (K.R. Norman, *Pāli Literature*, 110-111). The *Milindapañha* is included among the texts of the *Khuddaka-nikāya* in the Burmese tradition, but this is not the case in Sri Lanka. The material contained in the Chinese translation is regarded as the earliest .section of the *Milindapañha*. The definition of *cetanā* is found in this section (O. von Hinüber, *A Handbook of Pāli Literature*, 84).

[47] *Pahānāya yā cetanā ti ettha vivaṭṭagāminī maggacetanā veditabbā; sā hi kammakkhayāya saṁvattatī ti.* (AA. III. 213), *magga-cetanā akaṇha-asukkā ti āgatā* (MA. III. 105).

[48] The passage at A. V. 2-4 begins as follows:
Sīlavato bhikkhave sīlasampannassa na cetanāya karaṇīyam 'avippaṭisāro me uppajjatu' ti. Dhammatā esā bhikkhave, yaṁ sīlavato sīlasampannassa avippaṭisāro uppajjati (A. V. 2.).

The entire passage is repeated at A. V. 312-313. It is quoted in the *Nettippakaraṇa* (Nt. 144) with the following changes: *na cetanā karaṇīyā* for *na cetanāya karaṇīyam* and *jāyeyya* for *uppajjatu*.

[49] L.S. Cousins, A. Kunst, and K.R. Norman, *Buddhist Studies in Honour of I.B. Horner*, 184.

[50] *Iti kho bhikkhave dhammā ' va dhamme abhisandenti, dhammā ' va dhamme paripūrenti, aparā pāraṁ gamanāyā ti* (A. V. 3-4).

Whereas the verb *abhisandenti* (literally, "to cause to overflow") signifies that the effect is the "outflow" or outcome of the cause, the verb *paripūrenti* conveys that the effect is the development and completion or fulfilment of the set of conditions that constitute the cause.

[51] . . . *na cetanāya karaṇīyaṁ ti na cetetvā kappetvā pakappetvā kātabbam* (AA. V. 1).

[52] The commentary to the *Dīgha-nikāya* (DA. II. 432) explains *citta-niyama* with the statement that each mental factor conditions the arising of the immediately following mental factor. It is posited that mental factors do not arise in a random fashion but follow one another in accordance with conditioned origination. The commentary says: *Purimā purimā citta-cetasikā dhammā pacchimānaṁ pacchimānaṁ citta-cetasikānaṁ dhammānaṁ upanissaya-paccayena paccayo ti.* Each mental factor that goes before becomes the supporting

condition for a mental factor that follows. In this way, conditioned origination becomes the governing principle in the continuum of consciousness.

Jayatilleke seeks to establish that Theravāda Buḍdhism makes a distinction between causation in the physical realm and in the psychological realm (K.N. Jayatilleke, *Early Buddhist Theory of Knowledge*, 453-454). According to his interpretation, the order of things (*dhammatā*) can only indicate "a probability and not a necessity" where psychological states are concerned. However, the inclusion of *citta-niyama* among the five types of ordered processes in the commentary to the *Dīgha-nikāya* conveys that causal uniformity applies equally to physical and mental processes.

[53] . . . *atha khvāssa pubbe va tathā cittaṁ bhāvitaṁ hoti yam-taṁ tathattāya upanetīti* (M. I. 301).

This passage indicates that the *citta* naturally attains to that state for which it has been previously prepared.

[54] *Na kho . . . saññā-vedayita-nirodhaṁ samāpajjantassa bhikkhuno evaṁ hoti: ahaṁ saññā-vedayita-nirodhaṁ samāpajjissan-ti vā, ahaṁ saññā-vedayita-nirodhaṁ samāpajjāmīti vā, ahaṁ saññā-vedayita-nirodhaṁ samāpanno ti vā. . . .* (M. I. 301).

[55] *Bhāvanānuyogam anuyuttassa bhikkhave bhikkuno viharato kiñcāpi na evam icchā uppajjeya Aho vata me anupādāya āsavehi cittaṁ vimucceyyā ti. Atha kvāssa anupādāya āsavehi cittaṁ vimuccati* (S. III. 153-154).

[56] The same *sutta* with the three analogies occurs at A. IV. 125-127.

[57] The *Rathavinīta-sutta* (M. I. 145-151) is cast in the form of a dialogue between one of the Buddha's most advanced disciples, Sāriputta, who often appears in the role of instructor to other monks, and another much respected monk, Puṇṇa Mantāṇiputta, described as one who is skilled in instructing and motivating his companions. This *sutta* is described as a skilful dialogue between two "great beings" (*mahā-nāga*) enjoying each other's understanding of the *Dhamma*.

Chapter V
Dynamics of Motivation in the *Suttas*

In this chapter, four perspectives on the dynamics of motivation are extrapolated from the *Sutta* literature, and the modes of functioning of *citta*, *cetanā*, and *saṅkhāra* are explored within these perspectives. The first of these perspectives focuses on "motivational sequences" in the *Suttas*. Rune Johansson has shown in *The Dynamic Psychology of Early Buddhism* that the *Sutta* literature often describes motivation as a gradual process where each stage is marked by an attitude of mind that provides the motivating conditions for the emergence of the next stage. I refer to his interpretation in order to demonstrate that in the *Suttas*, volition is described as a purposive impetus that invariably emerges from a specific attitude of mind. One does not find in the *Sutta* literature a concept of volition that suggests a self-generating motivating energy. On the contrary, volition and the cognitive and emotive processes within which it is formed are shown to be mutually conditioning factors of the continuum of consciousness.

A second perspective on motivation comes from passages in the *Suttas* that view wholesome motivation as a struggle against unwholesome attitudes that prevail in the mind. The vivid imagery of heroically striving "against the current" suggests that the *Suttas* endorse the view that volition indeed is a controlling process that can change the orientation of the intellect and control emotions. However, an investigation of the passages where this notion of striving against the current is enunciated reveals that wholesome motivation becomes efficacious only when it is supported by the disciplines of the Eightfold Path and by a wholesome lifestyle that fits the personality and needs of the disciple. It is obvioius that wholesome motivation prevails against the unwholesome only because it "flows with the current" of the Eightfold Path. In the final analysis, therefore, these passages confirm the interpretation that regards volition in the *Suttas* to be a mental process that is conditioned by attitudes of mind that arise from the interplay of cognitive, emotive, and conative factors.

A third perspective on the *Sutta* view of volition is based on the discourses on the cultivation of mindfulness (*satipaṭṭhāna*). Mindfulness as a method of transforming the mind is based, not on evoking a controlling "conscience" or a sovereign "will", but on the affirmation that the mind has the capacity to observe its own present contents and to reflect on past processes. The practice of mindfulness confirms the view that in the *Suttas*, consciousness is regarded as an organic whole that can assess its own processes and bring about internal changes and adjustments.

A fourth perspective focuses on the motivating capacity attributed to understanding (*paññā*). Not only is understanding defined as intellectual acumen and judgment that can develop into liberating wisdom, but it is also regarded as having the impetus to rouse energy (*viriya*) and initiate goal-oriented action. The concept of *paññā* shows that cognition and volition are regarded as mutually conditioning processes in the *Suttas*. It follows that cognitive factors, such as attention (*manasikāra*), perception (*saññā*), and view (*diṭṭhi*) are seen to be capable of motivating action.

Motivational Sequences in the *Suttas*

In *The Dynamic Psychology of Early Buddhism*, Rune Johansson shows that in the *Suttas*, motivation is regarded as a causal process where one mental state motivates the next in accordance with conditioned origination, leading gradually to the goal.[1] He does not, however, focus on the question of what role is to be assigned to volition within a sequence of conditioned states. More specifically, since *cetanās* are regarded as purposive impulses carrying the impetus to initiate action, the relevant question is how they can function in a motivational process governed by conditioning. Johansson's interpretation of motivation in the *Suttas* is based on his view that all forms of motivation can be reduced to "needs" that are experienced in different dimensions of life.[2] His notion of motivational sequences implies that while each stage fulfils some of the needs that are experienced in the previous stages, it also sets up further needs that impel the process forward. Although Johansson has clearly demonstrated that in the *Suttas* motivation is regarded as a cumulative process where each stage is marked by a further development of what has gone before, his theory that all forms of motivation are driven by needs poses problems. His view that motivation is invariably based on needs does not neatly correlate with what is said in the *Suttas* about the motivating role of mindfulness (*sati*), systematic attention (*yoniso-manasikāra*), and understanding (*paññā*).

Following Johansson's line of argument that all motivation is ultimately driven by experiences of needs, one could interpret mindfulness and wisdom as motivational factors that arise out of experiences of insufficiency, frustration, and many-sided sorrow in daily life. Mindfulness and wisdom would then be viewed as motivational factors that arise from psychological needs, proceed to function as stimuli that set up physical and emotional tensions, and finally, motivate action to alleviate those needs. However, such an interpretation would be flawed. The *Satipaṭṭhāna-sutta* shows that *sati* and *paññā* do not intensify a sense of need. On the contrary, they bring about a re-examination and re-evaluation of experiences of need, lack, desire, and craving. The theory of motivation through needs on which Johansson bases his analysis assumes that the disciplines of the Eightfold Path are developed through skilful fulfilment of needs.

Furthermore, Johansson's view implies that the cultivation of the mind (*bhāvanā*) through mindfulness, calming, and wisdom proceeds along the same route as a mundane (*lokiya*) way of life, which is governed by goal-oriented purposive impulses (*mano-sañcetanā*) and the desire or need to fulfil them through purposive acts (*saṅkhāras*). However, the standard motivational sequences that demonstrate the steps leading to liberation point to a stage when the cultivation of virtue (*sīla*), meditation, and mindfulness leads to a sense of disenchantment (*nibbidā*) and dispassion (*virāga*) towards worldly objects (Charts 1 and 2). Non-attachment to objects and goals must include a reassessment of the intentions and purposive impulses (*cetanā*) that cause a person to form future goals and make them the focus of one's life. Renunciation requires a profound re-examination of all motivation, including wholesome motivation and ethically good purposive impulses. Renunciation, therefore, differs greatly from unexamined rejection and deluded repulsion. *Nibbidā* and *virāga* signify not only renunciation of unwholesome purposive impulses (*akusala-sañcetanā*), but renunciation of development through the fulfilment of needs that are based on desires and attachment to goals. Liberation is a mode of life that is characterized as "not dependent on forming goal-oriented deeds" (*asaṅkhata*) and "not based on acts motivated by purposive impulses" (*asañcetayita*).

One example of a motivational series that Johansson outlines[3] is taken from the *Aṅguttara-nikāya* (Chart 3). The first part of this passage (A. I. 264-265) describes the series of motivational conditions that produces acts with karmic consequences. The second part describes another type of motivational sequence that is opposed to the first. In the second case, wise understanding (*paññā*) ends attachment to objects, with the result that they not longer bring about deeds that entail karmic consequences. In the first part, the motive is passionate desire (*chanda-rāga*) for things. The Buddha explains that when a person ponders over (*anuvitakketi*) and repeatedly contemplates (*anuvicāreti*) objects that are greatly desired, then the impetus to act (*chanda*) arises and causes a person to become attached to these things (*tehi dhammehi saññutto hoti*). In this manner, an act with karmic consequences is shown to be initiated through a sequence of motivational conditions. In the second case, wholesome behaviour is motivated by understanding (*paññā*), which is said to arise from insight into the bitter consequences of pursuing objects of desire. The Buddha explains that insight causes a person to withdraw from objects of sensual desire, to feel no attachment towards them, to re-evaluate them through understanding, and to see them as impermanent configurations of conditionally arisen factors.

A detailed unwholesome motivational sequence is presented in the *Madhupiṇḍika-sutta* (Chart 4). The discourse at M. I. 109-110 begins with the statement that quarrels and violence is incited by the arousal of persistent unwholesome tendencies (*anusayas*). The Buddha goes on to say succinctly that these *anusayas* become manifest because a person enjoys, welcomes, and adheres to the causes that give rise to ideas and perceptions that provide the impetus for the mind to proliferate concepts (*papañca-saññā-saṅkhā*). Later, a senior monk, Mahākacchāna, gives the following detailed picture of the sequence of mental processes that lead to quarrels and violence. When the eye, "visual consciousness" or the capacity to see, and a visual object come together in a process of sensory stimulation, there is visual perception, followed by a feeling of pleasure, pain, or neither pleasure nor pain. When one feels (*vedeti*) something, one then perceives (*sañjānāti*) the object that caused the feeling, and proceeds to think (*vitakketi*) about it. Concepts and images of the visual object that preoccupies a person begin to diversify and grow in the mind, so that images of that same visual object as it was in the past, as it will be in the future, and as it presently exists, begin to obsess the mind. The whole process leads to attachment to the object, the desire to possess it, consequent quarrels, and violence. The *Madhupiṇḍika-sutta* maintains that the same motivational sequence with the same violent conclusion can occur with regard to the objects of the other sense organs and mental objects (M. I. 111-112).

This motivational series in the *Madhupiṇḍika-sutta* is significant because here the Buddha addresses the social and political violence that he witnessed around him. The narrative portions of the *Nikāyas*, especially the *Mahāparinibbāna-sutta* (D. II. 71-84), show that the Buddhist *Saṅgha* came into existence in the midst of political conflict and social unrest.[4] In the *Madhupiṇḍika-sutta* the Buddha makes the point that desire to acquire objects, coupled with a language of aggression based on the mind's craving to multiply concepts, ideas, and mental images, leads in gradual stages to cycles of personal and social violence.

A motivational series in the *Saṁyutta-nikāya* (S. II. 143-149), like the one in the *Madhupiṇḍika-sutta*, stresses the influence of the cognitive processes of the mind (such as the tendency to proliferate concepts) on the mind's capacity to initiate action (Chart 5). In the *Saṁyutta-nikāya* the Buddha maintains that the mind's desire to experience a greater and greater diversity (*nānattam*) of objects is the impetus that causes people to constantly increase their feverish quests for more and more possessions. This motivational series has the following stages: the diversity of elements (*dhātus*) in the natural universe leads to a diversity of perceptions and ideations, (*saññā-nānattam*); based on this diversity of perceptions, there arises a diversity of intentions or purposive thoughts (*saṅkappa-nānattam*); based on the diversity of intentions, there arises a diversity of action-oriented impulses (*chanda-nānattam*); based on the diversity of the impulses to act, there arises a diversity of feverish passions (*pariḷāha-nānattam*); and based on the diversity of obsessive passions, there arises a diversity of quests for objects (*pariyesanā-nānattam*). This motivational series that focuses attention on the diversity of passionate human quests for diverse objects is also found in the *Digha-nikāya* (D. III. 289). The *Saṁyutta-*

nikāya emphasizes that the sequential order of factors in this motivational series cannot be reversed (S. II. 144-145) because each factor "arises by depending on" the previous factor (*paṭicca uppajjati*). The repetition of the term *paṭicca* at each stage of the series by both the *Saṁyutta-nikāya* and the *Dīgha-nikāya* alerts the reader that this motivational sequence is to be linked to the definition of conditioned origination given in the *Nidāna-saṁyutta* (S. II. 25-26). Furthermore, the use of the term *paṭicca* (dependent on, conditioned by) with each factor of a motivational sequence reveals how deeply the concept of conditioned origination penetrates the psychological concepts in the Pāli texts. It should also be noted that when conditioned origination is affirmed, these motivational factors in the motivational sequences cannot be regarded as acting singly; in fact, each must be viewed as the most obvious condition in a configuration of mental conditions that constitutes a specific stage in a process of motivation.

These examples of motivational sequences leave unanswered the question why *cetanā* does not occur among the motivating factors. From the *Abhidhamma* perspective, this question is answered by pointing out that in the *Abhidhamma* lists of mental states, *cetanā* is placed among the rudimentary mental constituents that are present in all states of mind (*cittas*). According to the *Abhidhamma* system, *cetanā* functions in all *cittas* by coordinating concomitant mental factors (*cetasikas*), energizing them, and directing their functions towards a chosen goal. It follows then that from an *Abhidhamma* perspective, *cetanā* is present in every motivational factor in a motivational sequence as an action-initiating purposive impetus. By extrapolating from passages that refer to how *cetanās* arise and function, the inference can be drawn that in the *Suttas* also it is implied (though not overtly stated, as in the *Abhidhamma* literature) that *cetanā* is present as a component in every motivational factor. It was noted in Chapter IV that *cetanā* is regarded in the *Suttas* as a mental function that arises from the matrix of sensory and mental stimulation. It can be inferred that *cetanās* arise in a motivational sequence whenever there is contact (*phassa*) between the consciousness continuum and a sensory or mental object.

Cetanā does not appear as a separate motivational factor in any motivational sequence because it is not the function of *cetanā* to introduce a new thought or emotion into the motivational process. The function of *cetanā* is to give dynamic impetus to the thoughts and emotions that occur in motivational sequence by putting forth a purposive impulse that corresponds to their cognitive or affective features. In this way *cetanā* provides the purposive thrust that directs all the motivating factors in a motivational sequence towards the goal that the mind has chosen.

Furthermore, it is stated in the *Suttas* that intention (*cetanā*), aspiration (*patthanā*), and resolve (*paṇidhi*) arise and function within a universe of experience permeated by a specific world-view (*diṭṭhi*). There are two passages in the *Aṅguttara-nikāya* (A. I. 32, V. 212) where the argument is made that the world-view that a person holds casts its influence on intentions, aspirations, resolves, and all acts of body, speech, and mind. According to the interpretation of the Eightfold Path given in these two passages, the cognitive features of right view function as motivating factors that impel and direct a person to follow all the aspects of the Path. Right acts of body, speech, and mind (*kāya-kammam*, *vacī-kammam*, *mano-kammam*) are regarded as a fitting completion and fulfilment in concrete acts of the cognitive content of right view (*yathā-diṭṭhi-samattam samādinnam*). Conversely, wrong view is regarded as the primary motivating factor that leads to wrong acts of body, speech, and mind. The *cetanā*, *patthanā*, and *paṇidhi* that arise from the motivating influence of wrong view are described as leading to harmful and painful consequences. It follows that the motivational sequences described in this chapter must be viewed as processes that are further subject to conditioning by a person's view of the world.

Motivational Processes and the "Inclination of the Mind"

In other passages of the *Suttas*, motivational processes are depicted as a gradual inclining of the mind, stage by stage, towards a certain mode of behaviour. The phrase *cittaṁ namati* (the mind inclines or "bends") conveys the idea that motivation is a process of causing the entire mind to incline gradually towards a specific goal by providing conditions that are conducive to that inclination. The passages that refer to the "inclining" of the mind suggest that the inclination is often towards that which is more comfortable and less arduous (S. I. 137), or towards the fine things enjoyed by the senses (S. I. 92; A. IV. 392). On the other hand, it is affirmed that the mind inclines towards wholesome renunciation (*nekkhamma-ninnam*) when it is cleansed of the blemishes arising from attachment to sensory gratification (S. III. 232). When liberation from the unwholesome motivations of the *āsavas* is finally attained, the bent of the mind is towards seclusion (*viveka-ninnam cittaṁ hoti*), even when the liberated one dwells among a crowd of people (D. III. 283; A. IV. 233, V. 175). It is assumed that in the cases of both wholesome and unwholesome motivation, the direction in which the mind bends is dependent on the conditions that come together in the motivational process.

An example of wholesome bending of the mind is found in the *Caṅkī-sutta* (M. II. 171-174). In this passage the Buddha delineates the motivational stages by which an exemplary householder proceeds on the Path of liberation from sorrow. The householder chooses a teacher in the following way. He first studies (*samannesati*) that teacher carefully to make sure that he is free from greed (*lobha*), enmity (*dosa*), and delusion (*moha*). Having gained confidence in the purity of the teacher's character, the householder places faith (*saddhā*) in the teacher. He then listens to the teaching, remembers it, examines the meaning of the teaching, and finds pleasure in understanding its contents. Then zeal arises in him (*chandaṁ jāyati*), and he exerts himself (*ussahati*), examines (*tuleti*) the teaching, and strives (*padahati*) until he attains wisdom (*paññā*). The passage goes on to emphasize that the conditions present at each stage greatly serve (*bahu-kāra*) the arising of the next stage. It is said that in the course of the training, an understanding of the teaching does much (*bahu-kāra*) for the arising of the impetus to act (*chanda*), and the latter greatly aids the exertion of energy (*ussāha*). Energetic striving is very helpful for careful examination of the teaching (*tulanā*), and such investigation of the teaching does much to support intense striving (*padhāna*). Although there is a great deal of emphasis on sustained striving in this motivational sequence, the way to wisdom is not presented as a heroic struggle where volition plays the major role. Each stage facilitates and supports the arising of the next and, at the same time, becomes a fulfilment and culmination of all that goes before. At each stage the mind affirms and acquiesces in the process, and is transformed in such a way that its inclination is "naturally" towards wisdom. Energetic striving is not presented as the driving force in the motivational process, but as a conditioned factor that arises in conjunction with sustained and thoughtful examination and assessment of the teachings.

A typical example of a motivational sequence where the mind gradually inclines towards an unwholesome goal is given in the *Dīgha-nikāya* (D. III. 289) and is again repeated in the *Aṅguttara-nikāya* (A. IV. 400-401). This motivational sequence demonstrates how craving (*taṇhā*) urges a person to seek after and acquire goods and property, causing the mind to incline, stage by stage, towards conflict and violence (Chart 6). In the motivational series presented here, acquisition leads to processes of decision-making concerning one's possessions; these decisions become occasions for the arising of passionate desire (*chanda-raga*); and desire for objects is followed by attachment to one's possessions. Avarice and arrangements to safeguard one's goods follow in quick sequence, and the final outcome is conflict and violence in the course of protecting one's acquisitions. Again, the terminology of conditioned origination is evident in this passage, and each stage is described as arising by depending on (*paṭicca*) the one previous to it. It is implied that if any of the conditions is changed, the motivational sequence will move in a different direction.

These passages from the *Sutta* literature do not describe motivation as a process where either the intellect or emotions or volition play the dominant role in directing the personality. On the contrary, both wholesome and unwholesome motivations are described as processes where the entire mind is shown to incline (*namati*), stage by stage, towards a specific goal. The *Saṁyutta-nikāya* says that a *bhikkhu* who purifies and cultivates the mind inclines, slopes, and leans towards *nibbana* (*nibbāna-ninno, nibbāna-poṇo, nibbāna-pabbhāro*), just as the River Gaṅgā flows towards the east (S. V. 239, 244, 290, 307-308). At each stage, discursive thoughts, emotional attitudes, and conative energies condition each other in such a way that the entire mind comes to be in accord with the goal. The goal exerts a teleological "pull" on the mind and determines the direction in which the mind "bends". At the same time, it is the impulsion experienced at every stage that carries the process forward. The wholesome motivational sequences show that the Eightfold Path is conceived as a *sādhanā*, that is to say, a "method" through which a goal is accomplished. While the goal gives purpose to the motivational process as a whole, each stage has its own significance because it is both the culmination of the previous stages and the indispensable method through which the next stage is attained. Each stage marks a recapitulation of what has gone before, a renewal of energy, and the coming together of the conditions for reaching the next stage.

Motivation That Goes "Against the Current"

Unlike the motivational sequences, which depict the activating and directing of behaviour as a "natural" process where each stage produces the next in accordance with conditioned origination, there are other passages in the *Suttas* (for example, M. I. 168; S. I. 136; A. II. 5) where the emphasis is on the expending of energy towards a goal that is in sharp contrast to one's bent of mind. The idea that the practice of the Buddha's teachings goes against ordinary motivations that focus on thoughts of "I" and "my world" is illustrated in the imagery of a person "going upstream" and "moving against the current" (*paṭisota-gāmī*).[5] In such contexts, *chanda* (impetus to act), *viriya* (energy), and *padhāna* (striving, exertion) are the preferred terms to convey the struggle against the unwholesome impulses that prevail in the mind. The meaning of these terms does not focus on the cognitive features of purposive reflection or intention, but emphasizes the application of conative energy to initiate and direct action.

Of all the Pāli terms signifying conation, *chanda* is the one that covers the widest range and comes most readily to mind as the equivalent of "initiation of action". In a basic sense, *chanda* signifies the excitation or stimulation of the entire *citta.* C.A.F. Rhys Davids gave much importance to the fact that *cetanā, saṅkappa*, and *chanda* can function either as wholesome or as unwholesome motivational impulses. She designated them as factors of basic conation and pointed out that these motivational factors are clearly distinguished in the *Tipiṭaka* from craving (*taṇhā*). Johansson takes the same approach to these terms by describing them as "neutral" motivational factors that function in a wholesome manner in a wholesome motivational process, and in an unwholesome manner when they are conditioned by unwholesome factors. When *chanda* represents an unwholesome state of mind, its closest equivalent is *rāga* (passion) or *kāma* (desire). Unwholesome *chanda* becomes associated with *dosa* (aversion), *moha* (delusion), and *bhaya* (fear) to form four motives for wrong ways of behaviour (*agati-gamana*) (D. III. 228; A. II. 18). Unwholesome *chanda* is *asmīti chanda*, which indicates impulse to act based on the notion of "I" as an autonomous self (S. III. 131).

As a virtue, *chanda* manifests in the form of wholesome zeal directed towards what is good and right (*kusala dhamma-chanda*) (A. III. 441). Qualified by the adjective *tibba* (keen, eager), *chanda* represents the keen aspiration of a *bhikkhu* to cultivate higher virtue, higher thought, and higher insight (A. I. 229). "Right effort" (*sammā-vāyāma*), an aspect of the Eightfold Path, is defined as applying energy against the stubborn inclinations of a mind that is motivated by the unwholesome mental states called the "defilements" (*kilesas*). It is often repeated in the *Suttas* that a person who cultivates right effort generates zeal (*chandaṁ janeti*) and puts forth energy (*viriyam ārabhati*) by exerting the mind and striving (*padahati*) to fulfil four purposes: preventing the arising of unwholesome states, overcoming unwholesome states that have already arisen, producing wholesome states that have not yet arisen, and nourishing the wholesome states that are beginning to arise (D. III. 221; A. II. 15; S. V. 269). The imagery of striving mightily against the current and the description of "right effort" in the Eightfold Path signify the putting forth of powerful zeal and the exertion of heroic energy through volitional acts that counteract the defilements of the mind. However, the exertion of energy to renounce unwholesome states is set in the context of the Eightfold Path and is supported by "right view" (*sammā-dhiṭṭhi*) and "right resolve" (*sammā-saṅkappa*). Right effort goes against the defilements (*kilesas*) in the mind precisely because it is in harmony with the Eightfold Path. In this sense, right effort is conditioned by all the other aspects of the training. Although it goes against the current of the defilements, it goes along with the current of the Eightfold Path. In this context, right effort is seen as a wholesome condition within a larger process of conditioning that inclines the mind towards the disciplines and goals of the Eightfold Path.

It follows that the notion of "striving against the current" must be qualified by the following considerations. According to the Middle Way of the Buddha, to be fruitful (*saphala*), striving must be balanced with a clear, serene sense of purpose (M. II. 223-225). Furthermore, when conditioned origination is affirmed, sheer striving cannot be regarded as the sufficient condition for achieving the goal. On the contrary, determined effort should be viewed as one of a set of necessary conditions. Finally, it is significant that in a poem that opens the *Saṁyutta-nikāya* (S. I. 1), the Buddha says that he crosses the flood without holding on to supports (*appatiṭṭham*) and without striving for goals (*anāyūham*). Striving is fruitful when it moves towards the goal of "non-striving".

The term *viriya* is widely used in the *Suttas* to signify vigorous effort or energy. In the *Saṁyutta-nikāya*, the factors regarded as essential in the training of a *bhikkhu* are *yoga* (discipline, uninterrupted practice), *chanda* (enthusiasm, zeal), *ussoḷhi* (exertion), *appaṭivāni* (not turning back), *ātappa* (ardour), *viriya* (energy), *sātacca* (perseverance), *sati* (mindfulness), *sampajañña* (clear comprehension or discernment), and *appamāda* (vigilance, carefulness) (S. II. 131-132). Similarly, in the *Majjhima-nikāya*, the true disciple is described as steadfast in persevering, capable of steady striving, and not one to shrink from responsibility in cultivating wholesome states (M. I. 356). The term *ārabbha-vatthu* signifies an occasion when one should exert and make the following resolve: "Let me put forth energy to attain what has not been attained, to achieve what has not been achieved, to realize what has not been realized" (D. III. 256 = A. IV. 334-335).[6] *Viriya* is defined as the quality of the hero (*vīra*), and the one who has attained enlightenment is called a *mahāvīra* (S. III. 83).

Although the call to put forth energy is continually heard in the *Suttas*, there are passages where the Buddha explains that the application of energy can be successful in overcoming unwholesome mental states only when it is supported by wholesome conditions and wholesome attitudes of mind. For example, when the *bhikkhu* Meghiya is troubled by thoughts of sensual pleasure, hatred, and cruelty, the Buddha tells him that five wholesome conditions liberate the minds of those who are beginners in the monastic training: seeking out a good friend (*kalyāṇa-mitta*), living by the precepts and restraints of monastic life, helpful discussion, putting forth energy (*āraddha viriya*), and cultivating wisdom (A. IV. 357). Similarly, the *Anaṅgaṇa-sutta* explains at length that the attitude of mind and lifestyle of a person should be free from the hold of deceit, carelessness, laziness, lethargy, and lack of concentration, if energy is to be efficaciously applied in pursuing the disciplines of the Eightfold Path (M. I. 32). According to this teaching, the arduous effort of overcoming the unwholesome cannot be effective unless it is supported by one's entire way of life.

"Subduing the Mind by the Mind"

Theravāda Buddhism shares with the Upaniṣadic, Jaina, and Yoga traditions the unwavering confidence that it is possible, through sustained training, to cause unwholesome mental states to cease and to develop wholesome attitudes. In the *Aṅguttara-nikāya*, the Buddha assures his disciples that one can indeed rid oneself of the unwholesome[7] and cultivate the wholesome.[8] He tells them that he would not expect them to embark on an impossible or futile quest (A. I. 58). At the same time, the Theravāda tradition leaves the disciple with no illusions regarding the sheer magnitude of the effort called for in purifying and cultivating the mind. This section of the *Aṅguttara-nikāya* presents to the student, as a model of the determined exertion required, the Bodhisatta's vow that he will not rise from his seat of meditation with his goal unattained, even if the nerves and sinews of his body wither away. The Bodhisatta's quest is shown to be driven by a twofold effort: not to rest content with wholesome states that already have been attained and not to turn back from the effort of attaining the goal (A. I. 50).[9] The process of removing unwholesome mental states and cultivating wholesome factors is compared to the patient and skilful stages by which gold is refined (A. I. 253-254).

Although for the most part the cultivation of the mind through the disciplines of the Eightfold Path is seen as a gradual process, like a tree bearing fruit (A. IV. 99) or like small mountain streams gathering to form the rivers that swell the ocean (A. V. 115-116), there are other passages in the *Suttas* where the emphasis is on subduing a rebellious mind immediately, solely by means of relentless effort. The *Vitakkasaṇṭhāna-sutta* (M. I. 118-122) offers the following ways of dealing with thoughts rooted in greed (*lobha*), hatred (*dosa*), and delusion (*moha*). The first is a strategy of substitution whereby a person focuses attention on something that is wholesome until unwholesome thoughts cease to trouble the mind. If substitution does not work, the next method is to examine the danger that arises from unwholesome thoughts. If this investigation of the sorrowful consequences of unwholesome thoughts does not cause them to wane, the next technique is not to keep remembering those unwholesome thoughts and not to give them attention. If none of the above methods work, the next technique is to quieten the mind by practising meditation to "stop the configurations of thoughts" (*vitakka-saṅkhāra-saṇṭhāna*). If unwholesome thoughts still beset the mind, a person is advised to proceed, with clenched teeth and tongue pressed to the palate, to "subdue the mind by means of the mind", as a strong person may subdue one who is weak. The text says that the mind (*citta*) is to be restrained, crushed (*abhiniggaṇhitabbaṃ, abhinippīḷetabbaṃ*), and subjugated (*abhisantāpetabbaṃ*) by means of the mind (*cetasā*).

The instructions given here certainly sound as if the mind is to be controlled at any cost, even if its vitality is sapped, its creativity crushed, and its confidence in its own capacities broken. However, this passage has to be set in the context of the basic approach to training in the *Sutta-piṭaka* as a whole. In other discourses there is sharp criticism of the severe ascetic practices of the Nigaṇṭhas and their techniques of seeking to control the mind forcibly through fasting and other harsh methods (M. I. 237-240; II. 223-225). The Eightfold Path of the Buddha is characterized as the Middle Way (*majjhimā paṭipadā*) that avoids the two extremes: the way of attachment to sensual pleasure (*kāma-sukhallikānuyoga*), which is pursued by ordinary ignorant folk (*pothujjanika*); and the way of exhausting oneself by severe disciplines (*atta-kilamathānuyoga*). The Buddha characterizes both these extremes as sorrowful and unbeneficial (*anatthasaṁhita*) (S. IV. 330). It can be inferred from these passages in the *Suttas* that the technique of "subduing the mind by the mind" was never to be taken up as the sole means of self-control, without being supported by the well balanced factors of the Eightfold Path.

This idea of controlling the mind (*citta*) by the mind (*cetasā*) in the *Vitakkasaṇṭhāna-sutta* resonates with the statements in the *Therīgāthā* and the *Theragāthā* that compare bringing the mind under one's own control to taming an elephant. This technique of "crushing" and "subjugating" the mind with clenched teeth and tongue pressed to the palate also evokes the imagery of "striving against the current" and "going upstream". As in the case of "battling the current", it should be noted that the technique of "subduing the mind by the mind", cannot be interpreted to signify a division of consciousness into a controlling component and one that is controlled. We do not have here the picture of a *citta* where one "dimension" has become vitiated and unwholesome while another remains powerful and pure. When conditioned origination is affirmed, the *citta* is pictured as a network of interacting processes, and transformations can only be viewed as taking place in the *citta* as a whole through the interaction of thoughts, emotions, and conative energies. The instructions in the *Vitakkasaṇṭhāna-sutta* are given to *bhikkhus* who are committed to the Eightfold Path and its interrelated techniques, which simultaneously address a person's views, thoughts, intentions, outward behaviour, way of life, and aspiration for wisdom. The *Sabbāsava-sutta*, for example, advocates a comprehensive approach in training the mind to overcome the multiple distortions that are caused by the *āsavas* (M. I. 6-12). The method put forward in this discourse includes disciplines that simultaneously energize the mind with a strong resolve, clarify and sharpen thought processes, and calm emotional tensions through the cultivation of patience and fortitude.

Mindfulness and the Transformation of Mind

The description of the Foundations of Mindfulness (*satipaṭṭhāna*) in the *Suttas* (D. II. 290-315, M. I. 56-63) shows that the practice is based on the view that the mind has the capacity of reflexive awareness (*paccavekkhaṇa*), which enables it both to be cognizant of its own processes at the time they are occurring and also to review them retrospectively. The *Dhammasaṅgaṇi* explains that in the context of training and developing the mind, mindfulness signifies focusing attention and "bearing in mind" (*dhāraṇatā*) currently occurring physical and mental processes, as well as "recollecting" or "reviewing" (*paṭissati*) a physical or mental process that has already occurred (Dhs. 11). The *Visuddhimagga* lists mindfulness among the factors that are found in all wholesome states of mind and regards its defining characteristic to be the capacity to hold an object steadily in the mind in order to give attention to it (Vsm. XIV. 133). According to the vivid imagery of the commentary to the *Visuddhimagga*, mindfulness does not allow the object to "wobble" in the mind like a pumpkin bobbing up and down in water, but "sinks" into the object in a manner that contrasts with superficial attention.[10]

The practice of mindfulness (D. II. 298-299; M. I. 59-60) includes attentively observing one's feelings (*vedanānupassanā*) and states of mind (*cittānupassanā*). The disciple is instructed first to observe feelings and states of mind "internally" (*ajjhattam*). This implies becoming aware that these processes are private and intimate. Next, one observes feelings and states of mind are observed "externally" (*bahiddhā*) by becoming mindful that these processes are "shared", in the sense that similar processes occur in one's own mind and in the minds of others. The next step is to examine feelings and states of mind in the light of the principle of conditioned origination. One becomes aware that feelings and mental states originate as "arising states" (*samudaya-dhammā*), only to change and become "decaying states" (*vaya-dhammā*). And finally, one observes mental states solely as present facts, with the awareness that a certain feeling is present in the mind (*atthi vedanā*) or that a certain state of mind has come into existence (*atthi cittam*).

Mindfulness of states of mind (*cittānupassanā*) is described as precise and focused observation of whether or not the mind is affected by passion (*rāga*), hatred (*dosa*), or delusion (*moha*), and whether or not the mind has "expanded" by entering into a level of meditation (*jhāna*) (D. II. 299; M. I. 59). There is nothing in these instructions to suggest that mindfulness includes processes of volition whereby one makes a decision and deliberately initiates action either to produce wholesome states or to eradicate unwholesome states. The focus is solely on lucid awareness and steady observation of physical and mental states. Yet both of the *Satipaṭṭhāna-suttas* conclude with the statement that the practice of mindfulness leads to the purification of beings, the overcoming of sorrow and anguish, the cessation of suffering and sadness, and the attainment of *nibbāna* (D. II. 315; M. I. 63). It is simply assumed that the steady observation of the rise and fall of one's mental states will lead to such transformations in one's mind.

The instructions for the practice of mindfulness do not include a description of the process by which mindfulness cleanses the mind of unwholesome mental states and establishes wholesome states. However, some clues are offered. The *Satipaṭṭhāna-sutta* instructs the person who is engaged in mindfully observing feelings and states of the *citta* to become aware that mental states arise and cease in accordance with conditioned origination. It is clear that the emphasis here is not merely on becoming aware of mental states as factors of consciousness, but on observing them from the perspective of universal change and conditioning. According to the *Satipaṭṭhāna-sutta*, it is the direct experience of the body and mind in terms of change and impermanence that causes what could be designated as a "shift" in mental attitude or, in the language of the *Suttas*, an alteration in the way the *citta* "inclines" (*namati*). It can be inferred that the idea of conditioned origination gives to persons who are practising mindfulness a perspective from which they can directly observe, review, classify, and bear in mind physical and mental states. At the same time, conditioned origination ceases to be a mere idea and becomes a directly experienced fact for those who observe the fleeting nature of feelings and mental states. Through the practice of mindfulness, processes of change and conditioning become immediate and intimate experiences. The *Satipaṭṭhāna-sutta* maintains that the mindful observation of dependently arising, fragile, and impermanent physical and mental states leads to a radical change in attitude, so that those who devote themselves to the practice learn to live without seeking security in changing things (*anissito ca viharati*) and without clinging to anything in the world (*na ca kiñci loke upādiyati*).

Like the *Satipaṭṭhāna-sutta*, the *Atthasālinī* also maintains that direct awareness of conditioned origination will bring about changes in attitude, which will be followed by changes in behaviour (Asl. 129). The direct awareness of change becomes the condition for transformations in the mind, and no special interventions of reason or resolve are deemed necessary for these transformations to occur. According to the *Atthasālinī*, when a person becomes aware that all physical and mental states are impermanent, void of selfhood or autonomous individuality, and prone to cause sorrow, then transformations in attitudes come about, replacing greed, aversion, and delusion with generosity, friendliness, and understanding. The *Atthasālinī* asks:

> Clearly knowing a thing to be impermanent,
> who, indeed, would develop excessive fondness
> for it? Understanding conditioned things to be

> sorrow-ridden, who would further increase sorrow
> by expressing extremely violent anger? Realizing
> the emptiness of selfhood, who would fall into
> delusion? (Asl. 129).

It can be inferred that both the *Satipaṭṭhāna-sutta* and the *Atthasālinī* view these changes in attitude to be the fruits, not of volitional effort to cleanse the mind, but of suspending purposive thoughts and volitional effort in order to view physical and mental processes solely as facts of existence (*dhammas*) that come into being and pass away. The method of mindfulness requires steadfast application of energy, but the energy is focused on attentively observing one's own bodily and mental processes, not on deliberatively repressing or transforming these processes through strong resolve or sustained energy.

Wisdom and Motivation

The method of mindfulness is based on the understanding that the direct experience of change, conditioning, and sorrow in the processes of the mind and the body will influence consciousness in such a way as to make mental attitudes wholesome and behaviour beneficent. It is implied in the *Satipaṭṭhāna-sutta* that the method of mindfully observing the mind "as it actually is" transforms the mind precisely by holding in check any resolutions, any intentions, and any deliberate attempts at cleansing and concentrating the mind. The practice involves just observing both wholesome and unwholesome mental states and becoming clearly aware of both disturbance and concentration as changing stances of the mind, without striving to purify emotions or clarify thought processes. The *Satipaṭṭhāna-sutta* maintains that insight into conditioned origination "naturally" brings about radical changes in a person's attitudes and aspirations. There are other passages in the *Sutta* literature, however, where *paññā* (wisdom) and *viriya* (energy) are juxtaposed, and understanding the teachings of the Buddha is regarded as the motivation for putting forth energy and deliberate effort to cleanse the mind of unwholesome habits of thought.

In the Theravāda tradition, wisdom is viewed both as the aspired goal of the Eightfold Path and also as a mental function that has a significant role in daily living. The *Visuddhimagga* states that *paññā* develops out of perception (*saññā*) and cognitive discernment (*viññāṇa*) and functions as reasoning and intellectual acumen in everyday life.[11] This statement can be interpreted to mean that the partnership and mutual relationship between wisdom and energy that is posited in the supramundane (*lokuttara*) level of the Path of liberation develops out of the linking of sound understanding with beneficial energy in the course of experiences that fall within mundane (*lokiya*), *kamma*-bound life. However, in Theravāda, *paññā* represents more than well-utilized intelligence, even within the mundane boundaries of *kamma* and the five aggregates. "Wisdom" signifies gradually coming to see the world in terms of conditioned origination, and the beginnings of a commitment to the Eightfold Path that involves clarification of thought processes, purification of emotional responses, and a redirecting of conative energies towards the goal of freedom from sorrow. The Theravāda view that wisdom does not arise suddenly, but blossoms out of processes of cognition and emotion, once again demonstrates the holistic view of consciousness that this tradition upholds.

The relationship that Theravāda posits between wisdom and the putting forth of energy to cleanse and transform one's emotions becomes especially evident in the methods that are prescribed for changing behaviour that is motivated by "delusion" (*moha*). Delusion signifies not only a confused, bewildered, inattentive, or careless state of mind that is unable to come to terms with the impermanent and conditioned nature of all objects, but also infatuation caused by emotional attachment to specific persons and objects. Whereas greed (*lobha*) and aversion (*dosa*) direct the mind towards an object and away from it respectively, delusion clouds one's judgment regarding the nature and characteristics of objects and causes one to make unwise choices because of obsessively clinging to certain persons and objects. Giving systematic attention to the actual characteristics of persons and objects, and wisely exerting energy to cleanse the mind of infatuations are regarded as essential conditions for overcoming delusion. Wisdom, when it functions as non-delusion, signifies a calm and energetic state of mind that is free of enticements born of greed, prejudices generated by hatred, and infatuations produced by delusion. Serenity and freedom from vitiating and painful emotions are considered to be as much marks of wisdom as lucidity of thought.

The interconnection between wisdom, which knows the changing and conditioned nature of all things, and energy, which strives to overcome unwholesome mental states is most clearly demonstrated in the instructions for training the mind given in the *Anumāna-sutta* (M. I. 97-100) and the *Dvedhāvitakka-sutta* (M. I. 114-118). In the *Anumāna-sutta*, the senior monk Mahā Moggallāna gives instructions in self-training to the monks in his care. Mahā Moggallāna's method is designated as "valid inference" (*anumāna*) because it teaches a monk to infer that if certain patterns of behaviour are harmful and displeasing when they are found in others, he should not emulate such behaviour since it would bring sorrow and harm to himself. If the monk discovers such morally wrong and unwholesome thoughts and acts in his own mind and in the way he conducts himself, he is instructed to strive courageously in order to remove them. Mahā Moggallāna tells the monks that a monk should first observe himself (*bhikkhunā attanā va attānam evaṁ paccavekkhitabbam*), and then put forth valiant effort (*vāyamitabbam*) to remove the unwholesome factors that he sees in himself (M. I. 98). The implication here is that sound judgment can function as the primary motivating factor for the arousing of energy. It is to be noted that there is a difference between the method that is taught in the *Anumāna-sutta* and the method of mindfulness, though both begin with the practice of observing and reviewing the contents of the mind. In the method of mindfulness, goal-directed thoughts and volitional efforts are deliberately suspended, and no intentional effort is made to uproot unwholesome thoughts. Transformations of the mind are given room to come about "naturally", in accordance with to conditioned origination. The instruction given in the *Anumāna-sutta* is that the cognitive process of holding up a mirror to the mind should be a prelude to intense voluntary effort to remove unwholesome states.

In the *Dvedhāvitakka-sutta*, the Buddha tells his disciples of a method of cleansing the mind that he devised when he was striving for enlightenment. This method has the following steps: one should remain vigilant and fervent and resolute; as thoughts (*vitakkas*) arise, one should divide them into categories of wholesome and unwholesome; one should realize that whenever the mind constantly thinks about (*anuvitakketi*) and ponders over (*anuvicāreti*) an object, then the mind inclines towards that object (*nati hoti cetaso*); and finally, one should realize the unhappy consequences of unwholesome thoughts and put forth energy to purify the mind. The method of cleansing the mind in the *Dvedhāvitakka-sutta* is based on the idea that the wise recognition of sorrow-producing unwholesome thoughts will motivate a person to put forth energy to remove them. Both the technique taught by Mahā Moggallāna in the *Anumāna-sutta* and the method devised by the Bodhisatta for the removing of unwholesome thoughts rely on clear discernment and coherent reasoning. The Bodhisatta's method of classifying thoughts as wholesome and unwholesome relies on developing the capacity of reason to discern the characteristics of things and to recognize the distinction between two things that fall under the same general category. Mahā Moggallāna's method depends on the mind's capacity to form valid inferences. Nevertheless, far from relying solely on cognitive process of reasoning, both methods also recognize the power of the emotions to motivate behaviour and the need to put forth energy to cultivate wholesome emotions. In the Bodhisatta's method, unwholesome thoughts are defined as those that cause harm to oneself, or to others, or to both oneself and others. To clearly distinguish thoughts in this manner, one requires both good judgment and emotional maturity.

Neither the mind's capacity to observe its own processes (*paccavekkhaṇa*) nor the gradually maturing mental factor of wise understanding (*paññā*) can claim to transcend processes of conditioning; in fact, both come into being through the support of a network of thoughts, emotions, and goal-directed efforts. However by reflecting on its own contents, the mind becomes aware of how the networks of mental conditioning operate. The therapeutic value of observing one's own mind (*paccavekkhaṇa*) is referred to by Joanna Macy. She points out that in the practice of mindfulness, attention is directed "not to the things we see but to how we see them".[12] One's attention is radically shifted to the "co-arising nature" of feelings, perceptions, and thought processes. Wise insight into how the processes of change and mutual conditioning operate in one's own mind does not set aside, negate, or transcend the processes of conditioning. According to Theravāda, the conditioned order of mental processes (*citta-niyāma*) is a given fact. However, when the mind becomes aware of its own conditioning, this wise awareness itself becomes a dominant conditioning factor, and it casts its wholesome and enlightening influence on the other processes that constitute the mind. As the Buddha tells Rāhula, the source of the motivating power of understanding is the capacity of the mind to "hold a mirror" to its own processes of conditioning (M. I. 415). These passages in the *Suttas* do not claim that consciousness has the capacity to become aware of every detail of its processes. However, they do maintain that consciousness can become aware of its dominant features and observe the patterns of conditioning in the processes that constitute it.

Furthermore, Theravāda does not regard wisdom as a virtue that functions autonomously but views it as a participant in a constellation of mutually conditioning mental powers. Thus *paññā* is perceived to be one of five "controlling faculties" (*indriyas*), faith (*saddhā*), energy (*viriya*), mindfulness (*sati*), concentration (*samādhi*), and wisdom (*paññā*) (D. III. 239). These five are also known as the five "powers" (M. II. 12). The tradition emphasizes the need for balance in the mutual relationships of these five controlling faculties (*indriya-samatta*). In the practice of mindfulness, faith provides a counterbalance to wisdom and prevents the latter from anything approaching mere sophistry. Similarly, the calming power of concentration prevents energy from becoming a form of restlessness.[13] These five virtues are chosen out of an array of wholesome mental states and grouped together in this way because they are perceived to be capable of cleansing and training thoughts, emotions, and the mind's capacity to initiate action when their functions are interlinked. Since Theravāda perceives the mind to be an organic whole of mutually conditioning cognitions, emotions, and motivating impulses, the disciplines of the Eightfold Path are based on the idea that wholesome changes in any function of the mind will have a good influence on many other mental processes. Throughout the Eightfold Path, the emphasis is neither on cultivating a sovereign capacity of reasoning nor on establishing a controlling power of volition. The Eightfold Path aims at setting up helpful conditions so that wholesome states of mind follow one another in the continuum of consciousness. The training is based on the affirmation that when the state of mind (*citta*) is wholesome, the purposive impulse (*cetanā*) that arises from it will also be wholesome. A wholesome purposive impulse motivates other mental factors to come together to form a wholesome configuration of conditions (*abhisaṅkhāra*) that becomes expressed in a wholesome act.

Conclusion

In this chapter, the concept of volition in the *Suttas* has been approached from four different perspectives. None of these has yielded the notion of volition as a sovereign power that can control mental processes and transform behaviour. There is no indication that *cetanā* is viewed as a self-initiating mental capacity. There are passages in the *Suttas* that present "motivational sequences" wherein each stage is conceived to be an attitude of mind that can provide the conditions for the emergence of the next, in accordance with conditioned origination. In this context, the disciplines of the Eightfold Path are viewed as a gradual and cumulative process of training through which a person gradually "inclines" towards *nibbāna*. No interventions of purposive impulses (*cetanās*) are seen to be necessary, since each stage naturally leads to the next (A. V. 1-2).

The techniques of mindfulness are based on the affirmation that the mind has the capacity to view itself reflexively and assess its own contents. Cultivating this capacity of the mind to observe and review itself (*paccavekkhaṇa*) is not regarded as a release from conditioning, but as a method of becoming aware of how the processes of conditioning affect mental states. In the practice of mindfulness, no deliberate volitional effort is made to remove unwholesome thoughts and emotions. It is posited that an understanding of how processes of conditioning occur in oneself and others introduces into the continuum of consciousness fresh, wholesome conditions that gradually come to dominate over other conditioning factors.

In the *Suttas*, understanding (*paññā*) is defined,not only as the wisdom that ultimately liberates the mind from sorrow, but as a motivating "power" (*bala*) that is gradually developed through clarifying one's thought, purifying the emotions, and making the mind calm and attentive through meditation and mindfulness. The idea that there is a tragic split in the mind between the capacity to know and the competence to initiate action is emphatically rejected in the *Suttas*. At the same time, neither reason nor wisdom that develops out of sound judgment is conceived as a cognitive capacity that can act alone to transform the mind or effect changes in behaviour. Wisdom and energy become mutually conditioning factors: an understanding of the causes and consequences of unwholesome mental states is regarded as a powerful motivating impetus in seeking to uproot them.

When one first encounters the notion of "subduing the mind by the mind", it appears to be a form of self-determinism. "Subduing" suggests that the mind, acting autonomously, corrects and controls itself by deploying its own inherent capacity (*śakti*). However, such an interpretation would be based on a misunderstanding. In the *Suttas*, the *citta* is not viewed as an entity that can somehow transcend the processes that constitute it, nor is it posited that that some "part" or "level" of the mind remains uncorrupted and can take on a controlling role in purifying conscious processes. No part of the mind can claim to escape the pervading corruption of the *āsavas* and the *anusayas*. It is instructive to note that both the wholesome roots of action (non-greed, non-hate, and non-delusion) as well as the unwholesome roots that oppose them include thought processes, emotions and the motivating impulses that initiate action. Any of these aspects of the mind can be rendered either wholesome or unwholesome. It follows that all mental transformations are regarded as results either of mutual conditioning between processes that constitute the *citta* or of interactions between the *citta* functioning as an organic whole and one or more of its constituent processes.

Taking another approach, Johansson focuses on statements in the *Suttas* that suggest the affirmation of a self who guards and controls the *citta* (A. V. 92-94; M. I. 214; M. III. 32). According to Johansson's interpretation, a controlling "I" analogous to the superego of Freud is posited in the *Suttas*.[14] Johansson's interpretation does not take into account the fact that statements about an "I" directing the mind are placed within the context of the disciplines through which the mind as a whole is cleansed, nourished, developed, and transformed. The Eightfold Path is never described as a method of developing a superego to control the mind. On the contrary, notions of an autonomous and sovereign "I" are regarded as manifestations of a persistent tendency of conceit (*mānānusaya*).

Since the notion of an autonomous and unchanging "I" is rejected in the *Suttas*, references to an "I" who controls the mind should be taken as a way of speaking about the mind's ability to observe its present contents and recall its past experiences. The phrase "subduing the mind by the mind" refers, not to the action of an autonomous and inherently powerful dimension of the mind, but to wholesome processes that take place in a mind that is conditioned by training. The "subduing" refers to setting up conditions through which wholesome influences begin to act upon many aspects of the mind simultaneously. The training in the Eightfold Path begins by forming wholesome behaviour patterns that cast their good influence simultaneously on thought processes, emotions, and motivating factors.

ENDNOTES

[1] R.E.A. Johansson, *The Dynamic Psychology of Early Buddhism,* 119, 121, 136, 184, 209, 211.

[2] Ibid., 99-100.

[3] Ibid., 209.

[4] R.F. Gombrich, *Theravāda Buddhism,*, 55-59.

[5] For further discussion of this imagery of going "against the stream", see S. Collins, *Selfless Persons: Imagery and Thought in Theravāda Buddhism,* 249-251.

[6] . . . *handāhaṁ viriyam ārabhāmi appattassa pattiyā anadhigatassa adhigamāya asacchikatassa sacchikiriyāyāti* (D. III. 256). The following list specifies eight occasions when energy should be exerted in fulfilling the teaching of the Buddha: (1) before starting a task; (2) when one has completed a task; (3) prior to starting a journey; (4) after the journey is completed; (5) when a monk does not receive sufficient alms food, by reminding himself that he can focus his mind better because his stomach is not too full; (6) when a monk gets sufficient food, by realizing that he has the strength to exert energy; (7) when one is indisposed, by exerting oneself before the illness gets worse; (8) when one has recovered, by putting forth energy to accomplish what has yet to be accomplished. It is obvious that a life that is in accordance with the teaching of the Buddha is a life of energy (*viriya*).

[7] *Sakkā bhikkhave akusalaṁ pajahitum. No ce taṁ bhikkhave sakkā abhavissa akusalaṁ pajahituṁ nāham evaṁ vadeyyam "akusalaṁ bhikkhave pajahathā" ti* (A. I. 58).

[8] *Sakkā bhikkhave kusalaṁ bhāvetum* (A. I. 58).

[9] This vow to persevere in the Path of liberation is also found at M. I. 480-481 and S. II. 28.

[10] Pe Maung Tin, *The Expositor*, 194-195; Bhikkhu Ñāṇamoli, *The Path of Purification*, 524, n. 64.

[11] The *Visuddhimagga* (XIV. 3-4) holds that perception, cognitive discernment, and wisdom are related because cognitive processes (*viññāṇa*) presuppose processes of perception and ideation (*saññā*), and wise understanding (*paññā*) develops from cognitive discernment (*viññāṇa*). Nevertheless, since each of them approaches and knows the object differently, they are distinguishable. *Saññā* is like a child who perceives a coin but does not realize its monetary value. *Viññāṇa* is like a villager who knows that a coin is used in commerce, but cannot tell whether it is counterfeit or genuine. *Paññā* functions like a money-changer who knows what the child and the villager know about the coin but can also discern whether or not it is genuine. According to Buddhaghosa's explanation, *saññā* grasps the outward features of an object, for example, whether it is blue or yellow. *Viññāṇa* includes what is known through perception, but also grasps the three characteristics of all conditioned factors: impermanence, liability to cause suffering, and absence of an autonomous self. *Paññā* not only thoroughly understands these three characteristics, but makes the Eightfold Path a manifest fact in the life of an

individual by means of energetic striving (*lakkhaṇa-paṭivedhañca pāpeti, ussakitvā magga-pātubhāvañca pāpeti*). It is to be noted that here Buddhaghosa links the functioning of *paññā* with the putting forth of energetic endeavour (*ussāha*).

[12] J. Macy, *Mutual Causality in Buddhism and General Systems Theory: The Dharma of Natural Systems,* 136.

[13] Vsm. IV. 45-49; Nyanatiloka, *Buddhist Dictionary: Manual of Buddhist Terms and Doctrines,* 79.

[14] R.E.A. Johansson, *The Dynamic Psychology of Early Buddhism,* 160.

Chapter VI
Cetanā and Attitudes of Mind: *Abhidhamma* Perspectives

It is in the *Dhammasaṅgaṇi*, its commentary the *Atthasālinī*, and the *Visuddhimagga* that the relationship of purposive impulses (*cetanās*) to the continuum of consciousness (*citta*) and to the mind's goal-directed activities (*saṅkhāras*) is most fully described. These texts[1] present list after list of mental states that the reader must study and contemplate with care, for it is through the very format of these lists that the *Abhidhamma* view of consciousness is put forward.

It is generally agreed that the texts of the *Abhidhamma* were developed from summaries of topics (*mātikās*) that were considered to be central to the teachings of the Buddha.[2] *Mātikās* are found in all the books of the *Abhidhamma* except the *Kathāvatthu*. For example, an extensive *mātikā* that functions as a table of contents occurs at the beginning of the *Dhammasaṅgaṇi* (Dhs. 1-8). It is conjectured that these *mātikās*, along with additional explanations of the key terms that they contain, were already extant at the time of the third council. Although the Mahāyāna schools remain silent on this point, according to the Theravāda tradition,[3] the third council was held under the patronage of the emperor Aśoka, who reigned during the middle of the third century B.C.E.[4]

The main distinction between the *Sutta* and *Abhidhamma* system is the development of the theory of *dhammas*. In the *Abhidhamma*, *dhammas* are regarded as discrete physical and mental states from which the universe and all that inhabits it are formed. However, the idea of conditioned origination continues to be upheld, and every momentary *dhamma* is defined as a physical or mental state linked to the past and the future through processes of conditioning. According to interpreters of the *Abhidhamma* system, the distinction between the *Sutta* and the *Abhidhamma* methods of analysis is not radical, but stems only from the more detailed classification and the technical vocabulary of the *Abhidhamma*.[5] There are clear lines of continuity between the *Suttas* and the *Abhidhamma* system with regard to the interpretation of *cetanā*. As in the *Suttas*, in the *Abhidhamma* system also *cetanā* is regarded as arising in the matrix of sensory or mental contact (*phassa*) with an object and functioning as a constituent of a state of consciousness (*citta*); *cetanās* are defined as purposive impulses that function within the constructive activities of *saṅkhāras*; *cetanā* is identified with *kamma*; and *cetanā* is given more importance than the purposive act that it instigates with regard to assigning moral value. The difference between the *Suttas* and the *Abhidhamma* is that in the *Abhidhamma* system of analysis, purposive impulses or intentions, specific states of consciousness, contacts with objects, and the constructive activities of the mind are regarded as distinct analyzable factors (*dhammas*) that arise as constituents of the continuum of consciousness.

The *Dhammasaṅgaṇi* presents a compilation of all the *dhammas* (physical and mental states) that are recognized in the Theravāda tradition. The term *dhamma* includes the following factors in its range of reference: material quality (*rūpa*); the four primary material elements (*mahābhūtas*) consisting of fire, water, earth, and air; dependent material qualities (*upādāya-rūpas*); discrete states of consciousness (*cittas*); mental factors (*cetasikas*) that constitute the states of consciousness; and *nibbāna*, which is designated as the sole "unconditioned *dhamma*" (*asaṅkhata dhamma*). *Dhammas*, therefore, are the basic mental and physical factors that constitute the universe. *Cetanā* is regarded as a *dhamma* that is included in the category of mental factors (*cetasikas*) that form a specific state of consciousness (*citta*).

The *Atthasālinī* (Asl. 39) defines *dhammas* by stating that they carry "their own nature" (*attano pana sabhāvan dhārenti*),[6] but immediately qualifies this definition by adding, "or they are supported by causal conditions, or they are supported according to their own nature" (*dhāriyanti vā paccayehi dhāriyanti vā yathā sabhāvato*). Warder regards this definition of *dhamma* in terms of distinct nature (*sabhāva*) to be a new development of the *dhamma* theory in the commentaries. According to his analysis, this statement signifies that physical and mental factors have their own character "naturally" (*yathā sabhāvato*), that is to say, through causal conditions (*paccayehi*).[7] Warder's interpretation suggests that each discrete physical or mental state (*dhamma*) has its own specific nature (*sabhāva*) because of the distinctive manner in which it is conditioned by other *dhammas*. This explanation of the definition of *dhamma* in the *Atthasālinī* implies that the specific nature (*sabhāva*) of any physical or mental *dhamma* is not intrinsic to it, but is the product of its distinctive relationship to a network of objects. Warder's interpretation poses problems because the literal meaning of *sabhāva*, as well as the meaning given to this term in philosophical debates, is "inherent" or "intrinsic" nature. The definition in the *Atthasālinī* remains quite ambiguous. It is postulated that each physical and mental state has its own nature (*sabhāva*); at the same time, the attempt is made to hold on to the principle that the nature and characteristics of physical and mental states arise through causes and conditions (*paccayehi*).

Above all, in interpreting this definition of *dhamma*, it should be noted that the *Atthasālinī* states that one of the meanings of *dhamma* is "that which does not have the nature of an individual entity or individual self" (*nissatta-nijjīvatā*) (Asl. 38). The import of the above statement is that no physical or mental factor can claim to possess an inviolable selfhood or irreducible "essence". The idea of *nissatta-nijjīvatā* corresponds to the concept of *anattā* in the *Sutta* literature. On the basis of the idea of *nissatta-nijjīvatā*, it is possible to argue (as Warder does) that the definition of *dhamma* in the *Atthasālinī* does not imply that each physical and mental factor "carries" its own inherent nature independently and autonomously. The definition in the *Atthasālinī* can be interpreted to mean that though *dhammas* are neither separable from, nor independent of, processes of conditioning, each physical or mental state is a factor that belongs to a specific moment (*khaṇa*) in the psycho-physical continuum, distinguishable by its characteristic mark (*lakkhaṇa*). Conditioned origination entails that this recognizable characteristic must be regarded, not as something inherent to the *dhamma*, but as a product of the conditions that converge at the moment of the arising of the *dhamma*.

Holistic Approach to Consciousness in the *Abhidhamma*

It is posited in the *Abhidhamma* method of classification that the arising of each mental factor marks a distinct moment in the processes of conditioning. Consequently, each mental factor is considered to be recognizably endowed with distinct characteristics through the convergence of the necessary conditions at that moment. However, the mind is described, not as a collection of disparate momentary mental factors, but as a dynamic unity of mutually dependant processes. A study of the *Visuddhimagga* (Vsm. XIV. 131-184), for example, shows that the very manner in which the lists of mental states are conceived and arranged demonstrates that the *Abhidhamma* system views the continuum of consciousness as an organic unity of diverse dynamic components.

Not only is each momentary state of mind (*citta*) portrayed as an internally coherent whole, but it is also shown to be organically linked, through processes of mutual conditioning and interdependence, with states of mind that precede and follow it. Since conditioned origination entails compatibility between antecedent and consequent moments, a sequence of transitory *cittas* is experienced as a chain of associated thoughts, emotions, and motivating impulses that continues for a while, shaped by a dominant emotional mood and vitalized by compatible conative energies. Each *citta* in the chain is a unity of diverse factors, and the chain of *cittas* is perceived to be a complex continuum, rich with nuances that are linked by mutual conditioning.

According to the *Abhidhamma*, each transitory state of consciousness (*citta*) is flavoured, as it were, by a dominant type of feeling (*vedanā*) that is experienced as pain (*dukkha*), pleasure (*sukha*), or a neutral state that is characterized neither by pleasure nor by pain. Moreover, each *citta* is regarded as bearing a moral value produced precisely through the confluence and interrelationships of the mental factors (*cetasikas*) that constitute it. Every momentary state of mind can be assessed as wholesome (*kusala*), unwholesome (*akusala*), or morally indeterminate (*avyākata*). Guenther's designation of *cittas* as attitudes of mind is apt since each *citta* is marked by a dominant feeling and a specific moral value.

The *cetasikas* that make up a wholesome *citta*, for example, include: mental factors that make cognition possible; mental factors that can be characterized as wholesome emotions and sentiments; wholesome roots of action comprising non-greed, non-hate, and non-delusion; and mental factors such as flexibility, buoyancy, and adaptability in functioning, which make for facility and ease in initiating goal-oriented action (Chart 7). Each list of mental factors, in fact, can be shaped into a *maṇḍala*. The *Abhidhamma* system of classifying *cittas* is based on the notion that the nature of any mental factor (*cetasika*) is dependent on its function, and its function is dependent on its relationships with concomitant factors. It is implied that the more detailed the classification and the more minute the description of the interrelationships, the better the nature and function of any mental factor can be understood. The imagery of a *maṇḍala* is appropriate because the *cetasikas*, like the elements of a *maṇḍala*, are understood to be in vibrant motion, forming and changing relationships.[8] The way any mental factor manifests depends on the strength and variety of its interrelationships. Consciousness is like a large *maṇḍala* containing smaller *maṇḍalas*. In the lists of mental factors, there are sub-sets within sub-sets, like *maṇḍalas* within *maṇḍalas*, showing intricate cross-relationships.

Moreover, these lists of mental factors demonstrate that according to the *Abhidhamma* view, each state of mind (*citta*) in the continuum of consciousness is conceived, not as a closed system, but as an organic whole that is responsive to fresh influences. In fact, it is posited that each state of mind arises, together with the mental factors that constitute it, through a specific moment of contact with an object that stimulates the senses and the mind. The *Atthasālinī* (Asl. 63-64, 112) defines *citta* as the mental function that thinks of (*cinteti*) or cognizes (*vijānāti*) its object (*ārammaṇam*). It is in this context that the *Atthasālinī* (Asl. 64) portrays consciousness as a master-artist (*citta-kāra*) capable of seemingly endless creativity. The states of mind are said to be abundantly variegated, matching the diversity of objects and the diverse circumstances in which the processes of perception take place. The *citta* responds organically to the object that is perceived; consequently, its constituents are shaped and organized in relation to the object, and the *citta* as a whole experiences a transformation because of these internal adjustments.

A holistic view of consciousness is also evident in the fact that the lists of mental factors in the *Dhammasaṅgaṇi*, the *Atthasālinī*, and the *Visuddhimagga* are put together in such a way as to posit a continual mutual conditioning between the cognitive processes (*viññāṇa*) and the action-producing processes (*saṅkhāras*) in the series of states of mind (*cittas*). A study of these lists shows that the very same mental factors that occur as constituents (*cetasikas*) in a *citta* configuration also occur as the constituents of the *saṅkhārakkhandha* (Vsm. XIV. 131-184). It is posited that in their function as *cetasikas*, the mental factors constitute a state of mind (*citta*) whose chief feature is cognitive awareness. These same mental factors come together to form the dynamic configurations (*saṅkhāras*) of causal conditions (*paccayas*) that produce purposive acts of body, speech, and mind. Like other mental factors in the *maṇḍala* of consciousness, *cetanā* is regarded both as a *cetasika* (mental factor) in a *citta* configuration and as a causal condition in a dynamic formation (*saṅkhāra*). The same mental factors constitute both cognitive and motivational processes. According to the *Abhidhamma* system, when *cetanā* functions as a constituent of a *citta*, it directs the mind's attention towards objects that are selected because they are of interest to the organism. In this role of directing attention selectively, *cetanā* becomes associated with concomitant constituents of the *citta* in processes of cognition. As the primary constituent of the *saṅkhārakkhandha*, *cetanā* applies its function of directing the mind to selected objects in such a way as to bring together concomitant mental functions and "compose" (*abhisaṅkharoti*) purposive acts (*sañcetanika-kamma*) related to those objects. Like *cetanā*, all the mental factors in the lists of wholesome and unwholesome *cittas* are regarded as factors with a twofold function: they condition cognitive processes, and they also bring about the continual dynamic "composing" (*abhisaṅkharaṇa*) activity by which "composed" (*abhisankhata*) acts of body, speech, and mind are produced.

Emotions are counted among the mental factors (*cetasikas*) that constitute typical wholesome and unwholesome states of consciousness (*cittas*). Unwholesome *cittas* include emotions associated with greed, hate, and delusion, lack of shame at doing wrong, and lack of fear regarding the consequences of evil. Restless agitation and obsessive worry arise within unwholesome *cittas* in specific circumstances (see Charts 8-10). The list of mental factors (*cetasikas*) that constitute a wholesome *citta* includes emotions associated with the wholesome "roots of action" (non-greed or generosity, non-hate or friendliness, and non-delusion or wise understanding) as well as shame at doing wrong and fear of the consequences of evil. The presence of emotions among the *cetasikas* helps to transform the cognitive processes that arise when the mind makes contact with an object into an "attitude of mind". That is to say, the presence or absence of specific emotions determines the ethical value of a *citta* as well as whether it is associated with mental ease (*somanassa*), mental uneasiness (*domanassa*), or a neutral feeling characterized neither by pleasure nor by discomfort.

The inclusion of emotions in the *saṅkharakkhandha* implies that they are regarded as motivating impulsions that influence the choice of goals and the direction taken by the dynamic processes of the mind. At the same time, the placing of emotions within a configuration of factors that constitute a *citta* signifies that emotions are perceived to be interacting with concomitant cognitive states such as attention (*manasikāra*), initial thought (*vitakka*), and reflection (*vicāra*) within a specific attitude of mind. This interaction between cognitive processes and states of emotion implies that emotion does not function solely as a tension-producing, motivational "drive", but includes a cognitive evaluation of how an object or event affects one's own well-being. At the same time, the inclusion of emotion in the cognitive process implies that emotions influence the way objects are cognized and evaluated.

Cetanā Regarded as Common to All States of Consciousness

The relationship between *citta* and *cetanā* is most clearly expressed in the *Abhidhammattha-saṅgaha*, a late eleventh or early twelfth century student manual of *Abhidhamma* categories. In the *Abhidhammattha-saṅgaha*,[9] *cetasikas* are defined as mental factors that arise and perish together with the state of mind (*citta*) that they constitute. The definition goes on to say that *cetasikas* are linked with the *citta* by having the same object and the same "base" (*vatthu*). This definition of *cetasikas* reinforces the Theravāda position that consciousness always arises in relation to an object (Asl. 112-113). The term "base" in the definition of *cetasika* refers to the sensitive area of the sense organ where sensory stimulation occurs.[10] For example, according to the account given in the *Abhidhamma* system, when a beautiful visual object is seen, the conscious experience of seeing (*cakkhu-viññāṇa*) arises together with a constellation of cognitive, emotional and dynamic factors that interact to produce a specific state of consciousness (*citta*) that can be evaluated as ethically wholesome, unwholesome, or indeterminate.

The *Milindapañha* (Mil. 56), the *Dhammasaṅgaṇi* (Dhs. 17-18, 84-85, 118), the *Visuddhimagga* (Vsm. XIV. 133-180), the *Atthasālinī* (Asl. 107-112, 248) and the *Abhidhammattha-saṅgaha*[11] list *cetanā* with the basic mental factors that constitute basic conscious awareness and vitality. Among these basic *cetasikas*, *cetanā* takes its place as the fundamental dynamic capacity in the mind that makes all goal-oriented action possible, including the most rudimentary movements in relation to the environment.

According to the *Atthasālinī*, the following five mental factors are present in all states of consciousness:

sensory contact	(*phassa*)
feeling	(*vedanā*)
perception	(*saññā*)
purposive impulse	(*cetanā*)
consciousness	(*citta*)

H.V. Guenther points out that the term *citta*, which is "rather ambiguous", has been replaced in the *Visuddhimagga* and the *Abhidhammattha-saṅgaha* by the more precise term *manasikāra* (attention) in this list of fundamental factors.[12]

The *Milindapañha* (Mil. 56) and the *Abhidhammattha-saṅgaha*[13] leave out *citta* and add the following three basic *cetasikas* to the first four named above:

one-pointed concentration	(*ekaggatā*)
vitality	(*jīvitindriya*)
attention	(*manasikāra*)

In the *Abhidhammattha-saṅgaha* these seven are designated as *cetasikas* that are "common to all types of consciousness" (*sabba-citta-sādhāraṇa*). The presence of *cetanā* in this list of seven basic mental factors implies that a rudimentary sense of a goal, correlated with an equally rudimentary impulse to initiate goal-oriented action, characterizes even those basic states of consciousness where there is no fully developed affirmation of an intention.

Lama Govinda interprets these seven basic mental factors to be a constellation of mutually conditioning mental coefficients in *The Psychological Attitude of Early Buddhist Philosophy.*[14] It is posited in the *Suttas* and *Abhidhamma* texts that when sensory contact (*phassa*) occurs, even before the object is clearly recognized, a preliminary feeling (*vedanā*) arises that is either pleasant (*sukha*), or painful (*dukkha*), or neither pleasant nor painful. This feeling is regarded as conditioned both by the object and also by past wholesome and unwholesome experiences. Lama Govinda maintains that *cetanā* arises in this preliminary stage of sensory stimulation, not as a full-fledged "free will", but as "an instinctive volition" determined to some extent by aspects of the perceiver's "character". He obviously means that the manner in which *cetanā* first functions in response to the object is conditioned by the nuances of feeling (*vedanā*) that dominates this initial phase of perception and, more significantly, by the habits of mind that the subject brings to the object.

Lama Govinda makes the point that even in the initial stages of perception, *cetanā* fulfils its distinctive role of coordinating (*abhisaṅkharaṇa*) the functions of concomitant *cetasikas* (for example, concentration and attention) and directing their energies towards the object. According to Lama Govinda's interpretation, one-pointed concentration (*ekaggatā*) demarcates the object as the focus of mental activity, while attention (*manasikāra*) directs the mind to apply itself to that focal point. He stresses that at the initial stage of perception, *manasikāra* manifests as a "spontaneous attention" that is aroused, not by an ethical choice, but by the "pull" exerted by the dominant qualities of the object.

The *Abhidhamma* system, therefore, posits that the rudimentary function of *cetanā* in the initial stage of perception differs from its more complex function in relation to intentional acts. This variation in functioning attributed to *cetanā* points to what the *Abhidhamma* scholar S.Z. Aung describes in his *Compendium of Philosophy*[15] as "the protean character" of each of the constituents of a *citta*. By the term "protean" he means that each *cetasika* is viewed in the *Abhidhamma* as a mental factor whose basic characteristic (*lakkhaṇa*) remains the same, but whose mode of functioning varies according to the object with which it is associated or the circumstances in which it arises. Though *cetanā* functions by merely directing the mind to objects in the preliminary stages of perception, in other circumstances it can function as a fully developed purposive impulse or intention, and can put forth acts that carry karmic consequences. Furthermore, when a person enters the Eightfold Path, *cetanā* can function as the resolve to renounce all karmic fruitions, and can become "the *cetanā* of the Path" (AA. III. 213).

The *Abhidhammattha-saṅgaha* gives the following account of how *cetanā* fulfils its role of being the primary condition in producing purposive acts that have karmic consequences: [16] *cetanā* can function either as a "conascent *kamma*-condition" (*sahajāta-kamma-paccaya*) or as an "asynchronous *kamma*-condition" (*nānākkhaṇika-kamma-paccaya*). In the preliminary stages of perception, when *cetanā* operates as merely habitual inclination towards the object, it does not function as a fully developed purposive impulse or intention; hence it does not instigate a purposive act (*sañcetanika-kamma*) that carries moral value and entails karmic consequences. However, when *cetanā* acts upon concomitant physical and mental factors as a motivating impetus based on an intention and produces a wholesome or unwholesome act that immediately puts forth commensurate karmic consequences, then it becomes a conascent *kamma*-condition. In this context, "conascence" signifies that the karmic consequence of a purposive act occurs concurrently with the purposive impulse that initiated the act and is experienced in the present body and mind. If the concerted action of *cetanā* and its concomitants produces a wholesome or unwholesome act entailing consequences that are experienced in a future rebirth, then *cetanā* becomes an asynchronous *kamma*-condition. Obviously, in this case the purposive impulse and the karmic consequences it entails are not synchronized.

Definition of "Wholesome"

In the *Dhammasaṅgaṇi* (Dhs. 180), wholesome factors (*kusalā dhammā*) are defined as those that have as their "roots" (*mūlāni*) non-greed, non-hatred, and non-delusion (*alobha, adosa, amoha*). The four non-physical *khandhas*, comprising feeling (*vedanā*), perception (*saññā*), the mind's constructive activity (*saṅkhāra*), and conscious awareness (*viññāṇa*), are looked upon as wholesome when they are associated with these roots. Likewise, all acts (*kamma*) of body, speech, and mind that arise from these roots (*taṁ samuṭṭhānaṁ*) are regarded as wholesome. In the same way, physical, verbal, and mental acts are defined as unwholesome when they spring from the three unwholesome roots: greed, hatred, and delusion (Dhs. 180). Similarly, the non-physical aggregates and the acts that originate from them are considered unwholesome when they are associated with these three unwholesome roots (*taṁ sampayutto*). The *Atthasālinī* (Asl. 39) emphasizes that "unwholesome", far from conveying merely the absence of the wholesome and the good, signifies an act of body, speech, or mind that is actively opposed to the wholesome (*kusala-paṭipakkha*). According to the *Dhammasaṅgaṇi*, ethically indeterminate (*avyākata*) mental states are those that cannot be categorized as wholesome or as unwholesome. The *Atthasālinī* adds that ethically indeterminate states do not produce karmic consequences that are pleasant, painful, or neither pleasant nor painful (Asl. 39).[17] It becomes clear that the *Dhammasaṅgaṇi* (Dhs. 180) bases the criteria for moral evaluation on the wholesome or unwholesome quality that is manifested in the physical or mental state that is to be evaluated. Nevertheless, the idea of *kamma* forms the background for these statements in the *Dhammasaṅgaṇi*, and it is assumed that wholesome and unwholesome acts are also defined by the commensurate consequences that they produce.

The *Atthasālinī* (Asl. 38) explains that the term *kusala*, which is usually translated as "wholesome" or "skilful" or "good", has the following connotations: "good health" (*ārogya*), "faultless" or "blameless" (*anavajja*), "skilful" or "dextrous" (*cheka*), and "productive of felicitous consequences" (*sukha-vipāka*). Good health or vitality is interpreted to mean absence of the disease of mental defilements (*kilesa-vyādhi*) (Asl. 62-63), and "faultless" is explained as freedom from the fault, the blemish, and the distress of the same mental defilements. The text explains that when one is engaged in distinguishing wholesome, unwholesome, and ethically indeterminate mental states, the term *kusala* does not mean "skilful" or "dextrous", whereas it does have these connotations when the reference is to the actions of skilled craftsmen who make chariots or trained performers of music and dance (Asl. 38). However, in another passage (Asl. 63), the *Atthasālinī* holds that the meaning of "skilful" does apply in the case of wholesome mental states, provided "skill" is taken in the sense of "wisdom" or "understanding" (*paññā*).[18]

The *Atthasālinī* (Asl. 63), therefore, adds a new dimension to the definition of *kusala* in the *Dhammasaṅgaṇi* by interpreting skill (*kosallam*) as wise understanding (*paññā*). Furthermore, according to the *Atthasālinī*, wholesome mental states have systematic and thorough attention (*yoniso-manasikāra*) as their proximate cause (Asl. 293). The *Atthasālinī* (Asl. 39) utilizes the delightful didactic method of play on words to draw out the connotations that have gathered around the term *kusala*. It is stated that *kusala* mental states have that name because they cause bad (*ku*) mental factors to tremble (verb root *sal-*), to shake, to be agitated, and to be annihilated. Or *kusala* signifies bad (*ku*) states of mind being cut off, chopped off (verb root *lū-*). Or knowledge (*ñāṇa*) can be called *kusa* because through knowledge reprehensible (*ku*) mental states are curtailed (verb root *so-*); and *kusala* indicates that things should be taken (verb root *lā-*), grasped, set in motion by that knowledge (*kusa*). Alternatively, *kusala* factors are so named because, just as *kusa* grass can cut (verb root *lū-*) one's hand with both its sharp edges, so wholesome states cut off both unwholesome states that have already arisen and those that have not yet arisen.[19]

In an article entitled "Good or Skilful? *Kusala* in Canon and Commentary", L.S. Cousins concludes that *kusala* carries the meaning of "skill" in the very large number of passages where it is associated with *dhammas*. He takes the position that in the passages where there are references to *dhammas* that are characterized as *kusala*, the intention of the Pāli texts is to indicate, primarily, the *jhāna* states and the mental states that came to be designated as *dhammas* that conduce to awakening (*bodhi-pakkhiya*). Cousins makes the point that the term *kusala* is applied to these *dhammas* to indicate that they are special states, skilfully produced by wisdom. However, he holds that in later texts of the Pāli canon and in the commentaries, *kusala* refers in a general sense to ethically good acts and mental states. His argument is developed in response to Damien Keown, who maintains that translating *kusala* as "skilful" is misleading because the term "skilful" has no place in the "vocabulary of moral discourse" in the English language.[20] By taking a different approach from that of Cousins and Keown, it is possible to interpret *kusala* in such a way that it carries all three meanings (health, moral goodness, and skill) when it is applied to mental factors (*dhammas*), except in the case of *cittas* that are defined as "dissociated from knowledge" (*ñāṇa-vippayutta*). Such *cittas* are not regarded as skilful, since they are lacking in understanding or wisdom (*paññā*). When the commentary assigns a certain meaning to *kusala*, it is valid to question whether all the other meanings of this term are excluded in that context.

In the *Nikāyas*, *kusala-dhammas* are regarded as arising in the course of a comprehensive and integrated training that includes the practice of ethical goodness (*sīla*), the cultivation and concentration of the mind (*samādhi*), and the development of wisdom (*paññā*). It is affirmed that these disciplines are interdependent and should be cultivated simultaneously. The methods of training that gradually lead to liberation from sorrow are perceived as stages of a "way" that has to be navigated with skilfulness (*kosallam*). In this context, skill signifies both knowledge of a method and competence in applying it. When a purposive impulse that ensues in an ethically good act is referred to as *kusala-cetanā*, the term *kusala* can indicate that ethically good motivation is as much an expression of skill as entry into meditation (*jhāna*). Ethical goodness is regarded as a skill involving specific techniques that are to be learnt through regular practice and instruction from a beneficent teacher. Through practice, one becomes good at being good. By the same argument, when *jhāna* states are designated as *kusala*, the term *kusala* signifies not only that they are skilfully developed through wisdom, but also that they are ethically good in the sense that they prevent mental "hindrances" (*nīvaraṇas*), which block both moral virtue and concentration of mind. With reference to both mental states (*dhammas*) associated with moral virtue and *jhāna* states, *kusala* can include in its meaning health (*ārogya*), interpreted as absence of an unhappy state of mind (*domanassa*) and freedom from the sickness of mental defilements (*kilesas*). When these defilements are compared to poisoned darts (S. I. 40, 192; Sn. 51, 334), or the mind afflicted by defilements is pictured as a barren land (M. I. 101; A. IV. 460; D. III. 238), the implication is that *akusala* states bring about an unhealthy, unhappy and unproductive frame of mind.

It follows, then, that *kusala* carries all the connotations of "well" in the term "well-being", and more. *Kusala* connotes much more than mental health that frees the mind from emotional stress and prepares the way for personal growth and development; it includes, in addition, felicity based on the conviction that the mind is directed towards ethical goodness resulting from wisely renouncing morally wrong mental states that distort one's perceptions and produce sorrow. By including *paññā* with the other connotations of *kusala*, the *Atthasālinī* maintains that moral goodness, at its best, includes a wise understanding of conditioned origination and the causes of sorrow. As a term used in ordinary parlance, *kusala* signifies not only good health but also skill in human relationships and wisdom in choosing both one's goals and the methods of attaining them.

Though the *Atthasālinī* links the wholesome (*kusala*) with wise understanding (*paññā*), this text concedes that wholesome *cittas* are of two types: those associated with knowledge (*ñāṇa-sampayutta*) and those dissociated from knowledge (*ñāṇa-vippayutta*) (Asl. 63). Wholesome states of mind associated with knowledge are defined as wholesome in three senses: "salutary" (*ārogya*), "faultless" (*anavajja*), and "produced by skill" (*kosalla-sambhūta*). In this context, "skill" represents understanding or wisdom. When dissociated from knowledge, wholesome states are said to lack skill, though they are marked by good health and freedom from fault. Here, "lack of skill" conveys that a wholesome act dissociated from knowledge (*ñāṇa*) is not well thought out and is not supported by reasoned judgment, though it is free of harmful intentions. In *Compendium of Philosophy*, Aung explains that in the *Abhidhammattha-saṅgaha* the three terms *paññā*, *ñāṇa*, and *amoha* (non-delusion) are not different in meaning.[21] He interprets the term *ñāṇa* in the designation "wholesome mental-states associated with *ñāṇa*" to mean the "intellectual" element expressed in processes of "comparison and discrimination", especially in the "reasoning processes (*takka-vīthi*)". According to Aung's interpretation, wholesome mental states defined as "associated with *ñāṇa*" are not only characterized by non-greed, non-aversion, and non-delusion, but also include a measure of judgment, reasoning, or purposive reflection.

The *Atthasālinī* (Asl. 63) gives the following definition of *kusala*, in accordance with the *Abhidhamma* method of analysis:

lakkhaṇa characteristic	*anavajja-sukha-vipāka* Wholesome states have the characteristic of bringing about faultless, happy results.
rasa function	*akusala-viddhaṁsana-rasa* They have the basic function of destroying the unwholesome.
paccupaṭṭhāna mode of manifestation	*vodāna-paccupaṭṭhāna* Purification is their actual mode of manifestation.
padaṭṭhāna proximate cause	*yoniso-manasikāra-padaṭṭhāna* They have systematic attention as proximate cause.

It is evident that the *Atthasālinī* perceives cognitive, emotive, and conative aspects of the mind to be engaged interdependently in producing a wholesome (*kusala*) state of consciousness. The honing of cognitive processes in the cultivation of careful attention (*yoniso-manasikāra*) is not considered possible if the mind's capacity for understanding (*paññā*) is vitiated by unwholesome emotions. At the same time, this definition of *kusala* implies that the mind cannot be purified of unwholesome emotions unless its cognitive capacity of attentiveness is empowered by conative energy (*viriya*) to initiate and sustain acts of purification. By the same argument, according to this definition, merely practical purposes or intentions of achieving beneficial goals are not considered to be sufficient for setting in motion the wholesome function of destroying unwholesome states. It is implied here that the function of uprooting the unwholesome and manifesting the wholesome can only be brought about through the cognitive process of focusing attention vigilantly and wisely on the mind and its objects, here and now. Undistorted perception results in purification. Furthermore, in this context, purification of the mind through systematic attention (*yoniso-manasikāra*) implies that the mind has the capacity of observing its own contents (*paccavekkhaṇa*) in such a way as to separate the wholesome from the unwholesome. It is surprising that *kusala* is not defined as that which is associated with the three wholesome roots. However, the definition does say that *kusala* manifests itself as the process of cleansing the mind (*vodāna*), implying the removal of the unwholesome and the production of the wholesome. It is obvious that the three defining characteristics of *kusala* consisting of good health in the sense of freedom from unhealthy mental states, blamelessness achieved through removing these mental defilements, and skill manifested as systematic and wise attention are included in this definition.

The *Atthasālinī* and the *Visuddhimagga* make it clear that wholesome states of consciousness occur in the ordinary (*lokiya*) everyday life that is designated as "the sphere of sensory experience" (*kāmāvacara*). Wholesome mental states are said to be experienced by ordinary people, who are not free of persistent unwholesome tendencies (*anusayas*) and mental corruptions (*āsavas*). *Kusala*, therefore, is not necessarily *anāsava*. The wholesome does not imply entire absence of the unwholesome, and the defining characteristic of the wholesome is not fully accomplished purity but participation in the dynamic process of purifying (*vodāna*) the mind of the causes of sorrow. When *cetanā* is associated with a wholesome frame of mind, it represents purposive thought and conative impulse directed towards that process of purification. If the wholesome *citta* is associated with a degree of knowledge (*ñāṇa-sampayutta*), the wholesome purposive impulse (*cetanā*) emerging from that wholesome *citta* becomes conditioned by cognitive processes of discriminative judgment and discernment.

Wholesome and Unwholesome "Roots"

Despite their designation, the three unwholesome "roots" (greed, hatred, and delusion) and the wholesome ones (non-greed, non-hate, and non-delusion) are not conceived as lasting structures or subliminal blueprints within consciousness. Their mode of functioning is similar to that of the persistent unwholesome tendencies (*anusayas*) in that they arise again and again as conditions in the continuum of consciousness, producing behaviour that is marked by repeated patterns of habits. The inclusion of the roots in the lists of mental factors (*cetasikas*) that constitute wholesome or unwholesome *cittas* (Dhs. 9, 76; Vsm. XIV. 133, 159, 170, 176) signals that a wholesome or unwholesome root (for example, non-greed or greed) originates from mental conditions accompanying the same sensory and mental stimulation that produces the *citta* that contains the root. It follows that the roots are conceived as conditionally produced mental factors that come into being as the dominant constituents of a series of transitory states of mind (*cittas*). However, although these roots of action are placed among the mental factors that constitute a *citta*, it is acknowledged that their capacity to affect the inner dynamics of an attitude of mind exceeds the influence of concomitant mental factors. Each root determines what mental factors can arise under its influence and function compatibly with its own wholesome or unwholesome characteristics. A root condition, therefore, "stabilizes" a *citta* and renders all of its wholesome or unwholesome characteristics clearly manifest. In other words, though a *citta* exists only for a moment, the presence of wholesome or unwholesome roots establishes it, with all its components and accompaniments, as a clearly recognizable typical "stance" of the consciousness continuum.

Of the three unwholesome roots, since greed (*lobha*) and hate (*dosa*) represent, respectively, the polarity of attraction to the desirable and aversion to the undesirable, they cannot coexist in the same *citta*. Delusion (*moha*) is regarded as the mental factor that puts its distinctive mark on all unwholesome *cittas* and sustains them; therefore, without the presence of delusion, greed and hate are said to be incapable of fulfilling their function as roots.[22] Delusion, by contrast, is considered to be capable of functioning without the collaboration of the other two unwholesome roots and of developing into intense delusion (*momūha*) when it functions as the sole root. The definition of greed (Asl. 248-249; Vsm. XIV. 162) says that its distinguishing characteristic (*lakkhaṇa*) is to grasp objects, and compares its action of clinging to objects to meat sticking to a hot pan. The mode of manifestation of greed is described as not renouncing or not letting go (*apariccāga*) any physical or mental object, and its proximate cause is held to be finding enjoyment in objects that subsequently produce the unwholesome mental states that are designated as "fetters" (*saṁyojanāni*) that cause *kamma*.

According to the *Visuddhimagga* (Vsm. XIV. 171), hate has the characteristic of ferocity and the function of spreading and destroying the entire organism in which it arises and finds support, like a raging fire or a drop of poison. Delusion (*moha*) is shown to be much more complex in its functioning than greed or hatred (Asl. 249; Vsm. XIV. 163). The definition of delusion in the *Visuddhimagga* gives its characteristic as opposition to understanding, and its mode of functioning is portrayed as hiding the actual specific nature (*sabhāva*) of an object from the perceiver. The definition also states that delusion manifests as confusion or ignorance that opposes right conduct by preventing insight into the way things actually are. The proximate cause of delusion is specified as lack of thorough, systematic attention (*ayoniso-manasikāra*). *Moha* is succinctly defined as the root cause of all unwholesome attitudes of mind (Asl. 249).

The definition of the three wholesome roots in the *Visuddhimagga* (Vsm. XIV. 143) and the fuller explanation in the *Atthasālinī* (Asl. 127-129) make it clear that the terms non-greed (*alobha*), non-hatred (*adosa*), and non-delusion (*amoha*) do not connote the entire absence of greed, hate, and delusion, but rather, the presence of mental states that resist and oppose their unwholesome influence. The *Atthasālinī* (Asl. 127) says that non-greed and non-hate are opposites (*paṭipakkha*), respectively, of the impurities of avarice or stinginess and bad conduct. Non-delusion is said to oppose whatever prevents the cultivation of wholesome mental factors. The three wholesome roots are described as the causes, respectively, of generous giving (*dāna*), virtue (*sīla*), and the cultivation (*bhāvanā*) of mindfulness and concentration. The *Abhidhamma* method of classification of mental states, therefore, confirms the view of the *Suttas* that wholesome mental states can arise, even though the *āsavas* continue to condition thoughts, emotions, and acts. In Theravāda, ethical goodness (*kusala*) is conceived in two ways: on the one hand, it is an ideal to be attained; on the other hand, it is a vibrant motivating energy arising through causes and conditions in the continuum of consciousness. In the stages of the path of purification (*vodāna*), non-greed, which is first arises as generosity (*dāna*), is transformed into total absence of greed; non-hate, which first manifests as friendship (*mettā*), is transformed into total absence of hate; and non-delusion, which first functions as the cultivation of mindfulness (*sati*), is transformed into the entire absence of delusion. This interpretation implies that whereas generosity, friendship, and understanding can arise from time to time in the consciousness continuum of a beginner in the Eightfold Path, the unwholesome roots are entirely eradicated only in the enlightened life of an *arahant.* In the beginning stages of the Path, when generosity, friendship and mindfulness begin to burgeon, the roots of greed, hate and delusion are still threateningly present. In the heart of an *arahant,* there are no traces of greed, hate, or delusion whatsoever (S. IV. 251,261).

The *Atthasālinī* (Asl. 129) makes the profound statement that the cultivation of non-greed, non-hate, and non-delusion produce, respectively, insight into impermanence (*anicca-dassana*), direct and unmediated awareness of the sorrow experienced by all beings (*dukkha-dassana*), and clear perception of the absence of a separate and permanent self (*anatta-dassana*). These insights in turn are regarded as nourishment for the further development of non-greed, non-hate, and non-delusion. Here the *Atthasālinī* affirms a principle that is regarded as fundamental to all disciplines of *yoga*: wholesome attitudes and acts are viewed as the vehicles through which liberating wisdom is ultimately attained. Acts of friendship, for example, are seen as concrete expressions of insight into the sorrow (*dukkha*) that all beings feel, and such insight is perceived to be impossible to attain without experiencing genuine friendship in one's life. This passage in the *Atthasālinī* resonates with a statement in the *Saṁyutta-nikāya* (S. IV. 261) where Sāriputta defines *nibbāna* as the complete cessation of passion (*rāgakkhaya*), hate (*dosakkhaya*), and delusion (*mohakkhaya*). When non-greed, non-hate, and non-delusion become manifest not only as expressions of generosity, friendship, and mindfulness, but as the entire absence of greed, hate, and delusion, then *nibbāna* is attained.

The Composition of Wholesome States of Mind.

The *Abhidhamma* system of classifying mental states maintains that no purposive impulse (*cetanā*) can arise and become expressed in action (*kamma*) without the support of the cognitive, emotive, and conative components of a specific state of mind (*citta*). According to this view, greedy purposive impulses, for example, emerge from complex, many-faceted, greedy attitudes of mind. From the *Abhidhamma* perspective, then, it is necessary to see the inner dynamics of wholesome and unwholesome *citta*s in order to understand the nature of the *cetanā*s that emerge from them.

In its detailed classification of *citta*s, the *Visuddhimagga* (Vsm. XIV. 133) holds that there are thirty-six possible mental factors (*cetasika*s) that can enter into the composition of different types of wholesome states of mind. Each *cetasika* can be viewed as a "nuance in consciousness"—to borrow a phrase from Aung[23]—that interacts with its concomitants in such a manner as to form a wholesome (*kusala*) attitude of mind (Chart 7). The *Visuddhimagga* (Vsm. XIV. 133) divides the *cetasika*s of a wholesome *citta* into the following three groups: the "constant" factors (*niyata*), the "supplementary" factors (*yevāpanaka*),[24] and the "inconstant" factors (*aniyata*). The constant mental factors invariably occur as a set, and their presence is considered necessary either for the maintenance of conscious awareness or to give a *citta* its specific wholesome or unwholesome nature. The supplementary ones are mental factors (*cetasika*s) that may arise as constituents of a state of mind (*citta*) in response to a particular occasion. This category of "supplementary" factors implies that the list of mental factors forming a specific type of *citta* is not to be regarded as final and closed. In fact, any specific situation may become the occasion for the arising of more supplementary factors. Unlike the constant factors, the inconstant factors do not form a set, and their presence is not considered necessary to give a *citta* its wholesome or unwholesome character. Nevertheless, these inconstant factors do call attention to the variations that occur in specific types of *cittas*. For example, in the case of persons following the Eightfold Path, wholesome *cittas* include the mental factors of restraint of bodily misconduct, restraint of verbal misconduct, and abstaining from wrong livelihood. However, these mental facors may not be present in the wholesome *cittas* of those who are not committed to following the Eightfold Path. Likewise, in specific cases, mental attitudes dominated by hate may include the inconstant unwholesome factors of envy, avarice, and futile worry. It is obvious that these mental states can give an added dimension of unwholesomeness to hate, but they are not present in all *cittas* dominated by hate.

The *Atthasālinī* explains that the constant (*niyata*) *cetasikas* are so named because they are mentioned regularly as "constituents of consciousness" in the Pāli texts (Asl. 132). For the sake of clarification, the twenty-seven constant *cetasikas* in a wholesome *citta* can be divided into three sub-groups. First, there is the triad of sensory contact (*phassa*), purposive impulse imbued with the capacity to initiate action (*cetanā*), and vitality (*jīvitindriya*). These three are considered basic factors of sentience in the *Visuddhimagga*. They appear in all classes of consciousness: the wholesome, the unwholesome, and the ethically indeterminate. Next, there is a group of five *cetasikas*, some or all of which appear also in unwholesome *cittas*. For this reason, it can be inferred that these *cetasikas* are ethically "neutral" and become wholesome or unwholesome according to the ethical quality of the *citta* of which they are components. These include initial application of thought (*vitakka*), sustained thought (*vicāra*), zest, interest, or delight in the object (*pīti*), energy or exertion (*viriya*), and concentration of attention on the object (*samādhi*). Of these ethically neutral *cetasikas*, *viriya* is closest to *cetanā*, since it shares the latter's purposive thrust.

Next, the constant *cetasikas* include a group of mental factors that can be regarded as morally decisive, since they specifically oppose unwholesome factors and give to the *citta* its wholesome quality. The first of these, faith (*saddhā*), is described as having the function of cleansing the mind of pollutants and bringing forth serene, clear-minded commitment to a goal. Faith is said to manifest itself as the resolve based on trust (*adhimutti*) that motivates and empowers a person to undertake difficult tasks (Vsm. XIV. 140; Asl. 120). Faith is followed in the list by mindfulness (*sati*), which is regarded as indispensable for the cultivation of the wholesome roots of action. The next two wholesome *cetasikas*, namely shame (*hiri*) at the very thought of doing wrong, and dread (*ottappa*) of evil, show the influence of social and cultural ideals on concepts of "wholesome" and "unwholesome" in the *Suttas* and in the *Abhidhamma* system. These two mental factors are considered to be invariably present in all wholesome states of mind. *Hiri* is defined as conscientiousness based on training and a sense of respect for oneself; *ottappa* is said to be based on a healthy fear of the consequences of evil and on respect for others (Vsm. XIV. 142). The next three constant *cetasikas* are the three wholesome roots of action: non-greed, non-hate, and non-delusion.

Finally, the wholesome *citta* contains a group of *cetasikas* that ensure tranquillity (*passaddhi*), buoyancy (*lahutā*), flexibility (*mudutā*), adaptability or literally, readiness to be put to work (*kammaññatā*), proficiency (*pāguññatā*), and rectitude (*ujjukatā*) that opposes deceit and fraud (Vsm. XIV. 144-149). These mental factors that endow wholesome *cittas* with the capacity to function with mental ease and proficiency pertain both to the *citta* as a whole and to three of the mental aggregates: feelings, perceptions, and constructive activities (*saṅkhāras*). This group of factors of ease and proficiency demonstrates that the wholesome (*kusala*) is conceived as a blending of mental health, moral goodness manifested in body and mind, and skilfulness based on understanding. Guenther explains that the "functional ease" that arises from this group of mental factors is regarded as an inseparable feature of a wholesome attitude of mind.[25] If they are not present, a mental state would not be designated as "wholesome".

The supplementary, or *yevāpanaka* states are so named because, though their status as mental factors is not firmly established in the *Suttas*, they are named and described in various passages (Asl. 132). The four supplementary *cetasikas* in the wholesome *cittas* include impetus to act (*chanda*), resolution or decision (*adhimokkha*) in responding to the object, attention (*manasikāra*), and equipoise or wholesome balance of mind (*tatra-majjhattatā*). Of these four mental factors, impetus to act, decision, and attention to the object are also functions of unwholesome *cittas*. It follows that these *cetasikas* become wholesome or unwholesome in accordance with the ethical quality of the *citta* to which they belong. It is to be noted that two of the supplementary mental factors, namely impetus to act (*chanda*) and resolve (*adhimokkha*), resemble the constant factor that functions as energy (*viriya*) because, like *viriya,* they reinforce the purposive thought and motivating impulse of *cetanā.* In its simplest form, *adhimokkha* is the personal inclination that causes the mind to focus on one object rather than on others in the environment (Vsm. XIV. 151), but in a more developed form, this inclination grows into a strong faith and firm resolve that supports and upholds the commitment to pursue a chosen goal (Vsm. XIV. 140). Similarly, the basic impetus to act (*chanda*) manifests as zeal in pursuing an object and grows into either the unwholesome motivation directed to objects of pleasure (*kāma-chanda*) or the wholesome resolve to follow the teachings of the Buddha (*dhamma-chanda*).

The five inconstant (*aniyata*) mental factors in wholesome *cittas* are connected with specific Buddhist disciplines. Two of these disciplines comprise meditating on two "immeasurable" factors, namely endless compassion (*karuṇā*) and endless participation in the joy of others (*muditā*). Three factors of the Eightfold Path, namely, right action, right speech, and right livelihood, are also included in this category. They are designated as "inconstant factors" because they are not invariably present in wholesome *cittas* but arise only with the cultivation of the specific disciplines to which they are related.

Eight Types of Wholesome *Cittas* and *Cetanās*

The *Visuddhimagga* (Vsm. XIV. 156) classifies wholesome mental states that arise in the realm of ordinary sensory and rational experience (*kamāvacara*) into eight types (Chart 11). It is posited that these eight types of wholesome *cittas* produce the corresponding eight types of wholesome purposive impulses (*cetanās*) that become manifest as wholesome purposive acts bearing beneficent karmic consequences (*sañcetanika-kamma*). In this classification of wholesome *cittas* (Vsm. XIV. 83-85), the variables are whether the *citta* is prompted (*sasaṅkhāra*) or not prompted (*asaṅkhāra*), whether or not the *citta* is associated with knowledge (*ñāṇa*), and whether the *citta* is conjoined with joy (*somanassa*) or with a neutral state (*upekkhā*) defined as neither joy nor dejection. The *Visuddhimagga* (Vsm. XIV. 84) succinctly explains "prompting" as prior exertion (*pubba-payoga*) on the part of oneself or another person, depending on whether the instigation comes form oneself or from another. *Somanassa* is explained as a mental feeling of pleasure that is marked by excitation or stimulation.[26] In the *Abhidhamma* method of classification, wholesome *cittas* are perceived to be conjoined with joy (*somanassa*) or with a neutral mental state (*upekkhā*), but never with mental displeasure.[27] This reflects the Theravāda view that what is wholesome is in harmony with the aspiration of all beings to be at ease and free of sorrow. Wholesome *cittas* do not cause a rift in the mind since they are free of regret and agitation. In this classification of wholesome *cittas* into eight types, the other variable, knowledge (*ñāṇa*), represents a degree of understanding about the nature of the act and its consequences.

The *Visuddhimagga* (XIV. 84-85) gives the following examples of the eight types of wholesome *cittas*. When an appropriate gift is gladly made to the right person, without instigation and with an understanding of "right view", then the state of consciousness (*citta*) of the giver is associated with knowledge (*ñāṇa*) and with joy (*somanassa*), and the action is unprompted (*asaṅkhāra*). Right view signifies awareness of the conditioned and ephemeral nature of the gift and the transience of all beings. On the other hand, when a gift is made in the same manner as above, but with some prompting, the mind of the giver is associated with knowledge and joy, but the action is prompted (*sasaṅkhāra*). When children, imitating their parents, give gifts happily and spontaneously, but without yet having cultivated right view and an understanding of the significance of their action, their attitude of mind (*citta*) is associated with joy but is dissociated from knowledge, and their intention to give is unprompted. In the case of children who are prompted to offer gifts and do so cheerfully but without understanding, their act of giving proceeds from a state of mind that is associated with joy but is dissociated from knowledge and is prompted. If joy is replaced by a state of neither pleasure nor displeasure (*upekkhā*) in the four instances given above, then we have four corresponding types of wholesome *cittas* imbued with a neutral feeling rather than with joy.

In the case of any of these *cittas*, purposive thought becomes translated into purposive action through the purposive impulse of *cetanā*. In the examples given above, the intention to give (*dāna-cetanā*) and the manner of giving that it motivates match the dominant thoughts and emotional features of the wholesome attitude of mind (*citta*) from which the intention arises. Intention matches attitude of mind, and act matches intention.

The Inner Dynamics of Unwholesome States of Mind

Unwholesome states of mind are classified as those dominated by either greed or aversion or delusion.

Unwholesome citta dominated by greed (lobha)

The *Visuddhimagga* (XIV.159) reckons thirteen constant (*niyata*) mental factors and four supplementary (*yevāpanaka*) states to be the ingredients that constitute unwholesome *cittas* dominated by greed (Chart 8). Of the thirteen constant or invariably present factors, five give the *citta* its specific characteristic of greed and render it unwholesome, while eight ensure the continuance of conscious awareness and the efficient working of consciousness in relation to objects. These eight include sensory and mental contact with objects, purposive impulse (*cetanā*), vitality, initial application of thought, sustained thought, delight based on interest in the object, energy, and concentration of attention on the object. These factors occur also in wholesome *cittas*. The five morally decisive states that oppose wholesome factors and render consciousness greedy and unwholesome are the following: dishonourable lack of shame in doing wrong deeds (*ahirika*), absence of fear of the consequences of evil (*anottappa*), greed (*lobha*), delusion (*moha*), and wrong view (*micchā-diṭṭhi*). Unscrupulous lack of shame at doing wrong and absence of fear of the consequences of evil are regarded as mental states that arise through lack of integrity, absence of conscientiousness, and failure of training. Every *cetanā* that arises as a purposive impulse in unwholesome *cittas* is considered to be infected by these two mental states and, more fundamentally, by a deluded outlook on life (*moha*).

The supplementary (*yevāpanaka*) states in unwholesome *cittas* of greed are impetus to act (*chanda*), resolution or decision (*adhimokkha*) in focusing the mind on an object, attention (*manasikāra*) to the object, and restlessness or agitation (*uddhacca*). It is postulated that under the influence of deluded desire and restlessness, the ethically neutral mental factors of impetus to act, decisiveness, and attention manifest, respectively, as impetus to pursue sensory pleasure (*kāmacchanda*), weakness and wavering with regard to focusing on an object (*citta-vikkhepa*), and unsystematic, unwise attention (*ayoniso-manasikāra*).

The *Visuddhimagga* (Vsm. XIV. 167-168) goes on to say that there are two "inconstant" factors that can affect the entire emotional colour of a greedy state of consciousness. The first of these is a combination of sluggish dullness (*thīna*) and lethargy or laziness (*middha*) that arises from unsystematic, unwise attention (*ayoniso-manasikāra*) and blocks activity that is spontaneous and not instigated. The second is conceit (*māna*) that is said to manifest as obsessive concern with one's self-image. In its extreme form, self-obsessive conceit is compared to mental derangement.

Unwholesome citta associated with hate (dosa)

According to the *Abhidhamma* method of classification, greed (*lobha*) and hate or aversion (*dosa*) cannot co-exist in the same mental state (*citta*), because they are polar opposites: greed is based on attraction to the object and desire to acquire it, while aversion is based on rejection and repulsion that wishes to harm the object.

The *Visuddhimagga* regards a restless state of mind (*uddhacca*) to be common to both greed and hate (*dosa*). Envy, avarice, and worry based on blaming oneself are specified as the distinctive impelling forces of hate. Aversion (*paṭigha*), described as rejection stemming from ill will coupled with a wish to cause injury, is regarded as the mark of hate.[28] The *Visuddhimagga* (Vsm. XIV. 170) lists eleven constant, four supplementary, and three inconstant mental factors as the constituents of *cittas* dominated by hate (Chart 9). Like all other *cittas*, these *cittas* dominated by hate contain the constant, invariably present mental factors that maintain sentience and guarantee the basic cognitive and conative functions of consciousness. These factors comprise contact with an object, purposive impulse (*cetanā*), life-giving vitality, inception of thought, sustained thought, energy, and concentration of attention on an object. However, zest or delight (*pīti*) in experiencing an object is considered compatible with greed, but incompatible with hate, because hate arises from repulsion. The constant factors (*cetasikas*) also include the dominant emotional state of hate (*dosa*) and the three following factors that are deemed necessary to render a *citta* unwholesome: delusion (*moha*), lack of shame or scruple in doing wrong (*ahiri*), and lack of wholesome fear of the consequences of evil (*anottappa*).

The same four supplementary factors, namely impetus to act, decisiveness in turning to an object, attention, and a disturbing restlessness, are listed as constitutents of both *cittas* rooted in greed and *cittas* rooted in hate. The *Visuddhimagga* regards agitation or restlessness or disturbance of mind (*uddhacca*) to be a supplementary feature of all unwholesome states of mind, whether they are obsessed by greed, hate-ridden, or confounded by delusion. Three *cetasikas* are listed as inconstant, not always present, factors that may arise together or separately on specific occasions: envy (*issā*) marked by jealousy at the success of others, avarice (*macchariya*) manifested as shrinking from the very thought of sharing one's gains with others, and worry (*kukkucca*) that leads to regret and self-castigation regarding what one has done and left undone (Vsm. XIV. 172-174; Asl. 373-376). These factors are regarded as manifestations of hate.

The *Visuddhimagga* (Vsm. XIV. 175) goes on to say that a state of consciousness rooted in hate will manifest differently if a combination of dullness and laziness (*thīna-middha*) arises as an inconstant mental factor and enters into its constitution. It is posited that in spite of the repulsion produced by hatred, a mind pervaded by sluggish lethargy will act only when prompted (*sasaṅkhārika*).

Unwholesome citta rooted in delusion (moha)

Like the Upaniṣadic and Yoga traditions, Theravāda regards delusion (*moha*) to be the fundamental cause of unwholesome attitudes of mind. It is worth emphasizing again that *moha* includes both a cognitive component of ignorance (*avijjā*) manifested as a wrong view of life (*micchā-diṭṭhi*) as well as an emotive component, which consists of a passionate infatuation towards chosen objects. Such deluded obsession makes a person ignore the complex totality of a given situation. The *Visuddhimagga* (Vsm. XIV. 176, 178) holds that states of mind rooted in delusion (*moha*) can manifest in two ways: they can be marked either by indecision (*vicikicchā*) or by agitated restlessness (*uddhacca*). In this manner, the *Visuddhimagga* appears to reduce the range of nuances in the motivating capacity of delusion either to perplexed indecision or unsettling agitation. However, it can be expected that *moha* will put forth seemingly countless variations of confusion and bewilderment when its spell is intensified by the perplexed wavering of *vicikicchā* or the restless agitation of *uddhacca.* Restlessness (*uddhacca*) ranges from vague disturbance to violent turbulence caused by infatuation based on ignorance. Both perplexity and restlessness prevent a person from applying systematic attention (*yoniso-manasikāra*) to the network of causes and conditions that impinge on any situation, thereby intensifying delusion (*moha*).

In the *Visuddhimagga* classification (Vsm. XIV. 176), eleven constant mental factors and two supplementary mental factors are listed as possible components of deluded states of mind associated with perplexity (Chart 10). As in the case of wholesome *cittas* and *cittas* rooted in desire and in hate, several constant factors that ensure basic conscious awareness and the continuous functioning of consciousness are included in *cittas* rooted in delusion. According to the *Abhidhamma* method of classification, zest or delight in the object (*pīti*) does not occur in *cittas* rooted either in hate or in delusion. Whereas hatred is considered to be marked by a mental quality of unhappiness (*domanassa*) based on aversion to objects, delusion is associated with a neutral feeling (*upekkhā*) experienced as neither joy nor displeasure. This neutral feeling causes a person to remain oblivious of the actual qualities of an object and blocks any genuine, joyful appreciation of the object. The constant factors in mental states rooted in delusion include the following two that are considered signposts of unwholesome states of consciousness: dishonourable lack of shame (*ahirika*) in unethical behaviour and lack of fear (*anottappa*) of the consequences of wrongdoing. It was noted above that deluded states of mind are considered to be dominated by either perplexed indecision (*vicikicchā*) or restlessness (*uddhacca*). The *Visuddhimagga* (Vsm. XIV. 176) maintains that the mental factor of focusing attention (*samādhi*) on an object cannot occur in states of mind beset by the unsteadiness of indecision (*vicikicchā*). Only very brief and weak spans of concentration are considered capable of coexisting with indecision. Similarly, resoluteness or decisiveness (*adhimokkha*) in responding to the object is said to be inhibited by this doubt-ridden state of confused and deluded indecision.

According to the classification in the *Visuddhimagga* (Chart 10), indecision or perplexity (*vicikicchā*) is not present in deluded states of mind associated with restlessness (*uddhacca*). A deluded and restless state of mind is considered to be capable of accommodating the following factors: some degree of decisiveness (*adhimokkha*) regarding the object to be attended to, some measure of attention (*manasikāra*) to the object, and stronger mental concentration (*samādhi*) than is possible in a state of perplexed indecision. This description of how delusion functions as an unwholesome "root" implies that intentions and purposive impulses (*cetanās*) arising in a deluded state of mind will be trapped by indecisive wavering or by uneasy restlessness, with the result that steady resolve and persistent endeavour will become difficult, if not impossible, to attain.

Twelve Unwholesome *Cittas* and *Cetanās*

The *Visuddhimagga* classifies unwholesome *cittas*—all of which arise in the realm of sensory experience (*kāmāvacara*)—into twelve types: eight rooted in greed, two rooted in hate and two rooted in delusion (Chart 12). According to the *Abhidhamma* system, unwholesome mental states do not arise in levels of meditation. With regard to the processes of *kamma* and rebirth, the *Visuddhimagga* (Vsm. XVII. 44, 60) holds that unwholesome *cittas* condition twelve corresponding types of purposive impulses (*cetanās*) that become expressed in unwholesome goal-driven physical, verbal, and mental acts (*abhisaṅkhāras*). These acts are characterized by demerit and produce commensurate unpleasant karmic consequences.

In the list of the eight types of unwholesome *cittas* rooted in greed, the variables are the presence or absence of joy (*somanassa*), neutral feeling (*upekkhā*), speculative view (*diṭṭhi*), and prompting or instigation (*sasaṅkhāra*) (Vsm. XIV. 90). The *Visuddhimagga* (Vsm. XIV. 91) gives the following examples. When a person who is in a happy frame of mind (*somanassa*), but is controlled by wrong views (*micchā-diṭṭhi*), greedily seeks out sensory pleasures without being prompted (*asaṅkhāra*), then the first type of greedy consciousness arises. The second type of greedy mind is identical with the first, except that it is characterized by dullness and sluggishness (*thīna-middha*), and requires prompting (*sasaṅkhāra*). When a person is joyful (*somanassa*) and uninfluenced by wrong views but nevertheless engages in wrong and unwholesome greedy behaviour without being prompted to do so (*asaṅkhāra*), the third type of *citta* of greed arises. The fourth type of greedy *citta* exhibits a happy state of mind, but because it is lazy and lethargic, it acts only when prompted (*sasaṅkhāra*). This type of *citta* manages to remain uninfluenced by wrong views. When joy is absent in the four instances given above and is replaced by a neutral feeling (*upekkhā*) characterized neither by joy nor by displeasure, then the remaining four types of unwholesome states of mind rooted in greed arise. According to the analysis given in the *Visuddhimagga* (XIV. 168), a greedy mind is motivated either by wrong view (*micchā-diṭṭhi*) or by conceit (*māna*). In the *Sammādiṭṭhi-sutta* (M. I. 46-55), right view is regarded as including an understanding of which states of mind are wholesome and which are not, as well as a knowledge of the main Buddhist teachings: the Four Noble Truths, the Four Nutriments (*āhāra*), and the Twelve Links of conditioned origination. In Theravāda, a mind that is afflicted by a wrong view of life is considered to be prone to greed because of not acknowledging the transitory and conditioned nature of things. Nevertheless, a person who intellectually affirms conditioned origination may still be motivated by greed because of conceit (*māna*) that develops into pride and a self-centred approach to life.

The *Visuddhimagga* (Vsm. XIV. 92) describes states of mind rooted in hate (*dosa-mūla*) as those that bear the distinct marks of cheerlessness or displeasure (*domanassa*) and aversion (*paṭigha*). These hate-ridden states of mind are classified into two types: those that are characterized by laziness and dullness (*thīna-middha*), so that they produce action only when they are instigated; and those that are characterized by restless agitation (*uddhacca*) and have the capacity to act without being prompted.

States of mind rooted solely in delusion (*momūha-citta*) are also regarded as twofold: they are conditioned either by indecision arising from confused, perplexed thinking (*vicikicchā-sahagata*) or by restlessness (*uddhacca-sahagata*). The lists of *cetasikas* in the *Visuddhimagga* show that a disturbed, restless mind is a characteristic of all unwholesome *cittas*. However, according to the *Abhidhamma*, whereas restlessness is a secondary feature in other unwholesome *cittas*, in a deluded frame of mind it becomes a principal factor. The *Visuddhimagga* emphasizes that each of these twelve types of unwholesome attitudes of mind (eight rooted in greed, two in hatred, and two in delusion) is capable of generating a corresponding type of purposive impulse (*cetanā*) that leads to an unwholesome intentional act.

Relationship Between Feeling (*Vedanā*) and *Cetanā*

In the verses of the *Dhammapada*, various thoughts regarding wholesome and unwholesome mental states are strung together like a garland of flowers. In the scattered references to the criteria for assigning moral values to acts, judgments regarding how people ought to make ethical decisions become inseparably linked with the idea that all beings naturally desire happiness (*sukha-kāmāni bhūtāni*) and fear death (*sabbe bhāyanti maccuno*) (Dhp. 129-132). According to the teaching given in the *Dhammapada*, since one can see in one's own being an example of how all beings yearn for happiness (*attānam upamānaṁ katvā*), one ought neither to harm any being nor instigate others to cause harm. In this way, the *Dhammapada* bases its ethical judgment of how human beings ought to act on its psychological assessment of feelings that are "natural" to the human mind. This link between happiness (*sukha*) and moral goodness that the *Dhammapada* posits underlies the lists of wholesome and unwholesome *cittas* that the *Visuddhimagga* presents.

In the *Tipiṭaka*, the term *sukha* covers a whole range of feelings, from absence of physical pain to the complete bliss of *nibbāna*. A distinction is made between bodily sensation (*kayika-vedanā*) and mental feeling (*cetasika-vedanā*), and feelings are divided into five types: pleasant bodily sensation (*sukha*), painful bodily sensation (*dukkha*), mental joy (*somanassa*), mental dejection (*domanassa*), and a neutral mental state of neither joy nor dejection (*upekkhā*) (S. IV. 232). The neutral state can be transformed into a serene state of balanced equanimity through the cultivation of mindfulness and meditation. From this distinction between bodily sensation and mental feeling follows the practical teaching that a person can remain tranquil even while enduring severe physical pain or compassionately responding to the pain of others. The *Mahāparinibbāna-sutta* presents the example of the Buddha, whose luminous calm does not diminish as he faces physical weakness and dehydration, the knowledge of possible warfare and destruction in the familiar places where he had lived and taught, and the awareness of approaching death (D. II. 72-76, 102, 129-130).

The idea that all conditioned things (*saṅkhāras*) are capable of producing feelings of physical pain or mental dejection is a central tenet of Theravāda. The relationship between conditioned origination and sorrow (*dukkha*), however, requires further interpretation. It is postulated in Theravāda that all conditioned states—physical and mental—bear three marks (*lakkhaṇas*): impermanence, absence of inherent individuality or selfhood, and possibility of becoming a cause of sorrow. The first two of these *lakkhaṇas* constitute the very principle of conditioned origination. It would not be possible to affirm conditioned origination without implying, at the same time, that all things are subject to change and that nothing can claim an autonomous and separate individuality. In contradistinction to these two distinguishing marks, sorrow is defined as a factor that arises within the process of conditioned origination because of the presence of two necessary conditions: ignorance (*avijjā*) and craving (*taṇhā*).

Whereas impermanence (*anicca*) and the absence of inherent individuality (*anattā*) signify the actual nature of things (*yathā-bhūtam*) and are constitutive features of conditioned origination, sorrow (*dukkha*) ceases when the conditions that cause it to arise come to cessation. This notion of the conditioned nature of sorrow has to be taken into account in analysing the relationship between various attitudes of mind and the feelings that are associated with them.

There is a passage in the *Aṅguttara-nikāya* (A. II. 2) where the Buddha sets forth the four essential factors of his method of training: virtue (*sīla*), concentration (*samādhi*), wisdom (*paññā*), and release from sorrow (*vimutti*). The Buddha's discourse is followed by a verse which ends by joyfully proclaiming that the goal of happiness is attained by means of happiness (*sukhenānvāgataṁ sukham*). The verse signifies that virtue, concentration, and wisdom constitute the happy path that leads to the supreme happiness of *nibbāna*. The idea that experiences of happiness give momentum to those who cultivate the wholesome and seek ultimate freedom from sorrow is affirmed in the *Atthasālinī* and the *Visuddhimagga*. In the lists of mental states presented in these texts, one can clearly see the harmonizing of wholesome happiness and ethical goodness. These texts take the position that wholesome *cittas* are conjoined either with happiness (*somanassa*) or with a neutral state (*upekkhā*) characterized neither by pleasure nor by pain, but never with mental displeasure, unease, or dejection (*domanassa*) (Chart 11). Among the *cetasikas* that constitute a wholesome *citta* are factors that make for tranquillity (*passaddhi*), buoyancy (*lahutā*), and flexibility (*mudutā*) in the mind as a whole as well as in the aggregates of feelings (*vedanā*), perceptions (*saññā*), and constructive activities (*saṅkhāra*), which are included in the *citta*. It follows that *cetanās* proceeding from wholesome *cittas* must reflect a serene and happy state of mental health as well as moral goodness. In these lists of mental states, mental displeasure is the distinctive feature of the aversion or revulsion (*paṭigha*) that prevails in unwholesome states dominated by hate (*dosa*).

It is held that *cittas* rooted in sheer delusion (*momūha*) are always conjoined with a neutral feeling (*upekkhā*). Bhikkhu Bodhi explains that according to the *Abhidhamma*, the attitudes of restlessness (*uddhacca*) or indecision (*vicikicchā*) that beset delusion-based states of mind prevent a person from appreciating the actual nature of an object and responding to it either with joy or with displeasure.[29] It follows that purposive impulses (*cetanās*) that emerge from deluded *cittas* are similarly conjoined with neutral feelings that block genuine understanding and whole-hearted responses to objects. Restless agitation and indecision are seen as factors that can vitiate a person's entire life, and restlessness is regarded as having such a grip on the mind that its last traces are removed only at the final stages of the Path of liberation.[30]

As one contemplates the lists of wholesome and unwholesome mental states, it is startling to see that only the two types of mental states associated with hate (*dosa*) are deemed to be invariably associated with mental displeasure (*domanassa*). These are states of hate that are either prompted or unprompted (Chart 12). The idea that mental uneasiness (*domanassa*) invariably accompanies *cittas* and *cetanās* rooted in hate can be interpreted as an indication that the description of wholesome and unwholesome mental states in the *Visuddhimagga* and the *Atthasālinī* resonates with the link between happiness and ethical goodness that is upheld in the teaching of the *Dhammapada*. These teachings imply that purposive impulses based on hate go against the instinctive recognition that all beings, like oneself, aspire for happiness and security from harm. *Domanassa* carries a range of meanings, all linked to feelings of discomfort with oneself and alienation from others; it conveys sadness, uneasiness of mind, dejection, melancholy, disappointment and grief.

According to the *Visuddhimagga*, the *cetasika* of zestful interest or delight (*pīti*) in an object is missing both in *cittas* based on hate (Vsm. XIV. 170) and in *cittas* based on delusion (Vsm. XIV. 176). *Pīti*, associated with wholesome sense-sphere *cittas*, is described as a mental state that blossoms into various forms of refreshing joy and felicity. Guenther points out that in the *Atthasālinī* (Asl. 143), *pīti* is associated with the state of mind designated as *attamanatā*.[31] The latter term means, literally, "the state of being one's own mind". The *Atthasālinī* gives the explanation that when delight is absent, the mind becomes the proximate cause of pain (*dukkha*) and is not "one's own mind". According to Guenther's interpretation, lack of *attamanatā* refers to a sense of alienation from one's own mind and dissatisfaction with oneself. In the *Dīgha-nikāya* (D. I.46, 86, 223, II. 71, 315, III. 206) *attamanatā* describes the joyous and exalted frame of mind of those who listened to the discourses of the Buddha. The term is explained in the commentaries as "delighted mind" (*tuṭṭha-mano*) or "one's own mind" (*saka-mano*) (P.E.D. 23, col. 1). In the *Abhidhamma* system, *cetanās* that arise from *cittas* rooted in hate or delusion are perceived as purposive impulses that lack the motivational energy of zest or delight in the object that comes within one's range of experience. *Pīti*, however, is regarded as a "neutral" mental state: it is found not only in wholesome *cittas* but also in unwholesome *cittas* rooted in greed and conjoined with joy. *Pīti* takes on the moral quality of the *citta* in which it arises. *Cetanās* arising from greedy *cittas* are conditioned by joy (*somanassa*) and zestful interest in the object (*pīti*); nevertheless, they motivate attachment to the object and are regarded as causes of future grief.

Planes of Consciousness

The *Abhidhamma* system inherits from the *Sutta* literature traditional ideas of an ascending order of cosmic realms into which beings are reborn and where they become engaged in a range of new experiences. The *Suttas* also hand down concepts developed by practitioners of *yoga*, who speak of clearly demarcated and recognizable "planes of consciousness" that are attained and fully experienced through meditation. The *Abhidhamma* subscribes to the notion expressed in the *Suttas* that there are correlations between the ascending order of cosmic levels and the ascending planes of consciousness. It is posited that a person who attains to a certain plane (*bhūmi*) of consciousness through meditation can commune, in this very life, with a corresponding cosmic plane by experiencing the felicity of that cosmic plane in a state of *jhāna*. Though the cosmic planes are described in *Abhidhamma* literature,[32] the emphasis is not on trying to explain where they are located or how they become realms of individual rebirth, but on classifying planes of consciousness and defining the mental factors that are considered to be in tune with each cosmic plane. It follows that the concept of the ascending cosmic realms becomes a frame that holds together various *Abhidhamma* classifications of planes of consciousness.

The *Suttas* and the *Abhidhamma* system speak of three spheres of rebirth: the sphere of sensory experience (*kāmāvacara*) the "sphere of fine matter" (*rūpāvacara*), and the "non-material sphere" (*arūpāvacara*). Each of these three spheres is considered to be the proper home, as it were, of certain types of states of mind (*cittas*). The *Dhammasaṅgaṇi* assigns to the sphere of sensory experience not only certain cosmic realms and types of beings that inhabit them, but also the five aggregates, the sense organs and the mind, and all sensory and mental objects (Dhs. 223-224). Along with specific cosmic planes, all the *cittas* that arise within ordinary sensory and rational experience are contained within the "sphere of sensory experience". Similarly, after referring to the celestial realms that comprise the "sphere of fine matter" and the divine beings that live there, the *Dhammasaṅgaṇi* says that the states of mind (*cittas*) of those who have attained the lower planes of meditation (*rūpa-jhānas*) belong to this sphere (Dhs. 224). The non-material sphere is said to include exalted cosmic planes as well as the states of mind of those who have cultivated the higher planes of "formless" meditation (*arūpa-jhanas*).

These three "spheres", therefore, become categories for classifying types of consciousness, whereas the cosmic planes are regarded as planes of existence where beings dwell.[33] To these three spheres of consciousness that are considered "mundane" (*lokiya*), the *Suttas* and the *Abhidhamma* texts add a fourth, which is designated *lokuttara*, "the supramundane" (Dhs. 193, Vsm. XIV. 88). According to the definition in the *Dhammasaṅgaṇi*, the four Paths that culminate in enlightenment are factors of the supramundane. These are the Paths pertaining to the four stages leading to enlightenment: "stream entry", "once-returning", "non-returning", and finally, the stage that leads one to become an *arahant*. Also included in the supramundane are the fruits of the Paths and the goal of *nibbāna*. The states of mind of those who experience the stages of purification[34] and the gradual liberation from sorrow achieved in these Paths are designated as *lokuttara-cittas* (supramundane states of mind). The *Suttas* affirm that it is possible to follow these Paths and reach enlightenment in this very world, in the course of a single lifetime. The supramundane, therefore, is not a separate cosmic realm.

With regard to the relationship between attitudes of mind and the processes of *kamma* and rebirth, *cittas* are classified into four types: wholesome (*kusala*), unwholesome (*akusala*), resultant (*vipāka*), and purely functional (*kiriya*). Corresponding to these, there are four types of *cetanās*. Both wholesome and unwholesome states of consciousness condition purposive impulses that instigate purposive acts (*sañcetanika-kammas*) that lead to karmic consequences. Resultant *cittas* are pleasant, painful or neutral states of mind that arise as consequences of wholesome and unwholesome *kammas*. In the debates with their opponents, the Theravādins took the position that the term *vipāka* (karmic fruition) can be applied properly only to the subjective experiences resulting from *kamma*.[35] In *Points of Controversy*, Aung and C.A.F. Rhys Davids explain that karmic fruition (*kamma-vipāka*) is defined in the *Kathāvatthu* in terms of pleasant, unpleasant, and neutral feelings that arise in the consciousness continuum of the "doer" of the past deeds.[36]

The fourth class of *cittas*, designated *kiriya-cittas*, cannot be classified either as constituting *kamma* or as constituted by *kamma*: they are neither *kamma*-producing wholesome and unwholesome *cittas*, nor are they *kamma*-produced resultant *cittas*. They are called *kiriya* or functional *cittas* because they arise, perform a function, and pass away without setting up any conditions for producing karmic consequences. The beneficent acts of an *arahant* fall under the category of *kiriya*. When the eight wholesome sense-sphere *cittas* (Chart 11) arise in ordinary folk or in those who are trainees in the Eightfold Path, these *cittas* carry goal-oriented impulses and produce pleasant consequences. It is posited in the *Abhidhammattha-saṅgaha* that *arahants* do experience eight types of states of mind that are the counterparts of the eight types of wholesome *cittas* of ordinary folk. When these states arise in the mind of an *arahant*, they are not instigated by intentions and plans regarding present benefits, nor do they produce aspirations for the future. These *cittas* of *arahants* are called "functional" because they serenely fulfil a beneficent task and leave no traces that can give rise to karmic consequences.[37]

The Concept of "Ethically Indeterminate"

Resultant (*vipāka*) *cittas* and functional (*kiriya*) *cittas* are classified as ethically indeterminate (*avyākata*) strictly in the sense that they neither carry action-generating wholesome and unwholesome roots, nor produce karmic results that are characterized by pleasure, pain, or neutral feeling. The *Atthasālinī* (Asl. 39)[38] says that whereas wholesome states of consciousness produce ethically blameless pleasant results, and unwholesome *cittas* put forth ethically reprehensible unpleasant results, morally indeterminate *cittas* have the defining characteristic of producing no results (*avipāka-lakkhaṇa*).[39] It is important to note that ethically indeterminate factors became, for the Theravādins, a bulwark against interpretations of *kamma* that undermine the significance of human agency. Against their opponents, the Theravādins argued that if the results (*vipāka*) of past *kamma* became the causes (*hetu*) of future *kamma*, there will be an endless chain of cause and effect, which will negate all hope of release from rebirth. For this reason, they maintained that resultant states are indeterminate and produce no further results (Kvu. 357-358).[40] In the same manner, by maintaining that the four non-material *khandhas* arise as resultant states that do not produce further *kamma* (Dhs. 180), they sought to avoid the view that one's future is determined by the type of *khandhas* one has. According to Theravāda, moral values pertain to the acts that are performed through the *khandhas*, not to the *khandhas* themselves. Furthermore, by regarding the wholesome acts of an *arahant* as purely functional (*kiriya*) factors that have no relationship to the karmic process of merit and demerit, the Theravādins upheld the view that one who has attained enlightenment is not bound to future rebirth (Kvu. 542-543).

There is one more debate with their opponents where the Theravādins resort to the concept of ethically indeterminate states. The pivotal question in this debate is how wholesome roots can develop in an ordinary person, given that it is a cardinal teaching of the *Suttas* that unwholesome roots and *āsavas* persist until the attainment of liberating knowledge.[41] All parties in the debate upheld the principle that *paṭicca-samuppāda* implies compatibility between two coexisting states as well as between cause and effect. For this reason, all agreed that wholesome and unwholesome *cittas* can neither coexist nor follow each other in a causal series. In this debate, the Theravādins held that an ethically indeterminate (*avyākata*) mental state of the resultant (*vipāka*) category invariably intervened between an unwholesome and a wholesome state of consciousness, thereby preparing the way for the arising of the latter. The *Abhidhammattha-saṅgaha* thus postulates that ethically indeterminate *citta*s accompanied by a neutral feeling that is neither pleasurable nor painful to the mind arise and provide a buffer between unwholesome *citta*s rooted in hatred, which are invariably accompanied by displeasure (*domanassa*), and *citta*s conjoined with joy (*somanassa*).[42] The Theravāda position remains problematic because indeterminate states cannot provide the causal conditions for wholesome motivation. What is of importance, however, is that Theravāda avoids the type of deterministic view that precludes the arising of wholesome states in the *āsava*-ridden mind of an ordinary ignorant person or a beginner in the Eightfold Path.

The commentary to the *Aṅguttara-nikāya* lists four classes of *cetanā*s (*cattāro cetanā-rāsayo*) corresponding to the four classes of *citta*s (AA. II. 274). These consist of wholesome *cetanā*s, unwholesome *cetanā*s, resultant *cetanā*s, and functional *cetanā*s. The commentary also explains that eight types of wholesome *cetanā*s and twelve types of unwholesome *cetanā*s functioning as purposive impulses instigate acts (*kamma*) at the three "doors of action", thereby becoming the causes of pleasant and unpleasant consequences (AA. III. 144-145).[43] These *cetanā*s obviously correspond to the wholesome and unwholesome types of *citta*s of ordinary sensory experience (*kāmāvacara*) (Charts 11-12). The commentary clarifies that it is the intention or purposive impulse (*cetanā*) becoming expressed in a physical, verbal, or mental act, and not solely the act, that is the cause (*paccaya*) of painful or pleasant karmic consequences (AA. III. 144).[44] Similarly, the commentary to the *Majjhima-nikāya* defines "dark" *kamma* as action stemming from the twelve types of unwholesome *cetanā*s of the sensory sphere (MA. III. 105). It is postulated that unwholesome purposive impulses do not occur in levels of meditation. "Bright" *kamma*s are acts associated with the wholesome *cetanā*s of the three spheres of rebirth: the sensory sphere and sphere of fine matter, which correspond to the lower levels of meditation; and the non-material sphere, which corresponds to the levels of "formless" meditation. *Kamma* that is "neither dark nor bright" has neither pleasant nor unpleasant karmic consequences. It is identified as the behaviour that expresses the purposive impulse that renounces *kamma* and enters the Eightfold Path (*magga-cetanā*).[45] These examples demonstrate that in the commentarial literature, *cetanās* are regarded as the dynamic counterparts of *cittas*.

The content and organization of the lists of mental factors (*cetasikas*) that constitute wholesome, unwholesome, and ethically indeterminate states of mind show the invariable relationship between a state of mind and a purposive impulse: there can be no state of mind (*citta*) that is not associated with at least a rudimentary dynamic impulse (*cetanā*) directed towards an object. The lists show, furthermore, that the designations "wholesome", "unwholesome", "resultant", and "functional" can be applied equally to attitudes of mind (*cittas*), purposive impulses (*cetanās*), and acts (*kamma*). The fact that these designations can be utilized in this manner signifies that *citta*, *cetanā*, and *kamma* are actually inseparable even though they are conceptually distinguishable. Ultimately, it is the integral whole of purposive thought, purposive impulse, and purposive act that can be designated as wholesome, unwholesome, resultant, or functional. In the *Abhidhamma* system, *cetanā* is given the leading role in the translation of an attitude of mind (*citta*) into an intentional act (*sañcetanika-kamma*). *Cetanā* and the emotions that arise together with *cetanā* within a state of mind condition each other in such a way that the relative values which concomitant emotions place on objects influence the selection of objects towards which the purposive impulse is directed. Through these same modes of conditioning, *cetanā* coordinates concomitant emotions and directs their motivating capacities towards goals chosen by the cognitive processes of purposive thought in the *cittas*.

Cetanā and the Cognitive Process

In the *Abhidhamma* system, cognitive processes are described in terms of ordered sequences of states of mind (*cittas*), where each conditions the following one in such a way as to produce a distinctive type of experience. Not only the perception of pleasant and unpleasant objects, but the process by which a level of meditation (*jhāna*) is established, "entry" into each of the four Paths of liberation, the process of dying, and the rebirth process are all defined as courses charted by ordered sequences of *cittas* that arise and pass away one after another.[46] In this section, the focus is on the *cetanās* that participate in the sequence of states of mind (*cittas*) that forms the process of perception. In the *Suttas* and in the *Abhidhamma* literature, perception is not regarded as a process in which the mind passively receives the impact of an object. Although that can happen when the object is insignificant, every process of perception is considered to be an occasion when the *cittas* can begin to actively respond to the object on the basis of their own wholesome or unwholesome inner dynamics. In the *Abhidhamma* terminology, *citta-vīthi* (Chart 13) signifies that cognition is conceived as the occurrence of *cittas* that proceed as a series of cognitive moments "leading one to the other in a regular and uniform order".[47] The term *vīthi* signifies a well travelled road with clearly marked stages, and *citta-niyāma* refers to the regular order in which the *cittas* follow one another in the cognitive process. The order that governs the sequence of *cittas* is based on conditioned origination.

With regard to the functioning of *cetanā* and the putting forth of *kamma*, the *Atthasālinī* explains, with the help of several analogies, that the cognitive process consists of two stages: a preliminary stage when the object is received into the cognizing medium of the mind so that its nature is determined; and a second stage, designated as *javana*, when the mind cognizes the object fully and actively responds to it (Asl. 271-272). It is at the stage of *javana* that wholesome and unwholesome *cittas* and *cetanās* originate and produce *kamma.* In the preliminary stage of the process of perception, *cetanā* does coordinate concomitant states and incline them towards the object; however, it is not motivated by greed, hatred, and delusion or by wholesome roots of action, and its function cannot be classed as ethically wholesome or unwholesome. *Cetanā* operates as a "*kamma*-condition" (*kamma-paccaya*) only in the *javana* stage.

The *citta* moments of the *citta-vīthi* and the dynamics of the process by which a sensory object is cognized are delineated in the *Atthasālinī* (Asl. 270-272), the *Visuddhimagga* (Vsm. XIV. 115-122), and in the fourth chapter of the *Abhidhammattha-saṅgaha.* According to the explanation given in these texts, the cognitive process (*citta-vīthi*) comes into being through the "arrest" and interruption of the life continuum (*bhavaṅga*).[48] It is posited that the life continuum arises moment by moment when there are no cognitive processes—for example, in deep sleep—and continues as long as no mental processes interrupt its continuity (Vsm. XIV. 114). When sensory contact (*phassa*) occurs, the *bhavaṅga* process is "arrested" and interrupted, the appropriate sense organs and the mind attend to the object, and perception occurs. At the conclusion of the process of perception, the life continuum begins to arise again.

According to the description given in the *Visuddhimagga,* the entire cognitive process that occurs when an object is perceived by the senses and the mind lasts for seventeen "thought moments" (Chart 13).[49] The first three moments represent the impingement of the object on the flow of *bhavaṅga.* As one moment of *bhavaṅga* rises and passes away, in the second moment *bhavaṅga* "vibrates" with the impact of the object and becomes "arrested" in the third moment, giving way to an ordered cognitive process (*citta-vīthi*). The next phase consists of attending to the object and recognizing it. In the fourth moment, designated as the moment of "five-door advertence" (*pañca-dvārāvajjana*), the appropriate sense organ is directed to the object. As a consequence, in the fifth moment, one of the five types of sensory consciousness (*pañca-viññāṇa*) comes into existence; for example, if the ear has made contact with a sound, auditory consciousness (hearing) arises. The sixth moment is marked by the passive reception (*sampaṭicchana*) of the object into the cognitive process. This is followed, in the seventh moment, by a rapid investigation (*santīraṇa*) of the object. The eighth is the decisive moment of "determination"(*voṭṭhapana*) when the specific characteristics of the object are determined, and it becomes possible to distinguish and differentiate the object from its surroundings. The object is recognized and defined when the data becomes organized in such a manner that a definite object is discerned.[50] All these moments of the *citta-vīthi*, including the eighth, are reckoned as incapable of producing karmic consequences.

In the active phase of the *citta-vīthi*, the subject begins to react to the object with personal responses and processes of *kamma* begin to operate. Seven thought moments—starting with the ninth and ending with the fifteenth—constitute an impulsion designated as *javana*, wherein cognition becomes wholesome or unwholesome mental *kamma* that involves moral responsibility. The cognitive process becomes completed in the sixteenth and seventeenth moments through a process of "registration" (*tadārammaṇa*). During these two moments, if the stimulus is sufficiently strong, the object that has been cognized in the *javana* phase is fully identified and retained in consciousness.

The *Atthasālinī*[51] illustrates the cognitive process with an apt analogy (Asl. 271-272). A man sleeps under a mango tree, his head covered. A ripe mango falls, striking him. Aroused from sleep, he removes his head covering, picks up the mango and examines its distinctive smell, shape, and green-gold colour. Knowing it to be a mango, he eats it all and registers the distinctive taste it leaves in his mouth. Pulling on his head covering, he goes back to sleep. The sleeping man represents the moment of the life continuum that passes just before the object makes its impact. The mango striking the man is like moments two and three when the life continuum "vibrates" and is then arrested. The awakening from sleep is comparable to the directing of the mind to the object at moment four, and the removal of the head cover is like consciousness operating in one of the senses at moment five. Picking up the fruit is analogous to the reception (*sampaṭcchana*) of the object into the cognitive process at moment six, and examining it resembles the rapid investigation (*santīraṇa*) of the object at the seventh moment. Recognizing it as a mango represents the crucial eighth moment, during which the nature of the object is determined (*voṭṭhapana*). Eating the mango and reacting to its flavour and texture stands for the impulsion of *javana*, which extends in duration from moment nine to moment fifteen. Identifying and retaining the mango flavour in the mind is like the registration of the object at moments sixteen and seventeen.[52] Through this process of registration, the object that has been perceived is recognized with clarity and certainty to be that object and none other (*tadārammaṇa*). The subjective reactions to the object are also cognized and registered.

The transition between passively receiving the mango from the tree's bounty and actively biting into it aptly illustrates the transition that the *Abhidhamma* method posits between the two phases of the cognitive process: the passive preliminary phase, wherein the mind remains mostly in a receptive mode, allowing itself to be determined by the nature of the object; and the active *javana* phase, during which the mind produces mental acts that affect the future of the consciousness continuum. The *Visuddhimagga* maintains that all the *cittas* that constitute the *citta-vīthi* are devoid of karmic consequences,[53] except the seven *javana* moments (Vsm. XX. 44). Likewise, the *Abhidhammattha-saṅgaha* states that all the moments of the *citta-vīthi*, with the exception of the *javana* moments, consist of resultant states (*vipāka-cittas*) or functional states (*kiriya-cittas*), both of which carry no karmic consequences.[54] It follows that whereas *cetanās* are present in all the states of mind that constitute a cognitive sequence, only the *cetanās* that occur in the *javana* process can have the form of fully developed wholesome or unwholesome purposive impulses that produce *kamma.*[55]

Once *javana* is attained, *cetanā* can operate in one of two ways: as conascent *kamma* condition, by causing concomitant physical and mental functions to produce acts that bring forth karmic consequences in the present body and mind; or as asynchronous *kamma* condition, by producing acts entailing karmic results that will be felt in a future rebirth.[56]

Fusion of Perception and Purposive Impetus in Cognitive Processes

Modern interpreters of the *Abhidhamma* system emphasize that *javana* is to be perceived, not merely as a cognitive process, but as a manifestation of the dynamic aspect of the rebirth process (*kamma-bhava*). Aung comments that *javana* refers to "the active or conative factor (cetanā) in the act of cognition", rather than solely to the process of knowing the object through perception and intellection.[57] In her response to this comment, C.A.F. Rhys Davids notes that teachers in Sri Lanka associated *javana* with the term "dynamic". She further remarks that the "dominant interest" of *javana* for Western psychologists is "the fusion of intellect and will in Buddhist psychology".[58] Her statement balances Aung's by drawing attention to the fact that at every point in the *javana* process, a *cetanā* emerges as a component of a *citta* and interacts with concomitant cognitive and emotive mental factors. Through this interaction, as C.A.F. Rhys Davids notes, the impetus to initiate action that *cetanā* possesses becomes "fused" with the cognitive processes of purposive thought and intention that are constitutive features of the *citta.*

Aung himself, while stressing the "active" role of *cetanā* in the *javana* process, shows that the capacity of *cetanā* to instigate goal-oriented acts is circumscribed by the conditioning influence of the unwholesome and wholesome "roots" (greed, hate, and delusion; non-greed, non-hate, and non-delusion). In order to clarify how the emotion-based roots of action and the dynamic impulses of *cetanā* differ from each other in the production of *kamma*, Aung draws on the distinction that is made in the *Abhidhamma* system between root-condition (*hetu-paccaya*) and *kamma*-condition (*kamma-paccaya*).[59] An act with karmic consequences is compared to a seed because it perpetuates life and rebirth. Extending this analogy, Aung interprets the root to be the principal condition that affects the seed with respect to its germination, growth, and fruition. He takes the root-condition (*hetu-paccaya*)—for example, greed—to be the dominant factor that influences and shapes the manner in which *cetanā* (the *kamma*-condition) becomes expressed as an act that has karmic consequences. The roots of action support the purposive thrust of *cetanā*, give orientation to that purpose, and limit the effect that concomitant mental factors (*cetasikas*) have on *cetanā*. For example, the motivating intention (*cetanā*) of making a gift can be conditioned by genuine generosity rooted in non-greed, or by the hope of attaining worldly honour and karmic merit that is rooted in greed. The states of mind that arise in the cognitive process prior to *javana* are not conditioned by any of the six root-conditions; the interacting factors of cognition, emotion and motivation that constitute *javana*, however, are supported by fecund roots that nourish the desire for new goals, new purposive acts, prolongation of life, and further rebirth.

Bhikkhu Ñāṇamoli suggests that the origins of the notion of *citta-vīthi* (cognitive series) can be traced to some *Sutta* passages, such as the description of perception as an ordered series of mental states in the *Madhupiṇḍika-sutta* (M. I. 112).[60] I referred to this passage in Chapter V to illustrate motivational sequences in the *Suttas*. Here I turn to the same passage to show

how *cetanā* develops from a rudimentary directing of the mind to an object of interest in the preliminary stage of a cognitive series to a mature *kamma*-producing purposive impulse in the *javana* stage. The argument in the *Madhupiṇḍika-sutta* begins very simply by showing that "eye-consciousness" (seeing) arises through the coming together of conscious awareness, the eye, and a visual object. This meeting of these three factors is defined as contact (*phassa*). With contact as condition, feeling (*vedanā*) is said to arise. The passage then goes on to say that when one experiences feelings (*vedeti*) arising from contact with an object, then one perceives the object (*sañjānāti*); what one perceives one thinks about (*vitakketi*); and finally, what one thinks about one diversifies in thought, producing a proliferation of concepts (*papañceti*). In his work *Concept and Reality in Early Buddhist Thought: An Essay on Papañca and Papañca-Saññā-Saṅkhā*, Bhikkhu Ñāṇananda points out that the description of the process of perception in the *Madhupiṇḍika-sutta* falls into two parts: in the first part, up to the mention of the arising of feeling (*vedanā*), perception is presented as an "impersonal process" where the visual object is passively received into the cognizing medium of the mind; but in the second part, the verbs take on personal endings, suggesting that the mind begins to adopt an active, deliberate role.[61] This division of the process of perception into a passive and an active stage in the *Madhupiṇḍika-sutta* perhaps anticipates the *Abhidhamma* method of dividing the cognitive process into a preliminary receptive stage and a dynamic *javana* stage.

Moreover, the route of the process of perception is traced in the *Madhupiṇḍika-sutta* with the purpose of showing at which point unwholesome factors can sabotage the cognitive process. The argument here is that when one makes the perceived object the starting point for proliferating concepts (*papañceti*), then the mind is assailed by perceptions and reckonings based on proliferation (*papañca-saññā-saṅkhā*).[62] The *Madhupiṇḍika-sutta* maintains that such propagation of concepts leads one to delight in, welcome, and covet the object. As a result, one experiences the obsessive behaviour brought about by the mind's unwholesome tendencies (*anusayas*): tendency towards sensual desire (*rāga*), aversion (*dosa*), views (*diṭṭhi*), doubt (*vicikcchā*), conceit (*māna*), attachment to life (*bhava*), and basic ignorance (*avijjā*) (M.I. 113). The conclusion to the argument is that the fundamental cause for quarrelling and violence is to be found in conceptual proliferation. *Papañca* is viewed as an ever-present danger in every cognitive process. At the same time, it can be posited that wholesome roots act upon consciousness in such a way as to prevent passion, aversion, or a deluded frame of mind from casting their influence on the purposive thrust of *cetanā*. The unwholesome tendencies cannot become active in the presence of wholesome roots. The account of *javana* in the *Abhidhamma*, therefore, carries the implication that to see well is to see, not only correctly, but also in a wholesome manner. Seeing the object as it actually is (*yathā-bhūtam*) implies responding to it without sorrow-producing unwholesome purposes (*akusala-cetanās*), so that no sorrow is entailed.

Javana and "Freedom of Will"

Some modern interpreters of Theravāda maintain that *cetanās* begin to manifest as factors involving freedom of choice in the *javana* process. They point out that subjective responses to the object begin to take effect in the states of mind that constitute the motivating impulsion that characterizes the cognitive process of *javana*. In their interpretation of the *citta-vīthi*, Aung, Mahāthera Nārada, and Lama Govinda emphasize that the dual capacity both to gain knowledge of an object and to create *kamma* imbues *javana* with "free will". Aung argues that *javana* is "a determining, free, causal act".[63] Mahāthera Nārada maintains that free will "plays its part" at the eighth moment of the *citta-vīthi*, in which the nature and qualities of the object are determined (*voṭṭhapana*),[64] and he interprets this decisive moment to be the "gateway to a moral or immoral thought process". Lama Govinda stresses that *javana* is the active dimension of consciousness, "indicating the free will".[65]

However, Aung, Nārada, and Govinda qualify their claim that *javana* is a process of free will by defining what they mean by "freedom" in this context. Aung explains that by "free" he does not mean that any *javana* can be free of the influences of past *kamma* and present circumstances, with the exception of the *javanas* experienced by an *arahant.* Aung limits the term "free" to what he calls "free by reason of the balance of motives or conditions".[66] He holds that when a *cetanā* emerges from the earlier, pre-*javana* stages of the cognitive series and becomes "asynchronous"—capable not only of influencing concomitant mental factors, but also of producing future consequences—then its scope widens, so that its capacity to determine what choices are made by the *citta* increases. Aung holds that as a result of its expanding capacity at the *javana* stage, *cetanā* reaches a point in its function of forming goal-oriented purposes when it is no longer constrained solely by the wholesome or the unwholesome root-conditions, but is equally affected by both. In this restricted sense, he holds that *cetanā* is not compelled one-sidedly by either wholesome or unwholesome motivation. He does not explain how this "balance of motives" is achieved. In the *Abhidhamma* system, each *cetanā* is classified as wholesome, unwholesome, or ethically indeterminate, but is never described as motivated equally by both wholesome and unwholesome factors.

Another argument that Aung puts forward in support of "free will" in the *javana* process is more convincing. Aung argues that since a person can learn to view a disagreeable object with pleasure and to reject an agreeable object with displeasure, such "reversal of *javana*" demonstrates that *javana* is a "free" act. He holds that unlike the impulses of *javana*, the activities of the mental states in the preliminary stage of perception are "fixed".[67] Aung adds a simile: *javana* can be compared to an alligator with the capacity to swim against the current of habits, but the ethically indeterminate *cittas* in the preliminary stages of perception are like inanimate objects floating in the tide.

Mahāthera Nārada's line of argument is similar to Aung's. He holds that free will comes into play at the *voṭṭhapana* stage. According to Mahāthera Nārada's interpretation, if the object is viewed with undistorted, systematic, rightly-applied attention (*yoniso-manasikāra*) when the mind seeks to determine its nature at the *voṭṭhapana* stage, a wholesome *javana* will ensue, whereas careless, unsystematic attention (*ayoniso-manasikāra*) will result in an unwholesome *javana*.[68] Lama Govinda, on the other hand, holds that though *javana* is not a totally free, unconditioned act, it is free in the sense that it is less bound by the habit patterns of *saṅkhāras* than the mental states of the preliminary stages of perception. In spite of the arguments put forward by Aung and Mahāthera Nārada, it is difficult to see how *cetanā* can become free of the constraints and compulsions that prevail in the conscious processes of ordinary persons.

In yet another way, without claiming that *javana* is an expression of "free will", Bhikkhu Bodhi elaborates on Aung's statement regarding "the reversal of *javana*"[69] and reiterates the Theravāda position that cognitive processes can be controlled and changed through sustained cultivation (*bhāvanā*) of the mind. According to his interpretation, the same object can be perceived differently by different persons, depending on differences in "temperament and proclivities", and the *javanas* of viewers can show startling variations even when they are viewing the same object.[70] Though the tenacity of *āsavas*, *anusayas* and root conditions is emphasized in the *Sutta* literature and the *Abhidhamma* texts, the thrust of the teaching is that these unwholesome factors and the *javanas* they govern can be changed through persistent practice. Bhikkhu Bodhi refers to the *Indriya-bhāvanā-sutta*, where the Buddha tells Ānanda that the *arahant*, abiding in constant mindfulness (*sati*) and clear comprehension (*sampajañña*), is able to see what is repulsive as not repulsive and what is not repulsive as repulsive, or remain in a state of equanimity (M. III. 301-302). In the *Aṅguttara-nikāya*, the Buddha teaches young monks the method of mindfully reversing *javana* processes by changing one's way of life, attitudes and perspectives (A. III. 169-170). The monks are taught that by shifting one's frame of mind, it is possible to view what is distasteful (*paṭikkūla*) as not distasteful and what is not distasteful as distasteful. The point of this exercise is to uproot unwholesome roots by filling the mind with the thought: "May I not feel sensual passion (*rāga*) for things that arouse passion, may I not feel hatred (*dosa*) for things that excite hatred, and may I not feel delusion (*moha*) towards things that delude".

In order to explore the Theravāda view that *javana* can be changed through training, it is necessary to probe more deeply into the blending of cognition, emotion, and conation in *javana*. C.A.F. Rhys Davids refers to a fascinating discussion between Aung and herself regarding the nature of *javana* and the difficulties of translating the term.[71] Aung finds the rendering of *javana* as "apperception" inadequate, since this term would emphasize the cognitive side of *javana*, but would not convey the capacity of *javana* to initiate purposive acts. He maintains that *javana* refers to the purposive thrust that *cetanās* put forth within the cognitive process. In other words, the purposive impulse or orientation towards a goal that *cetanās* produce in the *javana* process is to be regarded, not as a factor added to the *citta-vīthi*, but as internal to the cognitive process. On the other hand, Aung finds the translation of *javana* as "conative impulse" inadequate, because it fails to do justice to the capacity of the *javana-cittas* to cognize the object and discern its features. It is in this context that C.A.F. Rhys Davids concludes that *javana* resembles *cetanā* by demonstrating the blending of "intellect and will" in Buddhist psychology.[72]

Javana becomes a complex process with cognitive and conative dimensions because the *citta-vīthi* comes into effect through the mutual interplay of the cognizing function of *cittas* and the action-producing function of *saṅkhāras*. When conditioned origination is affirmed, neither the cognitive nor the conative dimensions of *javana* can claim to be free of conditioning. It follows that the discriminating, defining, and discerning functions of the *citta* and the purposive impulse of *cetanā* are both conditioned by the emotion-charged influences of the root conditions and by the habit patterns generated by *saṅkhāras*. Nevertheless, a sound case can be made for the claim that the *cittas* that constitute the *javana* process exhibit an expansion in cognitive and conative capacities, when compared with the *cittas* of the pre-*javana* stage of cognition. In spite of the influence of persistent tendencies and habits, the *cetanās* in the *javana-cittas* are regarded as being capable of a sense of purpose and intention towards the object that earlier *cetanās* in the preliminary stage of perception lack. Likewise, it can be argued that the *javana-cittas* display an expansion in the capacity to know the object and experience its characteristics.

According to the *Abhidhamma* system, the *citta* has the capacity to become aware of its own processes.[73] *Javana* can be interpreted to be that point in the cognitive process where the mind exhibits a greater capacity to become aware of itself and cognize its contents. The mind's capacity of cognizing its own processes does not imply freedom from conditioning. Nor does it entail a "balancing" of the motivating impulses of wholesome and unwholesome root-conditions, as Aung avers.[74] However, the instruction that is given in the *Suttas* for the "reversal of *javana*" can be interpreted to mean that Theravāda upholds the view that the mind has the capacity to become retrospectively aware of the cross-currents of influence in any *javana* process. When the mind recognizes unwholesome patterns of conditioning in any *javana* process, it can begin to set up conditions to alter or "reverse" that process through sustained training. The mind's capacity to be trained to observe its own features with mindfulness and attention can become the dominant condition that influences, and gradually changes, the contents and orientation of the *javana* stage of any cognitive process.

Conclusion

The lists of mental states in the *Dhammasaṅgaṇi*, the *Atthasālinī*, and the *Visuddhimagga* demonstrate that *cetanā* neither comes into existence as a separate, self-contained factor in the continuum of consciousness nor carries out its function as a purposive impulse singly and independently. The lists show that a *cetanā* arises as a purposive impulse, conditioned by all the cognitive, emotive, and dynamic factors of a specific wholesome or unwholesome state of mind (*citta*). It can be posited, therefore, that the conative impetus of *cetanā* is transformed into a purposive impulse because it is influenced by the purposive thought or intention that arises in the cognitive factors of the *citta* and by the emotions that shape the attitude of mind displayed by the *citta*. In other words, the purposive dimension of *cetanā* is derived from its participation within the attitude of mind manifested in the *citta*.

Furthermore, the very format of the lists demonstrates that in Theravāda, the cognitive processes of the *citta* and the action-producing factors of *saṅkhāras* are regarded as interwoven and interdependent dimensions of the continuum of consciousness. The same mental factors that occur as the cognitive, emotive, and conative constituents (*cetasikas*) in the organic unity of the *citta* function as the causal conditions (*paccayas*) in the process by which the *saṅkharakkhandha* brings together mental factors and produces purposive acts. In the lists, emotions are not separated from cognitive and conative factors. Emotions function as constituent factors that endow a specific *citta* with a distinctive mental attitude and a distinct moral value and, simultaneously, as motivating factors within the action-producing factors of the *saṅkharakkhandha.* Like other mental factors (*cetasikas*) in the lists, *cetanā* plays a dual role. Having arisen as a factor of rudimentary awareness within a *citta*, *cetanā* then becomes the chief motivating factor in a corresponding *saṅkhāra* process that formulates and manifests intentional acts (*kamma*).

Cetanā is classified in the lists as a neutral mental factor that takes on the moral value of the *citta* within which it arises. The criteria for ethical evaluation depend on whether the wholesome roots (non-greed, non-hate, non-delusion) or the unwholesome roots (greed, hate, delusion) prevail in a state of mind, and whether that state of mind leads to beneficial or harmful consequences. Although every *citta* contains a *cetanā* as one of its basic constituents, it is only in wholesome or unwholesome *cittas* that *cetanās* function as fully developed purposive impulses or motivating intentions. When a *cetanā* functions as a purposive impulse, it translates the moral value of the *citta* within which it arises into a corresponding wholesome or unwholesome purposive act (*sañcetanika-kamma*).

Furthermore, according to the *Abhidhamma* system, every mental state is pervaded by a specific feeling (*vedanā*). Wholesome states of mind are considered to be imbued with joy (*somanassa*) or with a neutral feeling (*upekkhā*), but never with mental discomfort. Theravādins maintain that since wholesome purposive impulses are free of mental displeasure, they are in accord with the natural inclination of all beings to desire happiness and avoid pain. It is implied in Theravāda that purposive impulses rooted in hate (*dosa*) go against the happiness that all beings naturally seek. Hate is the only type of *citta* that is invariably linked with mental uneasiness (*domanassa*).

It can be inferred from the lists of wholesome and unwholesome *cittas* that feelings and emotions have a profound influence on the processes of purposive thought through which possible goals are assessed and decisions are made. When *cetanās* function as wholesome or unwholesome purposive impulses, corresponding emotions function as motivating impulses that influence the manner in which purposive activity is implemented. For example, when wholesome roots become manifest as generosity, goodwill, and intelligent understanding, they are correlated with wholesome emotions and purposive impulses. Wholesome *cittas* also include emotions associated with shame at doing wrong and healthy fear of the consequences of morally wrong acts. Moreover, wholesome *cittas* manifest zest and delight in objects that come within their range and easy flexibility in their mode of functioning. These joyous feelings and wholesome emotions affect the nature of wholesome purposive impulses and add their motivating energy to the processes by which wholesome *cetanās* produce wholesome acts. Unwholesome *cetanās*, on the other hand, are thoroughly affected by unwholesome emotions that pervade unwholesome *cittas*. All unwholesome *cittas* manifest emotions associated with delusion as well as lack of shame at doing wrong, lack of fear of the consequences of evil acts, and restless agitation (*uddhacca*) (Charts 8-10). Greed is partnered with restlessness and, above all, with the infatuations and ignorance associated with delusion. A frame of mind rooted solely in intense delusion is always associated with a neutral feeling of neither joy nor dejection that is devoid of any genuine appreciation of any object that is experienced. Delusion is considered to be conditioned by emotions linked with either restlessness (*uddhacca*) or confused perplexity (*vicikicchā*) (Chart 10). Most significantly, mental displeasure or discomfort (*domanassa*) is regarded as invariably present in *cittas* rooted in hate. It is posited that this unhappy state of hatred is always conditioned by restless agitation and is further aggravated by envy (*issā*), avarice (*macchariya*), or obsessive worry (*kukkucca*).

In the *Abhidhamma* method of classification, emotions are never separated from cognitive processes. Cognitive evaluations regarding the nature of an object and how it affects the organism are regarded as conditioning factors in the arising of emotions. At the same time, when emotions and purposive impulses are regarded as concomitant factors (*cetasikas*) that condition each other in a specific state of mind (*citta*), it is implied that emotions have a profound influence on the thought processes by which goals are evaluated. Once the goal is chosen, specific emotions condition the purposive impulses (*cetanās*) and other conative energies in *saṅkhāra* processes and motivate them towards the chosen goal. Simultaneously, specific goals become endowed with value because they satisfy wholesome or unwholesome emotions.

The *Abhidhamma* system posits that *cetanās* act in two ways in cognitive processes: in the preliminary stage, *cetanā* directs mental processes to the object, but does not function as a fully developed purposive impulse; in the stage of *javana* when the object is fully cognized, *cetanās* take the form of motivating intentions and put forth *kamma*. Some modern scholars have maintained that the *cetanās* of the *javana* process are associated with freedom of will. The arguments they put forward are not convincing. Nevertheless, they have shown that it is implied in the *Abhidhamma* system that it is possible to "reverse" a *javana* process through training. The thrust of the argument in the *Abhidhamma* system is that when a range of wholesome conditions are set up, through their conditioning influence distorted and unwholesome cognitive processes can be gradually removed and replaced by undistorted ways of seeing and wholesome ways of acting.

ENDNOTES

[1] Warder suggests that the third council was held towards the end of Aśoka's reign, probably in 237 B.C.E. (A.K. Warder, *Indian Buddhism*, 273). Whereas the first two councils are accepted by all Buddhist traditions, splits in the *Saṅgha* begin to occur after the second council, and only the Theravādins maintain that the third council was held during the time of Aśoka. It is probable that this council concerned only the Theravādins and that it ended with the Sarvāstivādins breaking away to form their own sect.

The third council provides a landmark for dating the Pāli *Abhidhamma* texts. The commentary to the *Kathāvatthu* (KvuA. 1) records a tradition that the *Kathāvatthu* was compiled by Moggaliputta Tissa during the reign of Aśoka and recited to the monks at the third council. In the preface to *Points of Controversy*, C.A.F. Rhys Davids notes that the *Kathāvatthu* includes references to passages from the *Dhammasaṅgaṇi* and the *Vibhaṅga* as well as references to topics that are treated in the *Paṭṭhāna*. This leads to the conclusion that portions of these three *Abhidhamma* texts were available before the third council and that they were held to be "orthodox" works by the compiler of the *Kathāvatthu*. (S.Z. Aung and C.A.F. Rhys Davids, *Points of Controversy*, xxix-xxx) There are no references to the *Dhātukathā* in the *Kathāvatthu*. On the basis of linguistic evidence, Norman argues that the compiler of the *Kathāvatthu* was using an old and stereotypical framework that is cast in the form of a dialogue between opponents. According to Norman, the oldest debates perhaps can be traced back to the time when the Buddha lived, or at least to the period of the second council.

The *Atthasālinī* (Asl. 6) maintains that a section of the *Dhammasaṅgaṇi* is a commentary (*aṭṭhakathā*) on an earlier chapter in the same text. This leads to the assumption that the chapter which is commented on must be considerably older, and that portions of the *Dhammasaṅgaṇi* must have been completed before the third council (K.R. Norman, *Pāli Literature*, 103-105).

The method of analysis in terms of *dhammas* that the *Dhammasaṅgaṇi* sets forth in great detail is further elaborated in the *Vibhaṅga*. In the introduction to his translation of the *Vibhaṅga*, Sayadaw U Thittila states that the aim of this text is to show that a statement of "general truth" could also be applied to a "particular truth". In this regard, the *Vibhaṅga* makes a distinction between the analytical methods and definitions that are found in the *Suttas* (*Suttanta-bhājanīya*) and the more detailed analysis in terms of the technical vocabulary relating to philosophical and psychological categories that is present in the *Abhidhamma* (*Abhidhamma-bhājanīya*) (U Thittila, *Book of Analysis*, xviii).

The *Kathāvatthu* differs from the other canonical *Abhidhamma* texts since it is concerned, not with the definition and classification of *dhammas*, but with the refutation of views within the Buddhist community that conflict with the teachings of Theravāda. The *Kathāvatthu* does not specify the schools that held the views that it opposes, but the commentary to the *Kathāvatthu* refers to them by name. It has been noted that some of these schools, in actual fact, originated after the time of Aśoka (B.C. Law, *The Debates Commentary*, v-vi). However, it is possible that many of the views refuted in the *Kathāvatthu* were current before the third council, though they had not been categorized as the doctrines of well defined schools. The *Kathāvatthu* employs a strictly logical method. The refutations are meant to demonstrate that the views introduced by the opponent are inconsistent with concepts accepted by all Buddhist schools and go against statements that all accept as the words of the Buddha. In several instances the argument makes the point that it is unreasonable of the opponent to accept a certain proposition, only to deny what that proposition so obviously entails (S.Z. Aung and C.A.F. Rhys Davids, *Points of Controversy*, xlviii-xlix).

The *Visuddhimagga*, majestic in the vastness of its scope and in the depth of its interpretation of Buddhist doctrines, was composed by Buddhaghosa in Sri Lanka during the early part of the fifth century (Bhikkhu Ñāṇamoli, *The Path of Purification*, xiv). Though the *Visuddhimagga* is not part of the Theravāda canon, its influence on the tradition has been continuous and profound. The commentary to the *Visuddhimagga*, called the *Paramattha-mañjūsā*, was composed by Dhammapāla in South India within two hundred years after the death of Buddhaghosa (Ibid., xxx). At the beginning of the commentaries to each of the first four *Nikāyas*, Buddhaghosa states that he will not refer to certain matters since they have already been expounded in the *Visuddhimagga*. He goes on to say that the *Visuddhimagga* is placed "in the middle" of the four *Nikāyas* (DA. I. 2; MA. I. 2; SA. I. 2; AA. I. 2). The *Visuddhimagga* can be perceived as a detailed manual of meditation elaborated under the three headings of *sīla*, *samādhi*, and *paññā*. The four foundations of mindfulness, the levels of *jhāna*, and the stages in the cultivation of *paññā* are minutely described and skilfully linked with extended explanations of the five *khandhas*, the process of perception, conditioned origination, and the implications of *kamma*. Detailed enumerations of wholesome, unwholesome, and morally indeterminate *cittas*, and the mental factors that constitute them are included in the descriptions of the *saṅkhārakkhandha* and the *viññāṇakkhandha*. The *Visuddhimagga* follows the *Abhidhamma* method of analyzing things and persons in terms of irreducible momentary *dhammas*. The system of classification of physical and mental states is based on the *Dhammasaṅgaṇi* and the *Vibhaṅga*.

It is important to note that both the *Visuddhimagga* and the *Atthasālinī* insist upon the continuity of the Theravāda tradition by quoting from the old Sīhaḷa commentaries (O. von Hinüber, *Handbook of Pāli Literature*, 125, 152). These commentaries were probably brought to Sri Lanka from India, translated into Sīhaḷa-bhāsā, and augmented with comments by Sri Lankan teachers. Additions to the commentaries probably ended after the first century C.E. (Bhikkhu Ñāṇamoli, *The Path of Purification*, xiii; A.K. Warder, *Indian Buddhism*, 322).

Short manuals of *Abhidhamma* continued to be written from the fifth century onwards. The most popular of these is the *Abhidhammattha-saṅgaha*, which was composed at the end of the eleventh or the beginning of the twelfth century (K.R. Norman, *Pāli Literature*, 151). I have referred to the *Abhidhammattha-saṅgaha* several times in this chapter and the next in order to elucidate what is said in the *Visuddhimagga* and the *Atthasālinī*.

[2] A.K. Warder, *Indian Buddhism*, 10, 219; K.R. Norman, *Pāli Literature*, 96.

[3] A.K. Warder, *Indian Buddhism*, 272-273.

[4] R.F. Gombrich, *Theravāda Buddhism*, 128. There is much controversy regarding the precise dates of Aśoka. Gombrich refers to Eggermont, who proposed 268-239 B.C.E. after studying the problem for many years.

[5] Sayadaw U Thittila, *The Book of Analysis*, xviii, xxiii-xxiv; A.K. Warder, *Indian Buddhism*, 218-219.

[6] Bhikkhu Ñāṇamoli's explanation shows that the term *bhāva* in the compound term *sabhāva* has at least two strands of meaning: first, coming into being (*bhavana*) in the sense of the state of existing (*vijjamānatā*); and second, individual characteristic (*lakkhaṇa*). Ñāṇamoli refers to the *Atthasālinī* (Asl. 63) where *lakkhaṇa* is defined as either the individual nature (*sabhāva*) of a *dhamma* or a general characteristic (*sāmaññam*) that it shares with other *dhammas*. Hardness or impenetrability is the individual characteristic of the earth element, but impermanence is a general characteristic that the earth element shares with other *dhammas* (Bhikku Ñāṇamoli, *The Path of Purification*, 317, n. 68)

[7] A.K. Warder, *Indian Buddhism*, 323.

[8] Lama Govinda, *The Psychological Attitude of Early Buddhist Philosophy*, 123-125.

[9] Bhikkhu Bodhi, *A Comprehensive Manual of Abhidhamma*, 76-77.

[10] Ibid., 144-145.

[11] Ibid., 77.

[12] H.V. Guenther, *Philosophy and Psychology in the Abhidharma*, 31, n. 2.

[13] Bhikkhu Bodhi, *A Comprehensive Manual of Abhidhamma*, 77.

[14] Lama Govinda, *The Psychological Attitude of Early Buddhist Philosophy*, 116.

[15] S.Z. Aung, *Compendium of Philosophy*, 237-238.

[16] Bhikkhu Bodhi, *A Comprehensive Manual of Abhidhamma*, 307. . . . *sahajātā cetanā sahajātānaṁ nāma-rūpānaṁ; nānākkhaṇikā cetanā kammābhinibbattānaṁ nāma-rūpānaṁ kammavasena.*

[17] Nyanatiloka explains *avyākata* as "karmically neutral" or "amoral" factors of consciousness (Nyanatiloka, *Buddhist Dictionary: A Manual of Buddhist Terms and Doctrines*, 32.)

[18] *Kosallaṁ vuccati paññā* (Asl. 63).

[19] Pe Maung Tin, *The Expositor*, 50; H.V. Guenther, *Philosophy and Psychology in the Abhidharma*, 7.

[20] D. Keown, *The Nature of Buddhist Ethics*, 119-120.
Buddhaghosa distinguishes three methods of exposition with regard to the term *kusala* (DA. III. 883). The first of these, the *Jātaka* method, attributes to *kusala* the meaning of *ārogya* (absence of illness, good health). The *Suttanta* method takes *anavajja* (not blameable, without fault) as the meaning of *kusala*. The *Abhidhamma* method maintains that *kusala* includes three meanings: *kosalla-sambhūta* (generated by skill or proficiency), *niddaratha* (absence of pain, freedom from distress), and *sukha-vipāka* (producing pleasant results).

[21] S.Z. Aung, *Compendium of Philosophy*, 40-41.

[22] Bhikkhu Bodhi, *A Comprehensive Manual of Abhidhamma*, 33.

[23] S.Z. Aung, *Compendium of Philosophy*, 230, 242.

[24] The term *yevāpanaka* has the literal meaning of "or whatsoever" and is an abbreviation for a phrase which recurs in the *Dhammasaṅgaṇi* (for example, Dhs. 9, 17). This phrase signifies: "Or whatever other non-physical, conditionally originated states there may exist on that occasion". *Yevāpanaka* suggests that a class of *cetasikas* is not limited to those named in the list, since it also includes an indefinite number of other such *cetasikas* that might arise in a wholesome, unwholesome, or ethically indeterminate *citta*, in any given situation. The phrase *yevāpanaka* can be interpreted to mean: "and other such mental states that may occur in a particular situation" (Thera Nyanaponika, *Abhidhamma Studies: Researches in Buddhist Psychology*, 94).

[25] H.V. Guenther, *Philosophy and Psychology in the Abhidharma*, 84.

[26] S.Z. Aung, *Compendium of Philosophy*, 277.

[27] In this context *upekkhā* signifies, not the serenity that is cultivated through the disciplines of the Eightfold Path, but a "neutral" feeling that is neither joy nor displeasure. *Upekkhā* includes two meanings: (1) "neutral" in the sense of being neither joyous nor dejected; and (2) serene equanimity of mind associated with meditation. Here, *uppekhā* carries the first meaning. According to the *Abhidhamma* classification of mental states, feelings (*vedanā*) arising from bodily contact (touch) can be classified as pleasure (*sukha*) or pain (*dukkha*), but never as "neutral" (S.Z. Aung, *Compendium of Philosophy*, 232, n. 1).

[28] Bhikkhu Bodhi, *A Comprehensive Manual of Abhidhamma*, 37.

[29] Ibid., 38.

[30] Ibid., 362.

[31] H.V. Guenther, *Philosophy and Psychology in the Abhidharma*, 53.

[32] Bhikkhu Bodhi, *A Comprehensive Manual of Abhidhamma*, 185-219.

[33] Ibid., 29-31.

[34] The *Dhammasaṅgaṇi* (Dhs. 193) defines the Supramundane as follows: *Katame dhammā lokuttarā? Apariyāpannā maggā ca maggaphalāni va asaṅkhatā ca dhātu—ime dhammā lokuttarā.*

Each of the four Paths is described in terms of the removal of specfic unwholesome states. These are removed through the cultivation of the disciplines that pertain to each Path. From a psychological perspective, the four Paths are interpreted to be stages in the purification of the mind and mental development (*bhāvanā*) through the disciplines of meditation and mindfulness.

[35] The *Kathāvatthu* (Kvu. 353-355) records a debate between the Theravādins and their opponents, in which the latter maintain that old age and death can be taken as fruition of *kamma* (*kamma-vipāka*). The Theravādins argue that old age and death cannot be reckoned as *kamma-vipāka*, since only conscious states (*cittas*) that arise as consequences of past *kamma* are included under *kamma-vipāka*. The commentary to the *Kathāvatthu* (KvuA. 101) explains that old age and death cannot be regarded as *kamma-vipāka* since they are not entirely mental experiences but occur, at least in part, as the results of the natural order (*utu*). The commentary concludes by holding that though a causal relation (*paccaya*) can be posited between unwholesome *kamma* and physical decay, the term *vipāka* refers solely to the mental states that result from *kamma* (J.P. McDermott, *Development in the Early Buddhist Concept of Kamma/Karma*, 87).

[36] S.Z. Aung and C.A.F. Rhys Davids, *Points of Controversy*, 205, n. 3.

[37] Bhikkhu Bodhi, *A Comprehensive Manual of Abhidhamma*, 50.

[38] *Tesu anavajja-sukha-vipāka-lakkhaṇā kusalā, sāvajja-dukkha-vipāka-lakkhaṇā akusalā, avipāka-lakkhaṇā avyākatā* (Asl. 39).

[39] The *Dhammasaṅgaṇi* (Dhs. 180) classifies the following as indeterminate: the results (*vipāka*) of previous wholesome and unwholesome acts, the four Paths of enlightenment and the fruits of the Paths, the non-physical aggregates (*vedanā, saññā, saṅkhāra, viññāṇa*), purely functional (*kiriya*) *cittas*, all material form (*rūpa*), the three realms of rebirth, and the "Unconditioned element", namely *nibbāna*.

[40] In the *Kathāvatthu* (Kvu. 357-359) the position of the opponents is summed up in the statement: "*vipākas* entail further *vipākas*" (*vipāko vipākadhammo ti*). The Theravādins point out that if karmic results were to become the causes of further karmic results in an endless series, there could be no cessation of sorrow (*n'atthi dukkhassa anta-kiriyā*), no cutting off of the round of rebirth (*n' atthi vaṭṭupacchedo*), and no attainment of *parinibbāna* without residual causes of rebirth (*n' atthi anupādā-parinibbāna*) (Kvu. 357).

[41] P.S. Jaini, "The Sautrāntika Theory of *bīja*", 238.

[42] Bhikkhu Bodhi, *A Comprehensive Manual of Abhidhamma*, 174-175.

[43] . . . *kāya-sañcetanā nāma kāya-dvāre cetanā-pakappanā; sā aṭṭha-kāmāvacara-kusalavasena aṭṭha-vidhā, akusalavasena dvādasa-vidhā ti vīsati-vidhā. Tathā vacī-sañcetanā, tathā mano-sañcetanā* (AA. III. 144).

[44] The commentary says that when ignorance is present, then *cetanā*—the cause (*paccaya*) of joy and sorrow—arises at the three "gates" of action (body, speech, and mind).

Avijjā-paccayā . . . tīsu dvāresu sukha-dukkhānaṁ paccaya-bhūtā cetanā uppajjati (AA. III. 144).

[45] *Idaṁ pana kammacatukkaṁ patvā dvādasa akusala-cetanā kaṇhā nāma. Tebhūmaka-kusala-cetanā sukkā nāma magga-cetanā akaṇha-asukkā ti āgatā* (MA. III. 105).

[46] Bhikkhu Bodhi, *A Comprehensive Manual of Abhidhamma*, 149-173.

[47] Ibid., 151.

[48] *Bhavaṅga* can be described as "subliminal" in the sense that it cannot be perceived by the senses or grasped by the ordinary processes of the mind. However, it is not postulated in the *Abhidhamma* that *bhavaṅga* is a "sub-plane" operating beneath the threshold of consciousness (S.Z. Aung, *Compendium of Philosophy*, 11; Mahāthera Nārada, *A Manual of Abhidhamma*, 163-165). Thus *bhavaṅga* differs from the *ālayavijñāna* of *Vijñānavāda* and the subliminal level of the *citta* in the Yoga tradition: it does not function as the repository of *vāsanas* from which *cittas* and *cetanās* arise and into which impressions lapse. The explanation given by Collins (S. Collins, *Selfless Persons: Imagery and Thought in Theravāda Buddhism*, 243-244) is that *bhavaṅga* processes alternate with *citta-vīthis* to constitute the continuity of individual existence. He stresses that *bhavaṅga* differs from the Unconscious of Freudian psychology since it is not conceived as an underlying "level" of consciousness. Mahāthera Nārada explains that *bhavaṅga* is so named because it is essential for the continuity of subjective experience and individual existence in the wheel of rebirth (Mahāthera Nārada, *A Manual of Abhidhamma*, 165). Guenther, however, takes

bhavaṅga to be "the sum total of all potentialities", and identifies *bhavaṅga* with the *ālaya-vijñāna* of Vijñānavāda (H.V. Guenther, *Philosophy and Psychology in the Abhidharma*, 44).

[49] This is the basic cognitive process delineated in the *Visuddhimagga* (Vsm. XX. 44, XIV. 114-122) and the fourth chapter of the *Abhidhammattha-saṅgaha*. Differences occur in the process. For example, there are differences depending on whether the object is very clear, clear, obscure, or very obscure (Bhikkhu Bodhi, *A Comprehensive Manual of Abhidhamma*, 163-166). *Citta-vīthis* related to the stages of meditation, to the four Paths and their fruition, to dying, and to rebirth differ from each other and from the basic cognitive process.

[50] S.Z. Aung, *Compendium of Philosophy*, 29.

[51] This extended simile is cited in S.Z. Aung, *Compendium of Philosophy*, 30; C.A.F. Rhys Davids, *Buddhist Psychology: An Enquiry into the Analysis and Theory of Mind in Pali Literature*, 180-181; W.F. Jayasuriya, *The Psychology and Philosophy of Buddhism*, 42-43; Lama Govinda, *The Psychological Attitude of Early Buddhist Philosophy*, 134-135; and S. Collins, *Selfless Persons: Imagery and Thought in Theravāda Buddhism*, 242-243. The version given by Aung differs in some details from the *Atthasālinī* version.

[52] Bhikkhu Bodhi, *A Comprehensive Manual of Abhidhamma*, 124, 175.

[53] The five-door adverting consciousness (*pañca-dvārāvajjana*), the five types of sense consciousness (*pañca-viññāṇa*), receiving consciousness (*sampaṭicchana*), investigating consciousness (*santīraṇa*), and determining consciousness (*voṭṭhapana*) are classified as *ahetuka*. They do not have wholesome or unwholesome roots (Ibid., 108, 120). Of these, the five-door adverting consciousness and determining consciousness are purely functional (*kiriya*) *cittas* and the others are resultant (*vipāka*) *cittas*. Registration (*tadārammaṇa*) also is performed by resultant *cittas* (Ibid., 126-127).

[54] Ibid., 124-129.

[55] *Javana* moments are defined as either wholesome, unwholesome, "fruitional" (*phala*), or purely functional (*kiriya*) *cittas*. The wholesome and unwholesome *javana* moments constitute the *kamma*-forming processes (*kamma-bhava*) of the rebirth continuum. The "fruitional" (*phala*) *javana-cittas*

are resultant (*vipāka*) states, and they are experienced as the fruits of the stages of the Path that culminates in liberating wisdom. Functional (*kiriya*) *javana-cittas* are experienced only by the liberated one (*arahant*), whose actions perform a beneficent function without leaving any karmic traces. Neither the cognitive processes that arise as the fruits of the stages of the Path of liberation nor the cognitive processes of an *arahant* have karmic consequences. The *cetanās* that arise in "fruitional" and "functional" *javana* processes perform their basic function of energizing and co-ordinating concomitant mental factors and directing them towards objects. However, these *cetanās* do not have the form of purposive impulses that aspire for future goals, and they do not carry karmic merit or demerit.

[56] Bhikkhu Bodhi, *A Comprehensive Manual of Abhidhamma*, 307.

[57] S.Z. Aung, *Compendium of Philosophy*, 247.

[58] Ibid., 249, n. 1.

[59] Vsm. XVII. 66,88.

[60] Bhikku Ñāṇamoli, *The Path of Purification*, 131, n. 13.

[61] Bhikkhu Ñāṇananda, *Concept and Reality in Early Buddhist Thought*, 5-6.

[62] Bhikkhu Ñāṇananda (Ibid., 4-6) notes that *papañca* conveys "spreading out", "expansion", "diffusion", and "manifoldness". He translates *papañca-saññā-sankhā* as "concepts characterized by the prolific tendency". *Papañca* also connotes obsession with the concepts that have been proliferated and the tendency to give free rein to one's imagination. Collins translates *papañca-saññā-sankhā* as "imaginings, ideas and estimations"(S. Collins, *Selfless Persons: Imagery and Thought in Theravāda Buddhism*, 141). I have followed Bhikkhu Bodhi who renders *papañca-saññā-saṅkhā* as "perceptions and notions tinged by mental proliferation"(Bhikkhu Bodhi, *Middle Length Discourses of the Buddha: A New Translation of the Majjhima Nikāya*, 202).

[63] S.Z. Aung, *Compendium of Philosophy*, 248.

[64] Mahāthera Nārada, *A Manual of Abhidhamma*, p. 33, p. 167.

[65] Lama Govinda, *The Psychological Attitude of Early Buddhist Philosophy*, 137.

[66] S.Z. Aung, *Compendium of Philosophy*, 43.

[67] Ibid., 249.

[68] Mahāthera Nārada, *A Manual of Abhidhamma*,. 33.

[69] Bhikkhu Bodhi, *A Comprehensive Manual of Abhidhamma*, 173.

[70] However, the Theravādins differ from the Yogācārins, who use the argument that different people perceive the same thing differently to support their view that all objects are mind-created manifestations of subliminal *vāsanās* contained in the *ālaya-vijñāna*. (E. Conze, *Buddhist Thought in India: Three Phases of Buddhist Philosophy*, 256).

[71] S.Z. Aung, *Compendium of Philosophy*, 247-248.

[72] Ibid., 248-249, n. 1.

[73] The *Abhidhammattha-saṅgaha* includes the following among the objects that are perceived by the mind: a momentary state of mind (*citta*), mental factors (*cetasika*) constituting a *citta*, *nibbāna*, and concepts (*paññatti*). Bhikkhu Bodhi states in his explanatory notes that a given momentary state of mind (*citta*) cannot be directly apprehended, since the cognizer cannot simultaneously become the cognized. However, Bhikkhu Bodhi goes on to explain that according to the *Abhidhamma*, a *citta* can review earlier *cittas* in the same mental continuum or a *citta* in another being. It still remains a problem how any *citta* can review an earlier *citta*, if *cittas* are momentary (Bhikkhu Bodhi, *A Comprehensive Manual of Abhidhamma*, 135-136).

[74] S.Z. Aung, *Compendium of Philosophy*, 43.

Chapter VII

Cetanā and the Mind's Dynamic Capacities

In the *Dhammasaṅgaṇi*, the *Atthasālinī*, and the *Visuddhimagga* the continuum of consciousness is described as a series of interdependent pulsating moments that can be viewed in two ways. Every momentary poise of consciousness (*citta*) is shown to be a rich whole of mutually conditioning cognitive, emotive, and conative factors (*cetasika*s) that arise and constitute an attitude of mind when consciousness makes contact with the environment. It is posited in the *Abhidhamma* system that every *citta* is a moment of conscious awareness that comes into existence when a sense organ or the mind makes contact with an object. When a *citta* arises in this way through sensory or mental stimulation, it is constituted of the four non-physical *khandha*s, namely feeling aroused by the object (*vedanā*), perception of the object (*saññā*), purposive action in relation to the object (*saṅkhāra*), and cognitive discernment of the nature and qualities of the object (*viññāṇa*). The inclusion of the *saṅkhārakkhandha* within the continuum of *citta*s signifies that the cognitive, emotive, and conative factors that constitute an attitude of mind can be transformed by the *saṅkhārakkhandha* into causal factors (*paccaya*s) for the formation of purposive acts. Thus, according to the interpretation given in the *Abhidhamma* system, each pulsation of consciousness is simultaneously an attitude of mind and a dynamic process in which purposive acts of body, mind, and speech are formed and put forth. *Cetanā* is defined in the *Abhidhamma* as a coordinating function that brings together and marshals concomitant mental factors (*cetasika*s) by directing their activities towards a chosen goal

(Asl. 111-112; Vsm. XIV. 135). This definition of *cetanā* provides it with a leading role in the interweaving of the knowledge-gaining processes and the action-initiating impulses of the continuum of consciousness.

What *saṅkhāras* are and how they function is not fully clarified in the *Suttas*, though their crucial and ubiquitous role in the continuum of consciousness is made abundantly evident. The *Khandha-saṁyutta* states that *saṅkhāras* are constituted of the six types of *cetanās* that arise when the five senses and the mind (*manas*) make contact with their respective objects (S. III. 63). This bond between *cetanās* and the *saṅkhārakkhandha*, which is again noted in the *Vibhaṅga* (Vbh. 40), can be interpreted to mean that *cetanās* arise when objects are perceived and function as purposive impulses that motivate purposive acts (*saṅkhāras*) in relation to those objects. There are passages in the *Suttas* where the goal-oriented activities of *saṅkhāras* and *cetanās* are described. What is not clarified, however, is precisely how the functions of *cetanās* and *saṅkhāras* differ from each other.

It was shown in Chapter IV that there are passages in the *Suttas* where the term *saṅkhāra* signifies an act of body, speech, or mind that leads to karmic consequences (M. I. 54; D. III. 217). There are also passages relating to the formation and fruition of *kamma* that describe how ordinary folk ignorantly "form" (*abhisaṅkharonti*) formations of conditions that produce acts (*saṅkhāras*) of body, speech, and mind, thereby becoming enslaved to future goals and the sorrow of rebirth (M. I. 389 = A. II. 231; S. II. 40 = A. II. 158; S. II. 82, V. 449). These passages give substance to the succinct definition which states that *saṅkhāras* are so named because they "form" (*abhisaṅkharonti*) something that is "formed" (*saṅkhatam*) (S. III. 87). Furthermore, it is stated in the *Saṁyutta-nikāya* that the category of the "formed" includes not only karmically significant acts (*kamma*) of body, speech, and mind but also the aggregates (*khandhas*) that constitute the "person" (S. III. 87). This statement can be interpreted to mean that the mind's function of forming and producing goal-oriented acts also brings about corresponding developments in the processes that form the physical and mental factors of the organism.

Although the concise definition of *saṅkhāra* in the *Saṁyutta-nikāya* states that *saṅkhāras* include both the act of forming as well as what is formed, there is no detailed description in the *Suttas* of either the ingredients that are utilized in the act of forming or the method by which the forming is done. The commentary to the *Saṁyutta-nikāya* (SA. II. 292) explains that each of the aggregates that form the personality is designated as *saṅkhata* because it is "formed" by the coming together of necessary conditions (*paccayas*). For example, when there is a confluence of the necessary causal conditions—including motivation leading to sensory experience, the presence of the object of interest, the unimpaired functioning of the appropriate sense organ, and sensory contact with the object—*saṅkhāra* processes produce or "form" the aggregate of feeling (*vedanā*) in the consciousness continuum. Similarly, the *Atthasālinī* defines the "formed" (*saṅkhata*) as that which is made or produced (*kata*) by the convergence of the necessary conditions (*paccayas*). According to the *Atthasālinī*, the ingredients for the "formed" are the conditions necessary for forming it, and the method of forming is the assembling (*samāgamana*) of the necessary conditions (Asl. 47). This definition of "formed" (*saṅkhata*)[1] can be interpreted to mean that *saṅkhāras* produce effects by facilitating the confluence of the necessary causal conditions. Therefore, the definition in the *Atthasālinī* implies that the *saṅkhārakkhandha* represents conditioned origination at work in the continuum of consciousness. The motivation to initiate action must be regarded as a function that arises when cognitive processes, emotions, and conative energies meet as necessary conditions (*paccayas*) for producing goal-directed activities.

In Chapter IV, the quest for *Sutta* passages that clarify the relationship between *saṅkhāras* and *cetanā* led to the *Sañcetanika-vagga* of the *Aṅguttara-nikāya* (A. II. 157-158). It is said here that because of the impetus of purposive impulses pertaining to body, speech, and mind (*kāya-sañcetanā-hetu, vacī-sañcetanā-hetu, mano-sañcetanā-hetu*), one experiences consequences of personal joy or sorrow. This statement implies that purposive impulses (*sañcetanās*) have the capacity to initiate acts that entail karmic consequences. It was pointed out in Chapter IV that in the *Sañcetanika-vagga* these same acts instigated by *sañcetanās* are also called *saṅkhāras* of body, speech, and mind (*kāya-saṅkhāra, vacī-saṅkhāra, mano-saṅkhāra*). However, the *Sañcetanika-vagga* does not clarify how the functions of *sañcetanā* and *saṅkhāra* differ with regard to the production of acts with karmic consequences.

Reference was also made in Chapter IV to passages where the two terms *abhisaṅkhata* and *abhisañcetayita* are applied to the same act (*kamma*) that carries karmic consequences. Besides the passages mentioned in Chapter IV, there are passages where the two terms *abhisaṅkhata* and *abhisañcetayita* are applied to "planes" of meditation (*jhāna*). In this context, *abhisaṅkhatam* indicates that specific mental factors come together to form a distinct and clearly recognizable plane of meditation (M.I 350-352; A.V. 343-346). *Abhisañcetayitam* signifies that the plane of meditation is brought about intentionally through the functioning of a purposive impetus. The crucial teaching in these passages is that since a plane of meditation is purposefully conceived and formed of many mental components, it is governed by temporal factors and causal principles. Since a *jhāna* state is governed by conditioned origination, it comes to an end when the conditions through which it was formed cease to be. These passages declare that when a *bhikkhu* attains clear insight into the conditioned and ephemeral nature of the planes of meditation (*jhānas*), he is released from the lasting power of the mental corruptions (*āsavas*). Similarly, in the *Aṅguttara-nikāya* (A. V. 188), the Buddha's householder disciple Anāthapiṇḍika, who feeds and protects the destitute, tells a group of debating ascetics that he has attained release from all sorrow by coming to the realization that whatever is composed (*saṅkhatam*), motivated by purposive thought (*cetayitam*), and governed by conditioned-origination (*paṭicca-samuppannam*) is transient (*anicca*). Like planes of meditation, speculative views are regarded as mental acts that are composed (*saṅkhatam*) of ideas and are purposefully conceived (*cetayitam*) (A. V. 187). In other contexts (S. II. 82; M. III. 244), an *arahant* is described as one who is no longer formulating (*anabhisaṅkharonto*) acts with karmic consequences or occupying the mind with purposive thoughts (*anabhicetayanto*). However, none of these passages distinguishes and defines *abhisaṅkhatam* and *abhisañcetayitam*.

It is in the commentaries (SA. II. 402; AA. V. 84) that *abhisaṅkhatam* is explained as that which is made or produced by means of the assembling and binding together of the necessary causal conditions, while *abhisañcetayitam* is interpreted as that which is planned or designed (*pakappitam*) by thought. The commentaries to the first four *Nikāyas* rely on the *Sutta* passage where *ceteti* and *pakappeti* are juxtaposed (S. II. 66-67) when they gloss *abhisañcetayitam* with *pakappitam*. Buddhaghosa's commentaries are based on an ancient tradition of interpretation that once existed in the Sīhaḷa-bhāsā, the language of Sri Lanka. The Theravāda tradition seeks to guard its own coherence throughout the passage of time by maintaining and developing consistent explanations of its key concepts. The commentarial and *Abhidhamma* explanations of *cetanā* and *saṅkhāra* must be understood and evaluated in the context of the aims and the methods of interpretation preserved by the Theravāda tradition.

Connotations of *Āyūhana* in the Definitions of *Cetanā* and *Saṅkhāra*

The *Visuddhimagga* defines *saṅkhāra* twice in order to distinguish its two roles. In an individual being, the constructive processes of the *saṅkhārakkhandha* bring together the resources of the mind and produce purposive acts that entail karmic consequences (Vsm. XIV. 131-132). In the chain of rebirth, *saṅkhāra* functions as the causal link (*paccaya*) whereby the wholesome and unwholesome purposive acts become the causal conditions for rebirth (Vsm. XVII. 51). The definition of *saṅkhāra* as *paccaya* states that *saṅkhāra* becomes manifest as *cetanā* in the causal chain. The definition of *saṅkhāra* as *khandha* is as follows:

lakkhaṇa (characteristic)	*abhisaṅkharaṇa-lakkhaṇa* *Ahisaṅkharaṇa* is explained as "composing" or "combining".
rasa (function)	*āyūhana-rasa* *Āyūhana* has two meanings: "striving" and "bringing forth *kamma*".
paccupaṭṭhāna (manifestation)	*vipphāra-paccupaṭṭhāna* *Vipphāra/vyāpāra* is explained as "engaging in profitable work".
padaṭṭhāna (proximate cause)	*sesakkhandhattaya-padaṭṭhāna* The other three non-material aggregates (feeling, perception, and consciousness) are said to constitute the proximate cause of *saṅkhārakkhandha*.

The *Visuddhimagga* glosses *abhisaṅkharaṇa* as *rāsi-karaṇa* (literally, "to pile up", "make a heap", or "form an aggregate") (Vsm. XIV. 131). It was shown in Chapter IV that the *Milindapañha* (Mil. 61-62) specifies *cetayita* and *abhisaṅkharaṇa* to be the characteristics of *cetanā* and explains that *abhisaṅkharaṇa* is the process of bringing together mental factors in such a way as to produce an act that has karmic consequences. It can be assumed that *abhisaṅkharaṇa* has the same meaning when it is presented in the *Visuddhimagga* as the defining characteristic of *saṅkhāra*.

The term *vipphāra* (diffusion, vibration, quivering), which the *Visuddhimagga* employs to indicate the specific mode of manifestation of *saṅkhāra*, is changed to *vyāpāra* (occupation, work) in the commentary to the *Visuddhimagga* (VsmA. 2:1032). It is to be noted that the commentary (VsmA. 2:1035) also holds that the nature (*bhāva*) of *cetanā* can be defined as "being engaged in work" (*vyāpāra-bhāva*). In the definition of *saṅkhāra*, *vipphāra* indicates the power of *saṅkhāra* to vitalize the organism and initiate goal-oriented movement. *Saṅkhāra*, therefore, is the function that displays the capacity of consciousness to set the organism "vibrating", "pulsating", or "throbbing" with incipient activity. *Saṅkhāra* can also extend that rudimentary pulsation and develop it into the capacity to produce an intentional act that has karmic consequences.

Āyūhana is a rare term in the *Suttas*. However, in a striking poem of the *Saṁyutta-nikāya* (S. I. 1), the Buddha says that he crosses the "flood" without support (*appatiṭṭham*) and without striving or straining (*anāyūham*). The commentary explains that the flood is fourfold: sensual desire (*kām' ogho*), prolongation of existence in the rounds of rebirth (*bhav' ogho*), speculative views (*diṭṭh' ogho*) and ignorance (*avijj' ogho*) (SA. I. 17). The term *appatiṭṭham* signifies that the Buddha crosses the flood "without being supported". The connotations of the term *appatiṭṭham* in this context become clearer when this verse is linked with the three passages in the *Saṁyutta-nikāya* that are entitled *Cetanā* (S. II. 65-67). These passages say that whenever a person intends (*ceteti*), plans (*pakappeti*), or has a persistent tendency towards something (*anuseti*), that becomes an object (*ārammaṇam*) that provides a goal or support (*patiṭṭhā*) for consciousness. The mind of the enlightened one does not need objects as supports for plans and intentions. An *arahant* does not project thought processes towards future goals in order to prolong the experience of being an agent who executes various plans of action and experiences their goals. The *Saṁyutta-nikāya* poem indicates that the three terms, namely *patiṭṭhā*, *āyūhana*, and *abhisaṅkharaṇa*, have associated meanings. *Āyūhana* connotes straining towards a goal. The commentary explains *anāyūhanto* as not making an effort, not exerting oneself (*avāyamanto*). *Abhisaṅkharaṇa* emphasizes bringing together the necessary conditions to put forth a purposive act. It is postulated that when consciousness is supported by purposive impulses (*cetanā*) or aspirations (*patthanā*) arising from ignorance and craving, it strains towards future goals and experiences sorrowful rebirth (A. III. 224).

In the commentaries to the *Suttas* (MA. V. 57; AA. II. 192, 318, III. 212; SA. II. 292), the term *āyūhana* includes in its meaning both "goal-oriented striving" and "producing and accumulating *kamma*". In these commentarial passages, the verb *āyūhati* is linked with *rāsiṁ karoti* (forms a heap) and *sampiṇḍeti* (combines), and these three terms are brought together to explain *abhisaṅkharoti*. *Āyūhati* represents the function by which *saṅkhāra* "builds up" or "accumulates" the necessary conditions and produces conditioned acts that entail the accumulation of karmic consequences. The *Dhammasaṅgaṇi* (Dhs. 189, 201) adds another dimension to the meaning of *āyūhana* by making it one of the synonyms of greed (*lobha*) and of covetousness (*abhijjhā*). Likewise, in the *Vibhaṅga* (Vbh. 361), *āyūhana* occurs as one of the terms by which *lobha* is explained. Clearly, in these contexts *āyūhana* signifies, not "collecting" or "composing", but an emotion-charged conative striving that initiates a goal-directed action and brings about karmic consequences. When *āyūhana* is linked with greed or covetousness, it is regarded as a fundamental cause of rebirth and is associated with ignorance (*avijjā*).

The *Visuddhimagga* (Vsm. XXI. 38) defines *āyūhana* as *āyatiṁ paṭisandhi-hetu-bhūtam kammam* (the *kamma* that causes future rebirth). In his translation of this section of the *Visuddhimagga*, Pe Maung Tin renders *āyūhana* as "exerting", thereby indicating that *āyūhana* is to be conceived as striving to put forth the type of action that becomes the condition for rebirth.[2] Ñāṇamoli, on the other hand, translates *āyūhana* as "accumulating" *kamma.*[3] Although he does not explain what connotation he gives to "accumulating", this term can be understood as the act of producing and "piling up" wholesome and unwholesome purposive acts (*saṅkhāras*) in such a way that they form a set of conditions that produces rebirth. Neither rendering, however, captures the full significance of *āyūhana*: "exerting" does not indicate that the exerting produces action that brings about karmic consequences, and "accumulation" does not cover the urgency to perform such action. Both of these notions are fundamental to the meaning of *āyūhana*, especially when the term represents the distinctive function (*rasa*) attributed to *saṅkhāra* and to *cetanā*. It is significant that the *Visuddhimagga* gives *āyūhana* as the synonym of *saṅkhāra* in passages (Vsm. XVII. 292, XIX. 13) that list the following five causal links which constitute the dynamic, *kamma*-forming dimension of the wheel of rebirth: ignorance (*avijjā*), the mind's capacity to bring together causal conditions and form purposive acts (*saṅkhāra*), craving (*taṇhā*), attachment to the causes of rebirth (*upādāna*), and prolongation of existence (*bhava*).[4] By making *āyūhana* synonymous with *saṅkhāra* in its role of causal link in the chain of rebirth, the *Visuddhimagga* draws attention to the energizing, motivating, action-producing functions of *saṅkhāra*.

The translation of *āyūhana* as "accumulation" is misleading because it suggests that the connotations of *upacaya* are transferred to *āyūhana*. It was shown in Chapter IV that the opponents of Theravāda postulated that a special factor of "accumulation" (*upacaya*) is needed to ensure that every act that carries karmic consequences is "accumulated" and conserved in the consciousness continuum of a "person" until the time is appropriate for the act to come to fruition (Kvu. 520-522). The Theravādins argued that no such linking factor of "accumulation" is required to connect the act (*kamma*), which functions as the cause, with its effects (*kamma-vipāka*). It follows that the translation of *āyūhana* as "accumulation" should be interpreted, not as appropriating and preserving something so that it continues to exist, but as the production of a multiplicity of deeds that entail manifold karmic consequences and bring about rebirth. One can conclude that in the *Atthasālinī* and the *Visuddhimagga*, the term *āyūhana* primarily signifies the performing of acts that entail karmic consequences. At the same time, *āyūhana* indicates that these acts are characterized by some degree of urgency and goal-oriented striving. Theravāda puts forward the argument that in the context of conditioned origination, wholesome and unwholesome purposive acts, just by the fact that they have been done, become causal conditions that produce effects in the consciousness continuum of the doer. In the *Visuddhimagga* (Vsm. XVII. 173-174), merely performing *kamma* is regarded as sufficient cause to bring forth commensurate consequences.[5]

The *Atthasālinī* (Asl. 291) makes a distinction between *āyūhana-kāla* and *vipaccana-kāla*. In this context, *āyūhana-kāla* refers to the time when an act of body, speech, or mind is performed, and *vipaccana-kāla* refers to the time of "fruition" when the karmic result of that act becomes manifest. The *Visuddhimagga* (Vsm. XVII. 61) defines the "moment of *āyūhana*" (*kammāyūhanakkhaṇa*) as the point in time when a *saṅkhāra* of merit (*puññābhisaṅkhāra*), or a *saṅkhāra* of demerit (*apuññābhisaṅkhāra*), or a *saṅkhāra* that pertains to the "imperturbable" level of meditation (*āneñjābhisaṅkhāra*) is brought into existence.[6] In this passage of the *Visuddhimagga*, these three types of *saṅkhāras* are defined as acts motivated by purposive impulses (*sañcetanā*) that become manifest at the "three doors" as intentional acts of body, speech, and mind (*kāya-sañcetanā, vacī-sañcetanā, mano-sañcetanā*). The term *āyūhana*, therefore, points to the bond between *cetanā* and *saṅkhāra*. *Āyūhana* signifies the mind's function of striving to garner the necessary metal resources in order to produce an abundance of goal-oriented acts. Such goal-oriented striving is the function of *saṅkhāra* processes. *Cetanās* are the intentions and purposive impulses that motivate, direct and give urgency to the goal-oriented striving that *āyūhana* represents. The *Atthasālinī* (Asl. 261) explains that when *kamma* is performed by unwholesome states of mind (*akusala-cittehi kamme ayūhite*), sorrowful consequences follow because of the unwholesome purposive impulse (*tāya cetanāya*) that is manifested in that karmic activity. Although the *Atthasālinī* makes this statement about unwholesome acts, it is clear that parallel statements can be made about performing (*āyūhana*) wholesome acts.

Cetanā in the Classification of *Saṅkhāras*

The *Visuddhimagga* (Vsm. XVII. 44-46) classifies *saṅkhāras* into four types: *saṅkhāras* characterized as "formed"; *saṅkhāras* that are formed by *kamma*; *saṅkhāras* that actively form *kamma*; and *saṅkhāras* that consist of impetus or activating impulse.

1. *Saṅkhāras* characterized as "formed" (*saṅkhata-saṅkhāra*) constitute the widest category, which includes all physical and mental factors that are produced through causal conditions (*sappaccaya-dhammas*) and are subject to change and decay (Vsm. XVII. 46). The *Visuddhimagga* adds that this widely inclusive category of *saṅkhāras* is referred to in such *Sutta* statements as: "*Saṅkhāras*, indeed, are impermanent" (S. I. 158; D. II. 157). In another passage of the *Saṁyutta-nikāya* (S. III. 96-97), *saṅkhāra*, craving (*taṇhā*) contact with objects (*phassa*), and ignorance (*avijjā*) are described as impermanent, composite, and arisen through causal conditions (*anicca saṅkhata paṭicca-samuppanna*). *Saṅkhāras* of this category can come into existence in situations that are outside the course of *kamma*. This can be seen from the fact that processes in the physical world are *saṅkhāras*, but they do not produce *kamma*.

2. *Saṅkhāras* formed by *kamma* (*abhisaṅkhata-saṅkhāra*) are described as the consequences of past *kamma*. They come into existence in the form of physical and mental factors that constitute the three realms of rebirth: the realm of sensory experience (*kāma-dhātu*), the realm of fine matter (*rūpa-dhātu*), and the non-material realm (*arūpa-dhātu*) (Vsm. XVII. 44, 46). The body and the senses, for example, are the consequences of "old *kamma*" (*purāṇa kamma*) and fall under the category of *abhisaṅkhata-saṅkhāra*. The *Visuddhimagga* regards this class as a subset of the large class of *saṅkhāras* that are characterized as "formed" (*saṅkhata-saṅkhāra*). However, the *saṅkhāras* of this category have the following features: they are characterized by ignorance (Vsm. XVII. 44); they come into existence dependent on past *kamma*; and they constitute the realms of rebirth. The *Visuddhimagga* (Vsm. XVII. 46) makes the interesting point that there is no passage in the *Suttas* where *kamma*-formed *saṅkhāras* are distinguished as a specific category.

3. *Saṅkhāras* that actively form *kamma* (*abhikaṅkharaṇa-saṅkhāra*) are conditioned and composite like all *saṅkhāras*. However, their ability to take on the karmic values of merit (*puñña*) and demerit (*pāpa*) and produce purposive acts that have karmic consequences establishes them as a special category (Vsm. XVII. 46). The *Visuddhimagga* makes it clear that these dynamic *kamma*-forming *saṅkhāras* are constituted of the *cetanās* that arise as *cetasikas* in wholesome and unwholesome *cittas* (Vsm. XVII. 60-61).

4. The *Saṅkhāra* that consists of the impulse that produces activity (*payoga-saṅkhāra*) is explained in the *Visuddhimagga* (Vsm. XVII. 46) as bodily and mental energy (*kāyika-cetasika-viriyam*). In order to explain the meaning of *payoga*, the *Visuddhimagga* refers to the extended simile of the perfectly cast chariot wheel. The wheel moves as far as the impetus that sets it in motion propels it (*yāvatikā abhisaṅkhārassa gati*), and then it stops, standing perfectly

upright and motionless (A. I. 112). The commentary explains "the range of movement produced by the *saṅkhāra*" (*abhisaṅkhārassa gati*) as "the span of movement produced by the application of energy" (*payogassa gamanam*). *Payoga-saṅkhāra*, therefore, connotes the motivating energy or "push" that brings about wholesome or unwholesome *kamma*. In the commentarial literature (AA. III. 142; DA. III. 1030; Asl. 156), the term *sasaṅkhāra* is explained as *sappayoga* (endowed with energy, with impetus). In the specific case of the term *sasaṅkhāra*, *payoga* and *saṅkhāra* indicate instigation or prompting.

Cetanā in relation to saṅkhata-saṅkhāras

It is evident that the following factors have common features: states of mind imbued with pleasant, unpleasant, or neutral feelings, which arise as results of past *kamma* (*vipāka-cittas*); *cetanās* that arise as constituents of such "resultant" states of mind, not as fully developed purposive impulses, but as factors that help to maintain basic conscious awareness (*vipāka-cetanās*); and configurations of mental and physical factors, such as the present body and sense organs, which are produced through past *kamma* (*abhisaṅkhata-saṅkhāras*). All three are characterized as consequences of *kamma*. As resultant states, they are ethically indeterminate (*avyākata*), and they do not produce purposive acts of body, speech, or mind that have karmic consequences. For example, states of mind that are results of past *kamma* come into existence in the preliminary pre-*javana* stages of the cognitive process. *Cetanās* that arise in the incipient stages of perception do not have the form of fully developed intentions; therefore, they do not bring about wholesome and unwholesome acts though they direct the mind in a rudimentary manner towards objects.

Cetanās in abhisaṅkharaṇa-saṅkhāras

The states of mind and purposive impulses of the *javana* process come under the category of *kamma*-forming goal-oriented activities (*abhisaṅkharaṇa-saṅkhāras*). They put forth the personal reactions of the subject, and they are conditioned by wholesome and unwholesome roots of action. *Cetanās* that arise as constituents of the *cittas* that form the *javana* process are fully developed wholesome and unwholesome purposive impulses, and they generate acts with karmic consequences that become manifest either immediately or at a future time. Wholesome and unwholesome purposive acts (*sañcetanika-kammas*) of body, speech, and mind, which arise though the motivating impetus of an intention or purpose (*cetanā*) are also designated as *saṅkhāras* or *abhisaṅkhāras* of body, speech and, mind. The wholesome and unwholesome *cetanās* that produce these purposive acts are constituents of *kamma*-forming *abhisaṅkharaṇa-saṅkhāras*.

Cetanās in payoga-saṅkhāras

Since *cetanā* initiates action when it takes the form of a full-fledged purposive impulse, it can be identified as the motivating energy or impetus (*payoga*) within a configuration of causal conditions that constitutes a *saṅkhāra*. In the preliminary pre-*javana* stage of the cognitive process, the impetus of *cetanā* merely coordinates concomitant mental functions and directs them towards objects without producing an intentional act (*abhisaṅkhāra*). It is by virtue of this motivating impetus (*payoga*) that *cetanā* and *saṅkhāra* possess the urgency (*āyūhana*) to produce an accumulation of goal-oriented acts that carry karmic consequences. In the case of purposive acts that are instigated (*sasaṅkhāra*), the instigation arises in the form of a strong purposive impetus (*cetanā*) in the mind of the person who performs the act or in the mind of the person who does the prompting.

The Identification of Purposive Impulse (*Cetanā*) with Morally Weighted Act (*Kamma*)

The key to interpreting the meaning given to *cetanā* in the *Abhidhamma* system is the unambiguous identification of a morally-weighted act (*saṅkhāra*) with the intention or purposive impulse that it manifests. The Buddha's definition of *kamma* (A. III. 415) is recast in the equation *cetanā* = *abhisaṅkhāra*. In the definitions given by the *Vibhaṅga* (Vbh. 135), different categories of purposive acts are distinguished on the basis of the different types of karmic consequences that they carry, and each category of acts is identified with the corresponding type of purposive impulse that motivates it. A wholesome act that carries karmic merit (*puññābhisaṅkhāra*) is unequivocally defined as a wholesome *cetanā* (*kusala-cetanā*). Wholesome purposive impulses arise in the course of ordinary sensory and rational experiences or during the lower planes of meditation. Specific opportunities for the arising of wholesome *cetanās* come in the course of the practice of giving gifts (*dāna*), the cultivation of virtue (*sīla*), or the training of the mind (*bhāvanā*) through mindfulness and meditation. An act of karmic demerit (*apuññābhisaṅkhāra*) is clearly defined as an unwholesome purposive impulse (*akusala-cetanā*) that arises in the course of ordinary sensory and rational experience. An "imperturbable" mental act (*āneñjābhisaṅkhāra*) that leads to rebirth in a cosmic sphere of imperturbable peace is unmistakably identified as a wholesome *cetanā* that arises in a plane of "formless" meditation and partakes of its imperturbable serenity. In all these cases, the purposeful act is defined as a purposive impulse rendered concrete.

The *Visuddhimagga* (XVII. 60-61), very precisely identifies bodily *saṅkhāra* with bodily *sañcetanā*, verbal *saṅkhāra* with verbal *sañcetanā*, and mental *saṅkhāra* with mental *sañcetanā*. For example, both *mano-saṅkhāra* and *mano-sañcetanā* denote the same thing, namely a mental act with karmic consequences. In the *Suttas*, although it may be implied, it is not openly stated that the two terms *sañcetanā* and *saṅkhāra* equally refer to an intentional act with karmic consequences. It becomes clear in the *Visuddhimagga* that wholesome and unwholesome acts of body, speech, or mind are *saṅkhāras* in the sense that they are causally conditioned formations that arise because of the confluence of the necessary conditions. At the same time, those very same acts are wholesome and unwholesome *sañcetanās* in the sense that they are bodily, verbal, and mental manifestations of purposive impulses that arise in specific wholesome and unwholesome attitudes of mind (*cittas*). Whereas the designation *saṅkhāra* indicates their causally dependent origination, the designation *sañcetanā* signals not only that they are concrete expressions of purposive impulses, but also that they carry moral values. Both designations show that they are goal-oriented acts and entail karmic consequences.

Since a purposive impulse (*sañcetanā*) takes concrete form in a conditionally arisen act (*saṅkhāra/abhisaṅkhāra*), and since a purposive impulse is the primary motivating condition for the arising of a goal-oriented act, purpose and act become totally identified. The *Visuddhimagga* gives specific details regarding the wholesome *cetanās* of the planes of meditation [7] and the wholesome- and unwholesome *cetanās* of the sensory sphere. *Saṅkhāras* of merit and *saṅkhāras* of demerit are identified, respectively, with wholesome purposive impulses (*cetanās*) that arise in wholesome states of mind (*cittas*), and unwholesome purposive impulses that are conditioned by unwholesome states of mind (Charts 11-12). The equation that the *Visuddhimagga* makes between acts that have karmic consequences (*saṅkhāras*) and wholesome and unwholesome purposive impulses (*cetanās*) is consistent with the *Abhidhamma* interpretations of the definition of *kamma* that the Buddha gives in the *Aṅguttara-nikāya* (A. III. 415). According to the *Visuddhimagga,* this definition signifies that acts are the very manifestations of corresponding purposes and are therefore completely identical with those purposes. The *Visuddhimagga* defines a wholesome bodily act (*kāya-saṅkhāra*), for instance, as the purposive impulse in a wholesome state of mind coming into existence concretely in the body as a bodily act (*kāya-dvārato pavattā . . . kusala-cetanā*) (Vsm. XVII. 61).

The *Visuddhimagga* makes the following equations between wholesome and unwholesome *kamma*-generating acts (*abhisaṅkharaṇa-saṅkhāras*) and wholesome and unwholesome *cetanās* (Vsm. XVII. 177, 177, 180, 181, 252).

Saṅkhāra of body	=	*Sañcetanā* of body
Saṅkhāra of speech	=	*Sañcetanā* of speech
Saṅkhāra of mind	=	*Sañcetanā* of mind
Saṅkhāras of merit	=	*Cetanās* in the 8 wholesome *cittas* of the sphere of sensory experience (Chart 11) and *cetanās* in the 5 wholesome *cittas* of the fine material sphere (corresponding to the five lower planes of meditation).
Saṅkhāras of demerit	=	*Cetanās* in the 12 unwholesome *cittas* of the sphere of sensory experience, which are rooted in greed, aversion, and delusion (Chart 12).
Imperturbable *saṅkhāras*	=	*Cetanās* in the 4 wholesome *cittas* of the non-material sphere (corresponding to the four higher planes of meditation).

By precisely identifying *saṅkharas* with *sañcetanās*, the *Visuddhimagga* presents the *Abhidhamma* interpretation of a passage in the *Khandha-saṁyutta* (S. III. 60) which says that *saṅkhāras* are the six groups of *sañcetanās* that arise in relation to the objects of the five senses and the mind. Precisely how the *Visuddhimagga* identifies *saṅkhāras* with *sañcetanās* can be shown, for example, in the case of the eight types of wholesome *saṅkhāras* that are concrete expressions of the eight types of wholesome *sañcetanās* (Chart 11). The first type of wholesome goal-oriented act is the bodily, verbal, or mental expression of a purposive impulse (*cetanā*) arising within a wholesome state of mind (*citta*). This *citta* is characterized by knowledge (*ñāṇa*) and joy (*somanassa*) and expresses itself spontaneously, without being prompted. The distinctive characteristics of the wholesome state of mind and the purposive impulse that arises within it are given concrete form in the corresponding type of act. The second type of wholesome act manifests a purposive impulse that arises in the second type of wholesome state of mind. Though endowed with knowledge and joy, this type of state of mind lacks initiative and does not act unless it is prompted. The act that arises as an expression of a wholesome *cetanā* of this type is characterized by a joyous state of mind and an understanding of the situation, but it arises either through self-instigation or instigation from another person.

Similarly, the twelve types of unwholesome acts demonstrate how unwholesome purposive impulses become expressed in unwholesome behaviour (Chart 12). Eight different types of unwholesome states rooted in greed become manifest in eight corresponding acts of greed. The ninth and tenth types of unwholesome acts give concrete expression to hate-filled purposive impulses through bodily behaviour, speech, or thought. These unwholesome purposive impulses emerge from states of mind that are characterized by hatred (*dosa*), unhappiness (*domanassa*), and aversion (*paṭigha*). The ninth type of unwholesome act is unprompted, but the tenth is the manifestation of a purposive impulse emerging from a lethargic state of mind that does not act without being prompted. The acts that express unwholesome hate-ridden motivating intentions or purposive impulses (*cetanās*) are characterized by an unhappy restlessness and aversion towards an object or person. The *cetanās* arising from deluded states of mind are marked by confusion and infatuation, and become expressed in acts that manifest the same ignorance and inability to grasp the actual nature of the object or person towards whom the act is directed.

The *Abhidhammattha-saṅgaha* explains how wholesome states of mind and corresponding wholesome *cetanās* arise in the lower and higher planes of meditation. When unenlightened persons, who are not liberated from ignorance and rebirth, attain the tranquillity and calm of these planes of meditation, they do experience wholesome *cittas* of serene concentration, but their minds are not cleansed of the aspiration for present benefits and future goals.[8] Though their intentions and purposive impulses partake of the wholesome calm of the planes of meditation that they have experienced, they have not gained release from aspiring for, and striving towards, further attainments. Since they have not renounced their yearning for the blissful calm of meditation, they are reborn in cosmic realms that correspond to the planes of meditation that they have cultivated. When *arahants* enter into planes of meditation, they experience only purely functional mental states (*kiriya-cittas*).[9] Their functional *cetanās* (*kiriya-cetanās*) become expressed in beneficent acts that produce no karmic traces because they are not motivated by the intention to fulfil a purpose or attain a goal.

Cetanā and the Process of Rebirth

In the *Sutta* literature, the way *kamma* operates to perpetuate rebirth is explained in terms of a chain of causation with twelve causal conditions (*paccaya*). Each *paccaya* represents a distinctive or compelling condition among the set of causal conditions necessary to bring about an effect.[10] The *Visuddhimagga* arranges the twelve links in such a way as to cover three successive lives (Chart 14). According to the interpretation given in the *Visuddhimagga*, the twelve links of the chain of causation exhibit the interplay of two dimensions in the rebirth process: the active *kamma*-generating dimension (*kamma-bhava*), and the resultant *kamma*-generated dimension (*upapatti-bhava*). The dynamic *kamma*-forming dimension is said to be brought about by five causal conditions: ignorance (*avijjā*), dynamic configurations (*saṅkhāras*) of motivating factors that produce acts with karmic consequences, craving (*taṇhā*), clinging (*upādāna*) to factors that cause rebirth, and existence within the process of rebirth (*bhava*). These causal conditions powerfully direct conscious processes towards the future by putting forth and multiplying urgent purposive impulses, fervent aspirations, and firm resolves (*cetanā*, *patthanā*, *paṇidhi*). Wholesome and unwholesome *cetanās*, therefore, are integral to the dynamic, *kamma*-forming dimension of the rebirth process. Since purposive impulses that operate within mental processes (*mano-sañcetanā*) in the form of ever-renewed hopes, ever-changing plans, and ever-enticing projects nourish the urge to prolong individual existence, they are regarded as the primary nutriment (*āhāra*) for the rebirth process.

The resultant dimension (*upapatti-bhava*) of the rebirth process is made of *kamma*-generated factors. Arising as fruition of past *kamma*, these factors make up the aggregates (*khandhas*) of the "person" who experiences the mental happiness (*somanassa*) and unhappiness (*domanassa*) of a specific sphere of experience (Vsm. XVII. 253). For example, the *khandhas* that make up the body and mind of a *deva* are necessary conditions for the celestial experiences of the *deva* realm. The *khandhas* of a human being contain the senses and the mind without which it is not possible to partake of the distinctively human experiences of bondage to sorrow and hope of *nibbāna*. The following five are regarded as the primary links in the resultant aspect of the chain of rebirth: consciousness (*viññāṇa*), mind-and-body (*nāma-rūpa*), the six senses (*saḷāyatana*), sensory contact (*phassa*), and feeling (*vedanā*). All these factors of the rebirth process arise through the fruition of *kamma* (*kamma-vipāka*). In the *Saṁyutta-nikāya* the body (S. II. 65) and the sense organs (S. IV. 132) are said to be produced as consequences of past *kamma* (*purāṇa-kamma*) and are described as *abhisaṅkhata* and *abhisañcetayita*. In this context, the term *purāṇa* is interesting because in common usage it refers to an ancient past and suggests that the present body and senses are linked with events that happened long, long ago. *Abhisaṅkhata* conveys that the body and senses are formed through the convergence of causal conditions. The idea that the body and mind are conditioned by mental processes that are motivated by intentions and purposive impulses (*sañcetanā*) is expressed by the term *abhisañcetayita* (SA. II. 402). The concept of a *kamma*-produced resultant dimension (*upapatti-bhava*) in the description of the rebirth process corresponds to the concept of *kamma*-formed *saṅkhāras* (*abhisaṅkhata-saṅkhāra*) in the description and classification of *saṅkhāras*.

The *Visuddhimagga* defines *abhisaṅkhata-saṅkhāras* as the material and non-material factors of the realms of rebirth, which are produced by *kamma* (Vsm. XVII. 46).[11] It follows that all the factors of the resultant dimension of the rebirth process are *abhisaṅkhata-saṅkhāras*. Though they are conditioned by past acts that were motivated by intentions and purposes, they do not produce further intentional acts that have karmic consequences. The *cetanā* that occurs in a mental state that arises as result of past *kamma* is a resultant (*vipāka*) *cetanā*. It functions as a factor of basic conscious awareness, but it does not have the characteristics of a fully developed purposive impulse, and it does not become expressed in a wholesome or unwholesome deed. The *cittas* that arise in the preliminary phase of the cognitive process, for example, are resultant states, and the *cetanās* that they contain do not produce further *kamma*.

Although *cetanā* is not specifically mentioned as one of the twelve causal links in the chain of rebirth, two of the links, namely *saṅkhāra* and *bhava*, are identified with *cetanā* (Chart 14). The *Visuddhimagga* (Vsm. XVII. 177-180) explains that in its role as the second link in the chain of rebirth, *saṅkhāra* represents the wholesome and unwholesome purposive impulses (*cetanās*) that become realized in acts (*saṅkhāras/abhisaṅkhāras*) that have karmic consequences. Acts that carry karmic merit, acts of demerit, and the imperturbable mental acts of the higher levels of meditation are included in the category of *kamma*-forming *saṅkhāras*. It is to be noted that the *Visuddhimagga* also designates the second link in the chain of rebirth as *āyūhana* (Vsm. XVII. 292, XIX. 13). This designation is appropriate, since *āyūhana* represents the distinctive function through which *saṅkhāras* and *cetanās* put forth energy to perform and accumulate deeds that have karmic consequences. *Saṅkhāra* as the second link in the chain of rebirth stands for the intentions and purposive impulses (*cetanās*) of a person's previous life, which motivated past wholesome and unwholesome acts that have produced consequences in the present life. *Cetanās* are like figures with two faces, for they look back to past experiences and they look forward, simultaneously, to future goals. Through its interpretation of rebirth as a process that covers past, present, and future lives, the *Visuddhimagga* suggests that the motivating capacity of *cetanās* resides in the fact that they simultaneously recapitulate the past and anticipate the future.

Cetanā is also identified with the tenth link in the chain of rebirth, namely *bhava*.[12] In this context, the *Visuddhimagga* (Vsm. XVII. 250) quotes the *Vibhaṅga* (Vbh. 137) to show that *bhava* is constituted of *saṅkhāras* laden with karmic merit, *saṅkharas* characterized by demerit, and *saṅkharas* pertaining to the imperturbable planes of meditation. These wholesome and unwholesome *saṅkhāras* that constitute *bhava* are the goal-oriented acts of the present life, which cast their conditioning influence on the future. The term *bhava* signifies the perpetuation of existence within the wheel of rebirth. Both the active dimension of the process of rebirth that provides the conditions for the perpetuation of existence and the resultant dimension in which those conditions come to fruition are included in *bhava*. The *Visuddhimagga* regards the purposive impulses (*cetanās*) that become concretely manifest in the goal-oriented acts (*saṅkhāras*) of the present life as the causal conditions that bring forth a new birth (*jāti*) and a new life (Vsm. XVII. 292). In the description of rebirth that the *Visuddhmagga* gives, *cetanās* constituting *saṅkhāra* (the second causal condition in the chain of rebirth) link past life with present life, and *cetanās* constituting *bhava* (the tenth causal condition in the chain of rebirth) link present life with future life. By identifying *saṅkhāra* and *bhava* with *cetanā*, the *Visuddhimagga* demonstrates that purposive impulses constitute the entirety of life and rebirth. Through the motivating power of purposive impulses, the past gives birth to the present, and the present gives birth to the future. This identification of *cetanā* with *saṅkhāra* and *bhava* can be seen as the *Abhidhamma* interpretation of the Buddha's statement that it is *cetanā* that he regards as *kamma*.

The Connecting Role of *Cetanās*

The range of the *citta* is "wider" than the *saṅkhārakkhandha* and is constituted of the four mental aggregates: feelings, perceptions, the mind's action-producing processes (*saṅkhāras*), and conscious awareness (Dhs. 209). However, *saṅkhāras* compose and produce the mental aggregates (S.111. 87), and condition all the cognitive, emotive, and conative mental factors that constitute the *cittas*. It is in this sense that the series of attitudes of mind presented by the *cittas* and the action-producing processes displayed by the *saṅkhāras* can be described as two inseparable and mutually conditioning dimensions of the same continuum of consciousness. *Cetanās*, functioning as purposive impulses, link the two dimensions of the continuum of consciousness: the knowledge-gaining processes of *cittas* and the action-initiating processes of *saṅkhāras*. Similarly, *cetanās* link recollections of past experiences with anticipations of future goals.

The lists of wholesome and unwholesome *cittas* in the *Dhammasaṅgaṇi*, the *Atthasālinī*, and the *Visuddhimagga* present each state of mind as a *maṇḍala* of mutually conditioning mental factors (*cetasikas*). To continue the imagery, when *cetanā* arises, it is affected by the colours, the intricate design, and the inner dynamics of the *maṇḍala*. Every momentary mental state comes into existence through the contact that consciousness makes with a sensory or mental object. The purposive impulse that a *cetanā* represents is conditioned by the object as well as by the interplay of thought processes, emotions, and motivating impulses that come together in the state of mind within which it arises.

The lists of mental factors are laid out in such a way as to demonstrate that the very same factors that occur as constituents (*cetasikas*) of wholesome and unwholesome states of mind are reckoned as the motivating conditions that generate the mind's goal-oriented wholesome and unwholesome activities. The same cognitive, emotive, and conative factors that constitute wholesome and unwholesome attitudes of mind also function in the dynamic *saṅkhāra* processes of consciousness as configurations of action-initiating energies that produce wholesome and unwholesome intentional acts. The definitions of *cetanā* in the *Visuddhimagga* (XIV. 135) and the *Atthasālinī* (Asl. 111-112) imply that it is because a *cetanā* takes the lead as a goal-directed impulse that the cognitive and emotive constituents (*cetasikas*) of a state of mind (*citta*) begin to function as motivating conditions (*paccayas*) that produce a goal-directed act (*saṅkhāra*). When *cetanā* presents a purpose that captures the mind, cognitive factors such as thought (*vitakka*) and reflection (*vicāra*), emotive factors such as non-greed (*alobha*) and non-hate (*adosa*), and conative factors such as energy (*viriya*) and impetus to act (*chanda*), which constitute an attitude of mind (*citta*), begin to function as a set of action-initiating forces.

These motivating conditions not only produce a goal-oriented act of body, speech, or mind, but they also endow the act with specific wholesome or unwholesome features. This mutual conditioning of the cognitive and dynamic dimensions of consciousness implies that motivating factors such as intentions, purposes, and the impetus to act influence cognitive processes, while cognitive factors such as attention and mindfulness, and emotive factors such as non-greed and non-hate become manifest in acts of body, speech, and mind.

The *Atthasālinī* and the *Visuddhimagga* define *cetanā* as a leader that energizes concomitant mental factors (*cetasikas*) and coordinates their functions in such a way as to produce goal-directed wholesome and unwholesome acts. This definition of *cetanā* can be interpreted to mean that *cetanā* infuses concomitant mental factors with a sense of purpose so that they function as motivating conditions that produce goal-oriented acts. *Cetanā* straddles the capacity to know an object, which characterizes the states of mind (*cittas*) that constitute the cognitive dimension of the continuum of consciousness, and the capacity to pursue and attain the object, which is the chief feature of the action-producing *saṅkhāra* processes that constitute the dynamic dimension. When *cetanā* functions as purposive impulse, the sense of purpose is derived from the thought processes of the continuum of consciousness, which assess various possibilities and choose a goal. The capacity of *cetanā* to initiate action to achieve a purpose or implement a plan is derived from the mind's dynamic processes, which assemble the action-initiating capacities of the continuum of consciousness and direct them towards the chosen goal.

Conclusion

On the basis of the view of consciousness presented in the *Abhidhamma* system, it is possible to argue that though *citta* processes and *saṅkhāra* processes are constituted of the same mental factors and operate as two dimensions of the same continuum of consciousness, they exhibit very different, and even incompatible, features. *Saṅkhāra* processes make evident the governance of conditioned origination and the inescapability of conditioning in all conscious processes. *Saṅkhāras* of body, speech, and mind are conditioned acts that manifest as habit patterns. On the other hand, the very term *citta* conveys the mind's function of producing endlessly variegated cognitive, emotive, and conative states (Asl. 64). *Citta* is that dimension of the consciousness continuum which displays two unique capacities: the ability to become aware of its own contents (*paccavekkhaṇa*) and the power to manifest itself in a vast diversity of ways in diverse circumstances, like a master-artist (S. III. 151). In brief, *citta* is the mind as master artist, and *saṅkhāra* is the mind as habit maker. In their most limited manifestations, *saṅkhāras* function within the closed circuits of habit formations. *Cittas*, in contrast, are open to new influences, since they can only come into manifestation through sensory or mental stimulation. Although *citta* processes are governed by conditioning no less than *saṅkhāra* processes, the conditions that operate in *citta* processes take on many variations, and consequently there is the appearance of creativity in the functioning of the mental factors that constitute *cittas*. It can be argued that *cetanās*, functioning as purposive impulses, become a conduit through which conservative and delimiting influences of habit-forming *saṅkhāras* act upon the cognitive and emotive processes of *cittas*. At the same time, by carrying into the conditioning processes of *saṅkhāras* influences from the capacity of *cittas* to variegate their responses to objects, *cetanās* can loosen the hold of habits.

Saṅkhāras are not defined in terms of habit formation either in the *Atthasālinī* or in the *Visuddhimagga*. However, the verb *abhisaṅkharoti* conveys the bringing together of the necessary conditions to produce an effect, and conditioning implies repetition. By repeatedly bringing together the same or similar mental conditions in response to various situations that the mind encounters, the *saṅkhārakkhandha* inevitably produces wholesome and unwholesome habits. In the *Suttas* and the *Atthasālinī*, unwholesome intentional acts (*saṅkhāras/sañcetanika kamma*) are described in such a way that they are shown to be harmful habits conditioned by persistent unwholesome tendencies (*anusayas*) and the obdurate corrupting influence of the *āsavas*. Wholesome intentional acts are good habits nurtured by training in virtue (*sīla*), mindfulness, and wise understanding. The capacity of *cetanā* to initiate action in pursuit of intended goals is derived from its participation in the motivating energy (*payoga*) through which the *saṅkharakkhandha* puts forth goal-oriented behaviour. As a consequence, the purposeful activity of *cetanā* is conditioned and restricted by the tendency to form habits, which becomes unavoidable in the processes of the *saṅkhārakkhandha*. This conditioning entails that the intentions and purposive impulses that *cetanās* represent are shaped to a greater or lesser degree by mental habits.

The lists of *cittas* and *saṅkhāras* in the *Visuddhimagga* imply that purposive impulses become the medium through which the capacity for variegation, which characterizes *citta* processes, and the tendency to form habits, which is a feature of *saṅkhāra* processes, condition each other. Since the purposes and intentions manifested by *cetanās* are conditioned by habits, they habitually direct thought processes to some objects rather than to others. Habitual acts (*saṅkhāras*) of body, speech, and mind restrict a person's range of experience; therefore, one's interest in objects and the intentions and purposes (*cetanās*) that one forms in response to objects become limited. Since *cittas* and the factors that constitute them arise when the mind makes contact with sensory and mental objects, when intentions and purposive impulses pertaining to objects become limited by habits, the range of the discursive thoughts and the variegation of the emotional responses that arise in *citta* processes become correspondingly limited. At the same time, the *Suttas* and the *Abhidhamma* system dwell on the capacity of the consciousness continuum to make contact with new objects and to form vastly diverse responses to the environment. Moreover, it is posited in the Theravāda tradition that because of the fruition of *kamma*, a person encounters varied, and often unexpected, experiences in the course of life. The new influences from the environment and the capacity in *cittas* for variegated responses to objects condition the *cetanās* that arise as constituents of these *cittas*. In this manner, the restrictive propensities of habits that circumscribe the purposive impulses of *cetanās* begin to be counteracted by the capacity for variegation that characterizes *cittas*.

ENDNOTES

[1] *Paccayehi samāgantvā katā ti saṅkhatā, na saṅkhatā ti asaṅkhatā* (Asl. 47).

[2] Pe Maung Tin, *The Path of Purity*, 793.

[3] Bhikkhu Ñāṇamoli, *The Path of Purification*, 757.

[4] The *Visuddhimagga* (Vsm. XVII. 292, XIX. 13) proceeds to quote the *Paṭisambhidāmagga* (Ps. I. 52) where the five causal conditions that form the *kamma*-forming process (*kamma-bhava*) are defined. The following five are the *kamma*-forming causes: (1) ignorance (*avijjā*) defined as delusion (*moha*); (2) *saṅkhāra* defined as *āyūhana*; (3) craving (*taṇhā*) defined as desire (*nikanti*); (4) clinging (*upādāna*) defined as approaching and experiencing objects (*upagamana*); and (5) perpetuation of existence (*bhava*) identified with wholesome and unwholesome *cetanās*, which instigate acts that have karmic consequences.

[5] The *Visuddhimagga* (XVII. 173-174) holds that *saṅkhāras* of body, speech, and mind become conditions for their own fruition (*saṅkhārā attano phalassa paccayā honti*). Purposive acts (*saṅkhāras*) put forth effects solely because they have been performed (*katattā yeva*), not because they continue to exist nor because they cease to exist. The notion of *upacaya* (accumulation) entails that the act is somehow conserved in the consciousness continuum until the time that it comes to fruition. Theravāda finds the notion of the continued existence and preservation of an act in any form untenable. The *Visuddhimagga* gives the following analogy: performing a transaction (such as buying some goods) leads to the completion of the transaction. The act of performing the

transaction need not continue as a condition for the transaction to come to fruition and yield results. In this example, the actual act of buying need not continue in order to ensure that the buyer can possess and enjoy the bought goods.

[6] The *Visuddhimagga* (Vsm. XVII. 61) says that at three specific moments of *āyūhana*, the *saṅkhāras* of body, speech, and mind become manifest at the "doors of action" as a *saṅkhāra* of merit, a *saṅkhāra* of demerit, or an imperturbable *saṅkhāra*:

Ayaṁ tiko kammāyūhanakkhaṇe puññābhisaṅkhārādīnaṁ dvārato pavatti-dassanatthaṁ vutto.

In this statement the term *saṅkhāra* signifies a wholesome or unwholesome purposive act that produces karmic consequences. The term *āyūhana* signifies the performance of such an act. The import of this statement is that the moment when a wholesome or unwholesome act of body, speech or mind is enacted, a commensurate process of karmic merit or demerit comes into existence.

[7] In the *Suttas*, the lower levels of meditation (*rūpa-jhānas*) are often classified as four in number (for example, D. I. 74-75). However, in the *Abhidhamma* texts, the *rūpa-jhānas* are classified as fivefold when the *cittas* of the realm of fine matter (*rūpāvacara-cittāni*) are enumerated (Vsm. XIV. 86; Bhikkhu Bodhi, *A Comprehensive Manual of Abhidhamma*, 52). There are five wholesome *rūpāvacara cetanās* corresponding to the *cittas*. The wholesome *cittas* and *cetanās* of the non-material realm (*arūpāvacara*) are four each in number.

[8] Bhikkhu Bodhi, *A Comprehensive Manual of Abhidhamma*, 54, 62.

[9] The *Anupada-sutta* of the *Majjhima-nikāya* (M. III. 25-29) states that all the levels of meditation—with the exception of the fourth of the higher levels (*arūpa-jhānas*) which is designated as "neither perception nor non-perception"— have the following mental factors: contact (*phassa*) with a sensory or mental object, feeling (*vedanā*), perception (*saññā*), purposive impulse (*cetanā*), conscious awareness (*citta*), zeal (*chanda*), decisiveness (*adhimokkha*), energy (*viriya*), mindfulness (*sati*), equanimity (*upekkhā*), and attention (*manasikāra*). These mental factors, including *cetanā*, are regarded as necessary to maintain the smooth working of the mind and ensure continued calm concentration.

[10] For example, the *Visuddhimagga* (Vsm. XVII. 108) gives the following explanation of why ignorance (*avijjā*) is posited as the *paccaya* of *saṅkhāra* in the chain of rebirth. The *Visuddhimagga* acknowledges that

***saṅkhāras* arise, not with ignorance as the sole cause, but through a set of causes, including the sensitive matter of the five sense organs where sensory stimulation occurs (*vatthu*), sensory and mental objects (*ārammaṇam*), and conascent mental factors (*sahajāta-dhammā*). Nevertheless, the *Visuddhimagga* holds that *avijjā* is regarded as the cause of *saṅkhāra* because it is the most evident one (*pākaṭattā*) among the causal conditions.**

[11] *Kamma-nibbattā tebhūmakā rūpārūpa-dhammā abhisaṅkhata-saṅkhārā* (Vsm. XVII. 46).

[12] Nyanatiloka, ***Buddhist Dictionary: A Manual of Buddhist Terms and Doctrines*, 157-158.**

Chapter VIII
Defining *Cetanā*

In the Introduction, it was stated that the central question in interpreting *cetanā* is whether in the Pāli texts *cetanā* is viewed primarily as a cognitive function of assessing possibilities and deciding on goals, or as a motivating function that initiates goal-oriented activity in the organism. If both these functions are synthesized in *cetanā*, it becomes necessary to investigate how this synthesis is described and explained. The *Dhammasaṅgaṇi* (Dhs. 10) merely lists the two associated terms, *sañcetanā* and *sañcetayitattam*, and says that *cetanā* is produced when the mind makes contact with objects. The *Vibhaṅga* (Vbh. 7, 8, 40) only adds that different classes of *cetanās* are produced when each of the sense organs and the mind make contact with their respective objects. The main definitions of *cetanā* in the *Atthasālinī* (Asl. 111-112) and the *Visuddhimagga* (Vsm. XIV. 135) support the interpretations of those modern scholars of Theravāda who view *cetanā* as a conative impetus that initiates activity in the body and the mind. These interpretations tend to focus on the relationship of purposive impulses (*cetanās*) to the mind's action-initiating processes (*saṅkhāras*); consequently, they fail to explore fully the relationship of *cetanās* to cognitive and emotive processes in the continuum of consciousness. C.A.F. Rhys Davids explains in an editorial note[1] in *Compendium of Philosophy* that it was largely because of these definitions in the *Visuddhimagga* and the *Atthasālinī* that she was persuaded by Burmese *Abhidhamma* scholars to render *cetanā* as "will" or "volition", despite the hesitations that she had earlier expressed in her article "On the Will in Buddhism". It was mainly these definitions that also led H.V. Guenther to draw the conclusion that *cetanā* signified a "stimulus, motive, or drive" that aroused and sustained "mass activity" in the organism.[2]

Whereas these definitions in the *Visuddhimagga* and the *Atthasālinī* connect *cetanā* with *saṅkhāras* that perpetuate the action-producing processes of consciousness, there is another section devoted to the elucidation of *kamma* in the *Atthasālinī* that stresses the relationship of *cetanās* to the cognitive aspects of purposive reflection, planning, and decision making in the *cittas* (Asl. 84-106). This extended section of the *Atthasālinī* includes the following: Discourse on the Door of Bodily *Kamma* (*Kāyakammadvārakathā*), Discourse on the Door of Verbal *Kamma* (*Vacīkammadvārakathā*), Discourse on Unwholesome *Kamma* (*Akusalakammapathakathā*), and Discourse on the Doors of Action (*Dvārakathā*). These discourses can be read as a commentary to passages in the *Suttas* where the lists of ten wholesome and ten unwholesome *kammas* of body, speech, and mind are delineated (for example, M. III. 209-210; A.V. 292-301). Furthermore, the definitions of bodily *kamma* (Asl. 84), verbal *kamma* (Asl. 87), and mental *kamma* (Asl. 88) included in this section of the *Atthasālinī* provide an interpretation, based on the *Abhidhamma* system, of the equation that the Buddha makes between *cetanā* and *kamma* in his succinct definition of *kamma* (A. III. 415). Descriptions of the mental processes that bring about wholesome and unwholesome acts accompany the definitions. These descriptions, which are based on the *Karajakāya-vagga*, provide an *Abhidhamma* view of how an attitude of mind (*citta*) and the purposive impulse (*cetanā*) that accompanies it interact in the course of producing a purposive act that has karmic consequences.

The other issue discussed in the discourses on *kamma* in the *Atthasālinī* concerns the interaction between *cetanā* and other motivating factors that have a role in the process of initiating and sustaining a purposive act. More specifically, the question is focused on the interaction between a purposive impulse and the potent mental states that constitute mental *kamma*. In the list of ten unwholesome acts of body, speech, and mind given in the *Suttas*, the following three are specified as unwholesome mental acts (*mano-kammas*): covetousness (*abhijjhā*), hate, ill will, or malevolence (*vyāpāda*), and wrong view (*micchā-diṭṭhi*). Absence of covetousness, absence of hate, and right view (*sammā-diṭṭhi*) are regarded as wholesome *kammas* performed by the mind. It is an experiential fact that wholesome and unwholesome mental *kammas*, such as covetousness and generosity, can themselves function as motivating impulses and initiate goal-directed acts of body and speech. It becomes, therefore, necessary to lay down criteria to distinguish mental *kamma* from *cetanā*. The *Atthasālinī* takes the position that whereas all intentional acts of body, speech, and mind that entail karmic consequences arise only as concrete expressions of purposive impulses, certain other forms of mental activity—such as mental *kammas*—enhance or delimit purposive impulses and radically condition the manner in which purposive acts are initiated and accomplished. According to the *Atthasālinī*, then, while *cetanās* have the primary role in initiating *kamma*, certain forms of wholesome and unwholesome mental activities play secondary motivating roles, especially because they include powerful emotions and persuasive cognitive elements. At the same time, the *Atthasālinī* holds that these motivating thoughts and emotions not only bring about further *kamma*, but in themselves constitute *kamma*. To consider these wholesome and unwholesome purposive thoughts and emotions, such as goodwill and ill will, to be mental *kamma* implies that one is morally responsible for them, whether or not they become expressed in acts of body and speech. According to the *Atthasālinī*, they bring about karmic consequences even when they remain in the mind and are not communicated to others.

Definitions of *Cetanā* in *Atthasālinī* and *Visuddhimagga*

The following definition of *cetanā* in the *Atthasālinī* (Asl. 111-112) adheres to the standard procedure in the commentaries to *Abhidhamma* texts of listing the characteristic, the function, the mode of manifestation, and the proximate cause of the factor that is to be defined:

lakkhaṇa (characteristic)	*cetayita-lakkhaṇa* *Cetayita* is explained as the function by which *cetanā* connects (*atisandahati*) mental states to itself and makes them the objects of its action.
rasa (characteristic)	*āyūhana-rasa* *Āyūhana* means "exertion of energy" and "bringing forth *kamma*".
paccupaṭṭhāna (manifestation)	*saṁvidahana-paccupaṭṭhāna* *Saṁvidahana* connotes coordinating and activating (associated states).
padaṭṭhāna (proximate cause)	————

The *Atthasālinī* and the *Visuddhimagga* do not explain why the proximate cause of *cetanā* is not specified in their definitions of *cetanā*. The *Dhammasaṅgaṇi*, however, postulates that *cetanā* arises through the contact of sensory and mental processes with their respective object (Dhs. 10). In the *Visuddhimagga*, the defining characteristic of *cetanā* is specified as *cetayita*, which is explained as *abhisandahati*,[3] a more correct form of the verb than *atisandahati*.[4] Though *cetayita* is derived from the verb *ceteti* (to think, to apply the mind), the *Atthasālinī* and the *Visuddhimagga* elucidate *cetayita* by connecting its meaning with the relatively uncommon verb *abhisandahati.* This verb indicates that *cetanā* links to itself the other mental factors that arise at the same time as itself in a *citta,* by making them the objects (*ārammaṇa*) of its motivating and energizing function.

Derived from the verb *dahati* (to place, to set up), the range of meanings of *abhisandahati* includes "to aim at", "to direct towards", "to accord to", and "to put together again" (C.P.D. 1: 376, col. 2). The *Atthasālinī* gives us the key to interpreting its definition of *cetanā* by stating that whereas the defining characteristic of *cetanā,* namely *cetayita,* is found in all cases of *cetanā,* the function of bringing forth *kamma* (*āyūhana-rasa*) is restricted to wholesome and unwholesome *cetanās* (Asl. 111). The *Atthasālinī,* therefore, explains the term *cetayita* in such a way as to extend its applicability not only to wholesome and unwholesome *cetanās* that produce acts with karmic consequences, but also to *cetanās* of the two following classes. The first consists of *cetanās* in the preliminary, pre-*javana* stages of the cognitive process, which are regarded as having the characteristic of *cetayita,* even though they merely direct the mind to an object but do not have the form of fully developed intentions and do not produce *kamma.* The second is constituted of the "functional" *cetanās* of fully enlightened *arahants,* whose thoughts are not bound to future goals and do not produce *kamma.* When one is seeking to understand the connotations of *cetayita* in the definition of *cetanā,* one should keep in mind that *cetanās* occur, without exception, in all *cittas.* If *cetayita* is held to be the defining characteristic found in all *cetanās, cetayita* cannot be interpreted as a thought process involving deciding on a purpose, since only one class of *cetanās,* namely *kamma*-producing wholesome and unwholesome *cetanās,* is associated with purposive thought. Thus, the *Atthasālinī* makes *cetayita* synonymous with *atisandahati/abhisandahati* and explains the latter term in such a way that it is applicable to all *cetanās.*

The *Atthasālinī* interprets *abhisandahati* as follows: "It [*cetanā*] connects (*abhisandahati*) associated mental states to itself as objects".[5] The import of this statement is that *cetanā* connects concomitant cognitive, emotive, and conative factors with itself by making them the objects of its motivating action and directing their functions toward a chosen object. The *Atthasālinī* goes on to say that this characteristic of *cetayita* is present in all *cetanās*: those that come into existence in the processes of sensory and rational experiences, those that are present in the levels of meditation, and those that operate in the stages of the path that leads to *nibbāna*.[6] Since *cetanā* is said to be present in all states of consciousness, this statement implies that wherever consciousness exists, *cetanā* manifests its defining characteristic by carrying out the function of bringing together and coordinating concomitant mental factors.

It is not easy to determine the meaning of *abhisandahati*. The commentary to the *Visuddhimagga*, the *Paramattha-mañjūsā*, explains *abhisandahati* with two terms: *pabandhati* (to bind, combine, prepare, put together) and *pavatteti* (to send forth, set in motion) (VsmA. 2:1035). When these two terms are combined, they yield the meaning that *cetanā* connects concomitant states to itself by focusing its motivating action on them and setting them in motion. Clearly, the explanation of *abhisandahati* given in the commentary to the *Visuddhimagga* moves away from the connection that *cetayita* has to the verb *ceteti*, which primarily signifies, "to think", "to reflect". The commentary views *cetanā* as an action-producing impulse rather than as a cognitive function based on purposive thinking and choosing between goals. Furthermore, the commentary to the *Visuddhimagga* goes on to define the nature of *cetanā* as *vyāpāra-bhāva* (VsmA. 2:1035). The term *vyāpāra* conveys "occupation, business, service, work" (P.E.D. 654, col. 1). By utilizing this term to elucidate the very nature (*bhāva*) of *cetanā*, the commentary holds that the distinctive characteristic (*lakkhaṇa*) of *cetanā* is to engage itself in goal-oriented action.

In his translation of the *Atthasālinī*, Pe Maung Tin renders *abhisandahati* as "closely binds". According to his translation, *abhisandahati* conveys that *cetanā* firmly connects concomitant states to itself and makes them the objects of its action.[7] On the other hand, in *Philosophy and Psychology in the Abhidharma*, Guenther interprets *abhisandahati* as the function by which *cetanā* "aims at associated factors", sets them in motion, and treats them as its objects.[8] He emphasizes that in the *Atthasālinī*, *cetanā* is viewed as the mental factor that acts upon, and activates, concomitant states. Of the two terms—*pavatteti* and *pabandhati*—that the commentary to the *Visuddhimagga* presents in order to elucidate the meaning of *abhisandahati*, Guenther's interpretation is closer to *pavatteti* (to set in motion). By preferring *pabandhati* (to bind), Pe Maung Tin interprets *abhisandahati* as the function by which *cetanā* links concomitant mental states (*sampayutta-dhammas*) to its own action of directing the mind towards a goal. The *Atthasālinī* goes on to explain that *cetanā* directs its own action towards a goal and induces associated mental states to turn in the same direction.

The *Visuddhimagga* gives *āyūhana* as the function (*rasa*) of both *cetanā* (Vsm. XIV. 135) and *saṅkhāra* (Vsm. XIV. 132), thereby affirming the bond between these two factors in the continuum of consciousness. *Āyūhana* is a complex term covering in its range of meaning two notions: "to strive or exert oneself" and "to accumulate *kamma*" (C.P.D. 2:140, col. 2). The *Atthasālinī* (Asl. 111-112) stresses that whereas the characteristic of *abhisandahati* is found in all occurrences of *cetanā*, the function of *āyūhana* is confined to the role of *cetanā* in producing wholesome and unwholesome *kamma*.[9] The definition makes it clear that the mental factors that are associated with *cetanā* as constituents of a mental state (*sampayutta-dhammā*) have but a restricted role, when compared with *cetanā*, in the putting forth of goal-oriented effort (*āyūhana*) to generate wholesome and unwholesome *kamma*. The following analogy is given in the *Atthasālinī* to illustrate what it declares to be the surpassing energy (*atireka-vāyāma*) of *cetanā*. The analogy portrays a land-owner who takes fifty-five strong men and goes to the field to reap a crop of grain. He puts forth double effort (*diguṇa-ussāha*) and doubles his exertion (*diguṇa-vāyāma*) by instructing the labourers and cheerfully encouraging them with food, drink, and rewards, while also completing his own share of the work. The land-owner is compared to *cetanā* and the fifty-five strong labourers are likened to the fifty-five wholesome mental states that arise within wholesome *citta* (*cittaṅga-vasena*) and function as cooperating conditions in bringing forth a wholesome act. The doubling of energy and effort by the land-owner is likened to the redoubled energy expended by *cetanā* when it both carries out its distinctive function of striving to produce wholesome and unwholesome purposive acts and also motivates concomitant mental states to perform their respective functions. The *Atthasālinī* expects the reader to understand that the mental states that arise in relation to unwholesome acts differ from the fifty-five mental states that are connected with wholesome acts.

Cetanā functions in the most basic states of cognition in such a way as to connect (*abhisandahati*) concomitant mental factors to itself and merely incline their attention towards an object of interest. By contrast, as a mental factor in a wholesome or an unwholesome state of mind, *cetanā* operates in such a manner as to instigate a purposeful act of body, mind, or speech that expresses the moral quality of that state of mind. This is the function of *āyūhana* attributed to *cetanā*.

In the *Visuddhimagga* and the *Atthasālinī*, the mode of manifestation of *cetanā* is defined as *saṁvidahana*. This term, like *abhisandahati*, is derived from the verb *dahati* and signifies "to arrange", "to prepare", "to provide" (D. I. 61; A. II. 35).[10] The role of *cetanā* in relation to the mental states that arise together with it in a *citta* is compared to that of a head pupil in relation to other pupils, a chief woodcutter in relation to other woodcutters, and a general in relation to his soldiers. Each of them not only does his own work, but also instigates those under his supervision to do their work. The *Atthasālinī* explains that when *cetanā* begins its work by engaging itself with an object, it motivates each of the mental states that arises together with it in a *citta* to perform its own function. It is emphasized that that when *cetanā* starts its own task, the concomitant states also become activated and perform their respective tasks.

The analogies in the *Atthasālinī* indicate that *saṁvidahana* is to be interpreted as a term that conveys the capacity of *cetanā* to instigate activity in several factors of consciousness and to direct all this activity towards a goal. The following differences in meaning between *āyūhana* and *saṁvidahana* can be inferred from the analogies. *Āyūhana* focuses on the *ussāha* (power, energy, strength) and the *vāyāma* (endeavour, effort, striving) that *cetanā* itself puts forth in straining towards a goal. *Saṁvidahana* conveys that *cetanā* sets in motion and directs concomitant mental states by virtue of its distinctive characteristic of energy (*ussāhana-bhāvena*). The *Atthasālinī* maintains that *cetanā* energizes and prompts concomitant mental factors, for example, by causing them to remember an urgent task. In accordance with these analogies, Pe Maung Tin renders the term *saṁvidahana* as "directing" in his translations of both the *Atthasālinī* and the *Visuddhimagga*.[11] However, in Bhikkhu Ñāṇamoli's *The Path of Purification*, *saṁvidahana* is translated as "coordinating" and is linked to the notion of "marshalling" or "driving" associated factors to attend to their tasks.[12]

Cetanā Defined as Motivating Impulse

Though these definitions of *cetanā* in the *Visuddhimagga* and the *Atthasālinī* utilize the method of classification and the technical vocabulary developed in the *Abhidhamma* texts, their portrayal of *cetanā* closely follows the statements pertaining to *cetanā* in the *Suttas*. According to the *Suttas*, *cetanā* functions differently in the two modes in which it manifests. As a factor of rudimentary sentience (*nāma*), *cetanā* joins sensory contact (*phassa*), feeling (*vedanā*), and attention (*manasikāra*) in making basic sensory awareness possible. Simultaneously, as the equivalent of *kamma*, *cetanā* motivates acts that bear moral values and bring forth commensurate consequences. The difference between these two modes of functioning of *cetanā* that the *Suttas* present is affirmed and explicated in the definition of *cetanā* given by the *Atthasālinī* and the *Visuddhimagga*. According to this definition, *cetanā* functions through its distinctive characteristic of *cetayita* in all *cittas* and through its distinctive activity of *āyūhana* only in *cittas* that carry moral values and are designated as wholesome or unwholesome. In the definitions given by the *Atthasālinī* and the *Visuddhimagga*, the term *cetayita* signifies, not the cognitive function of purposive deliberation or intention, but the motivating function of quickening the mind and setting it in motion. The analogies that the *Atthasālinī* includes in its definition imply that the powerful, specialized function of initiating wholesome and unwholesome acts (*āyūhana*) grows out of the basic characteristic of stirring the mind and making consciousness responsive to the environment, which *cetanā* invariably manifests.

The explanation of *cetayita* given in the commentary to the *Visuddhimagga* indicates that in the *Abhidhamma* tradition of interpretation, *cetanā* comes to be conceived as the capacity to energize the organism, to activate it, and motivate it towards goal-oriented action (VsmA. 2:1035). It is worth emphasizing again that the definitions in the *Atthasālinī* and the *Visuddhimagga* and the commentary to the *Visuddhimagga* do not attribute to *cetanā* the functions of thinking, reflecting, or planning that are indicated by the verb *ceteti*. Not only does the commentary to the *Visuddhimagga* describe the nature of *cetanā* as *vyāpāra-bhāva* (being engaged in purposive activity), but it also takes the two terms *āyūhanam* (striving to perform *kamma*) and *cetayanam* to be synonyms and explains them as *īriyanam* (setting in motion). The commentary goes on to say that *āyūhana* is to be understood as *ussāhana* (energy, endeavour). It follows, then, that by making *āyūhana* and *cetayana* synonymous terms, the commentary to the *Visuddhimagga* indicates that *cetayana* is to be understood as conative energy (*ussāhana*) put forth in striving towards a goal. *Iriyanā* conveys "moving forward" and the verb *iriyati* carries the meaning of "to set in motion, to stir" (P.E.D. 122, col. 2). This term is used in the *Dhammasaṅgaṇi* to define *jīvitindriya*, the faculty of life that vitalizes and makes possible the most rudimentary ongoing movement (*iriyanā*) of physical and mental factors (Dhs. 11-12). By explaining *cetayana* as *iriyanā*, the commentary to the *Visuddhimagga* interprets *cetayita*, the defining characteristic of *cetanā*, not as the capacity to apply thought, but as the capacity to activate consciousness (*citta*) and to ensure that it keeps on functioning. By making *āyūhana*, *cetayana*, and *iriyanā* have the same meaning, the commentary interprets the function of putting forth wholesome and unwholesome acts (*āyūhana*) to be a specialized development of the basic function of enlivening the mind with sentient awareness and setting it in motion.

Guenther maintains that all schools of Buddhism "are unanimous" in holding that *āyūhana* is the primary function of *cetanā*.[13] However, Guenther interprets *āyūhana*, not as the activity of producing wholesome and unwholesome *kamma*, but as the basic function of energizing concomitant mental states and making them effective in relation to an object. In this context, he refers to Yaśomitra's commentary on the *Abhidharmakośa-bhāṣya*. Yaśomitra explains *cetanā* as *citta-praspanda* (Abhk. II.24).[14] The term *praspanda* refers to a rudimentary movement that has the form of a "vibration" or "pulsation". This explanation of the function of *cetanā* resonates with the passage in the *Saṁyutta-nikāya* (S. II. 3) that includes *cetanā* among the factors of basic sentient awareness (*nāma*). In her study of the *Abhidharmakośa-bhāṣya*, Aruna Haldar explains *citta-praspanda* as "psychic inception or initial process of consciousness" that occurs as the precursor of any conative function.[15] She further comments that *cetanā* probably represents the "first stage of all conative functions", which has not yet fully developed into a goal-directed motivational impulse. *Citta-praspanda*, therefore, signifies a basic activation of the mind that makes it capable of putting forth effects.

Shwe Zan Aung's notion of the "protean character of each cetasika"[16] can illuminate how this wide range of functions—from the rudimentary energizing of the mind to the instigation of complex wholesome or unwholesome purposeful actions—can be regarded as belonging to *cetanā*. He argues that the meaning attached to a given *cetasika* (mental factor) in the *Abhidhamma* system differs in accordance with the varying circumstances in which that *cetasika* is regarded as functioning and the varying objects to which it is held to be related. When Aung's idea that varying meanings accrue to each *cetasika* is applied to *cetanā*, it entails that although the function of *cetanā* is invariably to coordinate concomitant states and cause their actions to "incline" towards a goal, the specific meaning attached to the term *cetanā* in different contexts varies in accordance with the way *cetanā* manifests in different circumstances. It follows that the meaning given to the term *cetanā* when it indicates a factor of basic sentient awareness (*nāma*) is different from the meaning attributed to the term when it refers to the specific function of intentionally instigating *kamma*.

Identifying *Cetanā* with *Kamma*

Whereas the definitions in the *Visuddhimagga* (Vsm. XIV. 135) and the *Atthasālinī* (Asl. 111-112) present *cetanā* as a conative function that manifests itself as a motivating energy that initiates and directs action, the discourses on *kamma* and the "doors of action" in the *Atthasālinī* (Asl. 84-106) stress the relationship of *cetanā* to the cognitive functions of the *citta*. In these discourses, *cetanā* is presented as intention or purposive thought that contains the impetus to become concretely manifest at the three doors of action: body, speech, and mind. In these discourses, the *Atthasālinī* describes *cetanā* as a purposive impulse that arises within a specific attitude of mind and renders the cognitive and emotive content of that attitude of mind into a dynamic motivating impetus. These discourses emphasize—far more strongly than the definitions discussed above—that when a *cetanā* performs its function of *āyūhana* and produces a wholesome or unwholesome purposive act, its motivating energy (*ussāhana*) is grounded in the purposive thought that participates in the cognitive and emotive features of a corresponding attitude of mind. In these discourses, *cetanā* is seen as the dynamic counterpart of a corresponding *citta*.

The many examples given in the *Atthasālinī* demonstrate that "door of action" indicates the medium through which a purposive thought or intention that participates in a specific state of mind (*citta*) becomes expressed in action. One of the examples is meant to show that the wholesome act of making an offering to the Three Jewels of Buddhism may be accomplished at any of the "three doors" of action: body, speech, or mind. The *Atthasālinī* holds that the offering may be made in three ways: through the physical act (*kāya-kamma*) of presenting a gift with one's own hands, through the verbal act (*vacī-kamma*) of instructing another to make a gift on one's behalf, or solely through the mental act (*mano-kamma*) of resolving to make an offering prior to actually accomplishing the act (Asl. 77). The moment when the mind thinks of making an offering (*manasā cintita-kāla*) is regarded as the moment of producing a mental *kamma* that can be judged as wholesome.

Moreover, the *Atthasālinī* takes the position that purposive deliberation or intention is the defining factor that distinguishes an act that has karmic consequences. With regard to the giving of gifts, for example, the *Atthasālinī* distinguishes between the views of the *Vinaya* and the *Abhidhamma*. According to the *Atthasālinī*, whereas the *Vinaya* maintains that the defining factor in an act of giving (*dāna*) consists of a verbal declaration of the resolve to give a gift, the *Abhidhamma* position is that a wholesome act of giving is performed when the resolve to make a specific gift arises in the mind (Asl. 77). The *Atthasālinī* goes on to say that whatever act of body or speech one does to complete the giving is regarded by the *Abhidhamma* as a consequence following from the definitive mental act of intending to give.[17] Furthermore, in the *Atthasālinī* the attitude of mind and the intention or purposive thought underlying an act become supremely important. This emphasis on purposive thought or intention is apparent in the following classification of acts of giving (Asl. 77-78). When an object is given with the sole purpose of making a gift, the *Atthasālinī* describes that as an act that is of the nature of giving (*dānamaya*). When one remembers the tradition of virtue (*sīla*) passed down in one's family and offers gifts out of a sense of duty, the *Atthasālinī* considers that act of giving to have the nature of virtue (*sīlamaya*). A person who is engaged in training the mind (*bhāvanā*) understands that the gift, like all conditioned things, is characterized by impermanence. When a gift is offered with mindfulness, then, according to the *Atthasālinī*, the act of giving has the nature of mental cultivation (*bhāvanāmaya*). Through this threefold classification of acts of giving, the *Atthasālinī* puts forward the view that the nature of an act is to be judged by the attitude of mind and the purposive thought that motivates the act.

Like the *Vibhaṅga*, the *Atthasālinī* phrases its definitions of *kamma* in such a way as to convey unambiguously that the act does not come into existence as the consequence of *cetanā*, but as the very manifestation of *cetanā* at one of the "doors of action". Since the Buddha's definition of *kamma* (A. III. 415) states that having exercised *cetanā* (*cetayitvā*), one performs acts of body, speech, and mind, it is possible to interpret this definition to mean that *cetanā* precedes and motivates purposive acts (*sañcetanika-kammas*). If that interpretation is accepted, *cetanā* would be regarded as a mental act that is clearly different from *kamma*.

To preclude any suggestion that the purposive impulse (*cetanā*) precedes, and is separate from, the act (*kamma*), the *Vibhaṅga* (Vbh. 285-286) avoids the grammatical form of the gerund *cetayitvā* in defining the "five precepts". These precepts refer to the following five wholesome acts that are regarded as essential factors of a Buddhist way of life: abstaining from taking life, from stealing, from dishonesty, from drinking intoxicating liquor, and from sexual misconduct. The *Vibhaṅga* defines the precepts in such a way that in each case the wholesome act is identified with a specific *cetanā*. For example, the act of abstaining from taking life is identified with the purpose or intention (*cetanā*) of abstaining from taking life, and the purpose itself is identified with a wholesome attitude of mind (*citta*). The *Vibhaṅga* defines the precept as follows: "The purposive impulse (*cetanā*) that a person has at the time of abstaining from killing a living being (*paṇātipātā viramantassa yā tasmin samaye cetanā*) . . . that (very purposive impulse) is said to be the precept of abstaining from killing living beings (*idaṁ vuccati pāṇātipātā veramaṇi sikkhāpadam*)".

This definition of the precepts adds to one's understanding of *cetanā* by conveying that the precept is to be understood as the call for a commitment based on a firm sense of purpose and intention to fulfil what is taught. The motivating intention or purposive impulse becomes concretely realized in the act of abstaining from a specific unwholesome deed. In this sense the purposive impulse to abstain from a specific immoral act is identical with the actual act of abstaining. In this definition of the precept to abstain from killing, the *Vibhaṅga* makes it clear that the precept refers to a motivating impetus (*cetanā*) that arises within a wholesome attitude of mind (*kusala-citta*) that is conjoined with mental happiness (*somanassa-sahagata*) and is associated with understanding (*ñāṇa-sampayutta*). The precept also emphasizes that the other mental factors in the state of mind within which the purposive impulse to abstain from killing arises are firmly linked to that purposive impulse (*avasesā dhammā cetanāya sampayuttā*). This implies that the purpose of abstaining from killing pervades the entire wholesome state of mind and that the motivating impetus to act corresponds to that state of mind.

Like the *Vibhaṅga*, in the Discourse on the Door of Bodily *Kamma*, the Discourse on the Door of Verbal *Kamma*, and the Discourse on Unwholesome *Kamma*, the *Atthasālinī* avoids the grammatical form *cetayitvā* and formulates the definition of *kamma* in such a way as to render the act identical with the intention or purposive thought to which it gives concrete expression. The definition of bodily *kamma* in the *Atthasālinī* says: "When *cetanā* becomes effective (*siddhā*) at the bodily door so that one injures living beings, steals, engages in sexual misconduct, or refrains from such acts, then that *cetanā* is said to be bodily *kamma*" (Asl. 84).[18] The definition of verbal *kamma* is similar: "When *cetanā* becomes effective at the door of speech, causing a person to engage in false, harsh, malicious, and frivolous speech, or to refrain from such speech, then that *cetanā* is called a verbal *kamma*" (Asl. 87).[19] Likewise, the definition of a mental *kamma* says: "When *cetanā* becomes effective at the mind door, causing one to engage in covetousness, ill will, and wrong views or in non-covetousness, absence of ill will, and right views, then that *cetanā* is known as mental *kamma*" (Asl. 88).[20] According to these definitions, when a person abstains from (*viramati*) certain forms of unwholesome physical, verbal, and mental acts, that abstaining is also included under the category of *kamma*. It is implied here that abstaining from unwholesome acts is not to be regarded as mere non-performance of certain acts. The examples given in the *Karajakāya-vagga* show that refraining from an unwholesome act implies performing a wholesome act that is opposed to the unwholesome. The opposite of the unwholesome bodily *kamma* of injuring living beings, for example, is wholesome behaviour expressing compassion towards all beings (A.V. 295).

Like the *Atthasālinī*, the commentaries to the *Suttas* also define *cetanā* as that which becomes effective and produces action at the three doors. For example, in order to distinguish *cetanā* from aspiration (*patthanā*) and resolve (*paṇidhi*), the commentary to the *Aṅguttara-nikāya* (AA. V. 69) defines *cetanā* as that which is "brought forth" or made manifest at the three doors of action (*tīsu dvāresu nibbattita-cetanā*). The same commentary defines a physical act with karmic consequences (*kāya-saṅkhāra*) as *cetanā* that is associated with the bodily door of action (*kāya-dvāra-cetanā*) (AA. III. 212). This definition of bodily *kamma* indicates that the body provides the medium for action to occur, and that *cetanā* is the purposive impulse becoming expressed through that medium. Similarly, in order to explain the Buddha's statement that he designates *cetanā* as *kamma* because a person acts through body, speech, or mind after engaging in a process of *cetanā* (*cetayitvā*), the commentary (AA. III. 408) elucidates *cetayitvā* as *cetanā* that has become operative at a door of action (*dvārappavatta-cetanā*). *Cetanā* is purposive thought imbued with the impetus for realization, *kamma* is the concrete realization of that purpose, and the doors of *kamma* provide the venue without which purposive thought could not become realized as purposive act.

Cetanā at the Beginning, Middle, and End of an Act

Another section of the *Atthasālinī* (Asl. 159-160) posits that *cetanā* supports all phases of an act: prior *cetanā* (*pubba-cetanā*) functions as the motivating cause of the act; accompanying *cetanā* initiates (literally, "releases") and supports the act; and subsequent *cetanā* reflects (*paccavekkhati*) on the act and affirms its completion. The *Atthasālinī* maintains that *cetanā* operates in these three modes of intending, initiating, and completing action with respect to a whole range of meritorious acts. For example, according to the *Atthasālinī*, the act of giving (*dāna*) has three "arisings": *dāna* comes into existence or arises (*uppajjati*) when a person has the intention of giving a gift; it arises when the person is actually offering the gift; and it arises for a third time when the person reflects that the giving has been accomplished (Asl. 159).[21] The prior *cetanā* has the form, "I will make a gift"; the "releasing" *cetanā* initiates the giving; and the confirming *cetanā* consists of the thought, "I have given the gift". It is posited in the *Atthasālinī* that when these three *cetanās* become unified (*ekato katvā*), an act of merit that has the nature of *dāna* comes into being. Thus not only a purposive act taken as a whole, but every phase of the act is perceived to be the actualization of a purposive impulse.

The *Atthasālinī* goes on to say that these three related types of *cetanā* can also be distinguished in relation to the practice of virtue (*sīla*), the training of the mind (*bhāvanā*), the discipline of listening to the *Dhamma*, the establishing of right view, and other wholesome acts.[22] It is posited that *sīla* (virtue), for example, is attained in three phases: when one has the intention or purpose (*cetanā*) of fulfilling the precepts; when the purpose is being realized through practising the precepts; and when one reflects that since the precepts have been fulfilled, the purpose has been attained. The *Atthasālinī* concludes that the three types of *cetanā* that become expressed in these three phases of the cultivation of *sīla* unite to constitute *sīla*.

According to the *Abhidhamma* method of interpretation, *cetanā* is the purposive impulse that becomes realized in an act; therefore, *cetanā* is the act. When *cetanā* functions as the motivating purpose that is prior to the act, it becomes the condition through which a *kamma* of thought, word, or mind is produced (*kamma-paccaya*). Operating as *kamma-paccaya*, *cetanā* makes it possible for the "roots" of action (greed or non-greed, hate or non-hate, and delusion or non-delusion) to begin their pervasive influence on the form that the deed takes. Because the deed is conditioned by wholesome or unwholesome roots, it becomes morally weighted as wholesome or unwholesome and produces commensurate karmic consequences. In its middle phase, the purposive act (*abhisaṅkhāra/sañcetanika-kamma*) is initiated and supported by the motivating capacity of the purposive impulse. In this phase, *cetanā*, functioning as purposive impulse, energizes concomitant mental factors and urges the mind to carry out the bodily, verbal, or mental processes that the deed involves. In the same manner, the concluding phase also is determined by the intention or sense of purpose that initiates, implements, and supports the deed. It is the intention or sense of purpose that provides the criteria by which one can know when the deed has been fully accomplished. Through reflecting (*paccavekkhaṇa*) on the deed, the agent decides either that the purpose for which the deed was initiated has been achieved, or that the purpose cannot be fulfilled through that specific deed. It should be noted, however, that the *Atthasālinī* maintains that if a purpose is fully conceived in the mind, that purpose already has the status of mental *kamma* and can produce happy or sorrowful karmic consequences, regardless of whether it is successfully accomplished in a physical or verbal act. For example, a wholesome intention of giving a gift is reckoned as a wholesome mental *kamma* (Asl. 81).

Moral Responsibility for Mental *Kamma*

A standard list of ten wholesome and ten unwholesome deeds that are characterized by karmic merit (*puñña*) or demerit (*pāpa*) occurs in several passages in the *Suttas* (for example, D. III. 269, M. I. 286-287). This list is preserved in the tradition and is repeated in the *Atthasālinī* (Asl. 97, 102). Covetousness (*abhijjhā*), ill will or malevolence (*vyāpāda*), and wrong view (*micchā-diṭṭhi*) are specified as unwholesome mental acts in this list, while absence of covetousness, absence of ill will, and right view are regarded as the three types of wholesome mental *kamma*. It is obvious that each type of mental *kamma* is a complex factor constituted of powerful emotions interacting with thought processes. In its lengthy analysis of wholesome and unwholesome acts of body, speech, and mind, the *Atthasālinī* emphasizes that these emotionally charged patterns of mental behaviour that comprise the six types of mental *kamma* resemble *cetanā* since they too have the capacity to motivate bodily *kamma* and *kamma* of speech.

By affirming that not only wholesome and unwholesome acts of body and speech, but also wholesome and unwholesome mental states are to be viewed as *kamma*, the *Atthasālinī* corroborates the Theravāda position that a person bears moral responsibility for thoughts and emotions that constitute intentions and purposes, even if these thoughts and emotions do not produce acts of body and speech. The *Atthasālinī*, therefore, affirms that *kamma* happens not only in the body and in speech, but also in the mind (Asl. 77, 81, 94, 95). When certain configurations of purposive thought and emotion—such as malevolence and benevolent goodwill or covetousness and generosity—are regarded as *kamma*, this implies that they produce commensurate karmic consequences, even when they remain private and hidden from others. According to the theory of *kamma*, these consequences are twofold. Wholesome and unwholesome *kamma* produce experiences of joy and sorrow, respectively, in the near or distant future. In this way, the fruition of *kamma* (*kamma-vipāka*) has an effect on whether one's life will be lived in pleasant or unpleasant circumstances. At the same time, it is posited that wholesome and unwholesome intentional acts produce consequences in the physical and mental factors of the personality. *Kamma* affects not only the types of experiences that one will encounter, but also the kind of person one is becoming. Thus, in interpreting the *Abhidhamma* approach to *kamma* and the dynamics of volition, it is important to stress that the *Atthasālinī* regards covetousness and generosity, malevolence and goodwill, wrong view and right view as intentional mental acts (*mano-kamma*) that are capable of producing joyful or sorrowful consequences and affecting one's personal growth and development, even when they do not motivate acts of body and speech.

The *Atthasālinī* maintains that whereas both bodily *kamma* and verbal *kamma* can manifest only through the two venues of bodily behaviour and speech, mental *kamma* can be produced at all three doors. (Asl. 90). To illustrate how an unwholesome physical *kamma* can occur at the door of speech, the *Atthasālinī* gives the example of a person inciting another, through persuasive speech, to kill, steal, or engage in sexual misconduct (Asl. 90). According to the analysis given in the *Atthasālinī*, in this case, the physical act of killing is implemented through speech: the spoken word kills. Theravāda maintains that a person who instigates another to act bears moral responsibility for that act (A. V. 305-307). It is postulated that the unwholesome *kamma* will produce commensurate consequences in the consciousness continuum of the instigator. As an example of how unwholesome verbal *kamma* can be performed through the body, the *Atthasālinī* gives the illustration of a person communicating falsehood, slander, harshness, or frivolity, not through speech, but through physical gestures and body language (Asl. 92). According to the *Atthasālinī*, in this case, unwholesome words are communicated through bodily signals.

The *Atthasālinī* then proceeds to give the following explanation of how bodily behaviour, verbal expression, or solely mental processes can become the medium for performing a mental act that entails karmic consequences (Asl. 92-94). For example, stealing may be instigated by covetousness, which is regarded as one of the factors that constitutes unwholesome mental *kamma*. According to the *Atthasālinī*, in this case the physical act of stealing becomes the medium for carrying out the unwholesome mental *kamma* of covetousness. In other words, an unwholesome mental *kamma*, namely covetousness, becomes a powerful motivating condition operating in conjunction with the purposive impulse (*cetanā*) that produces the act of stealing. Similarly, the wholesome mental *kamma* consisting of non-covetousness may condition and intensify a wholesome purposive impulse that finds concrete expression in the wholesome physical act of restraining oneself from stealing. In the same way, wholesome or unwholesome mental *kammas* may condition and aid specific wholesome or unwholesome purposive impulses that become actualized in wholesome or unwholesome speech. The *Atthasālinī* goes on to explain how mental *kamma* can be expressed solely in thought, without the intervention of physical acts or words. In this context the *Atthasālinī* gives the example of the intention to kill a living being arising in a person's mind (Asl. 90). The *Atthasālinī* maintains that the mere purposive impulse motivated by the thought of killing a living being (*vadhaka-cetanā*) is to be judged as unwholesome *kamma* even if it does not lead to actual killing. The argument is put forward that the purposive impulse that motivates killing becomes concretely realized, in this case, through the unwholesome mental *kamma* of cruel malevolence (*vyāpāda-vasena*) rising as an emotion in the mind, not through the unwholesome bodily *kamma* of taking life.[23] It is posited that malevolence operating in thought processes is as much a purposive act (*sañcetanika-kamma*) as the physical act of harming a living being. The *Atthasālinī* goes on to say that when a person sits alone without engaging in physical activity or speech and only fills the mind with thoughts of generosity and non-covetousness (*anabhijjhā*), those beautiful thoughts should be regarded as wholesome mental *kammas* enacted solely at the mind-door (Asl. 95).

The *Atthasālinī* (Asl. 101, 102) maintains that the six types of mental *kamma* (covetousness and non-covetousness, ill will and goodwill, wrong view and right view) are manifestations of the six roots of action (greed and non-greed, hate and absence of hate, delusion and non-delusion). Covetousness (*abhijjhā*) and ill will (*vyāpāda*) are said to be off-shoots of greed (*lobha*) and aversion (*dosa*), respectively, while wrong view (*micchā-diṭṭhi*) is regarded as an outgrowth of the double root of greed and delusion (*moha*). Absence of covetousness, absence of ill will, and right view are considered to be other "names" (*nāmāni*) for the three wholesome roots: non-greed, absence of hate, and non-delusion (Asl. 129). It is implied here that the capacity of the six types of mental *kamma* to motivate acts of body and speech can be explained in terms of their close relationship to the basic roots of action. Each of these roots, like each mental *kamma*, is a configuration of emotional and cognitive factors infused with the capacity to influence *cetanā* in its function of motivating action. By closely connecting the six types of mental *kamma* with the six roots of action, the *Atthasālinī* emphasizes its view that the complex mental states that constitute mental *kamma* have a profound effect on the constitution and the internal modifications of a state of mind (*citta*). As in the case of the roots, the presence or absence of covetousness, hate, and wrong view can make the entire state of mind wholesome or unwholesome and determine what other cognitive and emotive states can arise as concomitant factors in that state of mind.

The Fallacy of Two Purposive Impulses in a Single Purposive Act

There are statements in the *Atthasālinī* that seem to attribute to the six mental states that constitute mental *kamma* the same capacity to motivate wholesome and unwholesome *kamma* that is regarded as the distinctive feature of *cetanā*. The most striking evidence of the close connection that the *Atthasālinī* posits between mental *kamma* and *cetanā* is that it grants the same functions to both of them (Asl. 87-88). The *Atthasālinī* defines the functions of covetousness, non-covetousness, and each of the other factors of mental *kamma* as follows: "It strains to produce *kamma* (*āyūhati*), it produces goal-oriented acts that have karmic consequences (*abhisaṅkharoti*), it connects mental states and forms configurations (*piṇḍaṁ karoti*), it puts forth goal-oriented thoughts and intentions (*ceteti*), it makes and arranges (*kappeti*), and it plans and designs (*pakappeti*)" (Asl. 87). These same activities are listed as functions of *cetanā* in the same passage (Asl. 88).

The nature of the relationship between mental *kamma* and *cetanā* became a topic of controversy among the early Buddhist schools.[24] The problem arises because the mental states that constitute mental *kamma* are regarded as capable of becoming manifest not merely through mental functions such as thoughts and emotions, but also through bodily behaviour and verbal expression. When a mental *kamma* becomes expressed in a bodily or verbal act, it takes on the instigating role of *cetanā*. For example, when the mental *kamma* of non-hate (*avyāpāda*) functions as the motivating impetus that prevents an act of cruelty, it resembles the purposive impulse that initiates the wholesome bodily act of restraining from injuring a living being. At the same time, the six types of mental *kamma*, like bodily and verbal *kamma*, are held to be concrete manifestations of the purposive impulses that instigate them (Asl. 88).

Strictly speaking, two *cetanās* function simultaneously when a mental *kamma* becomes conjoined with a specific *cetanā* in motivating an act of body, speech, or mind. This can be illustrated by the case of the mental *kamma* of covetousness motivating the bodily *kamma* of stealing. The direct cause of the bodily *kamma* is the purposive impulse directed towards stealing (*theyya-cetanā*) that becomes concretely expressed in the physical act of stealing. The other *cetanā* that operates simultaneously is the purposive impulse actualized in the mental *kamma* of covetousness that is now motivating the act of stealing. This becomes a problem because, according to the *Abhidhamma*, two *cetanās* cannot operate at the same time. The problem can be rephrased in the following way. According to the *Abhidhamma*, each wholesome or unwholesome purposive act (*kamma*) is the concrete expression of a purposive impulse (*cetanā*) that emerges from a correspondingly wholesome or unwholesome state of mind (*citta*). The purposive impulse that motivates giving (*dāna-cetanā*), for example, arises in a state of mind characterized by emotions and cognitive factors that are intent on making a gift (*dāna-citta*). The act of giving is a concrete manifestation of the purposive impulse that motivates the giving of a gift. If the act of giving is also motivated by a mental *kamma*, such as absence of covetousness (*anabhijjhā*), that would imply that the purposive impulse that is manifest in the mental *kamma* of non-covetousness and the purposive impulse that motivates the giving of a gift become simultaneously expressed in the act of giving. The *Abhidhamma* questions how two purposive impulses (the purposive impulse that is directed towards giving a gift and the purposive impulse that is the impetus for non-covetousness) can produce one and the same act of giving. According to the theory of momentariness, each purposive impulse arises at a specific moment in time and its impetus is expended in a single purposeful act. Two purposive impulses cannot become manifest in the same act.

Padmanabh Jaini makes the point that some of the early Buddhist schools, such as the Vaibhāṣikas, maintained that the concept of mental *kamma* was untenable because it led to conclusions that went against the *Abhidhamma* teaching that two *cetanās* do not operate simultaneously. In order to avoid the problem of two *cetanās*, the Vaibhāṣikas accepted only two categories of *kamma*: bodily *kamma* and verbal *kamma*. They did not define covetousness, ill will, and wrong view as factors of mental *kamma*; on the contrary, they described them as *kilesas* (unwholesome, morally wrong emotional states) that motivate and condition unwholesome physical and verbal acts.[25]

Kamma Redefined as *Cetanā* and Associated Mental States

Unlike the Vaibhāṣikas who accepted only bodily *kamma* and verbal *kamma*, the *Atthasālinī* acknowledges a viable third category, namely mental *kamma*. However, the *Atthasālinī* holds that whereas a bodily or verbal act arises as the concrete realization of a specific *cetanā*, the six mental states that constitute mental *kamma* arise as motivating factors associated with specific *cetanās* in specific wholesome and unwholesome *cittas*. Arising as associated factors (*sampayuttakā dhammā*), the mental states that constitute mental *kammas* influence the manner in which *cetanās* produce bodily and verbal behaviour.

The *Atthasālinī* (Asl. 88) defines *kamma* as twofold:[26] *kamma* that arises as the actualization of a specific *cetanā*, and *kamma* motivated by certain mental factors associated with *cetanā* (*cetanā-sampayuttakā-dhammā*). When an act is motivated by a mental factor associated with a motivating intention or purposive impulse, the characteristics of the mental factor become actualized in the act. The mental *kamma* of non-hate, for example, become actualized in an act of friendship. It can be concluded that the *Atthasālinī* seeks to avoid the problem of two *cetanās* functioning simultaneously by making it clear that covetousness, non-covetousness, and the other mental states that comprise mental *kamma* do not function independently of *cetanā*. Only specific *cetanās*, for example the *cetanā* that is the impetus for false speech (*para-visaṁvādakā-cetanā*) or the *cetanā* that motivates harsh speech (*pharusa-cetanā*), are assigned the capacity to become "effective" (*siddhā*) and bring about corresponding behaviour. At the same time, the *Atthasālinī* affirms that the "factors associated with *cetanā*", such as wholesome and unwholesome mental *kamma*, cast their influence on the process by which a *cetanā* instigates an act of body or speech. It can be inferred from the *Atthasālinī* that covetousness and non-covetousness, ill will and goodwill, right view and wrong view function in two different ways. When they do not motivate bodily acts or acts of speech, they are regarded as purposeful mental acts (*mano-kamma*) motivated by purposive impulses (*cetanās*). When the same six types of mental *kamma* motivate physical or verbal acts, they are regarded as factors closely associated with *cetanā* (*cetanā-saṁpayuttakā-dhammā*) in motivating *kamma* of body and speech. Since they have powerful cognitive and emotive components, they condition the manner in which purposive impulses become manifest in acts of body and speech. For example, the intention of making a gift (*dāna-cetanā*) may be conditioned by a wholesome absence of covetousness or by an unwholesome wrong view that affirms an autonomous and controlling self who is the "giver". The "factors associated with *cetanās*" are defined as *kamma* in the sense that they infuse *cetanā* with their characteristics when *cetanā* becomes concretely realized as *kamma* of body or speech.

The *Atthasālinī* (Asl. 88-89) expands the category of "factors associated with *cetanās*" (*cetanā-sampayuttakā-dhammā*) to include the eight aspects of the Noble Eightfold Path and the seven wholesome mental states designated as "factors of wisdom" (*bojjhaṅgas*).[27] In order to explain the concept of "factors associated with *cetanās*", the *Atthasālinī* refers to the familiar classification of *kamma* into four types: "dark" unwholesome *kamma*, "bright" wholesome *kamma*, *kamma* that is "both dark and bright", and *kamma* that is "neither dark nor bright". The discourse on *kamma* in the *Aṅguttara-nikāya* defines the fourth type of *kamma* as the *cetanā* that renounces the other three types of *kamma*, along with the consequences that they entail (A. II. 232, 233). The *Aṅguttara-nikāya* goes on to explain that this fourth type of *kamma*, which actually causes the waning away of all *kamma*, can be identified with the eight aspects of the Noble Eightfold Path and the seven factors of wisdom (A. II. 236, 237). The *Atthasālinī* includes the eight aspects of the Noble Eightfold Path and the seven factors of wisdom together with the six mental states that comprise mental *kamma* in its list of "factors associated with *cetanā*". This designation signifies that these twenty-one factors condition the manner in which *cetanā* operates in bringing about acts of body, speech, and mind that have a bearing on the course of *kamma* (Asl. 89). The *Atthasālinī* makes it clear that though many other factors may influence the production of *kamma*, in the final analysis, it is a specific *cetanā* that produces a corresponding act that has karmic consequences.

Classification of Factors Associated with *Cetanā* in the *Nettippakaraṇa*

In the introduction to his translation of the *Nettippakaraṇa*, Bhikkhu Ñāṇamoli explains that this text puts forward a systematic method for interpreting the *Tipiṭaka*.[28] On the basis of the distinctive metre of the verses in the *Nettippakaraṇa*, it is suggested that at least those portions of the text that contain verses were composed in North India "before the beginning of the Christian era".[29]

Like the *Atthasālinī*, the *Nettippakaraṇa* holds that the complex, emotion-charged factors of mental *kamma* cast their influence on the formation of physical and verbal *kamma*. Bhikkhu Ñāṇamoli notes in *The Guide*[30] that the *Nettippakaraṇa* adopts the unique method of classifying *kamma* into *cetanā-kamma* and *cetasika-kamma* (Nt. 43, 96). According to the classification in the *Nettippakaraṇa*, *cetanā-kamma* comprises the seven wholesome and seven unwholesome acts of body and speech, and *cetasika-kamma* is constituted of the six factors (covetousness and non-covetousness, ill will and goodwill, wrong view and right view) that are regarded as mental *kammas* in the *Suttas* and the *Atthasālinī*. By not designating these mental factors as mental *kamma*, the *Nettippakaraṇa* holds that unlike *kamma* of body and speech, they are not directly instigated by intentions and purposive impulses (*cetanā*).

The *Nettippakaraṇa* makes the following distinction between *cetanā-kamma* and *cetasika-kamma*. The former are instigated by specific *cetanās* and have karmic consequences. The latter arise together with *cetanā* and other cognitive, emotive, and conative factors (*cetasikas*) within specific states of mind (*cittas*) when the senses and the mind make contact with objects. The *Nettippakaraṇa* does not specify in what sense the constituents of *cetasika-kamma* are to be regarded as *kamma*, but emphasizes that they become associated with wholesome and unwholesome roots of action. These roots do not directly produce *kamma*, but operate as powerful conditions in the process by which *cetanās* become manifest as acts that have karmic consequences. By becoming linked with roots of action, the mental factors that constitute *cetasika-kamma* influence the production of *kamma* of body and speech.

The concept of *cetasika-kamma* in the *Nettippakaraṇa* has some resemblance to the concept of *cetanā-sampayuttakā dhammā* in the *Atthasālinī*. However, there are two important differences. Under the category of "mental states associated with *cetanā*", the *Atthasālinī* includes not only the mental states designated as mental *kamma* in the *Suttas*, but also the eight factors of the Eightfold Path and the wholesome factors associated with wisdom (*bojjhaṅgas*). The *Nettippakaraṇa*, however, limits factors associated with *cetanā* in producing *kamma* to covetousness, non-covetousness, and the other mental states that are classified as mental *kamma* in the *Suttas*. Moreover, the *Nettippakaraṇa* affirms only two categories of *kamma* (*kamma* of body and *kamma* of speech) and omits mental *kamma*. As a consequence, the *Nettippakaraṇa* does not give the same strong emphasis that the *Atthasālinī* gives to the idea that certain wholesome and unwholesome mental states can be regarded as purposeful mental acts that entail consequences. By affirming that mental states such as covetousness and ill will constitute mental *kamma*, the *Atthasālinī* insists that a person bears moral responsibility for wholesome and unwholesome thoughts and emotions, even if these do not ensue in corresponding acts of body and mind.

By defining covetousness and non-covetousness, ill will and absence of ill will, wrong view and right view as alternate forms of the powerful "roots" of action, the *Nettipakaraṇa* affirms that they support the formation of purposive bodily and verbal acts that entail karmic consequences. The *Nettippakaraṇa* (Nt. 43) identifies covetousness with the unwholesome root of greed (*lobha*), and ill will with the root of hate (*dosa*). Wrong view is identified with wrong path (*micchā-magga*). The text goes on to say that the unwholesome deeds of killing living beings, slander, and harsh speech are rooted in hate (*dosa*). Stealing, sexual misconduct, and lying are regarded as arising from greed (*lobha*). Frivolous speech is viewed as an outgrowth of delusion (*moha*). This bare list of identifications between *cetasika-kammas* and the powerful roots of action encodes many aspects of Theravāda's "psychological ethics". Theravāda maintains that since every wholesome and unwholesome act arises in a network of causes and conditions, it has multiple sources and produces effects in multiple dimensions of the personality. The comprehensive training of the Eightfold Path takes into account the multiple layers of wholesome and unwholesome conditioning that shape the consciousness continuum of a person.

The concept of motivating factors associated with purposive impulses (*cetanā-sampayuttakā-dhammā*) in the *Atthasālinī* implies, for example, that in the case of a hate-dominated act, the immediate purposive impulse (*cetanā*) that causes it is not only rooted in hate (*dosa-mūla*), but is also linked with a plethora of thoughts and emotions that take shape in the mind as the mental *kamma* of malevolence, ill will, or repulsion (*vyāpāda).* These supporting conditions (*cetanā-sampayuttakā-dhammā*) themselves are viewed as concrete realizations within thoughts and emotions of motivating intentions or purposive impulses (*cetanās*). It is posited that a tangled net of wholesome and unwholesome conditioning is created through the interlinking of purposive impulses, roots of action, and the factors associated with purposive impulses in the formation of wholesome and unwholesome deeds. The network of conditioning is continually widened because purposive impulses, the potent emotive and cognitive mental factors associated with purposive impulses, and the powerful roots of action are impelled to keep on functioning by the urgent striving to produce goal-oriented acts (*āyūhana*) that characterizes *saṅkhāra* processes.

The *Nettippakaraṇa* confirms the notion of multiple motivating factors cooperating with *cetanās* in producing *kamma.* Avaricious behaviour is regarded in the *Nettippakaraṇa* as the actualization of purposive impulses that are rooted in greed and strengthened by the emotion-charged motivating thoughts that constitute covetousness (*abhijjhā*). By acting in conjunction with the purposive impulse that produces avaricious behaviour, covetousness performs the role of *cetasika-kamma.* Similarly, all forms of infatuated, confused behaviour rooted in delusion (*moha*) are regarded as concrete expressions of purposive impulses that become linked with the emotion-fuelled thought processes that form a deluded, poorly reasoned view of life (*micchā-diṭṭhi*). At the same time, wholesome forms of behaviour rooted in non-greed, absence of hate, and non-delusion are seen to be the manifestations of purposive impulses that do not act alone, but are energized and made robust by the cognitive and emotive components of generosity, goodwill, and insight. Here these wholesome factors function as *cetasika-kamma.* One can presume that the *Nettippakaraṇa* adopts the method of classifying mental *kamma* as *cetasika-kamma* in order to avoid the problem of two *cetanās* functioning simultaneously in the instigation of any specific act of body or speech. At the same time, through the concept of *kamma*-motivating factors arising together with *cetanā* in the same *citta* (*cetasika-kamma*), the *Nettippakaraṇa,* like the *Atthasālinī,* affirms that *cetanā* is not an autonomous function but stands in mutual relationship with a network of cognitive and emotional processes. The threefold training that constitutes the Eightfold Path (training in virtue, mental development, and wisdom) seeks to address simultaneously the many layers of conditioning that a wholesome or unwholesome deed produces on the cognitive, emotive, and action-generating dimensions of the personality.

Purposive Impulse as the Dynamic Mode of an Attitude of Mind

The definitions of *cetanā* in the *Milindapañha* (Mil. 61-62), the *Visuddhimagga* (Vsm. XIV. 135), and the *Atthasālinī* (Asl. 111-112) maintain that wholesome and unwholesome *cetanās* coordinate concomitant mental factors and direct their functions towards performing wholesome and unwholesome goal-oriented acts. However, these definitions do not make it clear how the conative impetus of *cetanā* becomes infused with a sense of purpose, and how *cetanā* acquires its wholesome or unwholesome characteristics. A clearer picture of how wholesome and unwholesome *cetanās* originate comes into view in the Discourse on Unwholesome *Kamma* and the Discourse on the Doors of Action in the *Atthasālinī* (Asl. 87-105). These discourses interpret each *cetanā* as a purposive impulse that gives a dynamic turn to the cognitive and emotive content of a specific wholesome or unwholesome attitude of mind. It becomes evident in these discourses that alternative choices are assessed, goals are chosen, and purposes are formed through the interplay of the cognitive, emotive, and motivational factors (*cetasikas*) constituting states of mind (*cittas*). The function of *cetanās* is to render these purposes into purposive impulses, to energize intention with impetus (*payoga*), and to translate the cognitive and emotive features displayed in these *cittas* into corresponding acts of body, speech, and mind. The purpose is formed through the organic interrelationship of thought processes and emotions in a state of mind. *Cetanā* is the dynamic mode of that purpose. In the *Abhidhamma*, classification of mental states, a *cetanā* is regarded as a "neutral" purposive impulse that becomes wholesome or unwholesome because it is conditioned by the wholesome or unwholesome constituents of the *citta* within which it arises.

The *Atthasālinī* states its view of the bond between attitude of mind (*citta*), purposive impulse (*cetanā*), and act (*kamma*) most clearly in the Discourse on Unwholesome *Kamma* (Asl. 97-106). This discourse is based on the description of the ten wholesome and ten unwholesome types of *kamma* in the *Karajakāya-vagga* of the *Aṅguttara-nikāya*. Each of these acts is designated as a *sañcetanika-kamma* of body, speech, or mind in the *Karajakāya-vagga* (A. V. 292-303). Though what constitutes a *cetanā* or *sañcetanā* is not explained in the *Karajakāya-vagga*, the narrative portions include statements of intentions, wishes, and aspirations that motivate a wholesome or unwholesome act. Deliberate lies (*sampajāna-musāvāda*), for example, are described as dishonest words spoken to serve one's own ends (*atta-hetu*) or the purposes of another (*para-hetu*). The *Karajakāya-vagga* gives examples of malicious words (*pisuṇā-vācā*) spoken with the motive of dividing people (*bhedāya*), of covetousness (*abhijjhā*) motivated by the longing to possess what belongs to others, and of ill will (*vyāpāda*) based on the evil wish to see others suffer.

The *Atthasālinī* identifies each of the three types of unwholesome physical acts and the four types of unwholesome acts of speech with a corresponding purposive impulse. Moreover, each purposive impulse is shown to be conditioned by a corresponding state of mind. The purposive impulse that produces wholesome and unwholesome acts can be described as an intention or purposive thought imbued with the impetus to initiate action. The following list can be extrapolated from the *Atthasālinī* (Asl. 97-101):

> The unwholesome physical act of taking the life of living beings is identical with the purposive impulse that motivates killing (*vadhaka-cetanā*), and this purposive impulse is based on a state of mind that is disposed to kill (*vadhaka-citta*).

The unwholesome physical act of appropriating the property of another is identical with the purposive impulse that motivates stealing (*theyya-cetanā*), and this purposive impulse is based on a state of mind that is disposed to steal (*theyya-citta*).

The unwholesome physical act of sexual misconduct is identical with the purposive impulse that motivates trespassing (*vītikkama-cetanā*), and this purposive impulse is based on a state of mind that has the intention to commit a morally wrong and unlawful act (*asaddhammādhippāya*).

The unwholesome act of deceit is identifical with the purposive impulse that motivates deceiving others (*para-visaṁvādakā cetanā*), and this purposive impulse is based on a state of mind that has the intention of deceiving (*visaṁvādanādhippāya*).

The unwholesome act of malicious speech is identical with the purposeful impulse (*cetanā*) that initiates bodily movement and speech with the purpose of causing dissension among others (*paresam bhedāya*). This purposive impulse is based on a corrupt state of mind (*saṅkiliṭṭha citta*).

The unwholesome act of harsh speech is identical with the purposive impulse that motivates extreme harshness (*ekanta-pharusa-cetanā*), and this purposive impulse is based on harshness of mind (*citta-pharusatā*).

The unwholesome act of frivolous talk is identical with the unwholesome purposeful impulse (*akusalā cetanā*) that initiates physical movement and speech with the purpose of communicating useless things.

> The three unwholesome mental acts are associated with the three unwholesome roots of action: covetousness with greed, (*lobha*), ill will with aversion (*dosa*), and wrong view with greed and delusion (*lobha, moha*).

Confluence of Purpose and Conative Impetus in *Cetanā*

The *Atthasālinī* gives many examples to demonstrate that the mind's capacity to initiate any action emerges from, and is conditioned by, a corresponding attitude of mind (*citta*). The bond that is posited between an attitude of mind and the purposive impulse that arises within it is shown, for example, in the account of how an unwholesome act is constituted (Asl. 97). The following five are delineated as the factors that make up an unwholesome act: the presence of the object or person affected by the misdeed; knowledge on the part of the doer of the misdeed that this object or person is present and will be affected; the purposive attitude of mind or intention that motivates the deed; the expending of effort in doing the misdeed; and the evil consequence that follows. The *Atthasālinī* (Asl. 97) maintains that unless the following factors come together, an act cannot be regarded as an unambiguous act of killing: the presence of a living being (*pāṇa*); awareness of the presence of a living being (*pāṇa-saññitā*); a state of mind that entertains killing (*vadhaka-citta*); carrying out the act (*upakkama*); and death caused by that act (*tena maraṇam*). Similarly, the constituents of the act of stealing are enumerated as the presence of the property of another, awareness that it belongs to another, a state of mind intent on stealing (*theyya-citta*), carrying out the act (*upakkama*), and theft as a consequence of that act (*tena haraṇam*) (Asl. 98).

In these accounts of the factors that constitute specific unwholesome physical acts, *cetanā* is not mentioned, and nothing is said about precisely how the unwholesome state of mind produces the correspondingly unwholesome act. However, in an earlier section of this discourse on unwholesome acts, the *Atthasālinī* (Asl. 96) identifies *cetanā* as the purposive impulse that links the purpose or intention that arises in a specific attitude of mind (*citta*) with the actual implementation of the act (*upakkama*). In the absence of a link to the cognitive processes of the mind that formulate the purpose, the act could not be regarded as that which is purposefully accomplished. *Cetanā* gives dynamic impetus to the purpose that is formulated in the *citta* and links purpose with act by virtue of its function of motivating action. Thus, it is posited that without a link to the wholesome or unwholesome sentiment—for example, greed or non-greed, hate or non-hate— present in the attitude of mind, the act would not have moral value. *Cetanā* gives active expression to the cognitive and emotive content of a specific state of mind and "actualizes" or makes concrete the moral values that reside in the state of mind.

In its account of how unwholesome acts of speech are constituted, the *Atthasālinī* further elucidates the view that moral values reside primarily in a state of mind and become expressed in a corresponding act. According to this view, an act is judged as reprehensible, not solely on the basis of the harmful, unhappy consequences that it entails, but primarily because it reflects an unwholesome and harmful state of mind. An attitude of mind that is intent on deceiving (*visaṁvādana-citta*) is regarded as the basis of deceitful speech (Asl.99). Slander is described as the verbal expression of an attitude of mind that is intent on causing disharmony among others or winning affection for oneself by maligning others (Asl. 100). Speech is considered to be genuinely harsh only when it expresses a harsh frame of mind (*citta-pharusatā*) (Asl. 100).[31] In this context, the *Atthasālinī* relates the charming story of a mischievous child who insisted on running into the forest to play. Unable to stop him, his mother said, "All right, let the wild buffalo chase you". As the child ran into the forest, he saw the wild buffalo coming towards him. Being as intelligent as he was mischievous, the boy concentrated on the thought: "Let what my mother really intended in her mind come into effect; let not what my mother said in her words come to pass". Immediately the wild buffalo stood absolutely still. The *Atthasālinī* maintains that the mother's words cannot be reckoned as harsh speech since her mind is tender. The conclusion reached is that just as spoken words cannot be judged as harsh if the heart is gentle, so also speech cannot be characterized as gentle if the mind of the speaker is cruel. The *Atthasālinī* points out that if a murderer with cruel intent gently tells the victim to rest comfortably, those words can hardly be characterized as free of harshness. A purposive impulse marked by extreme harshness (*ekanta-pharusa-cetanā*) is the channel through which the harshness that resides in an attitude of mind (*citta-pharusatā*) is brought into the act of harsh speech (*pharusā vacā*). Though gently spoken, the words of the murderer are to be judged as morally reprehensible because they proceed from a cruel heart.

The *Atthasālinī* further clarifies its view of how *cetanā* becomes manifest in acts of body, speech and mind by stating emphatically that *cetanā* is not merely an intention or purposive thought, but a purposive impetus endowed with the capacity to initiate action. For example, the *Atthasālinī* (Asl. 97-98)[32] states quite unambiguously that the *cetanā* that motivates stealing (*theyya-cetanā*) includes both the intention to steal and the capacity to initiate action to fulfil the intention. Thus, the *cetanā* that motivates stealing is regarded as having two defining features: first, the *cetanā* includes the cognitive awareness that the object to which the intention to steal is directed belongs to another person (*para-pariggahīta-saññitā*); and second, the *cetanā* has the conative capacity to initiate the act of appropriating that object (*tadādāyaka-upakkama-samuṭṭhāpikā*). Lying is defined as the *cetanā* that aims at deceiving others (*para-visaṁvādakā*) and is capable of putting forth effort of body and speech (*kāya-vacīppayoga-samuṭṭhāpikā*) in order to achieve its goal (Asl. 98-99).[33] The *cetanā* that instigates slander is said to be related to a corrupt frame of mind (*saṅkiliṭṭha citta*) (Asl. 99).[34] As its other aspect, this *cetanā* is considered to be capable of initiating acts of body and speech to achieve its goal of malicious slander.

It is obvious that the *Atthasālinī* conveys the capacity of *cetanā* to initiate action by describing *cetanā* as "that which sets up effort of body and speech" (*kāya-vacīppayoga-samuṭṭhāpikā*). This phrase occurs in relation to the *cetanās* that motivate lying (Asl. 98), slander (Asl. 99), harsh speech (Asl. 100), and frivolous talk (Asl. 100). A similar description, "that which sets up action" (*upakkama-samuṭṭhāpikā*), occurs in the portrayal of the *cetanās* that become expressed in the unwholesome acts of killing living beings (Asl. 97) and stealing (Asl. 98). Thus, the *Atthasālinī* not only maintains that every *cetanā* originates from a specific state of mind, but also emphasizes that every *cetanā* functions as an impetus that initiates action and directs that action towards a goal.

Cetanā and Moral Responsibility for Action

By interpreting a wholesome or unwholesome act as the concrete expression of a corresponding purpose in a specific state of mind (*citta*), the *Atthasālinī* rejects the view that posits a sharp distinction between inward intention and outward act. However, where there is a discrepancy between purpose and act, the *Atthasālinī* makes it clear that moral value lies primarily in the intention or purpose that motivates the act.

The *Kathāvatthu* records a debate where the Theravādins uphold the view that *kamma* signifies only activity that is produced as a physical, verbal, or mental expression of a specific purposive impetus. They argue that *kamma* does not include any incidental activity of body, speech, or mind that happens to occur while a wholesome or unwholesome intentional act is being performed. For example, a point of debate was whether mere physical occurrences, such as movements of the body and the lips that happen to take place during wholesome states of mind, are to be regarded as wholesome acts in their own right, even though they are not directly expressive of wholesome purposes (Kvu. 380-394). The Theravādins quote the Buddha's definition where *cetanā* is made synonymous with *kamma* (A. III. 415) in order to substantiate their argument that if physical movements or mental states are separated from a wholesome or unwholesome configuration comprising mental attitude, purpose, and act, they cannot carry moral import. In the debate, the Theravādins maintain that an act cannot be assessed as morally good or bad if it is not related to an object (*ārammaṇam*) and does not possess certain mental attributes that make moral evaluation possible. The mental attributes that the *Kathāvatthu* (Kvu. 380) specifies in this context are the following: directing (*āvaṭṭanā*) the mind to the object, experiencing the object (*ābhoga*), concentrating on the object (*samannāhāra*), attending to the object (*manasikāra*), motivation by a purposive impulse (*cetanā*), wishing for the goal (*patthanā*), and resolving to attain the goal (*paṇidhi*). This list of prerequisites for moral evaluation once again affirms the Theravāda position that moral evaluation is not possible unless there is a clearly recognized object that is recognized as the goal to be attained, a clearly affirmed purpose of attaining that goal, and a purposive impulse that motivates action towards that goal. *Cetanā* endows the act not only with purpose but also with the moral qualities of the state of mind in which the purpose is formed.

In a controversy that revolves around the question of the merit that accrues from the giving of gifts (*dāna*), the Theravādins further emphasize their view that the moral value of an act stems not solely from what the act achieves, but from the fact that the act is the manifest expression of a wholesome or unwholesome purposive impetus (Kvu. 339-347). The opponents maintain that the merit that is generated by the giving of gifts increases with increase in the enjoyment that the gift brings to the recipient. The Theravādins argue that merit does not accrue to the giver if the act of giving is not characterized by attention to the act of giving, a purposive impulse directed towards making a gift, the wish to give, and the aspiration to express generosity (Kvu. 343). Furthermore, the Theravādins insist that the merit gained by the person who makes the gift cannot be dependent solely on the benefit experienced by the recipient. They demonstrate that the view of their opponents entails the untenable position that karmic merit can be gained by a giver of gifts who harbours unwholesome thoughts (*akusala-vitakkas*) of sensual passion, malevolence, and cruelty (Kvu. 344).

Nevertheless, in the course of this debate concerning what constitutes the giving of gifts (*dāna*), the Theravādins make it clear that though they hold that moral value resides primarily in the purpose that is formed in a specific state of mind, and not solely in the act, they do not accept the idea that wholesome and unwholesome *kamma* can be distinguished and defined exclusively in relation to the motivating purposive impulse (*cetanā*), without any reference to physical, verbal, or mental activity. For this reason, they reject the view of other opponents who hold that *dāna* denotes, not the actual gift, but only the generosity in the mind of the giver. For the Theravādins, just the thought is not enough. The *Kathāvatthu* seeks to establish that the giving of gifts (*dāna*) includes both the mental state of generosity and the thing that is to be given (*deyya-dhamma*). The commentary to the *Kathāvatthu* (KvuA. 95-96) goes much further in showing the bond between the mental state (*citta*) of generosity, the purposive impulse (*cetanā*) that initiates the act of giving, and the gift itself. The commentary interprets *dāna* to be threefold (*tividham*), comprising the following factors: the purposive impulse that motivates a person to renounce, or part with, an object (*cāga-cetanā*); the act of abstaining (*virati*), which cuts off (*dāti*) the purposive impulse that can initiate morally bad behaviour (*dussīlya-cetanā*) and obstruct the intention to give; and the actual gift (*deyya-dhamma*). The commentary then reduces these three factors to two: the mental state (*cetasika*) that is the basis of giving and the object that is given. The conclusion to the argument is that the opponent incorrectly defines the giving of gifts solely in terms of the intention of giving, while ignoring the significance of what is actually given.

The commentary to the *Kathāvatthu*, however, proceeds to emphasize the primacy of the mental factors involved in the act of giving by pointing out that even the giving of an unpleasant thing, such as bitter medicine, must be regarded as a morally good act, provided that it has its source in a beneficent state of mind (*hita-citta*) and produces good consequences. According to the commentary, if the act of giving is initiated by the purposive impulse that motivates a person to part with something for the sake of the benefit of others (*hita-pharaṇa-cetanā*), then it must be regarded as a wholesome act, even if the recipient does not get immediate pleasure out of the gift. These debates between the Theravādins and their opponents illustrate the Theravāda position that a person's attitude of mind (*citta*), the purposive impulse (*cetanā*) that emerges from that attitude of mind and the act (*kamma*) in which the purpose becomes concretely realized define and give meaning to each other. Theravādins maintain that moral value resides in the integral whole that they form.

Conclusion

The definitions in the *Sutta* and *Abhidhamma* literature attribute to *cetanā* the following features. *Cetanā* is always associated with a specific state of mind (*citta*) that arises through the confluence of causal conditions in the continuum of consciousness. *Cetanā* always functions as a motivating impulse with the capacity to coordinate the functions of concomitant mental states and direct them towards a goal. Interest in an object and the purpose of attaining it are marked features of *cetanā*. Furthermore, purposive acts that entail karmic consequences (*sañcetanika-kammas*) are defined as "actualizations" or concrete realizations in bodily behaviour, verbal expression, or mental processes of motivating intentions or purposive impulses. In this sense, *cetanā* is identified with *kamma*.

The principal definitions of *cetanā* in the *Atthasālinī* (Asl. 111-112) and the *Visuddhimagga* (Vsm. XIV. 135) present *cetanā* primarily as a motivating impetus with the capacity to initiate goal-directed action. In these definitions, a distinction is made between the defining characteristic of *cetayita* that is attributed to all *cetanās*, and the function of *āyūhana* that is limited to *cetanās* that put forth wholesome and unwholesome *kamma*. Strictly speaking, in this definition the meaning of *cetayita* is not derived from the verb *ceteti* (to think, to intend), to which *cetayita* is linked grammatically, but from the cultural tradition that views *cetanā* as the rudimentary consciousness that quickens the organism, endows it with sentient awareness, and causes it to respond to the environment (Mt. U. III. 3-6; S. III. 143; M. I. 296). These definitions do not conceive of *cetanā* as a cognitive function of purposive reflection and decision-making, but emphasize its conative role of motivating concomitant mental states and initiating action in the organism. Whereas these definitions of *cetanā* in the *Atthasālinī* and the *Visuddhimagga* stress the capacity of *cetanās* to motivate the organism and initiate goal-oriented activity, in another extended section comprising the discourses on *kamma*, the *Atthasālinī* follows the *Karajakāya-vagga* of the *Aṅguttara-nikāya* and focuses on the relationship of *cetanā* to concomitant thought processes and emotions within a typical attitude of mind (*citta*). In these discourses, the *Atthasālinī* maintains that each *cetanā*, arising as a constituent of a specific state of mind, participates in the purposive thoughts and dominant emotional features of that state of mind and takes on the moral value that it exhibits.

Although a *cetanā* arises and functions as one of the constituents of a state of mind (*citta*), its energizing impetus links it to the *saṅkhārakkhandha*, which is the dynamic dimension of consciousness that brings together the resources of the mind and produces goal-oriented activities. The sense of purpose or thought of a goal that is at the core of *cetanā* gives direction to the capacity of the *saṅkhārakkhandha* to assemble the mental factors necessary to produce acts of body, speech, and mind. In this way, *cetanās* mediate between the cognitive and conative dimensions of the continuum of consciousness. *Cetanās*, as it were, carry the purposes and intentions that are formed by the cognitive and emotive factors (*cetasikas*) of the series of states of mind (*cittas*) into the action-producing processes of the *saṅkhārakkhandha*. Through the motivating impetus of purposive impulses (*cetanās*), purposes that are conceived in the cognitive processes of the states of mind (*cittas*) that form the continuum of consciousness become concretely realized in purposive acts that are composed and put forth by the *saṅkhārakkhandha*, which constitutes the dynamic dimension of the same continuum of consciousness. At the same time, the moral values that reside in the *cittas* become manifest in concrete acts through the motivating impetus of *cetanās*. It is said in the *Visuddhimagga* (Vsm. XVII. 60) that acts of karmic merit, for example, are concrete manifestations of wholesome purposive impulses (*kusala-sañcetanās*) that arise in wholesome states of mind (*kusala-cittas*) and become active and effective (*pavattā*) through the practice of virtue, mindfulness, and meditation.

Despite the emphasis on the conative impetus of *cetanā* in the definitions given in the *Atthasālinī* (Asl. 111-112) and the *Visuddhimagga* (Vsm. XIV. 135), when one reflects on the definitions of bodily, verbal, and mental *kamma* in the *Atthasālinī* (Asl. 84, 87, 88), one is led to the conclusion that *cetanā* is conceived in Theravāda as the dynamic rendering of a purposive thought that arises through the interplay of the cognitive, emotive, and conative factors (*cetasikas*) of a specific attitude of mind (*citta*). At the same time, it becomes clear that *cetanā* functions within the *saṅkhārakkhandha* as the mental factor that gives purpose and direction to the constructive processes by which configurations of causal conditions are formed and acts of body, speech, and mind are composed, in accordance with the principle of conditioned origination.

The definitions of the precepts in the *Vibhaṅga* (Vbh. 285-286) are phrased in such a way as to clearly identify each act of restraining from doing what is unwholesome and morally wrong with the purposive impulse that motivates the restraint. Similarly, the definitions in the *Atthasālinī* (Asl. 84, 87, 88) precisely identify each wholesome or unwholesome act (*kamma*) with a *cetanā* that becomes effective (*siddhā*) at a specific door of action: body, speech, or mind. In the *Abhidhamma* literature, the state of mind (*citta*) in which a wholesome or unwholesome purpose is conceived, the purposive impulse (*cetanā*) that gives dynamic expression to that state of mind and the act (*kamma*) that concretely manifests the purposive impulse are conceived as a dynamic unity. The *Abhidhamma* view is that moral value resides in this organic whole of *citta*, *cetanā*, and *kamma*. From the thrust of the argument in the *Atthasālinī*, the conclusion can be drawn that through the concept of *cetanā*, the *Abhidhamma* system seeks to avoid the notion of a habitual rift between purposive thought and act. It is postulated that when the wholesome or unwholesome "roots" that support a state of mind are strong, then the correspondingly wholesome or unwholesome purpose that arises within the state of mind will be well-established. The argument is made that when the purpose is strongly affirmed, it will give rise to a strong purposive impulse through which the purpose will become concretely realized. A well executed purposive act, in turn, will have a strengthening effect on the roots.

Although the *Atthasālinī* and the *Nettippakaraṇa* emphasize the motivating role of *cetanās*, these texts clarify that *cetanās* are supported not only by the roots of action, but also by the mental factors that are designated as mental *kamma* in the *Suttas*. The *Atthasālinī* maintains that the six mental factors that constitute mental *kamma*, the "seven factors of wisdom", and the factors of the Eightfold Path all function as factors associated with *cetanā* (*cetanā-sampayuttakā-dhammā*) in motivating purposive acts. In the *Abhidhamma* view, the cognitive and emotive roots of action, the states of mind that stem from these roots, the purposive impulses that emerge from these states of mind, and the purposive acts in which the purposive impulses find concrete manifestation are linked together by a network of mutual conditioning. It can be concluded that in the *Abhidhamma* view, when a rift appears between purpose and act, the cause can be found in a weak link in this net of interdependent relationships. The Eightfold Path seeks to establish a network of wholesome conditioning through which the mind can become gradually established in goodness, serenity, and wisdom.

ENDNOTES

[1] S.Z. Aung, *Compendium of Philosophy*, 236, n. 3.

[2] H.V. Guenther, *Philosophy and Psychology in the Abhidharma*, 44.

[3] *Cetayatī ti cetanā; abhisandahatī ti attho* (Vsm. XIV. 135).

[4] Pe Maung Tin, *The Expositor*, 147.

[5] *Cetayatī ti cetanā. Saddhiṁ attanā sampayutta-dhamme ārammaṇe atisandahatī ti attho* (Asl. 111).

The term *sampayutta-dhammā* (associated mental states) refers to mental factors that arise together as constituents of the same momentary state of consciousness (*citta*). They are causally associated with each other and have the same object, though they differ from each other in their characteristics (Bhikkhu Bodhi, *A Comprehensive Manual of Abhidhamma*, 76-77).

[6] ... *catu-bhūmaka-cetanā hi no cetayita-lakkhaṇā nāma n'atthi* (Asl. 111).

The *Atthasālinī* declares that there is no *cetanā* in the four planes of existence that does not have *cetayita* as its defining characteristic. These four planes are the realm of sensory experience, the realm of fine matter, the formless realm, and the "supramundane" realm.

[7] Pe Maung Tin, *The Expositor*, 147-148.

[8] H.V. Guenther, *Philosophy and Psychology in the Abhidharma*, 42.

[9] *Sabbā cetayita-lakkhaṇā va āyūhana-rasatā pana kusalākusalesu eva hoti* (Asl. 111).

[10] Commenting on the phrase at A. II. 35, "what is proper to do, what is proper to arrange" (*alaṁ kātum alaṁ saṁvidhātum*), the Buddhaghosa maintains that whereas *kātum* signifies what is to be done by oneself (*attanā kātum*), *samvidhātum* conveys an act that one causes to be done by another person (*parehi kārāpetum*) (AA. III. 247). This explanation of the verb *saṁvidahati* is helpful because it corroborates the meaning assigned to *saṁvidahana* in the definition of *cetanā* given in the Atthasālinī. The definition says that when *cetanā* begins its work with regard to its object, it causes each of the concomitant mental states (*cetasikas*) to commence its own work (*esā pi attano kiccena ārammaṇe vattamānā aññe pi sampayutta-dhamme attano attano kiriyāya pavatteti*) (Asl. 112).

[11] Pe Maung Tin, *The Expositor*, 148; *The Path of Purity*, 542.

[12] Bhikkhu Ñāṇamoli, *The Path of Purification*, 523.

[13] H.V. Guenther, *Philosophy and Psychology in the Abhidharma*, 42, n. 2.

[14] Yaśomitra makes the following comment on *Abhidharmakośa-bhāṣya*, II. 24: *Cetanācittābhisaṁskāra iti citta-praspandaḥ. Praspanda iva praspanda ityarthaḥ* (AbhkA. 1:187).

[15] A. Haldar, *Some Psychological Aspects of Early Buddhist Philosophy Based on Abhidharmakośa of Vasubandhu*, 84.

[16] S.Z. Aung, *Compendium of Philosophy*, 237.

[17] *Abhidhamma-pariyāyaṁ patvā pana vijjamānaka-vatthuṁ ārabbha dassāmī ti manasā cintita-kālato paṭṭhāya kusalaṁ hoti apara-bhāge kāyena vā vācāya vā kattabbaṁ karissatī ti vuttaṁ* (Asl. 77).

[18] *Yā pana tasmiṁ dvāre siddhā cetanā yāya pāṇaṁ hanti adiṇṇam ādiyati micchā carati pāṇātipātādīhi viramati, idaṁ kāya-kammaṁ nāma* (Asl. 84).

[19] *Yā pana tasmiṁ vacī-dvāre siddhā cetanā yāya musā katheti, pesuññaṁ katheti pharusaṁ katheti samphappalapati musā-vādādīhi viramati idaṁ vacī-kammaṁ nāma* (Asl. 87).

[20] *Yā pana tasmiṁ mano-dvāre siddhā cetanā yāyaṁ abhijjhā-vyāpāda micchā-dassanāni c'eva anabhijjhā-avyāpāda-sammādassanāni va gaṇhāti idaṁ mano-kammaṁ nāma* (Asl. 88).

[21] The *Atthasālinī* (Asl. 159) maintains that the *cetanās* that produce the meritorious act that has the nature of giving (*dāna*) arise on three occasions: *'dānaṁ dassāmī ti' cintentassa uppajjati, dānaṁ dadato uppajjati, 'dinnaṁ me ti' paccavekkhantassa uppajjati.* The text then goes on to say that when these three *cetanās* come together, then the act of giving comes into existence: *Evam pubba-cetanā muñcana-cetanā ti tisso pi cetanā ekato katvā dānamayam puñña-kiriya-vatthu nāma hoti.*

[22] The *Atthasālinī* (Asl. 157-160) maintains that the three *cetanās* (prior *cetanā*, *cetanā* at the time of acting, subsequent *cetanā*) come into play in ten meritorious acts: (1) charity, (2) virtue, (3) cultivating the mind, (4) respect for elders, (5) dutifulness, (6) sharing of merit, (7) giving thanks, (8) teaching, (9) learning the *Dhamma*, and (10) establishing right views (Pe Maung Tin, *The Expositor*, 209).

[23] *Mano-dvāre pana vadhaka-cetanāya uppanna-mattāya eva kamma-patha-bhedo hoti, so va kho vyāpāda-vasena na pāṇātipāta-vasena* (Asl. 90). The *Atthasālinī* here emphasizes that the mere arising of the intention to kill in the mind is sufficient to constitute *kamma*. According to the *Atthasālinī*, in this case, the processes of *kamma* are set in motion because of the mental *kamma* of ill will, not because murder has actually been committed.

[24] P.S. Jaini, "Sautrāntika Theory of *bīja*", 237-238.

[25] Ibid., 237.

[26] *Kim pan' etaṁ kammaṁ nāma? Cetanā c'eva ekacce va cetanā-sampayuttakā dhammā* (Asl. 88).

[27] In the *Aṅguttara-nikaya* (A. II. 236, 237), the eight aspects of the Eightfold Path and the seven *bojjhaṅgas* are described as "*kamma* that leads to the waning away of *kamma*". In the *Atthasālinī*, *cetanā-sampayuttakā dhammā* are reckoned as twenty-one in number: six factors of mental *kamma*, seven *bojjhaṅgas*, and eight aspects of the Eightfold Path (Asl. 89).

[28] Bhikkhu Ñāṇamoli, *The Guide*, vii-x. In his work as commentator, Buddhaghosa followed the method of interpretation given in the *Nettippakaraṇa*. The *Nettippakaraṇa* instructs the commentator that the explanation of any individual "thread" (*sutta*) of the Buddha's teaching must be in agreement with the teaching as a whole and must be true to the final aim of liberation from suffering. Elaborate details of procedure are laid out to guide the commentator in this method of interpretation. According to Bhikkhu Ñāṇamoli, the aim of the method taught in the *Nettippakaraṇa* is to find clarity by "re-wording" an idea that is already well known to the commentator.

[29] K.R. Norman, *Pāli Literature*, 110.

[30] Bhikkhu Ñāṇamoli, *The Guide*, 68, n. 239/1.

[31] The *Atthasālinī* is emphatic that gently spoken words cannot necessarily be classified as "absence of harsh speech": *Yathā ca citta-saṇhatāya pharusavācā na hoti evaṁ vacana-saṇhatāya apharusavācā pi na hoti* (Asl. 100). The point is made here that absence of harsh speech is to be defined in terms of a gentle attitude of mind (*citta-saṇhatā*).

[32] *Tasmin pana parapariggahīte saññino tadādāyaka-upakkama-samuṭṭhāpikā theyya-cetanā adinnādānam* (Asl. 97-98).

Theft is defined as the purposive impulse that produces the conative effort to steal in a person who has the thought of stealing.

[33] *Visaṁvādanādhippāyena pan' assa para-visaṁvādakā kāya-vacīppayoga samuṭṭhāpikā cetanā musāvādo* (Asl. 98-99).

[34] *Tattha saṅkiliṭṭhassa cittassa paresaṁ vā bhedāya attapiyakamyatāya vā kāya-vacī-payoga-samuṭṭhāpikā cetanā pisuṇā vācā* (Asl. 99).

Chapter IX
Cetanā and Other Pāli Terms Indicating Motivation

In this chapter, the focus is on two sets of Pāli terms pertaining to motivation: those that signify intention or resolve to pursue a goal, and those that indicate the capacity to initiate action to fulfil that goal. Of the many terms that connote purpose or intention to act, the most significant are *adhimokkha* (conviction with regard to choosing an object), *chanda* (desire to act), and *saṅkappa* (resolve, decision). The term that occurs most often in the *Sutta*s in relation to the mind's capacity to initiate goal-oriented action is *viriya*. However, in the debate against *sàmaṇa* teachers who advocated a deterministic view of human nature, the Buddha chose another term—*ārambha-dhātu* (the capacity to initiate action in oneself). A comparison of these terms with *cetanā* will demonstrate the distinctive features of *cetanā*.

This survey of terms related to the mind's capacity to form a purpose and initiate purposive action shows once again that according to Theravāda, no single mental factor is capable by itself of producing acts of body, speech, or mind. Only a confluence of necessary factors is regarded as sufficient for the initiation of action. *Cetanā* is first compared here with four Pāli terms that signify intention to pursue a goal: *adhimokkha*, *chanda*, *saṅkappa*, and *ārambha-dhātu*. This comparative survey shows that the distinctive function of *cetanā* is to activate conscious awareness by directing the mind towards an object of interest. By doing so, *cetanā* motivates concomitant mental factors to concentrate attention on that object.

Adhimokkha

In the *Suttas*, the verb *adhimuccati* indicates "to feel attached to", "to make up one's mind", "to become convinced", "to have faith" (P.E.D. 29, col. 2). In the *Atthasālinī* (Asl. 133) and the *Visuddhimagga* (XIV. 151), *adhimokkha* is defined as follows:

lakkhaṇa (characteristic)	*sanniṭṭhāna-lakkhaṇa* Its defining characteristic is ascertainment or decisiveness.
rasa (function)	*asaṁsappana-rasa* Its distinctive function is to avoid [indecisive] "crawling".
paccupaṭṭhāna (mode of manifestation)	*nicchaya-paccupaṭṭhāna* It manifests as conviction.
padaṭṭhāna (proximate cause)	*sanniṭṭhātabba-dhamma-padaṭṭhāna* Its proximate cause is the presence of something to be ascertained or decided.

When it is linked with the verb "to trust" (*saddahati*), *adhimuccati* conveys making a firm dedication to the teaching of the Buddha (*Dhamma*) (S. III. 225). In *The Buddhist Path to Awakening: A Study of the Bodhi-Pakkhiyā Dhammā*, Gethin explains that *adhimokkha* carries the meaning of commitment when it is associated with *saddhā*.[1] However, *adhimuccati* can also connote a strong unwholesome inclination towards a pleasant sense object (S. IV. 184-185). In its rudimentary form *adhimokkha* signifies a strong personal inclination towards an object and an impulse to focus attention on it; in its developed form, it manifests as commitment to pursue a chosen goal. *Adhimutti* remains a neutral term in the *Suttas*. When it pertains to worldly life, it signifies "being intent on" or "devoted to" worldly affairs (*lokāmisādhimutti*) (M. II. 253). The definition goes on to compare the decisiveness (*nicchaya*) of *adhimokkha* to the unshakeable (*niccala*) nature of a stone pillar demarcating a boundary. The commentary to the *Visuddhimagga* (VsmA. 2:1043) explains that the function of *adhimokkha* is to free the mind of perplexity (*vicikicchā*) and to avoid zigzagging from side to side like a creeping serpent. Here the snake's movement symbolizes childish indecision regarding the nature of an object and inability to decide whether to act or not to act in relation to the object.

In its rudimentary form[2] *adhimokkha* is one of the basic mental factors that brings about the preliminary stages of the cognitive process. In this context, *adhimokkha* functions, not as a full-fledged certainty based on judgment, but as a preliminary freeing of the mind from uncertainty when faced with a plurality of objects. *Adhimokkha* acts as inclination towards, and interest in, a certain object. The functioning of *adhimokkha* enables the mind to begin to direct its attention to one object and to set the others aside. In its developed form, *adhimokkha* shows itself as firm faith and commitment to a chosen goal. It then takes the form of a conviction based on discipline and cultivation of the mind, and it becomes expressed in wholesome action. *Adhimutti*, when it functions as trust in the Eightfold Path and unswerving commitment to the goal, develops into the manifestation of firm faith (Vsm. XIV. 140).

The meaning that *adhimokkha* came to acquire in Buddhist circles can be seen in Yaśomitra's commentary to the *Abhidharmakośa-bhāṣya* (AbhkA. 1.187).[3] This passage shows the two aspects of *adhimokkha*: in its incipient form, *adhimokkha* signifies personal inclination towards an object, but in its mature form it is associated with states of mind characterized by conviction and dedication in the pursuit of a goal.

Chanda

The term *chanda* is much more directly related to the initiation of action than *adhimokkha*. Of all the Pāli terms signifying conation, *chanda* is the one that covers the widest range and comes most readily to mind as the equivalent of "initiative to act". Like *cetanā*, *chanda* is a neutral term indicating basic conation spanning intention to act and capacity to initiate action. When *chanda* is linked with qualifying terms, it can signify either wholesome or unwholesome conation. When associated with *rāga* (passion, greed), *chanda* acquires the sense of unwholesome excitement of desire. Unwholesome *chanda* is said to be the root of sorrow (*chando hi mūlaṁ dukkhassa*) (S. IV. 328). The role of *chanda* in wholesome motivation is best seen in the definition of right effort (*sammā-vāyāma*) as a factor of the Eightfold Path. In several passages of the *Suttas*, a monk's ardent effort to cultivate wholesome mental states and uproot what is unwholesome is described as follows: *chandaṁ janeti* (he arouses zeal), *vāyamati* (strives), *viriyaṃ ārabhati* (begins to put forth energy), *cittaṁ paggaṇhāti* (exerts his mind), *padahati* (and endeavours) (for example, D. II. 312, III. 221; A. II. 15). In this context, *chanda* signifies wholesome ardour, fervour, zeal, or enthusiasm pervading the impulse to initiate an action. *Chanda* is associated with *ussoḷhi* (exertion), *appaṭivāni* (unflagging effort), *ātappa* (ardour), *viriya* (energy), and *sātacca* (perseverance) in a passage of the *Saṁyutta-nikāya* (S. II. 132) that describes the exertion that is required of a disciple in the process of training.

In the *Vibhaṅga* (Vbh. 216) *chanda* is defined as desire to act (*kattukamyatā*). The more detailed definition of *chanda* in the *Visuddhimagga* (Vsm. XIV. 150) is as follows:

lakkhaṇa (characteristic)	*kattukāmatā-lakkhaṇa* Its defining characteristic is "desire to act".
rasa (function)	*ārammaṇa-pariyesanā-rasa* Its function is searching for an object.
paccupaṭṭhāna (mode of manifestation)	*ārammaṇena-atthikatā-paccupaṭṭhāna* It manifests as need for an object.
padaṭṭhāna (proximate cause)	*tad ev' assa padaṭṭhānam* That same object functions as its proximate cause.

The definitions of *chanda* in the *Visuddhimagga* and the *Atthasālinī* (Asl. 132-133) vividly compare the mental act of seeking an object—which is specified as the function of *chanda*—to the physical act of reaching out one's hand (*hatthappasāraṇam*) to grasp an object.

The following differences between *cetanā* and *chanda* emerge from the definitions of the two terms. At the outset it can be seen that *cetanā*, unlike *chanda*, is posited as a basic mental factor essential for the maintenance of even the most rudimentary sentient awareness. In the lists of mental factors given in the *Dhammasaṅgaṇi*, the *Atthasālinī*, and the *Visuddhimagga*, *cetanā* appears among those factors that are fundamental and constantly present in all states of consciousness. From what is said in the *Abhidhammattha-saṅgaha*,[4] it can be inferred that *chanda* is regarded as a function that operates only in states of mind where there is some sense of the nature of the object, and where no perplexity (*vicikicchā*) or restlessness (*uddhacca*) rooted in delusion (*moha*) prevents the mind from directing itself towards the chosen object.

Moreover, the definitions show that though both *cetanā* and *chanda* are goal-oriented impulses, there is a difference in their manner of functioning. Arising within a specific state of consciousness (*citta*), *cetanā* exercises its capacity to initiate action by relating itself to a purpose that is conceived through the interaction of thoughts and emotions in that *citta*. Furthermore, the function of *cetanā*, as the analogies in the definitions of *cetanā* demonstrate, is to arouse concomitant mental states to perform their functions by associating themselves with its own purposive action. In other words, *cetanā* instigates activity in different aspects of the mind and directs all the efforts garnered in this manner towards the object. The function of *chanda* is to maintain the orientation of the mind towards the goal, once that orientation has been established by *cetanā*, and to strengthen the mind's enthusiasm in pursuing the goal. As a consequence, unwholesome *chanda* becomes passionate desire (*chanda-rāga*) for the goal and wholesome *chanda* becomes a noble zeal in cultivating the disciplines of the Eightfold Path (*dhamma-chanda*). The commentary to the *Visuddhimagga* defines *chanda* as the function that persistently turns concomitant mental factors towards the object and maintains their relationship to the object (VsmA. 2:1042).

Furthermore, *chanda*, functioning as intention to pursue a goal, becomes one of the four dominant factors (*adhipatis*) that determine the manner in which the disciplines of the Eightfold Path are pursued. The four dominant factors are: *chanda* in the aspect of zeal in following the Eightfold Path (*dhamma-chanda*); energy (*viriya*); consciousness (*citta*) itself, especially when it is developed through meditation and mindfulness; and investigation (*vīmaṁsā*) of physical and mental states (*dhammas*). It is posited that any one of these dominant factors can lead the consciousness continuum to persevere in a difficult task, especially in relation to the Eightfold Path (Dhs. 56, Vbh. 216-226).[5] To some extent, the concept of "*cetanā* of the Path" (*magga-cetanā*) is similar to the concept of *dhamma-chanda.* However, whereas there are details of how *chanda* functions in its role of *adhipati*, there are no comparable descriptions of how *cetanā* of the Path functions. Whereas *dhamma-chanda* is portrayed as taking a leading role by imbuing the mind with enthusiasm and zeal, *cetanā* is not described in this way.

The most important difference between *cetanā* and *chanda* is that *cetanā* is identified with the processes of *kamma* in a way that *chanda* is not. In brief, *chanda* is the enthusiasm in pursuing the object, which comes after *cetanā* has established the initial connection between the mind and an object. *Cetanā* performs the more basic function of stirring the mind and directing it to an object.

Saṅkappa

Whereas *adhimokkha* functions as decisiveness with regard to focusing attention on an object and *chanda* operates as the wish to pursue an object, *saṅkappa* manifests as intention based on cognitive processes of purposive reflection. The passages in the *Suttas* where these two terms are found imply that while the impetus to act represented by *chanda* is conditioned primarily by the nature and qualities of the object, the intention or resolve that constitutes *saṅkappa* is governed by the cognitive processes of decision-making in the continuum of consciousness. A passage in the *Dīgha-nikāya* that lists a sequence of motivating conditions helps to clarify how *saṅkappa* and *chanda* function as factors of motivation (D. III. 289). This passage seeks to explain why people engage in different types of quests and end up with different kinds of gains. It is posited that because people perceive objects differently, there are wide differences in the intentions (*saṅkappas*) they form. The passage goes on to say that differences in intention lead to differences in the manner in which people desire to act (*chanda*). Differences in *saṅkappa* and *chanda* are regarded as causes that lead, stage by stage, to differences in the feverish passion for objects, differences in the search for objects, and differences in what is gained. The causal bond that this passage posits between *saṅkappa* and *chanda* implies that *saṅkappa*, in its role of purposive deliberation or intention, opens the way for the action-oriented impetus of *chanda* to come into effect.

The relationship posited between *saṅkappa* and thought or intellection (*vitakka*), both in the *Suttas* and in the *Abhidhamma*, shows that *saṅkappa* is closer to purpose, design, intention, and goal-oriented thought than to the conative impulsion that actually implements the purpose.[6] The term *adhippāya* captures this meaning of *saṅkappa* in the *Suttas* (S. I. 124, V. 108; A.II. 81). In the *Saṅgīti-sutta* it is shown that both *saṅkappa* and *vitakka* carry moral values and can be classified as wholesome or unwholesome (D. III. 215). Unwholesome *saṅkappas* and *vitakkas* are both defined identically as manifestations of sensual desire (*kāma*), ill will (*vyāpāda*), and cruelty (*vihiṁsā*); and both wholesome *saṅkappas* and *vitakkas* are regarded as expressions of renunciation (*nekkhamma*), non-aversion, and absence of cruelty. In the *Dhammasaṅgaṇi* (Dhs. 10, 12) the same definition serves both *sammā-saṅkappa* (right resolve) and *vitakka* (thought, reflection): both are defined in terms of "fixing and focusing" and "applying the mind" to the object (*cetaso abhiniropanā*).[7] In *A Buddhist Manual of Psychological Ethics*, C.A.F. Rhys Davids comments that *abhiniropanā* signifies not only "attending to the object" in order to discern its defining characteristic, but also "aspiration, intention, purpose, design" in relation to the object.[8] Although *vitakka* includes in its meaning intellection and reasoning, this term, like *saṅkappa*, can also connote intention or purpose. When thought becomes goal-directed, it becomes conditioned by emotions that arise in relation to the object and it takes on moral values of wholesome and unwholesome.

The definition of *saṅkappa* in the *Vibhaṅga* is identical with the definition in the *Dhammasaṅgaṇi.* In both cases, the definition begins by characterizing *saṅkappa* as *takka, vitakka.* (Vbh. 237, 238; Dhs. 10).[9] These two terms, *takka* and *vitakka* signify "ratiocination" and "discursive thought". On the other hand, the description of *cetanā* in the *Atthasālinī* shows it to be a combination of intention or purposive thought and the capacity to initiate action directed towards a goal (Asl. 111-112). At first glance it appears that the difference between *saṅkappa* and *cetanā* is that the latter has the capacity to initiate goal-oriented action. However, especially when *saṅkappa* functions as an aspect of the Eightfold Path, it acts as an overarching resolve that has the motivating power to express itself in action. The main difference between *saṅkappa* and *cetanā* is that whereas *cetanā* is regarded as a basic factor that is present even in the most rudimentary states of conscious awareness, *saṅkappa* develops out of conceptualization and discursive thought. *Saṅkappa* is the preferred term in the *Suttas* and the *Abhidhamma* to convey a resolve based on ethical values and a world-view (*diṭṭhi*).

Though the intention that *saṅkappa* represents can come to dominate a state of mind, the implementation of the intention is dependent on the more basic function of *cetanā* to coordinate the resources of the mind and direct them towards a goal. *Cetanā* is conceived as a basic purposive impulse with conative energy that makes an attitude of mind into an effective act. *Saṅkappa* develops as an intention based on thought, but it does not necessarily become translated into action unless it is nurtured and supported by other factors such as *viriya* (energy) and *padhāna* (sustained effort). More significant for an understanding of the dynamics of volition in Theravāda is the fact that whereas *saṅkappa* is conceived as an intention that arises within a *citta* and conditions the attitude of mind displayed by the *citta, cetanā* is regarded as a function that reflects the purpose that finally becomes dominant in the *citta* as a whole. For example, when a benevolent intention (*avyāpāda-saṅkappa*) arises in a *citta,* it is influenced by concomitant cognitive and emotive states in the *citta*. However, it is possible that the benevolent intention may be counteracted by other factors within the *citta*. *Cetanā*, on the other hand, reflects and gives dynamic impetus to the purpose that comes to the fore in the *citta* through the mutual conditioning of all the factors within the *citta*. *Cetanā* functions as the dynamic aspect of the *citta* as a whole. For example, *dāna-cetanā* signifies *dāna-citta* rendered dynamic. The purposive impetus to give a gift (*dāna-cetanā*) is the dynamic mode of an attitude of mind (*dāna-citta*) in which the purposive thought of giving becomes dominant through the mutual conditioning of all the factors in the mind at that time. The term *saṅkappa* does not carry the same significance.

Cetanā Compared with Terms That Indicate Capacity to Initiate Goal-Directed Action

It is not *cetanā* or *chanda* but the special term *ārambha-dhātu* (capacity to initiate action in oneself) that the Buddha chooses in arguing against the deterministic view of human nature put forward by the Ājīvakas. Against their rigid determinism, the Buddha argues that all individuals are endowed with the capacity to activate themselves and to initiate such acts as stepping forth, stepping forward, halting, standing, and stepping towards any object (A. III. 337-338).[10] The Ājīvaka teacher Makkhali Gosāla taught that there is neither "self agency" (*atta-kāra*), nor "agency of another" (*para-kāra*), nor "human agency" (*purisa-kāra*) of any kind (D. I. 53). He also denied that there were such qualities as strength, energy, human stamina, and human vigour. The commentary interprets "self-agency" as action initiated by oneself and "agency of another" as action based on the instigation or instruction of another (DA. I. 161). The Buddha teaches that because all people are endowed with *ārambha-dhātu*, initiating one's own action and acting on the prompting of another become viable possibilities.

There are other contexts (S. V. 66, 104) where *ārambha-dhātu* does not signify initiative to act in a general sense, but is specifically linked to the cultivation of energy (*viriya*) as an aspect of wisdom (*bojjhaṅga*). The *Saṁyutta-nikāya* names inception of energy (*ārambha-dhātu*), exertion (*nikkama-dhātu*), and striving (*parakkama-dhātu*) as the "nutriments" or conditioning factors for the arising and development of energy (*viriya*) as a wholesome and powerful factor of wisdom. The commentary interprets *ārambha-dhātu* as the arousal of energy and the other two factors as the intermediate and fully developed stages in the application of energy in following the Eightfold Path (SA. III. 141). Similarly, in the *Visuddhimagga* (Vsm. IV. 53) *ārambha-dhātu* is interpreted to mean the initial arousal of energy (*paṭhama-viriya*) for the cultivation of systematic attention (*yoniso-manasikāra*).

Ārambha-dhātu is not given the status of a distinctive mental factor (*cetasika*) in the *Vibhaṅga* or in the lists of mental states that appear in the *Dhammasaṅgaṇi*, the *Atthasālinī*, and the *Visuddhimagga*. The passages where the term occurs do not clarify how *ārambha-dhātu* functions in the more complex processes of choosing one's goals and intending to pursue them.

Viriya

Viriya is the Pāli term that most clearly indicates the arousal and application of energy. Whereas *saṅkappa* represents an intention or decision in the mind, and *chanda* conveys desire to act, *viriya* is the term that is most often utilized to indicate the actual application of energy to initiate and sustain an act. The term *viriya* indicates both energy in initiating an act and perseverance in directing activity towards a goal. The lists of mental factors in the *Abhidhamma* literature indicate that *viriya* is a "neutral term". *Viriya* signifies energy that can function in a wholesome or unwholesome manner.

Gethin points out that when *viriya* functions as a wholesome mental factor, it is considered to be closely linked with *sammappadhāna* (right effort) and *sammā-vāyāma* (right striving).[11] In the *Saṁyutta-nikāya* (S. V. 198) wholesome *viriya* is defined as the four modes of right effort: effort to produce wholesome mental states, effort to nourish wholesome mental states that have already arisen, effort to prevent the arising of unwholesome mental states, and effort to uproot unwholesome mental states that have already arisen. The association of wholesome *viriya* with the application of energy is spelt out in the definition of *viriya* in the *Dhammasaṅgaṇi* (Dhs.22). In this definition, *viriya* in its role of one of the "Five Strengths" or "Five Faculties" is connected with exertion of effort (*vāyāma*), vigour (*parakkama, ussāha, ussoḷhi*), firmness, and fortitude (*dhiti, thāma*). *Viriya* in its fully developed wholesome form is also defined as the state of mind of a hero. Courage and unflagging determination are associated with *viriya*. The *Atthasālinī* (Asl. 146) explains that *viriya* is exemplified in the words of the Bodhisatta when he vows that he will not get up from his seat under the Bodhi tree until he attains his goal, even if his skin, his sinews, and his bones wither away (S. II. 28). When a *bhikkhu* has put away mental hindrances and his energy is aroused, when his body is calmed and his mind is concentrated, then he is said to be "ardent, conscientious, constantly and consistently putting forth energy (*satataṁ samitam āraddha-viriyo*), and resolute in mind" (A. II. 14-15). In the *Suttas*, when *viriya* is conjoined with strong endeavour, vigorous exertion, and eager striving, it has the meaning of steady perseverance in seeking a chosen goal.

Wholesome *viriya* is defined as the effort that one puts forth to remove unwholesome mental states and cultivate wholesome ones (A. IV. 363). However, *viriya* is not always wholesome but appears among the basic mental factors that participate in both wholesome and unwholesome mental attitudes (Dhs. 17-18, 84-85; Vsm. XIV. 133, 170, 176). In the *Abhidhammattha-saṅgaha*, *viriya* is included among the list of secondary mental factors (*pakiṇṇaka*) that become wholesome or unwholesome, depending on the moral quality of the *cittas* in which they participate.[12] In the *Atthasālinī*, *viriya* is defined as "that which is to be set in motion (*īrayitabbam*) or brought into effect through an appropriate method or by skilful means (*nayena upāyena*)" (Asl. 120). This definition shows the relationship that Theravāda posits between vigorous energy and discipline. Though vigour (*viriya*) is celebrated as the nature of a hero (*vīra*), vigour is also defined as a quality that can be cultivated by every *bhikkhu* or *bhikkhunī* through disciplined means. Rightly deployed vigour, in its turn, is regarded by the *Atthasālinī* as the basis of all achievements (Asl. 121). In the *Atthasālinī* (Asl. 121) *viriya* is again defined as follows:

lakkhaṇa (characteristic)	*ussāhana-lakkhaṇa* "Energizing" is its defining characteristic.
rasa (function)	*sahajātānam upatthambhana-rasa* Its function is to uphold conascent mental states.
paccupaṭṭhāna (mode of manifestation)	*asaṁsīdana-bhāva-paccupaṭṭhāna* It manifests as not losing heart.
padaṭṭhāna (proximate cause)	*saṁvega-padaṭṭhāna* Its proximate cause is a feeling of urgency (*saṁvega*) or an occasion that calls for the arousal of energy (*viriyārambha-vatthu vā*).

The definition of *viriya* in the *Visuddhimagga* (Vsm. XIV. 137) is identical. The *Atthasālinī* compares the revitalizing role of *viriya* to a king sending reinforcements to a small besieged army, or to a householder buttressing an old home with supporting pillars. The commentary to the *Visuddhimagga* says that *viriya* prevents concomitant mental states from falling into laziness, and provides them with support, additional strength, and uplift (VsmA. 2:1036).

There are two basic differences between *cetanā* and *viriya*. Wholesome and unwholesome *cetanā*s include purposive thought and the intention to pursue a specific goal. The function of *viriya* is concerned not so much with forming a purpose as with energy and perseverance in pursuing the purpose that has already been formed. Moreover, the analogies of the landlord's role at harvest time and the head pupil's role in the classroom in the definition of *cetanā* demonstrate that the function of *cetanā* is to initiate rudimentary activity in concomitant mental states and direct that activity towards a wholesome or unwholesome end. The role played by *viriya* in energizing the mind and all its functions becomes possible once *cetanā* accomplishes its basic task of stirring the organism to action and directing mental processes towards a goal. When *cetanā*, functioning as a purposive impulse, stimulates the mind by directing it to an object of interest, the functions of *adhimokkha*, *chanda*, *saṅkappa*, and *viriya* become coordinated, purposeful, and goal-oriented. The motivating functions of these mental factors are assembled as necessary conditions by *saṅkhāra* processes in producing wholesome and unwholesome intentional acts (*sañcetanika-kamma*). *Cetanā* performs the basic function of transforming a purposive thought or intention that arises in the mind into a purposive impulse or intention imbued with motivating impetus. The qualities of heroic ardour and unfaltering fortitude that characterize wholesome *viriya* are not regarded as attributes of *cetanā*.

Differentiating Craving (*Taṇhā*) from *Cetanā*

It is to be noted that *cetanā*, *adhimokkha*, *saṅkappa*, and *viriya* are all classified as neutral terms in the *Abhidhamma* classification of mental states. It is posited that they take on the ethical values of the *citta* within which they arise. Craving (*taṇhā*), by contrast with these "neutral" mental factors, is regarded as unwholesome and as the cause of sorrow. *Cetanā* arises as a purposive impulse within a specific state of mind and is supported by the thought of a goal that exerts a teleological "pull" on the continuum of consciousness. Craving, however, is closer to the experience of hunger or thirst and it is caused by the sense of a need that "pushes" or impels the mind towards an object that it feels will assuage that need. It is associated with emotional tension that persists until the need is temporarily satisfied. According to the analysis of mental states in the *Visuddhimagga*, the proximate cause of craving is a feeling (*vedanā*) of pleasure or pain arising from sensory or mental stimulation (Vsm. XVII. 51). *Cetanā*, on the other hand, is inseparably linked in its mode of functioning to a state of mind (*citta*) that includes cognitive processes through which choices are weighed and a goal is chosen. For this reason, wholesome and unwholesome *cetanās* exhibit a sense of purpose and are not governed solely by the need to satisfy a feeling or remove emotional tension.

In the *Suttas* craving is defined as the origin of sorrow and rebirth (D. II. 308; M.I. 48, III. 250, 287). The definition goes on to say that craving is characterized by delight and passion, and by jubilation in the experience of objects, now here, now there (*tatra-tatrābhinandinī*). Terms connoting delight, merriment, or sensual excitement—for example, *nandi-rāga* and *abhinandana*—do not appear in the definitions of *cetanā*, *adhimokkha*, *saṅkappa*, and *viriya*. *Nandi* signifies utter delight, ardent joy, and pleasure, while *raga* conveys desire for sensory enjoyment or more intense sensual passion. This sense of sheer pleasure, excitement, or passion for things that delight the senses and the mind is not necessarily associated with the basic conative capacity to initiate action that characterizes both *cetanā* and *chanda* in its role of a simple wish to act (*kattu-kāmatā-chanda*). Neither is pleasure or enjoyment a necessary element of the function of energizing and sustaining goal-directed activity, which is attributed to *viriya*. *Cetanā*, *adhimokkha*, *saṅkappa*, and *viriya* become associated with passion for objects only when they function in *citta*s rooted in greed (*lobha*).

According to the definition of *taṇhā* put forward in the *Visuddhimagga*, the function of *taṇhā* is "enjoying" or "taking delight" (*abhinandana-rasa*) (Vsm. XVII. 51). The mode of manifestation of *taṇhā* is "remaining devoid of satisfaction" or "insatiability" (*atitta-bhāva-paccupaṭṭhāna*). Feeling of pleasure or pain that arises from contact with objects is considered to be the proximate cause of craving. The term *atitta* conveys that craving, by definition, is that which cannot be fulfilled or satisfied. The definition of greed (Asl. 249; Vsm. XIV. 161) puts the emphasis on tenacious grasping of objects (*ārammaṇa-gahaṇa*), whereas the definition of craving stresses insatiability (*atitta-bhāva*). Greedy adherence to an object is compared to meat sticking to a hot frying pan, and greed manifesting itself as "not letting go" of the object (*apariccāga*) is likened to the irremovable quality of dye prepared from lampblack. The fixation attributed to greed and the insatiability attributed to craving indicate that addiction to an object is regarded as the basic nature of both of these mental states.

The *Mahānidāna-sutta*, in the midst of its lofty discussion of the great chain of causation related to rebirth, pauses at the causal link of craving and offers a very down-to-earth excursus on the everyday chain of motivation leading from craving to cruel combat (D. II. 58-59). This passage presents the following "motivational series". Craving (*taṇhā*) conditions constant search (*pariyesanā*) for objects, and searching leads to acquisition of objects (*lābha*). Acquisition necessitates decision (*vinicchaya*) regarding what has been acquired, decision generates sensual passion (*chanda-rāga*), and sensual passion produces attachment (*ajjhosāna*). Attachment brings about appropriation of property (*pariggaha*) and ownership, appropriation develops into avarice (*macchariyam*), avarice manifests as the need for guarding (*ārakkha*) what has been acquired, and guarding of possessions ends in quarrel, strife, and combat (Chart 6). The commentary to the *Dīgha-nikāya* maintains that craving can be regarded from two different points of view (DA. II. 499): past experiences of craving function as a causal link in the chain of causation leading to rebirth (*vaṭṭa-mūla-bhūtā purima-taṇhā*); at the same time, craving also affects habitual behaviour or conduct (*samudācāra-taṇhā*) here and now, in this lifetime. The commentary goes on to say that when craving conditions conduct in the course of one's daily life, it does so both by motivating one's search (*esana-taṇhā*) for a desired object and by energizing one's action in holding on to what has been searched for (*esita-taṇhā*) and gained. Like *taṇhā*, *cetanā* functions in two ways. In the rounds of rebirth, *cetanā* is associated with two causal links: *saṅkhāra* and *bhava*. In the course of daily living, *cetanā* functions as a basic mental factor (*cetasika*) in every state of consciousness.

An analysis of the definitions of *cetanā* and *taṇhā* points to some clear differences between these two mental functions. At the outset, it is posited that craving, in its role of a causal link in the chain of rebirth, continues to condition the consciousness continuum (along with ignorance) as long as the factors that cause bondage to *kamma* and rebirth are present. Nevertheless, it is to be noted that in the lists of wholesome and unwholesome mental states, greed (*lobha*), which is a form of craving (*taṇhā*), occurs as a mental factor only in an unwholesome *citta* rooted in greed (Chart 8). The definitions of greed in the *Atthasālinī* (Asl. 249) and *Visuddhimagga* (Vsm. XIV. 162) state that greed swells into the river of craving and carries beings into sorrowful states of rebirth. However, wholesome *cittas* and unwholesome *cittas* rooted in aversion (*dosa*) and delusion (*moha*) do not include greed as a mental factor. The *Abhidhamma* classification of mental states implies that craving arises as a conditioning factor in a person's current conduct and lifestyle (*samudācāra-taṇhā*) only when that person is under the influence of greed. One can draw the conclusion that according to the *Abhidhamma* classification of mental states, although *taṇhā* as a causal link (*paccaya*) in the chain of rebirth operates in association with ignorance (*avijjā*) until liberating wisdom is attained, craving as a factor of daily living (*samudācāra-taṇhā*) operates only in *cittas* rooted in greed. While *samudācāra-taṇhā* can be interpreted as a mental factor that is specific to certain unwholesome *cittas*, *cetanā* is said to occur in all *cittas*: wholesome, unwholesome, those that arise as the effects (*vipāka*) of past *kamma*, and those that have no karmic effects since they are purely "functional" (*kiriya*). *Cetanā* as a neutral purposive impulse functioning in all *cittas* is clearly distinguished in the *Abhidhamma* classification of mental states from desire (*kāma*), passion (*rāga*), greed (*lobha*), and craving (*taṇhā*).

The definition of craving in the *Visuddhimagga* names feeling (*vedanā*) arising from contact with objects as the proximate cause of craving. However, the *Visuddhimagga* stresses that though feelings caused by sensory and mental stimulation condition the arising of *taṇhā*, without the operation of the persistent tendencies designated as the *anusayas*, craving will not arise (Vsm. XVII. 238). According to the definition in the *Visuddhimagga*, when pleasant feelings become vitiated by the *anusayas*, then a person clings to the object of enjoyment and ultimately suffers because the craving for the enjoyable feelings remains insatiable. By contrast, the lengthy discussion on the relationship between *cetanā* and *kamma* in the *Atthasālinī* (Asl. 84-104) shows that feelings and emotions are not considered to be the sole cause—or even the primary cause—of *cetanā*. The examples given in the *Atthasālinī* demonstrate that specific *cetanās* are conditioned in a holistic manner by the dominant features of the cognitive processes, emotions, and conative energies of the attitudes of mind (*cittas*) within which those *cetanās* arise. A sense of purpose derived from its association with the cognitive processes of a state of mind (*citta*) characterizes *cetanā*. Craving, on the contrary, is linked to feelings and emotions and is motivated by the sense of a need.

Greed and craving are regarded as factors that bind a person to the course of *kamma* and rebirth. *Cetanā*, however, is held to be a mental function that can either bind a person to *kamma* or facilitate the processes of release from *kamma* and sorrowful rebirth. It is posited in the *Suttas* that *cetanā* can be associated with four types of *kamma*. The first three types of *kamma* are described as acts that are wholesome, unwholesome, or characterized by both wholesome and unwholesome features. The *Aṅguttara-nikāya* stresses that when *cetanā* arises from a state of mind that regards the world with serene non-attachment, it becomes identified with the fourth type of *kamma* and takes the form of the intention to renounce the effects of the three previous types of *kamma* (A. II. 232). It follows that whereas craving is regarded as a factor that binds a person to the course of acts and consequences, *cetanā* can either bind or bring about release from such bondage. Because of its defining characteristic of insatiability (*atitta-bhāva*) craving is regarded as invariably unwholesome and sorrow-producing. A *cetanā* can be either wholesome or unwholesome because it participates in the wholesome or unwholesome quality of the *citta* within which it arises.

Conclusion

Unlike other *Sutta* and *Abhidhamma* terms that connote the intention to pursue a goal or the initiation of intentional action, *cetanā* refers to a more rudimentary mental state that brings about a basic quickening and goal-directed impetus of consciousness even in the most fundamental states of awareness. To be without *cetanā* is to be inanimate or dead. Moreover, *cetanā* is made distinctive by its special relationship to both the cognitive and the dynamic dimensions of the continuum of consciousness. The purposive thrust that *cetanā* brings to the knowledge-gaining processes and the emotional excitations experienced by the *citta*, and the goal-oriented impetus that *cetanā* gives to the action-initiating processes of the *saṅkhārakkhandha* can be viewed as developments arising from its basic function of stimulating consciousness and rendering the mind responsive to the environment.

When the definition of *cetanā* in the *Abhidhamma* literature is compared with the definition of *saṅkappa* (Dhs. 12), *chanda* (Vsm. XIV. 150), and *viriya* (Asl. 121), it becomes evident that the distinctive feature of *cetanā* is its basic function of giving a dynamic form to a state of mind (*citta*) and causing it to engage with the environment. *Saṅkappa*, which manifests as intention or resolve, is closely associated with discursive thought (*vitakka*); thus the definition in the *Dhammasaṅgaṇi* does not assign to *saṅkappa* the capacity to initiate action. *Saṅkappa* is purposive thought, not purposive impulse. The definitions in the *Dhammasaṅgaṇi*, the *Visuddhimagga*, and the *Atthasālinī* do not endow *viriya* and *chanda* with purposive thought and participation in the cognitive process of choosing a goal. By contrast, as the discourses on *kamma* in the *Atthasālinī* show, when *cetanā* puts forth wholesome and unwholesome *kamma*, it functions as a purposive impulse that is governed by the purposive thought or intention that arises within the cognitive and emotive factors of a specific state of consciousness.

The special relationship that *cetanā*s have to the states of consciousness (*citta*s) in which they arise is shown by the fact that *citta*s and *cetanā*s are designated similarly. For example, a *cetanā* that arises within a (*citta*) that is characterized by harshness (*citta-pharusatā*) is designated as the impetus to speak harshly (*pharusa-cetanā*), and the *cetanā* that belongs to a *citta* that is intent on stealing (*theyya-citta*) is called the impulse to steal (*theyya-cetanā*). By designating *cetanās* in accordance with the *cittas* within which they arise, the *Abhidhamma* method of classification puts forward the view that *cetanās* are motivating impulses that derive their sense of purpose from the attitude of mind in which they participate. At the same time, a *cetanā* is regarded as the basic mental factor that energizes the entire state of consciousness (*citta*) of which it is a component. Thus *cetanā* provides consciousness with the impetus for goal-oriented action. This basic function of giving dynamic impetus to the dominant attitude and purposive thought manifested in a *citta* distinguishes *cetanā* from other mental factors (*cetasikas*) such as desire to act (*chanda*) and vigour (*viriya*). According to the definition in the *Atthasālinī* (Asl. 111-112), *cetanā* functions as the "leader" and the other conative factors in the continuum of consciousness become directed towards a goal because they become linked to the purposive impulse of *cetanā*.

In the same manner, a special relationship to the *saṅkhārakkhandha* distinguishes *cetanā* from *chanda*, *viriya*, and other conative mental factors. The definitions in the *Sutta* and *Abhidhamma* literature maintain that *saṅkhāras* are constituted of *cetanās*. It is made clear in the *Abhidhamma* and commentarial texts that the *saṅkhārakkhandha* is the action-initiating, dynamic dimension of the continuum of consciousness, which assembles (*abhisaṅkharoti*) the causal conditions (*paccayas*) necessary to produce wholesome and unwholesome purposive acts that have karmic consequences. *Cetanās* are identified with goal-oriented acts that have karmic consequences since every such act is viewed as a concrete bodily, verbal, or mental manifestation of a pruposive impulse. These karmically operative acts are also designated as *saṅkhāras*, signifying that they are composed through the confluence of various mental factors. *Chanda, viriya, ārambha-dhātu,* and *saṅkappa,* came together with other mental factors and function as causal conditions to produce purposive acts that have karmic consequences. However, what factors will assemble at any moment in the continuum of consciousness and the mode of assembling are determined by the type of purpose that is contained in the purposive thrust of *cetanā*. For this reason, *cetanā* is regarded as the foremost component of the *saṅkhārakkhandha* and the fundamental motivating factor in putting forth *kamma* (*kammāyūhana*).

ENDNOTES

[1] R.M.L. Gethin, *The Buddhist Path to Awakening: A Study of the Bodhi-Pakkhiyā Dhammā*, 114-115.

[2] The *Abhidhammattha-saṅgaha* holds that *adhimokkha* is a constituent of all *cittas* except the following two: the rudimentary state of consciousness when the object is first "contacted" through one of the senses (*pañca-viññāṇa*); and the unwholesome state of consciousness rooted in delusion (*moha*) and accompanied by perplexity (*vicikicchā*) (Bhikkhu Bodhi, *A Comprehensive Manual of Abhidhamma*, 93).

[3] *Adhimuktistadālambanasya guṇato' vadharāraṇam. Rucirityanye. Yathāniṣcayam dhāraṇeti yogācāracittāḥ* (AbhkA. 1.187).

[4] The *Abhidhammattha-saṅgaha* states that *chanda* does not arise in *cittas* that do not produce the roots of wholesome and unwholesome action (*ahetuka*) and in unwholesome *cittas* that are motivated by the sole root of delusion (*momūha*). The *ahetuka-cittas* that do not carry wholesome or unwholesome roots include the *cittas* that occur in the preliminary, pre-*javana* stage of a cognitive process (*citta-vīthi*) and the purely functional (*kiriya*) *cittas* of a liberated *arahant*. In the preliminary stages of perception, the nature and characteristics of an object have not yet been fully determined. *Chanda* does not arise in the pre-*javana* stage of perception because its function is to initiate action in pursuit of an object. States of mind rooted solely in delusion (*momūha*) are marked by confusion with regard to the object and are dominated by either indecision and wavering (*vicikicchā*) or by restless agitation (*uddhacca*). *Chanda* cannot perform its function of goal-oriented action where there is confusion and indecision with regard to the object. *Cetanā*, on the other hand, arises as a constituent of pre-*javana cittas*, *cittas* rooted in *moha*, and in *kiriya cittas* (Bhikkhu Bodhi, *A Comprehensive Manual of Abhidhamma*, 93)

[5] Bhikkhu Bodhi, *A Comprehensive Manual of Abhidhamma*, 274.

[6] Gethin explains that the term *saṅkappa* is used in the Pāli texts to indicate "a clearly formed thought or idea". He agrees with those who maintain that it conveys "intention" or "purpose" in the *Suttas* and in the *Abhidhamma* (R.M.L. Gethin, *The Buddhist Path to Awakening: A Study of the Bodhi-Pakkhiyā Dhammā*, 193).

[7] The *Dhammasaṅgaṇi* gives the following definition of *saṅkappa*: *Katamo tasmiṁ samaye sammā-saṅkappo hoti? Yo tasmiṁ samaye takko vitakko saṅkappo appanā vyappanā cetaso abhiniropanā sammā-saṅkappo—ayaṁ tasmiṁ samaye sammā-saṅkappo hoti* (Dhs. 12). The definition of *vitakka* (Dhs. 10) is identical.

[8] C.A.F. Rhys Davids, *A Buddhist Manual of Psychological Ethics*, 17, n. 4.

[9] *Yo takko vitakko saṅkappo appanā vyappanā cetaso abhiniropanā . . . ayam vuccati sammā saṅkappo* (Vbh. 237).

[10] *Yaṁ kho brāhmaṇa arabbhadhātuyā sati ārabbhavanto sattā paññāyanti, ayaṁ sattānam attakāro, ayaṁ parakāro* (A. III. 338).
The Buddha points out that since there is such a factor as the capacity to initiate action, and living beings are known to possess this capacity, it follows that people have the capacity to initiate their own actions and to instigate others to act.

[11] R. M. L. Gethin, *The Buddhist Path to Awakening: A Study of the Bodhi-Pakkhiyā Dhammā*, 72-73.

[12] Bhikkhu Bodhi, *A Comprehensive Manual of Abhidhamma*, 81.

Conclusion

In the Introduction, I said that the purpose of this work was to explore whether, within the boundaries of conditioned origination, *cetanā* performs the three following functions: forming a purpose, initiating action to pursue the goal specified by that purpose, and directing action towards that goal. As a starting point for this exploration, in the Introduction "volition" was defined as a complex mental factor comprising intending, initiating action, and directing action towards the intended goal. The investigation of whether *cetanā* fulfils these three functions that constitute volition led to a delineation of the relationship that *cetanā* has to the cognitive processes of purposive reflection and to the conative dynamism that Theravāda attributes to the consciousness continuum. Further focus for the work was provided by the Buddha's definition of *kamma:* "I name *cetanā* as *kamma*; having exercised *cetanā*, one performs action through body, speech, and mind" (A. III. 415).

In the *Abhidhamma* classification of mental factors, cognitive processes are subsumed under the series of states of mind (*cittas*) that constitute the continuum of consciousness, while the processes of motivational energy, which produce purposive acts, are included in the *saṅkhārakkhandha*. The two terms *citta* and *cetanā* are related grammatically to the verb *ceteti* (to think, to intend), and *cetanās* are described as coming into existence in the form of mental factors within *cittas*. Nevertheless, both in the *Khandha-saṁyutta* (S. III. 60) and in the *Vibhaṅga* (Vbh. 144,173), it is the relationship of *cetanās* to the action-producing processes of *saṅkhāras* that is given predominance: *saṅkhāras* are defined as factors that are constituted of different kinds of *cetanās*. In this work, *saṅkhāras* are shown to include both the conditioned and conditioning processes of consciousness as well as the purposive acts of body, speech, and mind that are produced through these processes. Given the boundaries of conditioned origination, it follows that the series of states of mind (*citta*) that arise in the continuum of consciousness cannot claim an existence apart from the mental factors that constitute them. Similarly, the conditioning and compounding activities (*saṅkhāras*) in the continuum of consciousness cannot claim to possess an autonomous energy that can flourish apart from the concrete activity of composing and forming (*abhisaṅkharaṇa*) conditioned and composed acts (*saṅkhata-saṅkhāra*) of body, speech, and mind. As a consequence, the *cetanās* that constitute *saṅkhāras* cannot claim a volitional capacity that can function apart from the processes of conditioned origination that are at work in the mind and the body.

Since conditioned origination entails compatibility—if not resemblance—between causes and effects, certain patterns of similarity begin to be exhibited both within the processes of causal conditioning in the continuum of consciousness and in the series of conditioned acts that *saṅkhāras* produce by assembling causal conditions. These similarities often take the form of habits of body, patterns of speech, and mental dispositions. However, though the term *saṅkhāra/abhisaṅkhāra* often refers to an act that is habitual, this is not always the case. It is worth noting that *saṅkhāra* is not defined as habitual behaviour in the *Suttas* and in the *Abhidhamma* literature. The *Saṁyutta-nikāya* (S. III. 87) defines *saṅkhāra* in terms of its capacity to assemble the necessary conditions in such a manner as to "form" different types of "formations". These formations include both the aggregates that constitute the "person" who experiences rebirth as well as the purposive acts through which the person finds self-expression. According to this definition, the emphasis is on the compounding and conditioning activity of *saṅkhāras* (*saṅkhatam abhsaṅkharonti*). The *Visuddhimagga* (Vsm. XIV. 131-132) specifies the defining characteristic of *saṅkhāra* as the capacity of producing purposive acts through processes of conditioning and composing (*abhisaṅkharaṇa*). The basic function of *saṅkhāra* is described as the urge to produce and amass *kamma* (*āyūhana*). Neither of these definitions regards forming habit patterns or producing persisting mental dispositions as a basic characteristic of *saṅkhāras*.

While it is implicitly acknowledged that the conditioning activity of *saṅkhāras* tends to form habits, not all *saṅkhāras* are regarded as habitual acts. For this reason, it is not entirely correct to translate *saṅkhāra* as "mental disposition" or "habit formation". Furthermore, it is significant that the adjectives and phrases associated with *anusayas* and *āsavas* to indicate their persistent and habitual nature are seldom used in speaking of *saṅkhāras*. In one of the debates recorded in the *Kathāvatthu* (Kvu. 405-408), the Theravādins insist that *anusayas* are to be included under *saṅkhāras*. Nevertheless, specific qualities are assigned to *anusayas* that make them a special class of *saṅkhāras*. The *Visuddhimagga* (Vsm. XXII. 60) maintains that the distinctive characteristic of *anusayas* is their intransigence or power of resisting opposition (*thāmagata*) and their capacity to repeatedly (*punappunam*) cause unwholesome mental states to arise. *Saṅkhāras*, however, are not described as possessing the characteristic of persistence or tenacity, and their function is not defined in terms of repeatedly causing the same patterns of behaviour. It follows that when *cetanās* function as the primary constituents of *saṅkhāras*, their motivating impetus is not invariably directed towards producing habitual behaviour.

The classification of mental states in the *Dhammasaṅgaṇi*, the *Visuddhimagga*, and the *Atthasālinī* can be interpreted to demonstrate that *cetanā* functions as the link between the cognitive and emotive processes of the series of mental states (*cittas*) that constitute the continuum of consciousness and the conditioning and composing activities (*saṅkhāras*) that form the dynamic dimension of consciousness. The *Dhammasaṅgaṇi*

(Dhs.209) defines the relationship between *cittas* and the motivational dynamism of *saṅkhāras* by explaining that the feelings, perceptions, and motivational activities that constitute the *vedanākkhandha*, the *saññākkhandha*, and the *saṅkhārakkhandha* are included as indispensable components (*cetasikas*) within the continuum of *cittas*. By virtue of its two distinctive functions of coordinating (*abhisandahati*) concomitant mental states and producing (*āyūhati*) wholesome and unwholesome purposive acts, *cetanā* performs the crucial role of linking the thought processes and the range of emotions that arise within the continuum of *cittas* with the capacity of *saṅkhāras* to initiate activity in the organism. According to the *Abhidhamma* system, a *cetanā* arises as a purposive impulse in a specific state of mind and motivates action by coordinating the mind's conative capacities around this purposive core. Through the functioning of *cetanās* the conditioning and conditioned processes of the *saṅkhārakkhandha* become transformed into purposive acts characterized with moral values. *Cetanās* infuse the processes of the *saṅkhārakkhandha* with the sense of purpose and the wholesome and unwholesome moral values that arise within *cittas*. It is in this sense that *cetanā* is *kamma*.

A sense of purpose as such can remain as an intention (*saṅkappa*), a mental aspiration (*patthanā*), or a resolve (*paṇidhi*) in the mind. In *cetanā*, however, the cognitive processes of purposive thinking are integrated with the action-producing processes in the *saṅkhārakkhandha*. Although *cetanā* is often associated with *patthanā* and *paṇidhi* (for example, A. I. 32, 224, V. 212; S. II. 99, 154), it differs from them and from *saṅkappa* in two ways. First, the function of *cetanā* is regarded as more basic. In association with other basic mental factors, *cetanā* performs the function of maintaining rudimentary sentient awareness and directing the mind, in the incipient stage of perception, towards an object of interest. Second, unlike *saṅkappa*, *patthanā*, and *paṇidhi*, *cetanā* is endowed with the impetus to initiate action to attain a goal. At the same time, *cetanā* differs from *chanda* (desire to act), *viriya* (vigour), *padhāna* (putting forth effort) and other mental factors that have the capacity to motivate physical and mental action. Unlike these dynamic mental factors, *cetanā* is described as the fundamental conscious awareness that gives vitality to the organism and stirs it to rudimentary action. Thus, *cetanā* is viewed as performing a basic energizing function on which *chanda*, *viriya*, and *padhāna* base their dynamic capacities. The *Suttas* affirm the Upaniṣadic notion that to be without *cetanā* is to be dead.

Once *cetanā* develops into a full-fledged wholesome or unwholesome purposive impulse, it differs from *chanda*, *viriya* and *padhāna* because of its essential link with the purpose that dominates a state of mind (*citta*). *Cetanā* also differs from mental factors that represent purpose but do not possess the impetus to initiate action to implement that purpose. Whereas *saṅkappa*, *patthanā*, and *paṇidhi* represent specific intentions, aspirations, and resolves that arise within a *citta*, *cetanā* is the dynamic counterpart of the purpose that becomes prominent in the *citta* as a whole. It is implied that the purpose to which *cetanā* gives dynamic impetus rises to prominence in the *citta* through the mutual conditioning of the cognitive, emotive, and conative factors in a specific attitude of mind.

It is striking that in the classification of mental states provided by the *Dhammasaṅgaṇi* the *Visuddhimagga*, and the *Atthasālinī*, the very same cognitive and emotive mental factors (*cetasikas*) that constitute the wholesome and unwholesome *cittas* also constitute the motivating conditions (*paccayas*) through which the mind produces its wholesome and unwholesome activities (*saṅkhāras*). On the basis of these lists, the purposive impulse provided by *cetanā* can be interpreted as the key factor through which the cognitive and emotive components (*cetasikas*) of a state of mind (*citta*) begin to function as configurations of causal conditions that put forth purposive acts of body, speech and mind. When a *cetanā* arises as a wholesome purposive impulse in a wholesome attitude of mind, for example, it links (*abhisandahati*) concomitant cognitive and emotive factors to its own wholesome function. As a result of interacting with the wholesome purposive thrust of *cetanā*, the cognitive factors in a wholesome *citta*, such as initial application of thought (*vitakka*), sustained thought (*vicāra*), concentration on an object (*samādhi*), and mindfulness (*sati*) become goal-oriented conditions for the initiation of wholesome action. At the same time, the purposive impetus of *cetanā* intensifies and directs the motivating capacity of the emotive components of the wholesome roots of action. Through this purposive impetus, non-greed, non-hate, and non-delusion become motivating conditions for generosity, goodwill, and understanding. Likewise, the emotive features of joyful interest in the object (*pīti*), which is a component of a wholesome *citta*, and mental factors such as flexibility (*mudutā*) and proficiency (*pāguññatā*), which endow a wholesome *citta* with skilful ease in functioning, become strong motivating forces through the energy of purpose provided by *cetanā*.

Since *cetanās* are related to knowledge-seeking processes of *cittas*, as well as to the habit-forming processes of *saṅkhāras*, purposive impulses are shaped by two modes of functioning in the continuum of consciousness. As a causal condition (*paccaya*) in the conditioning and conditioned processes of *saṅkhāras*, the motivating capacity of *cetanās* becomes limited by habit formations. However, the habit-making activities of *saṅkhāras* are continually modified by the cognitive processes and emotions that prevail in the *cittas*. The continuum of consciousness that is constituted of the series of states of mind (*cittas*) is constantly receiving, and responding to, fresh sensory and mental stimulations. The narrow and repetitive habit-forming activities of the mind are challenged by the mind's capacity to vastly vary its emotional responses and its thought processes without overstepping the boundaries of conditioned origination. The purposive impulses or motivating intentions manifested by *cetanās* can be interpreted as the focal points where habitual acts interact with the thoughts and emotions arising in the series of states of mind that constitute the consciousness continuum. The forming and implementing of a purpose provides an opportunity when and the mind's capacity for variegations can influence its habit-forming activities. For example, when *cetanā* arises in a wholesome *citta* its motivating impulsion is influenced by such undistorted and liberating cognitive processes as systematic attention (*yoniso-manasikāra*), mindfulness (*sati*), and wise understanding (*paññā*). Similarly, within a wholesome *citta*, a purposive impulse becomes imbued with wholesome emotions such as non-greed and non-hate. When wholesome purposive impulses carry these wholesome influences into the conditioning processes of the *saṅkhārakkhandha*, the hold that habits have on the body and mind begin to loosen. On the other hand, the purposive impulses of *cetanās* provide the opportunities for the habit-forming characteristics of the *saṅkhārakkhandha* to exert their wholesome or unwholesome influences on the thoughts and emotions that arise within *cittas*. Wholesome habits of body and speech, for example, aid the development of mindfulness and wisdom.

The definitions of *cetanā* found in the *Visuddhimagga* (Vsm. XVII. 135) and the *Atthasālinī* (Asl. 111-112), and the description of the "cognitive series" (*citta-vīthi*) through which perception takes place (Vsm. XIV. 115-122; Asl. 270-272), make it evident that the mode of functioning of a *cetanā* was not regarded as uniform in all *cittas*. On the contrary, it is posited that the manner in which *cetanā* functions differs according to the dominant characteristics of the state of mind within which it arises. In every state of mind, *cetanā* is present as a factor of basic sentience and invariably functions as the capacity that stimulates and vitalizes the organism and stirs the mind to action. The close link between vitality and consciousness awareness that is posited both in the Upaniṣadic tradition and in the *Suttas* becomes apparent in the functioning of *cetanā*. In the preliminary stages of perception when the mind is guided by the qualities of the object and its own habitual reactions, *cetanā* functions, not as a fully developed purpose or intention, but as the mental factor that coordinates and energizes concomitant mental states and inclines the mind towards the object. However, in the advanced stage of perception (*javana*), when the mind begins to respond to the object with wholesome or unwholesome attitudes, *cetanā* assumes the role of a full-fledged purposive impulse and instigates goal-oriented acts (*kamma*) of body, speech, and mind in relation to the object. Moreover, when *cetanās* are conditioned by obdurate, habit-forming mental corruptions (*āsavas*) and by persistent unwholesome tendencies (*anusayas*), they take the form of purposive impulses that become "food" (*āhāra*) for the processes of rebirth. Under the influence of the *āsavas*, *cetanā* functions as *kamma-bhava* and prolongs the process of rebirth by providing the continuum of consciousness with newer goals and more exciting purposes.

Furthermore, Theravāda maintains that virtuous states of mind carrying wholesome *cetanās* can arise as factors of "mundane virtue" (*lokiya-sīla*) in ordinary folk, even though the mental corruptions (*āsavas*) and the persistent unwholesome proclivities (*anusayas*) have not been eradicated from their minds. As factors of mundane virtue, *cetanās* perform a twofold function: they provide the wholesome motivating impetus for acts of merit that entail a happy rebirth; simultaneously, under the good influence of virtuous states of mind, they provide momentum, urging the mind towards the Eightfold Path that leads to liberation from rebirth (Vsm. I. 32). When the mind turns towards the Eightfold Path, *cetanā* arises as the purposive impulse that pertains to the Path (*magga-cetanā*). In this role *cetanā* manifests as the "fourth type of *kamma*", which renounces the processes and the fruits of *kamma*. *Cetanās* of the Path come into existence as motivating factors within wholesome *cittas*. These *cetanās* are pervaded by energy, wise understanding, and serenity that arise through the cultivation of the eight factors of the Path and the seven factors of wisdom (*bojjhaṅga*) (A. II. 236-237). Finally, in the minds of liberated *arahants*, *cetanās* arise not as goal-oriented intentions that carry karmic consequences but as factors of conative dynamism that simply fulfil a present beneficent function (*kiriya-cetanā*).

In all these modes of functioning, *cetanā* exhibits its two distinctive characteristics: it becomes imbued with the attitude and the dominant features of the state of mind within which it arises, and it also engages in coordinating concomitant mental states and directing their energies towards acts of body, speech, and mind. *Cetanā*, therefore, functions as a factor of basic sentience that stirs the organism to turn to objects of interest in the environment, as the purposive impulse that becomes concretely manifest in wholesome and unwholesome acts, as a nutriment for the prolongation of life and rebirth, as the liberating impetus that facilitates entry into the Eightfold Path, and as the purely functional conative dynamism that enables as *arahant* to act without karmic consequences.

The concept of *cetanā* as purposive impulse that directs action towards an intended goal is illustrated in the *Puggala-paññatti*. This *Abhidhamma* text is based on the Theravāda view that the term "person" (*puggala*) does not indicate an existent individual but functions as a mere concept (*paññatti*) or conventional designation. The purpose of this text is to classify "persons" into different types according to their qualities and capacities, so that they represent different stages of progress in the Eightfold Path. One type of *puggala* is described as a person who becomes able to attain and sustain states of meditation through the exercise of *cetanā* (*cetanā-bhabbo*). The person who gains competence in the practice of meditation through the exercise of *cetanā* is distinguished from two other types of persons: the type who arrives at *jhāna* states with much difficulty only to lose these attainments through lack of mindfulness (*parihāna-dhammo*); and the type who is enabled through the cultivation of virtue and wisdom to enter *jhāna* states effortlessly and to abide in them securely (*Puggala-paññatti*, 11-12). In this context, the former type of person is not able to form a firm purpose with a strong impetus to act, and the latter type of person has attained a stage where the impulsion of a motivating intention is no longer necessary. This passage of the *Puggala-paññatti* can be interpreted to mean that the type of "person" called "enabled by *cetanā*" gains the ability to practice calming meditation and mindfulness through the functioning of a strong purposive impulse. The concept of *cetanā-bhabbo* in the *Puggala-paññatti* is significant because it shows that though *cetanā* arises within a *citta,* and is conditioned by concomitant mental factors, it also profoundly influences the series of *citta*s that constitute the continuum of consciousness. A strong *cetanā* empowers a series of *citta*s to move towards a chosen goal.

It follows that *cetanā* can be called "volition" in accordance with the definition of volition put forward in the Introduction because it performs the combined functions of intending, initiating action, and directing action towards the fulfilment of the intention. However, since the capacities and the mode of functioning of *cetanā* are governed by conditioned origination, *cetanā* cannot function as "will" in the sense of an autonomous, controlling power. In this context, it is significant that the early Jainas categorized the teaching of the Buddha as a form of *akriyāvāda* (doctrine of non-action). Jacobi explains that the early Jainas defined *kriyāvāda* as the view that affirms the self to be both the agent of action and the recipient of the fruits of ethically good and bad acts.[1] Since there is no room in Buddhism for an autonomous self with inherent powers of agency and control, the early Jainas regarded the Buddha's teachings as a doctrine of non-action. In Chapter II it was shown that the Jainas attribute to the self an energy (*vīrya*) that is the ultimate source of all the capacities and functions that operate in the body and mind, including the capacity to know and be aware.[2] In *Harmless Souls,* Johnson interprets the Jaina concept of *vīrya* as the "will" that enables the soul within to express in action its own nature of consciousness (*caitanya*) and bliss (*sukha*).[3] In the Buddha's time the early Jainas arrived at the same conclusion that C.A.F. Rhys Davids reached at the end of the nineteenth century: Buddhism cannot have an adequate concept of "will" and agency, since "will" presupposes the self as "willer".

In his response to the view that Buddhism lacks an adequate concept of will, Kalupahana maintains that in Buddhism the "dispositions" (*saṅkhāras*) are at the basis of all decision-making functions.[4] He argues that in the *Suttas*, the decision to perform a goal-directed act involves two factors: "volition" (*cetanā*), which represents the immediate decision to act; and the "character" of a person, which has been gradually shaped over a period of time by dispositions or habits of mind. Kalupahana is quick to add that the dispositions themselves are generated by acts that proceed from "volitions" (*cetanā/sañcetanā*). In his work *The Principles of Buddhist Psychology*, Kalupahana focuses on what he calls the function of "selectivity" performed by mental dispositions (*saṅkhāras*) in the processes of perception.[5] The thrust of his argument is that due to the conditioning of the mind by the dispositions, consciousness selects objects that it finds to be of "interest". According to Kalupahana's interpretation, Buddhism maintains that the ability of a human person to "choose, think, and act" arises from this "selectivity in consciousness".

Kalupahana interprets *cetanā* to be the volition or immediate decision to act that is conditioned by the "mental dispositions" that have been formed over a period of time. His interpretation of *cetanā* is not satisfactory for at least two reasons: whereas he emphasizes the conditioning influence of *saṅkharas* on the formation of *cetanās*, he does not take note of the passages in the *Suttas* and the *Abhidhamma* texts that describe the influence of thought processes and emotions on the formation of *sañcetanika-kammas* (purposive acts). Moreover, he does not explain how habit-based mental dispositions, which function strictly within processes of conditioning, can effect transformations in the personality. Kalupahana does not take into account that in the *Suttas* and the *Abhidhamma*, the function of *cetanā* is inseparably connected, not only to the conditioned and conditioning process of the *saṅkhāras*, but also to the processes of intellection, discernment, and reflection that arise in the states of mind (*cittas*) that constitute the continuum of consciousness. While the principle of conditioned origination precludes the notion of a sovereign autonomous will, it would be incorrect to say that in Theravāda the mental function of making decisions is explained solely in terms of mental dispositions or habits of thought.

The *Karajakāya-vagga* of the *Aṅguttara-nikāya* (A. V. 292-297) demonstrates the *Sutta* view that a decision to act is influenced both by the conditioning processes of *saṅkhāras* and also by the processes of discursive thought and ethically wholesome or unwholesome emotions that constitute an attitude of mind (*citta*) Whereas the term *cetanā* does not occur in the *Karajakāya-vagga*, the wholesome and unwholesome acts are designated as acts motivated by *sañcetanā* (*sañcetanika-kammas*). The relationship between attitude and act is illustrated, for example, in the case of a person who does not injure living beings. Such a person is described in the *Karajakāya-vagga* as one who feels compassion towards all that lives and breathes. Since this person is described as habitually compassionate, the influence of the habit-forming *saṅkhāras* is clearly implied. Nevertheless, a difference is maintained in the *Suttas* and the *Abhidhamma* between the cognitive and emotive features of the *citta* and the conditioning activities of the *saṅkhārakkhandha*. The compassionate state of mind is not reduced to mental habits conditioned by past experiences. The *Suttas*, the *Atthasālinī*, and the *Visuddhimagga* emphasize that wholesome attitudes need to be sustained by systematic attention, mindful awareness, and continual exercise of wisdom. A reciprocal relationship is posited between attitude of mind (*citta*) and intentional act (*sañcetanika-kamma*): a wholesome or unwholesome attitude supports and motivates a corresponding act by endowing it with a purpose, and the act gives concrete expression to the thought, emotion, and purpose that are distinctive to the attitude of mind.

In the *Vinaya-piṭaka* (Vin. III. 73), the close correlation between a state of mind (*citta*) and the purposive thought that expresses the dominant cognitive processes and distinctive emotive features of that state of mind is indicated by the phrase *iti-citta-mano*, which Horner translates: "As the mind so the thought".[6] This phrase is put forward to explain the deliberate offence committed by a monk who incites a lay follower to commit suicide by describing life after death as a far happier state than life on earth. The offence is said to be deliberately committed because the state of mind (*citta*) of the monk who commits the offence and his purposive thought or intention (*mana*) correspond to each other: both the state of mind and the purposive thought are focused on causing death. Horner quotes the commentary to the *Vinaya-piṭaka*, where it is emphasized that in the case of a deliberate act, there is no disparity whatsoever between the mind-set or state of mind (*citta*) of a person and that person's purposive thought or intention. According to this explanation, the deliberate act (*sampajāna-kamma*) reflects the purposive thought, and the purposive thought or intention reflects the state of mind or mind-set. The commentary goes on to say that the two are as one and that the purposive thought expresses the state of mind.[7] Conversely, it is implied that no such match between a specific state of mind and a purposive thought or intention can be shown in the case of an act that is done without attention or without sufficient knowledge of the act and its probable consequences (*asampajāna-kamma*).

The *Vinaya* view, therefore, maintains that unlike an unintentional act, every deliberate act (*sampajāna-kamma*) arises from a thought that has its basis in a specific state of mind or mind-set. This view is reiterated and further developed in the *Visuddhimagga*, the *Atthasālinī*, and the commentaries to the *Suttas*. The *Atthasālinī* makes a purposive impulse (*cetanā*) identical with a wholesome or unwholesome act (*kamma*) by defining such an act as the very expression or concrete manifestation of a purposive impulse (Asl. 84, 87, 88). In the definitions of bodily, verbal, and mental *kamma*, the *Atthasālinī* deliberately avoids the sentence structure in the Buddha's definition of *kamma* (A. III. 415). In the second part of this definition, it is stated that "having exercised *cetanā* (*cetayitvā*), one performs action (*kamma*) through the body, speech or mind". Here, the gerund *cetayitvā* could be interpreted to signify that *cetanā* precedes *kamma*, and that *kamma* can be separated from *cetanā* since it comes into existence as the consequence of *cetanā*. Instead, in the definition of bodily *kamma*, for example, the *Atthasālinī* makes it clear that the very purposive impulse (*yā cetanā*) through which (*yāya*) one performs unwholesome bodily acts or refrains from doing so is identical with the act performed by the body (*idaṁ kāya-kammaṁ nāma*). The definitions of *kamma* of body, speech, and mind in the *Atthasālinī* leave no doubt that attitude of mind, purposive impulse, and goal-oriented act form a single integral whole which serves as the basis of ethical values and produces commensurate consequences. In another context, the *Atthasālinī* (Asl. 63-64) portrays the continuum of consciousness (*citta*) as the artist (*citta-kāra*) and the intentional act (*kamma*) as the work of art (*citta/citra*) that expresses the mind of the artist.

Surprisingly, there is no sustained discussion of how memory occurs in the *Dhammasaṅgaṇi*, the *Visuddhimagga*, the *Atthasālinī*, or the *Abhidhammattha-saṅgaha*. However, the analysis of *saṅkhāra* in these texts suggests the following conclusions regarding the nature of memory. Both the past experience that is remembered and the remembrance of it are composite and conditioned events (*saṅkhāras*), and the act of remembering arises in the consciousness continuum in accordance with conditioned origination. The account of the relationship between causal condition and conditioned effect presented in the *Visuddhimagga* (Vsm. XVII. 173-174) can be extended to explain processes of memory. Buddhaghosa maintains that given conditioned origination, there is no need for a third factor to link cause and effect: although the cause has passed away, the effect follows in due course. According to this interpretation of the theory of conditioned origination, when a remembered event functions as the cause, no third factor—such as a residual "impression" of the event in the mind—is required to link the remembered event and the moment of remembering. When the causal conditions are present, the effect follows in due course, taking the form of a memory of the event. However, the act of remembering is conditioned, not only by the attitude of the subject at the time of remembering, but also by the environment in which the remembering occurs. What is remembered cannot be compared to a photograph of the original, and the act of remembering is not like the retrieval of an unchanged photograph. Furthermore, the notion that the body itself is "past *kamma*" (*purāṇa kamma*) suggests that the body is regarded as the living evidence of vast processes of past conditioning, most of which are forgotten. The act of remembering can be seen as a psychophysical *saṅkhāra*, a composite and conditioned event in which physical and mental processes are combined. Every habitual act is a remembering and a recapitulation, in which body and mind participate.

Given conditioned origination, it follows that living and remembering overlap. Every conditioned, goal-oriented act (*saṅkhāra/abhisaṅkhāra*) of body, speech, and mind is a remembrance of the past and an anticipation of the future. When these processes of conditioning that link the present to the past and to the future are consciously experienced, remembering occurs. *Cetanā*, in its role of intention imbued with capacity to act, has an important role in the processes of memory. Every intention is a response to past experiences and an anticipation of a future time when the intention will become an actuality. Recollections of the past, often encoded in habits of body, speech, and mind, are integral to the formation of *cetanās*.

While upholding conditioned origination as their central principle, Theravādins affirm that it is possible to cleanse, train, and transform the mind, and they reject those forms of determinism that they regard as inimical to the idea that liberation from sorrow can be achieved. They oppose the *Sāṁkhya* view that the effect is already potentially present in the cause, regarding this view as a form of determinism that discourages a person from striving to establish the conditions that will bring enlightenment and freedom from suffering. At the outset, the Buddha rejects the idea that present experiences are determined totally by past deeds (*pubbe-kata-hetu*) on the practical grounds that such determinism leads to attitudes of mind where there is neither the impetus to act (*chanda*), nor striving (*vāyāma*), nor the sense that one should perform certain deeds and refrain from other deeds (A. I. 173). It is implied here that intentions and purposive impulses (*cetanās*) arise out of the interaction between influences from the past and fresh stimulations from present experiences. The verses of the *Theragāthā* and *Therīgāthā* show that present experiences of joy and sorrow, the presence or absence of a beneficent friend (*kalyāṇa-mitta*), and training in virtue (*sīla*) or the lack of it are considered to be crucial present factors that interact with past experiences in shaping the intentions (*cetanā*), aspirations (*patthanā*), and resolves (*paṇidhi*) that guide the course of one's life.

Theravāda also rejects the view that thought processes and behaviour are totally determined by latent tendencies in the mind. Chapters III and IV show that it is difficult to find passages in the *Suttas* and the *Abhidhamma* texts to substantiate the idea of "unconscious motivation". Padmasiri de Silva is one of the modern interpreters of Theravāda who maintain that *anusayas* and *āsavas* are latent tendencies in the sense that they can act upon the mind without the mind being aware of their motivating influence. The debates in the *Kathāvatthu* show that Theravādins did not always find it easy to explain how *anusayas* and *āsavas* can repeatedly and obsessively influence the continuum of consciousness (Kvu. 405-408) Even so, they reject the view that *anusayas* and *āsavas* somehow remain latent and intact in the midst of changing mental processes. As this debate about the nature and function of *anusayas* continues among modern scholars of Theravāda, Johansson, for example, acknowledges that there are some passages in the *Suttas* (especially in the *Mahāmāluṅkya-sutta*) that seem to regard *anusayas* as factors that remain dormant in the mind till the conditions are appropriate for them to be activated (M. I. 433-437). However, Johansson makes a strong case for the position that there is no evidence in the *Suttas* that *anusayas* were considered to be capable of initiating unwholesome behaviour while they remained in the mind in a latent state. Johansson argues that there is no passage in the *Suttas* that unambiguously asserts that *anusayas* can operate on the mind without the mind being aware of their presence in the consciousness continuum.[8]

One can find support for Johansson's interpretation of *anusayas* in the *Satipaṭṭhāna-sutta* (D. II. 290-315; M. I. 55-63). The instructions for the practice of mindfulness do not demonstrate a concern to discover and dismantle hidden sources of motivation. The discipline of mindfully observing mental processes does include giving careful attention to processes of conditioning present in the mind. However, no attempt is made to causally connect a particular mental syndrome pertaining to the present with a specific event in the past. In the *Satipaṭṭhāna-sutta*, mindfulness (*sati*) is interpreted as "bearing in mind" what is currently occurring and not allowing the present to go unheeded. Mindfulness is never interpreted as the practice of delving into the past or seeking to uncover motivating factors of which the mind is not conscious.

Another fonn of determinism that Theravāda rejects is the view that wholesome mental states that pertain to the Eightfold Path cannot arise in a mind that is beset with *anusayas* and *āsavas*. The description of the factors of the Path given in the *Mahācattārīsaka-sutta* of the *Majjhima-nikāya* (M. III. 72-73), for example, upholds the view which maintains that even an ordinary person bound to ignorance (*avijjā*) and afflicted by the *āsavas* can begin to practice the disciplines of the Eightfold Path. According to the teaching given in this *sutta*, five factors of the Eightfold Path, namely, right view, right intention, right speech, right action and right livelihood, in fact, are cultivated by people in two ways: *sāsava* and *anāsava*. A *sāsava* mode of cultivating these factors of the Path is considered to be the characteristic of those who are still bound by aspirations for karmic merit and a happy rebirth. Those whose only aspiration is to cultivate the Path and to be established in it are regarded as those who practise an *anāsava* mode of training the mind. The *Mahācattārīsaka-sutta* goes on to say that the cultivation of right view, right effort, and right mindfulness will lead to the right way of cultivating the Eightfold Path. This *sutta* can be interpreted to mean that right view, right effort, and right mindfulness will guide those who are striving to follow the Path. It is affirmed that by cultivating these disciplines, they will gradually go from a deluded, self-serving *āsava*-ridden manner of cultivating the factors of the Path to freedom from the *āsavas* .

A similar approach to the cultivation of the Path of liberation is found in a brief, but significant, passage of the *Visuddhimagga* (Vsm. I. 32). Here a distinction is made in between "mundane" virtue (*lokiya-sīla*) and "supramundane" virtue (*lokuttara-sīla*). It is stated that whereas "mundane" virtue still keeps a person bound to the processes of *kamma* and can only lead to a happier state of rebirth, "supramundane" virtue (*lokuttara-sīla*) can bring release from the bonds of *kamma* and the sorrow of rebirth. It is implied here that those who practice mundane virtue do so with the hope of acquiring benefits in the present life and a happy rebirth in the future. Though the *Visuddhimagga* makes this distinction between mundane and supramundane virtue, it does not posit a rift between them. Mundane virtue is taken to be a preparation and pre-requisite or necessary condition (*sambhāra*) for complete liberation from ignorance and rebirth. The implication is that most *āsava*-ridden ordinary folk need mundane virtue as a stepping-stone to the cultivation of supramundane virtue.

The question still remains how transformations can be effected within conscious processes if there is no agent to choose what is to be transformed or decide upon the direction in which changes should proceed. There are several passages in the *Suttas*, especially in the poems of the *Theragāthā* and the *Therīgāthā*, which describe the processes by which tensions are resolved and changes are effected in the continuum of consciousness. These descriptions sometimes suggest that when consciousness functions as an organic whole, it can subdue and alter those of its constituents that cause tension and conflict. However, given conditioned origination, it follows that the whole and its constituents condition each other, and the whole cannot claim the status of a sovereign controller. When it functions as an organic whole, the *citta* does not acquire a controlling energy (*śakti*) that it can exert over the cognitive processes, emotions, and conative energies of which it is formed. Any transformation in the continuum of consciousness, therefore, must take place either through adjustments in the mutual conditioning among the parts that constitute the whole or between the whole and its parts. The phrase "the mind should be subjugated by the mind" (*cetasā cittaṁ abhiniggaṇhitabbam*) does not mean that the continuum of consciousness develops into a "willer" possessing "will power" by which it can control its processes. Theravāda does not put forward a form of self-determinism according to which the mind has the autonomous capacity to control and determine its own processes. It is the trained and guarded mind that is regarded as capable of assessing and transforming its processes. The training itself is seen as a process of wholesome conditioning involving changes in one's entire way of life (S. IV. 70; A. III. 6). Given conditioned origination, it is implicit that the transformation does not follow from the training, but coincides with it. Every moment of the training conditions the next, and every physical or mental factor (*dhamma*) that is transformed widens the network of transformations. According to the *Suttas* and the *Abhidhamma*, that is the way of nature (*dhammatā*).

From a psychological perspective, the *Saṁyutta-nikāya* (S. IV. 251, 261) defines *nibbāna* as complete liberation from the three unwholesome roots of action: greed (*lobha/rāga*), hatred (*dosa*), and delusion (*moha*). Throughout the *Suttas* and the *Abhidhamma* literature, there is the strong affirmation that non-greed, non-hatred, and non-delusion can function as wholesome roots of action and generate wholesome *cittas* in a continuum of consciousness that is still conditioned by the corrupting influence of the *āsavas* and the obsessive urges of the *anusayas*. The *Atthasālinī* (Asl. 127-129) describes how non-greed inhibits covetousness, encourages generosity and opens the mind to the impermanence (*anicca*) of all physical and mental states; non-hate renders friendship (*mettā*) possible and makes a person see the sorrow (*dukkha*) of others; and non-delusion prepares the way for the cultivation of mindfulness (*bhāvanā*) and brings insight into the absence of permanent and autonomous selfhood (*anattā*) in conditioned physical and mental states. This statement of encouragement in the *Atthasālinī* maintains that though *cittas* of greed, hatred, and delusion do arise even when one is practising generosity, friendship, and mindfulness, faithful practise can lead gradually to the cessation of the corrupting influence of the *āsavas* and, finally, to the total absence in the mind of greed, hatred, and delusion. It is implied here that virtue (*sīla*) and wisdom (*paññā*) support each other, so that generosity, friendship, and mindfulness can gradually open the way for total absence of greed, hatred, and delusion. This statement in the

Atthasālinī affirms what is implied in the motivational sequences in the *Suttas*: development towards the goal is gradual and cumulative. The continuum of consciousness grows towards the purity and wisdom of an *arahant*, neither by the exertion of a sovereign will nor by the guidance of a faculty of reason that can control all aspects of consciousness. Freedom from sorrow is attained though a process of gradual training wherein ethical virtue, the cultivation of the mind through meditation and mindfulness, and the development of wisdom mutually condition and buttress each other.

It is a basic *Abhidhamma* tenet that wholesome (*kusala*) mental states are never conjoined with mental displeasure and discomfort. Moreover, among the components of wholesome *cittas* are included mental factors that manifest as tranquillity (*passaddhi*), buoyancy (*lahutā*), and flexibility (*mudutā*). Thus, wholesome *cittas* are regarded as combining a joyous state of mental health with moral goodness. Many unwholesome *cittas*, by contrast with wholesome states of mind, are associated with uneasy restlessness and agitation (*uddhacca*) in the *Abhidhamma* classification of mental states. *Cittas* rooted in hate (*dosa*) constitute the only type of state of mind that is classified as invariably associated with mental displeasure and lack of ease (*domanassa*). The significance of the *Abhidhamma* view that wholesome mental states are never associated with an unhappy frame of mind can be seen when this view is juxtaposed with a statement in the *Dhammapada* which points out that all beings aspire for happiness, preservation of life, and freedom from fear (Dhp. 129-132). The *Dhammapada* goes on to say that taking one's own desire for freedom from pain as an example of the aspiration for happiness in all beings, one should never cause pain to others. The classification of mental states in the *Abhidhamma* implies that wholesome *cittas* are never conjoined with mental displeasure because the mental factors that constitute them and the purposive impulses that emerge from them are in harmony with the natural inclination of all beings for happiness.

The idea that mental states of hate are invariably associated with restlessness and mental displeasure can be interpreted to signify that *cittas* and *cetanās* rooted in hate go against the aspiration of all beings for mental ease and freedom from pain.

Bhikkhu Bodhi explains that the functional *cittas* of an *arahant* resemble the wholesome *citta* of those ordinary people who are motivated by non-greed, non-hate, and non-delusion.[9] These wholesome roots are manifested in those who are not *arahants* as the wholesome mental *kamma* of generosity based on non-covetousness (*anabhijjhā*), goodwill based on non-hate (*avyāpāda*), and right view rooted in non-delusion (Asl. 104). The difference is that whereas the wholesome mental states of ordinary people are directed towards presents benefits and future goals, the beneficent mind of an *arahant* is entirely free from the desire for results and is entirely at ease. The functional conative impulses (*kiriya-cetanās*) in functional states of mind (*kiriya-cittas*) merely perform their function (*kiriya*) of coordinating (*saṁvidahana*) the energies and operations of concomitant states by directing them to appropriate objects. In wholesome and unwholesome states of mind *cetanās* function as purposive impulses that put forth effort (*āyūhana*) in producing acts of body, speech, and mind. *Kiriya-cetanās*, however, are free of any form of straining (*anāyūhana*). Unlike the *cetanās* of ordinary people (*puthujjana*), the *kiriya-cetanās* of an *arahant* are not directed toward objects of interest and goals that one hopes to attain. The *kiriya-cittas* and *cetanās* of an *arahant*, therefore, are unsupported (*appatiṭṭham*) by objects of interest, goals, plans, and projects. The beneficent acts of an *arahant* cannot be designated as *saṅkhāras* because they are not governed by purposes. It is in this sense that *saṅkhāras* are calmed and brought to cessation (M. I. 167, 436; Sn. 731).

From those passages in the *Suttas*, the *Abhidhamma* texts and the commentarial literature that define and describe the *citta* and its components, the conclusion can be drawn that according to Theravāda, the continuum of consciousness is able to liberate itself from unwholesome roots of action, obdurate underlying tendencies (*anusayas*), and long-lasting mental corruptions (*āsavas*) because of its two unique capacities: the capacity for variegation and the capacity for self-awareness. The capacity of the *citta* to "colour" itself variously by varying its responses to a variety of external influences and internal tensions is compared to the skill of a master artist. The "colours" of the *citta* are its seemingly endless variety of thoughts, purposes, emotions, and motivations, and the dramatic scenes that it portrays are its experiences in the various realms of rebirth (S. III. 151; Asl. 63-64). This capacity for variegation implies that the continuum of consciousness does not merely react to situations, but is capable of responding creatively by varying the patterns of mutual conditioning among the factors that constitute the mind. The *Madhupiṇḍika-sutta* (M. I. 109-110) describes how this capacity in the mind to multiply and vary mental factors produces perceptions and ideas conditioned by conceptual proliferation (*papañca-saññā-saṅkhā*), which results in sorrow for the individual and conflict among peoples. The imagery of the artist is found also in a passage of the *Saṁyutta-nikāya* (S. II. 98-102) that contains a description of how the four "nutriments" keep the continuum of consciousness bound to the wheel of rebirth. This passage says that just as an artist can create various portraits if paints and a proper surface are available, so also, if there is passion for the four nutriments, if a person delights in them and craves for them, then the processes of *kamma* are prolonged and rebirth becomes inevitable. In this passage, *kamma* is the artist and the various paintings portray the fruitions of *kamma* that are ultimately sorrowful.

In all these passages, the image of the artist and the mind's capacity for variegation are associated with multiplication of desires, sorrow, conflict, and the prolongation of bondage to *kamma*. Nevertheless, one could make the argument that this same capacity for variegation can free the mind from bondage to habits and open the way for fresh influences to act upon consciousness. Throughout the *Suttas*, experiences of life, especially experiences of sorrow, are seen as opportunities for the mind to rethink and re-evaluate its own development. This capacity for diversity makes it possible for the continuum of consciousness to vary its purposive impulses (*cetanās*) and its goal-oriented projects (*saṅkhāras*). The artist-like flexibility of the *citta*, therefore, can be seen as the factor that counteracts the tendency of *saṅkhāras* to manifest as habits. If the mind did not have the capacity to vary its thoughts, emotions, and responses to diverse situations, it would be bound to the habits formed by the conditioning processes of the *saṅkhāras* and would not be able to gain wisdom from its experiences. This concept of the *citta* as a master artist capable of richly varied responses to changing conditions makes it possible for Theravāda to affirm that transformations can occur in the continuum of consciousness, without violating its central principle of conditioned origination.

Theravāda offers the techniques of mindfulness (*satipaṭṭhāna*) and insight (*vipassanā*) as the methods by which the mind can liberate itself from greed, hatred, and delusion. These disciplines are based on the affirmation that the mind has the capacity of reflecting (*paccavekkhaṇa*) on its own contents. This reflexive awareness does not prevent processes of conditioning from occurring in the mind, but it does make the mind aware of how the networks of conditioning are formed. *Saṅkhāras* continue to produce fresh configurations of conditioning factors, but the *cittas* that constitute the continuum of consciousness become aware of how these configurations follow each other and form dynamic processes. Moreover, according to Theravāda, through the capacity of reflexive awareness, the continuum of consciousness becomes directly aware that the configurations (*saṅkhāras*) of mental states are impermanent (*anicca*), that they have no claim to autonomous selfhood (*anattā*), and that they are liable to cause sorrow (*dukkha*). The techniques of *vipassanā* are based on the principle that unwholesome purposive impulses (*cetanās*) marked by greed, hatred, and delusion can gradually be brought to cessation through the wholesome conditioning influence of these insights.

It follows, therefore, that Theravāda views the mind's capacity for reflexive awareness, not as a device by which processes of conditioning can be inhibited, but as a powerful influence that can begin to condition and transform all the processes of the continuum of consciousness. The idea that cognitive processes (*javanas*) can be "reversed" is based on the affirmation that the capacity to see into its own processes can influence and change the way the mind responds to objects. Through the practice of mindfulness, *javana* processes motivated by purposive impulses (*cetanās*) that desire to possess an object can gradually be "reversed", so that the mind puts forth *javana* processes based on joyful appreciation of the object. This "reversal" is possible because consciousness has the capacity not only to review and its contents, but also to vary its responses to objects.

A constantly recurring theme throughout this work has been the integral unity of an attitude of mind (*citta*), the purposive impulse (*cetanā*) that arises within the attitude of mind and the act (*kamma*) that "actualizes" the purposive impulse. *Cetanā* cannot act on its own since its function is to bring to concrete realization the contents of an attitude of mind. Changes in behaviour cannot occur without changes in the contents of the series of *cittas* that constitute the continuum of consciousness. The thrust of the argument in the Pāli texts is that a strong volition neither arises nor becomes effective unless it is supported by a mind-set and a lifestyle. At the same time, the impact of volition on attitudes of mind is emphasized throughout the texts. *Cetanā* plays a dual role by functioning as nutriment within the process of *kamma* and as empowerment within the disciplines of the Eightfold Path. One is enabled by *cetanā* (*cetanā-bhabbo*) to cultivate the factors of the Path.

In the final analysis, however, the dynamic impetus of *cetanā* is not regarded as intrinsic to itself or to the purpose that it contains. It is posited that acts of body, speech, and mind can arise through the confluence of causes and conditions within the natural process of conditioned origination, whether or not *cetanā* operates as a wholesome or unwholesome purposive impetus. Through the momentum of conditioned origination, wholesome and unwholesome attitudes of mind can become concretely realized in corresponding acts, as naturally as eggs hatch and trees bear fruit (M. I. 301-302; S. III. 153-154). The training of the Eightfold Path utilizes the dynamism of conditioned origination.

The *Aṅguttara-nikāya* (A. V. 2-3) declares that when a sequence of wholesome mental states begins to occur in the Eightfold Path, there is no need for special interventions of *cetanā* to "pull" the mind from one stage to the next. Purposive impulses, goal-oriented thoughts, and determinations become redundant. The mind's need to strain for achievements begins to cease. It is affirmed that the wholesome stages that gradually change all aspects of one's life will follow naturally, from one to the other, in accordance with conditioned origination. At the beginning of this work, reference was made to a verse of the *Dhammapada* (Dhp. 183) that emphasized the need for volitional effort in the pursuit of cleansing the mind from greed, hatred, and delusion. It is appropriate to close this work with a reference to this passage in the *Aṅguttara-nikāya* where the affirmation is made that the cultivation of the Eightfold Path leads naturally to release from volitional striving (A. V. 2-4). In the beautiful words of the *Aṅguttara-nikāya*, there is no need to put forth a purposive impulse (*na cetanāya karaṇīyam*) because it happens naturally (*dhammatā esā*) that each wholesome stage fulfils what has gone before and prepares the way for what is yet to come.

ENDNOTES

[1] H. Jacobi, *Jaina Sutras*, 2: xxv.

[2] P.S. Jaini, *The Jaina Path of Purification*, 105.

[3] W.J. Johnson, *Harmless Souls*, 99, 101.

[4] D. Kalupahana, *Ethics in Early Buddhism*, 49-53.

[5] Ibid., *The Principles of Buddhist Psychology*, 89.

[6] I.B. Horner, *The Book of the Discipline*, 1:127.

[7] Ibid., 1:126, n. 1.

[8] R.E.A. Johansson, *The Dynamic Psychology of Early Buddhism*, 110.

[9] Bhikkhu Bodhi, *A Comprehensive Manual of Abhidhamma*, 50.

Charts

Chart 1

Stages in the cultivation (*bhāvanā*) of the disciplines of the Path of liberation develop "naturally", in accordance with conditioned origination (A. V. 2).

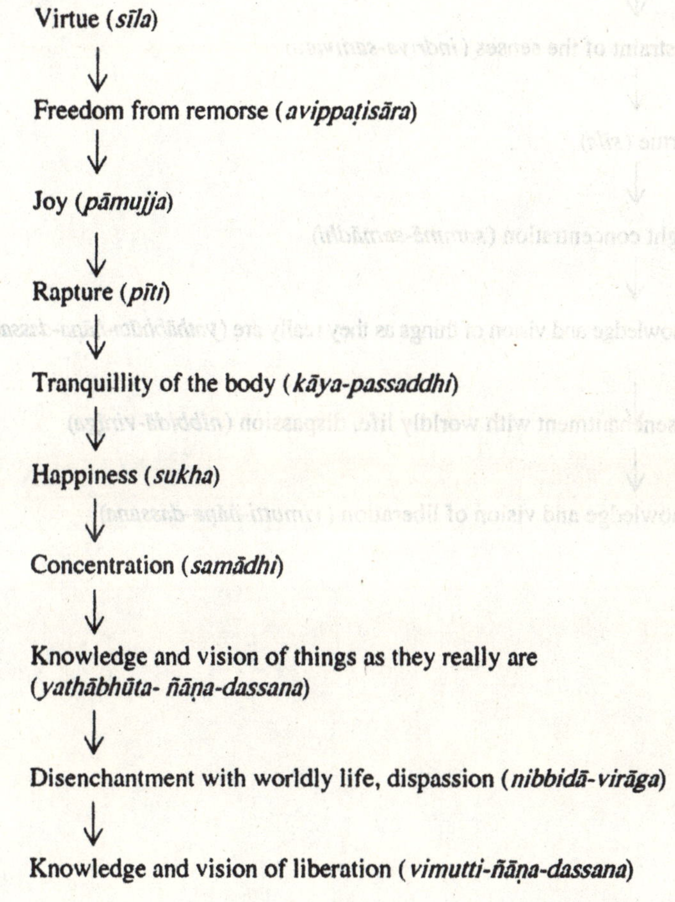

* Charts 1-6 are modelled after those found in R.E.A. Johansson, *The Dynamic Psychology of Early Buddhism* (Scandinavian Institute of Asian Studies Monograph Series, no. 37, London: Curzon Press Ltd., 1979). See Figures 4, 14, and 15.

Chart 2

Stages of the Path of liberation develop "naturally", in accordance with conditioned origination (A. IV. 99).

Shame at doing wrong and fear of the consequences of harmful acts (*hiri-ottappa*)

↓

Restraint of the senses (*indriya-saṁvara*)

↓

Virtue (*sīla*)

↓

Right concentration (*sammā-samādhi*)

↓

Knowledge and vision of things as they really are (*yathābhūta-ñāṇa-dassana*)

↓

Disenchantment with worldly life, dispassion (*nibbidā-virāga*)

↓

Knowledge and vision of liberation (*vimutti-ñāṇa-dassana*)

Chart 3

Two motivational sequences: one where conditioning factors cause the *citta* to incline towards acts with karmic consequences, and one where such action is avoided (A. I. 264).

A *bhikkhu* ponders over (*anuvitakketi*) and reflects on (*anuvicāreti*) objects that cause desire and passion (*chanda-rāga*).	A *bhikkhu* understands the future consequences of objects that cause desire and passion (*āyatiṁ vipākaṁ pajānāti*).
↓	↓
Desire is produced (*chando*[1] *jāyati*).	He turns away from such objects (*abhinivaṭṭeti*).[2]
↓	↓
He is fettered by these things. (*saññutto hoti*)	He becomes detached towards them (*abhivirājeti*).
↓	↓
Origination of *kamma* (*kammānaṁ samudaya*).	He understands the objects thoroughly and sees them clearly (*paññāya ativijjha passati*).
	↓
	Desire is not produced *(chando na jāyati*).

[1] In this context *chanda* is not a morally "neutral" term indicating impetus to act, but is closer to *rāga* (sensual pleasure).

[2] The text has *abhinivaddheti*, but the commentary gives *abhinivaṭṭeti* (AA. II. 368).

Chart 4

Mental processes leading in stages to discord and violence (M. I. 111-113).

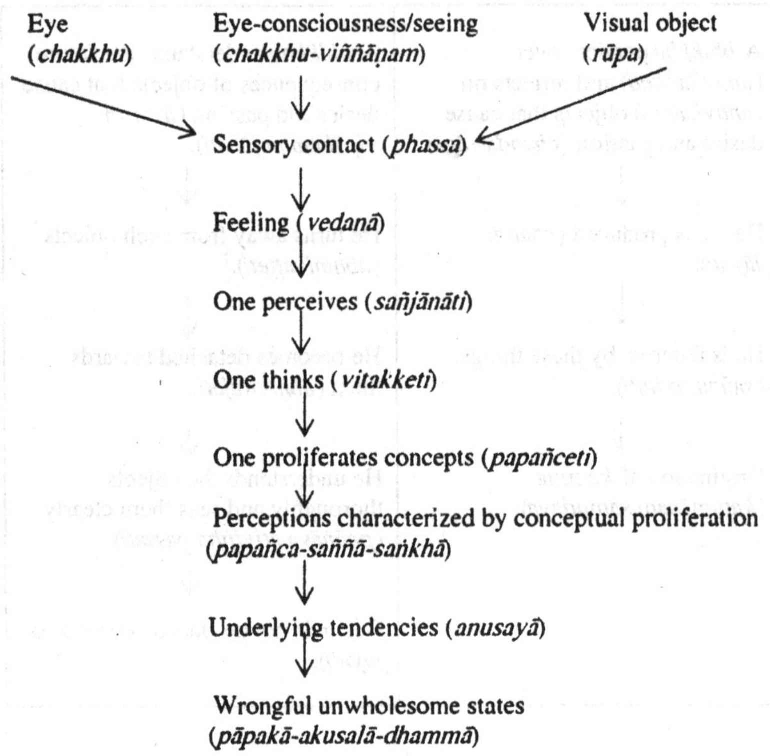

Chart 5

This chart illustrates the place of *saṅkappa* and *chanda* in a motivational series leading to a variety of quests for objects. *Cetanā* is not specifically mentioned as a separate factor in this motivational process (S. II. 142-143; D. III. 289). Each stage in the sequence arises by depending on the preceding one (*paṭicca uppajjati*).

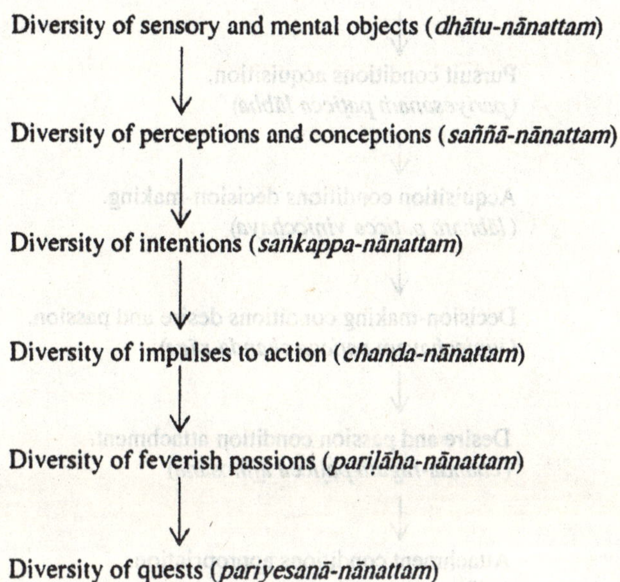

Chart 6

The terminology of conditioned origination is evident in the following motivational series (D. III. 288-289; A. IV. 400-401). *Cetanā* does not occur here to indicate a specific stage in the motivational process.

Craving conditions pursuit.
(*taṇhaṁ paṭicca pariyesanā*)

↓

Pursuit conditions acquisition.
(*pariyesanaṁ paṭicca lābha*)

↓

Acquisition conditions decision-making.
(*lābhaṁ paṭicca vinicchaya*)

↓

Decision-making conditions desire and passion.
(*vinicchayaṁ paṭicca chanda-rāga*)

↓

Desire and passion condition attachment.
(*chanda-rāgaṁ paṭicca ajjhosāna*)

↓

Attachment conditions appropriation.
(*ajjhosānaṁ paṭicca pariggaha*)

↓

Appropriation conditions avarice.
(*pariggaham paṭicca macchariya*)

↓

Avarice conditions safeguarding possessions.
(*macchariyaṁ paṭicca ārakkha*)

↓

Safeguarding possessions conditions conflict, violence, and unwholesome mental states.

Chart 7, (continued on the next page.)
Visuddhimagga XIV. 133

First sense-sphere wholesome consciousness, unprompted:
Kamāvacara-kusala-asaṅkhārika

Twenty-seven "constant" factors (niyata-cetasikas)

1. Contact with the object (*phassa*)
2. Purposive impulse (*cetanā*)
3. Initial application of thought (*vitakka*)
4. Sustained thought (*vicāra*)
5. Zest, joyful interest in the object (*pīti*)
6. Energy (*viriya*)
7. Vitality, faculty of life (*jīvitindriya*)
8. Concentration (*samādhi*)
9. Faith (*saddhā*)
10. Mindfulness (*sati*)
11. Shame at doing wrong (*hiri*)
12. Fear of wrongdoing (*ottappa*)
13. Non-greed (*alobha*)
14. Non-hate (*adosa*)
15. Non-delusion (*amoha*)
16. Tranquillity of the mental "group" (*kāya-passaddhi*)*
17. Tranquillity of the mind (*citta-passaddhi*)
18. Buoyancy of the mental "group" (*kāya-lahutā*)*
19. Buoyancy of the mind (*citta-lahutā*)
20. Flexibility of the mental "group" (*kāya-mudutā*)*
21. Flexibility of the mind (*citta-mudutā*)
22. Adaptability of the mental "group" (*kāya-kammaññatā*)*
23. Adaptability of the mind (*citta-kammaññatā*)
24. Proficiency of the mental "group" (*kāya-pāguññatā*)*
25. Proficiency of the mind (*citta-pāguññatā*)
26. Rectitude of the mental "group" (*kāyujjukatā*)
27. Rectitude of the mind (*cittujjukatā*)

Chart 7,(continued.)

Four supplementary factors corresponding to the occasion (yevāpanaka-cetasikas)

28. Impetus to act (*chanda*)
29. Decisiveness (*adhimokkha*)
30. Attention (*manasikāra*)
31. Balance of mind, equanimity (*tatra-majjhattatā*)

Five "inconstant" factors (aniyata-cetasikas)

32. Compassion (*karuṇā*)
33. Responsive joy (*muditā*)
34. Abstaining from bodily misconduct (*kāya-duccarita-virati*)
35. Abstaining from verbal misconduct (*vacī-duccarita-virati*)
36. Abstaining from wrong livelihood (*micchājīva-virati*)

* The term *kāya* is used here in the sense of "group" or "collection". Here the term refers to three of the mental aggregates: *vedanā, saññā,* and *saṅkhāra* (*Kāyo ti c'ettha vedanādayo tayo khandhā*) (Vsm. XIV. 144).

The *Visuddhimagga* (XIV. 83, 156) enumerates eight types of sense-sphere wholesome states of consciousness (Chart 11).

Chart 8
Visuddhimagga XIV. 159

First unwholesome consciousness rooted in greed, unprompted:
Akusala-lobhamūla-asaṅkhārika

Thirteen "constant" factors (niyata-cetasikas)

1. Contact with object (*phassa*)
2. Purposive impulse (*cetanā*)
3. Initial application of thought (*vitakka*)
4. Sustained thought (*vicāra*)
5. Zest, joyful interest in the object (*pīti*)
6. Energy (*viriya*)
7. Vitality, faculty of life (*jīvitindriya*)
8. Concentration (*samādhi*)
9. Lack of shame at doing wrong (*ahirika*)
10. Lack of fear at doing wrong (*anottappa*)
11. Greed (*lobha*)
12. Delusion (*moha*)
13. Wrong view (*micchā-diṭṭhi*)

Four supplementary factors corresponding to the occasion (yevāpanaka-cetasikas)

14. Impetus to act (*chanda*)
15. Decisiveness (*adhimokkha*)
16. Restlessness (*uddhacca*)
17. Attention (*manasikāra*)

The *Visuddhimagga* (Vsm. XIV. 166-169) classifies *cittas* associated with greed into eight types (Chart 12).

Cittas associated with greed that are prompted (*sasaṅkhārika*) include sluggishness (*thīna*) conjoined with lethargy (*middha*) among the inconstant factors. *Cittas* associated with greed but dissociated from wrong view (*micchā-diṭṭhi*) are described as having conceit (*māna*) among the inconstant states. The *Abhidhammattha-saṅgaha* explains that wrong view and conceit are incompatible and cannot coexist. One of them becomes dominant and leaves no room for the other (Bhikkhu Bodhi, *A Comprehensive Manual of Abhidhamma*, 95-96).

Chart 9, (continued on the next page.)
Visuddhimagga XIV. 170

First unwholesome consciousness rooted in hatred, unprompted:
Akusala-dosamūla-asaṅkhārika

Eleven "constant" factors (niyata-cetasikas)

1. Contact with objects (*phassa*)
2. Purposive impulse (*cetanā*)
3. Initial application of thought (*vitakka*)
4. Sustained thought (*vicāra*)
5. Energy (*viriya*)
6. Vitality, faculty of life (*jīvitindriya*)
7. Concentration (*samādhi*)
8. Lack of shame at doing wrong (*ahirika*)
9. Lack of fear at doing wrong (*anottappa*)
10. Hate (*dosa*)
11. Delusion (*moha*)

Four supplementary factors corresponding to the occasion (yevāpanaka-cetasikas)

12. Impetus to act (*chanda*)
13. Decisiveness (*adhimokkha*)
14. Restlessness (*uddhacca*)
15. Attention (*manasikāra*)

Three "inconstant" factors (aniyata-cetasikas)

16. Envy (*issā*)
17. Stinginess, avarice (*macchariya*)
18. Worry (*kukkucca*)

The *Visuddhimagga* (Vsm. XIV. 166-167) classifies *cittas* associated with hate into two types (Chart 12). The second differs from the first in being prompted (*sasaṅkhārika*). Like prompted *cittas* associated with greed, this second type of *cittas* associated with hate has sluggishness (*thīna*) conjoined with lethargy (*middha*) as an inconstant factor.

Chart 9, (continued.)

The *Visuddhimagga* (Vsm. XIV. 92) holds that *cittas* rooted in hate are always associated with the attitude of aversion (*paṭigha*) and conjoined with the feeling of displeasure (*domanassa*). Bhikkhu Bodhi explains that, according to the *Abhidhamma* system, whereas displeasure is not associated with *cittas* rooted in greed or delusion, hate is always accompanied by the mental feeling of unpleasantness (Bhikkhu Bodhi, *A Comprehensive Manual of Abhidhamma,* 37).

Chart 10
Visuddhimagga XIV. 176

First unwholesome consciousness rooted in delusion, conjoined with indecision: *Mohamūla vicikicchā-sampayutta*

Eleven "constant" factors (niyata-cetasikas)

1. Contact with objects (*phassa*)
2. Purposive impulse (*cetanā*)
3. Initial application of thought (*vitakka*)
4. Sustained thought (*vicāra*)
5. Energy (*viriya*)
6. Vitality, faculty of life (*jīvitindriya*)
7. [Momentary] steadiness of consciousness (*cittaṭṭhiti*)
8. Lack of shame at doing wrong (*ahirika*)
9. Lack of fear at doing wrong (*anottappa*)
10. Delusion (*moha*)
11. Indecision (*vicikicchā*)

Two supplementary factors corresponding to the occasion (yevāpanaka-cetasikas)

12. Restlessness (*uddhacca*)
13. Attention (*manasikāra*)

The *Visuddhimagga* (Vsm. XIV. 178) classifies *cittas* associated with delusion into two types (Chart 12). The second differs from the first in being conjoined with restlessness (*uddhacca*) rather than indecision (*vicikicchā*). Since indecision is absent in *cittas* that are associated with delusion and conjoined with restlessness, decisiveness (*adhimokkha*) arises as a supplementary mental factor (*yevāpanaka-cetasika*). With the arising of decisiveness, momentary steadiness of consciousness (*cittaṭṭhiti*) is strengthened and develops into concentration (*samādhi*).

Chart 11
Visuddhimagga XIV. 83. 156.

Eight types of sense-sphere wholesome consciousness

1. **Accompanied by joy (*somanassa*), associated with knowledge (*ñāṇa*), unprompted (*asaṅkhārika*).**

2. **Accompanied by joy, associated with knowledge, prompted.**

3. **Accompanied by joy, dissociated from knowledge, unprompted. Non-delusion or understanding (*amoha*) does not arise among the constant factors.**

4. **Accompanied by joy, dissociated from knowledge, prompted. Non-delusion does not arise.**

5. **Accompanied by equanimity (*upekkhā*),* associated with knowledge, unprompted. Zest or joyful interest in the object (*pīti*) does not arise.**

6. **Accompanied by equanimity, associated with knowledge, prompted. Joyful interest in the object does not arise.**

7. **Accompanied by equanimity, dissociated from knowledge, unprompted. Joyful interest in the object does not arise. Non-delusion does not arise.**

8. **Accompanied by equanimity, dissociated from knowledge, prompted. Joyful interest in the object does not arise. Non-delusion does not arise.**

*** *Upekkhā* here represents, not the serene balance of mind that is attained by cultivating the Eightfold Path, but feeling characterized as "neither pleasure nor pain".**

Chart 12, (continued on the next page.)
Visuddhimagga XIV. 89-93, 166-169, 175-178.

Twelve types of unwholesome consciousness

Eight types rooted in greed

1. Accompanied by joy (*somanassa*), associated with wrong view (*diṭṭhi*), unprompted.

2. Accompanied by joy, associated with wrong view, prompted. Sluggishness (*thīna*) conjoined with lethargy (*middha*) is present.

3. Accompanied by joy, dissociated from wrong view, unprompted. Wrong view is absent. Conceit (*māna*) arises among the inconstant factors.

4. Accompanied by joy, dissociated from wrong view, prompted. Wrong view is absent. Sluggishness conjoined with lethargy is present. Conceit arises among the inconstant factors.

5. Accompanied by equanimity (*upekkhā*),* associated with wrong view, unprompted. Zest or pleasurable interest (*pīti*) in the object is absent.

6. Accompanied by equanimity, associated with wrong view, prompted. Zest or pleasurable interest in the object is absent. Sluggishness conjoined with lethargy is present.

7. Accompanied by equanimity, dissociated from wrong view, unprompted. Zest or pleasurable interest in the object is absent. Conceit is present among the inconstant states.

8. Accompanied by equanimity, dissociated from wrong view, prompted. Zest or pleasurable interest in the object is absent. Conceit is present among the inconstant states. Sluggishness conjoined with lethargy is present.

Chart 12, (continued.)

Two cittas rooted in hate (dosa)

1) Accompanied by displeasure (*domanassa*), conjoined with aversion (*paṭigha*), unprompted.

2) Accompanied by displeasure (*domanassa*), conjoined with aversion, prompted. Sluggishness conjoined with lethargy is present as an inconstant state.

Two cittas rooted in delusion (moha)

1) Accompanied by equanimity (*upekkhā*), associated with indecision (*vicikicchā*). Concentration (*samādhi*) is weak and takes the form of mere steadiness of consciousness (*cittaṭṭhiti*).

2) Accompanied by equanimity, associated with restlessness (*uddhacca*). Concentration is stronger because of the presence of decisiveness (*adhimokkha*) among the supplementary (*yevāpanaka*) states.

* *Upekkhā* associated with unwholesome *cittas* is not a serene balance of mind, but feeling that is neither pleasant nor unpleasant (*adukkhamasukhā vedanā*). A *citta* that is pervaded by indecision (*vicikicchā*) is considered incapable of concentration. *Cittaṭṭhiti* is explained in the commentary as stability at the present moment, with no guarantee of the continuity of steady attention (Bhikkhu Ñāṇamoli, *The Path of Purification*, 533, n.70).

Chart 13

Citta-vīthi

Cognitive process when an object is presented to the mind through one of the senses.

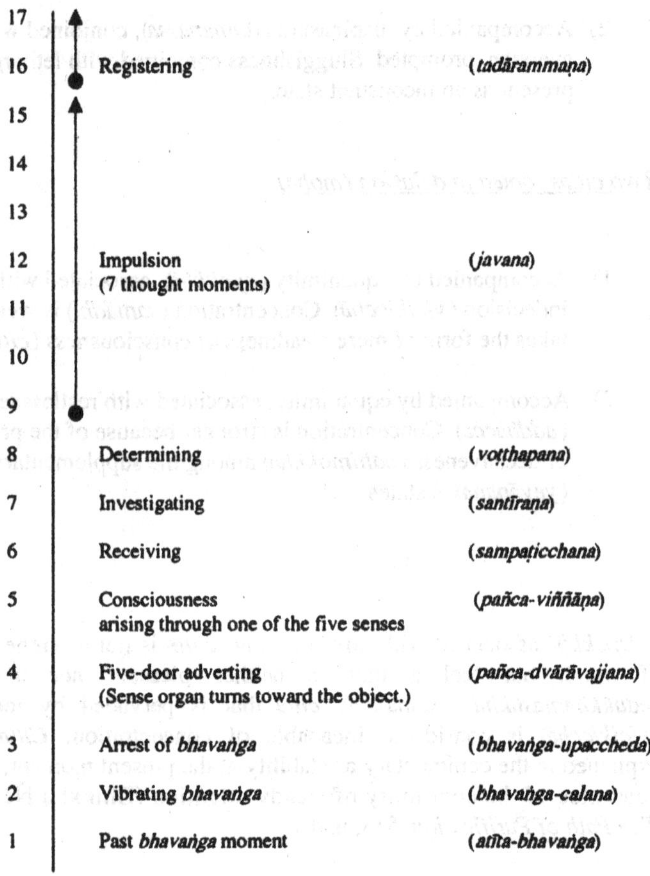

Chart 14
Visuddhimagga XVII. 284-298.

Three successive lives in the rebirth process.

PAST LIFE	1. Ignorance (*avijjā*) 2. Acts with karmic consequences (*saṅkhāra*) (*defined in terms of cetanā*)	*Kamma* process (*kamma-bhava*) with 5 causes: 1, 2, 8, 9, 10.
PRESENT LIFE	3. Consciousness (*viññāṇa*) 4. Mind-and-body (*nāma-rūpa*) 5. Six senses (*āyatana*) 6. Sense-contact (*phassa*) 7. Feeling (*vedanā*)	Rebirth process (*upapatti-bhava*) with 5 results: 3, 4, 5, 6, 7.
	8. Craving (*taṇhā*) 9. Grasping (*upādāna*) 10. Becoming (*bhava*) (*defined in terms of cetanā*)	*kamma* process (*kamma-bhava*) with 5 causes: 1, 2, 8, 9, 10.
FUTURE LIFE	11. Rebirth (*jāti*) 12. Old age and death (*jarā-maraṇa*)	Rebirth process (*upapatti-bhava*) with 5 results 3, 4, 5, 6, 7, occurring between birth and death.

Glossary

abhijjhā	covetousness
abhisañcetayita	motivated by a purposive impulse or intention
abhisaṅkhāra	conditioned purposive act with karmic consequences
abhisaṅkhāra-viññāṇa	consciousness imbued with karma-forming activities leading to rebirth
abhisaṅkhata	produced by the mind's capacity to bring together mental factors that function as causal conditions
acetana	insentient, lacking basic conscious awareness
adhimokkha	personal inclination, decision regarding the object, resolve leading to firm faith
āhāra	nutriment, causal conditions that prolong rebirth: (1) food that nourishes the body; (2) contact with sensory and mental objects; (3) purposive impulses in the mind; (4) the continuum of conscious awareness
ahetukavāda	doctrine of non-causality
akusala	unwholesome, morally reprehensible
anusaya	persistent unwholesome tendency
ārambha-dhātu	mental capacity to initiate action in oneself
asampajāna	not deliberate, unknowing, unintended

āsava	four mental corruptions manifesting as persistent addictive habits: (1) desire for sensual pleasure; (2) desire for rebirth; (3) speculative views; and (4) ignorance
avijjā	ignorance, basic cause of rebirth
avyākata	ethically indeterminate, neither karmically wholesome nor unwholesome
āyūhana	striving; producing and accumulating *kamma*
bhāvanā	development of the mind through meditation and mindfulness
bojjhaṅga	factor of enlightenment comprising mindfulness, investigation of *dhammas*, energy, delight, tranquillity, concentration, and equanimity
cetanā	purposive impulse, intention imbued with impetus to act
cetasika	cognitive, emotive, and motivational mental factors constituting a *citta*
chanda	desire to act, which can manifest as desire for sensory objects (*kāma-chanda*) or zeal in following the Eightfold Path (*dhamma-chanda*)
chanda-rāga	sensual passion
citta	(1) state of mind constituted of *cetasikas*; (2) attitude of mind arising through the mutual conditioning of *cetasikas*; (3) continuum of consciousness

cittaṁ namati	the mind "inclines" (towards a chosen goal)
citta-niyāma	conditioned order of mental states forming the continuum of consciousness
citta-vīthi	ordered sequence of *citta*s in mental processes, especially the process of perceiving an object
dhamma	(1) natural order, law; (2) basic, classifiable physical or mental state; (3) object perceived by the mind (*manas*); (4) quality
Dhamma	teaching of the Buddha
dhammatā	natural order based on conditioned origination
dhammikaṁ sukham	pleasure that is in accordance with virtue
diṭṭhi	philosophical view, speculative theory
domanassa	unhappy or uneasy state of mind, especially associated with hate
dosa	aversion, repulsion, hate
dukkha	pain, lack of mental ease, sorrow
hiri	shame in doing wrong, based on training and respect for oneself
hṛd	heart regarded as the centre of emotions
indriya	faculty: (1) the six sense faculties; (2) the five "spiritual faculties" comprising faith, energy, mindfulness, concentration, wisdom

javana	karmically active impulsion: the active phase of the cognitive process, wherein intentions are formed and *kamma* is generated
kāma	(1) desire for sensual pleasure; (2) object of sensory enjoyment
kamma	wholesome or unwholesome purposive act of body, speech, or mind, which entails karmic consequences
kamma-bhava	active, kamma-forming dimension of the rebirth process
kilesa	mental impurity, afflicted state of mind
kiriya	merely "functional" mental process that performs a function without entailing karmic consequences; the acts of an *arahant* are *kiriya* processes
kiriyavāda	doctrine of action
kratu	purpose, resolve
kusala	wholesome, morally good, skilful, producing beneficial consequences
lobha	greed
lokiya	mundane sphere comprising physical and mental states that are not included in the supramundane
lokuttara	supramundane: the four paths that constitute the stages leading to freedom from rebirth, the four fruitions of the paths, and *nibbāna*

manas	(1) the dynamic unity of consciousness constituted of thoughts, emotions, and motivational states; (2) faculty of thought and intellection; (3) faculty that perceives mental objects and coordinates sensory data
manasikāra	attention
mano-sañcetanā	purposive impulses in the mind, one of the nutriments of rebirth
moha	delusion
momūha	sheer delusion
mūla	root of action: wholesome roots comprising non-greed, non-hate, and non-delusion; unwholesome roots comprising greed, hate, and delusion
nāma	(1) factors of basic sentience: feeling, perception, purposive impulse, contact with objects, attention; (2) mental "aggregates": feelings, perceptions, the mind's constructive activities, the continuum of conscious awareness
ottappa	fear of doing wrong
paccavekkhaṇa	the mind's capacity to observe and review its own processes
paccaya	causal condition
pamāda	carelessness, lack of vigilance, negligence
paṇidhi	aspiration, resolve

paññā	understanding, wisdom
pāpa	(1) moral wrongdoing; (2) karmic demerit
pariyuṭṭhāna	obsessive, overpowering emotions caused by the activation of *anusayas*
passaddhi	tranquillity
paṭicca-samuppāda	causal theory of conditioned origination
paṭigha	aversion
patthanā	aspiration, prayer, request
payoga	(1) means, preparatory undertaking; (2) impetus
puñña	(1) morally good action; (2) karmic merit
purāṇa-kamma	past acts that entail karmic consequences
rāga	desire, passion
sabhāva	distinctive nature, intrinsic nature
saddhā	faith
samādhi	concentration of mind
sampajāna	deliberate, knowingly done
sañcetanā	purposive impulse, intention imbued with impetus (see *cetanā*)
sañcetanika-kamma	wholesome or unwholesome purposive act carrying karmic consequences
saṅkappa	intention, purposive thought

saṅkhāra	(1) the mind's conditioning processes that motivate purposive acts; (2) wholesome and unwholesome purposive acts that entail karmic consequences
saphalam padhānam	fruitful striving
sasaṅkhāra	prompted, instigated
sati	mindfulness
sīla	ethical virtue
somanassa	joy, happy state of mind
sukha	pleasant feeling, pleasure
taṇhā	craving
thīna-middha	lethargy and sluggishness
uddhacca	agitation, restlessness
upacaya	"accumulation" of *kamma* in the continuum of consciousness
upapatti-bhava	rebirth-process: resultant dimension of the course of rebirth, wherein the pleasant and unpleasant consequences of *kamma* are experienced
upekkhā	(1) "neutral" state of mind characterized neither by pleasure nor by displeasure; (2) equanimity: one of the factors of wisdom
viññāṇa	conscious awareness
viññāṇa-sota	stream of consciousness

vipāka	fruition, result
vipallāsa	distorted cognition
vipassanā	insight
viriya	energy, vigour, exertion
vitakka	application of the mind, discursive thought, reasoning
yathā-bhūtam	"as it actually is", "in its real nature"
yoniso-manasikāra	systematic, careful, wise, attention

Selected Bibliography

Primary Sources (Pāli and Saṁskṛt texts) and Dictionaries

Abhidhammatthasaṅgaha and Abhidhammatthavibhāvinī-ṭīkā. Edited by H. Saddhātissa. Oxford: Pali Text Society (P.T.S.), 1989.

Abhidharmakośa and Bhāṣya of Vasubandhu with Sphuṭārthā Commentary of Ācārya Yaśomitra. Edited by Swami D. Shastri. 4 vols. Varanasi: Bauddha Bharati, 1970-1973.

Abhidharmakośabhāṣyam of Vasubandhu. Edited by P. Pradhan. Revised by A. Haldar. 2d rev. ed. Patna: K.P. Jayaswal Research Institute, 1975. First edition, Patna: K.P. Jayaswal Research Institute, 1967.

Aṅguttara-nikāya. Edited by R. Morris and E. Hardy. 5 vols. Vol. 1, 2d rev. ed., London: P.T.S., 1961; first edition, London: P.T.S., 1885. Vols. 2-5, London: P.T.S., 1888-1900.

Atthasālinī. Edited by E. Müller. Rev. ed. London: P.T.S., 1979. First edition, London: P.T.S., 1897.

A Critical Pāli Dictionary. By V. Trenckner. Continued by D. Anderson, H. Smith, and others. Work in progress. Copenhagen: Royal Danish Academy of Sciences and Letters, 1924-.

Dhammansaṅgaṇi. Edited by E. Müller. London: P.T.S., 1885.

Dhātu-kathā Pakaraṇa and Its Commentary. Edited by E.R. Gooneratne. London: P.T.S., 1892.

Dīgha-nikāya. Edited by T.W. Rhys Davids and J.E. Carpenter. 3 vols. London: P.T.S., 1890-1911.

Itivuttaka. Edited by E. Windisch. London: P.T.S., 1889.

Kathāvatthu. Edited by A.C. Taylor. 2 vols. (combined). London: P.T.S., 1979. First edition, London: P.T.S. 1894 and 1897.

Kathāvatthuppakaraṇa-Aṭṭhakathā. Edited by N.A. Jayawickrama. London: P.T.S., 1979.

Majjhima-nikāya. Edited by V. Trenckner and R. Chalmers. 3 vols. London: P.T.S., 1888-1899.

Manorathapūraṇī. Edited by M. Walleser and H. Kopp. 5 vols. Vol. 1, 2d ed., London: P.T.S., 1973; first edition, London: P.T.S., 1924. Vol. 2, 2d rev. ed., London: P.T.S., 1967; first edition, London: P.T.S., 1930. Vols. 3-5, London: P.T.S., 1936-1956.

Milindapañho with Milinda-ṭīkā. Edited by V. Trenckner. London: P.T.S., 1986. First edition, London: Williams and Norgate, 1880.

Nettippakaraṇa. Edited by E. Hardy. London: P.T.S., 1902.

Pali-English Dictionary. Edited by T.W. Rhys Davids and W. Stede. New Delhi: Oriental Books Reprint Corp., 1975. Original edition, London: P.T.S., 1921-25.

Papañcasūdanī. Edited by J.H. Woods, D. Kosambi, and I.B. Horner. 4 vols. London: P.T.S., 1922-1938.

Paṭisambhidāmagga. Edited by A.C. Taylor. 2 vols. London: P.T.S., 1905 and 1907.

Puggalapaññatti. Edited by R. Morris. London: P.T.S., 1883.

Rig-veda Samhitā: The Sacred Hymns of the Brāhmans together with the Commentary of Sāyaṇāchārya. 2d ed. Edited by M. Müller. 4 vols. Chowkhamba Sanskrit Series Work, no. 99. Varanasi, India: Chowkhamba Sanskrit Series Office, 1966. First edition, n.p., 1849-1874.

Sammohavinodanī. Edited by A.P. Buddhadatta Thero. London: P.T.S., 1923.

Saṁyutta-nikāya. Edited by L. Feer. 5 vols. London: P.T.S., 1884-1898.

A Sanskrit-English Dictionary. By M. Monier-Williams. Oxford: Clarendon Press, 1899.

Sāratthappakāsinī. Edited by F.L. Woodward. 3 vols. London: P.T.S., 1929-1937.

Sumaṅgalavilāsinī. Edited by T.W. Rhys Davids, J.E. Carpenter, and W. Stede. 3 vols. Vol. 1, 2d ed., London: P.T.S., 1968; first edition, London: P.T.S., 1886. Vol. 2, 2d ed., London: P.T.S., 1971; first edition, London: P.T.S., 1931. Vol. 3, 2d ed., London: P.T.S., 1971; first edition, London: P.T.S., 1932.

Sutta-nipāta. Edited by D. Andersen and H. Smith. London: P.T.S., 1913.

Thera- and Therī-gāthā. Edited by K.R. Norman and L. Alsdorf. 2d ed. London: P.T.S., 1966. First edition, ed. H. Oldenberg and R. Pischel, London: P.T.S., 1883.

Udāna. Edited by P. Steinthal. London: P.T.S., 1885.

Vibhaṅga. Edited by C.A.F. Rhys Davids. London: P.T.S., 1904.

Visuddhimagga. Edited by H.C. Warren. Revised by D. Kosambi. Harvard Oriental Series, vol. 41. Cambridge, Mass: Harvard University Press, 1950.

Visuddhimaggo with Paramatthamañjūsāṭīkā. Edited and revised by Dr. Rewatadhamma. 3 vols. Varanasi: Research Institute, Varanaseya Sanskrit Vishwavidyalaya, 1969-1972.

Secondary Sources and Translations

Allport, G.W. *Pattern and Growth in Personality.* New York: Holt, Rinehart, and Winston, 1961.

Aung, S.Z., trans. *Compendium of Philosophy.* Revised and edited by C.A.F. Rhys Davids. London: P.T.S., 1910.

Aung, S.Z., and C.A.F. Rhys Davids, trans. *Points of Controversy.* London: P.T.S., 1915.

Baba, Bangali, trans. *Yogasūtra of Patañjali with the Commentary of Vyāsa.* Delhi: Motilal Banarsidass, 1976.

Balasooriya, S., A. Bareau, R. Gombrich, S. Gunasingha, U. Mallawarachchi, and E. Perry, eds. *Buddhist Studies in Honour of Walpola Rahula.* London: Gordon Fraser, 1980.

Basham, A.L. *History and Doctrines of the Ājīvikas.* London: Luzac and Co., 1951.

Bastow, D. "An Example of Self-change: The Buddhist Path". *Religious Studies* 24 (1988):157-172.

Bechert, H. "The Date of the Buddha Reconsidered". *Indologica Taurinensia* 10 (1981): 29-36.

_______. "The *Nikāyas* of Mediaeval Sri Lanka and the Unification of the *Sangha* by Parākramabāhu I." In *Studies in Buddhism in Honour of Professor A.K. Warder*, ed. N.K. Wagle and F. Watanabe, 11-21. Toronto: University of Toronto Centre for South Asian Studies, 1993.

Bergaigne, A. *Vedic Religion According to the Hymns of the Ṛgveda.* Vol. 3. Translated by V.G. Paranjpe. Poona: Āryasaṁskṛti Prakāśana, 1973. First Published in French as *La Religion Vedique*, 4 vols. Paris: F. Vieweg, 1887-1897.

Bhagat, M.G. *Ancient Indian Asceticism.* New Delhi: Munshiram Manoharlal, 1976.

Bhargava, D. *Jaina Ethics.* Delhi: Motilal Banarsidass, 1968.

Bodhi, Bhikkhu, ed. *A Comprehensive Manual of Abhidhamma.* Kandy, Sri Lanka: Buddhist Publication Society, 1993. Originally edited and translated by Mahāthera Nārada, Colombo, Sri Lanka: Vajirārāma, 1956.

_______, ed. *The Middle Length Discourses of the Buddha: A New Translation of the Majjhima-nikāya.* Based on original translation by Bhikkhu Ñāṇamoli. Boston: Wisdom Publications, 1995.

_______, trans. *The Connected Discourses of the Buddha: A New Translation of the Saṁyutta Nikāya.* 2 vols. Boston: Wisdom Publications, 2000.

Boisvert, M. *The Five Aggregates: Understanding Theravāda Psychology and Soteriology.* Canadian Corporation for Studies in Religion, vol. 17. Waterloo, ON: Wilfrid Laurier University Press, 1995.

Bond, G.D. "The Nature and Meaning of the Netti-pakaraṇa". In *Studies in Pali and Buddhism: A Memorial Volume in Honour of Bhikkhu Jagdish Kashyap*, ed. A.K. Narain, 29-39. Delhi: B.R. Publishing Corporation, 1979.

_______. "The Netti-pakaraṇa: A Theravāda Method of Interpretation". In *Buddhist Studies in Honour of Walpola Rahula*, ed. S. Balasooriya et al., 16-28. London: Gordon Fraser, 1980.

Buitenen, J.A.B. van, trans. *The Bhagavadgītā in the Mahābhārata: Text and Translation.* Chicago: University of Chicago Press, 1981.

Carter, J.R. *Dhamma: Westerm Academic and Sinhalese Buddhist Interpretations.* Tokyo: Hokuseido Press, 1978.

Chauduri, S. *Analytical Study of the Abhidharmakośa.* Sanskrit College Research Series, no. 114. Calcutta: Sanskrit College, 1976.

Collins, S. "On the Very Idea of the Pali Canon". *Journal of the Pali Text Society* 21 (1990): 301-393.

_______. *Selfless Persons: Imagery and Thought in Theravāda Buddhism.* First paperback edition. Cambridge: Cambridge University Press, 1990. Original edition. Cambridge: Cambridge University Press, 1982.

Conze, E. *Buddhist Thought in India: Three Phases of Buddhist Philosophy.* First Edition as Ann Arbor Paperbacks. Ann Arbor: University of Michigan Press, 1967. Original edition, George Allen & Unwin Ltd., 1962.

Cousins, L.S. "Dhammapāla and the Ṭīkā Literature". *Journal of Religion and Religions* 2 (1972): 159-169.

_______, "The *Paṭṭhāna* and the Development of the *Theravādin* Abhidhamma". *Journal of the Pali Text Society* 9 (1981): 22-46.

_______, "Good or Skilful? *Kusala* in Canon and Commentary". *Journal of Buddhist Ethics* 3 (1996): 136-164.

Cousins, L.S., A. Kunst, and K.R. Norman, eds. *Buddhist Studies in Honour of I.B. Horner.* Dordrecht, Holland: D. Reidel Publishing Co., 1971.

Dasgupta, S. *A History of Indian Philosophy.* Vol. 1. Cambridge: Cambridge University Press, 1932.

Davies, J., trans. *The Sankhya Karika of Iswara Krishna: An Exposition of the System of Kapila.* 2d ed. Calcutta: Susil Gupta, 1957. First edition, n.p., 1881.

Deussen, P. *The Philosophy of the Upanishads.* Translated by A.S. Geden. New York: Dover Publications, 1966. First published in German as *Philosophie der Upanishads,* n.p.: T. and T. Clark, 1906.

Dixit, K.K. *Jaina Ontology.* Lalbhai Dalpatbhai Series, ed. D. Malvania and N.J. Shah, no. 31. Ahmedabad, India: L.D. Institute of Indology, 1971.

_______. *Early Jainism.* Lalbhai Dalpatbhai Series, ed. D. Malvania and N.J. Shah, no. 64. Ahmedabad, India: L.D. Institute of Indology, 1978.

Dube, S.N. *Cross Currents in Early Buddhism.* New Delhi: Manohar Publications, 1980.

Edgerton, F., trans. *The Bhagavad Gītā.* Cambridge, Mass.: Harvard University Press, 1972. First edition, Harvard Oriental Series, vols. 38-39, Cambridge, Mass.: Harvard University Press, 1944.

Erdosy, G. "The Archaeology of Early Buddhism". in *Studies on Buddhism in Honour of Professor A.K. Warder,* ed. N.K. Wagle and F. Watanabe, 40-56. Toronto: University of Toronto Centre for South Asian Studies, 1993.

Ewan, R.B. *An Introduction to Theories of Personality.* 2d ed. Orlando, Fla.: The Academic Press, 1984.

Feuerstein, G. *The Yoga-sūtra of Patañjali: An Exercise in the Methodology of Textual Analysis.* New Delhi: Arnold-Heinemann, 1979.

_______, trans. *The Yoga-sūtra of Patañjali: A New Translation and Commentary.* Folkestone, U.K.: William Dawson and Sons, 1979.

_______. *The Philosophy of Classical Yoga.* Manchester: Manchester University Press, 1980.

Folkert, K.W. *Scripture and Community: Collected Essays on the Jains.* Edited by J.E. Cort. The Harvard University Center for the Study of World Religions: Studies in World Religions, no. 6. Atlanta, Ga.: Scholars Press, 1993.

Frauwallner, E. *The Earliest Vinaya and the Beginnings of Buddhist Literature.* Serie Orientale Roma, vol. 8. Roma: Istituto Italiano per il Medio ed Estremo Oriente, 1956.

_______. *History of Indian Philosophy.* Translated by V.M. Bedekar. 2 vols. Delhi: Motilal Banarsidass, 1973. First published in German as *Geschichte der Indischen Philosophie,* Salzburg: Otto Muller Verlag, 1953.

______. *Studies in Abhidharma Literature and the Origins of Buddhist Philosophical Systems.* Translated by S.F. Kidd. Albany, N.Y.: State University of New York, 1995.

Gethin, R.M.L. *The Buddhist Path to Awakening: A study of the Bodhi-Pakkhiyā Dhammā.* Brill's Indological Library, ed. Johannes Bronkhorst, vol. 7. Leiden, The Netherlands: E.J. Brill, 1992.

Glasenapp, H. von. *The Doctrine of Karman in Jain Philosophy.* Translated by B. Gifford. Bombay: Bai Vijibai Jivanlal Panalal Charity Fund, 1942. First published in German as *Die Lehre vom Karman in der Philosophie der Jainas,* Leipzig: Otto Harrassowitz, 1915.

Gombrich, R.F. *Theravāda Buddhism.* London and New York: Routledge and Kegan Paul, 1988.

Gómez, L.O. "Some aspects of the free-will question in the Nikāyas". *Philosophy East and West* 25, no. 1 (1975): 81-90.

Gonda, J. *The Vision of the Vedic Poets.* The Hague: Moutan and Co., 1963.

Govinda, Lama Anagarika. *The Psychological Attitude of Early Buddhist Philosophy.* London: Rider, 1961.

Griffith, R.T., trans. *The Hymns of the Ṛgveda.* Rev. ed. Delhi: Motilal Banarsidass, 1973. First edition, n.p., 1889.

Griffiths, P. "Notes Towards a Critique of Buddhist Karmic Theory". *Religious Studies* 18 (1982): 277-291.

______. "Karma and Personal Identity: A Response to Professor White". *Religious Studies* 20 (1984): 481-485.

Guenther, H.V. *Philosophy and Psychology in the Abhidharma.* Berkeley, Calif.: Shambala Publications, 1976. Original edition, Lucknow, India: Buddha Vihara, 1957.

Haldar, A. *Some Psychological Aspects of Early Buddhist Philosophy Based on Abhidharmakośa of Vasubandhu.* The Asiatic Society Monograph Series, vol. 25. Calcutta: The Asiatic Society, 1981.

Hamilton, S. *Identity and Experience: The Constitution of the Human Being According to Early Buddhism.* London: Luzac Oriental, 1996.

Harvey, P. *The Selfless Mind: Personality, Consciousness and Nirvāṇa in Early Buddhism.* Richmond, Surrey, U.K.: Curzon Press, 1995.

Hinüber, O. von. *A Handbook of Pāli Literature.* New Delhi: Munshiram Manoharlal, 1997. Original edition, Berlin: Walter de Gruyter & Co., 1996.

Horner, I.B., trans. *The Collection of the Middle Length Sayings.* 3 vols. London: P.T.S., 1954-1959.

_______, trans. *The Book of the Discipline.* 6 vols. The Sacred Books of the Buddhists, vols. 10, 11, 13, 14, 20, 25. London: P.T.S., 1938-1975.

_______, *The Early Buddhist Theory of Man Perfected.* New Delhi: Oriental Books Reprint, 1979. Original edition, London: Routledge and Kegan Paul, 1936.

Hume, R.E., trans. *The Thirteen Principal Upanishads.* 2d rev. ed. Madras: Oxford University Press, 1931. First edition, London: Oxford University Press, 1921.

Jacobi, H., trans. *Jaina Sutras.* Parts 1 and 2. Dover Books, New York: Dover Publications, 1968. Original edition, Sacred Books of the East, vols. 22 and 45, Oxford: Clarendon Press, 1884 and 1895.

Jain, B. *Jainism in Buddhist Literature.* Nagpur, India: Alok Prakashan, 1972.

Jaini, J. *Outlines of Jainism.* Cambridge: Cambridge University Press, 1940.

Jaini, J.L., trans. *Tattvarthadhigama Sutra.* New York: AMS Press, 1974. Original edition, Sacred Books of the Jainas, ed. S.C. Ghoshal, vol. 2, Arrah, India: Central Jaina Publishing House, 1920.

Jaini, P.S. "The Sautrāntika Theory of *bīja*". *Bulletin of the School of Oriental and African Studies, University of London* 22, no. 2 (1959): 236-249.

_______. *The Jaina Path of Purification.* Berkeley: University of California Press, 1979.

James, W. *The Principles of Psychology.* 2 vols. New York: Dover Publication, 1950. First edition, n.p.: Henry Holt and Co., 1890.

Jayasuriya, W.F. *The Psychology and Philosophy of Buddhism.* Colombo, Sri Lanka: YMBA Press, 1963.

Jayatilleke, K.N. "Some Problems of Translation and Interpretation, I and II". *University of Ceylon Review* 7 (1949): 208-224; 8 (1950): 45-55.

_______. *Early Buddhist Theory of Knowledge.* London: George Allen and Unwin, 1963.

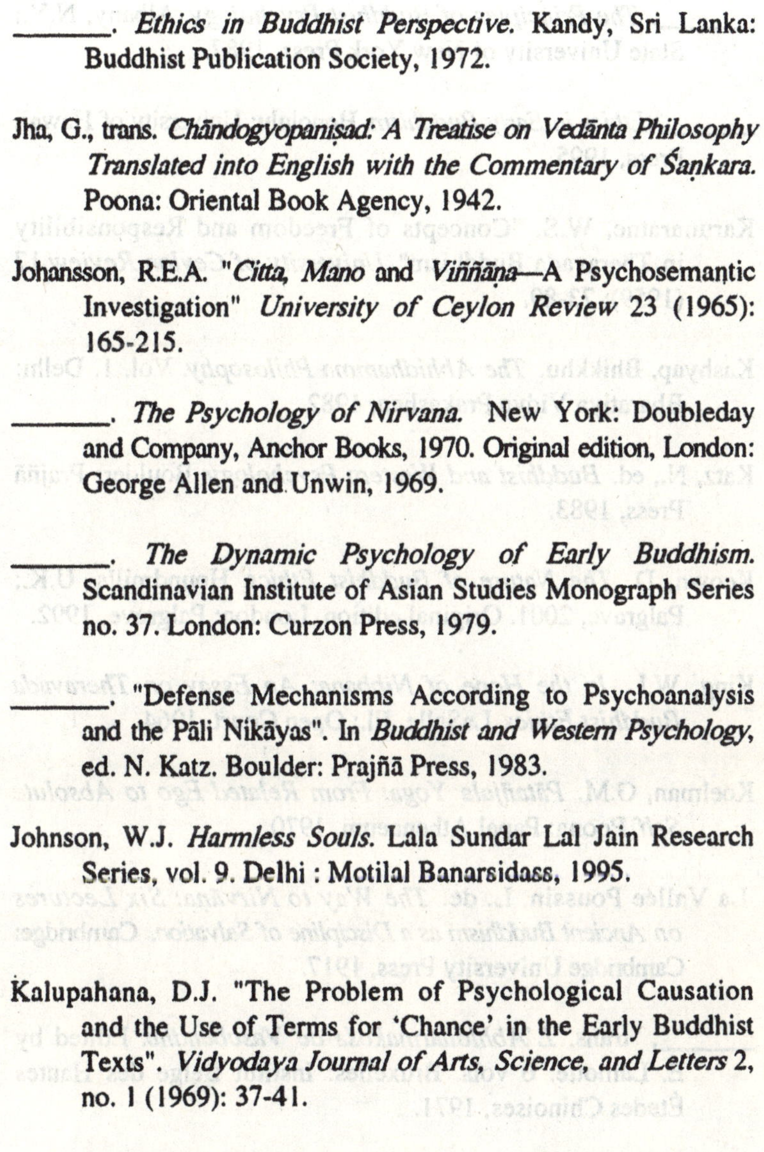

_______. *Ethics in Buddhist Perspective.* Kandy, Sri Lanka: Buddhist Publication Society, 1972.

Jha, G., trans. *Chāndogyopaniṣad: A Treatise on Vedānta Philosophy Translated into English with the Commentary of Śaṇkara.* Poona: Oriental Book Agency, 1942.

Johansson, R.E.A. "*Citta, Mano* and *Viññāṇa*—A Psychosemantic Investigation" *University of Ceylon Review* 23 (1965): 165-215.

_______. *The Psychology of Nirvana.* New York: Doubleday and Company, Anchor Books, 1970. Original edition, London: George Allen and Unwin, 1969.

_______. *The Dynamic Psychology of Early Buddhism.* Scandinavian Institute of Asian Studies Monograph Series no. 37. London: Curzon Press, 1979.

_______. "Defense Mechanisms According to Psychoanalysis and the Pāli Nikāyas". In *Buddhist and Western Psychology,* ed. N. Katz. Boulder: Prajñā Press, 1983.

Johnson, W.J. *Harmless Souls.* Lala Sundar Lal Jain Research Series, vol. 9. Delhi : Motilal Banarsidass, 1995.

Kalupahana, D.J. "The Problem of Psychological Causation and the Use of Terms for 'Chance' in the Early Buddhist Texts". *Vidyodaya Journal of Arts, Science, and Letters* 2, no. 1 (1969): 37-41.

_______. *Causality: The Central Philosophy of Buddhism.* Honolulu: University Press of Hawaii, 1975.

_______. *The Principles of Buddhist Psychology.* Albany, N.Y.: State University of New York Press, 1987.

_______. *Ethics in Early Buddhism.* Honolulu: University of Hawaii Press, 1995.

Karunaratne, W.S. "Concepts of Freedom and Responsibility in Theravada Buddhism" *University of Ceylon Review* 17 (1959): 73-89.

Kashyap, Bhikkhu. *The Abhidhamma Philosophy.* Vol. 1. Delhi: Bharatiya Vidya Prakashan, 1982.

Katz, N., ed. *Buddhist and Western Psychology.* Boulder: Prajñā Press, 1983.

Keown, D. *The Nature of Buddhist Ethics.* Houndmills, U.K.: Palgrave, 2001. Original edition, London: Palgrave, 1992.

King, W.L. *In the Hope of Nibbana: An Essay on Theravada Buddhist Ethics.* LaSalle, Ill.: Open Court, 1964.

Koelman, G.M. *Pātañjala Yoga: From Related Ego to Absolute Self.* Poona: Papal Athenaeum, 1970.

La Vallée Poussin, L. de. *The Way to Nirvāṇa: Six Lectures on Ancient Buddhism as a Discipline of Salvation.* Cambridge: Cambridge University Press, 1917.

_______, trans. *L'Abhidharmakośa de Vasubandhu.* Edited by E. Lamotte. 6 vols. Bruxelles: Institut Belge des Hautes Études Chinoises, 1971.

Lamotte, E. "Conditioned Co-production and Supreme Enlightenment". In *Buddhist Studies in Honour of Walpoḷa Rahula*, ed. S. Balasooriya et al., 118-132. London: Gordon Fraser, 1980.

_______. *History of Indian Buddhism: From the Origins to the Śaka Era*. Translated by S. Webb-Boin. Louvain-la-Neuve: Université Catholique de Louvain, 1988. First published in French as *Histoire du Bouddhisme Indien, des origines à l' ère Śaka*, Louvain: Bibliothèque du Muséon 1958.

Larson, G.J., trans. *Classical Sāṁkhya: An Interpretation of its History and Meaning*. Delhi: Motilal Banarsidass, 1969.

Law, B.C., trans. *Designation of Human Types*. London: P.T.S., 1924.

_______, trans. *The Debates Commentary*. London: P.T.S., 1940.

Ledi, Sayadaw. *The Manual of Insight (Vipassanā Dīpani)*. Translated by U Nyāṇa Mahā-Thera. Kandy, Sri Lanka: Buddhist Publication Society, 1961.

Macy J. *Mutual Causality in Buddhism and General Systems Theory: The Dharma of Natural Systems*. Albany, N.Y.: State University of New York Press, 1991.

Madanayake, B.W. "The Study of *Saṅkhāras* in Early Buddhism". Ph. D. dissertation, University of Toronto, 1978.

Mādhavānanda, Swāmi, trans. *The Bṛhadāraṇyaka Upaniṣad: With the Commentary of Śaṅkarācārya*. 4th ed. Calcutta: Advaita Ashrama, 1965. First edition, n.p., 1934.

Mainkar, T.G., trans. *Sāṁkhyakārikā of Īśvarakṛṣṇa with the Commentary of Gauḍapāda*. 2d rev. ed. Poona: Oriental Book Agency, 1972.

Manne, J. "Categories of Sutta in the Pāli Nikāyas and Their Implications for Our Appreciation of the Buddhist Teaching and Literature". *Journal of the Pali Text Society* 15 (1990): 29-87.

Masefield, P., trans. *The Udāna.* Oxford: P.T.S., 1994.

Matthews, B. *Craving and Salvation: A Study in Buddhist Soteriology.* Waterloo, Ontario: Canadian Corporation for Studies in Religion, 1983.

McDermott, J.P. *Development in the Early Buddhist Concept of Kamma/Karma.* New Delhi: Munshiram Manoharlal, 1984.

Mehta, M.L. *Jaina Psychology.* Amritsar, India: Sohanlal Jaindharma Pracharak Samiti, 1955.

Nakamura, H. "The Theory of 'Dependent Origination' in Its Incipient Stage." In *Buddhist Studies in Honour of Walpola Rahula,* ed. S. Balasooriya et al., 165-172. London: Gordon Fraser, 1980.

Ñāṇamoli, Bhikkhu, trans. *The Guide.* London: P.T.S., 1962.

_______, trans. *The Path of Purification.* 2d. ed. Colombo, Sri Lanka: A. Semage, 1964. First edition, Colombo, Sri Lanka: A. Semage, 1956.

_______, trans. *The Path of Discrimination.* London: P.T.S., 1982.

Ñāṇananda, Bhikkhu. *Concept and Reality in Early Buddhist Thought: An Essay on "Papañca" and "Papañca-Saññā-Saṅkhā".* Kandy, Sri Lanka: Buddhist Publication Society, 1976.

Nārada, Mahāthera, trans. *A Manual of Abhidhamma.* 3d. rev. ed. Kandy, Sri Lanka: Buddhist Publication Society, 1975. First edition, Colombo, Sri Lanka: Vajirārāma, 1956.

Nārada, U, trans. *Discourse on Elements.* London: P.T.S., 1962.

Norman, K.R., trans. *The Elders' Verses I: Theragāthā.* London: P.T.S., 1969.

_______, trans. *The Elders' Verses II: Therīgāthā.* London: P.T.S., 1971.

_______. "Māgadhisms in the Kathāvatthu". In *Studies in Pali and Buddhism: A Memorial Volume in Honour of Bhikkhu Jagdish Kashyap,* ed. A.K. Narain, 279-287. Delhi: B.R. Publishing Corporation, 1979.

_______. *Pāli Literature.* A History of Indian Literature, ed. J. Gonda, vol. 7. Wiesbaden: Otto Harrassowitz, 1983.

_______, trans. *The Rhinoceros Horn.* With alternative translations by I.B. Horner and W. Rahula. London: P.T.S., 1984.

_______. "Theravāda Buddhism and Brahmanical Hinduism: Brahmanical Terms in a Buddhist Guise". In *The Buddhist Forum Volume II: Seminar Papers 1988-90,* ed. T. Skorupski, 193-201. New Delhi : Heritage Publishers, 1992.

Nyanaponika, Thera. *Abhidhamma Studies: Researches in Buddhist Psychology.* 3d ed. Kandy, Sri Lanka: Buddhist Publication Society, 1976. First edition, Colombo, Sri Lanka: Frewin and Co., 1949.

______. *The Four Nutriments of Life.* The Wheel Publication, nos. 105-106. Kandy, Sri Lanka: Buddhist Publication Society, 1967.

Nyanatiloka. *Buddhist Dictionary: Manual of Buddhist Terms and Doctrines.* Edited by Nyanaponika. 4th rev. ed. Kandy, Sri Lanka: Buddhist Publication Society, 1980. First edition, n.p., 1952.

Ohira, S. *A Study of Tattvārthasūtra with Bhāṣya.* Lalbhai Dalpatbhai Series, no. 86. Ahmedabad, India: L.D. Institute of Indology, 1982.

Oldenberg, H. *Buddha: His Life, His Doctrine, His Order.* Translated by W. Hoey. Delhi: Indological Book House, 1971. Original edition, London: Williams and Norgate, 1882. First published in German as *Buddha, sein Leben, seine Lehre, sein Gemeinde.*

Olivelle, P., trans. *Upaniṣads.* Oxford World's Classics. Oxford: Oxford University Press, 1998. Originally published as a World's Classics paperback, Oxford: Oxford University Press, 1996.

Pe Maung Tin, trans. *The Expositor.* 2 vols. London: P.T.S., 1920-1921.

______, trans. *The Path of Purity.* 3 parts. London: P.T.S., 1923-1931.

Pieris, A. "The Notions of Citta, Attā and Attabhāva in the Pāli Exegetical Writings". In *Buddhist Studies in Honour of Walpola Rahula,* ed. S. Balasooriya et al., 213-222. London: Gordon Fraser, 1980.

Pio, E. *Buddhist Psychology: A Modern Perspective.* New Delhi: Abhinav Publications, 1988.

Prasāda, R., trans. *Patañjali's Yoga Sūtras: With the Commentary of Vyāsa and the Gloss of Vāchaspati Miśra.* New York: AMS Press, 1974. Original edition, The Sacred Books of the Hindus, ed. Major B.D. Basu, vol. 4, Allahabad: Panini Office, 1912.

Prebish, C.S. "Recent Progress in Vinaya Studies". In *Studies in Pali and Buddhism: A Memorial Volume in Honour of Bhikkhu Jagdish Kashyap*, ed. A.K. Narain, 297-306. Delhi: B.R. Publishing Corp., 1979.

Radhakrishnan, S., trans. *The Principal Upaniṣads.* London: George Allen and Unwin, 1953.

______, trans. *The Dhammapada.* Madras: Oxford University Press, 1966. Original edition, London: Oxford University Press, 1950.

Rahula, W. "Wrong notions of *Dhammata* (*Dharmatā*)". In *Studies in Honour of I.B. Horner*, ed. L.S. Cousins, A. Kunst, and K.R. Norman, 181-191. Dordrecht, Holland: D. Reidel Publishing Co., 1974.

Reat, N.R. *The Origins of Indian Psychology.* Berkeley, Calif.: Asian Humanities Press, 1990.

Rukmani, T.S., trans. *Yogavārttika of Vijñānabhikṣu: Text with English Translation and Critical Notes along with the Text and English Translation of the Pātañjala Yogasūtras and Vyāsabhāṣya.* Vols. 1-4. New Delhi: Munshiram Manoharlal, 1981-1989.

Rhys Davids, C.A.F. "On the Will in Buddhism". *Journal of the Royal Asiatic Society of Great Britain and Ireland* 10 (1898): 47-59.

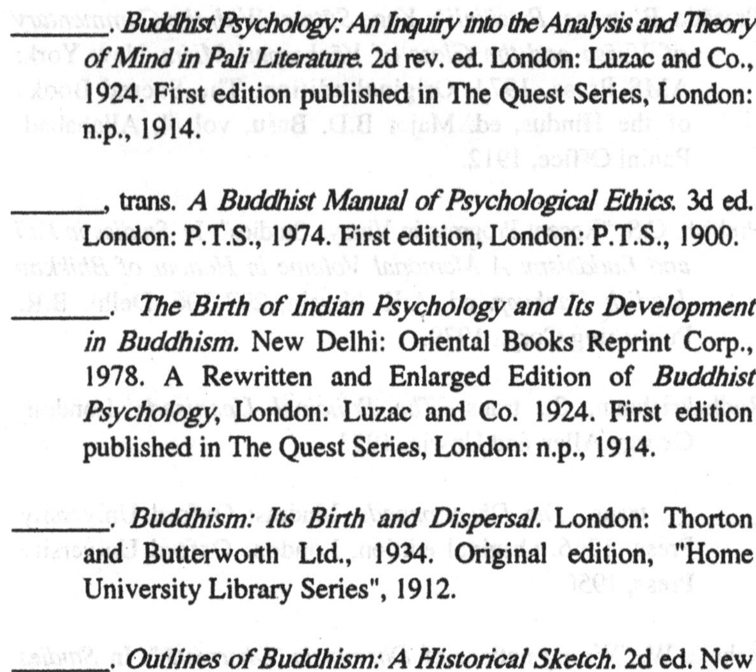

_______. *Buddhist Psychology: An Inquiry into the Analysis and Theory of Mind in Pali Literature.* 2d rev. ed. London: Luzac and Co., 1924. First edition published in The Quest Series, London: n.p., 1914.

_______, trans. *A Buddhist Manual of Psychological Ethics.* 3d ed. London: P.T.S., 1974. First edition, London: P.T.S., 1900.

_______. *The Birth of Indian Psychology and Its Development in Buddhism.* New Delhi: Oriental Books Reprint Corp., 1978. A Rewritten and Enlarged Edition of *Buddhist Psychology*, London: Luzac and Co. 1924. First edition published in The Quest Series, London: n.p., 1914.

_______. *Buddhism: Its Birth and Dispersal.* London: Thorton and Butterworth Ltd., 1934. Original edition, "Home University Library Series", 1912.

_______. *Outlines of Buddhism: A Historical Sketch.* 2d ed. New Delhi: Oriental Books Reprint Corporation., 1978. First edition, London: Methuen and Co., 1938.

Rhys Davids, C.A.F., and F.L. Woodward, trans. *The Book of the Kindred Sayings.* 5 vols. London: P.T.S., 1917-1930.

Rhys Davids, T.W., trans. *The Questions of King Milinda.* 2 vols. New York: Dover Publications, 1963. Original edition, Sacred Books of the East, ed. F.M. Müller, vols. 35 and 36, Oxford: Clarendon Press, 1890 and 1894.

Rhys Davids, T.W., and C.A.F. Rhys Davids, trans. *Dialogues of the Buddha.* 3 vols. Sacred Books of the Buddhists, ed. F.M. Müller, vols. 2-4. London: P.T.S., 1889-1921.

Sarathchandra, E.R. *Buddhist Psychology of Perception.* Colombo, Sri Lanka: Ceylon University Press, 1958.

Schubring, W. *The Doctrine of the Jainas, Described after the Old Sources.* Translated by W. Beurlen. Delhi: Motilal Banarsidass, 1962. First published in German as *Die Lehre der Jainas, nach dem alten Quellen dargestellt*, Berlin: De Gruyter, 1935.

Siderits, M. "Beyond Compatibilism: A Buddhist Approach to Freedom and Determinism". *American Philosophical Quarterly* 24, no. 2 (1987):149-159.

Silburn, L. *Instant et Cause: Le Discontinu dans la Pensée Philosophique de l'Inde.* Paris: Librairie Philosophique J. Vrin, 1955.

Silva, P. de. *Buddhist and Freudian Psychology.* Colombo, Sri Lanka: Lake House Investments, 1973.

_______. *Tangles and Webs: Comparative Studies in Existentialism, Psychoanalysis and Buddhism.* Kandy, Sri Lanka: T.B.S. Godamunne and Sons, 1974.

_______. *An Introduction to Buddhist Psyohology.* London: Macmillan Press, 1979.

_______. "Two Paradigmatic Strands in the Buddhist Theory of Consciousness". In *The Metaphors of Consciousness*, ed. R.S. Valle and R. von Eckartsberg, 275-285. New York: Plenum Press, 1981.

_______. "Emotions and Therapy: Three Paradigmatic Zones". In *Buddhist and Western Psychology*, ed. N. Katz, 111-136. Boulder: Prajñā Press, 1983.

Sinha, J. *Indian Psychology.* 2 vols. 2d ed. of vol. 1 and 1st ed. of vol. 2. Calcutta: Sinha Publishing House, 1958-1961. First edition of vol. 1, n.p., 1933.

Stcherbatsky, T. *Buddhist Logic.* 2 vols. New York: Dover Publications, 1962. Original edition, Bibliotheca Buddhica Series, vol 26, parts 1-2, Leningrad: circa 1930.

_______. *The Central Conception of Buddhism and the Meaning of the Word "Dharma".* Delhi: Indological Book House, 1970. Original edition, London: Royal Asiatic Society, 1923.

Stein, Nancy L., Bennett Leventhal, and Tom Trabasso, eds. *Psychological and Biological Approaches to Emotion.* Hillsdale, N.J.: Lawrence Erlbaum Associate Publishers, 1990.

Sumegi, A.D. "Mara: Death and Desire in the Pāli Nikāyas". M.A. Dissertation, Carleton University, 1984.

Swāhānanda, Swāmī, trans. *The Chāndogya Upaniṣad.* 2d. ed. Madras: Sri Ramakrishna Math, 1965. First edition, Madras: Sri Ramakrishna Math, 1956.

Tart, C.T. *States of Consciousness.* El Cerrito, Calif.: Psychological Processes, Incorporated, 1983.

Thittila, U, trans. *The Book of Analysis.* London: P.T.S., 1969.

Thomas, E.J. *The History of Buddhist Thought.* 2d. ed. London: Routledge and Kegan Paul, 1951.

Veidlinger, D. "Paṭiccasamuppāda, Kamma and Freedom of Choice: A Study of the Nikāyas and Some Modern Interpretations." M.A. dissertation, Carleton University, 1994.

Walshe, M., trans. *Thus Have I Heard: The Long Discourses of the Buddha.* London: Wisdom Publications, 1987.

Warder, A.K. *Introduction to Pali.* 2d. rev. ed. London: P.T.S., 1974. First edition, London: Luzac and Co., 1963.

_______. *Indian Buddhism.* Delhi: Motilal Banarsidass, 1970.

_______. "Some Problems of the Later Pali Literature". *Journal of the Pali Text Society* 9 (1981): 198-207.

Whicher, I. *The Integrity of the Yoga Darśana: A Reconsideration of Classical Yoga.* Albany, N.Y.: State University of New York Press, 1998.

White, J.E. "Is Buddhist Karmic Theory False?" *Religious Studies* 19 (1983): 223-228.

Whitney, W.D. *Sanskrit Grammar.* 2d. ed. London: Oxford University Press, 1967. First edition, Cambridge: Cambridge University Press, 1879.

Woods, J.H., trans. *The Yoga-System of Patañjali.* 3d ed. Delhi: Motilal Banarsidass, 1966. First edition, Harvard Oriental Series, vol. 17, Cambridge, Mass.: Harvard University Press, 1914.

Woodward, F.L., trans. *The Minor Anthologies of the Pali Canon, Part 2.* London: P.T.S., 1935.

Woodward, F.L., and E.M. Hare, trans. *The Book of Gradual Sayings.* 5 vols. London: P.T.S., 1932-1936.

Zydenbos R.J. *Mokṣa in Jainism, According to Umāsvāti.* Wiesbaden: Franz Steiner Verlag, 1983.

General Index

The Glossary provides translations of Pāli terms in the General Index. References to endnotes are given by page number and the character "n" followed by the number of the note.